1KBW on International Child Abduction

1KBW on International Child Abduction

Richard Harrison QC
Nicholas Anderson
Jennifer Perrins
Katy Chokowry
Samantha Ridley
Thomas Dance
Elle Tait

Bloomsbury Professional
LONDON • DUBLIN • EDINBURGH • NEW YORK • NEW DELHI • SYDNEY

Bloomsbury Professional
Bloomsbury Publishing Plc

41–43 Boltro Road, Haywards Heath, RH16 1BJ, UK

BLOOMSBURY and the Diana logo are trademarks of Bloomsbury Publishing Plc

British Library Cataloguing-in-Publication Data

A catalogue record for this book is available from the British Library.

ISBN:	PB	978 1 52651 282 6
	ePDF	978 1 52651 284 0
	ePub	978 1 52651 283 3

Typeset by Evolution Design and Digital Ltd (Kent)

Preface

This book is intended to be a practical guide to international child abduction proceedings in England and Wales. The book is written from our perspective as litigators operating in this field and our emphasis has been on practice as much as principle. 1KBW hosts an annual child abduction conference and we thought it would be useful to amalgamate our knowledge and experience into a book.

Since the 1980 Hague Convention was incorporated into English law by the enactment of the Child Abduction and Custody Act 1985, this field has spawned literally hundreds of authorities. To those who are new to the subject, it can seem a minefield, peppered with terms that carry specialist meanings. Our aim has been to write a book which serves as an accessible and comprehensive guide for all practitioners, not just those who specialise in this area.

Although there are many people we should thank for the shared pool of knowledge that we have acquired over the years, we would like to give particular thanks to James Turner QC and Anthony Kirk QC, who were among the pioneers in this field in the early days of the Hague Convention and have acted in numerous leading cases since that time. They have each helped us enormously in the development of our own practices. We would also like to thank Susan Wilkins for assisting with the writing of several chapters of the book, and Kate Harrison for her help with Chapter 2.

Finally, we would like to express our gratitude to the publishing team at Bloomsbury for their expertise, encouragement and professional support.

RH, NA, JP, KC, SR, TD and ET
August 2020
1 King's Bench Walk

Contents

Table of Cases

[All references are to paragraph numbers]

X

Y

Z

Table of Statutes

[All references are to paragraph numbers]

Table of Statutory Instruments

[All references are to paragraph numbers]

Table of European Legislation

[All references are to paragraph numbers]

CHAPTER 1

Introduction

Content at a Glance:

A. **Preliminary**

B. **Brussels IIA**

C. **The 1980 European Convention**

D. **Covid-19 and the remote court**

A. PRELIMINARY

1.1 We started writing this book in the Autumn of 2019. At the time, Parliament was in a state of deadlock over the withdrawal of the United Kingdom from the European Union ('Brexit'). There was talk of a second referendum and a real possibility that Brexit would end up either being revoked or made subject to a lengthy implementation period with close alignment to the rules of the single market and the customs union.

1.2 The previous uncertainty ended on 12 December 2019 when a general election was held and the Conservative Party was elected with an overall majority of 80 seats. Following the election, the European Union (Withdrawal Agreement) Act 2020 ('EUWAA 2020') was enacted. It received royal assent on 23 January 2020.

1.3 The EUWAA 2020 amends the European Union (Withdrawal) Act 2018 ('EUWA 2018') and needs to be read in conjunction with it. As a consequence of the two Acts and the relevant statutory instrument[1], the United Kingdom ceased to be a Member of the European Union at 11 pm on 31 January 2020, referred to in the legislation as 'exit day'. The European Communities Act 1972 was repealed on exit day, although it continues substantially to have effect during 'the implementation period' which will come to an end on 'IP completion day', defined as 11 pm on 31 December 2020[2].

1 The European Union (Withdrawal) Act 2018 (Exit Day) (Amendment) (No 3) Regulations 2019, reg 2 amends the definition of 'exit day' in the EUWA 2018, s 20 to 11 pm on 31 January 2020.

2 EUWAA 2020, s 39.

1.4 From the perspective of international children lawyers, the most immediately significant consequence of Brexit will be that the European Regulation known as Brussels IIA ('BIIA')[3], which was revoked on exit day[4], will cease to have effect at 11 pm on 31 December 2020, subject to transitional provisions in Art 67 of the EU Withdrawal Agreement which apply in relation to applications issued before the end of the implementation period.

1.5 The European Regulation known as Brussels IIA Recast ('BIIA Recast')[5] will come into effect in all EU Member States except Denmark on 1 August 2022; as a consequence of Brexit it will not have effect in the United Kingdom. BIIA Recast contains important modifications to BIIA. Notably, Art 21 enshrines the right of a child who is the subject of proceedings and is capable of forming his or her own views to have '*a genuine and effective opportunity*' to express those views; this article applies also in proceedings for the return of the child under the 1980 Hague Convention[6] ('HC80')[7]. Article 21, which may indirectly have an impact upon domestic procedures in England and Wales, is considered in **Chapter 7** of this book. The new Chapter III of BIIA Recast is specifically concerned with international child abduction and reinforces the need for proceedings under HC80 to be concluded expeditiously, as well as imposing an obligation on the courts of the Member States to invite the parties to consider mediation or other forms of alternative dispute resolution[8].

1.6 The majority of child abduction cases are brought under HC80, which is given effect in the law of England and Wales by the Child Abduction and Custody Act 1985 ('CACA 1985'). Section A of this book (**Chapters 2 to 8**) is concerned almost exclusively with the substantive law of HC80.

1.7 In Section B (**Chapters 9 and 10**) we consider abduction outside the 1980 Hague Convention. **Chapter 9** deals with applications for the return of the child under the inherent jurisdiction. **Chapter 10** is concerned with the 1996 Hague Convention[9] ('HC96'). To date, applications under HC96 are relatively rare although, after BIIA has ceased to have effect, it is expected that it will become the key international instrument to which the United Kingdom is a party for determining jurisdiction in relation to children proceedings and for the recognition and enforcement of orders made in other Contracting States (which include the Member States of the European Union).

3 Council Regulation (EU) No 2201/2003 of 27 November 2003 concerning jurisdiction and the recognition and enforcement of judgments in matrimonial matters and matters of parental responsibility, repealing Regulation (EC) No 1347/2000.
4 The Jurisdiction and Judgments (Family) (Amendment etc) (EU Exit) Regulations 2019, reg 3.
5 Council Regulation (EU) No 2019/1111 of 25 June 2019 on jurisdiction and enforcement of decisions in matrimonial matters and the matters of parental responsibility, and on international child abduction (recast).
6 The 1980 Hague Convention on the Civil Aspects of International Child Abduction.
7 Article 26.
8 Article 25.
9 The 1996 Hague Convention of 19 October 1996 on Jurisdiction, Applicable Law, Recognition, Enforcement and Co-operation in Respect of Parental Responsibility and Measures for the Protection of Children.

1.8 Section C is concerned with issues of procedure. **Chapter 11** deals with the procedures for making applications in incoming and outgoing cases. **Chapter 12** is concerned with steps that can be taken to find and protect children within child abduction proceedings. **Chapter 13** addresses the enforcement of orders. **Chapter 14** deals with appeals.

B. BRUSSELS IIA

1.9 We had originally intended to devote two chapters of this book to BIIA: one to the scheme for recognition and enforcement of orders in Chapter III; and another to the procedure under Art 11(7)–(8) of BIIA whereby a Member State with jurisdiction in respect of a child has the ability to override another Member State's refusal to make a return order on one of the grounds in Art 13 of HC80.

1.10 It is now clear that, within a few months of this book being published, BIIA will become of historic interest only so far as the law of England and Wales is concerned (and indeed in the other jurisdictions of the United Kingdom). We have therefore decided merely to summarise in this introductory chapter the main provisions of BIIA, from a child abduction perspective.

1.11 Recital 17 of BIIA specifies that, in a case involving the wrongful removal or retention of a child, the return of the child should be obtained without delay and that, to this end, the provisions of HC80 continue to apply 'as complemented' by the provisions of BIIA. The complementary provisions are contained in Art 11 and can be summarised as follows:

Article 11 of BIIA complementing HC80	
Art 11(2)	Child must be given opportunity to be heard unless inappropriate having regard to age and degree of maturity[10].
Art 11(3)	HC80 proceedings must be conducted expeditiously and concluded within 6 weeks of issue unless exceptional circumstances make this impossible[11].
Art 11(4)	No refusal to return on the basis of Art 13(b) of HC80 (grave risk of harm) if it is established that adequate arrangements have been made to secure the protection of the child after return[12].
Art 11(5)	No refusal to return unless person seeking return is given an opportunity to be heard[13].

10 In England and Wales this principle has been extended to all proceedings under HC80, whether or not involving another EU Member State: see *Re D (A Child) (Abduction: Rights of Custody)* [2006] UKHL 51, [2007] 1 AC 619, [2007] 1 FCR 1, [2007] 1 FLR 961 and **Chapter 7**.

11 This reinforces Art 11 of HC80; there is unlikely to be any change in the current practice in the High Court whereby applications are dealt with speedily and given listing priority.

12 It is unlikely that there will be any change to the existing law in England and Wales whereby the courts seek to mitigate any potential risk under Art 13(b) of HC80 by requiring undertakings or other protective measures to be in place before a return order is made: see **Chapter 6**.

13 This accords with the domestic law in any event and will not be subject to change after Brexit.

Art 11(6)–(8)	Procedure whereby a Member State which refuses to return a child on one of the grounds in Art 13 of HC80 must, within a month, notify and provide relevant documents to the court in the Member State with substantive welfare jurisdiction. The latter court has the ability then to examine the question of custody, and any decision it makes requiring the return of the child will be automatically enforceable[14].

1.12 Chapter III of BIIA contains a scheme for the recognition and enforcement of orders made in one EU Member State in all another Member States (with the exception of Denmark). Article 21 provides that a judgment given in a Member State shall be recognised in other Member States without any special procedure being required. However, an interested party may make an application for the judgment to be recognised or not recognised as the case may be.

1.13 There are limited grounds upon which a court can refuse to recognise a judgment relating to parental responsibility. These are set out in Art 23 of BIIA and can be summarised as follows:

Article 23 of BIIA: non-recognition of judgments on parental responsibility	
Art 23(a)	Judgment manifestly contrary to public policy[15].
Art 23(b)	Except in case of urgency, child not given opportunity to be heard, in violation of fundamental principles of procedure[16].
Art 23(c)	No service of application on respondent in sufficient time to arrange defence (unless judgment unequivocally accepted).
Art 23(d)	Judgment infringes parental responsibility of person not given opportunity to be heard.
Art 23(e)	Judgment irreconcilable with later judgment in Member State where recognition sought.
Art 23(f)	Judgment irreconcilable with later judgment given in (a) another Member State or (b) a non-Member State of habitual residence of the child, provided the later judgment is recognisable in the Member State where recognition sought.
Art 23(g)	The procedure for placing a child in institutional care in Art 56 of BIIA has not been complied with.

1.14 Section 2 of Chapter III of BIIA sets out the procedure known as '*exequator*' for making applications for a declaration of enforceability of a

14 This procedure has been considered in a number of cases at first instance: see, for example, *HA v MB (Brussels II Revised: Article 11(7) Application)* [2007] EWHC 2016 (Fam), [2008] 1 FLR 289; *M v T (Abduction: Brussels II Revised, Art 11(7))* [2010] EWHC 1479 (Fam), [2010] 2 FLR 1685.

15 This ground is 'a high hurdle': see, for example, *Re L (Brussels II Revised: Appeal)* [2012] EWCA Civ 1157, [2013] 2 FCR 195, [2013] 1 FLR 430; see also **Chapter 10** for consideration of the equivalent provision under HC96.

16 It is a fundamental principle of procedure in England and Wales that the court must give consideration to hearing the voice of the child: see *Re D (A Child) (International Recognition)* [2016] EWCA Civ 12, [2016] 1 WLR 2469, [2016] 2 FCR 1, [2016] 2 FLR 347; see also **Chapter 7**.

judgment[17]. Article 27(2) provides that, in the United Kingdom, judgments 'shall be enforced' if they have been registered. In England and Wales, applications for registration must be made to the Principal Registry of the High Court in accordance with the procedure in Family Procedure Rules 2010 ('FPR'), Part 31. Appeals against the registration lie to the High Court, Family Division.

1.15 Section 4 of Chapter III sets out two categories of judgment which '*shall be recognised and enforceable ... without the need for a declaration of enforceability and without any possibility of opposing its recognition*' if the judgment has been certified under Art 41 of and Annex III to, or Art 42 of and Annex IV to, BIIA. The two categories of judgment are:

- judgments in relation to rights of access (Art 41); and
- judgments for the return of a child given pursuant to Art 11(8) of BIIA[18] (Art 42).

1.16 With effect from IP completion day, BIIA will cease to apply in the United Kingdom. Thereafter, applications for the recognition and enforcement of overseas orders will need to be made pursuant to either HC96 or the 1980 European Convention[19] ('EC80'). HC96 is addressed in detail in **Chapter 10**.

C. THE 1980 EUROPEAN CONVENTION

1.17 EC80 is a treaty prepared by the Council of Europe. It was given domestic effect in the United Kingdom as a schedule to the CACA 1985[20]. Since BIIA came into effect, EC80 has fallen into disuse[21] and there are very few reported cases that deal with this Convention. Although there is no hierarchy between EC80 and HC96, it is expected that after IP completion day the vast majority of applications for the recognition and enforcement of overseas decisions will be brought under HC96, for essentially two reasons:

- HC96 applies in a greater number of States than EC80[22]; and
- the grounds upon which a court can refuse to recognise decisions under EC80 are more extensive than those under HC96. Where there is a choice, it will be advantageous to applicants to proceed under HC96.

17 BIIA Recast will abolish entirely the procedure of exequatur for all decisions in matters of parental responsibility (Arts 34 and 35).

18 See footnote 14 above.

19 The 1980 European Convention of 20 May 1980 on Recognition and Enforcement of Decisions Concerning Custody of Children.

20 Schedule 2.

21 Article 60 of BIIA provides that BIIA takes precedence over the 1980 European Convention insofar as it concerns matters governed by BIIA.

22 See www.coe.int/en/web/conventions/full-list//conventions/treaty/105/signatures for a list of States which have ratified EC80.

1.18 EC80 includes the following grounds for non-recognition which have no equivalent in HC96:

EC80 grounds for non-recognition without equivalent in HC96	
Art 10(1)(b)	By reason of a change of circumstances including the passage of time but not including a mere change in residence, the effects of the original decision are manifestly no longer in accordance with the welfare of the child.
Art 10(1)(c)(i)	At the time proceedings were instituted in the State of origin, the child was a national of the State addressed or habitually resident there and no such connection existed with the State of origin.
Art 10(1)(c)(ii)	At the time proceedings were instituted in the State of origin, the child was a national of both the State of origin and the State addressed and was habitually resident in the State addressed.

1.19 Article 10(2) of EC80 sets out grounds on which a court can adjourn proceedings for recognition and enforcement. Article 11(2) entitles the authorities in the State addressed to 'fix the conditions' for the implementation and exercise of rights of access. These are further reasons why applicants are more likely to opt to enforce orders under HC96, which contains no equivalent to those provisions.

D. COVID-19 AND THE REMOTE COURT

1.20 By the end of 2019, it seemed clear that 2020 would come to be remembered above all as the year of Brexit. As matters have transpired, the United Kingdom – and indeed the rest of the world – has ended up being dominated by the biggest crisis since the end of the Second World War as a result of the Covid-19 pandemic.

1.21 At the time of writing, Covid-19 has had such a dramatic effect on the way in which proceedings are being conducted through remote court hearings that we have decided to summarise those provisions in this introduction. It may be that current remote court procedures will prove to be of relatively short duration. On the other hand, it may well be the case that they endure in some form or other for a significant period of time. **Chapter 11** of this book describes the procedures for making incoming and outgoing applications and **Chapter 14** deals with procedures on appeal. Those chapters and the existing 2018 Practice Guidance[23] for the conduct of child abduction proceedings (see paras **11.26–11.52**), at least for the time being, have been partially superseded by the temporary Practice Guidance issued in the light of Covid-19[24] ('the Covid-19

23 Practice Guidance 13 March 2018: Case Management and Mediation of International Child Abduction Proceedings.

24 COVID-19: Temporary Amendments to the Practice Guidance on Case Management and Mediation of International Child Abduction Proceedings. The procedural changes effected are discussed in detail at para **11.48** below.

Guidance'). The changes made by the Covid-19 Guidance (also summarised at para **11.48**) are as follows:

ICACU

- Working remotely
- All applications by email
- Documents sent by post, DX or fax will not be received

Legal Aid Agency

- Operating a normal service
- Provision of evidence to prove financial means has been amended

Issue Procedure - All Applications

- All applications issued as, in effect, without notice applications (paras 2.1, 2.2, 9 and 10 of the 2018 Practice Guidance suspended)
- Applications issued electronically and the email subject line should be: "URGENT: NEW 1980 HAGUE CONVENTION APPLICATION FOR ISSUE"
- All applications accompanied by proposed directions order in draft in Word document format

Service

- Permitted to serve orders prior to sealing, which have been endorsed by court
- Endorsed orders are effective without sealing
- Personal service only effected if safe. Service by email or posting through letterbox is sufficient in the first instance
- Copy of Temporary Guidance will be included with the order for service on the respondent

Child Abduction Mediation Scheme

- Suspended only insofar as to prevent face-to-face mediation at court
- Each party to contact reunite prior to first on-notice hearing: reunite@dircon.co.uk or 0116 2555 345

Child's Participation

- Children can be interviewed remotely by Cafcass High Court
- Cafcass can receive electronic papers
- Email: highcourtgm.cafcass.gov.uk

Hearings

- Take place in accordance with President's Guidance of 19 March 2020: "COVID 19: National Guidance for the Family Court"
- Each order must prominently state that the next hearing will take place 'remotely'
- Immediate steps must be taken to obtain/ensure access to technology for the next hearing
- No less than 48 hours before hearing, applicant's solicitor to contact respondent/solicitor to arrange remote hearing
- If respondent has no computer, hearing by telephone

Tipstaff

- Orders available in the usual way
- Tipstaff will discharge his responsibilities, subject to operational constraints imposed by Government
- Tipstaff requires sealed order to discharge port alerts and/or passport orders

1.22 As the table above shows, remote hearings are being conducted in accordance with the President's Guidance of 19 March 2020[25], which relates to the entirety of the Family Court. The types of 'remote' hearing identified are[26]:

25 COVID 19: National Guidance for the Family Court 19 March 2020, Sir Andrew McFarlane, President of the Family Division and Head of Family Justice.

26 Also read the document titled 'the Remote Access Family Court' by Mr Justice MacDonald, at the time of writing on its fourth version dated 20 April 2020, in particular the 'Protocol for Remote Hearings' at Appendix 1. 'CVP' refers to Court Video Platform, a new video-conferencing platform in its infancy at the time of writing.

In the various pieces of guidance, several issues must be considered in advance of and during a remote hearing:

Recording of the hearing

- Remote hearings must be recorded
- The party who has arranged the remote hearing is responsible for the recording (often the court)
- If a legal representative is conducting the recording, it must be uploaded to secure cloud storage immediately after the hearing
- It is a criminal offence for a party to record privately the hearing (Coronavirus Act 2020)

Applicant's solicitors

- Must make the technical arrangements, unless the court indicates it will do so
- Must confirm the details to the court / parties at least 24 hours before hearing
- Must file by email with the court an electronic PDF bundle the day before the hearing

Electronic bundle

- Must include: case summary and chronology; position statements of parties; relevant previous orders; all essential documents the court requires to determine the issues; and a draft order
- Must be searchable
- Must contain computer-generated pagination
- Must be bookmarked

Professional decorum must be maintained

- Advocates must dress as if attending court
- Background to the video must be appropriate
- Ensure no interruptions during the hearing
- No one may move away from the screen without the court's permission
- No eating or drinking, save for water
- Take all reasonable steps to maintain confidentiality
- Use of earphones encouraged
- Address the judge and advocates as if in court

At the start of the hearing

- The court will identify the case, remind the parties that it is a court of law
- The court will warn the parties about private recording and confidentiality

During the hearing

- All participants must keep camera on
- Microphones must be on mute, unless speaking
- If advocates need to take instructions, time will be provided to do so
- Any witness will be sworn or affirmed 'remotely' prior to evidence.

1.23 We are going through exceptional times. We all hope to be able to return as soon as possible to our familiar working practices. Until that becomes possible, practitioners will need to adapt to the new circumstances. There will inevitably be changes to the technology we use, and further guidance will be issued reflecting the shared experience of practitioners and judges as we 'learn on the job'.

CHAPTER 2

Background and overview of the 1980 Hague Convention

Content at a Glance:

A. The Hague Conference on Private International Law
- Introduction
- The Founding Statute of HCCH
- Child Law Conventions

B. The background and structure of the 1980 Hague Convention
- Background
- Objectives of HC80
- The welfare of the child is a primary consideration
- Structure and key provisions of HC80
- The role of Central Authorities
- Need for expedition
- Rights of access

A. THE HAGUE CONFERENCE ON PRIVATE INTERNATIONAL LAW

Introduction

2.1 The 1980 Hague Convention on the Civil Aspects of International Child Abduction ('HC80') is an international treaty which was concluded at the fourteenth session of the Hague Conference on Private International Law ('HCCH'[1]). HC80 is published in English and French, the two official languages of HCCH.

2.2 HCCH describes itself as 'The World Organisation for Cross-border Co-operation in Civil and Commercial Matters'. At the time of writing, HCCH has 85 Members including 84 States (the other Member is the European Union).

2.3 HCCH was first convoked as a diplomatic conference in 1893 by Tobias Asser, a Dutch lawyer who was later awarded the Nobel Peace Prize for his work in the field of private international law. Its aim was to work towards

1 The Hague Conference on Private International Law is usually abbreviated to HCCH which stands for 'Hague Conference / Conférence de la Haye', reflecting the fact that its official languages are English and French.

the unification of rules and principles of private international law through the conclusion of multilateral conventions in relation to different aspects of civil law, including family law.

2.4 The meetings of the Hague Conference are referred to as 'sessions'. At the first session in 1893 there were 12 participating States[2] which did not include the United Kingdom. The fourth session was held in 1904, after which the Conference did not meet again until after the First World War. At the fifth and sixth sessions held in 1925 and 1928, HCCH concluded a Protocol to recognise the competence of the Permanent Court of International Justice[3] to interpret its Conventions. Following the sixth session, no further sessions were held until after the Second World War.

The Founding Statute of HCCH

2.5 The seventh session of HCCH was held in 1951 between 16 States[4] including the United Kingdom. At this session, steps were taken to formalise HCCH by establishing it as an intergovernmental organisation. A treaty called The Statute of the Hague Conference on Private International Law ('the Founding Statute') was adopted during the session and entered into force on 15 July 1955. It was later amended in 2005, with the amendments coming into force in 2007.

2.6 The preamble to the Founding Statute records the aim of the signatory States to stress the permanent character of HCCH. Article 1 states that its purpose is to work for the progressive unification of the rules of private international law. Article 2 requires States to accept the Founding Statute in order to be admitted as members of HCCH. The United Kingdom became a member on 15 July 1955.

2.7 Articles 4 and 5 of the Founding Statute provide for the creation of a Council on General Affairs and Policy ('the General Council') to be composed of all members with responsibility for the operation of HCCH. This responsibility is designated to a Permanent Bureau which shall have its seat in The Hague. Article 4 sets out an expectation that ordinary sessions will be convened every four years, while allowing for the possibility of an extraordinary session to be convened. The General Council meets annually.

2.8 Article 7 of the Founding Statute of HCCH requires each Member State to designate a 'national organ' with a view to facilitating communication between

2 Austria-Hungary, Belgium, France, Germany, Italy, Luxembourg, Netherlands, Portugal, Romania, Russia, Spain and Switzerland.

3 The Permanent Court of International Justice was attached to the League of Nations and existed between 1922 and 1946. Following the Second World War the League of Nations and its associated court ceased to exist and were replaced by the United Nations and the International Court of Justice.

4 Austria, Belgium, Denmark, Finland, France, the Federal Republic of Germany, Italy, Japan, Luxembourg, Norway, the Netherlands, Portugal, Spain, Sweden, Switzerland and the United Kingdom.

Members and the Permanent Bureau. The national organ in the United Kingdom is the Ministry of Justice.

Child Law Conventions

2.9 The members of HCCH have concluded a number of Conventions in the field of children law:

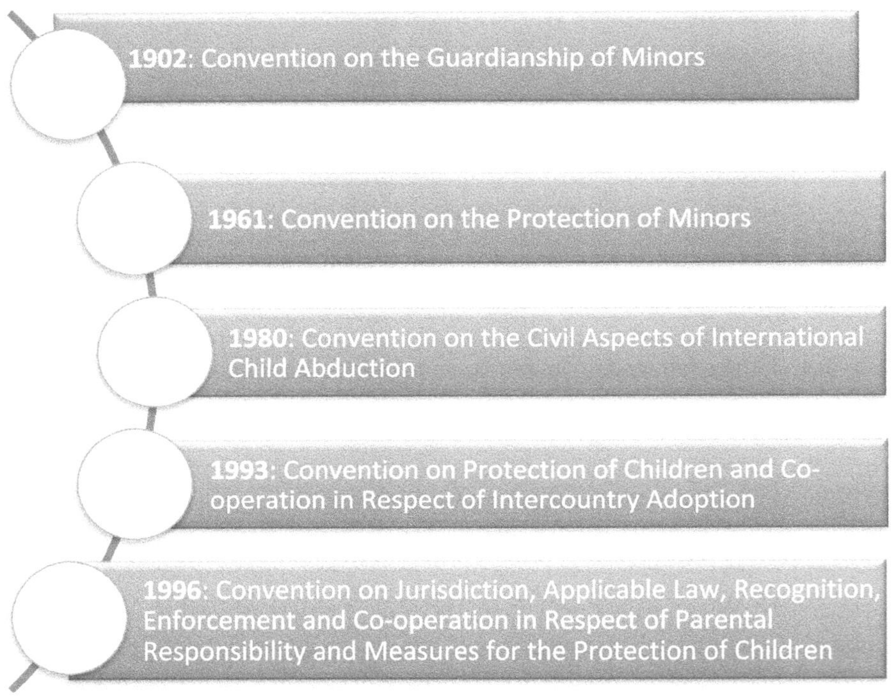

2.10 Under the 1902 Convention on the Guardianship of Minors, the nationality of the child was the primary connecting factor for the establishment of jurisdiction (see Art 1). This remained the case until the 1902 Convention was eventually replaced by the 1961 Convention on the Protection of Minors. The impetus for change resulted from a well-known case in the International Court of Justice about a child called Marie Elizabeth Boll.

Case Summary: *Netherlands v Sweden ('the Boll case')*[5]

Facts:

In 1958 the Netherlands took legal action against Sweden in relation to the guardianship of Marie Elizabeth Boll, whose mother had died. The father was of Dutch nationality and the mother was Swedish. The child lived in Sweden before the mother's death but, under the existing rules of nationality at the time, was solely entitled to the Dutch nationality of her father. In spite of her residence in Sweden, her guardianship was assigned by the Dutch authorities in favour of the father in accordance with the Dutch Civil Code. However, the Swedish authorities placed Marie under a protective public care order as she was residing with her maternal grandparents in Sweden.

The Netherlands brought proceedings against Sweden in the International Court of Justice, claiming that the actions taken in Sweden interfered with the guardianship assigned to the father under Dutch law and were contrary to the rules of jurisdiction under the 1902 Convention.

Held by the ICJ:

The ICJ determined that, under the Guardianship of Minors Convention 1902, the Swedish intervention by taking the child into 'care' was permissible as the decisions taken did not concern the guardianship of the child and therefore fell outside the ambit of the Convention. This meant that, in practice, States in which a child was residing could overrule the guardianship orders of other States with presumptive jurisdiction, through the execution of public laws in that State.

2.11 The result of the *Boll* case led to calls for a review of the rules of jurisdiction in the 1902 Convention, which ultimately resulted in the conclusion of the 1961 Convention on the Protection of Minors. The ambit of the 1961 Convention was extended to include public law measures. Significantly, Art 1 of the 1961 Convention made the habitual residence of the child the primary basis for jurisdiction. Habitual residence has remained the main basis for jurisdiction in children proceedings since 1961, both in Hague Conventions and in Regulations promulgated by the European Union. For habitual residence, see **Chapter 4**.

2.12 The 1961 Convention was eventually replaced by the 1996 Hague Convention[6] ('HC96'). For HC96, see **Chapter 10**.

5 [1958] ICJ 8.

6 Convention of 19 October 1996 on Jurisdiction, Applicable Law, Recognition, Enforcement and Co-operation in Respect of Parental Responsibility and Measures for the Protection of Children.

B. THE BACKGROUND AND STRUCTURE OF THE 1980 HAGUE CONVENTION

Background

2.13 On 24 October 1980, at the fourteenth session of the HCCH, the 23 Member States[7] unanimously adopted HC80; it was signed the following day, 25 October 1980, by four Member States and bears this date. It entered into force as between the signatory States on 1 December 1983, although it did not acquire the force of law in individual Member States until steps were taken to implement it into domestic law. It was concluded in response to what had been identified as an increasing problem of cross-border parental child abduction.

2.14 HC80 was implemented in the United Kingdom as a Schedule[8] to the Child Abduction and Custody Act 1985 ('CACA 1985'), which came into force on 1 August 1986. As between Member States of the European Union, it is complemented by the provisions of Council Regulation (EC) 2201/2003[9] ('BIIA'), in particular Art 11. Following the departure of the United Kingdom from the European Union, BIIA will cease to be applicable in the UK at the conclusion of the implementation period on 31 December 2020, unless an agreement is reached through which it continues to have effect.

2.15 The Convention is accompanied by an Explanatory Report prepared by Professor Eliza Pérez-Vera, who held the position of 'Reporter' to a small sub-committee, described as the First Commission, to whom the task of preparing the Convention was entrusted. The Explanatory Report is often relied upon by the court as an aid to the interpretation of HC80 although, as Professor Pérez Vera points out, the report was prepared at the end of the fourteenth session based upon the *procès-verbaux*[10] of the proceedings and her own notes[11]. The Explanatory Report was not formally approved by HCCH.

2.16 As is explained by Professor Pérez-Vera in the Explanatory Report[12], the Convention was the product of drafting by several committees during the course of the fourteenth session which was held between 6 and 25 October 1980. The report drew upon research undertaken by Adair Turner, the First Secretary of the Permanent Bureau, and a draft convention prepared by a Special Commission of HCCH in 1979.

7 Argentina, Australia, Belgium, Canada, Czechoslovakia, Denmark, Finland, France, the Federal Republic of Germany, Greece, the Republic of Ireland, Italy, Japan, Luxembourg, Norway, the Netherlands, Norway, Portugal, Spain, Sweden, Switzerland, the United Kingdom and Yugoslavia.

8 Schedule 1 to CACA 1985 does not replicate the entirety of HC80 but omits the following Articles: Arts 1, 2, 6, 20, 23, 25, 33–45.

9 Council Regulation (EC) No 2201/2003 of 27 November 2003 concerning jurisdiction and the recognition and enforcement of judgments in matrimonial matters and the matters of parental responsibility, repealing Regulation (EC) No 1347/2000. For a limited summary of BIIA, see **Chapter 1**.

10 The official written records of proceedings.

11 See para 8 of the Explanatory Report.

12 Paragraphs 1 to 4.

2.17 The final form of the Convention represented a compromise between different perspectives articulated by various delegations. The Member States had previously been unable to reach agreement as to the recognition and enforcement of foreign decisions in relation to custody. Certain delegations advocated a clear rule of recognition subject only to limited exceptions; others favoured a more flexible approach which would allow courts being asked to recognise a foreign decision to exercise a discretion which accorded with the interests of the child[13]. Those who favoured greater rigidity believed that a more flexible approach would be ineffective in combating child abduction.

2.18 The eventual compromise abandoned earlier attempts to conclude a Convention based upon the recognition and enforcement of foreign decisions. Instead, the central premise of HC80 is that, following the abduction of a child, steps should be taken to ensure the swift restoration of the child to the country of his or her habitual residence to enable the courts in that 'home' country to take any necessary decisions about substantive issues of custody.

2.19 The habitual residence of the child is a central concept which underpins HC80. It is not defined in the Convention. At para 66 of the Explanatory Report it is described as '*a well-established concept in the Hague Conference, which regards it as a question of pure fact*'. For habitual residence, see **Chapter 4**.

Objectives of HC80

2.20 The aims and objectives of HC80 are recorded in its preamble and in Art 1. They can be summarised as follows:

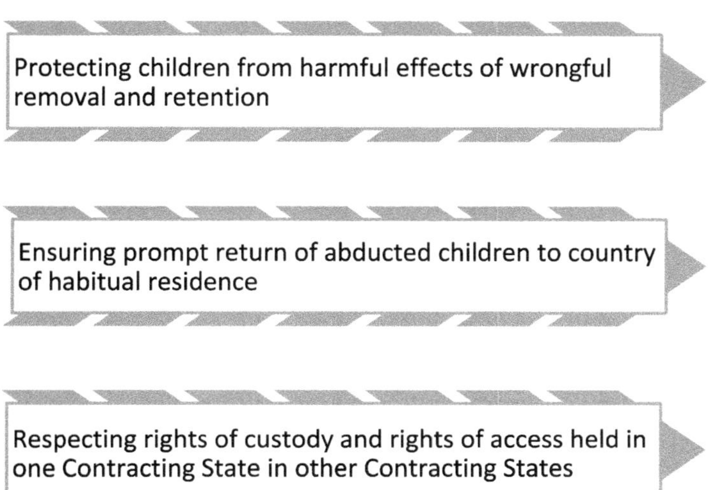

13 See Brigitte M Bodenheimer *The Hague Draft Convention on International Child Abduction* Family Law Quarterly Vol 14, No 2 (summer 1980).

Neither the preamble nor Art 1 is contained in the abbreviated version of HC80 which comprises Schedule 1 to CACA 1985. Nevertheless, it has been held that they are relevant to its construction: *Re H and Others (Minors) (Abduction: Acquiescence)*[14].

2.21 The Explanatory Report to HC80 emphasises that one of the ways in which the Convention secures its objectives is by deterring would-be abductors from wrongfully removing or retaining children: see para 16.

The welfare of the child is a primary consideration

2.22 The welfare of the child is not 'the paramount consideration' in proceedings under HC80 and, indeed, is not referred to in any of its articles. However, the preamble records the general principle that '*the interests of children are of paramount importance in matters relating to their custody*'.

2.23 Article 3.1 of the United Nations Convention on the Rights of the Child 1989 ('UNCRC') provides that:

> 'In all actions concerning children … the best interests of the child shall be a primary consideration.'

The United Kingdom is a party to the UNCRC which creates binding obligations in international law. Although it has not been formally incorporated into the law of England and Wales by statute, it has been held that its 'spirit' has been translated into our national law[15]. Article 3.1 requires the Hague Convention to be applied in a way which is consistent with the welfare of the child being a primary consideration[16].

2.24 In *Neulinger and Shuruk v Switzerland*[17] it was held by the European Court of Human Rights that, in determining whether a decision made in proceedings under HC80 was in breach of a person's right to family life under Art 8 of the European Convention on Human Rights[18] ('ECHR'), the decisive issue was whether a fair balance had been struck between the various rights at stake, bearing in mind that the interests of the child must be the primary consideration.

2.25 In *Re E (Children) (Abduction: Custody Appeal)*[19] it was held by the Supreme Court that each of the following is '*a primary consideration*' in HC80 proceedings:

14 [1998] AC 72, [1997] 2 FCR 257, [1997] 1 FLR 872.
15 *ZH (Tanzania) v Secretary of State for the Home Department* [2011] UKSC 4, [2011] 2 AC 166, [2011] 1 FCR 221, [2011] 1 FLR 2170.
16 *Re E (Children) (Abduction: Custody Appeal)* [2011] UKSC 27, [2012] 1 AC 144, [2011] 2 FCR 419, [2011] 2 FLR 758.
17 (2012) 54 EHRR 31, [2011] 2 FCR 110, [2011] 1 FLR 122.
18 The Convention for the Protection of Human Rights and Fundamental Freedoms.
19 [2011] UKSC 27, [2012] 1 AC 144, [2011] 2 FCR 419, [2011] 2 FLR 758.

- the best interests of the children subject to the proceedings; and
- the best interests of children generally.

2.26 The policy objectives of HC80 are designed, in part, to deter abduction and thus safeguard the interests of children generally. These will often be consistent with the best interests of the children in the individual case under consideration, but in some cases they may not be.

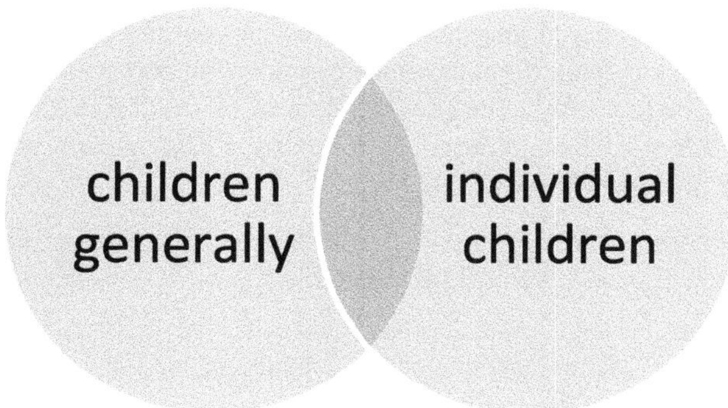

The outcome of proceedings will not necessarily be that which would be reached if the best interests of the children were the court's paramount consideration. Article 19 of HC80 emphasises that a decision under the Convention shall not be taken to be a determination on the merits of any custody issue.

Structure and key provisions of HC80

2.27 HC80 is divided into six 'Chapters' shown in the table below (articles in square brackets do not appear in the version of HC80 contained in Schedule 1 to CACA 1985 and have therefore not been implemented into domestic law).

Chapter	Title	Articles
I	Scope of the Convention	[1–2], 3, 4, 5
II	Central Authorities	[6], 7
III	Return of Children	8–19, [20]
IV	Rights of Access[20]	21
V	General Provisions	22, [23], 24, [25], 26–32, [33–36]
VI	Final Clauses	[37–45]

20 Article 21 places an obligation upon Contracting States to secure rights of access held in other Member States. However, it does not provide any specific means by which this is to be achieved. A party seeking to enforce access rights held pursuant to an order of the court should make an application to recognise and enforce the order in question under either HC96 or, while it remains in force, BIIA.

Key provisions

2.28 From the perspective of child abduction practitioners, the most important articles are:

- **Articles 3–5**: these define the scope of HC80 and set out when the removal or retention of a child is to be considered wrongful: see **Chapter 3**.
- **Article 12**: this requires the authorities in Contracting States to order the return of a child 'forthwith' where the child has been the subject of a wrongful removal or retention and proceedings have been commenced within a period of less than a year from the date of that removal or retention. Exceptionally, a return may be to a third state (not the state of habitual residence): see *O v O* [2014] 1 FLR 1405, considered in *Re B (A Child) (Abduction: Habitual Residence)* [2020] EWCA Civ 1187.

  Where proceedings are commenced after a year, the return of the child must also be ordered unless the child is settled in his or her new environment: see **Chapter 8**.
- **Article 13**: this sets out limited exceptions to the requirement under Art 12 to order the return of the child forthwith:
  (a) Consent, acquiescence and non-exercise of rights of custody: see **Chapter 5**.
  (b) Grave risk that the child will be exposed to harm or placed in an intolerable situation: see **Chapter 6**.
  (c) The child objects to returning and has attained an age and degree of maturity at which it is appropriate to take account of his or her views: see **Chapter 7**.

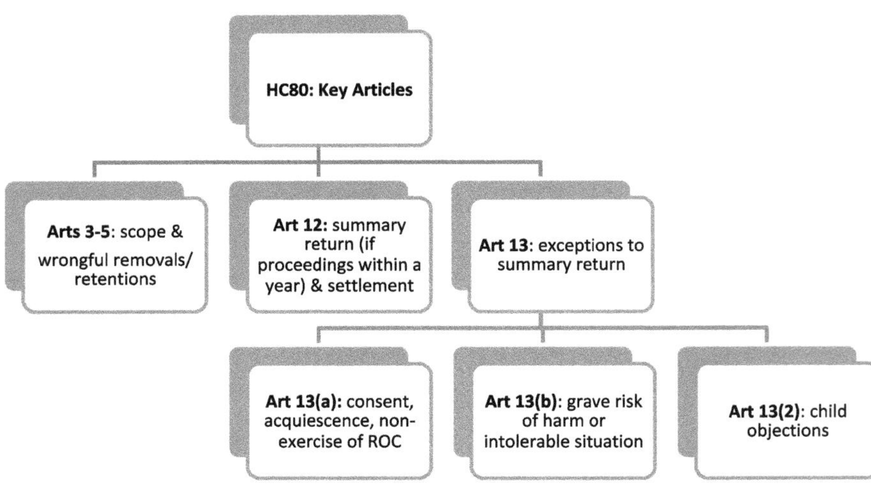

2.29 The following diagram illustrates the decision-making process in HC80 proceedings:

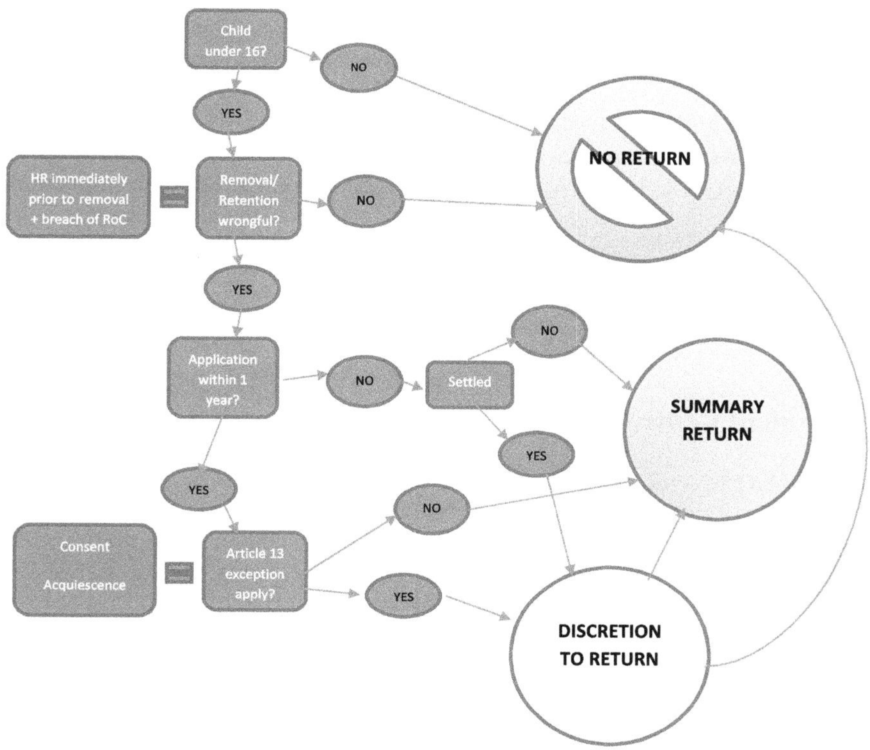

No custody decision following notice of wrongful removal or retention

2.30 Article 16 of HC80 prevents the courts in a State to which a child has been removed, or in which it has been retained, from making any merits-based decision on issues relating to rights of custody after receiving notice of the wrongful removal or retention unless and until:

(a) a decision is made not to order the return of the child under HC80; or

(b) no application under HC80 is lodged within a reasonable time following the receipt of notice.

Returns outside HC80

2.31 Article 18 of HC80 provides that the terms of the Convention do not prevent the authorities in Contracting States from making an order for the return of a child at any time. This allows the court to make an order for the return of a child under the inherent jurisdiction if it is in the best interests of the child to do so: see **Chapter 9**.

Human rights and asylum

2.32 Article 20 of HC80 provides that the return of the child may be refused if this would not be permitted by the fundamental principles in the Requested State relating to the protection of human rights and fundamental freedoms. This article was not included in Schedule 1 to the CACA 1985 and therefore does not have effect under the domestic law of England and Wales. However, the Human Rights Act 1998, s 3 requires the court, so far as it is possible to do so, to read and give effect to legislation in a manner which is compatible with rights under the ECHR.

Where a child has been granted refugee status or has a pending claim for asylum, the court cannot implement a return order to the state from which the child has sought asylum: *E v E* [2018] Fam 24.

The role of Central Authorities

2.33 Article 6 of HC80 requires Contracting States to designate a Central Authority with responsibility for discharging the duties imposed by the Convention. Although Art 6 has not been incorporated into the domestic law of the United Kingdom, relevant Central Authorities have been designated. In England and Wales the Central Authority is the International Child Abduction and Contact Unit (known informally as 'ICACU') at the Office of the Official Solicitor and Public Trustee.

2.34 ICACU's details are as follows:

ICACU CONTACT DETAILS	
Address	The International Child Abduction and Contact Unit Office of the Official Solicitor Victory House 30-34 Kingsway LONDON WC2B 6EX DX 141423 Bloomsbury 7 United Kingdom
Telephone	+44 (203) 681 2608
Fax	+44 (203) 681 2762
Email	ICACU@ospt.gov.uk
Website	www.gov.uk/government/publications/icacu-referral-list-information-and-application-details/international-child-abduction-and-contact-unit-information-for-solicitors

2.35 Article 7 of HC80 sets out the responsibility of Central Authorities to co-operate with each other and promote co-operation amongst the competent authorities in their respective States to secure the prompt return of children and to achieve the other objectives of this Convention. In particular, either directly or through an intermediary, they are required to take all appropriate measures to take various steps which can be summarised as follows:

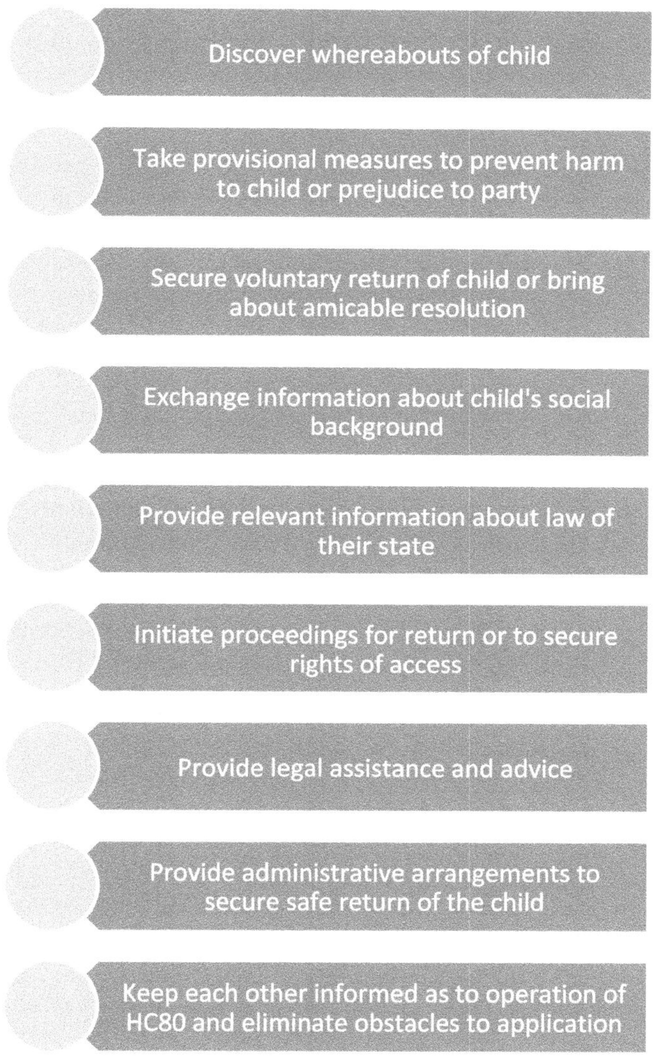

Thus it can be seen that Central Authorities are not neutral as between parties to proceedings: one of their main responsibilities is to secure the return of the child, either on a voluntary basis (Arts 7(c) and 10) or by instituting proceedings (Art 7(f)).

2.36 In *Re S (A Child)*[21] Moylan LJ referred to the Guide to Good Practice in respect of the 1980 Convention, published by The Hague Conference on Private International Law, which includes guidance as to the roles of Central Authorities based in part on Art 27 of HC80. In particular the Central Authority in the country where the applicant is based can be assumed to have checked that any application

21 [2018] EWCA Civ 1453, [2018] 3 FCR 394, [2019] 1 FLR 354.

satisfies Convention requirements, carefully scrutinising outgoing applications to ensure they come within HC80. The fact that an application has been issued means that it has been considered by the Central Authorities in both the outgoing State and in the UK.

2.37 Article 8 of HC80 allows a person, institution or other body claiming that a child has been wrongfully removed or retained to make an application for the return of the child to any Central Authority. Under Art 9, where it is believed that a child has been taken to another State, the Central Authority to whom the application is made will transmit the application to the Central Authority in the State where the child is located. The latter will then attempt to secure the return of the child or initiate proceedings for return.

2.38 In England and Wales, ICACU does not directly initiate proceedings for the return of a child. It appoints specialist solicitors to do so on its behalf.

2.39 There is no requirement for an applicant to commence proceedings through ICACU; they can initiate proceedings directly. A possible advantage of making the application through ICACU is that such applicants are automatically entitled to legal aid which is not means-tested or merits-tested (although it may also be possible to obtain legal aid if an application is issued directly). The procedure for making applications is dealt with in **Chapter 11**.

Need for expedition

2.40 Article 11 of HC80 places an obligation on Contracting States to act expeditiously in proceedings. If a decision has not been reached within 6 weeks of the date of commencement of proceedings, the applicant and the Central Authority in the Requesting State have the right to ask for an explanation for the delay.

2.41 In proceedings between Member States of the European Union[22] the requirement for expedition is reinforced by Art 11(3) of BIIA which *requires* proceedings under HC80 to be concluded within 6 weeks of the date upon which the application was lodged unless exceptional circumstances make it impossible to comply with this timescale[23]. The Court of Appeal has held that this 6-week timescale should also apply to appeals[24]: for appeals, see **Chapter 14**.

2.42 The need for expedition, including in relation to the enforcement of any order, has been repeatedly emphasised by the European Court of Human

22 Also the United Kingdom for so long as BIIA remains in force; unless its provisions are extended by agreement, BIIA will cease to be applicable after 31 December 2020.

23 See *Vigreux v Michel* [2006] EWCA Civ 630, [2007] 3 FCR 196, [2006] 2 FLR 1180.

24 *Klentzeris v Klentzeris* [2007] EWCA Civ 533, [2007] 3 FCR 580, [2007] 2 FLR 996.

Rights as '*the passage of time can have irredeemable consequences*' for relations between the child and a parent[25].

Rights of access

2.43 Article 21 of HC80 places an obligation upon Contracting States to secure rights of access in other Contracting States. Rights of access are defined in Art 5(b) as including the right to take a child for a limited period of time to a place other than the child's habitual residence. Article 21 applies even after a child has ceased to be habitually resident in the Contracting State in which rights of access were awarded: *Re G (A Minor) (Enforcement of Access Abroad)*[26].

2.44 HC80 does not provide any specific means by which rights of access are to be secured. It has been held that the obligations imposed by Art 21 are of an administrative non-mandatory nature and are directed to Central Authorities rather than the courts[27]. Such obligations may be discharged by the provision of appropriate assistance to an applicant such as an introduction to legal services. HC80 does not provide a means of enforcing a foreign contact order; unless there exists an alternative route for recognition or enforcement, an application to secure rights of access must proceed as an application for contact under Children Act 1989 ('CA 1989'), s 8, in which the welfare of the child will be the court's paramount consideration[28].

2.45 A party seeking to enforce access rights held pursuant to an order of the court can make an application to recognise and enforce the order in question under either HC96 or, while it remains in force, BIIA[29]. The advantage of pursuing such a remedy is that there are only limited circumstances in which a court can refuse to recognise a foreign order: for HC96, see **Chapter 10**.

2.46 The expression 'rights of access' also features in BIIA. In *Valcheva v Babanarakis (Case C-335/17)*[30] it was held by the Court of Justice of the European Union, in the context of BIIA, that the definition does not impose any limitation in regard to the persons who may benefit from rights of access. Accordingly, it encompasses rights of persons, other than a parent, held by family members

25 See *Sylvester v Austria* (2003) 37 EHRR 17, [2003] 2 FCR 128, [2003] 2 FLR 210; *Shaw v Hungary* (2015) 61 EHRR 15, [2012] 2 FLR 1314.

26 [1993] Fam 216, [1993] 2 FCR 485, [1993] 1 FLR 669.

27 *Re G (A Minor) (Enforcement of Access Abroad)* [1993] Fam 216, [1993] 2 FCR 485, [1993] 1 FLR 669, approved by the Supreme Court in *Re C and another (Children) (International Centre for Family Law, Policy and Practice Intervening)* [2018] UKSC 8, [2019] AC 1, [2018] 2 FCR 733, [2018] 1 FLR 861 at para 33.

28 Re G (A Minor) (Enforcement of Access Abroad) [1993] Fam 216, [1993] 2 FCR 485, [1993] 1 FLR 669, approved by the Supreme Court in Re C and another (Children) (International Centre for Family Law, Policy and Practice Intervening) [2018] UKSC 8, [2019] AC 1, [2018] 2 FCR 733, [2018] 1 FLR 861 at para 33.

29 For a limited summary of BIIA, see **Chapter 1**.

30 [2019] 1 FLR 302.

'*with whom it is important for the child to maintain a personal relationship*', including the child's grandparents.

2.47 In *A v C (Hague: Rights of Access)*[31] it was held that the principle in *Valcheva v Babanarakis*[32] also applied in the context of HC80 and that, for the purposes of Art 21, 'rights of access' include rights not contained in a court order. The significance of the decision is that it enables foreign applicants to make an application for contact with a child through the Central Authority under Art 21 of HC80. Such applicants are entitled to legal aid which is not means-tested or merits-tested. By contrast, a person pursuing a freestanding application for contact under CA 1989, s 8 (not via the Central Authority) may not be entitled to legal aid at all under the current regulations.

31 [2018] EWHC 2048 (Fam), [2019] FLR 429.
32 *Valcheva v Babanarakis (Case 315/17)* [2019] 1 FLR 302.

CHAPTER 3

Wrongful removals and retentions and rights of custody

Content at a Glance:

A. WRONGFUL REMOVALS AND RETENTIONS

Overview

3.1 In order to obtain a summary return order under Art 12 of the 1980 Hague Convention[1] ('HC80') the applicant must demonstrate that the child has been subject to either a wrongful removal or a wrongful retention[2]. Article 3 provides that the removal or retention of a child will be considered wrongful where:

> '(a) it is in breach of rights of custody attributed to a person, an institution or any other body, either jointly or alone, under the law of the State in which the child was habitually resident immediately before the removal or retention; and
>
> (b) at the time of the removal or retention, those rights were actually exercised, either jointly or alone, or would have been so exercised but for the removal or retention.'

If the removal or retention or the child is wrongful and proceedings have been issued within a year, Art 12 of HC80 provides that the court 'shall' order the return of the child forthwith (subject to the exceptions in Art 13). Exceptionally, a return may be to a third state (not the state of habitual residence): see *O v O* [2014] 1 FLR 1405, considered in *Re B (A Child) (Abduction: Habitual Residence)* [2020] EWCA Civ 1187.

3.2 The position can be summarised by the following graphic:

3.3 It is for the courts of the Requested State to determine whether a removal or retention is 'wrongful' (*Re J (A Minor) (Abduction: Custody Rights)*[3]). In order to answer this question, the court will need to determine:

(a) the State of habitual residence of the child at the date of the alleged wrongful removal or retention: see **Chapter 4**;

(b) whether the removal or retention was in breach of rights of custody in that State: see para **3.19** below; and

1 The Convention on the Civil Aspects of International Child Abduction signed at the Hague on 25 October 1980.

2 If the child has not been subject to a wrongful removal or retention, it may still be possible to secure a summary return by making an application under the inherent jurisdiction or applying for a specific issue order under Children Act 1989, s 8: see **Chapter 9**.

3 [1990] 2 AC 562 (per Lord Donaldson MR in the Court of Appeal at 568F and Lord Brandon of Oakbrook at 578A), [1991] FCR 129, [1990] 2 FLR 442.

(c) whether those rights of custody were actually exercised or would have been but for the wrongful removal: see para **3.80** below.

Removals and retentions are single events

3.4 A removal or a retention under HC80 is a single event which occurs on a specific occasion, as opposed to a continuing state of affairs: *Re H; Re S (Minors) (Abduction: Custody Rights)*[4]; *Re C (Children) (International Centre for Family Law, Policy and Practice intervening)*[5] at para 51(v); Re *H (Abduction: Retention in non-Contracting State)*[6]. It is a common misconception that a child who has been wrongfully removed from one State will thereafter be wrongfully retained (in a continuing sense) in the State to which they have been removed. This is not the case.

3.5 A child who has been removed from country A to country B may be the subject of either a wrongful removal or a wrongful retention but cannot be the subject of both: *Re H; Re S (Minors) (Abduction: Custody Rights)*[7]. It is necessary for the court to identify when a wrongful removal or retention has taken place in order to ensure that the application for a summary return order has been issued within a year of that date: *Re H; Re S (Minors) (Abduction: Custody Rights)*[8]. If the application is issued after a year has elapsed from the date of the wrongful removal or retention, the court will need to consider whether the child has become settled in their new environment: see **Chapter 8**.

Case Summary: *Re H; Re S (Minors) (Abduction: Custody Rights)*[9]

Facts:

Two cases involving children who were removed from Canada before HC80 came into force in that jurisdiction. This meant that the removals could not be wrongful as HC80 did not apply at the time. It was argued however that the continuing failure to return the children amounted to wrongful retentions.

Held by the House of Lords:

Removal and retention under HC80 were events occurring on a specific occasion and were mutually exclusive concepts. The children had been the subjects of removals rather than retentions. As the removals occurred before the Convention came into force, the court had no jurisdiction to make a return order.

4 [1991] 2 AC 476, [1991] 3 WLR 68, [1991] 2 FLR 262, [1992] FCR 45.
5 [2018] UKSC 8, [2019] AC 1, [2018] 2 FCR 733, [2018] 1 FLR 861.
6 [2019] EWCA Civ 672, [2019] 3 WLR 1143, [2019] 3 FCR 113, [2019] 2 FLR 563.
7 [1991] 2 AC 476, [1991] 3 WLR 68, [1991] 2 FLR 262, [1992] FCR 45.
8 [1991] 2 AC 476, [1991] 3 WLR 68, [1991] 2 FLR 262, [1992] FCR 45.
9 [1991] 2 AC 476, [1991] 3 WLR 68, [1991] 2 FLR 262, [1992] FCR 45.

3.6 It may not be possible to identify the exact date on which a wrongful removal or, more particularly, a wrongful retention has taken place. In such circumstances, it will be sufficient for the court to find that it has occurred not later than a particular date: *Re C (Children) (International Centre for Family Law, Policy and Practice intervening)*[10] at para 51(v).

Removals and retentions are international

3.7 A wrongful removal for the purposes of HC80 can only occur is a child is taken out (ie across the frontier) of the State of its habitual residence. The Convention is not concerned with removals from a parent which occur within the borders of the child's State of habitual residence[11]. The removal of a child from one part of the UK to another does not give rise to an application under HC80, even if the removal is to a part of the UK with a different legal system (such as a removal from England and Wales to Scotland or Northern Ireland)[12].

3.8 A wrongful retention occurs when a child has been removed lawfully from the State of habitual residence and subsequently retained wrongfully (eg in breach of a court order or contrary to an agreement between the parents)[13]. A removal or retention will not be wrongful under HC80 if, by the date it occurs, the child has ceased to be habitually resident in the State from which it was removed and become habitually resident in the State where the application is lodged: *Re C (Children) (International Centre for Family Law, Policy and Practice intervening*[14].

Removals and retentions in non-Hague States

3.9 It is possible for a child to be wrongfully removed to or wrongfully retained in a country that is not a Contracting State to HC80[15]. Where that occurs and the child is then brought to an HC80 Contracting State, the courts have jurisdiction to order a summary return to the jurisdiction where the child was habitually resident immediately prior to the wrongful removal or retention which took place in the non-Contracting State[16].

10 [2018] UKSC 8, [2019] AC 1, [2018] 2 FCR 733, [2018] 1 FLR 861.

11 *Re H; Re S (Minors) (Abduction: Custody Rights)* [1991] 2 AC 476, [1991] 3 WLR 68, [1991] 2 FLR 262, [1992] FCR 45.

12 In such cases, if a court order has been made, it may be possible to seek recognition and enforcement of the order under Family Law Act 1986, Part I, Chapter V.

13 *Re H; Re S (Minors) (Abduction: Custody Rights)* [1991] 2 AC 476, [1991] 3 WLR 68, [1991] 2 FLR 262, [1992] FCR 45.

14 [2018] UKSC 8, [2019] AC 1, [2018] 1 FLR 861.

15 *Re H (Abduction: Retention in Non-Contracting State)* [2019] EWCA Civ 672, [2019] 3 WLR 1143, [2019] 3 FCR 113, [2019] 2 FLR 563.

16 *Re H (Abduction: Retention in Non-Contracting State) [2019]* EWCA Civ 672, [2019] 3 WLR 1143, [2019] 3 FCR 113, [2019] 2 FLR 563.

Case Summary: Re H *(Abduction: Retention in Non-Contracting State)*[17]

> **Facts:**
>
> The parties lived in Australia and went on holiday to Uganda with the child. M refused to return to Australia and travelled instead to England.
> F applied under HC80 for a summary return to Australia. M argued that HC80 did not apply as the retention had taken place in Uganda which was not a Contracting State.
> Mostyn J rejected the argument and held that HC80 applies even in cases where the retention takes place in a non-Contracting State.
>
> **Held by the Court of Appeal:**
>
> Appeal dismissed. Decision upheld. Article 4 of HC80 provides that the Convention applies to any child habitually resident in a Contracting State immediately prior to the removal or retention. Therefore there is no need for a removal to be to a Contracting State or a retention to take place in a Contracting State in order for it to be wrongful.

Repudiatory retention

3.10 Where it has been agreed or authorised by a court that a parent can take a child to another jurisdiction for a defined period (for example, a year), and before the expiry of that period the parent decides that they do not intend to return the child, the question arises as to whether such decision amounts to a breach of rights of custody and therefore a wrongful retention.

3.11 The issue is important for three reasons:

(a) If a *decision* to retain a child beyond the end of an authorised period amounts to a wrongful retention, the left-behind parent can thereafter issue proceedings immediately without waiting for the authorised period to elapse.

(b) For the purposes of Art 12 of HC80, the 12-month period within which (subject to Art 13) the court is bound to order the summary return of the child starts to run from the date of the wrongful retention. The date of expiry of an authorised period of retention will not be material for these purposes if a wrongful retention has occurred on an earlier date.

(c) In cases where the authorised period of retention is relatively long (for example, a year or more) the child may cease to be habitually resident[18] in

17 [2019] EWCA Civ 672, [2019] 3 WLR 1143, [2019] 3 FCR 113, [2019] 2 FLR 563.
18 For habitual residence, see **Chapter 4**.

the State from which it was removed by the time that period expires. In such circumstances a failure to return the child at the conclusion of the period will not be a *wrongful* retention under HC80.

3.12 The issue was considered by the Supreme Court in *Re C and another (Children) (International Centre for Family Law, Policy and Practice intervening)*[19]. It was held (by a majority) that where, before the expiry or an agreed period of absence, the travelling parent denied or 'repudiated' the custody rights of the left-behind parent by unilaterally deciding where the child would live, this could amount to a repudiatory retention.

3.13 A repudiatory retention normally requires two elements to be established (*Re C* at para 51):

- A subjective intention not to honour the agreed arrangement

- Some objectively identifiable act or statement which manifests the repudiation of custody rights

3.14 A purely internal, unmanifested thought by the travelling parent does not amount to a repudiatory retention. It is not necessary, however, for the repudiation to be communicated to the other parent (*Re C* at para 51). The exact date of the repudiation does not need to be identified (*Re C* at para 51).

Case Summary: *Re C and another (Children) (International Centre for Family Law, Policy and Practice intervening)*[20]

Facts:

In May 2015 with the consent of F, M brought two children from Australia to England for an 8-week holiday when the marriage was in difficulty. F agreed to a 4-week extension of the stay and then agreed to M and the children remaining in England until the end of June 2016.

19 [2018] UKSC 8, [2019] AC 1, [2018] 2 FCR 733, [2018] 1 FLR 861.
20 [2018] UKSC 8, [2019] AC 1, [2018] 2 FCR 733, [2018] 1 FLR 861.

M resigned from her job in Australia and enrolled the children in pre-school in England. In November 2015, without informing F, she applied for British citizenship for the children. She stated in the application that the marriage had irretrievably broken down, and that she could not return to Australia. M's case was that by April 2016 she had decided not to return.

At first instance the Judge found that (a) in November 2015, M did not have an intention to remain in the UK, and (b) by the end of the authorised period in June 2016 the children were no longer habitually resident in Australia and therefore there was no wrongful retention.

The CA allowed the appeal on the basis that the Judge had not addressed the evidence of 'anticipatory retention' on a date earlier than June 2016.

Appeal allowed by the Supreme Court:

(1) The Hague Convention cannot be invoked if, by the date of an alleged wrongful removal or retention, the child has become habitually resident in the State where the request for return is made.

(2) The concept of repudiatory retention was possible in law. The travelling parent must (a) intend not to return the children to the State of habitual residence, and additionally (b) manifest a denial, or repudiation, of the rights of the left-behind parent by some objectively identifiable act or statement, or combination of such. However, that did not mean that the repudiation had to be communicated to the left-behind parent.

(3) There was insufficient evidence to overturn the Judge's finding that, in November 2015, M did not intend to remain in the UK. If she had had such an intention in November, the application to the immigration authorities would have been capable of amounting to an objective manifestation of her repudiation. Even though M gave evidence that, by the end of April 2016, she had resolved not to return, M's internal thinking could not, without an objective act, amount to a repudiatory retention. There was no basis for criticising the Judge's decision that, by June 2016, the children were habitually resident in England.

3.15 In *Re I-L (Children) (1996 Hague Child Protection Convention: Inherent Jurisdiction)*[21] it was held by the Court of Appeal that an application to the court during the course of an agreed time-limited stay could amount to a repudiatory retention, although the judge had been entitled to conclude that this was not so on the facts of the case.

21 [2019] EWCA Civ 1956, [2020] 1 FCR 35.

Case Summary: *Re I-L (Children) (1996 Hague Child Protection Convention: Inherent Jurisdiction)*[22]

Facts:

The family was an international family, moving between Russia, the UK and the USA.

M proposed that the children should be with F in England for three weeks until the end of May 2019 and then with her in England for four months from June. M then indicated that she planned to move to the USA from October. On 31 May 2019, F commenced proceedings in the family court in E&W seeking a child arrangements order. M argued that issuing proceedings amounted to a repudiatory retention.

The judge decided that F's actions did not amount to a repudiatory retention. Commencing proceedings in England by F had been 'reactive' to M's proposal to move with the children to the USA. The judge concluded: '*I consider that the fact of his application to his local family court evinces a desire to prevent sudden change in the lives of the children, to achieve stability via a legal process. He was not "insisting on unilaterally deciding where the child will live". He was not demonstrating a wish not to honour "the temporary nature of the stay abroad". He was not setting "about making [the temporary stay] indefinite, often putting down the child's roots in the destination State with a view to making it impossible to move him home". He was not acting in order to prevent a return to Russia. He had just been informed, by inference, that M had no wish to return to Russia*'.

Held by the Court of Appeal:

Appeal dismissed. Peter Jackson LJ held that '*the making of an application to court might of itself amount to a breach of rights of custody. However, the judge carefully analysed the circumstances of this case and, in my view, reached a conclusion that was open to him on the evidence and which is supported by his conclusion as to the father's intentions. There is no basis on which this court could interfere with that determination*'.

3.16 In *Re G-E (Children: Hague Convention 1980: Repudiatory Retention and Habitual Residence)*[23], M and the children arrived in the UK from Australia on 21 July 2017 on six-month return tickets. In December 2017, M instructed solicitors in England (but did not issue proceedings) and, on 27 March 2018, M told F that she did not intend to return to Australia. The judge found that M had not made up her mind about whether to return to Australia in December

22 [2019] EWCA Civ 1956, [2020] 1 FCR 35.
23 [2019] EWCA Civ 283, [2019] 1 FCR 908, [2019] 2 FLR 17.

2017 but had '*both options clearly in her mind*'. Her thoughts were '*internal unmanifested considerations*'. The intention not to return to Australia was formed in mid-March 2018, by which time the children were habitually resident in England and Wales. The decision was upheld by the Court of Appeal.

Burden and standard of proof

3.17 The burden of proof is on the applicant to establish that there has been a wrongful removal or retention. Once that has been demonstrated, the burden then falls upon the respondent to satisfy the court that the child should not be summarily returned on one of the grounds in Art 13 (or, if appropriate, Art 12(2) of HC80): *Re P (A Child) (Abduction: Custody Rights)*[24].

3.18 The standard of proof is the ordinary civil standard, the balance of probabilities: *C v H (Abduction: Consent)*[25].

B. RIGHTS OF CUSTODY

Relevant law is the law of the State of the child's habitual residence

3.19 The court must consider whether the removal or retention of the child is in breach of *relevant* rights of custody. The relevant rights for the purposes of Art 3 are those which arise under the law of the State in which the child was habitually resident *immediately prior to* the removal or retention relied upon for the purposes of the application. The meaning of habitual residence is considered in **Chapter 4**.

3.20 For the purposes of establishing the wrongfulness of a removal or retention, it is *not* relevant to consider the habitual residence of the child at the date of the application or the date of the hearing.

3.21 Some Contracting States – Spain, for example – apply the personal law of the child to determine issues of parental rights. In such cases, as is explained by Professor Pérez-Vera at para 68 of the Explanatory Report to HC80, the court may thus be required to consider a parent's rights under English law in order to decide their rights under the law of the home State: see, for example, *Re JB (Child Abduction: Rights of Custody: Spain)*[26].

24 [2004] EWCA Civ 971, [2005] Fam 293, [2004] 2 FCR 698, [2004] 2 FLR 1057 at para 22.
25 [2009] EWHC 2660 (Fam), [2010] 1 FLR 225 at paras 9 and 10.
26 [2003] EWHC 2130 (Fam), [2004] 1 FLR 976. It is noteworthy that, in *Re K (Children) (Rights of Custody: Spain)* [2009] EWCA Civ 986, the court reached a different conclusion about Spanish law (on different expert evidence) from that arrived at in *Re JB*. In the latter case, it was held that the Spanish courts would be likely to reject English law of parental responsibility as discriminatory against unmarried fathers.

Definition of 'rights of custody' under the Convention

3.22 Article 5 of HC80 provides a partial definition of rights of custody as follows:

> '"rights of custody" shall include rights relating to the care of the person of the child and, in particular, the right to determine the child's place of residence.'

3.23 It can be seen that two specific categories of right fall within the definition:

Rights relating to the care of the person of the child

The right to determine the child's place of residence

The definition is deliberately wide and leaves it open to courts to determine that other rights – not within these two categories – amount to rights of custody.

3.24 Article 5 must be read in to Art 3 and may extend the concept of custody rights beyond the ordinarily understood domestic approach: *C v C (Abduction: Rights of Custody)*[27]; see also *Re F (A Minor) (Abduction: Custody Rights Abroad)*[28].

3.25 Rights of custody can be contrasted with 'rights of access'. Article 5 of HC80 provides that the latter '*shall include the right to take a child for a limited period of time to place other than the child's habitual residence*'.

Autonomous concept

3.26 Rights of custody is an '*autonomous*' concept for the purposes of HC80. This means that it is not necessary to demonstrate that a person has '*custody*' of a child under domestic law in order to establish that they hold '*rights of custody*' for the purposes of the Convention. This was underlined in the Report of the Second Special Commission which reviewed the operation of HC80 in 1993:

> 'The key concepts which determine the scope of the Convention are not dependant for their meaning on any single legal system. Thus the expression "rights of custody", for example, does not coincide with any particular concept of custody in domestic law, but draws its meaning from the definitions, structure and purpose of the Convention.'

27 [1989] 1 WLR 654 at 663, [1989] FCR 197, [1989] 1 FLR 403.
28 [1995] Fam 224, [1995] 2 FLR 31.

The same point was made by Lord Donaldson in *C v C (Abduction: Rights of Custody)*[29]; see also *Re F (A Minor) (Abduction: Custody Rights Abroad)*[30].

Case Summary: *Re F (A Minor) (Abduction: Custody Rights Abroad)*[31]

Facts:

In July 1994, M removed the child from Colorado, USA, where he was habitually resident, to England. Under Colorado law, in the absence of a court order each parent had equal and separate rights of custody. Each parent could act independently of the other and there was no prohibition on removal of the child from the jurisdiction by one parent against the wishes of the other if not prevented by court order. It was argued by M that, as the removal of the child was not contrary to Colorado law, it was not wrongful.

Held by the Court of Appeal:

(1) It is the duty of the court to construe HC80 in a purposive way to make it work.

(2) 'Rights of custody' within the Convention are broader than an order of the court; parents have rights in respect of their children without the need to have them declared by court order.

(3) The removal of the child interfered with the rights of custody of F, in that he was prevented from exercising them in the USA, and was therefore a breach of such rights under Art 3, notwithstanding that the removal was not in breach of Colorado law.

Who can hold rights of custody?

3.27 Art 3(a) of HC80 provides that rights of custody may be attributed to:

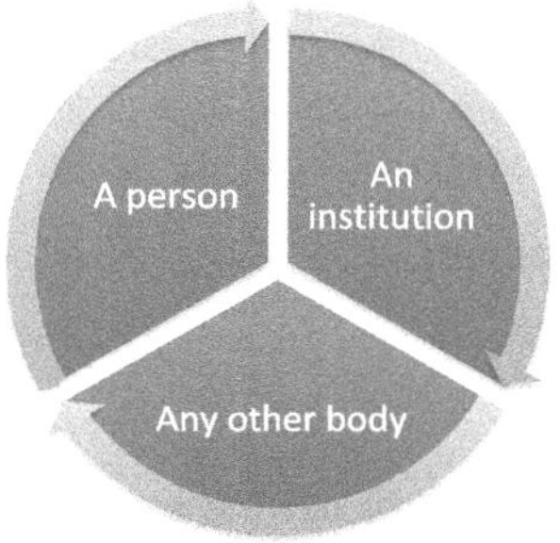

29 [1989] 1 WLR 654 at 663, [1989] FCR 197, [1989] 1 FLR 403.
30 [1995] Fam 224, [1995] 2 FLR 31.
31 [1995] Fam 224, [1995] 2 FLR 31.

3.28 Moreover, rights of custody may be held:

- jointly; or
- alone.

Rights of care/custody and joint custody

3.29 A parent who has a legal right to the day-to-day care of the child (pursuant to a court order or otherwise) has a right of custody for the purposes of HC80: *Re D (A Child) (Abduction: Rights of Custody)*[32]. The same is true if a parent holds joint or shared custody or where bundle of rights and responsibilities in relation to the child inhere in both parents: *ibid*[33].

Rights of access

3.30 A parent who *merely* holds 'rights of access' does not have rights of custody under HC80: *Re D (A Child) (Abduction: Rights of Custody)*[34]. This is so even where the rights of access are very extensive: *Hunter v Murrow*[35].

3.31 It is, however, possible that a parent with rights of access will also have other rights – such as parental responsibility – which do amount to rights of custody: *Re D (A Child) (Abduction: Rights of Custody)*[36].

Case Summary: *Hunter v Murrow*[37]

Facts:

M removed child from New Zealand to England without F's knowledge or consent. F had been having regular visiting contact twice a week but did not have parental responsibility. The NZ court determined under Art 15 of HC80 that F's contact meant that he had 'rights of custody'.

F applied to the English court for a summary return order. His application was dismissed by Singer J on the basis that – contrary to the NZ decision – rights of contact were not rights of custody under the Convention.

Held by the Court of Appeal:

Appeal dismissed.

32 [2006] UKHL 51, [2007] 1 AC 619, [2007] 1 FCR 1, [2007] 1 FLR 961 at para 29.
33 [2006] UKHL 51, [2007] 1 AC 619, [2007] 1 FCR 1, [2007] 1 FLR 961; *NT v LT (Return to Russia)* [2020] EWHC 1903 (Fam).
34 [2006] UKHL 51, [2007] 1 AC 619, [2007] 1 FCR 1, [2007] 1 FLR 961.
35 [2005] EWCA Civ 976, [2005] 3 FCR 1, [2005] 2 FLR 1119.
36 [2006] UKHL 51, [2007] 1 AC 619, [2007] 1 FCR 1, [2007] 1 FLR 961.
37 [2005] EWCA Civ 976, [2005] 3 FCR 1, [2005] 2 FLR 1119.

It was for the courts of the Requested State (ie England) not the Requesting State (ie NZ) to determine whether an applicant had rights of custody. That question involved considering:

(1) what rights the applicant enjoyed under the law of the Requesting State; and then

(2) determining whether those rights were rights of custody under the autonomous law of HC80.

Despite the contrary view of the NZ courts, rights of access were not rights of custody.

Where a father does not hold parental responsibility, particular regard should be paid to 'the sharing arrangements' in operation at the date of the child's removal.

Rights of veto

3.32 A right to veto the removal of a child to another jurisdiction amounts to a right of custody: *Re D (A Child) (Abduction: Rights of Custody)*[38]; *Abbott v Abbott*[39].

Case Summary: *Re P (Abduction: Custody Rights)*[40]

Facts:

M removed the child from New York to England without F's consent. Under a court order, F had been granted rights of visitation (not custody). The order also provided that neither party could remove the child from the State of New York without the prior written consent of the other party or a court order.

Held by the Court of Appeal:

The '*ne exeat*' clause in the court order conferred a right of custody upon F as it gave him the right to determine the child's place of residence. The decision was later approved by the House of Lords in *Re D (A Child) (Abduction: Rights of Custody)*[41].

3.33 In some cases, the lack of a right of veto to the removal of a child under domestic law will mean that the left-behind parent does not have rights of custody

38 [2006] UKHL 51, [2007] 1 AC 619, [2007] 1 FCR 1, [2007] 1 FLR 961.
39 560 U.S. 1 (2010).
40 [2004] EWCA Civ 971, [2004] 2 FCR 698, [2004] 2 FLR 1057.
41 [2006] UKHL 51, [2007] 1 AC 619, [2007] 1 FCR 1, [2007] 1 FLR 961.

under HC80: see, for example, *Re D (A Child) (Abduction: Rights of Custody)*[42]. In other cases, the left-behind parent may hold other rights under domestic law (such as equal custody) which are sufficient to confer rights of custody under HC80 even though the parent has no domestic law right to veto a removal. In *Re F (A Minor) (Abduction: Custody Rights Abroad)*[43], the mother was entitled as a matter of Colorado law to remove the child from the jurisdiction without the consent of the father, as each parent was entitled to exercise their custodial rights independently of the other. Nevertheless, it was held that the father held equal and separate rights of custody to the mother under Colorado law and that the removal of the child breached those rights for the purposes of HC80, despite being lawful in Colorado.

Case Summary: *Re D (A Child) (Abduction: Rights of Custody)*[44]

Facts:

In December 2002, M brought the child (then aged 4) from Romania to England without F's consent. In February 2003, F made an application for the child's return under HC80. Each side instructed an expert to report as to the effect under Romanian law of court orders in existence at the date of removal. The experts disagreed and the English court requested the Romanian court to determine the issue pursuant to Art 15 of HC80. In June 2005 the final Court of Appeal in Romania ruled that the removal was not wrongful. The English court directed further evidence from a single joint expert ('SJE') who reached the opposite conclusion from the Romanian court. In February 2006 the court ordered the child to be returned to Romania. M's appeal to the Court of Appeal was dismissed. She appealed to the House of Lords (by the time of this appeal, the child was aged 7).

Held by the House of Lords:

The absence of a '*ne exeat*' clause in the court order meant – as the Romanian court had ruled – that F did not have rights of custody, as he did not have the right to determine the child's place of residence. The court had been wrong to direct evidence from an SJE when it had requested a declaration under Art 15 as to the wrongfulness of the removal. The court should only decline to follow an Art 15 declaration in limited circumstances (see paras **3.50–3.52** and **3.73–7.76** below).

This case is also considered in detail in **Chapter 7** as it is a leading authority on the importance of hearing the voice of the child in HC80 proceedings.

42 [2006] UKHL 51, [2007] 1 AC 619, [2007] 1 FCR 1, [2007] 1 FLR 961.
43 [1995] Fam 224, [1995] 2 FLR 31. See also *NT v LT (Return to Russia)* [2020] EWHC 1903 (Fam).
44 [2006] UKHL 51, [2007] 1 AC 619, [2007] 1 FCR 1, [2007] 1 FLR 961.

3.34 A *potential* right of veto – ie the right to go to court to seek orders to prevent a removal – does not amount to a right of custody: *Re D (A Child) (Abduction: Rights of Custody)*[45].

3.35 A right to be 'informed' or 'consulted' about a proposed removal from the jurisdiction (without a right of veto) is not a right of custody: *Re V-B (Abduction: Custody Rights)*[46].

Inchoate rights of custody

3.36 In *Re K (A Child) (Reunite International Child Abduction Centre intervening)*[47] it was held that in limited circumstances it is possible for a person to hold 'inchoate' rights of custody for the purposes of HC80, even though they do not have any formal legal rights in relation to the child.

3.37 In *Re K* the child had lived with his grandmother in Lithuania from the time of his birth until the age of 7. When he was aged 1 the mother had moved to live in Northern Ireland with her partner. The child had not seen the mother in that period apart from once when he was aged 20 months. When he was aged 7 the mother travelled to Lithuania and removed the child to live with her in Northern Ireland, using force to achieve her aims.

3.38 The Supreme Court (by a majority) allowed the grandmother's appeal, holding that she had inchoate rights of custody. In order to preserve the essential distinction between rights of custody and rights of access, Baroness Hale (at para 59) emphasised that inchoate rights could only arise in limited circumstances:

45 [2006] UKHL 51, [2007] 1 AC 619, [2007] 1 FCR 1, [2007] 1 FLR 961 at para 38.
46 [1999] 2 FCR 371, [1999] 2 FLR 192.
47 [2014] UKSC 29, [2014] AC 1401, [2014] 2 FCR 231, [2014] 2 FLR 629.

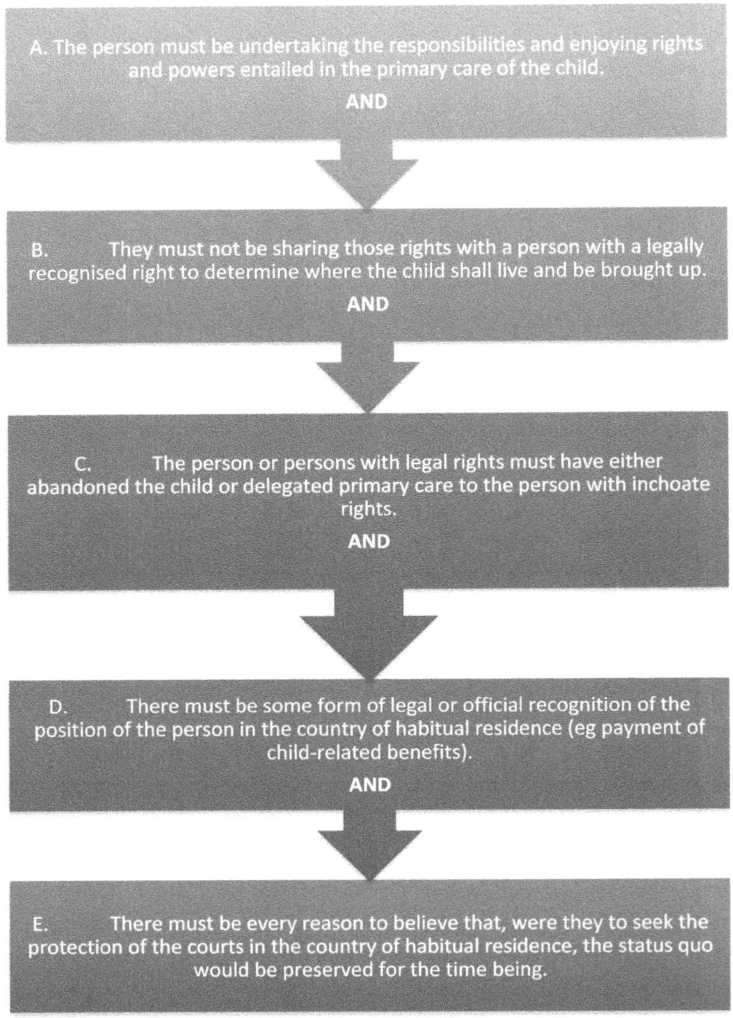

Rights of custody in the court

3.39 There are a number of cases in which a parent without rights of custody has made an application to court but, before the application has been determined, the other parent has abducted the child to another jurisdiction. In those cases, the question arises as to whether the court holds rights of custody under HC80.

3.40 The leading authority on this issue is *Re H (A Minor) (Abduction: Rights of Custody)*[48]. The father had applied to the Irish court for guardianship and access orders but, before the proceedings could be determined, the mother removed the children to England. The House of Lords held that a court could

48 [2000] 2 AC 291, [2000] 1 FCR 225, [2000] 1 FLR 374.

be an 'other body' under Art 3 of HC80 and thus possess rights of custody so as to found an application for summary return. A parent was entitled to rely upon rights of custody in the court in support of his own application under HC80. The Court further held *obiter dicta* that:

(a) The application before the court must raise matters of custody within the meaning of HC80.

(b) Generally the court will become vested with rights of custody at the time the application is served on the other party.

(c) In cases where interim orders are made before service, the court will acquire rights of custody at the time the order is made: see also *A v B (Abduction: Rights of Custody: Declaration of Wrongful Removal)*[49], where an ex parte order was held to vest the court with rights of custody.

(d) Once seised, the court's jurisdiction will be treated as 'continuously invoked' until the application is disposed of, unless the proceedings are stayed or some equivalent action taken.

3.41 In *X County Council v B (Abduction: Rights of Custody in the Court)*[50] it was held that a court seised of care proceedings had rights of custody.

3.42 It is possible for a court which holds rights of custody to acquiesce in the retention of a child if it has the opportunity to make orders requiring the child to remain in the country of habitual residence but does not do so: see *NM v SM (Rights of custody in foreign court; acquiescence by that court)*[51].

Case Summary: *NM v SM (Rights of custody in foreign court; acquiescence by that court)*[52]

Facts:

After F issued and served proceedings in Ireland, M removed the child to England. The removal was wrongful as it was in breach of rights of custody in the court, even though F himself did not have rights of custody at the time. M returned to Ireland with the child and attended a hearing. At that

49 [2008] EWHC 2524 (Fam), [2009] 1 FLR 1253.
50 [2009] EWHC 2635 (Fam), [2010] 1 FLR 1197.
51 [2017] EWHC 1294 (Fam); practitioners should be cautious about placing too much reliance upon this decision. In a recent unreported case involving very similar facts, the trial judge declined to hold that the Irish court had acquiesced in a wrongful removal, as the court had been advised that the father intended to make an application to the English court for the return of the child to Ireland under HC80 and had made interim welfare orders in the knowledge that such an application was to be pursued. The court made a summary return order and permission to appeal was refused by the Court of Appeal.
52 [2017] EWHC 1294 (Fam).

hearing the court refused F's oral application for an order restraining M from removing the child from Ireland; M accordingly returned to England.

Held by Holman J:

Although the original removal was wrongful, the Irish court had acquiesced in that removal by refusing to make an order preventing further removal when it had the opportunity to do so. M had returned the child to Ireland following the original removal and thus the purpose of the Hague Convention had been fulfilled; F could not continue to rely upon that removal. The later removal was not wrongful as it had been authorised by the Irish court.

Rights falling short of rights of custody

3.43 In the following cases the applicant fathers were held not to have rights of custody:

Case	Father's rights
Re J (A Minor) (Abduction: Custody Rights)[53]	F lived with M in Australia and shared de facto care of the child without any legal 'right'.
S v H (Abduction: Access Rights)[54]	F had rights of access and a right under Italian law to 'watch over' the child's education and living conditions.
Re V-B (Abduction: Custody Rights)[55]	F had rights of contact under Dutch law and the right to be 'informed' / 'consulted' about where the children would live.
Hunter v Murrow[56]	F had the right to have extensive contact with the child several times a week in New Zealand.
Re D (A Child) (Abduction: Rights of Custody)[57]	F had the right under Romanian law to have contact with the child and 'watch over' the child's upbringing.
A v H[58]	F had gone through a Muslim ceremony of marriage which was a 'non-marriage' under English law and had registered the birth of the child without the attendance of the mother, believing this gave him PR.

C. RIGHTS OF CUSTODY UNDER THE LAW OF ENGLAND AND WALES

3.44 As a matter of English and Welsh domestic law, the following confer rights of custody for the purposes of HC80:

53 [1990] 2 AC 562, [1991] FCR 129, [1990] 2 FLR 442.
54 [1998] Fam 49, [1997] 3 FCR 450, [1997] 1 FLR 971.
55 [1999] 2 FCR 371, [1999] 2 FLR 192.
56 [2005] EWCA Civ 976, [2005] 3 FCR 1, [2005] 2 FLR 1119.
57 [2006] UKHL 51, [2007] 1 AC 619, [2007] 1 FCR 1, [2007] 1 FLR 961.
58 [2009] EWHC 636 (Fam), [2009] 3 FCR 95, [2010] 1 FLR 1.

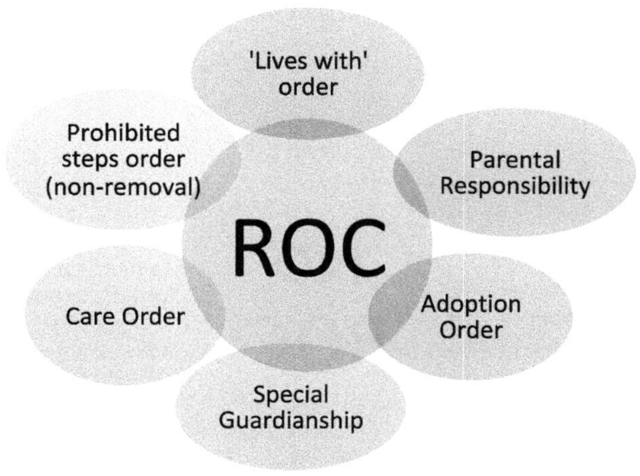

3.45 One reason why parental responsibility confers rights of custody is that it gives a person the right to determine the child's place of residence: see *Re W (Minors) (Abduction: Father's Rights); Re B (A Minor) (Abduction: Father's Rights)*[59], per Hale J. Section 1 of the Child Abduction Act 1984 makes it a criminal offence to remove a child without the consent of the child's mother, or the child's father if he has parental responsibility. A right to veto the removal of a child to another jurisdiction amounts to a right of custody: *Re D (A Child) (Abduction: Rights of Custody)*[60]; *Abbott v Abbott*[61]: see also para **3.32** above. It is not a criminal offence under English law to retain a child outside the jurisdiction without the consent of a person with parental responsibility. Nevertheless, such a retention would be wrongful under HC80, as two parents who share parental responsibility share '*all the rights, duties, powers, responsibilities and authority which by law a parent of a child has in relation to the child and his property*'[62]. Such rights amount to rights of custody.

3.46 It should not be assumed that concepts in other jurisdictions similar to parental responsibility – for example, 'parental authority' – *necessarily* confer rights of custody on a left-behind parent, although it is likely that they will do so: see, for example, *BK v NK*[63] which concerns 'parental authority' under Polish law. Practitioners need to focus on the precise nature of the rights in question and, in particular, upon whether these include the right to veto the removal of the child.

59 [1999] Fam 1, [1998] 2 FCR 549, [1998] 2 FLR 146.
60 [2006] UKHL 51, [2007] 1 AC 619, [2007] 1 FCR 1, [2007] 1 FLR 961.
61 560 U.S. 1 (2010).
62 Children Act 1989, s 3(1).
63 [2016] EWHC 2496 (Fam).

3.47 The following do not confer rights of custody as a matter of English law:

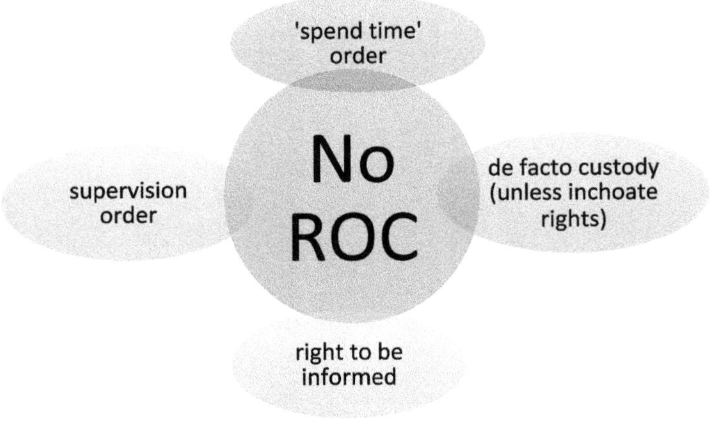

D. DETERMINING RIGHTS OF CUSTODY

The courts in the Requested State make the decision

3.48 In order to determine whether an applicant has a right of custody, the court must engage in a two-stage process (see *Re D (A Child) (Abduction: Rights of Custody)*[64]; *Re P (A Child) (Abduction: Custody Rights)*[65]; *Hunter v Murrow*[66]):

3.49 Therefore, an expert instructed to report about rights held in another jurisdiction should identify the relevant rights without expressing an opinion as to whether these amount to rights of custody. This is not a matter for expert evidence, but a point for the English court to determine: *Re F (A Minor) (Abduction: Custody Rights Abroad)*[67]; *Re P (A Child) (Abduction: Custody Rights)*[68].

64 [2006] UKHL 51, [2007] 1 AC 619, [2007] 1 FCR 1, [2007] 1 FLR 961.
65 [2004] EWCA Civ 971, [2005] Fam 293, [2004] 2 FCR 698, [2004] 2 FLR 1057.
66 [2005] EWCA Civ 976, [2005] 3 FCR 1, [2005] 2 FLR 1119.
67 [1995] Fam 224, [1995] 2 FLR 31.
68 [2004] EWCA Civ 971, [2005] Fam 293, [2004] 2 FCR 698, [2004] 2 FLR 1057.

3.50 A decision by the courts of the Requesting State that a father's rights amount to rights of custody is not binding on the English court which must determine the question as a matter of English law, applying the autonomous law of the Convention: see *Re J (A Minor) (Abduction: Custody Rights)*[69]; *Re D (A Child) (Abduction: Rights of Custody)*[70]. That remains the case even if the decision is made following a request under Art 15 of HC80: *Hunter v Murrow*[71]; *Re D (A Child) (Abduction: Rights of Custody)*[72].

3.51 However, a foreign court is much better placed than an English court to understand the true meaning and effect of its own laws in Convention terms. The English court should only decline to follow an Art 15 ruling that rights do or do not amount to rights of custody if the foreign court's '*characterisation of the parent's rights is clearly out of line with the international understanding of the Convention's terms*': *Re D (A Child) (Abduction: Rights of Custody)*[73].

3.52 Save in exceptional circumstances such as cases of fraud or breach of natural justice, a determination by the courts of the Requesting States as to the content of a parent's rights under their domestic law is conclusive: *Re D (A Child) (Abduction: Rights of Custody)*[74].

How rights of custody may arise

3.53 Article 3 of HC80 provides that rights of custody may arise in one of the following ways: (i) by operation of law; (ii) by judicial or administrative decision; or (iii) by an agreement having legal effect.

69 [1990] 2 AC 562, [1991] FCR 129, [1990] 2 FLR 442.
70 [2006] UKHL 51, [2007] 1 AC 619, [2007] 1 FCR 1, [2007] 1 FLR 961.
71 [2005] EWCA Civ 976, [2005] 3 FCR 1, [2005] 2 FLR 1119.
72 [2006] UKHL 51, [2007] 1 AC 619, [2007] 1 FCR 1, [2007] 1 FLR 961.
73 [2006] UKHL 51, [2007] 1 AC 619, [2007] 1 FCR 1, [2007] 1 FLR 961 at para 44.
74 [2006] UKHL 51, [2007] 1 AC 619, [2007] 1 FCR 1, [2007] 1 FLR 961.

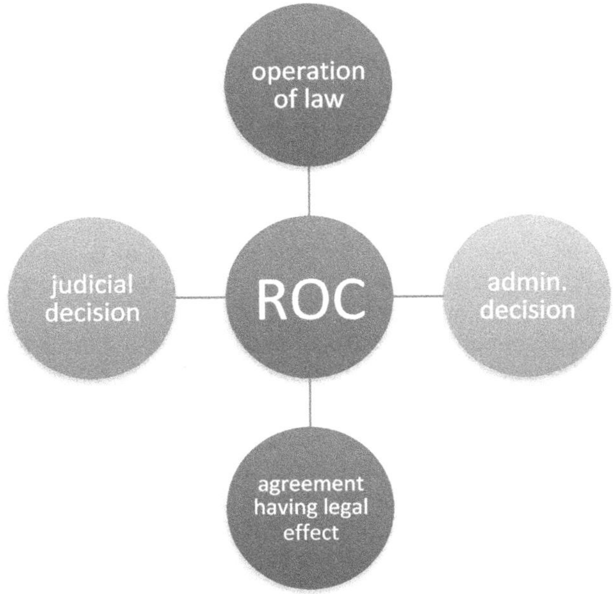

3.54 Article 3, however, does not provide an *exhaustive* list of the circumstances in which rights of custody may arise[75]. It has been held that they may also arise in other ways not specified by the article which can include 'inchoate rights': *Re K (A Child) (Reunite International Child Abduction Centre Intervening)*[76]: see para **3.36** above.

Operation of law

3.55 The removal or retention of a child will often take place around the same time as the breakdown of the parental relationship; in some cases it occurs before the parties have been to court or even consulted lawyers. One of the features of HC80 which makes it effective in combating child abduction is that, by contrast with other international instruments, it can be relied upon in cases where there has been no prior court involvement at all[77]. In the absence of a decision about custody or an agreement having legal effect, it will be necessary to consider whether relevant rights of custody arise by operation of law.

3.56 In order to answer this question, unless the respondent makes an admission as to the existence of rights of custody, it will be necessary to examine the law of the State in which the child was habitually resident immediately prior to the removal or retention in order to determine what rights the applicant parent

75 Explanatory Report to HC80 at para 67.
76 [2014] UKSC 29, [2014] AC 1401, [2014] 2 FCR 231, [2014] 2 FLR 629.
77 Explanatory Report to HC80 at para 68.

held under that law: *Re D (A Child) (Abduction: Rights of Custody)*[78]. For the means by which rights of custody may be established, see para **3.65** below.

Judicial decision

3.57 In some cases the applicant may rely upon a judicial decision as a basis for asserting that they hold relevant rights of custody.

3.58 It will usually be necessary to consider the terms of the decision in combination with information about the relevant law in order to determine whether the effect of the decision is such as to confer rights of custody upon the applicant.

3.59 For example, in *Re V-B (Abduction: Rights of Custody)*[79] there was a Dutch court order which conferred rights of custody on the father. The mother was granted sole parental responsibility but had given an undertaking to inform the father of '*any matter of importance relating to the children*' including specifically a decision to reside abroad. The Court of Appeal held that this right *to be consulted* about a removal without an associated right *to object* did not amount to a right of custody.

3.60 The issue for the court is whether the parental rights conferred by a judicial decision amount to rights of custody under the autonomous law of the Hague Convention; how such rights may be classified under the domestic law of the foreign State is not determinative of that issue: *Hunter v Murrow*[80].

3.61 It is not necessary for the judicial decision which confers custody rights to have been issued in the State of the child's habitual residence, or even for it to have been '*formally recognised*', so long as it contains '*certain minimum characteristics which are necessary for setting in motion the means by which it may be confirmed or recognised*' in the State of habitual residence[81].

Administrative decision

3.62 The inclusion of '*administrative decisions*' as a basis for asserting rights of custody reflects the fact that, in a number of jurisdictions, decisions about children are made by administrative bodies rather than the judiciary. It might be argued that a long-term foster parent has rights of custody as a result of an administrative decision taken by a local authority, but such an argument is unlikely to succeed as the legal '*rights*' in relation to the child would remain vested in the local authority holding a care order for the child.

78 [2006] UKHL 51, [2007] 1 AC 619, [2007] 1 FCR 1, [2007] 1 FLR 961.
79 [1999] 2 FCR 371, [1999] 2 FLR 192.
80 [2005] EWCA Civ 976, [2005] 3 FCR 1, [2005] 2 FLR 1119.
81 Explanatory Report to HC80 at para 69.

Agreement having legal effect

3.63 There are a number of cases decided in overseas jurisdictions in which the courts have considered the meaning of '*agreements having legal effect*' for the purposes of Art 3. These are discussed by the Supreme Court in *Re K (A Child) (Reunite International Child Abduction Centre Intervening)*[82]at para 34 onwards. New Zealand law, for example, expressly recognises parental agreements about children. Baroness Hale at para 40 raised the possibility (without deciding the issue) that agreements having legal effect could be concluded under English law as a result of Children Act 1989, s 2(9), which provides that:

> 'A person who has parental responsibility for a child may not surrender or transfer any part of that responsibility to another but may arrange for some or all of it to be met by one or more persons acting on his behalf.'

Other

3.64 The means by which rights of custody may arise identified in Art 3 of HC80 are not exhaustive. As explained at para **3.36** above, in certain circumstances a person may hold 'inchoate' rights of custody.

Establishing rights of custody

3.65 There are various means, evidentially, by which the courts may consider the issue of rights of custody under the law of another jurisdiction. These include the following which were identified in *Re D (A Child) (Abduction: Rights of Custody)*[83] at para 80:

(i) direct evidence of foreign law (see para **3.67** below);

(ii) expert evidence (see para **3.70** below); and

(iii) Art 15 declaration (see para **3.73** below).

3.66 Additionally, there may be circumstances in which a court can rely upon a presumption that foreign law is the same as English law (see para **3.77** below).

Direct evidence of foreign law

3.67 Article 14 of HC80 provides that, in ascertaining whether there has been a wrongful removal or retention, the courts may take notice directly of the law of the State of the child's habitual residence without recourse to the specific procedures for the proof of that law that would otherwise be applicable. As Professor Pérez Vera states in para 119 of the Explanatory Report to HC80:

82 [2014] UKSC 29, [2014] AC 1401, [2014] 2 FCR 231, [2014] 2 FLR 629.
83 [2006] UKHL 51, [2007] 1 AC 619, [2007] 1 FCR 1, [2007] 1 FLR 961.

> 'There is no need to stress the practical importance this rule may have in leading to the speedy decisions which are fundamental to the working of the Convention.'

3.68 Details of the relevant law may be submitted with the application by means of an affidavit or a certificate provided by the Central Authority of the Requesting State responsible for transmitting the application or by 'a qualified person': HC80, Art 8(f).

3.69 In the majority of cases, the information provided by the Central Authority is likely to be sufficiently clear to enable the court to rely upon and avoid the delay and expense involved in obtaining further evidence. In *Re D (A Child) (Abduction: Custody Rights)*[84] Lord Hope emphasised (at para 5) that:

> 'A court cannot make a finding that the child's removal was wrongful unless it is provided with a basis for doing so. But if it is to deal with the case summarily the court must not seek perfection. It has to do the best it can on the information that has been made available, as Butler-Sloss LJ indicated in *C v C (Abduction: Rights of Custody)* [1989] 1 WLR 654, 658A.'

Expert evidence

3.70 The court may only order expert evidence to be obtained to resolve an issue as to the existence of rights of custody if it is satisfied that it is 'necessary' to assist the court to resolve the proceedings: Family Procedure Rules 2010 ('FPR 2010'), r 25.4. In *Re H-L (A Child)*[85] the Court of Appeal held that:

> '["necessary"] has a meaning lying somewhere between 'indispensable' on the one hand and "useful", "reasonable" or "desirable" on the other hand, having the connotation of the imperative, what is demanded rather than what is merely optional or reasonable or desirable.'

3.71 If a party wishes to make an application for expert evidence, the procedure in FPR 2010, Part 25 must be followed. Where two or more parties wish to put expert evidence before the court in relation to rights of custody, the court may direct that the evidence should be given by a single joint expert ('SJE'): FPR 2010, r 25.11. Given the summary nature of HC80 proceedings, it is preferable to direct expert evidence from a single joint expert rather than permitting each party to instruct its own expert: *Re P (A Child) (Abduction: Custody Rights)*[86].

84 [2006] UKHL 51, [2007] 1 AC 619, [2007] 1 FCR 1, [2007] 1 FLR 961.
85 [2013] EWCA Civ 655, [2014] 1 WLR 1160, [2013] 2 FLR 1434.
86 [2004] EWCA Civ 971, [2005] Fam 293, [2004] 2 FLR 1057 at para 25.

3.72 Where a court has obtained a declaration pursuant to HC80 as to the wrongfulness of the removal or retention, it is inappropriate then to obtain expert evidence on the issue of rights of custody: *Re D (A Child) (Abduction: Rights of Custody)*[87].

Article 15 determination

3.73 Article 15 of HC80 provides as follows:

> 'The judicial or administrative authorities of a Contracting State may, prior to the making of an order for the return of the child, request that the applicant obtain from the authorities of the State of the habitual residence of the child a decision or other determination that the removal or retention was wrongful within the meaning of Article 3 of the Convention, where such a decision or determination may be obtained in that State. The Central Authorities of the Contracting States shall so far as practicable assist applicants to obtain such a decision or determination.'

3.74 The last sentence in Art 15 indicates that a 'determination' for these purposes means something other than the assertion or certificate of a central authority. It is the determination by the authorities having the power within the Requesting State to make authoritative decisions relating to rights over children[88].

3.75 Save in exceptional circumstances, such as where an Art 15 determination has been obtained by fraud or in breach of the rules of natural justice, it will be conclusive as to the rights of the parties under the law of the Requesting State[89].

3.76 A foreign court's ruling under Art 15 as to the wrongfulness of a removal or retention is not binding on the courts of the Requested State. However, the court should only decline to follow such a ruling if it is clearly out of line with the international understanding of the terms of HC80[90]; an example of such a case is *Hunter v Murrow*[91].

87 [2006] UKHL 51, [2007] 1 AC 619, [2007] 1 FCR 1, [2007] 1 FLR 961 at paras 7 and 81.

88 *Re D (A Child) (Abduction: Custody Rights)* [2006] UKHL 51, [2007] 1 AC 619, [2007] 1 FCR 1, [2007] 1 FLR 961 at para 39.

89 *Re D (A Child) (Abduction: Custody Rights)* [2006] UKHL 51, [2007] 1 AC 619, [2007] 1 FCR 1, [2007] 1 FLR 961 at para 43.

90 *Re D (A Child) (Abduction: Custody Rights)* [2006] UKHL 51, [2007] 1 AC 619, [2007] 1 FCR 1, [2007] 1 FLR 961 at para 44.

91 [2005] EWCA Civ 976, [2005] 3 FCR 1, [2005] 2 FLR 1119; see *Re D (A Child) (Abduction: Custody Rights)* [2006] UKHL 51, [2007] 1 AC 619, [2007] 1 FCR 1, [2007] 1 FLR 961 at para 44.

Presumption that foreign law is the same as English law

3.77 It has been suggested in cases not concerned with HC80 that, until the contrary is proved, there is a presumption that foreign law is the same as English law[92].

3.78 However, to speak of *a presumption* in this context may overstate the position. In *Global Multimedia International Limited v ARA Media Services and ors*[93] it was held that the more accurate proposition is that '*as foreign law is a question of fact to be proved by evidence, in the absence of such evidence the court has no option but to apply English law*'.

3.79 There is no reported decision in which an issue as to rights of custody under HC80 has been decided by reference to such a presumption.

E. EXERCISING RIGHTS OF CUSTODY

3.80 In order to establish that a removal or retention is wrongful, it is necessary to demonstrate that, at the time of the removal or retention, the rights of custody which have been breached:

(a) were actually exercised; or

(b) would have been so exercised but for the removal or retention.

3.81 The requirement merely to prove that rights of custody 'would have been exercised' but for the removal or retention makes it almost impossible for a respondent to argue that this is not established.

3.82 In *Re A (A Child) (Abduction: Rights of Custody: Imprisonment)*[94], the mother removed the child from Australia to England while the father was serving a prison sentence for assaulting her. She argued that he was not actually exercising his rights of custody as a result of his circumstances. However, the father successfully argued that the relevant right of custody was his right to veto the removal of the child; but for the mother's actions, he 'would have' exercised that right. *Re A (A Child)* was followed in *Re L (A Child)*[95] and cited with approval in *Re EE (Children) (Habitual Residence)*[96].

92 *Mansour v Mansour* [1989] 1 FLR 418; *Re J (A Child) (Custody Rights: Jurisdiction)* [2005] UKHL 40, [2006] 1 AC 80, [2005] 2 FCR 381, [2005] 2 FLR 802 at para 15; *O (A Child) v Rhodes & ors* [2014] EWCA Civ 1277, [2015] EMLR 4, [2015] 1 CL 276.

93 [2006] EWHC 3612 (Ch), [2007] 1 All ER (Comm) 1160.

94 [2004] 1 FLR 1.

95 [2005] EWHC 1237 (Fam), [2006] 1 FLR 843.

96 [2016] EWHC 3363 (Fam), [2017] 1 FCR 500.

CHAPTER 4

Habitual residence

Content at a Glance:

A. INTRODUCTION

4.1 The concept of habitual residence ('HR') lies at the heart of international family law. Any application under the 1980 Hague Convention[1] ('HC80') will involve a determination as to where the child was habitually resident immediately before any alleged wrongful removal or retention.

4.2 The concept of HR is central to the determination of the jurisdiction of the court to deal with applications relating to children both in international and domestic jurisprudence.

1 The Convention on the Civil Aspects of International Child Abduction signed at the Hague on 25 October 1980.

The 1980 Hague Convention

Preamble

The States signatory to the present Convention, firmly convinced that the interests of children are of paramount importance in matters relating to their custody, desiring to protect children internationally from the harmful effects of their wrongful removal or retention and *to establish procedures to ensure their prompt return to the State of their habitual residence*, as well as to secure protection for rights of access, have resolved to conclude a Convention to this effect, and have agreed upon the following provisions …

Article 3

The removal or the retention of a child is to be considered wrongful where–

(a) it is in breach of rights of custody attributed to a person, an institution or any other body, either jointly or alone, *under the law of the State in which the child was habitually resident immediately before the removal or retention* …

Article 4

The Convention shall apply to any child *who was habitually resident in a Contracting State immediately before any breach* of custody or access rights. The Convention shall cease to apply when the child attains the age of 16 years.

The 1996 Hague Convention[2]

Chapter II – Jurisdiction

Article 5

(1) The judicial or administrative authorities of the Contracting State *of the habitual residence of the child have jurisdiction* to take measures directed to the protection of the child's person or property.

(2) Subject to Article 7, in case of a change of the child's habitual residence to another Contracting State, the authorities of the State of the new habitual residence have jurisdiction.

Brussels IIA[3]

Article 8

General jurisdiction

1. The courts of a Member State shall have jurisdiction in matters of parental responsibility over a child who is habitually resident in that Member State at the time the court is seised.

Article 13

Jurisdiction based on the child's presence

1. Where a child's habitual residence cannot be established and jurisdiction cannot be determined on the basis of Article 12, the courts of the Member State where the child is present shall have jurisdiction.

2 Hague Convention of 19 October 1996 on Jurisdiction, Applicable Law, Recognition, Enforcement and Co-operation in Respect of Parental Responsibility and Measures for the Protection of Children.

3 Council Regulation (EC) No 2201/2003 of 27 November 2003 concerning jurisdiction and the recognition and enforcement of judgments in matrimonial matters and the matters of parental responsibility, repealing Regulation (EC) No 1347/2000.

Domestic law: the Family Law Act 1986

Section 2 – Jurisdiction: general

(1) A court in England and Wales shall not make a [*welfare*] order with respect to a child unless–
  (a) it has jurisdiction under the Council Regulation or the [*1996*] Hague Convention, or
  (b) neither the Council Regulation nor the [*1996*] Hague Convention applies[4], but–
    (i) the question of making the order arises in or in connection with matrimonial proceedings … or
    (ii) the condition in section 3 of this Act is satisfied.

Section 3 – Habitual residence or presence of child

(1) The condition referred to in section 2(1)(b)(ii) of this Act is that on the relevant date the child concerned–
  (a) is habitually resident in England and Wales, or
  (b) is present in England and Wales and is not habitually resident in any part of the United Kingdom …

B. WHAT IS HABITUAL RESIDENCE?

4.3 Although the phrase is widely used, 'habitual residence' is not defined in any of the Acts or treaties in which it is mentioned. The meaning of 'habitual residence' has been considered in six cases before the Supreme Court since 2013:

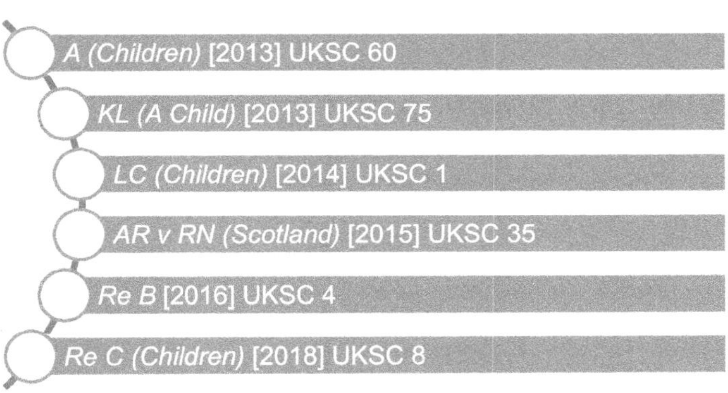

4 This should be read with the inclusion of the words 'so as to give the court jurisdiction' per Baker J in *AG and AB* [2018] EWHC 381 (Fam), [2019] Fam 1, [2018] 2 FCR 313, [2018] 2 FLR 439.

4.4 In *A (Children)*[5], the Supreme Court decided that the domestic tests to determine the HR of children were no longer applicable. Instead, it adopted the approach of the European courts, in particular the rulings from the CJEU in *Mercredi v Chaffe*[6] and the CJEU case *Proceedings brought by A*[7].

Case Summary: *Mercredi v Chaffe* CJEU Case C-497/10[8]

Facts:

A child was born in the UK to unmarried parents: M (French) from Réunion (a French *départment*) and F (British). A few weeks after the birth, M took the child to Réunion. F did not have parental responsibility, so lacked rights of custody. A day after removal, a duty judge made a location order. F then applied for welfare orders and a judge (*ex parte*) ordered M to return the child to England.

M then applied in Réunion for sole parental responsibility. F applied for a return under HC80; his application was dismissed as he did not have rights of custody. In the English proceedings, it was held that the English courts were seised and acquired rights of custody[9] when F telephoned the duty judge. The child was habitually resident in England at that time.

M was then granted sole parental responsibility in Réunion. She appealed the English decisions. The Court of Appeal requested a preliminary ruling from the CJEU to clarify the test for determining the HR of a child.

Held by the CJEU:

- HR is a matter of fact to be resolved in each case;
- to be 'habitual', residence must have 'a certain permanence[10] or regularity';
- a uniform EU-wide interpretation of HR was required;
- jurisdictional issues were to be shaped in the light of the best interests of the child and, in particular, on the criterion of proximity;
- HR corresponds to the place which reflects some degree of integration by the child in a social and family environment;

5 *A v A and another (Children: Habitual Residence) (Reunite International Child Abduction Centre intervening)* [2013] UKSC 60, [2014] AC 1, [2013] 3 WLR 76, [2013] 3 FCR 559, [2014] 1 FLR 111.

6 CJEU, Case C-497/10, [2012] Fam 22, [2011] 1 FLR 1293.

7 CJEU, Case C-523/07, [2010] Fam 42, [2009] 2 FLR 1.

8 [2012] Fam 22, [2011] 1 FLR 1293.

9 For rights of custody in the court, see para **3.39** above.

10 See *DL v EL* [2013] FLR 163 and *AR v RN (Scotland)* in which it was held that 'permanence' in this context means 'stability'.

- reference must be made to the conditions and reasons for the child's stay, as well as to his nationality;
- in addition to physical presence, other factors must make it clear that the child's presence is not in any way temporary or intermittent; the intention of the person with parental responsibility to settle permanently with the child in another Member State may constitute an indicator of the transfer of HR;
- to distinguish HR from temporary presence, there must be a duration which reflects an adequate degree of permanence[11], although there is no minimum duration; the duration of a stay can only be an indicator in the assessment of the permanence of the residence; and
- a child's social and family environment is fundamental in determining their HR; age is also likely to be of particular importance. An infant necessarily shares the social and family environment of the people on whom they are dependent.

Guidance:

Where an infant has been removed to a new Member State and has been there only a matter of days, the factors to be taken into consideration when determining the child's HR include: (i) the duration, regularity, conditions and reasons for the stay in the territory of that Member State and for the parent's move; and (ii) the child's age, the parent's geographic and family origins and the family and social connections which the parent and child had with the new Member State.

4.5 In *A (Children)*[12], the Supreme Court preferred the European test to the test formerly adopted by the English courts. The determination was:

A child is HR in "the place which reflects some degree of integration ... in a social and family environment"

HR is a question of fact, not a legal concept

There must be consistency between the Hague Conventions, European law and domestic jurisprudence

The purposes and intentions of parents is merely one of the relevant factors

11 See *DL v EL* [2013] FLR 163 and *AR v RN (Scotland)*.

12 [2013] UKSC 60, [2014] AC 1, [2013] 3 FCR 559, [2014] 1 FLR 111.

4.6

Case Summary: *A (Children)*[13]

Facts:

The proceedings related to four children, the oldest three of whom were born in the UK. After the birth of the third child, the parents separated. M took the three children to Pakistan for a 3-week holiday. Under pressure from F and from family members, she agreed to reconcile with F on the basis that the family would return to England.

In fact, M and the children were forced to remain in Pakistan; the children were enrolled into local schools and F removed M's and the children's passports. M then became pregnant and was beaten, threatened and abused by F and his family.

Following the birth of the child, M managed to retrieve her passport and was able to return to England. F commenced custody proceedings in Pakistan.

On her arrival in the UK, M obtained an order from the English High Court for the immediate return of the children. The order was made in wardship, on the basis that all the children were habitually resident in England and Wales.

The Court of Appeal held that the youngest sibling was not habitually resident in England and Wales. The Court upheld the determination that the three older siblings remained habitually resident in England and Wales after being retained in Pakistan.

Held by the UKSC:

The Supreme Court unanimously confirmed that English law retained a discretionary, residual basis of jurisdiction over children, based on their British nationality.

The Supreme Court also provided detailed guidance on the test for ascertaining a child's HR, rejecting previous tests and adopting a simple test: a child is habitually resident in the place which reflects some degree of integration by the child in a social and family environment.

13 *A v A and another (Children: Habitual Residence) (Reunite International Child Abduction Centre intervening)* [2013] UKSC 60, [2014] AC 1, [2013] 3 WLR 76, [2013] 3 FCR 559, [2014] 1 FLR 111.

The test to determine habitual residence

4.7 In a summary, Baroness Hale stated at para 54 of *A (Children)*:

'(i) All are agreed that habitual residence is a question of fact and not a legal concept such as domicile. There is no legal rule akin to that whereby a child automatically takes the domicile of his parents.

(ii) It was the purpose of the 1986 Act to adopt a concept which was the same as that adopted in the Hague and European Conventions. The Regulation must also be interpreted consistently with those Conventions.

(iii) The test adopted by the European Court is "**the place which reflects some degree of integration by the child in a social and family environment**" in the country concerned. This depends upon numerous factors, including the reasons for the family's stay in the country in question.

(iv) It is now unlikely that that test would produce any different results from that hitherto adopted in the English courts under the 1986 Act and the Hague Child Abduction Convention.

(v) In my view, the test adopted by the European Court is preferable to that earlier adopted by the English courts, being focussed on the situation of the child, with **the purposes and intentions of the parents being merely one of the relevant factors**. The test derived from *R v Barnet London Borough Council, ex p Shah*[14] should be abandoned when deciding the habitual residence of a child.

(vi) The social and family environment of an infant or young child is shared with those (whether parents or others) upon whom he is dependent. Hence it is necessary to assess the integration of that person or persons in the social and family environment of the country concerned.

(vii) The essentially factual and individual nature of the inquiry should not be glossed with legal concepts which would produce a different result from that which the factual inquiry would produce.

(viii) As the Advocate General pointed out in para AG45 and the court confirmed in para 43 of *Proceedings brought by A*[15], it is possible that a child may have no country of habitual residence at a particular point in time[16].'

14 [1983] 2 AC 309, [1983] 2 WLR 16.
15 CJEU, Case C/523/07, [2010] Fam 42, [2009] 2 FLR 1.
16 See para **4.13** in relation to a child having no HR.

C. GAINING AND LOSING HABITUAL RESIDENCE

Parental intention

4.8 Parental intention is a relevant consideration to the determination of a child's HR. However, the factual and individual nature of the inquiry should not be glossed with legal concepts which would produce a different result from that which the factual inquiry would produce. In *AR v RN (Scotland)*[17], the Supreme Court upheld the earlier decision of the Court of Appeal of England and Wales in *Re H (Children) (Reunite International Child Abduction Centre intervening)*[18] that there is no *rule* to prevent one parent changing, or bringing about the change of, the HR of a child on a unilateral basis.

Case Summary: *AR v RN*[19]

Facts:

The case concerned two girls who lived in France; F was French and M was British and Canadian. The mother and children moved to Scotland for an agreed one-year period; whilst in Scotland they sold the family home in France and the older child started school in Scotland.

On the parents' separation after months in Scotland, M sought a custody order from the Scottish courts and F applied under HC80 for the return of the children to France.

At first instance, the court held that the children had been habitually resident in France immediately before the alleged wrongful retention and ordered their return to France. This decision was overturned on appeal.

Held by the UKSC:

The Appeal court was correct in its determination that the children were habitually resident in Scotland at the time of the alleged wrongful retention.

The UKSC summarised the factors that must be taken into account in determining the HR of the child, noting that its guidance was consistent with that of the Court of Justice of the European Union (CJEU). It adopted the CJEU definition of HR as '[corresponding] to the place which reflects some degree of integration by the child in a social and family environment'.

In establishing HR, factors relating to the duration, regularity, conditions and reasons for the stay / move to the new State, as well as the school attendance, languages, nationality and family and social relationships of the child, should

17 [2015] UKSC 35, [2016] AC 76, [2015] 2 FCR 570, [2015] 2 FLR 503.
18 [2014] EWCA Civ 1101, [2015] 1 WLR 863, [2014] 3 FCR 405, [2015] 1 FLR 1132.
19 *AR v RN (Scotland)* [2015] UKSC 35.

be considered. This must be a factual determination, made on a case-by-case basis.

It is necessary to consider the primary carer's integration in a social and family environment, where the child is an infant. Where the child is dependent on one parent, the child will share the environment in which that person has integrated.

Passages from *Mercredi v Chaffe* 'appeared to import a requirement of permanence for residence to be habitual', but the French version of the judgment referred to '*stabilité*' rather than 'permanence'; '[i]t is therefore the stability of the residence that is important, not whether it is of a permanent character'.

For a child to be habitually resident in a given State, the parent(s) do not necessarily need to have intended to remain there permanently. The intentions of the parents are only one of many factual considerations that require evaluation in every individual case.

4.9 In *MB v GK*[20] the court's findings as to the intentions of the parents proved decisive in the determination of HR.

Case Summary: *MB v GK*[21]

Facts:

The child moved to Singapore, for education, to live with grandparents. F refused to return the child to England, contending that the parties agreed that the child would remain in the care of the grandparents indefinitely. He asserted that in any event, by the time of M's application for a return order, the child was habitually resident in Singapore.

Held by Russell J:

While the child must have been dependent on the care of the grandparents and must necessarily share their social and family environment, '*it does not mean that the purpose and intention of the parents (as those with parental responsibility) becomes immaterial*'. The judge concluded that the child's integration into the social and family environment in Singapore was temporary in nature, in fact and by intention. The father was ordered to return the child to this jurisdiction.

20 [2014] EWHC 963 (Fam).
21 [2014] EWHC 963 (Fam).

Simultaneous gaining and losing of habitual residence

4.10 In *Re B (A Child) (Habitual Residence: Inherent Jurisdiction)*[22] it was determined that, in general, a child will lose a pre-existing HR at the same time as gaining a new HR. It is only in exceptional cases that a child will be 'in limbo' and be found to have no HR at a given time. The position was explained by Lord Wilson at para 45:

> 'I conclude that the modern concept of a child's habitual residence operates in such a way as to make it highly unlikely, albeit conceivable, that a child will be in the limbo in which the courts below have placed B. The concept operates in the expectation that, when a child gains a new habitual residence, he loses his old one. Simple analogies are best: consider a see-saw. As, probably quite quickly, he puts down those first roots which represent the requisite degree of integration in the environment of the new State, up will probably come the child's roots in that of the old State to the point at which he achieves the requisite de-integration (or, better, disengagement) from it.'

4.11 The seamless transfer of a child's HR from one State to another is illustrated by the following graphic:

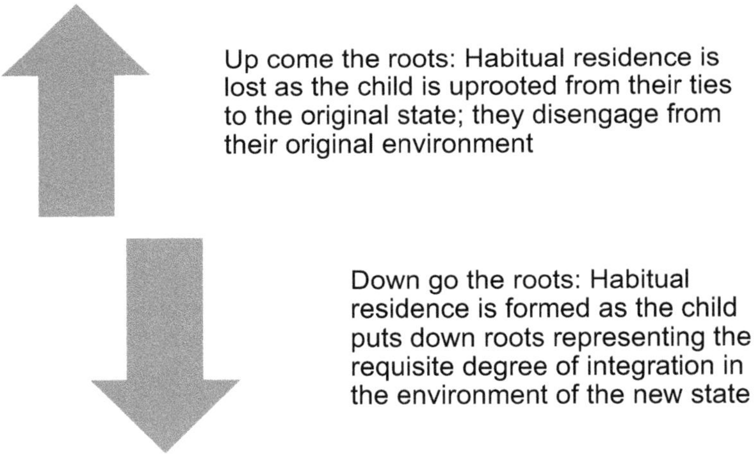

4.12 In *Re B*[23] Lord Wilson also considered the circumstances which could cause a child to lose HR and gain a new one. A question was posed as to whether a child can lose HR in one country and gain it in another in a single day.

Lord Wilson offered three examples of the matters a court will take into account when determining the point at which HR has been lost and gained:

22 [2016] UKSC 4, [2016] AC 606, [2016] 2 FCR 307, [2016] 1 FLR 561.

23 *Re B (A Child) (Habitual Residence: Inherent Jurisdiction)* [2016] UKSC 4, [2016] AC 606, [2016] 2 FCR 307, [2016] 1 FLR 561.

The deeper the child's integration in old state, probably the less fast his achievement of requisite degree of integration in new state

The greater the pre-planning of the move, probably the faster the child's achievement of that requisite degree

Where all central members of the child's life have moved with him, probably the faster his achievement of a new HR and, conversely, if any of them have remained behind, probably the less fast his achievement of it

This reflects an observation made by Baroness Hale in *Re LC (Children) (International Abduction: Child's Objections to Return)*[24], at para 63:

> 'Some habitual residences may be harder to lose than others and others may be harder to gain. If a person leaves his home country with the intention of emigrating and having made all the necessary plans to do so, he may lose one habitual residence immediately and acquire a new one very quickly. If a person leaves his home country for a temporary purpose or in ambiguous circumstances, he may not lose his habitual residence there for some time, if at all, and correspondingly he will not acquire a new habitual residence until then or even later.'

No habitual residence

4.13 In exceptional circumstances the English court may make a finding that a child has no HR, or an HR which cannot be established[25]. This can provide the court with jurisdiction pursuant to BIIR Art 13 and Family Law Act 1986, s 3(1)(b), both of which confer jurisdiction on the court based on the physical presence of a child.

4.14 *Re F (Habitual Residence: Peripatetic Existence)*[26] is an example of a case in which the court was unable to determine the child's HR.

24 [2014] UKSC 1, [2014] AC 1038, [2014] 1 FCR 491, [2014] 1 FLR 1486.
25 *Re B (A Child) (Habitual Residence: Inherent Jurisdiction)* [2016] UKSC 4, [2016] AC 606, [2016] 2 FCR 307, [2016] 1 FLR 561.
26 [2014] EWFC 26, [2015] 1 FLR 1303.

Case Summary: *Re F (Habitual Residence: Peripatetic Existence)*[27]

Facts:

The child had been removed from her family in Zimbabwe to the USA by F. She remained in the USA for 20 months before spending just over six months travelling with F – at least in part to evade M.

Held by Peter Jackson J:

For the entire period since she left Zimbabwe, the child had no HR. F lived an '*incessant peripatetic existence*' which meant that the child's '*overall position was a precarious one, reflected in the degree of exclusive control that had to be asserted by one parent*'.

The child's HR could not be determined at the date of commencement of care proceedings; she was not habitually resident anywhere and the English court had jurisdiction to deal with the application.

Guidance for determining the habitual residence of a child

4.15 A number of helpful checklists and tests have been put forward in the following cases[28] to assist in the factual assessment of HR.

27 [2014] EWFC 26, [2015] 1 FLR 1303.

28 *Re R (A Child) (Jurisdiction: Habitual Residence)* [2015] EWCA Civ 674, [2016] 1 FLR 1119 (see paras 37–40); *Re B (A Child) (Custody Rights: Habitual Residence)* [2016] EWHC 2174 (Fam), [2016] 4 WLR 156 (at para 17); *Re J (A Child) (Finland: Habitual Residence)* [2017] EWCA Civ 80, [2017] 2 FCR 542; *Re S (A Child) (Article 16 and 18 BIIA and Article 19 EU Service Regulation)* [2017] EWHC 3768 (Fam), [2018 2 FCR 480, [2019] 1 FLR 194; *Re G (Children)* [2017] EWHC 2111 (Fam); *AB v CD* [2018] EWHC 1021 (Fam).

4.16 The checklist adopted by Hayden J in *Re B*[29] sets out the factors which a court may consider, and upon which practitioners must focus, when dealing with the factual determination of a child's HR. These are summarised below:

- Child's HR requires some degree of integration in social and family environment
- Factual enquiry centred on circumstances of child's life likely to illuminate his HR
- Meaning of HR shaped in light of best interests, in particular 'practical connection' between child and country concerned
- Parent may unilaterally change HR by removing the child without the consent of the other parent
- Child usually has same HR as the caring parent(s) but it is the child's HR and intergration under consideration, not parent's
- Parental intention is relevant, but not determinative
- Highly unusual for child to have no HR. Usually a child loses pre-existing HR at the same time as gaining a new one
- In assessing whether a child has gained new HR, the judge must weigh connection between child and the state where resided before move
- *Stability* of residence as opposed to *permanence* is relevant
- Question is ***some degree of*** integration in social / family environment; not whether *fully* integrated before becoming HR
- Requisite integration can develop quickly; possibly in a day
- HR is question of fact focused on child; purposes / intentions of parents merely relevant factors. No requirement of intention by parents to reside permanently or indefinitely

In *Re M (Children) (Habitual Residence: 1980 Hague Child Abduction Convention)* [2020] EWCA Civ 1105 it was held that, while a child's historical connection with another jurisdiction may be relevant, it is not the primary focus; a requirement to weigh a child's connection with the state of residence before a move should not be part of the checklist. A child with deep roots in state A may very quickly gain a new habitual residence in state B following a pre-planned move: *Re B (A Child) (Abduction: Habitual Residence)* [2020] EWCA Civ 1187.

Retention and the date of habitual residence

4.17 In *Re C and another (Children) (International Centre for Family Law, Policy and Practice intervening)*[30], the Supreme Court dealt with the issue of

29 *Re B (A Child) (Custody Rights: Habitual Residence)* [2016] EWHC 2174 (Fam), [2016] 4 WLR 156 at para 17.

30 [2018] UKSC 8, [2019] AC 1, [2018] 2 FCR 733, [2018] 1 FLR 861.

'repudiatory retention' and considered the important issue of the circumstances in which HR may transfer from one jurisdiction to another during an agreed time-limited stay overseas.

Case Summary: *Re C and another (Children) (International Centre for Family Law, Policy and Practice intervening)*[31]

Facts:

A couple who lived in Australia were experiencing difficulties in their marriage. F agreed to move to the UK for an eight-week stay. F then agreed to the children staying for up to a year. M gave notice to her Australian employer and sought work in England.

The elder child began at pre-school in England and M applied for British citizenship for both children. M's solicitors wrote a letter to the immigration authorities indicating that she and the children could not return to Australia for fear of domestic abuse.

Eventually, M said that she would not return the children to Australia at the expiry of a year. F brought proceedings under HC80. At first instance, the judge determined that, by the time of M's decision not to return to Australia, the children were habitually resident in England so HC80 could not apply.

Held by the UKSC:

Held (by a majority) that where, before the expiry of an agreed period of absence, the travelling parent denied or 'repudiated' the custody rights of the left-behind parent by unilaterally deciding where the child would live, this amounted to a repudiatory retention.

A repudiatory retention normally requires two elements to be established:

- a subjective intention not to honour the agreement to return to the country where the children had been HR; and
- an objectively verifiable act or statement which manifests the repudiation of custody rights.

In this case, by the time the retention became 'wrongful', as a matter of fact, the children were no longer habitually resident in the original State. As such, there was no remedy under HC80; the retention was not wrongful because the children were no longer habitually resident in Australia at the date of the retention.

31 [2018] UKSC 8, [2019] AC 1, [2018] 2 FCR 733, [2018] 1 FLR 861.

4.18 Lord Hughes said at [12]:

> 'In some cases, however, it is possible that by the time of the act relied upon as a wrongful removal or retention, the child may have acquired habitual residence in the destination State. It is perhaps improbable in the case of removal, but it is not in the case of retention. It may particularly happen if the stay in the destination State is more than just a holiday and lasts long enough for the child to become integrated into the destination State. It is the more likely to happen if the travelling parent determines, however improperly, to stay, and takes steps to integrate the child in the destination State. Even in the case of wrongful removal it may be possible to imagine such a situation if, for example, there had been successive periods of residence in the destination State, followed by a removal from the State of origin which infringed the rights of custody of the left-behind parent.'

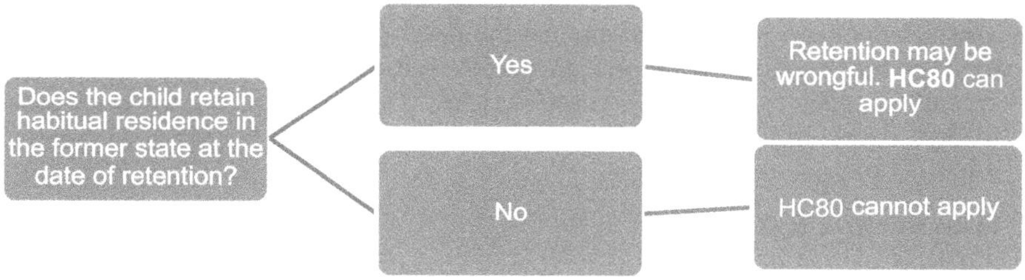

Habitual residence and the age of a child

4.19 In *Proceedings brought by A*[32], *Mercredi v Chaffe* and *A (Children)* the courts were concerned with young infants. It was determined that the social and family environment of an infant or a young child is shared with those on whom he or she is dependent, whether parents or others. In *LC (Children)*[33], Lord Wilson giving the majority judgment held that, when a child moves lawfully to reside with a parent in a State where that parent is habitually resident, it would be highly unusual for that child not to acquire HR there. However, in assessing the degree of integration in relation to an adolescent child, the court may have regard to that child's state of mind during her period of residence in relation to the nature and the quality of that residence.

32 CJEU, Case C/523/07, [2010] Fam 42, [2009] 2 FLR 1.
33 [2014] UKSC 1, [2014] AC 1038, [2014] 1 FCR 491, [2014] 1 FLR 1486.

Case Summary: *Re LC (Children)*[34]

Facts:

The parents and the four children, who were all born in the UK, moved to Spain where they lived with M and the MGM. After a few months in Spain, the parents agreed that the children would travel to the UK for a holiday to stay with F for two weeks. Shortly before they were due to return, the two older boys hid the family's passports and missed the plane. M made an application under HC80 for the children's return to Spain.

Cobb J ordered the return of the children to Spain, despite the eldest child objecting.

The CA dismissed the appeal against the finding that the children's HR was in Spain but reversed the judge's decision to return the oldest child; her views should be given 'very considerable weight'. The CA remitted the question whether it would be intolerable to return the younger children to Spain without their sister.

Held by the UKSC:

The UKSC unanimously found that the eldest child's statements about her state of mind during her residence in Spain in 2012 were relevant to a determination whether her residence there was habitual. The UKSC remitted the factual issue of the eldest child's HR to the High Court for fresh consideration. The finding of HR in respect of the other three children was set aside so that the issue could be reconsidered in relation to all four children.

The views of (particularly) older children can be relevant in the determination of their HR.

Rehearing before Roderic Wood J[35]:

The judge found that none of the children had been habitually resident in Spain, despite their presence there for six months. The children had been removed from their English schools without warning; they took few of their possessions; their emails showed a desire to come 'home'; and M was ignoring the children's wishes because of her desire to start a new life in Spain.

The judge also addressed the children's objections to a return and found that the prospect of separation between the eldest child and her brothers was 'almost too painful to comprehend'. The judge had 'no doubt' the defence under Art 13(b) would have been made out in the event that the children had been habitually resident in Spain at the time of their retention.

34 [2014] UKSC 1, [2014] AC 1038, [2014] 1 FCR 491, [2014] 1 FLR 1486.
35 *LC v RRL & Others* [2014] EWFC 8.

4.20 There is a sliding scale between a new-born, who will almost inevitably take on the HR of their primary carer, and an adolescent child who will form their own sense of integration in the new State. As Peter Jackson J put it in *F (Habitual Residence)*[36]:

> '... the relevance of the actions and intentions of parents or carers depends on the age of the child. In a silhouette of a mother and new-born baby, the baby may not appear at all, but as a child grows, its silhouette will become increasingly distinct and distant from the parent ... A child [on the threshold of primary age schooling] has a degree of independence in the day-to-day, but is otherwise dependent on her carer. The actions and intentions of the parent are therefore of real relevance, but they will not predominate as they would with a new-born. This is particularly the case where there are two parents with different intentions and philosophies of life.'

Physical presence of the child

4.21 In *UD v XB*[37], the CJEU considered the HR of a new-born child. The court was required to determine whether presence is a prerequisite to HR: could a new-born baby be habitually resident in a State in which they had never been present, based on the HR of the mother?

The CJEU, differing from the opinion of the Advocate General, held:

(i) In order to determine where a child is habitually resident, *in addition to* the physical presence of the child in a Member State, other factors must also make it clear that that presence is not in any way temporary or intermittent.

(ii) Physical presence in the Member State in which the child is allegedly integrated is a condition which necessarily must be satisfied before assessing the stability of that presence and that 'habitual residence', for the purposes of Brussels II Revised, may not be established in a Member State to which the child has never been.

(iii) Circumstances such as the fact that the father's coercion of the mother had the effect of her giving birth to their child in a third country where she has resided with that child ever since, and, secondly, the breach of the mother's or the child's rights, do not have any bearing on the requirement for the physical presence of a child as a pre-requisite to habitual residence.

4.22 This is an important decision in the context of cases in which a mother travels to the UK to give birth and then decides to remain here. If the father seeks the return of the child to the home State, HC80 cannot apply and an application must be made on welfare grounds under the inherent jurisdiction. Following *UD v XB* the requirements for establishing HR may now be summarised by the following graphic:

36 [2014] EWFC 26, [2015] 1 FLR 1303 at paras 46–47.
37 (Case C-393/18 PPU), [2019] 1 WLR 3083, [2019] 1 FLR 289.

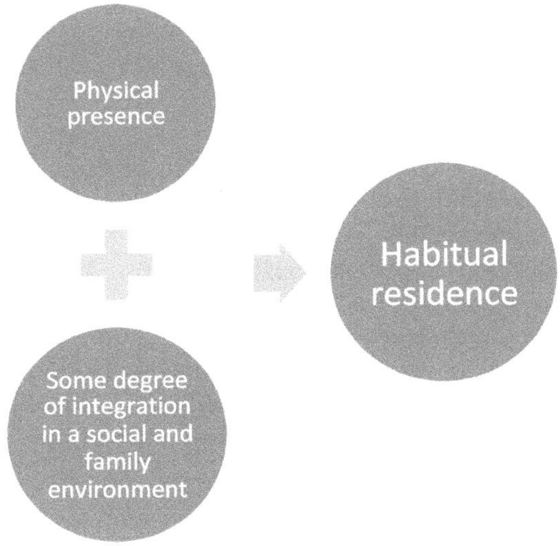

4.23 If a mother travelled to the UK with an older sibling and gave birth in the UK, the court would be faced with two different applications, to which different tests could apply: a welfare-based analysis in relation to the new-born baby, and an application under HC80 for the summary return of the older child.

Relocation subject to appeal

4.24 In *Re KL*[38] the Supreme Court rejected a submission that where a child is permitted to live in a foreign country pursuant to a return order, *which is under appeal*, the child would not acquire HR in the country in which he was living until the appeal was determined.

This would be to place a legal gloss on the factual concept: a child's HR could change despite the opposition of one parent, particularly when the relocation had been permitted by order of a court.

The Supreme Court also confirmed that there is no legal rule, similar to that in the law of domicile, whereby a child automatically took the HR of his parents: HR is a question of fact. The proposition that a young child in the sole lawful custody of his mother would necessarily have the same HR as she did was a helpful generalisation, which would usually but not invariably be true, rather than a proposition of law.

38 [2013] UKSC 75; also reported as *Re L (A Child) (Custody: Habitual Residence) (Reunite International Child Abduction Centre intervening)* [2014] AC 1017, [2014] 1 FCR 69, [2014] 1 FLR 772.

Case Summary: *Re KL*[39]

Facts:

The proceedings concerned a child born in the USA. F was a US citizen; M had indefinite leave to remain in the UK. The parents entered into an agreement in Texas which provided that M had the authority to determine the child's residence 'without regard to geographic location'. M subsequently took the child to the UK.

In 2010, M took the child to Texas for court proceedings, as a result of which the child stayed with F for 18 months. M appealed against an order that F had custody of the child, but the appeal was never heard. M commenced proceedings in the Texas court under HC80 for the return of the child to the UK. She was successful and she was allowed to return to the UK with the child.

F's appeal against the Texas HC80 order was allowed, the Appeal court finding that the child had remained habitually resident in the United States of America, and that the mother had consented to the Texas court's final resolution of the issue of custody[40]. M was required to return the child to F in the USA.

F brought proceedings in England arguing that the removal of the child from Texas was wrongful in the light of the US Appeal court's ruling. These applications were dismissed[41]. F's appeal to the Court of Appeal was unsuccessful[42]. F was given permission to appeal to the Supreme Court.

Held by the UKSC:

Appeal allowed; return ordered. The removal was not wrongful and HC80 was not engaged as the child was habitually resident in England and Wales on the relevant date.

The Supreme Court ordered a return under the inherent jurisdiction: it was in the child's best interests to return so a Texan court could make welfare determinations.

4.25 *Re KL* is consistent with the later decision of the CJEU in *C v M*[43]. In *C v M* the CJEU confirmed that, where the removal of a child has taken place

39 [2013] UKSC 75; also reported as *Re L (A Child) (Custody: Habitual Residence) (Reunite International Child Abduction Centre intervening)* [2014] AC 1017, [2014] 1 FCR 69, [2014] 1 FLR 772.

40 *Larbie v Larbie*, 690 F.3d 295 (5th Cir. 2012) [INCADAT Reference: HC/E/USf 1236].

41 [2013] EWHC 49 (Fam), [2013] 2 FLR 163.

42 [2013] EWCA Civ 865, [2013] 3 FCR 69, [2014] 1 FLR 570.

43 Case C-376/14 PPU [2015] 1 FLR 1.

in accordance with a judgment which was provisionally enforceable and which was thereafter overturned, the child's habitual residence must be determined by undertaking an assessment of all the circumstances of fact. Whilst it was possible the child's habitual residence may have changed, account must be taken of the fact that the judgment authorising the removal was only provisionally enforceable and that an appeal had been brought.

4.26 The court of the Requested State, dealing with an application for the return of the child, must determine as a fact whether the child was still habitually resident in the Member State of origin immediately before the alleged wrongful retention. The court must consider all the circumstances of fact specific to the individual case. Account must be taken of the fact that the judgment authorising the removal could be provisionally enforced and that an appeal had been brought against it.

D. BURDEN AND STANDARD OF PROOF

4.27 The burden of establishing a wrongful removal lies on the applicant, which means that in general the burden will be on the applicant to demonstrate that the child was habitually resident at the relevant time in the Requesting State. Where it is asserted that there has been a change of HR, the burden of proof is on the person asserting that the change has taken place (see *Re R (Wardship: Child Abduction)*[44] and *F v S (Wardship: Jurisdiction)*[45]).

4.28 The standard of proof is the balance of probabilities. The majority of applications under HC80 are dealt with on the basis of submissions only, without hearing any oral evidence. Older authorities suggest that, where oral evidence is not called, there needs to be '*compelling*' evidence before a judge is entitled to reject the affidavit evidence of one of the parties; see *Re F (A Minor) (Child Abduction)*[46].

4.29 An example of a case in which (in a different context) the trial judge was held to have been entitled to make findings on the basis of evidence that was either not disputed or, in the case of email exchanges, was '*incontrovertible*' is the decision of the Supreme Court in *Re S (A Child) (Abduction: Rights of Custody)*[47].

4.30 The issue of HR is a question of fact for the trial judge. It is therefore important that, if there is a clear factual conflict which goes to the issue of HR, the person on whom the burden of proof falls should seek a direction for oral evidence.

44 [1992] 2 FLR 481.
45 [1993] 2 FLR 686.
46 [1992] FCR 269, [1992] 1 FLR 548.
47 [2012] UKSC 10, [2012] 2 AC 257, [2012] 1 FCR 493, [2012] 2 FLR 442.

CHAPTER 5

Consent and acquiescence

Content at a Glance:

A. INTRODUCTION

Consent and acquiescence

5.1 Article 13(a) of HC80 provides that the court in the Requested State *may* refuse to order the return of a child that has been wrongfully removed or retained within the meaning of the Convention if it is established by the person opposing return that the applicant had consented to or subsequently acquiesced in the removal or retention.

The 1980 Hague Convention

> Art 13(a)
>
> Notwithstanding the provisions of the preceding Article, the judicial or administrative authority of the requested State is not bound to order the return of the child if the person, institution or other body which opposes its return establishes that–
>
> (a) the person, institution or other body having the care of the person of the child was not actually exercising the custody rights at the time of removal or retention, *or had consented to or subsequently acquiesced in the removal or retention*

Thus Art 13(a), if made out, confers *a discretion* on the court not to order a summary return.

5.2 This chapter will consider the consent[1] and acquiescence[2] 'defences', and also the possibility of arguing that the applicant was 'not actually exercising custody rights'[3] at the time of the wrongful removal or retention. Finally, this chapter will also discuss the approach the court takes to the discretionary exercise once a defence is established[4].

The difference between consent and acquiescence

5.3 The essential difference between consent and acquiescence is one of timing. Consent arises before a removal or retention, whereas acquiescence follows afterwards: *Re A (Minors) (Abduction: Custody Rights)*[5]. It follows that[6]:

> A respondent can oppose a return on the basis of consent and aquiescence as alternatives

> *Re H*, the leading case on acquiescence, is also relevant to consent

1 See paras **5.5–5.11**.
2 See paras **5.12–5.20**.
3 See para **5.21**.
4 See paras **5.22–5.27**.
5 [1992] Fam 106 at 123, [1992] 2 FCR 9, [1992] 2 FLR 14 at 29, CA.
6 *Re H (Minors) (Abduction: Acquiescence)* [1998] AC 72, [1997] 2 FCR 257, [1997] 1 FLR 872.

Burden and standard of proof

5.4 The burden of establishing consent or acquiescence is on the respondent[7]. The standard of proof is the ordinary civil standard, the balance of probabilities. Previous case law[8] suggested that evidence of consent needed to be clear, compelling and unequivocal. That must now be read in the light of Munby J's decision in *C v H*[9], in which he noted that evidence was needed to establish consent on the 'balance of probabilities, pure and simple'.

B. CONSENT

Article 3 or Article 13(a)?

5.5 As a matter of logic, it is difficult to describe as 'wrongful' a removal or retention which has taken place with the consent of both parents. Thus, it has been argued that, where a removal or retention is consensual, this is relevant to the question of whether it is wrongful for the purposes of Art 3 of HC80[10]. However, it has been conclusively determined that issues of consent fall to be considered under Art 13(a) and not Art 3 of HC80[11].

Key citation: *Re P (Abduction: Consent)*[12]

> 'Consent did not fall to be considered for the purpose of establishing the wrongfulness of a removal or a breach of rights of custody pursuant to Art 3 of the Hague Convention, but only for the purpose of invoking an exercise of the court's discretion pursuant to Art 13 of the Hague Convention …'

The essential elements of consent

5.6 Consent does not need to be in writing[13] but it must be informed, clear, unequivocal and real[14]:

7 *Re H (Minors) (Abduction: Acquiescence)* [1998] AC 72, [1997] 2 FCR 257, [1997] 1 FLR 872.
8 *D v S (Abduction: Acquiescence)* [2008] EWHC 363 (Fam), [2008] 2 FLR 293; *Re R (Child Abduction: Acquiescence)* [1995] 2 FCR 609, [1995] 1 FLR 716.
9 *C v H (Abduction: Consent)* [2009] EWHC 2660 (Fam), [2010] 1 FLR 225.
10 See, for example, *Re P-J (Children) (Abduction: Habitual Residence: Consent)* [2009] EWCA Civ 588, [2010] 1 WLR 1237, [2010] 1 FCR 32, [2009] 2 FLR 1051.
11 *Re P (Abduction: Consent)* [2004] EWCA Civ 971, [2005] Fam 293, [2004] 2 FCR 698, [2004] 2 FLR 1057; *Re P-J (Children) (Abduction: Habitual Residence: Consent)* [2009] EWCA Civ 588, [2010] 1 WLR 1237, [2010] 1 FCR 32, [2009] 2 FLR 1051.
12 [2004] EWCA Civ 971, [2005] Fam 293, [2004] 2 FCR 698, [2004] 2 FLR 1057.
13 *Re M (Abduction) (Consent: Acquiescence)* [1998] 9 WLUK 98, [1999] 1 FCR 5, [1999] Fam Law 8, [1999] 1 FLR 171.
14 *Re P-J (Abduction: Habitual Residence: Consent)* [2009] EWCA Civ 588, [2010] 1 WLR 1237, [2010] 1 FCR 32, [2009] 2 FLR 1051.

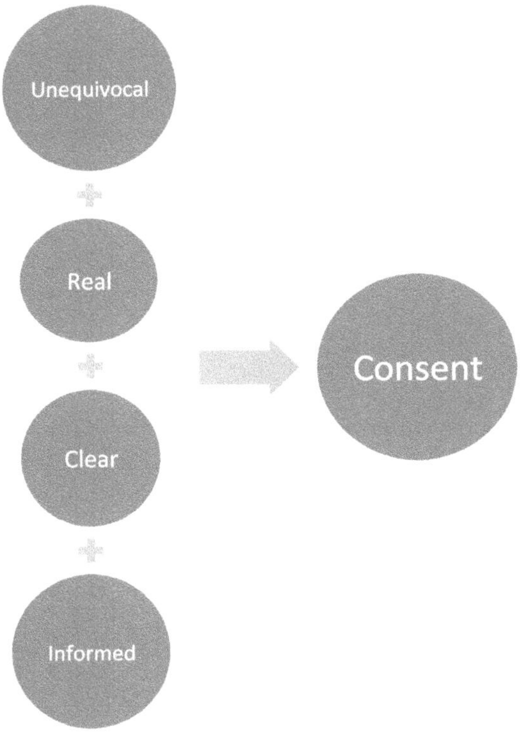

By contrast, purported consent which is vaguely expressed or uncertain, or subject to conditions which are not met, will not amount to consent for the purposes of HC80. The question of consent is fact-specific.

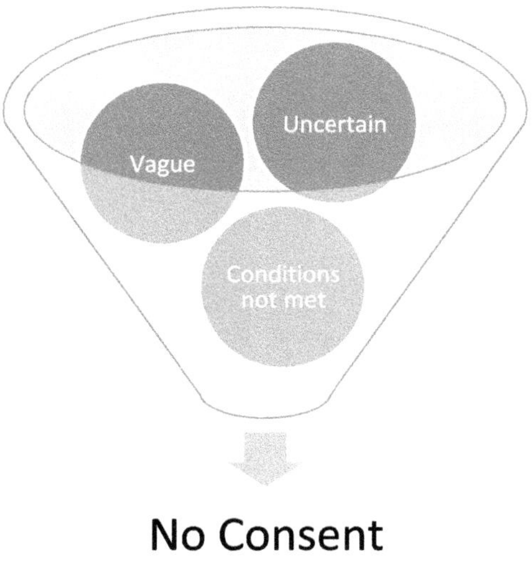

The courts adopt a common sense approach to the question of whether a person has consented, as is illustrated by the following citation:

Key citation: *Re P-J (Abduction: Habitual Residence: Consent)*[15]

> '… when intimate human relationships break down, our emotions lead us – whether in anger, jealousy, pain or a wish to wound – to say things which we do not mean and/or which are entirely inconsistent even from one hour to the next. Take a father who has clearly consented to a removal of the children with the mother to England. Is he to be taken to have withdrawn his consent because he rushes to the airport and there shouts "You can't go"? Of course not.
>
> Or take a father who has clearly not consented to a removal to England. Is he to be taken to have consented because, when the mother is piling the children into the taxi which will take them to the airport, he unexpectedly returns home and, in his shocked distress, tells her, in his vernacular, that she can take them wherever she pleases? Of course not.
>
> So the task of the judge in weighing a defence that an advance consent subsisted can prove difficult; and he will need to call upon his understanding of how, with all our imperfections, we human beings operate. Thus if, as here, the defendant asserts the other's advance consent to a removal, the judge has to persuaded that in reality it subsisted at the time of removal.'

5.7 Evidence of consent may be in writing but that is not essential. Consent may be inferred from conduct.

Key citation: *P v P (Abduction: Acquiescence)*[16]

> 'The parties agree that the onus is on the mother to establish this, that it should be shown in a manner similar to that which is required now for acquiescence in the light of the House of Lords' decision in *Re H (Abduction: Acquiescence)* [1998] AC 72, [1997] 1 FLR 872. The task of the court is to find as a fact whether the father subjectively intended to and did give unconditional consent to the removal of the child.'[17]

Third party consent

5.8 For the purposes of HC80, a third party cannot give consent on behalf of the parent even if, under the law of the foreign State, such consent is permissible[18].

15 [2009] EWCA Civ 588, [2010] 1 WLR 1237, [2010] 1 FCR 32, [2009] 2 FLR 1051 per Wilson LJ at para 56.
16 [1998] 3 FCR 550, [1998] 2 FLR 835.
17 Ward LJ at p 836.
18 *C v H (Abduction: Consent)* [2009] EWHC 2660 (Fam), [2010] 1 FLR 225.

Consent obtained by fraud or deception

5.9 Consent obtained by a trick or misrepresentation or upon a misunderstanding as to relevant intentions will be ineffective[19]. In *T v T (Abduction: Consent)*[20] Charles J held:

> '… such a misunderstanding or non-disclosure … would exist if the [abductor] knew that the father was proceeding on the basis of a misunderstanding, or she had not told him something, and in either case she knew or ought to have known that such misunderstanding, or non-disclosure, would or would be likely to, affect the father's decision to consent to her taking [the child] to England …'

Case Summary: *M v T (Abduction)*[21]

Facts:

F (Spanish) and M (British) entered into an agreement that the elder child should live with F in Spain and the younger child with M in England. There was to be extensive contact between both parents and both children. Immediately after relocating to England, M failed to facilitate contact between the younger child and F, and then later wrongfully retained the older child in England. F issued proceedings under HC80.

Held by Pauffley J:

On the evidence, M had never had the slightest intention of complying with the terms of the signed agreement. M's deception of the father and all of the children had been cruel and serious and had had the effect of vitiating F's consent to removal.

Conditional and future consent

5.10 Consent to the removal of a child may be valid, even if it is dependent on a future event, provided it is not too vague, uncertain or subjective and the facts at the time are not wholly or manifestly different from those prevailing at the time of removal.

19 See *T v T (Abduction: Consent)* [1999] 2 FCR 2, [1999] 2 FLR 912, per Charles J and *D v S (Abduction: Acquiescence)* [2008] EWHC 363 (Fam), [2008] 2 FLR 293 per Charles J.
20 [1999] 2 FCR 2, [1999] 2 FLR 912.
21 [2008] EWHC 1383 (Fam), [2009] 1 FLR 1309.

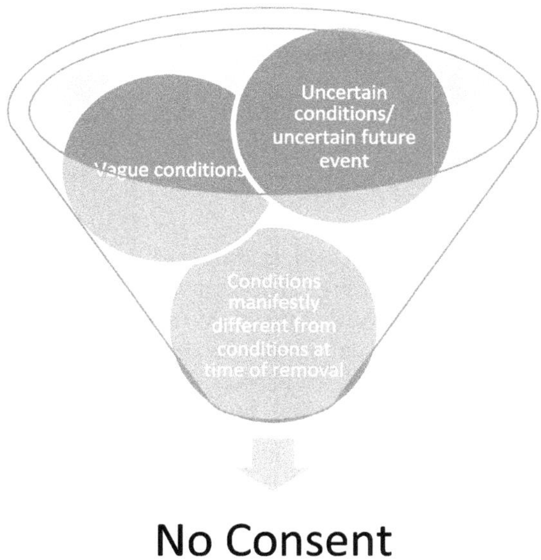

The condition, in essence, must be objectively verifiable[22].

Case Summary: *Re L (Abduction: Future Consent)*[23]

Facts:

The family moved to Florida and F told M that, if she did not like living there, she could relocate to England. M later removed the children from the US to England for the purposes of a holiday and then sought to rely on the father's earlier 'consent'.

Held:

F was held not to have consented.

22 *Re P-J (Abduction: Habitual Residence: Consent)* [2009] EWCA Civ 588, [2010] 1 WLR 1237, [2010] 1 FCR 32, [2009] 2 FLR 1051.

23 [2007] EWHC 2181 (Fam), [2008] 1 FLR 914.

Case Summary: *BT v JRT (Abduction: Conditional Acquiescence and Consent)*[24]

Facts:

M had previously brought the child to England and had returned when F had threatened HC80 proceedings. Thereafter the parties had reconciled. Approximately one year later, M and the child (aged 2) returned to England for a holiday and thereafter M wrongfully retained the child in England. In the course of discussions between the parents, F agreed that M could remain in England for a period of five years on condition that M took the child to Australia once a year for contact. F surrendered the lease to the matrimonial home on the basis that the mother was not returning. F subsequently sought to withdraw his consent and issued a Hague Convention summons.

Held by Sumner J:

Consent and acquiescence could be conditional provided the terms were clear, readily determined and that the consent was not vitiated by fraud, misunderstanding or deceit. F was held to have acquiesced.

Withdrawal of consent

5.11 Advance consent must be operative and in force at the time of the removal. Consequently, consent can be withdrawn at any time before actual removal.[25]

Key citation: *Re P-J (Abduction: Habitual Residence: Consent)*[26]

'Once we allow arguments to the effect that, although the left-behind parent had, prior to removal, clearly purported to withdraw an earlier consent, he was not *entitled* to do so, legal concepts crowd in upon the straightforward inquiry; and the stance taken by parents on the ground becomes rewritten as the stance which the law deems them to have taken. Decisions about children are best taken without such artifice.'

However, the right to withdraw consent is not absolute – it can be too late:

24 [2008] EWHC 1169 (Fam), [2008] 2 FLR 972.

25 *Re P-J (Abduction: Habitual Residence: Consent)* [2009] EWCA Civ 588, [2010] 1 WLR 1237, [2010] 1 FCR 32, [2009] 2 FLR 1051 per Ward LJ at para 48.

26 Ibid per Wilson LJ at para 55.

Re P-J (Abduction: Habitual Residence: Consent) per Wilson LJ:

"Take a father who has clearly consented to a removal of the children with the mother to England. Is he to be taken to have withdrawn his consent because he rushes to the airport and there shouts 'You can't go'? Of course not."

VK v JV (Abduction: Consent) per Moor J:

"I do, however, accept that it can become too late to withdraw consent as was suggested by Wilson LJ ... My conclusion is that it is too late once the parent who was given permission has begun to depart – in other words, the consent must be withdrawn prior to the other parent leaving."

It is clear from Wilson J's judgment in *Re P-J* that not every utterance of agreement, or dissent, will amount to something sufficient to be a reliable statement of views. For example:

Case Summary: *GC v RD (Children: Abduction)*[27]

Facts:

M lived in France with the children. F lived in England, where the children were spending time. In the midst of a long argument by email, M wrote to F: "*OK take custody ... You must still be in Paris? Pop round to pick up the rest of their belongings*". F thereafter did not return the children to France. His case was that he regarded the email as M genuinely and unequivocally consenting to the children moving back to England to live with him. M described the email as "*a slip of full thought and in anger*"; it was absolutely not the case that she wanted the children to remain in England.

Held by Baker J:

M's words were not '*a clear and unequivocal consent*'. Plainly what she said in those emails was said in the heat of the moment. Per *Re P-J*: '*Consent, or the lack of it, must be viewed in the context of the realities of ... the disintegration of family life*'. The exchange took place '*in the course of a heated conversation in which M was becoming frustrated and angry about F's unreasonable behaviour*'. In any event, M had clearly withdrawn any consent prior to the date for the children's return.

27 [2015] EWHC 3990 (Fam).

C. ACQUIESCENCE

5.12 The leading case on acquiescence is the House of Lords decision in *Re H and Others (Minors) (Abduction: Acquiescence)*[28]. Before *Re H* it had been held that it was possible for acquiescence to be either 'active' or 'passive'. The old authorities were overruled in favour of a new approach to acquiescence, whereby the court is primarily concerned, not with the question of the other parent's perception of the applicant's conduct, but with the question of whether the applicant acquiesced *in fact*. The approach can be summarised by the following graphic:

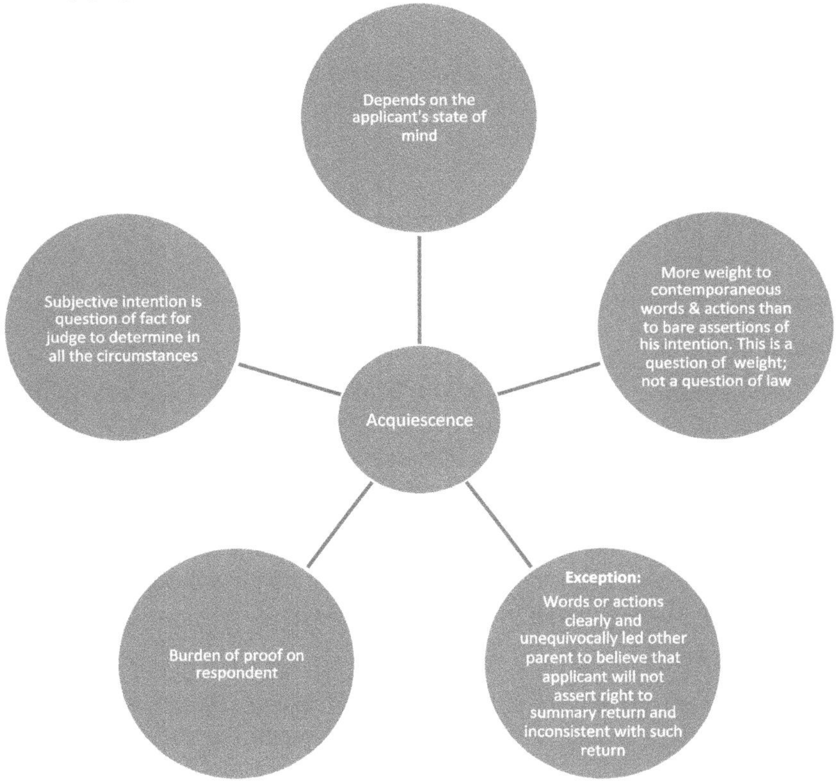

Case Summary: *Re H and others (Minors) (Abduction: Acquiescence)*[29]

Facts:

M took the children (3, nearly 2, and 9 months) to England from their home in Israel. Following the removal, F sought to secure the return of the children

28 [1998] AC 72, [1997] 2 FCR 257, [1997] 1 FLR 872.
29 [1998] AC 72, [1997] 2 FCR 257, [1997] 1 FLR 872.

through established orthodox Jewish procedures. After several months and many failed attempts, he was given permission by the Rabbinical Court to take whatever steps he saw fit. In May 1996 he applied under HC80. The High Court ordered the return of the children. The Court of Appeal reversed this decision, finding that F had acquiesced in the removal. It based its decision on a distinction, long relied on by the courts, between 'active' and 'passive' acquiescence. The distinction dictated that, where an act of acquiescence existed, the subjective intention of the applicant was irrelevant to the question of acquiescence. F appealed to the House of Lords.

Held by the House of Lords:

Acquiescence is a matter of the actual subjective intention of the wronged parent, save only in exceptional cases where his words or actions clearly showed, and had led the other parent to believe, that he was not asserting or going to assert his right to summary return and were inconsistent with such return.

Acquiescence is a question of fact, the burden of proof being on the abducting parent. Judges should be slow to infer an intention to acquiesce from attempts by the wronged parent to effect a reconciliation or to reach an agreed voluntary return of the abducted child. The father's faith required him to pursue his claim in the Beth Din; this was not acquiescence.

Subjective acquiescence

5.13 As the House of Lords held in *Re H*, save in exceptional cases the respondent has to establish that the applicant has acquiesced in the removal or retention in 'a subjective sense'. In other words, the left-behind parent must genuinely intend to permit the child to remain in the overseas country notwithstanding the actions of the abducting parent. This is a question of fact to be determined on the evidence. The following table sets out examples of cases in which the courts have considered the question of acquiescence.

Case	Acquiescence?
De L v H[30]	The child objected to a return and claimed to have burned his travel documents. F, who had retained the child, made serious attempts to secure replacement documents, but was thwarted by a lack of co-operation from M, without whose consent replacement documents could not be issued.
	Held by Sir Mark Potter P: M's failure to co-operate was not acquiescence. She did not agree to the child not being returned and F had no grounds on which to doubt that the mother wished the child to be returned.

30 [2009] EWHC 3074 (Fam), [2010] 1 FLR 1229.

Case	Acquiescence?
Re W (Acquiescence: Children's Objections)[31]	Post wrongful retention in England, the parties attempted a reconciliation over a period of months in England, including co-habitation.
	Held by Black J: F had not acquiesced in the wrongful retention. The arrangements he had helped to make for the family were explicable on the basis that he wanted the children to be comfortable while he attempted to reconcile with M. If F had at any stage agreed to the children remaining in England, it had been on the conditional basis that he would be part of the family. When ultimately the reconciliation failed, it could not be found that F had clearly and unequivocally acquiesced.
Re H, R and E (Abduction: Consent: Acquiescence)[32]	The parents had lived in the Netherlands with their 3 children. M claimed that, during a period of reconciliation, F had consented to her bringing the children to England. F waited a further 3 months after the removal before issuing Hague Convention proceedings, hoping to allow time for a reconciliation.
	Held by Keehan J: F's willingness to do whatever he could to achieve a reconciliation did not amount to either consent or acquiescence.

Objective acquiescence

5.14 It follows from the speeches in *Re H*[33] that a parent may be held to have acquiesced by virtue of his conduct whilst not having acquiesced as a matter of subjective intention[34]. Such cases of 'objective acquiescence' were described by the House of Lords as *strictly exceptional* and will arise where the parent seeking return, *knowing of his rights*, has so conducted himself towards the other parent and the children that he cannot be heard to go back on what he has done and seek to persuade the judge that, all along, he has secretly intended to claim the summary return of the children.

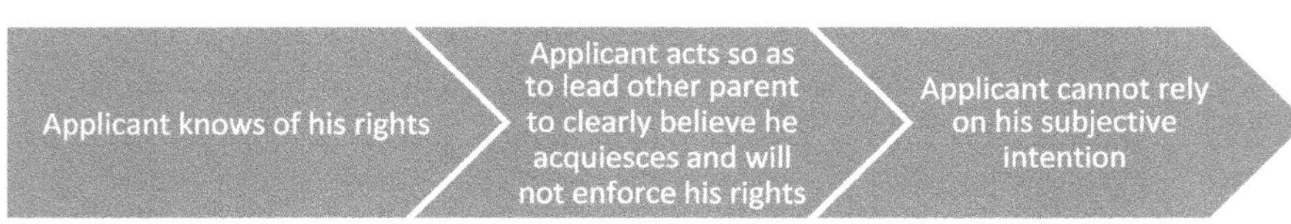

5.15 Cases in which a parent has not subjectively acquiesced but is nevertheless found to have acquiesced on the basis of the 'objective acquiescence' exception are rare. This was made clear in *Re H*[35] at pp 89H–90C:

31 [2010] EWHC 332 (Fam), [2010] 2 FLR 1150.
32 [2013] EWHC 3857 (Fam), [2014] 2 FLR 385.
33 [1998] AC 72, [1997] 2 FCR 257, [1997] 1 FLR 872.
34 At p 89F and p 883E.
35 [1998] AC 72, [1997] 2 FCR 257, [1997] 1 FLR 872.

> "… these exceptional circumstances can only arise where the words or actions of the wronged parent show clearly and unequivocally that the wronged parent is not insisting on the summary return of the child: it must be wholly inconsistent with a request for the summary return of the child. Such clear and unequivocal conduct is not normally to be found in passing remarks or letters written by a parent who has recently suffered the trauma of the removal of his children. Still less is it to be found in a request for access showing the wronged parent's desire to preserve contact with the child in negotiations for the voluntary return of the child or in the parent pursuing the dictates of his religious beliefs …"

Knowledge of legal rights

5.16 Before the House of Lords decision in *Re H*[36] it was held that a parent should know of his or her rights in order to acquiesce, but this did not necessarily mean that they needed to be specifically aware of HC80:

AZ (A Minor) (Abduction: Acquiescence) [1993] 1 FLR 682 ◆ *Re S (Abduction: Acquiescence)* [1998] 2 FLR 115

Reliance by the wronged parent on incorrect advice could not be regarded as acquiescence to a removal, but acting on '*adequate and realistic advice*' could.

Case Summary: Re S *(Abduction:Acquiescence)*[37]

Facts:

Following a removal by M from Australia, F was not told about HC80 by his first solicitor. He shipped the child's and the mother's belongings to the UK. His second solicitor advised that HC80 proceedings would be a waste of time as the Australian court would allow the mother to return to the UK. The father issued after seeing a third solicitor.

Held by the Court of Appeal:

The failure to issue after the second advice amounted to acquiescence.

36 [1998] AC 72, [1997] 2 FCR 257, [1997] 1 FLR 872.
37 [1998] 3 FCR 113, [1998] 2 FLR 115.

5.17 In more recent cases, the manner in which the issue of legal advice has been dealt with by the courts has been less clear.

Case Summary: *D v S (Abduction: Acquiescence)*[38]

Facts:

The parents had moved from Mexico to England where they shared the care of the child whilst living in separate houses. The parties had agreed that the family would live in England for 3 years, after which F would be able to choose the country of their residence for the next 3 years. M came to England having a private intention not to leave at the end of three years, and then issued divorce and CA 1989 proceedings. F delayed the issue of an HC80 application, having initially been advised that he had little prospect of success. He eventually issued an application before 12 months had elapsed.

Held by Charles J:

M had knowingly misled F by not telling him that she never intended to return to Mexico. If he had known that, he would never have consented to the move and therefore he had not consented to the move. However, F had later acquiesced by not immediately initiating HC80 proceedings. Subjective acquiescence was established as F had consulted solicitors shortly after the move to England and, although the evidence was unclear as to precisely what advice he had received, he knew of the existence of the Convention and decided not to bring proceedings under it at that time. The second limb was satisfied by F's conduct in relation to the Mexican divorce proceedings, which indicated that he was not reserving the right to argue that the welfare issues should be dealt with only by the Mexican courts.

Acquiescence need not be a continuing state of affairs

5.18 Unlike consent, once given, acquiescence cannot be withdrawn: *Re S (Abduction: Acquiescence).*[39]

Doing nothing

5.19 The following table demonstrates other examples of cases where it was submitted that a failure to act amounted to acquiescence:

38 [2008] EWHC 363 (Fam), [2008] 2 FLR 293.
39 [1998] 3 FCR 113, [1998] 2 FLR 115 at para 122.

Case	Failure to act = acquiescence?
Re F (Abduction: Rights of Custody)[40]	The fact that F delayed for a year in making an application was insufficient to establish acquiescence.
B-G v B-G (Abduction: Acquiescence)[41]	F saw 3 different lawyers in France, none of whom advised him about his HC80 rights. M issued Children Act proceedings in the UK which were heard over a number of months until a judge at one of the hearings transferred the matter to the High Court. Attendance notes showed that, despite being aware that there were proceedings he could pursue in France for the children's return there, F had decided to allow the family to remain in the UK. That was sufficient for acquiescence, despite having no precise awareness of HC80.
Re G (Abduction: Withdrawal of Proceedings, Acquiescence and Habitual Residence)[42]	This was a second set of proceedings, the first having been resolved by consent so that the parties could attempt reconciliation. The court held that this was insufficient to establish subjective acquiescence. The exception in *Re H* was not at play as F did not lead M to believe that he would not pursue an application if reconciliation failed. None of his subsequent conduct when reconciliation failed was sufficient to amount to acquiescence.

Acquiescence by the court

5.20 It is possible for a 'body or institution' – which includes a court – to acquiesce in a wrongful removal or retention. This was held to be the case in *Re M*[43].

Case Summary: *Re M (A Child)*[44]

Facts:

M applied for the return of a child to Ireland, in circumstances where the child had been returned to the jurisdiction of Ireland since the removal for the purpose of proceedings there. Following the removal, there had been two court hearings in Ireland, in which both parties had taken part. The Irish court, for reasons that were unclear, declined to make an injunctive order ensuring the child was retained in Ireland until the conclusion of proceedings.

40 [2008] EWHC 272 (Fam), [2008] Fam 75, [2008] 2 FCR 120, [2008] 2 FLR 1239.
41 [2008] EWHC 688 (Fam), [2008] 2 FLR 965.
42 [2007] EWHC 2807 (Fam), [2008] 1 FCR 1, [2008] 2 FLR 351.
43 [2017] EWHC 1294 (Fam).
44 [2017] EWHC 1294 (Fam).

Held by Holman J:

The Irish court had acquiesced in the wrongful removal and consented to the child remaining in the UK.

D. NOT ACTUALLY EXERCISING RIGHTS OF CUSTODY

5.21 Rights of custody are discussed in detail in **Chapter 3** of this book. Article 3 of HC80 is the focus in that chapter but the exercise of rights of custody is also explicitly referred to in Art 13 of the Convention.

It is worth comparing the texts of each Article:

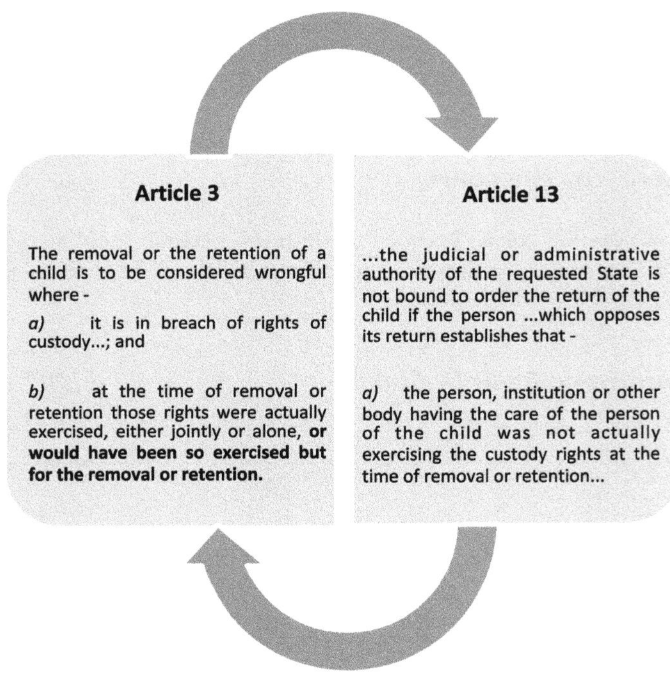

The highlighted text in Art 3 does not appear in Art 13. Article 3 therefore appears to provide an added layer of 'protection' to the applicant claiming that a retention or removal was wrongful. Specifically, although that party was not actually exercising rights of custody at the time of the removal or retention, those rights *would have been so exercised but for the removal or retention*: see, for example, *Re A (A Child) (Abduction: Rights of Custody: Imprisonment)*[45] (referred to at para **3.83** above).

45 [2004] 1 FLR 1.

That, arguably, leaves open the prospect that, although a court could find that a retention (for example) was wrongful as it was in breach of an applicant's rights of custody (although not exercised), the respondent might successfully defend the application for summary return on the basis that the applicant was not actually exercising his rights of custody, pursuant to Art 13.

E. DISCRETION

5.22 The essential difference between the discretion in a wider child welfare case and the ambit of the discretion in the context of HC80 proceedings was explained by the House of Lords in the leading case of *Re M and another (Children) (Abduction: Rights of Custody)*[46] (at para 32), in which the following passage from *Cannon v Cannon*[47] was approved, save for the description of the Convention objectives as being 'overriding'[48]:

> 'the exercise of a discretion under the Hague Convention requires the court to have due regard to the overriding objectives of the Convention whilst acknowledging the importance of the child's welfare ... whereas the consideration of the welfare of the child is paramount if the discretion is exercised in the context of our domestic law.'

The objectives or 'policy considerations' of the Convention include securing the swift return of abducted children, deterring abduction in the first place, comity between Contracting States and respect for the judicial processes in other Contracting States[49].

5.23 If the respondent proves that consent or acquiescence is established, the court must then go on to consider whether or not to order a return pursuant to Art 12 of HC80. There is no test of '*exceptionality*'[50]. A court may well find it convenient to start from the proposition that '*it is likely to be better for a child to return to his home country for disputes about his future to be decided there*', although '*the weight to be given to that factor will vary from case to case*'[51]. The court's discretion has been said to be '*at large*'[52], which means that the court can take into account:

46 [2007] UKHL 55, [2008] 1 AC 1288, [2008] 1 FCR 536, [2008] 1 FLR 251.
47 [2004] EWCA Civ 1330, [2005] 1 WLR 32, [2005] 1 FLR 169.
48 *Re M (Children) (Abduction: Rights of Custody)* [2007] UKHL 55, [2008] 1 AC 1288, [2008] 1 FCR 536, [2008] 1 FLR 251 at para 43.
49 *Re M (Children) (Abduction: Rights of Custody)* [2007] UKHL 55, [2008] 1 AC 1288, [2008] 1 FCR 536, [2008] 1 FLR 251 at para 42.
50 *Re M (Children) (Abduction: Rights of Custody)* [2007] UKHL 55, [2008] 1 AC 1288, [2008] 1 FCR 536, [2008] 1 FLR 251 at para 40.
51 *Re M (Children) (Abduction: Rights of Custody)* [2007] UKHL 55, [2008] 1 AC 1288, [2008] 1 FCR 536, [2008] 1 FLR 251 at para 39.
52 *Re M (Children) (Abduction: Rights of Custody)* [2007] UKHL 55, [2008] 1 AC 1288, [2008] 1 FCR 536, [2008] 1 FLR 251.

- the various aspects of Convention policy;
- the circumstances which gave the court a discretion in the first place; and
- wider considerations of the child's rights and welfare.

5.24 In consent and acquiescence cases, '*general considerations of comity and confidence, particular considerations relating to the speed of legal proceedings and approach to relocation in the home country, and individual considerations relating to the particular child might point to a speedy return so that her future can be decided in her home country*'[53].

5.25 In *Re S (Abduction: Acquiescence)*[54] it was held by the Court of Appeal that some of the factors to be taken into account in an acquiescence case included:

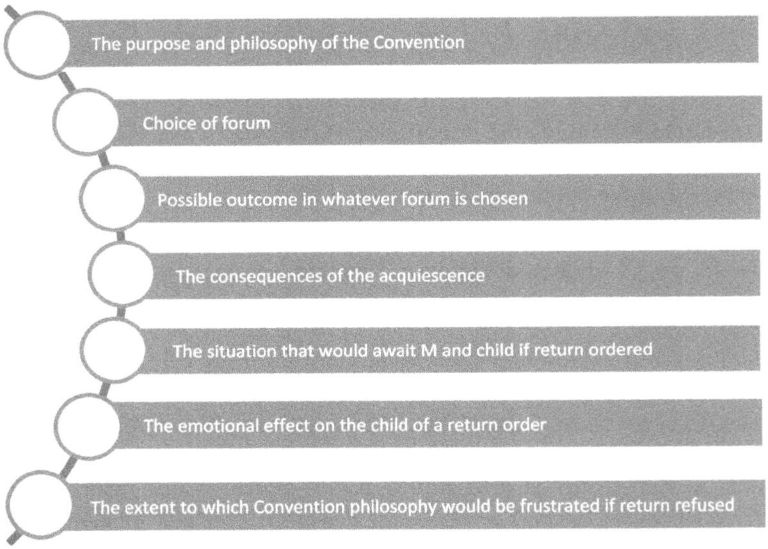

5.26 The fact that acquiescence, once given, is then swiftly withdrawn will affect the weight that is to be given to it in the exercise of the court's discretion[55].

53 *Re M (Children) (Abduction: Rights of Custody)* [2007] UKHL 55, [2008] 1 AC 1288, [2008] 1 FCR 536, [2008] 1 FLR 251 at para 45.

54 [1998] 3 FCR 113, [1998] 2 FLR 115.

55 *Re A (Minors) (Abduction: Custody Rights)* [1992] Fam 106, [1992] 2 FCR 9, [1992] 2 FLR 14; *Re R (Child Abduction: Acquiescence)* [1995] 2 FCR 609, [1995] 1 FLR 716.

5.27 In *BT v JRT (Abduction: Conditional Acquiescence and Consent)*[56] factors which were taken into account in exercising discretion *not* to order a return included:

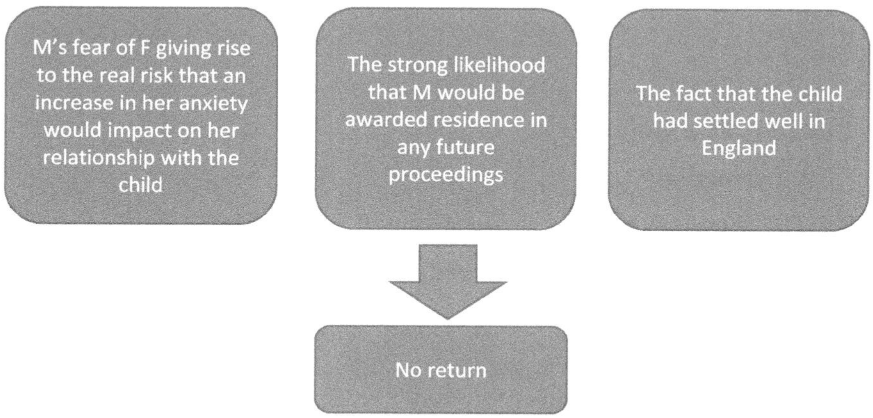

56 [2008] EWHC 1169 (Fam), [2008] 2 FLR 972.

CHAPTER 6

Article 13(b) – grave risk of harm

Content at a Glance:

A. **Introduction**

B. **The summary process versus disputed issues of fact**

C. **Do the assumed (or established) facts give rise to an Article 13(b) situation? *Re E***
- Domestic violence
- Mental health of the parent with care
- Reaction of the child to a return
- Separation from parent with care
- Separation from parent with care: refusal to return with the child
- Separation from siblings or half-siblings
- Potential arrest of the abducting parent
- Political unrest in the State of habitual residence
- Delay / Settlement for a period of time

D. **Protective measures**
- Brussels IIA, Art 11(4)

E. **Doing 'the best' the court can: oral evidence?**

A. INTRODUCTION

6.1 Article 13(b) of the 1980 Hague Convention[1] ('HC80') provides another so-called 'defence' or 'exception' to the otherwise mandatory requirement for the return of a child to the jurisdiction of his/her habitual residence, from which he/she has been wrongfully removed and/or wrongfully retained[2].

6.2 The wording of Art 13(b) is as follows:

Article 13(b) – 1980 Hague Convention

'Notwithstanding the provisions of the preceding Article [*ie a child must be returned forthwith where a wrongful removal or retention has been*

1 1980 Hague Convention on the Civil Aspects of Child Abduction.
2 For wrongful removals and retentions see **Chapter 3**.

established], the judicial or administrative authority of the requested State is not bound to order the return of the child if the person, institution or other body which opposes its return establishes that:

(a) [*defence of consent or acquiescence* – see **Chapter 5**]

(b) There is a grave risk that his or her return would expose the child to physical or psychological harm or otherwise place the child in an intolerable situation.

[*defence of child objections* – see **Chapter 7**]

In considering the circumstances referred to in this Article, the judicial and administrative authorities shall take into account the information relating to the social background of the child provided by the Central Authority or other competent authority of the child's habitual residence.'

6.3 The Supreme Court considered the Art 13(b) exception in *Re E (Abduction: Custody Appeal)*[3]:

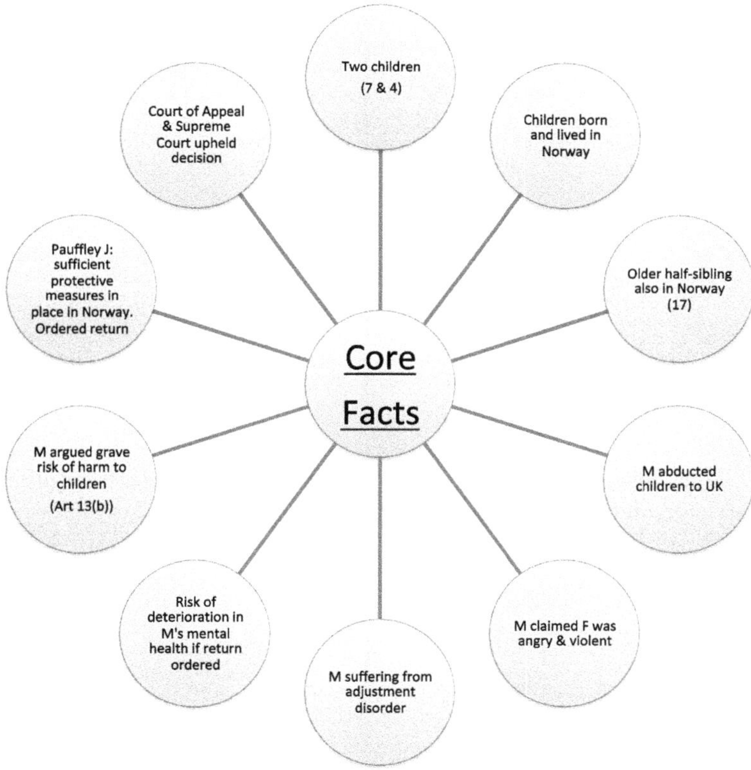

3 *Re E (Children) (Abduction: Custody Appeal)* [2011] UKSC 27, [2012] 1 AC 144, [2011] 2 FCR 419, [2011] 2 FLR 758.

6.4 Baroness Hale addressed the principles underlying the Art 13(b) exception at paras 31 to 36 of *Re E*[4]:

para 31

- Art 13(b) need not be 'narrowly construed'. By its terms it is of restricted application.
- The words require no elaboration or gloss.

para 32

- Burden of proof lies with the person opposing the return.
- Evidence must be produced to substantiate the exception.
- Standard of proof = balance of probabilities.
- Summary process means it will rarely be appropriate to hear oral evidence of the allegations.

para 33

- Risk to the child must have reached such a level of seriousness as to be "grave".
- Although "grave" characterises the risk of harm, rather than the harm itself, there is a link between the two concepts.

para 34

- "Intolerable" is a strong word, but must mean "a situation which this particular child in these particular circumstances should not be expected to tolerate".
- Those words can apply to physical or psychological harm.
- Every child has to put up with a certain amount of "rough and tumble, discomfort and distress" but "there are some things which it is not reasonable to expect a child to tolerate".
- If a risk exists sufficient to ground an Art 13(b) exception, the source of the risk is irrelevant.
- Thus, the risk can stem from a party's "subjective perception of events [which] leads to a mental illness which could have intolerable consequences for the child".

para 35

- Art 13(b) looks to the future: the situation as it would be on a return to the home country.
- The situation depends crucially on "the protective measures which can be put in place" to ensure that the child does not face an intolerable situation when she gets home.

para 36

- There is a tension betweeen the inability of the court to resolve factual disputes between the parties and the risks that the child will face if the allegations are true.
- Eg allegations of domestic abuse.

6.5 Thus, when considering a case where one party seeks to argue that the Art 13(b) exception applies, the following must be noted:

4 *Re E (Children) (Abduction: Custody Appeal)* [2011] UKSC 27, [2012] 1 AC 144, [2011] 2 FCR 419, [2011] 2 FLR 758. See also the speech of Baroness Hale in *Re D (A Child) (Abduction: Rights of Custody)* [2006] UKHL 51, [2007] 1 AC 619, [2007] Fam Law 102, [2007] 1 FCR 1, [2007] 1 FLR 961.

The burden of proving an Art 13(b) exception rests upon the person opposing the return

The burden of proof is the ordinary civil standard: the balance of probabilities

The 'exception' must be supported by evidence which establishes facts alleged to create a risk sufficient for Art 13(b)

It will seldom be appropriate to hear oral evidence

6.6 An issue arises in many cases involving Art 13(b) where the respondent makes factual allegations which are denied by the applicant. How is the court to resolve the tension between the summary nature of an application under HC80 and the need fairly to resolve Art 13(b) allegations? Given that a full investigation of disputed factual issues (eg by way of a full fact-finding hearing with oral evidence) is inconsistent with the object of the Convention, how should the court properly consider an Art 13(b) defence founded on disputed issues of fact (eg the perpetration of domestic violence)? The solution is found in para 36 of *Re E*[5]. This is considered in paras **6.7–6.12** below; specific examples of potential Art 13(b) exceptions are addressed at para **6.13** below.

B. THE SUMMARY PROCESS VERSUS DISPUTED ISSUES OF FACT

6.7 The '*sensible and pragmatic*' solution to the tension identified in para **6.6** above is as follows (para 36 of Baroness Hale's speech in *Re E*)[6]:

5 *Re E (Children) (Abduction: Custody Appeal)* [2011] UKSC 27, [2012] 1 AC 144, [2011] Fam Law 919, [2011] 2 FCR 419, [2011] 2 FLR 758.

6 *Re E (Children) (Abduction: Custody Appeal)* [2011] UKSC 27, [2012] 1 AC 144, [2011] Fam Law 919, [2011] 2 FCR 419, [2011] 2 FLR 758. In *Re C (Children) (Abduction: Article 13(b))* [2018] EWCA Civ 2834, [2019] 2 FCR 218, [2019] 1 FLR 1045, Lewison LJ said, obiter dicta, at paras 69–70 that the approach set out in para 36 of *Re E* may be 'unprincipled' and '… may be open to reconsideration by the Supreme Court one day'.

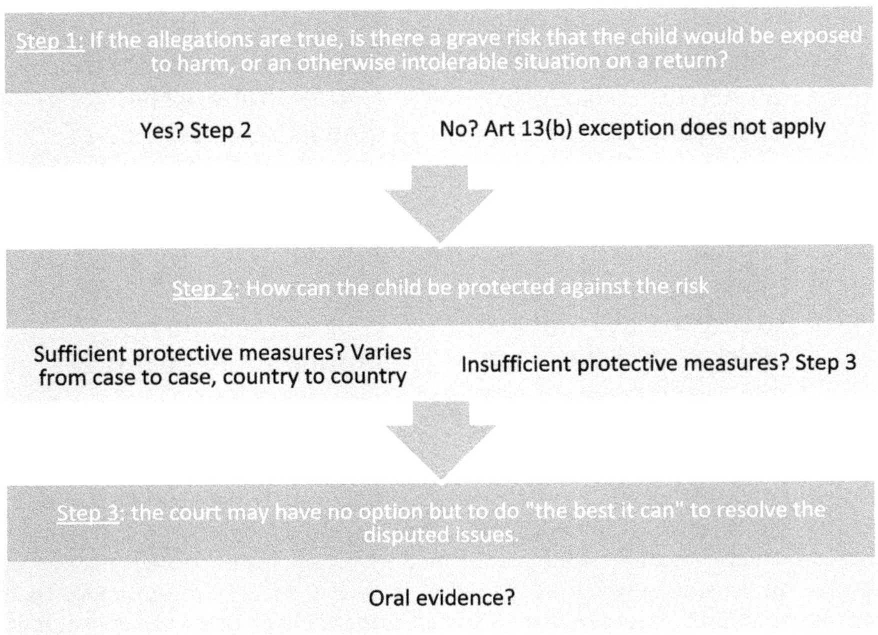

6.8 The approach identified above was considered by the Supreme Court in *Re S (A Child)*[7] and held to be appropriate in cases involving key disputed allegations of fact. However, the Supreme Court also said:

Key citation: Lord Wilson in *Re S (A Child)*[8] at para 22

> 'First, at a general level, the approach commended in [*Re E*] should form part of the court's general process of reasoning in its appraisal of a defence under the article and does not require formal identification as a preliminary point. Second, and more importantly, the guidance given in para 36 of [*Re E*] relates to factual "disputes" and to resolution of the "disputed" issues.'

6.9 *Re S*[9] can be distinguished factually from *Re E*[10], in that much of the relevant evidence before the court was either not in dispute or not capable of being disputed as it consisted of written communications.

7 *Re S (A Child) (Abduction: Rights of Custody)* [2012] UKSC 10, [2012] 2 AC 257, [2012] 1 FCR 493, [2012] 2 FLR 442.
8 *Re S (A Child) (Abduction: Rights of Custody)* [2012] UKSC 10, [2012] 2 AC 257, [2012] 1 FCR 493, [2012] 2 FLR 442.
9 *Re S (A Child) (Abduction: Rights of Custody)* [2012] UKSC 10, [2012] 2 AC 257, [2012] 1 FCR 493, [2012] 2 FLR 442.
10 *Re E (Children) (Abduction: Custody Appeal)* [2011] UKSC 27, [2012] 1 AC 144, [2011] 2 FCR 419, [2011] 2 FLR 758.

6.10 The court is not bound to follow the *Re E*[11] process through in a structured way if, for example, it is quite clear on the evidence before the court that the allegations enable a judge confidently to discount the possibility of a successful Art 13(b) defence. A good example of this is *Re K*[12].

Case Summary: *Re K (1980 Hague Convention) (Lithuania)*[13]

Facts:

M wrongfully retained a child, E, in England from Lithuania. She argued, *inter alia*, that there was a grave risk that a return would expose the child to an intolerable situation pursuant to Art 13(b) of HC80. There were disputed allegations about violent and abusive behaviour by F dating back several years.

Hogg J rejected the Art 13(b) ground: E had had a difficult time; she was suffering badly because of the influence of M and the maternal family; counselling would probably be very sensible if she were returned. E was not at grave risk of harm as M's allegations about F lacked substance: '*the mother has done nothing to corroborate her own evidence*' and, despite allegations dating back to 2002, she had allowed E to remain in the care of the father.

Held by the Court of Appeal (Black LJ):

On the criticism that Hogg J failed to follow the *Re E* approach (see para **6.7** above):

> '53. I do not accept that a judge is bound to take this approach if the evidence … enables him or her confidently to discount the possibility that the allegations give rise to an Article 13(b) risk. That is what the judge did here. It was for the mother, who opposed the return, to substantiate the Article 13(b) exception … and for the court to evaluate the evidence within the confines of the summary process. Hogg J found the mother's evidence about what had happened to be inconsistent with her actions in that she had continued her relationship with the father and allowed him to have the care of E … The Article 13(b) argument had therefore not got off the ground in the judge's view. The judgment about the level of risk was a judgment which fell to be made by Hogg J and we should not overturn her judgment on it unless it was not open to her …'.

11 *Re E (Children) (Abduction: Custody Appeal)* [2011] UKSC 27, [2012] 1 AC 144, [2011] 2 FCR 419, [2011] 2 FLR 758.

12 *Re K (1980 Hague Convention) (Lithuania)* [2015] EWCA Civ 720, per Black LJ at paras 52–53.

13 [2015] EWCA Civ 720, per Black LJ at paras 52–53.

6.11 The Court of Appeal in *Re C (Children)*[14] considered further the *Re E*[15] process in the context of disputed allegations of domestic violence; it is important to address whether the allegations of past domestic violence give rise to a risk of *future* violence capable of grounding a defence under Art 13(b).

Case Summary: Re C (Children)[16]

Facts:

M, F and their two children lived in South Africa. In May 2018 the family travelled to England. There was a dispute as to the purpose of the trip. F said it was for a holiday, and M said it was to consider a permanent move. The parties argued, the police were called, and F returned to South Africa alone.

F commenced proceedings under HC80 for the summary return of the children to South Africa. He offered undertakings, including to vacate the family home. He proposed to lodge the undertakings in South Africa.

M relied on Art 13(b), alleging that she had been the victim of significant domestic violence. She disputed the efficacy of F's proposed undertakings as protective measures. She argued that she would suffer psychologically if she had to return.

HHJ Bellamy dismissed the application. He concluded that: (1) if true, M's allegations would give rise to a grave risk of harm if the children were returned, and (2) it was apparent that a return would aggravate the fear and distress already experienced by M. It was not possible, without fact-finding, to determine whether M's anxieties had an objectively proven foundation, but they were nevertheless real.

Held by Court of Appeal (Moylan LJ) allowing the appeal:

Considered *Re E*[17], in particular para 36[18], and paras 52–53 of R*e K*[19] before saying:

> 'in adopting this proposed solution[20], it was not being suggested that no evaluative assessment of the allegations could or should be undertaken

14 *Re C (Children) (Abduction: Article 13(b))* [2018] EWCA Civ 2834, [2019] 2 FCR 218, [2019] 1 FLR 1045.

15 *Re E (Children) (Abduction: Custody Appeal)* [2011] UKSC 27, [2012] 1 AC 144, [2011] Fam Law 919, [2011] 2 FCR 419, [2011] 2 FLR 758.

16 *Re C (Children) (Abduction: Article 13(b))* [2018] EWCA Civ 2834, [2019] 2 FCR 218, [2019] 1 FLR 1045.

17 *Re E (Children) (Abduction: Custody Appeal)* [2011] UKSC 27, [2012] 1 AC 144, [2011] 2 FCR 419, [2011] 2 FLR 758.

18 See para **6.5** above.

19 *Re K (1980 Hague Convention) (Lithuania)* [2015] EWCA Civ 720. See para **6.10** above.

20 At para 36 of *Re E (Children) (Abduction: Custody Appeal)* [2011] UKSC 27, [2012] 1 AC 144, [2011] 2 FCR 419, [2011] 2 FLR 758.

> by the court. Of course a judge has to be careful when conducting a paper evaluation but this does not mean that there should be no assessment at all about the credibility or substance of the allegations.' (para 39)
>
> '... the judge did not sufficiently address the situation as it would be' (para 49)
>
> '[T]he judge appears to relate the risk to the mother's allegations of abuse she has suffered rather than to the situation as it would be if she and the children returned ... The failure by the judge to address the nature of the risk of domestic violence occurring in the future and to answer why this would not be sufficiently ameliorated by the measures proposed by the father are ... fundamental gaps in the reasoning ...' (para 50)

6.12 With the caveat that it may be permissible for a judge to take a more holistic evaluation of an Art 13(b) argument and to reject it on the basis described in *Re K*[21] and *Re C*[22], this chapter will now follow the structure of the steps set out in para 36 of *Re E*[23] to consider:

(1) the assumed (or established) facts that might give rise to an Art 13(b) exception;

(2) protective measures; and

(3) doing 'the best it can' – when might the court hear oral evidence?

C. DO THE ASSUMED (OR ESTABLISHED) FACTS GIVE RISE TO AN ARTICLE 13(B) SITUATION? *RE E*[24]

6.13 If one assumes the allegations made by the person resisting a return to the home country to be true, when do they give rise to a grave risk of harm to the child, or an otherwise intolerable situation sufficient to ground an exception under Art 13(b)? Each case will turn on its own facts. The case law shows that allegations of grave risk under Art 13(b) fall into a number of different categories (illustrated by the following graphic):

21 *Re K (1980 Hague Convention) (Lithuania)* [2015] EWCA Civ 720.

22 *Re C (Children) (Abduction: Article 13(b))* [2018] EWCA Civ 2834, [2019] 2 FCR 218, [2019] 1 FLR 1045.

23 *Re E (Children) (Abduction: Custody Appeal)* [2011] UKSC 27, [2012] 1 AC 144, [2011] 2 FCR 419, [2011] 2 FLR 758.

24 *Re E (Children) (Abduction: Custody Appeal)* [2011] UKSC 27, [2012] 1 AC 144, [2011] 2 FCR 419, [2011] 2 FLR 758.

Domestic violence

6.14 The Art 13(b) exception can be established where there is a risk of harm to the child from exposure to domestic violence likely to be inflicted upon the caring parent. This is the most common allegation raised in HC80 proceedings but, unless combined with other risk factors[25], the level of risk to the child arising from such exposure to violence will probably need to be very high for a court to be satisfied that a return cannot be ordered with protective measures in place.

6.15 Rare examples of a successful defence to a return order founded purely on a risk of violence are the old cases of *Re F*[26] and *Re D (Children)*[27].

25 For instance, clear evidence that a return would cause a drastic deterioration in the mental health of the abducting parent with care (see below).

26 *Re F (A Minor) (Abduction: Custody Rights Abroad)* [1995] Fam 224, [1995] Fam Law 534, [1995] 2 FLR 31, pp 233–235.

27 *Re D (Children) (Article 13(b): Non Return)* [2006] EWCA Civ 146, [2006] Fam Law 438, [2006] 2 FLR 305. See also *TB v JB (formerly JH) (abduction: Grave Risk of Harm)* [2001] Fam Law 576, [2001] 2 FCR 497, [2001] 2 FLR 515.

Case Summary: *Re D (Children) (Article 13(b): Non Return)*[28]

Facts:

The family lived in Caracas, Venezuela. In June 2005, M was the victim of a targeted firearm assault. She was shot at close range in the face and right shoulder, having been identified before she was shot. The person who shot her alleged that he was hired to do so. The person who 'contracted' the shooting was unknown and at large.

M already had permission from the court in Caracas to come to England for a summer holiday. She applied, without notice to F, to bring forward her holiday, was granted permission to do so, arrived in England and cancelled her return flight.

F applied for a summary return. The judge at first instance made serious findings as to the risk posed to M, possibly F, and the children directly (as opposed to merely a generalised risk of violence posed by the State of Venezuela). She upheld M's objection to a return based on Art 13(b).

Held by the Court of Appeal (appeal dismissed):

> '… the judge having found the real risks of physical danger to the children as vivid and as oppressive as she did, it is hard to see how the alleviating potential of security measures could cast doubt on the validity of the mother's Article 13(b) case founded on physical risk. … on the judge's findings, her concluding sentence necessarily had to be more strongly expressed, namely that the physical risks alone would have been sufficient to establish the defence and that would have been the end of the case.' (para 29)

6.16 By contrast, in *Re M (Children)*[29] the Court of Appeal overturned the first instance judge's refusal to order a return to the United States on the basis of the mother's Art 13(b) 'defence' based on contested allegations of physical, sexual and emotional abuse by the father, alleged to have been witnessed by the children[30]. Notwithstanding the gravity of the allegations, there was evidence before the court that sufficient protective measures could be afforded to the mother to make a return order[31].

28 [2006] EWCA Civ 146, [2006] 2 FLR 305. See also *TB v JB (formerly JH) (abduction: Grave Risk of Harm)* [2001] Fam Law 576, [2001] 2 FCR 497, [2001] 2 FLR 515.

29 *Re M (Children) (Hague Convention: Article 13(b))* [2016] EWCA Civ 942, [2018] 2 FCR 181, [2017] 2 FLR 556.

30 Reported as *Re J (A Child)* [2016] EWHC 1282 (Fam).

31 See paras 21–24 of the judgment of Macur LJ (discussed at para **6.38** below).

Mental health of the parent with care

6.17 Where a parent with care is suffering from mental ill-health and an order for return to the home country would lead to a deterioration in that condition (and thus their ability to provide adequate care for the children), this may result in a grave risk for Art 13(b) purposes. However, the evidence must be substantial and a successful argument will be highly unusual. The key authority is *Re S (Abduction: Rights of Custody)*[32].

Case Summary: *Re S (Abduction: Rights of Custody)*[33]

Facts:

The parents lived together in Australia until February 2011 when M removed the child ('W') to England without F's knowledge or consent. M's only 'defence' to F's application for a summary return was pursuant to Art 13(b). She made a large number of serious allegations against F, linking them with evidence as to the state of her psychological health whilst in Australia.

Charles J dismissed the application. Witness statements and 300 text messages revealed that important allegations were admitted (or could not be realistically denied) by F (see paras 7–15). M had been prescribed medication for anxiety and depression. She had had extensive psychotherapy in Australia and in England. There was evidence from her treating psychologist and an SJE psychiatrist who reported that M suffered from PTSD and that the likely psychiatric and psychological impact on M of a return to Australia was significant and severe.

The Court of Appeal allowed the appeal.

Held by the UKSC allowing the appeal (Lord Wilson):

> 'In [*Re E*][34] this court considered the situation in which the anxieties of a respondent mother about a return … were not based upon objective risk to her but nevertheless were of such intensity as to be likely, in the event of a return, to destabilise her parenting of the child to the point at which the child's situation would become intolerable. No doubt a court will look very critically at an assertion of intense anxieties not based upon objective risk; and will, among other things, ask itself whether they can be dispelled. But in [*Re E*] it was this court's clear view that such anxieties could in principle found the defence …'. (para 27)

32 *Re S (A Child) (Abduction: Rights of Custody)* [2012] UKSC 10, [2012] 2 AC 257, [2012] 1 FCR 493, [2012] 2 FLR 442.

33 *Re S (A Child) (Abduction: Rights of Custody)* [2012] UKSC 10, [2012] 2 AC 257, [2012] 1 FCR 493, [2012] 2 FLR 442.

34 *Re E (Children) (Abduction: Custody Appeal)* [2011] UKSC 27, [2012] 1 AC 144, [2011] Fam Law 919, [2011] 2 FCR 419, [2011] 2 FLR 758.

> 'Charles J sought faithfully to follow the guidance [at para 36 *Re E*] … Thus–
>
> (a) he began by assuming that the mother's allegations against the father were true;
>
> (b) he concluded that, on that assumption, and in the light of the fragility of the mother's psychological health, the protective measures offered by the father would not obviate the grave risk that, if returned to Australia, W would be placed in an intolerable situation; so
>
> (c) he proceeded to consider, as best he could in the light of the absence of oral evidence and the summary character of the inquiry, whether the mother's allegations were indeed true; and
>
> (d) following a careful appraisal of the documentary evidence … the mother had "made out a good prima facie case that she *was* the victim of significant abuse at the hands of the father".
>
> In the light of his conclusion at (d) … it was unnecessary … to address the mother's subjective perceptions. For the effect of his conclusion was that the mother's anxieties were based on objective reality.' (para 29)
>
> '… we must make clear the effect of what this court said in [*Re E*]. The critical question is what will happen if, with the mother, the child is returned. If the court concludes that, on return, the mother will suffer such anxieties that their effect on her mental health will create a situation that is intolerable for the child, then the child should not be returned. It matters not whether the mother's anxieties will be reasonable or unreasonable. The extent to which there will, objectively, be good cause for the mother to be anxious on return will nevertheless be relevant to the court's assessment of the mother's mental state if the child is returned.' (para 34)

6.18 Following on from this analysis, in a case which involves arguments about the respondent's mental health, the crucial question to ask is this (para 27 of *Re S*[35])[36]:

35 *Re S (A Child) (Abduction: Rights of Custody)* [2012] UKSC 10, [2012] 2 AC 257, [2012] 1 FCR 493, [2012] 2 FLR 442.

36 For example, see paras 51–52 of Moylan LJ's judgment in *Re C (Children) (Abduction: Article 13(b))* [2018] EWCA Civ 2834, [2019] 2 FCR 218, [2019] 1 FLR 1045, where he concluded that there was insufficient evidence to support the conclusion that a return would be '*potentially psychologically disabling*' for the mother.

Are the anxieties of the respondent about a return with the child to the state of habitual residence of such intensity as to be likely, in the event of a return, to destabilise his / her parenting of the child to the point at which the child's situation would become intolerable or cause them psychological harm?

This is a high threshold to satisfy[37]. There will need to be a detailed consideration of what, if any, protective measures can ameliorate the risk of harm to the parent with care (and thus the child).

6.19 In the event of an Art 13(b) 'defence' being run on the basis of the respondent's mental ill-health, consideration must be given at the commencement of proceedings as to the need for expert psychiatric evidence to report on the following:

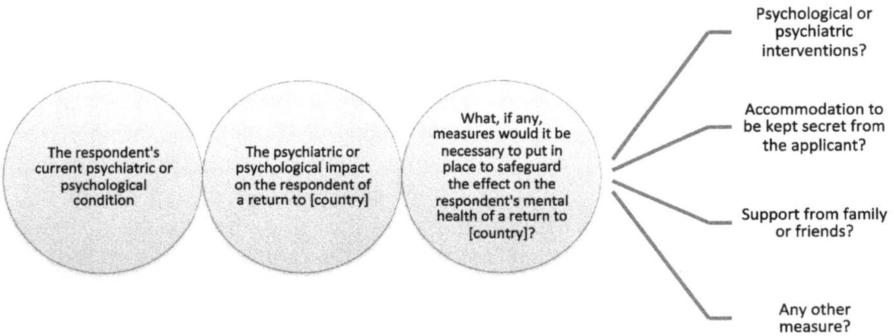

6.20 Depending on the contents of the expert report as to the parent with care's current psychiatric condition and/or the need for ongoing treatment, consideration should also be given to the need for expert evidence from a psychiatrist / psychologist in the country to which the return order would be made, to report on what resources and treatments are available, and the ease with which they can be accessed by the parent (eg cost and availability).

37 See the comments by (1) Holman J in *KS v MK* [2015] EWHC 3276 (Fam), [2016] Fam Law 152 at paras 20 and 21: *'[21] Patently, if the effect of … an enforced return … would be at all likely to induce a mother actually to kill herself, the effect on the child, both immediately and frankly lifelong, could be devastating.*', and (2) the judgment of MacDonald J in *T v E (Refusal to Order Return)* [2016] EWHC 3148 (Fam), [2017] 4 WLR 18. See also *Uhd v McKay* [2019] EWHC 1239 (Fam), [2019] 2 FLR 1159 (discussed at para **6.21** below).

6.21

Case Summary: *Uhd v McKay*[38]

Facts:

F and M lived in Australia. They separated prior to the birth of the child in July 2015. There were continuous proceedings in Australia: (1) injunction proceedings, equivalent to those under the Family Law Act 1996 in this jurisdiction, and (2) F's application for parental responsibility and shared care. Within these proceedings, M had made many serious allegations against F, which had not been found proven.

In September 2018, M abducted the child from Australia to England. F commenced proceedings for summary return under HC80 and to enforce the orders of the Australian court under the 1996 Hague Convention[39] ('HC96'). M and the child were located subsequent to an order publicising the case[40].

M relied on Art 13(b) as a defence to a return to Australia, contending that her mental health would deteriorate – whatever the objective level of risk – such as to expose the child to a grave risk of physical or psychological harm.

An SJE forensic psychiatrist concluded that the symptoms as described by M were consistent with a diagnosis of complex PTSD, but that this was dependent on the traumatic events as alleged by M having taken place.

Held by MacDonald J (ordering return):

The judge analysed the expert evidence. After setting out the relevant passages from *Re E*[41], *Re K*[42] and *Re C*[43] he accepted that:

> '[73] ... in evaluating the extent to which the anxieties of a respondent about a return with the child that are not based upon objective risk to the respondent but are nevertheless of such intensity as to be likely, in the event of a return, to destabilise the respondent's parenting of the child to a point where the child's situation would become intolerable, the court should consider, amongst other factors, the objective evidence (if any) that the

38 [2019] EWHC 1239 (Fam), [2019] 2 FLR 1159.

39 Convention of 19 October 1996 on Jurisdiction, Applicable Law, Recognition, Enforcement and Co-Operation in Respect of Parental Responsibility and Measures for the Protection of Children.

40 See **Chapter 15**.

41 *Re E (Children) (Abduction: Custody Appeal)* [2011] UKSC 27, [2012] 1 AC 144, [2011] Fam Law 919, [2011] 2 FCR 419, [2011] 2 FLR 758.

42 *Re K (1980 Hague Convention) (Lithuania)* [2015] EWCA Civ 720.

43 *Re C (Children) (Abduction: Article 13(b))* [2018] EWCA Civ 2834, [2019] 2 FCR 218, [2019] 1 FLR 1045.

> respondent will have good cause to be anxious if the child were returned to the jurisdiction of habitual residence, as well as the protective factors that may ameliorate such a situation.'

The Australian court had already made findings which were binding on the English court (para 83) and M relied on allegations already dismissed during that fact-finding process. After a detailed analysis of the particular facts of the case, the judge concluded that M had not made out her case.

Reaction of the child to a return

6.22 The situation where a child's objection to and obstruction of a return to his/her home State can result in difficulties (and sometimes a wholesale failure) in enforcing the order to return is discussed in **Chapter 15**. However, it is also the case that in certain circumstances the child's negative reaction to the prospect of a return, founded on having witnessed domestic violence, can lead to a finding that to order a return would expose the child to psychological harm, even where the domestic violence itself is insufficient to ground an Art 13(b) exception.

Case Summary: *Klentzeris v Klentzeris*[44]

Facts:

The parties and children lived in Athens, Greece. The relationship was extremely fraught and on M's evidence there was one episode of violence which resulted in the arrival of the police and other occasions when she was subjected to some abuse.

The children were wrongfully removed to England and F applied for a summary return. The children were interviewed by a Cafcass officer, who recorded strong objections to a return. The oldest child recalled witnessing an incident of violence by F against M, had a panic attack during the interview and said he would kill himself if he went back to Greece. M reported that he had had a number of panic attacks.

M defended the application on the basis of (1) the children's objections, and (2) the grave risk of psychological harm to the children if ordered to return (Art 13(b)). **Held:**

The judge (upheld by CA) was ambiguous in his conclusion on the child objections 'defence'. However, after recognising that the allegations of domestic violence would – ordinarily – fail to provide a defence to a

44 *K v K* [2007] EWCA Civ 533, [2007] 3 FCR 580, [2007] 2 FLR 996.

summary return, in light of protective measures available and the aims of HC80 he concluded that:

> '… I have great difficulty in taking a course with these children that I have been warned will be likely to cause them psychological harm. It is, in my experience, extremely unusual for a judge to receive so stark a warning. I cannot overlook it and I find that I cannot persuade myself that it is unreal or overstated. It is because of the likelihood of psychological harm in the particular and special circumstances of this case and for that reason alone that I exercise my discretion not to award the return of the children to Greece …'

6.23 In *Re E (A Child) (Abduction: Article 13(b): Deferred Return Order)*[45] the subject child had been placed with foster parents in the interim[46]; the foster mother described her as 'the most traumatised child she had cared for'. The judge found the Art 13(b) exception to be established in circumstances where she had:

> '[82] … clear and unequivocal [evidence] about the profound emotional and psychological harm in both the short and long term which might flow from any move of E from her foster carer at this current time.'

Separation from parent with care

6.24 There may be circumstances in which the abducting parent is unable to return to the home country with the child, in the event of a return order. Each case will turn on its facts, but an Art 13(b) argument was rejected by the Court of Appeal in *Re W (A Child)*[47], a case in which the mother had serious mental health issues and the child was ordered to be returned to the USA to live with the father.

Separation from parent with care: refusal to return with the child

6.25 What of the situation where the abducting parent refuses to return to the country of habitual residence and relies on this refusal as generating an intolerable situation for the child[48]? These cases are not easy to resolve, as there is an obvious tension between the need to protect the child from a grave risk of harm generated by the separation from the parent with care and the need to

45 *Re E (A Child) (Abduction: Article 13(b): Deferred Return Order)* [2019] EWHC 256 (Fam), [2019] 2 FLR 615.

46 Pursuant to the Child Abduction and Custody Act 1985, s 5: see **Chapter 11**.

47 *Re W (A Child)* [2017] EWCA Civ 2152.

48 As distinct from the situation whereby the parent with care refuses to return on the basis of his/her own psychological issues.

avoid allowing that parent to frustrate the return order. The issue has not been addressed in a consistent manner in the reported cases, which are not easy to reconcile.

6.26 The starting point must always be the decision in *Re E*[49], discussed above, in which it was said that if a risk of harm exists its source is irrelevant[50]. However, that was *obiter dicta* and was not the subject either of full argument or discussion in the Supreme Court. It is notable that in *Neulinger v Switzerland*[51], discussed in *Re E*, the European Court of Human Rights had concluded that the mother's refusal to return to Israel was 'objectively justifiable'[52] before overturning the decision to return on the basis (as found by the Swiss court) that to separate the mother and child would cause the latter 'major psychological harm'[53]. This was not, said Baroness Hale in *Re E*, anything more than an acknowledgment that guarantees under the European Convention on Human Rights had to be interpreted in light of HC80[54].

Key citation: Baroness Hale in *Re E*[55]

> '[27] It is possible to imagine other, highly unusual, cases in which a return might be in violation of the ECHR. … a person cannot be expelled to a country where he will face a real risk of torture or inhuman or degrading treatment or punishment or the flagrant denial of a fair trial … That could, in theory, arise where the abducting parent would face such a risk and the child could not safely be returned without her. In such a case … it would be unlawful for the court, as a public authority, to act incompatibly with the Convention rights. But that is a far cry from the suggestion that article 8 "trumps" the Hague Convention: in virtually all cases, as the Strasbourg court has shown, they march hand in hand.'

The following examples and extracts from case law illustrate the approach which has been adopted at different times to cases where a parent refuses to return with

49 *Re E (Children) (Abduction: Custody Appeal)* [2011] UKSC 27, [2012] 1 AC 144, [2011] 2 FCR 419, [2011] 2 FLR 758.
50 At para 34.
51 *Neulinger v Switzerland (41615/07)* (2012) 54 EHRR 31, [2011] 2 FCR 110, [2011] 1 FLR 122.
52 At paras 144–150.
53 At para 44.
54 *Re E (Children) (Abduction: Custody Appeal)* [2011] UKSC 27, [2012] 1 AC 144, [2011] 2 FCR 419, [2011] 2 FLR 758, at para 26.
55 *Re E (Children) (Abduction: Custody Appeal)* [2011] UKSC 27, [2012] 1 AC 144, [2011] 2 FCR 419, [2011] 2 FLR 758.

a child (NB *Re C (A Minor)*[56] was decided before *Re E*[57] and therefore needs to be considered with caution[58]):

Re C (A Minor) (Abduction) - Butler-Sloss LJ

- "The grave risk of harm arises not from the return of the child, but the refusal of the mother to accompany him... Is a parent to create a psychological situation, and then rely upon it? If the grave risk of psychological harm to a child is to be inflicted by the conduct of the parent who abducted him, then it would be relied upon by every mother of a young child who removed him out of the jurisdiction and refused to return." (p.661)
- Cited with approval by the Court of Appeal in *Re S (A Child)* [2002] EWCA Civ 908 at para 31.

C v S - Pauffley J

- "If his mother failed to accompany him, reneging upon her assurances, doubtless there would be an impact upon L. He would be entitled to feel resentful and betrayed. But considering the factual background as to how L's relationship with his father has been promoted throughout his life and the positives noted by Mr McGavin, it is really quite impossible to conclude that a return into the father's household would fulfil the criteria for the establishment of an Article 13B exception" (para 49)

AT v SS - MacDonald J

- Ordered a return to Netherlands, where the child would be placed termporarily in foster care given M's refusal to return
- "Were the court to conclude that on return to Holland separation from his mother and placement in care *would* expose S to a grave risk of physical or emotional harm or would otherwise place him in an intolerable situation then it is correct that it matters not whether the separation and all that follows is due to the mother's contumelious attempt to frustrate the Convention process or an involuntary inability to travel or something between those two extremes. The mother's conscious refusal to return is nevertheless relevant to the court's assessment of *whether* the situation for S should he be returned to Holland falls within the tightly drawn boundaries of Art 13(b)." (para 44)
- See also paras 34, 42 and 47: "The significance for the situation the child will face upon return of a parent's refusal to return must in each case be evaluated in the context of the protective measures that can be put in place to mitigate the impact of the same."

R v P - Theis J

- Real risk that the M would not return to Lithuania due to (i) new baby with partner, and (ii) repeated failures by F to comply with court orders in Lithuania (paras 126-129)
- If the child had to return without M "it is very likely, in my judgment, such a situation would result in her suffering from a grave risk of psychological harm and it would place her in an intolerable situation."

56 *Re C (A Minor) (Abduction)* [1989] 1 WLR 654, [1989] 1 FLR 403.

57 *Re E (Children) (Abduction: Custody Appeal)* [2011] UKSC 27, [2012] 1 AC 144, [2011] 2 FCR 419, [2011] 2 FLR 758.

58 *Re C (A Minor) (Abduction)* [1989] 1 WLR 654, [1989] 1 FLR 403; *C v S (Child Abduction: Hague Convention: Article 13)* [2014] EWHC 3799 (Fam); *AT v SS (Abduction: Article 13(b): Separation from Carer)* [2015] EWHC 2703 (Fam), [2016] 2 FLR 1102; *R v P* [2017] EWHC 1804 (Fam).

Separation from siblings or half-siblings

6.27 There is no definitive answer to the question as to whether the separation of the subject child from his/her siblings or half-siblings will successfully ground an Art 13(b) exception. There are numerous examples of reported cases; in some, Art 13(b) has been established whereas, in others, the defence has been rejected [59]. The majority of these cases pre-date *Re E*[60] and need to be approached with caution.

Case Summary: *Re S (Child Abduction: Joinder of Sibling: Child's Objections)*[61]

Facts:

M and F lived in France with their two children, S (aged 13) and R (aged 17). In late 2015, M wrongfully removed the children to England. F applied for the summary return of S to France. Due to her age, R could not be the subject of the application. R had expressed the intention to remain in England.

M accepted that the removal was wrongful, but defended the summary return of S on the basis of (1) her objection to a return, and (2) a grave risk of psychological harm founded, in the main, on the likely separation of S from her sibling, R.

Held by Cobb J (ordering a return):

R should be joined as a party. R was a non-subject child and had to demonstrate that she had '*sufficient interest in the welfare of* [the subject child]' (FPR 2010, r 12.3(1)) and that it was in her best interests to be joined (r 16.2). Those tests were made out.

Rejecting M's Art 13(b) defence (based on separation from R) (paras 22–23):

> 'I accept the evidence that R and S are close; however the girls are 3½ years apart in age. They are at a very different stage of their emotional

59 *B v K (Child Abduction)* [1993] Fam Law 17, [1993] 1 FCR 382; *Re C (Abduction: Grave Risk of Psychological Harm)* [1999] Fam Law 371, [1999] 2 FCR 507, 1 FLR 1145; *Re C (Abduction: Grave Risk of Physical or Psychological Harm)* [1999] Fam Law 520, [1999] 3 FCR 510, [1999] 2 FLR 478; *Re T (Abduction: Child's Objections to Return)* [2000] Fam Law 594, [2000] 2 FCR 159, [2000] 2 FLR 192; *Zaffino v Zaffino (Abduction: Children's Views)* [2006] EWCA Civ 1012, [2006] 1 FLR 410; *Re E (Abduction: Intolerable Situation)* [2008] EWHC 2112 (Fam), [2009] Fam Law 472, [2009] 2 FLR 485; *Re H (Abduction)* [2009] EWHC 1735 (Fam), [2009] Fam Law 656, [2009] 2 FLR 1513; *WF v FJ and Others* [2010] EWHC 2909 (Fam), [2001] Fam Law 124, [2011] 1 FLR 1153; *Re S (Child Abduction: Joinder of Sibling: Child's Objections)* [2016] EWHC 1227 (Fam), [2016] Fam Law 1075, [2017] 2 FLR 384.

60 *Re E (Children) (Abduction: Custody Appeal)* [2011] UKSC 27, [2012] 1 AC 144, [2011] Fam Law 919, [2011] 2 FCR 419, [2011] 2 FLR 758.

61 [2016] EWHC 1227 (Fam), [2016] Fam Law 1075, [2017] 2 FLR 384.

and educational development. In the event that S is returned to France, the sisters will be able to see each other in holidays, for significant periods [and occasional weekends] … The separation may … be only temporary.

… R has declared a choice to be in England … That is a matter over which I have no influence let alone jurisdiction. R could just as easily decide to return to France to return to school there at least for the next year; she is after all nearly at the end of her education, and may ultimately decide to complete it within a curriculum which she has thus far followed for all her school life.'

Although S objected to a return, discretion exercised to order a return (para 36).

Potential arrest of the abducting parent

6.28 The risk of the abducting parent being arrested and prosecuted for the abduction (or indeed for any previous offence) is unlikely to be an argument, by itself, sufficient to establish an Art 13(b) exception[62]. However, that is not to say that the argument can simply be dismissed out of hand; consideration must be given (as discussed at paras **6.34–6.45** below) as to what effect a parent's arrest will have on the child and what, if anything, should be done about it. Recently the issue has been referred to in the following cases[63]:

Re GP

- Risk and consequences of M's arrest not fully explored.
- What situation would face the child "in concrete terms" on a return?
- Appeal allowed and rehearing directed.
- See **6.42** below.

Re B (Children)

- M posed a potential risk to the children.
- But "even if the father were to be imprisoned … arrangements to protect the children could easily be devised …".

H v K

- "a parent who chooses to abduct a child … must expect to be the subject of arrest and prosecution … It sits ill in the mouth of a parent who has abducted a child to complain about the consequent risk of arrest and prosecution."

62 See *Re L (Abduction: Pending Criminal Proceedings)* [1999] 1 FLR 433; and *H v K* [2017] EWHC 1141 (Fam), [2018] 1 FLR 700.

63 *Re GP (A Child) (Abduction: Consideration of Evidence)* [2017] EWCA Civ 1677, [2018] 1 FCR 638, [2018] 1 FLR 892; *Re B (Children) (Return of Children)* [2018] EWCA Civ 614, [2018] 2 FLR 663; *H v K (Abduction: Undertakings)* [2017] EWHC 1141 (Fam), [2018] 1 FLR 700.

Political unrest in the State of habitual residence

6.29 In exceptional cases it may be possible to argue that life in the State from which the child is being wrongfully retained is so dangerous, or poses such a grave risk of harm to that child, that a return should be prevented under Art 13(b). In *TB v JB*[64] Hale LJ said at para 42:

> 'It is possible to hypothesize circumstances in which events since the departure have created such a risk: obvious examples are the outbreak of civil war or the destruction of the children's home and livelihood.'

6.30 However, in practice it is more difficult to establish that the risk actually exists on the ground, as opposed to in theory or in the newspapers. In *Re S (A Child)*[65] the mother argued that the return of the child to Israel would expose her to physical or psychological harm as a result of the political situation. The Court of Appeal said[66]:

> '[37] … These terrorist attacks are events over which neither she nor the father have control and over which the courts in Israel have no control. They are external to the family dynamic and in our judgment a reactive illness which arguably impairs the mother's ability fully and properly to cope with her child of whom she is the primary carer can amount to an Article 13(b) defence if as a result of her disabilities there is a grave risk of physical or psychological harm to the child or if the situation to which the child is being returned is intolerable within the meaning of that Article …
>
> [64] … [the judge] correctly asked herself what was the actual risk to this child of returning to Israel. She correctly asked whether the risk fell within the tests established by this court. She took account of the worsening situation. She recognised that "there must be anxieties and uncertainties in everyone's mind who live in [Israel]", but she concluded that "the risk of direct harm befalling [the child] as a result of acts of terrorism is not as great as the mother would wish me to believe". On the evidence before her that was a conclusion to which she was entitled to come.'

64 *TB v JB (Formerly JH) (Abduction: Grave Risk of Harm)* [2001] 2 FCR 497, [2001] 2 FLR 515.
65 *Re S (A Child)* [2002] EWCA Civ 908, [2002] 3 FCR 43, [2002] 2 FLR 815.
66 Per Ward LJ.

6.31 In *Re M & Another*[67] the House of Lords rejected an argument that '*the moral and political climate in Zimbabwe is such that any child would be at grave risk of psychological harm or should not be expected to tolerate having to live there*'[68].

6.32 However, there may be a grave risk of harm arising from actions of others in the home country which are specific to the parties and which successfully establish an Art 13(b) situation, for example where the mother has been shot and remains at great personal risk (see *Re D (Children) (Article 13(b): Non Return)*[69].

Delay / Settlement for a period of time

6.33 A long delay in resolving HC80 proceedings could in principle give rise to an intolerable situation for the child were a return to the 'home' country to be ordered. However, care must be taken with any argument that is founded entirely on the delay[70].

Re D (A Child) - House of Lords

- "...a delay of this magnitude [four years in this case] in securing the return of the child must be one of the factors in deciding whether his summary return, without investigation of the facts, will place him in a situation which he should not be expectd to tolerate" [para 53]
- However, this element was not the subject of the appeal and no view was expressed on how much weight should be placed on the delay in an Art 13(b) 'defence' [para 55]

Re KS - Macur J

- "L is integrated so completely within his new life in time, location and physical and social environment that he could only be described as 'settled'" [para 43]
- "He has known no other life and has had to make no conscious adjustment to a change in his geographical circumstances. He has no cognitive recognition of an earlier and different life or community." [para 44]
- "I consider that to disrupt L's present living arrangements would have more far reaching consequences and adverse impact than in the case of an older and less sensitive child able to comprehend a sudden departure from one routine and community and the prospect of the next ..." [para 46]
- Article 13(b) 'defence' allowed [para 46]. However, note the decision of *Re L-S.*

Re L-S (A Child) - Court of Appeal

- "*Re KS* was a strong case on its own facts" as the child had been in the UK for two years. In *Re D*, the child had been in the UK for 4 years. [para 78]
- "[the judge] was entirely correct in sounding a strong note of caution with respect to the extent to which the mere passage of time may be deployed in establishing an intolerable situation sufficient to satisfy Article 13(b) ... Where a period of settlement is to be relied upon in support of an 'intolerable situation' claim under Article 13(b) the judicial evaluation is of a wholly different character. The passage of time in that context, rather than being a simple matter of calculation, must, as Mr Scott submitted, be viewed through the lens of the requirements of Article 13(b)." [para 80]
- See also para 82.

67 *Re M & Another (Children)* [2007] UKHL 55, [2008] AC 1288, [2008] 1 FCR 536, [2008] 1 FLR 251.

68 At para 55.

69 [2006] EWCA Civ 146, [2006] 2 FLR 305.

70 Case references for the graphic below: *Re D (A Child) (Abduction: Rights of Custody)* [2006] UKHL 51, [2007] 1 AC 619, [2007] 1 FCR 1, [2007] 1 FLR 961; *Re KS (Abduction: Wrongful Retention)* [2009] EWHC 1494 (Fam), [2010] 1 FCR 338, [2009] 2 FLR 1231; *Re L-S (A Child) (Abduction: Custody Agreement: Acquiescence)* [2017] EWCA Civ 2177, [2018] 1 FCR 429, [2018] 1 FLR 1373.

D. PROTECTIVE MEASURES

6.34 The Supreme Court in *Re E*[71] was clear that undertakings given by the party seeking a return and/or other protective measures which can be put in place in the home country will play a crucial role in the operation of HC80. Even if it is considered that the assumed facts, as alleged by the party objecting to the return, would create an intolerable situation under Art 13(b), the court must then consider what, if any, protective measures are available to mitigate the risk sufficiently to enable the court to make an order for the child's return.

6.35 The breadth and extent of protective measures required in any particular case will vary depending on the nature of the risk, but consideration should be given to the following issues, designed to remove any perceived risk that a child will suffer harm (or an intolerable situation) on a return to the home jurisdiction:

Mechanics of the return?

- Who will accompany the child?
- What mode of transport?
- Who will fund the travel?
- When? Any conditions imposed?

What happens when the child gets off the plane/train?

- Is the other parent to stay away from the airport?

Where will the child live?

- How and when is the accommodation to be secured and funded?

With whom will the child live?

- Will there be contact with the other parent?
- Should the applicant undertake not to remove the child from the abductor's care pending a first hearing?
- Should the applicant undertake not to enforce an order awarding them the care of the child pending the matter returning to court?

Finances?

- Should the applicant pay maintenance pending the home courts being seised of maintenance jurisdiction?
- What should the maintenance cover? Accommodation? General living? Transport? Legal fees?

Will the abductor be arrested on arrival?

- Is there anything that can be done to prevent / minimise this?
- Should the applicant undertake not to institute / support any proceedings (criminal or civil) relating to the abduction?

Any risk of domestic violence?

- How can the risk be mitigated / prevented?
- Undertakings along the lines of a non-molestation injunction? Mirror order?

Risk of the deterioration of a parent's mental health?

- What services are available in the home jurisdiction?
- Can that parent receive the necessary treatment if he/she returns with the child?
- What will be the effect on the parent's mental health?

71 *Re E (Children) (Abduction: Custody Appeal)* [2011] UKSC 27, [2012] 1 AC 144, [2011] 2 FCR 419, [2011] 2 FLR 758.

6.36 There is an important difference in principle between (1) protective measures designed to protect a child from an Art 13(b) risk, and (2) practical arrangements designed to facilitate a smooth return for the child on arrival in the home State. Practical arrangements can be directed as a means of implementing a return order, whereas the court can only insist upon protective measures as a precondition to making a return order if these are necessary to eliminate a grave risk which would otherwise exist. It is clear from the decisions in *Re D*[72] and *Re E*[73] that the protective measures must be '*effective*' to secure the protection of the child. The court must '*examine in concrete terms*' the situation facing a child on return and whether the protective measures proposed negate the intolerability of that situation[74]. In *Re S (A Child)*[75] Moylan LJ drew attention to the distinction between practical arrangements, on the one hand, and protective measures, on the other (paras 55–56):

Practical arrangements versus protective measures

> 'The Hague Conference on Private International Law is expected soon to be publishing a Guide to Good Practice on Article 13(b) of the 1980 Convention. This is likely to refer to the need to consider whether, when undertakings are being relied upon, they can be made enforceable in the Requesting State and, if not, that they should be used with caution when being relied on as measures to protect against an Article 13(b) risk. It will also draw attention to the difference between protective measures and practical arrangements. The latter are put in place to ensure an orderly return so are directed towards facilitating and implementing the child's return by, for example, providing who will pay for flights. They might be described as arrangements which are more light touch.
>
> Clearly, protective measures designed or relied on to protect a child from an Article 13(b) risk are in a different category. If the court is considering such measures in the context of determining whether the risk has been established or whether, as in the present case, such measures will sufficiently ameliorate an identified grave risk, the efficacy of the measures will need to be addressed with care. Clearly, the more weight placed by the court on the protective nature of the measures when determining the application, the greater the scrutiny required in respect of their efficacy.'

72 *Re D (A Child) (Abduction: Rights of Custody)* [2006] UKHL 51, [2007] 1 AC 619, [2007] Fam Law 102, [2007] 1 FCR 1, [2007] 1 FLR 961.

73 *Re E (Children) (Abduction: Custody Appeal)* [2011] UKSC 27, [2012] 1 AC 144, [2011] Fam Law 919, [2011] 2 FCR 419, [2011] 2 FLR 758.

74 *Re GP (A Child) (Abduction: Consideration of Evidence)* [2017] EWCA Civ 1677, [2018] 1 FCR 638, [2018] 1 FLR 892, at para 61.

75 *Re S (A Child) (Hague Convention 1980: Return to Third State)* [2019] EWCA Civ 352, [2019] 2 FCR 539, [2019] 2 FLR 194.

6.37 Thus, whilst the precise terms of the protective measures will be tailored to address the issues arising in the particular circumstances of the case, practitioners must consider the '*broad potential scope of the exercise*'[76], including the following:

Laws of the home country

- What is the law in the foreign jurisdiction? Are there legal mechanisms to prevent the type of harm/risk of harm identified by the Art 13(b) exception? Eg laws against domestic violence?
- How are those laws enforced? Can/should protective orders be obtained in that jurisdiction before a return?
- Is there a need for expert evidence from a foreign lawyer? Can one rely on the principle of comity?

State facilities in the home country

- Social security
- Social housing
- Education
- Medical (including psychological and psychiatric) facilities, care and cost
- Can any of the above be guaranteed on a return?

Undertakings / assurances given by the other party

- In what terms?
- Are they enforceable in the foreign jurisdiction?
- Should they be accepted without more? Are they better expressed as an order made under the 1996 Hague Convention?
- Should mirror provisions be obtained in the foreign court prior to a return?

6.38

Case Summary: *Re M (Children)*[77]

Facts:

At first instance, Russell J refused to order a return of the children to the United States on the basis of the mother's Art 13(b) 'defence' stemming from disputed allegations of physical, sexual and emotional abuse by the father, alleged to have been witnessed by the children.

Held by the Court of Appeal (Macur LJ):

Notwithstanding the gravity of the allegations, there was evidence before the court that sufficient protective measures could be put in place to enable a return order to be made (paras 21–23).

> 'I would direct the children's immediate return to the USA provided that the father provides evidence first of all that a consent order has

76 Moylan LJ at para 51 of *Re S (A Child) (Hague Convention 1980: Return to Third State)* [2019] EWCA Civ 352, [2019] 2 FCR 539, [2019] 2 FLR 194.

77 *Re M (Children) (Abduction: Hague Convention: Article 13(b))* [2016] EWCA Civ 942, [2018] 2 FCR 181, [2017] 2 FLR 556.

been entered into the Superior Court of New Jersey and secondly that the landlord of his present accommodation consents to the subletting or assignment of the tenancy to the mother, or otherwise her exclusive occupation of the same.' (para 24)

6.39 If the other jurisdiction is one in which HC96[78] has effect[79] then the protective measures may be expressed as being '*necessary measures of protection*' by reference to Art 11 of HC96, provided they fall within the scope of HC96 (see Arts 3 and 4); issues relating to maintenance are expressly excluded under Art 4. Measures of protection ordered pursuant to Art 11 will be enforceable until the authorities of the State to which the child is returned have taken '*the measures required by the situation*' (see Art 11(2)).

6.40 If the case is one in which undertakings are offered / required of the applicant parent, thought must be given to their effectiveness and enforceability in the State to which the child is to be returned. In some cases the English court may be willing to accept the undertakings without more, but in others it may require effective and enforceable 'mirror' assurances in the courts of the foreign jurisdiction.

Case Summary: *Re S (A Child) (Hague Convention 1980: Return to Third State)*[80]

Facts:

Cobb J ordered the summary return of a child to Hungary. An annex to the order contained 14 undertakings given by F, but for which Cobb J would have decided that the mother had established the grave risk exception under Art 13(b) due to the allegations of domestic violence made by M. Unusually, Hungary was not the State of the child's habitual residence prior to his wrongful removal; he had been habitually resident in Germany.

Held by the Court of Appeal, allowing the appeal (Moylan LJ):

(1) The focus in respect of protective measures was on the undertakings F was willing to provide and not on protective measures more generally. However, the expression '*protective measures*' has a wide meaning. (para 50)

78 Convention of 19 October 1996 on Jurisdiction, Applicable Law, Recognition, Enforcement and Co-Operation in Respect of Parental Responsibility and Measures for the Protection of Children. For HC96 see **Chapter 10**.

79 See the status table at https://www.hcch.net/en/instruments/conventions/status-table/?cid=70.

80 [2019] EWCA Civ 352, [2019] 2 FCR 539, [2019] 2 FLR 194.

(2) Care must be given to the scope of HC96; some matters are excluded from the scope of HC96, eg 'maintenance obligations' in Art 4. (para 53)

(3) There is a '*need for caution when relying on undertakings*' (per para 43 of *Re C*[81]). The '*efficacy*' of protective measures is essential and this will vary from case to case and from country to country. (para 54)

(4) The effectiveness of the undertakings accepted from F was questionable:

> '[61] ... the judge provides no explanation for his conclusion (at [58]) that the father's undertakings are "*effective ... to neutralise*" the grave risk. Is this based on a conclusion simply that the father can be relied upon to comply with them or is it based on them in some manner being effective in Hungary? The recitals to the Order would certainly indicate that the judge viewed the undertakings as being enforceable ... but, for the reasons given above ... I struggle to see how [Art 11 of HC96] would apply to the maintenance obligations covered by the undertakings ...'

6.41 As regards the laws of other jurisdictions, reliance can be placed in some cases on the principle of comity, such that '*the court should accept that, unless the contrary is proved, the administrative, judicial and social services in the requesting State are as adept at protecting children as they are in the requested State*'[82]. However, it is always necessary to show that any protective measures are actually going to be effective in that country in securing the protection of the child against an intolerable situation. Therefore, if there is any doubt as to whether the courts or law in the foreign jurisdiction will be effective in, say, protecting a mother with care against future domestic violence, it is essential to ensure that there is sufficient evidence before the court as to the mechanisms available in that jurisdiction. It may be necessary to instruct a foreign lawyer to report on this issue and on the enforceability of any undertakings / orders which may be made by the English courts.

6.42 The importance of the efficacy of protective measures was emphasised by the Supreme Court in *Re E*[83] (above) and restated more recently by the Court

81 *Re C (Children) (Abduction: Article 13(b))* [2018] EWCA Civ 2834, [2019] 1 FLR 1045.

82 *AT v SS (Abduction: Article 13(b): Separation from Carer)* [2015] EWHC 2703 (Fam), [2016] 2 FLR 1102; *R v P* [2017] EWHC 1804 (Fam), per Moylan J at para 34. Moylan J refers later in the paragraph to the following authorities: *Re H (Abduction: Grave Risk)* [2003] EWCA Civ 355, [2003] 2 FCR 151, [2003] 2 FLR 141; *Re M (Abduction: Intolerable Situation)* [2000] 1 FLR 930; and *Re L (Abduction: Pending Criminal Proceedings)* [1999] 2 FCR 604, [1999] 1 FLR 433.

83 *Re E (Children) (Abduction: Custody Appeal)* [2011] UKSC 27, [2012] 1 AC 144, [2011] Fam Law 919, [2011] 2 FCR 419, [2011] 2 FLR 758.

of Appeal in *Re GP*[84], *Re C*[85] and *Re S*[86]. In *Re GP* the Court of Appeal held that the first instance judge had failed properly to consider the situation which would subsist for the child if she were to be returned to her State of habitual residence.

Case Summary: *Re GP (A Child)*[87]

Facts:

In 2011, M moved GP (aged 11) to Northern Italy without the consent of F. M was prosecuted in Italy, found guilty in 2014 and sentenced to one year in prison. She appealed and the sentence was not activated pending appeal. The appeal was dismissed by the Italian Court of Appeal in 2017, by which time M had abducted GP to England (in breach of an Italian shared care order).

F applied for GP's return to Italy under HC80. Hayden J ordered a return to Italy, rejecting M's Art 13(b) defence. M appealed.

M's Art 13(b) argument:

M argued that Art 13(b) applied because of the likelihood of immediate imprisonment and consequential issues regarding finances and accommodation. There was limited evidence: an email from F's Italian lawyer stated it was possible to commute a prison sentence to community service. The judge:

- did not consider whether community service was likely to be applied;
- did not consider whether M would in any event be held in custody in the short term pending a decision being made on commuting her sentence;
- observed the removal to England was not the subject of prosecution; and
- accepted an undertaking from F not to voluntarily support any proceedings to punish M for the internal abduction, or the abduction to England.

Held by the Court of Appeal, allowing the appeal (Henderson LJ):

> '[the judge] was unduly influenced by considerations of comity and the underlying policy of [HC80], combined with his understandable wish not to let the mother profit from her deplorable behaviour, while paying insufficient regard to the predicament which was actually likely

84 *Re GP (A Child) (Abduction: Consideration of Evidence)* [2017] EWCA Civ 1677, [2018] 1 FCR 638, [2018] 1 FLR 892.

85 *Re C (Children) (Abduction: Article 13(b))* [2018] EWCA Civ 2834, [2019] 2 FCR 218, [2019] 1 FLR 1045.

86 *Re S (A Child) (Hague Convention 1980: Return to Third State)* [2019] EWCA Civ 352, [2019] 2 FCR 539, [2019] 2 FLR 194.

87 *Re GP (A Child) (Abduction: Consideration of Evidence)* [2017] EWCA Civ 1677, [2018] 1 FCR 638, [2018] 1 FLR 892.

> to face GP on her return to Italy with her mother, and which needed to be considered with some care on the alternative assumptions that the mother would, or would not, be imprisoned.' (para 59)
>
> 'it was … necessary … to examine in concrete terms the situation that would actually face GP on her return to Italy. What would happen when she and her mother stepped off the plane? Would her mother be arrested? Where would they go, and what would they live on?' (para 61)
>
> 'If the judge felt that he had insufficient information to answer these questions, he should … have adjourned the hearing so that more detailed evidence could be obtained, for example about the financial position of the mother and the practicalities of an application to commute the mother's sentence of imprisonment to community service …' (para 63)

6.43 In *Re C*[88], discussed more fully in para **6.11** above, Moylan LJ said (at para 43):

Key citation: Moylan LJ in *Re C*[89]

> '… in deciding what weight can be placed on [undertakings], the court has to take into account the extent to which they are likely to be effective. This applies both in terms of compliance and in terms of consequences, including remedies, in the absence of compliance. The issue is their effectiveness which is not confined to their enforceability: see for example, *H v K*[90] … I make clear that I am not saying that enforceability is not an issue, only that it forms one element of the court's assessment.'

Brussels IIA, Art 11(4)

6.44 At the time of writing, Britain has left the European Union ('EU') but is still subject to the implementation period which is due to end on 31 December 2020[91]. With that caveat, where the proceedings concern a country in which the Brussels IIA Regulation[92] ('BIIA') is in force, there is additional emphasis placed

88 *Re C (Children) (Abduction: Article 13(b))* [2018] EWCA Civ 2834, [2019] 2 FCR 218, [2019] 1 FLR 1045.

89 *Re C (Children) (Abduction: Article 13(b))* [2018] EWCA Civ 2834, [2019] 2 FCR 218, [2019] 1 FLR 1045.

90 *H v K and Others (Abduction: Undertakings)* [2017] EWHC 1141 (Fam), [2018] 1 FLR 700.

91 See **Chapter 1**.

92 Council Regulation (EC) No 2201/2003 concerning jurisdiction and the recognition and enforcement of judgments in matrimonial matters and the matters of parental responsibility, repealing Regulation (EC) No 1347/2000.

on the protective measures available in the home country by virtue of Art 11(4) of the Regulation.

> Article 11(4) BIIA
>
> A court cannot refuse to return a child on the basis of Article 13(b) of the 1980 Hague Convention if it is established that adequate arrangements have been made to secure the protection of the child after his or her return.

6.45 While the Art 13(b) exception is even harder to satisfy as regards a return to a Member State of the EU, as Baroness Hale said in *Re D*[93]:

Key citation: Baroness Hale in *Re D*[94]

> '… it has to be shown that those arrangements will be effective to secure the protection of the child. With the best will in the world, this will not always be the case.'

E. DOING 'THE BEST' THE COURT CAN: ORAL EVIDENCE?

6.46 Where the court has:

(i) assumed alleged facts to be true and found an Art 13(b) risk to exist on that assumption; and

(ii) failed to identify any protective measures which could negate the risk,

the Supreme Court in *Re E*[95] held that a court must do '*the best it can*' to resolve the allegations (see para **6.7** above). What does this mean in practice? In most cases involving disputed allegations, the court is unlikely to hear oral evidence. Thorpe LJ in *Re W (A Child)*[96] said this (para 23):

93 [2006] UKHL 51, [2007] 1 AC 619, [2007] Fam Law 102, [2007] 1 FCR 1, [2007] 1 FLR 961, at para 52.

94 [2006] UKHL 51, [2007] 1 AC 619, [2007] Fam Law 102, [2007] 1 FCR 1, [2007] 1 FLR 961, at para 52.

95 *Re E (Children) (Abduction: Custody Appeal)* [2011] UKSC 27, [2012] 1 AC 144, [2011] Fam Law 919, [2011] 2 FCR 419, [2011] 2 FLR 758.

96 *Re W (A Child) (Abduction: Conditions for Return)* [2004] EWCA Civ 1366, [2005] Fam Law 200, [2004] 3 FCR 559, [2005] 1 FLR 727.

Key citation: Thorpe LJ in *Re W (A Child)*[97]

> 'The authorities do restrain the judges from admitting oral evidence except in exceptional cases. The authorities do restrain the judges from making too ready judgments upon written statements that set out conflicting accounts of adult relationships. What the authorities do not do is to inhibit the judge from himself or herself requiring oral evidence in a case where the judge conceives that oral evidence might be determinative. The judge's conduct of the proceedings is not to be restricted by tactical or strategic decisions taken by the parties. However, to warrant oral exploration of written evidence, the judge must be satisfied that there is a realistic possibility that oral evidence will establish an Article 13(b) case that is only embryonic on the written material.'

6.47 In *Re K (1980 Hague Convention) (Lithuania)*[98] Black LJ rejected the argument that the first instance judge should have made provisional findings on allegations made as part of an Art 13(b) 'defence':

Key citation: Black LJ in *Re K (1980 Hague Convention) (Lithuania)*[99]

> '[45] … A judge trying a Hague abduction case has a difficult job deciding what to do about factual disputes … [T]he authorities are punctuated with reminders of the summary nature of these proceedings … Oral evidence is rightly rare in such proceedings and … it seems to me … that it is very much a matter for the judge whether it is necessary and/or possible, on the facts of the particular case, to make findings.'

6.48 In *Re C*[100] (discussed at paras **6.11** and **6.43** above) the judge had not heard oral evidence and had not made findings as to the allegations made by M. However, the Court of Appeal criticised the trial judge's refusal to make a return order based on an inference of future risk drawn from M's allegations of past

97 *Re W (A Child) (Abduction: Conditions for Return)* [2004] EWCA Civ 1366, [2005] Fam Law 200, [2004] 3 FCR 559, [2005] 1 FLR 727.

98 *Re K (1980 Hague Convention) (Lithuania)* [2015] EWCA Civ 720, [2015] 2 All ER (D) 187, per Black LJ.

99 *Re K (1980 Hague Convention) (Lithuania)* [2015] EWCA Civ 720, [2015] 2 All ER (D) 187, per Black LJ.

100 *Re C (Children) (Abduction: Article 13(b))* [2018] EWCA Civ 2834, [2019] 2 FCR 218, [2019] 1 FLR 1045.

violence. Addressing the process identified by the Supreme Court in *Re E*[101], Moylan LJ said this (para 39):

Key citation: Moylan LJ in *Re C*[102]

> '… in adopting this proposed solution, it was not being suggested that no evaluative assessment of the allegations could or should be undertaken by the court. Of course a judge has to be careful when conducting a paper evaluation but this does not mean that there should be no assessment at all about the credibility or substance of the allegations.'

6.49 There have been rare cases in which courts have heard oral evidence on contested issues relevant to Art 13(b). An example is *DT v LBT (Abduction: Domestic Abuse)*[103].

Case Summary: *DT v LBT (Abduction: Domestic Abuse)*[104]

Facts:

M objected to a return of the child to Italy. Her 'defence' under Art 13(b) was founded on very serious allegations of: (i) emotional abuse; (ii) threats of violence, including threats to kill; (iii) physical violence, including whilst M was pregnant; and (iv) sexual abuse, including multiple occasions of rape.

Held by Peter Jackson J:

'*it is not usually necessary for oral evidence to be taken, as this works against the essentially summary nature of the proceedings and may lead to a loss of focus on the essential question.*' (para 23(5)). However, in order to assess the truth of the allegations, and in the absence of expert evidence as to the effect of a return on M's mental health, the judge heard oral evidence. He found (para 10) the Art 13(b) exception established.

101 *Re E (Children) (Abduction: Custody Appeal)* [2011] UKSC 27, [2012] 1 AC 144, [2011] 2 FCR 419, [2011] 2 FLR 758.
102 *Re C (Children) (Abduction: Article 13(b))* [2018] EWCA Civ 2834, [2019] 2 FCR 218, [2019] 1 FLR 1045.
103 [2010] EWHC 3177 (Fam), [2011] 1 FLR 1215, Peter Jackson J.
104 [2010] EWHC 3177 (Fam), [2011] 1 FLR 1215, Peter Jackson J.

6.50 The need for oral evidence to be heard in an Art 13(b) case is highly unusual and, in the absence of an exceptionally serious factual dispute such as existed in *DT v LBT*[105], it is almost inevitable that the court's attempt to do '*the best it can*' will involve an evaluation of the evidence on the papers in support of any argument that a return would expose the child to a grave risk. It is, thus, crucial that a practitioner representing a respondent seeking to run such arguments obtains all possible evidence available, whether in England or the foreign jurisdiction.

105 *DT v LBT (Abduction: Domestic Abuse)* [2010] EWHC 3177 (Fam), [2011] 1 FLR 1215.

CHAPTER 7

The voice of the child and child objections

Content at a Glance:

A. INTRODUCTION

7.1 Article 13(2) of the 1980 Hague Convention[1] ('HC80') provides one of the exceptions to the mandatory summary return of a child who has been wrongfully removed or retained away from a Contracting State. It states:

> The judicial or administrative authority may also refuse to order the return of the child if it finds that the child objects to being returned and has attained an age and degree of maturity at which it is appropriate to take account of its views.

1 The Convention on the Civil Aspects of International Child Abduction signed at the Hague on 25 October 1980.

7.2 However, it is necessary to *consider* whether and how to hear 'the voice of the child' in *every* case under HC80 – not just those in which a 'defence' under Art 13(2) is being pursued. This was made clear by Baroness Hale in 2006 in *Re D (A Child) (Abduction: Rights of Custody)* (*'Re D'*)[2]. Where a child is capable of forming his or her own views, the child has a *right* to express those views in matters which affect him or her by virtue of Art 12 of the United Nations Convention on the Rights of the Child 1989 ('UNCRC').

The remainder of this chapter will address:

- the impact of the decision of the House of Lords in *Re D*[3];
- the different ways in which a court may 'hear the voice of the child'; and
- the specific 'defence' under Art 13(2) of HC80.

B. THE IMPACT OF *RE D*

7.3

Case Summary: *Re D (A Child) (Abduction: Rights of Custody)*[4]

Facts:

The application related to a boy born in Romania in July 1998. The parents were divorced and M was granted the primary role of care for the child by the Romanian court. In the autumn of 2002, M moved to the UK and formed a new life, including remarrying. The child lived with the maternal grandparents in Romania. In December 2002, M brought the child to England.

On 14 February 2003, F commenced proceedings under HC80. The court ordered that an Art 15 declaration[5] be sought from the Romanian authorities. On 25 May 2004 the Romanian court ruled that F did not have rights of custody.

F appealed the Romanian determination; meanwhile, the English court directed an expert opinion to clarify the Romanian judgments. There were further procedural hearings before ultimately the court ordered the summary return to Romania. This decision was upheld by the CA[6].

M was granted leave to appeal to the House of Lords and the child was granted leave to intervene and be separately represented.

2 [2006] UKHL 51, [2007] 1 AC 619, [2007] 1 FCR 1, [2007] 1 FLR 961.
3 [2006] UKHL 51, [2007] 1 AC 619, [2007] 1 FCR 1, [2007] 1 FLR 961.
4 [2006] UKHL 51, [2007] 1 AC 619, [2007] 1 FCR 1, [2007] 1 FLR 961.
5 For Art 15 Declarations, see **Chapter 3**.
6 *Deak v Deak* [2006] EWCA Civ 830.

Held by the House of Lords:

Appeal allowed. The inferior courts had erred in rejecting the Art 15 determination of the Romanian court. F had no rights of custody for Convention purposes and the removal of the child was not wrongful (see **Chapter 3**).

Children are capable of being moral actors in their own right and their voices should be heard in HC80 proceedings. The rule under Brussels IIA[7] ('BIIA') – that children should be heard unless this was inappropriate having regard to their age and maturity – should apply to all HC80 proceedings. This would lead to children being heard more frequently than previously. It was no longer sufficient to say that the abductor could present the child's views.

The usual means of hearing the child would be through a Cafcass officer, although in some cases the child could meet the judge, particularly if the child requested this. Whenever it seemed likely that the child's views and interests may not be properly presented to the court, and in particular where there were legal arguments which the adult parties were not putting forward, then consideration should be given to the separate representation of the child.

7.4 Prior to 2006, the courts did not routinely allow children to express a meaningful view in HC80 proceedings. The object of the Convention is to secure the *prompt return* of abducted children to the country of their habitual residence. In order to achieve that objective, the courts generally applied a policy-driven approach whereby children wrongfully removed or retained were returned in all but the most exceptional of cases. This robust approach was applied even to relatively mature teenagers expressing forceful objections to returning[8]. One of the main justifications for dealing with cases in this way was that it would deter others from abducting children in future; thus it was consistent with the aims of the Convention and with the welfare of children throughout the world generally.

7.5 In contrast to the previous approach, in *Re D*[9] Baroness Hale underlined the importance of hearing the voice of the child[10]. She referred to Art 11(2) of BIIA, and to Art 12 of the 1989 United Nations Convention on the Rights of the Child ('UNCRC'):

7 Council Regulation (EC) No 2201/2003 of 27 November 2003 concerning jurisdiction and the recognition and enforcement of judgments in matrimonial matters and the matters of parental responsibility, repealing Regulation (EC) No 1347/2000,

8 See, for example, *TB v JB (Abduction: Grave Risk of Harm)* [2001] 2 FCR 497, [2001] 2 FLR 515; *Vigreux v Michel and M* [2006] EWCA Civ 630, [2007] 3 FCR 196, [2006] 2 FLR 1180; and *JPC v SLW and SMW* [2007] EWHC 1349 (Fam), [2007] 3 FCR 243, [2007] 2 FLR 900; these were cases in which the strong objections of children aged 14 were not followed.

9 [2006] UKHL 51, [2007] 1 AC 619, [2007] 1 FCR 1, [2007] 1 FLR 961.

10 See, in particular, paras 57–62.

7.6 *The voice of the child and child objections*

Art 11(2) BIIA

- ..., it shall be ensured that the child is given the opportunity to be heard during the proceedings, unless this appears inappropriate having regard to his or her age or degree of maturity.

Art 12 UNCRC

- States parties shall assure to the child who is capable of forming his or her own views the right to express those views freely in all matters affecting the child, the views of the child being given due weight in accordance with the age and maturity of the child.
- ...the child shall in particular be provided the opportunity to be heard in any judicial ... proceedings affecting the child, either directly, or through a representative or an appropriate body...

7.6 Baroness Hale emphasised the following propositions:

Art 11(2) BIIA places a duty to hear the child in cases involving the Regulation.

↓

The Art 11(2) principles are of *universal* application, to be applied in *every* HC80 case.

↓

There is a presumption that the child will be heard in every case unless inappropriate having regard to age or degree of maturity.

↓

This presumption applies whether or not a specific defence of child objections has been raised.

↓

There is no minimum age before a child's views will be heard. In *Re D* the child should have been heard at age 7, but not at the outset of the proceedings when aged 4.

↓

There are **three ways** in which a child can be heard:

Interview by a Cafcass officer.	Meeting with the judge.	Separate representation.

7.7 Following *Re D*[11] it has been emphasised that in *every* case, the court must address *at the outset*, and at all subsequent hearings (including on appeal), the question of whether and how the child is to be given the opportunity to be heard[12]. See also the *Practice Guidance of 13 March 2018 on the Case Management and Mediation of International Child Abduction Proceedings*[13], in particular paras 2.5(g), 2.9(i), 2.11(h) and 3.5, which make clear the importance of case-managing issues concerning the child's participation from the very beginning of HC80 proceedings.

7.8 The requirement to 'hear the child' does *not* necessarily mean that the child needs to be a party to the proceedings. As Baroness Hale pointed out at para 60 of *Re D*[14], there are *three potential ways* in which a child may be heard:

- interview by a Cafcass officer;
- meeting with the judge;
- separate representation[15].

Although full-scale legal representation of a child will only be necessary '*in a few cases*', applications for the joinder of children are now much more common than they were before *Re D*[16].

7.9 The joinder of a child gives rise to other questions, such as the manner in which the child should participate in the proceedings – see also *Re M (Republic of Ireland) (Child's Objections) (Joinder of Children as Parties to Appeal)*[17]. Such issues must be addressed at an early stage of proceedings, in addition to the question of whether the case raises a 'child objections' defence under Art 13(2). In *Re D*[18], the child was given leave to intervene in the House of Lords; Baroness Hale was critical of the refusal of joinder in the Court of Appeal[19].

C. HEARING THE VOICE OF THE CHILD

Interview by a Cafcass officer

7.10 The most common method of canvassing a child's views is through a Cafcass officer. A direction is typically given to the Cafcass High Court team

11 [2006] UKHL 51, [2007] 1 AC 619, [2007] 1 FCR 1, [2007] 1 FLR 961.
12 See, for example, *Re F (Abduction: Child's Wishes)* [2007] 2 FLR 697; and the court must also consider how this can be done within the 6-week time limit.
13 See **Chapter 11**.
14 [2006] UKHL 51, [2007] 1 AC 619, [2007] 1 FCR 1, [2007] 1 FLR 961.
15 This involves the child being represented by solicitors through a Guardian (usually an officer of the Cafcass High Court team).
16 [2006] UKHL 51, [2007] 1 AC 619, [2007] 1 FCR 1, [2007] 1 FLR 961.
17 [2015] EWCA Civ 26, [2016] Fam 1, [2015] 2 FLR 1074 per Black LJ at para 140.
18 [2006] UKHL 51, [2007] 1 AC 619, [2007] 1 FCR 1, [2007] 1 FLR 961.
19 'When the proceedings began, it might well have been considered inappropriate to hear [the child]'s views. When the proceedings should have been completed, in August 2005, this may still have been the case. But once the proceedings were prolonged beyond then, [the child] had reached an age where it could no longer be taken for granted that it was inappropriate for him to be given the opportunity of being heard.' (para 62).

to prepare a report. The officers in the High Court team have experience of international cases, including those under HC80, and are aware that the role performed by Cafcass in such cases is more limited than in domestic cases where a full welfare enquiry is necessary.

7.11 The following sets out specimen directions from the Compendium of Standard Orders[20] relating to the decision whether or not to involve Cafcass:

Recitals

- The court has considered whether and how the voice of the child should be heard
- The court has determined that [the child] is too young for his/her views to be ascertained by a Cafcass officer [*to be used where a Cafcass report is not required*]

Orders

- **Cafcass/Child's participation**
- An officer of the Cafcass High Court team shall provide a report on the issue of:
  - [the child/ren's] views, wishes and feelings in respect of returning to [requesting state] and the [child/ren's] maturity
  - whether they are settled in England & Wales [only where settlement under Art 12 HC80 is raised]
  - whether the child/any of the children should be separately represented
  - whether the child/any of the children wish to meet the trial judge [if appropriate]

Where the child's 'state of mind', whether current or historical, may have an impact on issues of habitual residence[21], the report may cover this also.

7.12 Reports are usually conducted on the basis of a single interview with the child at the Cafcass offices in the Royal Courts of Justice. Cafcass usually require a minimum of 21 days, but in urgent cases, this timetable can be expedited. There should be liaison with the Cafcass High Court team whenever the court is considering ordering a report. If there is no time to prepare a written report, the officer can be asked to report orally to the court. In the most urgent cases, a direction can be given for the child to be brought to court the same day and interviewed immediately.

7.13 In settlement cases, the ambit of the report will usually be wider and may include, for example, input from the child's school and other significant people (although the report will not be as wide as a full welfare report). In such cases, Cafcass will normally require longer than 21 days to complete their task.

20 https://www.judiciary.uk/publications/practice-guidance-standard-children-and-other-orders/.
21 See para **4.19**.

The role of the Cafcass officer

7.14 Some Cafcass officers will express a view on whether or not the child '*objects*' to a return (often adding the phrase '*for Convention purposes*') or whether the child's expressed views merely amount to a '*preference*'. It is probably inappropriate for the officer to express an opinion in such terms. The Cafcass officer's role is to be the '*eyes and ears*' of the court, reporting on what the child has said, their demeanour, their maturity, the strength of their feelings, and whether the child's view was coloured by manipulation or external influence from the abducting parent or some other person. The overarching question of whether or not Art 13(2) is satisfied is a decision for the judge.

7.15 In *Re F (Child's Objections)*[22], the Court of Appeal commented on the role of a Cafcass officer in the context of determining whether a child objects[23]:

> *The Cafcass officer's task is to ascertain what the children are thinking and to convey that to the judge so that he can evaluate it with a view to making his factual finding as to whether they object. A Cafcass officer does not normally ask the children in terms whether they object to a return, but instead talks around the subject with them, letting them voice their views and their feelings in whatever way they wish.*

Meetings between the judge and the child

7.16 Before *Re D*[24], meetings between a child and the judge took place only rarely in HC80 cases. It became more common following the decision of the Court of Appeal in *Re G (Abduction: Children's Objections)*[25].

7.17 According to the April 2010 *Guidelines for Judges Meeting Children who are Subject to Family Proceedings*[26] ('the 2010 Guidelines'), the purpose of a meeting between a child and the Judge is *not* for evidence gathering. The preamble to, and para 5 of, the 2010 Guidelines make clear the following:

22 [2015] EWCA Civ 1022, [2016] 1 FCR 168.
23 See paras 39–40.
24 [2006] UKHL 51, [2007] 1 AC 619, [2007] 1 FCR 1, [2007] 1 FLR 961.
25 [2010] EWCA Civ 1232, [2011] 1 FLR 1645.
26 [2010] 2 FLR 1872.

The purpose ... is ... to enable children to feel more involved and give them an opportunity to satisfy themselves that the judge has understood their wishes and to understand the judge's task.

... the meeting is to benefit the child. However, it may also benefit the judge and other family members.

The meeting is not for gathering evidence. That is the responsibility of the Cafcass officer.

7.18 Despite the 2010 Guidelines, there are reported cases (see para **7.19** below) in which it is apparent that the content of a child's meeting with the judge has had a real impact upon the ultimate decision made. This does not sit easily with the principle that such meetings are not to be used for 'evidence gathering'. Moreover, if the meeting cannot be used for gathering evidence, it is difficult to see how it can ever be an effective means by which a child's voice can be heard.

7.19 It is illustrative to compare *Re G (Abduction: Children's Objections)*[27] and *Re J (Abduction: Children's Objections)*[28] with the later case of *Re KP (Abduction: Child's Objections)*[29]. In the former two cases, the trial judges were criticised for *not* meeting with the children, in circumstances where orders for return had been made against the children's wishes. In *Re KP*[30], the trial judge *did* meet the child, but a return was ordered despite the child's objections. That order was overturned on appeal, largely because of the judge's conduct of the meeting. In *Re KP*[31] the child was questioned at length by the judge, and the Court of Appeal held that the meeting had '*fallen on the wrong side of the line*' with regard to the principle that it should not be used for evidence-gathering.

7.20 A difficulty with this area of the law is that it is hard to discern where 'the line' lies. For example, in *Re G*[32] the Court of Appeal was directly influenced, in its decision not to return the child, by the content of their meeting with her. Similarly, in *Re J*[33], the Court of Appeal stated that judges need to have one eye on enforceability, and a direct meeting between judge and child might allow the judge to gauge any likely problems. By contrast in *Re KP*[34] the appeal was

27 [2010] EWCA Civ 1232, [2011] 1 FLR 1645.
28 [2011] EWCA Civ 1448, [2012] 1 FCR 161, [2012] 1 FLR 457.
29 [2014] EWCA Civ 554, [2014] 1 WLR 4326, [2014] 2 FCR 545, [2014] 2 FLR 660.
30 [2014] EWCA Civ 554, [2014] 1 WLR 4326, [2014] 2 FCR 545, [2014] 2 FLR 660.
31 [2014] EWCA Civ 554, [2014] 1 WLR 4326, [2014] 2 FCR 545, [2014] 2 FLR 660.
32 [2010] EWCA Civ 1232, [2011] 1 FLR 1645.
33 [2011] EWCA Civ 1448, [2012] 1 FCR 161, [2012] 1 FLR 457.
34 [2014] EWCA Civ 554, [2014] 1 WLR 4326, [2014] 2 FCR 545, [2014] 2 FLR 660.

allowed because the judge reached her conclusions based on what she saw and heard during her meeting with the child.

7.21 These cases demonstrate that the manner in which meetings should be conducted in HC80 cases remains unclear. Indeed, in *Re KP*[35] the Court of Appeal appeared to acknowledge this, when Moore-Bick LJ said that the concept of hearing the voice of the child is still '*in its infancy*', and that the judgment was not intended to set anything in '*concrete*' regarding the conduct of such meetings[36].

7.22

Case Summary: *Re G (Abduction: Children's Objections)*[37]

Facts:

The judge at first instance canvassed the views of the children (13 and 9) through Cafcass; both objected to returning to Canada. A letter from the older child explained why she did not want to return. The judge ordered a return despite finding that the children objected.

By the date of the appeal, the older child had written a further letter, making it clear that her position had hardened, and that she would not comply with a return order. The Court of Appeal took the unusual course of speaking to her in chambers.

Held by the Court of Appeal:

The CA referred to the '*growing perception*' that the court should hear the voice of the child, as a result of HC80 and UNCRC. Thorpe LJ acknowledged that, traditionally, children have been heard via Cafcass; but the Family Justice Council had expressed 'forceful' views that judges ought to meet children and hear their voices directly.

The CA declined to say that the judge below had been wrong, but allowed the appeal on the basis of fresh evidence, which *included what the child communicated to them in chambers*. Thorpe LJ said it was a pity the trial judge had not met the child, given that she was expressing a wish to see the decision maker. He said that the trial judge may well have refused to order a return if he had met with her; courts needed to be '*alive to the difficulty of implementing a return order which involved an articulate, naturally determined and courageous adolescent*'.

35 [2014] EWCA Civ 554, [2014] 1 WLR 4326, [2014] 2 FCR 545, [2014] 2 FLR 660.
36 Paragraph 52.
37 [2010] EWCA Civ 1232, [2011] 1 FLR 1645.

7.23

Case Summary: *Re J (Abduction: Children's Objections)*[38]

Facts:

Under a Polish order, the children (15, 13 and 10) lived with F in Poland, and had contact with M in England. Following a holiday, M retained the children. F sought a return. M's defence was that all three children objected to a return. M did not invite the judge to consider meeting with the children.

The Cafcass officer noted that the children's objections were very strong. Roderic Wood J nevertheless made a return order. The judgment was unclear as to whether he found that they did not object, or whether he was exercising a discretion to return them having found that Art 13(2) applied.

The children appealed and were granted party status.

Held by the Court of Appeal:

The appeal was allowed, in part on the basis of the judge's failure to meet the children, or at least to raise and consider this possibility with counsel.

Thorpe LJ said that the '*flow of authority pointed towards a meeting*'. He emphasised what he had said in *Re G*[39] and held that the 2010 Guidelines were applicable in HC80 proceedings: '*Practitioners and judges have the responsibility to consider in what way and to what extent the Guidance applies during preparations for trial and at the trial itself*'. He referred to the potential for enforcement problems where a child is objecting: meetings '*give the judge an opportunity directly to assess where the return order will lead if enforcement will be resisted*'. The case was remitted for rehearing.

7.24

Case Summary: *Re KP (Abduction: Child's Objections)*[40]

Facts:

A child (13) was brought to England by M from Malta, in a clandestine abduction. M relied on the child's objections (as well as Art 13(b)). The Cafcass officer reported that the child was articulate and confident, and had

38 [2011] EWCA Civ 1448, [2012] 1 FLR 457.
39 [2010] EWCA Civ 1232, [2011] 1 FLR 1645.
40 [2014] EWCA Civ 554, [2014] 1 WLR 4326, [2014] 2 FCR 545, [2014] 2 FLR 660.

strong objections to a return. The judge met the child for an hour, during which the child was asked 87 questions. The child later said that she had felt intimidated by the process.

The judge accepted that the child objected, but ordered a return despite the objections. She was influenced by the content of her meeting; in particular she had not been impressed by the rationality/objectivity of the child's views.

Held by the Court of Appeal:

Appeal allowed. The CA emphasised that judicial meetings with children were governed by the guidelines and therefore had a limited purpose, which did not include information/evidence gathering. The judge's meeting had clearly fallen on the '*wrong side of the line*'. The judge had actively probed the child's views, rather than acting as a '*passive recipient*' of information. The content of the meeting went to the heart of the judge's analysis and conclusions, and therefore could not stand.

The interview in this case had strayed into the arena of evidence gathering, and had given the child the wrong impression that the purpose was for her to '*argue her case*' – the judge had in effect allowed the child to make submissions to her about her objections. The judge then relied on information adduced during that meeting to inform her analysis and decision.

The CA considered a number of authorities on meeting with children to '*draw together a number of themes*'[41]. They gave general guidance as to the conduct of meetings[42].

The *Guidelines in Relation to Children Giving Evidence in Family Proceedings*[43] are not directly applicable, as they are concerned with children giving evidence in an adversarial trial[44] and not to the different context of a judge meeting with a child.

7.25 If a meeting between a judge and a child is being considered, it is essential to have regard to the 2010 Guidelines, and for discussions to take place regarding the conduct of the proposed meeting. It is impossible to anticipate every eventuality, but some examples of the likely questions that will arise in the planning of such a meeting are set out in the following graphic:

41 Paragraph 53.

42 Paragraph 56.

43 [2012] Fam Law 79.

44 The guidelines were issued following *Re W (Children) (Family Proceedings: Evidence)* [2010] UKSC 12, [2010] 1 WLR 701, [2010] 1 FCR 615, [2010] 1 FLR 1485.

Separate representation of children

7.26 Rule 16.2 of the Family Procedure Rules 2010 ('FPR 2010') provides that a court may grant a child party status if it is in the best interests of the child to do so. In *Re LC (Children) (Reunite International Child Abduction Centre intervening)*[45] ('*Re LC*'), Lord Wilson described '*best interests*' as the threshold condition which opens up the gateway to discretion. As he pointed out, it is a discretion that is more theoretical than real. If the court finds that it is in a child's best interests to be joined as a party, that will '*almost always*' be the result.

FPR 2010, Practice Direction 16A

7.27 FPR 2010, PD16A provides further guidance as to when a child may be joined as a party. Paragraph 7.1 of PD 16A provides that joinder should only occur in cases which involve an issue of significant difficulty, and consequently

45 [2014] UKSC 1, [2014] AC 1038, [2014] 1 FCR 491, [2014] 1 FLR 1486.

will occur in only a minority of cases. Paragraph 7.1 also provides that, before taking the decision to make the child a party, consideration should be given to whether an alternative route might be preferable.

7.28 In *Re LC*[46] Lord Wilson said that FPR 2010, PD16A, para 7.1 was '*well reflected by the court's current practice of inviting an officer in the Cafcass High Court team to see the child before it decides whether to make her a party to Convention proceedings*'. Arguably, however, this practice is inconsistent with the need to avoid delay in HC80 proceedings. Much may depend on the timing of an application for joinder, but it is not an invariable rule that a full Cafcass report must be obtained first.

7.29 FPR 2010, PD16A, para 7.2 makes it clear that joinder is always a matter for the court. It is not open to the parties to join a child by agreement without court approval. Paragraph 7.2 sets out a non-exhaustive list of circumstances which may justify making an order for joinder. These include:

- Joinder recommended by Cafcass.
- Child has standpoint or interest incapable of being represented by any adult party.
- Views and wishes of child cannot be adequately met by Cafcass report.
- Older child opposing a proposed course of action (but note in *Re LC* Lord Wilson emphasised this does not mean routine grant of party status to older children who object).
- International complications outside child abduction, in particular where it may be necessary for there to be discussions with overseas authorities or a foreign court.
- Proceedings concern more than one child and the welfare of the children is in conflict or one child is in a particularly disadvantaged position.

7.30 FPR 2010, PD16A, para 7.3 provides that:

> *'It must be recognised that separate representation of the child may result in a delay in the resolution of the proceedings … the court will take into account the risk of delay or other facts adverse to the welfare of the child.'*

In *Re LC*[47] it was held that this factor has a particular relevance in HC80 proceedings – however, there is a tension between the need to avoid delay, and the guidance stating that a Cafcass officer's opinion should first be sought (see paras 52–53 of *Re LC*).

46 [2014] UKSC 1, [2014] AC 1038, [2014] 1 FCR 491, [2014] 1 FLR 1486.
47 [2014] UKSC 1, [2014] AC 1038, [2014] 1 FCR 491, [2014] 1 FLR 1486.

Guidance from the House of Lords and Supreme Court

7.31 In *Re D*[48] Baroness Hale expressed the view that, although in most cases an interview with a specialist Cafcass officer should be sufficient, the child should be separately represented:

> *whenever it seems likely that the child's views and interests may not be properly presented to the court, and in particular where there are legal arguments which the adult parties are not putting forward.*

7.32 In *Re M (Children) (Abduction: Rights of Custody)*[49] Baroness Hale stated*:*

> *To order separate representation in all cases ... might be to send them the wrong messages. But it would not send the wrong messages in the very small number of cases where settlement is argued ... These are the cases in which the separate point of view of the children is particularly important ... In all other cases, the question ...is whether separate representation ...will add enough to the court's understanding of the issues that arise under [HC80] to justify the intrusion, the expense and the delay that may result.*

7.33 In *Re LC*[50] Lord Wilson questioned the proposition that settlement cases are more child-centric than, say, child objections cases, and he implicitly challenged the notion that children should routinely be joined as parties in such cases. He also emphasised that[51]:

> *The intrusion of the children into the forensic arena, which enables a number of them to adopt a directly confrontational stance towards the applicant parent, can prove very damaging to family relationships even in the long term and definitely affects their interests. So does delay in the resolution of the issue whether they should be ordered to return, albeit perhaps only temporarily, to the requesting state.*

7.34 In *Re LC*[52] Lord Wilson further identified that cases involving habitual residence were in some ways analogous to settlement cases and that:

> 'to both inquiries an older child may in particular be able to contribute relevant evidence not easily given by either of the parents, namely about her state of mind during the period in question.'

He emphasised, however, that this should not be taken to mean that children should be routinely joined in habitual residence cases.

48 [2006] UKHL 51, [2007] 1 AC 619, [2007] 1 FCR 1, [2007] 1 FLR 961.
49 [2007] UKHL 55, [2008] 1 AC 1288, [2008] 1 FCR 536, [2008] 1 FLR 251, at para 57.
50 [2014] UKSC 1, [2014] AC 1038, [2014] 1 FCR 491, [2014] 1 FLR 1486.
51 At para 48.
52 [2014] UKSC 1, [2014] AC 1038, [2014] 1 FCR 491, [2014] 1 FLR 1486.

Joinder of children at appellate stage

7.35 Ideally, the question of joining a child would be considered long before the appeal stage. Nevertheless, such applications may still be granted where necessary, including where a child was too young to be joined at first instance but is old enough by the time of the appeal. There are reported examples of this occurring, albeit not always with much judicial enthusiasm[53].

7.36 The need to join a child on appeal may arise where, for example, the child ought to have been joined at first instance, but no application for joinder was made, or an application was wrongly refused. Sometimes an older child will be spurred into action by the decision of the lower court; or the interests of the child will only crystallise after the conclusion of the first instance trial[54].

7.37 The FPR 2010 do not apply once a case reaches the Court of Appeal. If the question of joining a child as a party arises at the appeal stage, any order for joinder will be made pursuant to the Civil Procedure Rules 1998 ('CPR'), Part 52. Considerations of welfare are not paramount but are '*by no means out of place*'[55]. Pursuant to the CPR, a child should act through a litigation friend; but in HC80 proceedings this is a status most likely to be conferred upon the child's solicitor[56].

7.38 In *Re F (Abduction: Acquiescence: Child's Objections)*[57], two children were granted party status for the first time at the appeal stage by Ryder LJ and were represented in the substantive appeal. In *Re F (Children)*[58], an older child was joined for the first time at the appellate stage, an earlier application for her joinder having been refused before the first instance trial.

53 See, for example, Black LJ in *Re M (Republic of Ireland) (Child's Objections) (Joinder of Children as Parties to Appeal)* [2015] EWCA Civ 26, [2016] Fam 1 [2015] 2 FLR 1074.

54 As to a child's status to bring an appeal where s/he was not a party, see *Re LC* at para 11, in which Lord Wilson referred to the principle set out in *George Wimpey UK Ltd v Tewkesbury Borough Council* [2008] 1 WLR 1649: as the child had been adversely affected by the decision, she had the requisite status to bring an appeal.

55 *Re M (Republic of Ireland) (Child's Objections) (Joinder of Children as Parties to Appeal)* [2015] EWCA Civ 26, [2015] 2 FLR 1074 at para 149 per Black LJ.

56 *Re M (Republic of Ireland) (Child's Objections) (Joinder of Children as Parties to Appeal)* [2015] EWCA Civ 26, [2015] 2 FLR 1074 at paras 148–157 per Black LJ.

57 [2015] EWCA Civ 1022, [2016] 1 FCR 168.

58 [2016] EWCA Civ 354 and [2016] EWCA Civ 546, [2016] 3 FCR 255.

7.39

Case Summary: Re F *(Abduction: Acquiescence: Child's Objections)*[59]

Facts:

The parents were British and were living in England when the children were born. The family emigrated to Australia; shortly after arriving, the parents separated. M remained in Australia and F returned to England.

After a holiday with F, the children did not return. F accepted that he had wrongfully retained the children. The children expressed a strong desire to remain with F in England.

The judge found that, while all the children had a preference to remain in England, they did not object to returning to Australia within the meaning of Art 13(2). The judge met with the children (by video link) on the same day, but before, he delivered judgment without giving the parties the opportunity to address this in submissions.

F appealed, and the children, though not parties at first instance, were given permission to appeal out of time.

Held by the Court of Appeal (appeal allowed):

The word 'object' should have been treated as an ordinary English word, but that the trial judge had given it a special meaning:

> *'In this [Hague] context an "objection" means a wholesale objection to returning to the country of habitual residence. Invariably such a child cannot think of anything positive to say about that other country.'*

This placed an unwarranted gloss upon Art 13. Per Black LJ at para 33:

> *'an over-prescriptive or over-intellectualised approach is to be discouraged … a straightforward and robust process is required. The judge must ask him or herself simply, "Does the child object to being returned to his or her country of habitual residence?".'*

The children clearly objected to a return to Australia. The trial judge's conclusion was not one open to him on the basis of the evidence.

A meeting between a judge and children needs very careful planning: *'it is important that whenever there is a meeting … care is taken to ensure that the parties have the opportunity to make submissions about what emerges'*.

59 [2015] EWCA Civ 1022, [2016] 1 FCR 168.

Manner of representation– through Cafcass Guardian or otherwise

7.40 There are a number of HC80 cases in which children separately represented were permitted to instruct a solicitor directly (as opposed to having to act through a Guardian); this is what occurred in the House of Lords in *Re D*[60] (where the child was aged 7) and in the Court of Appeal in *Re M (Republic of Ireland) (Child's Objections) (Joinder of Children as Parties to Appeal)*[61].

7.41 In *Re C (Abduction: Separate Representation of Children)*[62] it was held that Family Proceedings Rules 1991, r 9.2A (which permitted children to act without a Guardian) did not apply to HC80 proceedings, and that children in such proceedings who are separately represented must act through a Guardian.

This has been described as a '*lacuna*'; and it has not been remedied in the FPR 2010: see rr 16.4 and 16.6. In *Re LC*[63] Lord Wilson said that he could not understand why, in certain other proceedings (including applications for a summary return under the inherent jurisdiction), children are able to instruct a solicitor directly whereas in HC80 proceedings they are not. He pointed out, however, that it was permissible for a solicitor also to assume the role of Guardian to the child[64]. Appointing a solicitor as the child's Guardian was the solution preferred by Black LJ in *Re M (Republic of Ireland) (Child's Objections) (Joinder of Children as Parties to Appeal)*[65].

7.42 What if the child and the Guardian disagree? This happened in *Re C (Abduction: Setting Aside Return Order: Remission)*[66]. The child was permitted for the purposes of the appeal to dispense with her Guardian and to instruct her own solicitor in circumstances where she and the Guardian had a disagreement about what was in her best interests. It was held (at a hearing prior to the substantive appeal) that FPR 2010, r 12.48(g) conferred a discretion on the court whether to appoint a Guardian when a child is joined as a party, and having regard to the overriding objective this interpretation should prevail over the lacuna in FPR 2010, rr 16.4 and 16.6. This was a 'pragmatic' decision; if the situation should arise again, following *Re LC*[67], the court would be more likely simply to appoint the child's new solicitor as her Guardian. The same *'pragmatic'* decision to appoint a solicitor Guardian was made by Baker J in *WF v RJ*[68].

60 [2006] UKHL 51, [2007] 1 AC 619, [2006] 3 WLR 989, [2007] 1 FLR 961.
61 [2015] EWCA Civ 26, [2016] Fam 1, [2015] 2 FLR 1074.
62 [2008] 2 FLR 6.
63 [2014] UKSC 1, [2014] AC 1038, [2014] 1 FCR 491, [2014] 1 FLR 1486.
64 [2014] UKSC 1, [2014] AC 1038, [2014] 1 FCR 491, [2014] 1 FLR 1486 at para 46.
65 [2015] EWCA Civ 26, [2016] Fam 1, [2015] 2 FLR 1074.
66 [2012] EWCA Civ 1144 [2013] 1 FLR 403.
67 [2014] UKSC 1, [2014] AC 1038, [2014] 1 FCR 491, [2014] 1 FLR 1486.
68 [2010] EWHC 2909 (Fam), [2011] 1 FLR 1153 at paras 19–22.

Manner of participation in the proceedings by a separately represented child

7.43 There are a number of High Court first instance authorities dealing with the issue of joining children, and the manner of their representation. Different approaches can be found in the reports: see, for example, *Ciccone v Ritchie (No 1)*[69], and *C v V*[70].

Case Summary: *Ciccone v Ritchie (No 1)*[71]

Facts:

Rocco, son of Madonna and Guy Ritchie, opposed a return to New York. He had been to see a solicitor before proceedings were issued, and had taken part in pre-proceedings mediation as well. At the first hearing, he attended court with counsel and solicitors, and applied to be joined as a party.

Held by Macdonald J:

Rocco should be joined. The judge was influenced by: (i) Rocco had already been fully involved in the issues between the parents and had been 'instrumental' in the efforts to mediate; and (ii) his age. Rocco's 'active rather than passive involvement' should be permitted.

Usually a Cafcass report would be prepared before making the decision, but in this case such a step would cause undue delay.

The judge permitted the solicitor to be the Guardian, to get around the 'lacuna' in FPR 2010 which prevented Rocco from instructing a solicitor directly; but he *also* ordered a Cafcass report, so that the alleged issue of parental influence could be assessed. He did not say that this should always be the procedure in such a case, but he commented on the likely difficulty for a solicitor acting as Guardian in dealing with that type of allegation.

Case Summary: *C v V*[72]

Facts:

Two boys (14 and 11) had been retained in England by F. F had arranged for his sons to see a solicitor following his decision to retain them, but before

69 [2016] EWHC 608 (Fam), [2016] 4 WLR 60, [2016] 3 FCR 419, [2017] 1 FLR 795.
70 [2016] EWHC 559 (Fam).
71 [2016] EWHC 608 (Fam), [2016] 4 WLR 60, [2016] 3 FCR 419, [2017] 1 FLR 795.
72 [2016] EWHC 599 (Fam).

HC80 proceedings had been issued. The boys had a lengthy interview with the solicitor.

When M issued HC80 proceedings for the return of the boys to Spain, an application was made for the children to be joined as parties. A Cafcass report was ordered first, but the children were subsequently joined. The younger child was represented via a Cafcass guardian; the solicitor was appointed as solicitor Guardian for the elder child.

Held by Parker J:

Order made for the return of both children. The judge was critical of the role the solicitor had taken. She referred in particular to an article published in Family Law[73], and said that she '*shared [the authors'] unease*' about the '*bypassing*' of Cafcass in HC80 cases. She noted the '*obvious problems*' for solicitors being the first port of call, as they cannot analyse or comment upon the child's views in the way that a trained Cafcass officer would.

The judge concluded that there had been parental influence by F, in particular of the elder child, and that the children's views were not '*authentically their own*'. Although the children objected to a return and had attained an age and degree of maturity such that the court should take account of their views, the child objections 'defence' failed at the discretionary stage.

Role of child in proceedings where separate representation directed

7.44 In *Re LC*[74] Lord Wilson identified that, once a child has been joined, the court has a wide discretion to determine the role she should play in the proceedings. On the facts of that case, he held that it would have been inappropriate for the court to hear conventional oral evidence from the child (aged 12). The most that should have been permitted, if the evidence might prove determinative and needed to be further explored, was cross-examination away from court which could be recorded. In all probability, the reasonable course would be to confine her participation to filing a statement (or a report by her Guardian) and permitting her advocate to cross-examine the other party and make submissions on her behalf.

7.45 In *Re LC*[75] Lord Wilson said that it would be for the court to determine whether the child should be present in court for the hearing, but for her Guardian to determine what documents she should be shown.

73 By Gill Honeyman & John Mellor (formerly of the Cafcass High Court team) [2011] Fam Law 613.

74 [2014] UKSC 1, [2014] AC 1038, [2014] 1 FCR 491, [2014] 1 FLR 1486.

75 [2014] UKSC 1, [2014] AC 1038, [2014] 1 FCR 491, [2014] 1 FLR 1486.

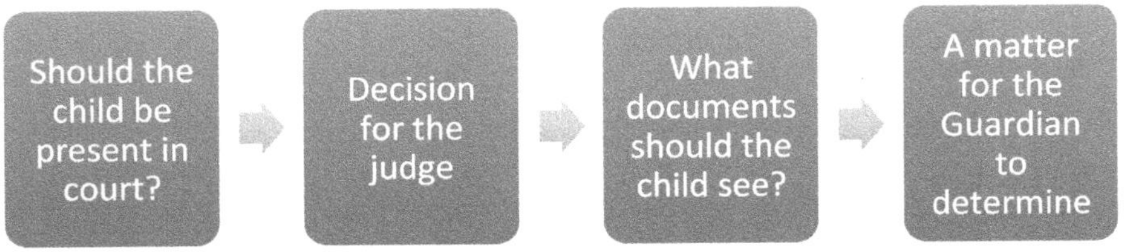

Children giving oral evidence

7.46 The circumstances in which children should give oral evidence in proceedings which concern them was considered by the Supreme Court in the context of care proceedings in *Re W (Children) (Family Proceedings: Evidence)*[76]. Paragraphs 22 to 30 of that decision set out the court's conclusions, which are summarised in the following graphic:

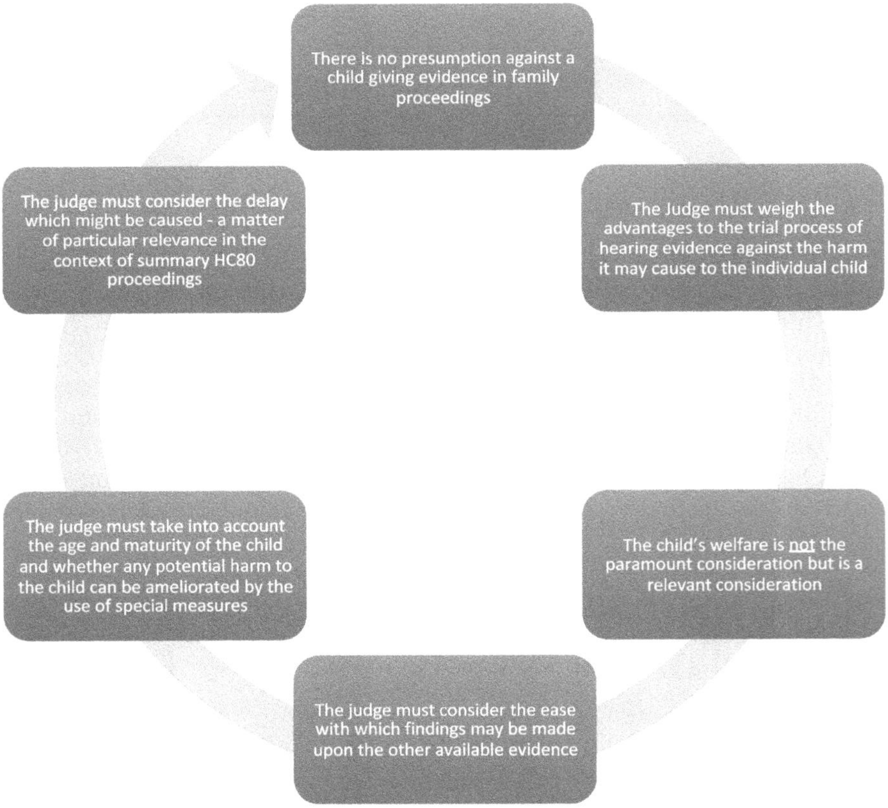

76 [2010] UKSC 12, [2010] 1 WLR 701, [2010] 1 FCR 615, [2010] 1 FLR 1485.

7.47 In *Re F (Children)*[77], Munby P stated that the courts have been too slow to acknowledge the 'sea-change' in attitudes towards '*hearing the child*' and in hearing evidence from children, in light of the guidance in *Re W*[78]. The '*proper adherence*' to that guidance will see increasing numbers of children giving evidence. As meetings with the judge are not for evidence-gathering, '*there are likely … to be more cases in future … where the child either gives evidence, without being joined as a party, or is joined as a party*'[79].

7.48 Given that oral evidence is very much the exception in HC80 litigation, it is unlikely that there will be many cases in which children give evidence. However, the guidance in *Re W*[80] must be borne in mind in the rare cases where it might be appropriate. The court *might* need to consider hearing oral evidence from a child in the following situations:

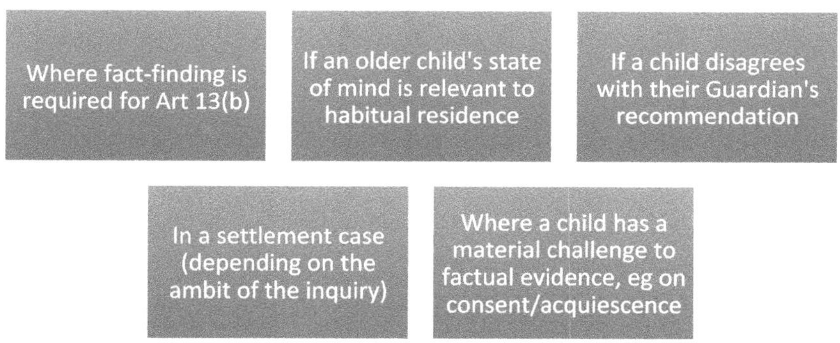

Separate representation of non-subject children

7.49 The question of joining a non-subject child may arise in the following situations:

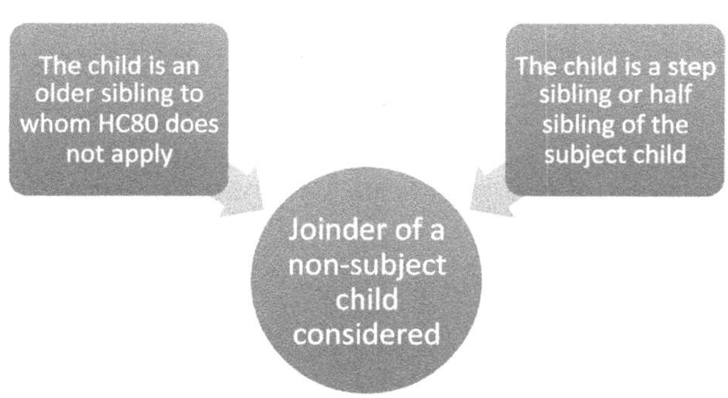

77 [2016] EWCA Civ 546, [2016] 3 FCR 255 at paras 35–44.
78 [2010] UKSC 12, [2010] 1 WLR 701, [2010] 1 FCR 615, [2010] 1 FLR 1485.
79 See also the report of the Children & Vulnerable Witnesses Working Group [2015] Family Law 443, and *Re E (A Child)* [2016] EWCA Civ 473, [2016] 4 WLR 105, [2016] 3 FCR 499, [2017] 1 FLR 1675 per McFarlane LJ in which similar comments were made.
80 [2010] UKSC 12, [2010] 1 WLR 701, [2010] 1 FCR 615, [2010] 1 FLR 1485.

FPR 2010, r 12.3 sets out the respondents to an application under HC80, which includes:

> 'any … person who appears to the court to have sufficient interest in the welfare of the child'.

7.50 In *Re E (Children) (Abduction: Custody Appeal)*[81] the Supreme Court referred to the joinder of non-subject children under FPR 2010, r 12.3 stating that it is a question for the judge in every individual case to decide whether or not that child has sufficient interest to be joined.

7.51 In *S v B (Abduction: Human Rights)*[82] it was argued that the child's older half-sibling was a person who had '*an interest in the welfare of the child*', and that he was therefore a mandatory party. Sir Mark Potter, P rejected this argument, holding that the rule covered people with a *direct* interest in the welfare of a child by:

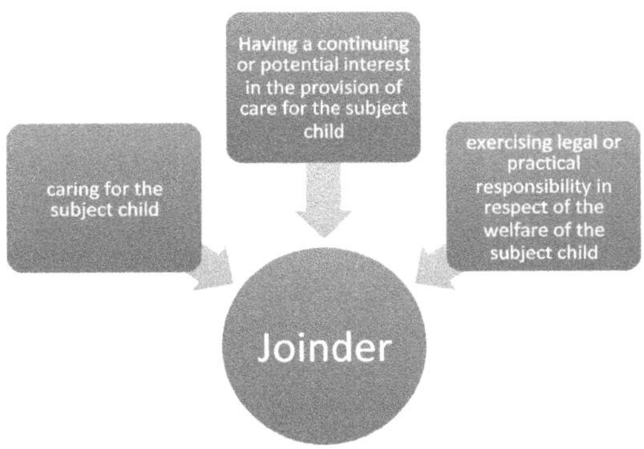

He held that the court retains the discretion to join a person who would not be an automatic party, although cases in which such a joinder will be justified will be rare indeed[83]. The law has developed since this decision, as can be seen from the cases referred to below.

7.52

Case Summary: *W v W (Abduction: Joinder of Party)*[84]

Facts:

In an application for the summary return of the child to Australia, the subject child was 11; the sibling was 17, rising 18. Neither parent supported the

81 [2011] UKSC 27, [2012] 1 AC 144, [2011] 2 FCR 419, [2011] 2 FLR 758.
82 [2005] EWHC 733 (Fam), [2005] 2 FLR 878.
83 *S v B (Abduction: Human Rights)* [2005] EWHC 733 (Fam), [2005] 2 FLR 878 at para 68.
84 [2009] EWHC 3288 (Fam), [2010] 1 FLR 1342.

application for joinder (F opposed it; M did not support it). The older sibling instructed a solicitor who filed a detailed statement setting out factual matters, and issues relevant both to their own and the subject child's welfare in opposition to the application for return; the older sibling argued that she was a mandatory party to the proceedings relating to her brother.

Held by Baker J:

Applying the decision in *S v B*[85], the older sibling was a mandatory party to the proceedings. Baker J commented:

> 'the President's definition is capable of encompassing everyone, or nearly everyone, who is likely to be able to demonstrate an interest in the welfare of the child sufficient to be heard on the question whether to order a return of the child to the country from which he has allegedly been wrongfully removed … [the sibling] is directly concerned in [the child]'s welfare in the sense that she has a continuing and potential interest in the provision of his care, and has some practical, albeit not legal, responsibility for his welfare.'

Baker J also suggested (obiter) that, in view of more recent decisions such as *Re D*[86], *Re M*[87] and *Mabon v Mabon*[88], there was some justification, in an appropriate case, for reconsidering the President's remarks about the 'rare' circumstances in which non-subject children would be joined.

7.53 In *Re S (Child Abduction: Joinder of Sibling: Child's Objections)*[89], Cobb J granted party status to the subject child's elder sister (aged 17 and not subject to the application under HC80), holding that:

(i) she had *'sufficient interest in the welfare of the subject child'* (per FPR 2010, r 12.3), and

(ii) it was in her best interests to be joined (per FPR 2010, r 16.2).

He said it would be 'rare' for the sibling of a subject child in HC80 proceedings *not* to meet the 'sufficient interest' test. In *AH v CD*[90] it was held that, whenever joinder is considered, the court must 'have regard' to *S v B (Abduction: Human Rights)*[91] and *W v W (Abduction: Joinder of Party)*[92].

7.54 The issue of joining a non-subject child arose on appeal in *Re M (Republic of Ireland) (Child's Objections) (Joinder of Children as Parties to Appeal)*[93].

85 [2005] EWHC 733 (Fam), [2005] 2 FLR 878.
86 [2006] UKHL 51, [2007] 1 AC 619, [2006] 3 WLR 989, [2007] 1 FLR 961.
87 [2007] UKHL 55, [2008] 1 AC 1288, [2008] 1 FCR 536, [2008] 1 FLR 251.
88 [2005] EWCA Civ 634, [2005] Fam 366, [2005] 2 FCR 354, [2005] 2 FLR 1011.
89 [2016] EWHC 1227 (Fam), [2017] 4 WLR 216, [2017] 2 FLR 384.
90 [2018] EWHC 1643 (Fam).
91 [2005] EWHC 733 (Fam), [2005] 2 FLR 878.
92 [2009] EWHC 3288 (Fam), [2010] 1 FLR 1342.
93 [2015] EWCA Civ 26, [2016] Fam 1, [2015] 2 FLR 1074.

Black LJ declined to resolve the debate as to whether the decisions in *S v B*[94] and *W v W*[95] '*might have been too restrictive an interpretation of the plain wording of the rule*'.

D. THE CHILD OBJECTIONS 'DEFENCE' UNDER ARTICLE 13(2)

7.55 Article 13(2) of HC80 provides:

> The judicial or administrative authority may also refuse to order the return of the child if it finds that the child objects to being returned and has attained an age and degree of maturity at which it is appropriate to take account of its views.

7.56 There are three 'limbs' to the objections defence. A respondent must demonstrate that the first two elements – often referred to as the 'gateway' stage – are satisfied. Satisfaction of the 'gateway' stage allows the court then to exercise its discretion to return the child or not. This can be illustrated as follows:

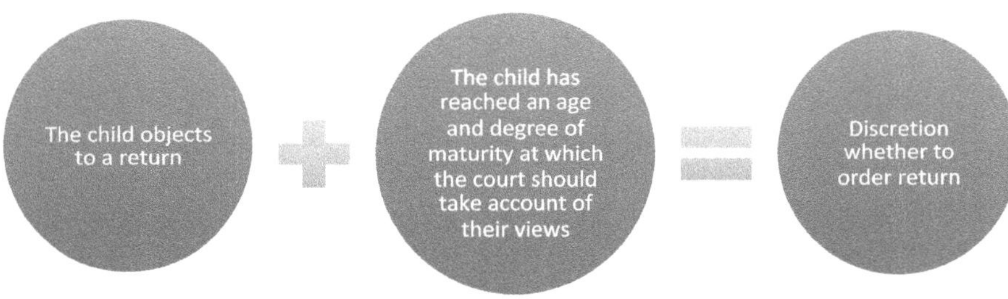

If either gateway limb is not made out, the court will have no jurisdiction to consider whether or not to order the child's return; the 'defence' will fail.

The child objects to being returned

7.57 The law has been clarified by the decisions of the Court of Appeal in *Re M (Republic of Ireland) (Child's Objections) (Joinder of Children as Parties to Appeal)*[96] and *Re F (Abduction: Acquiescence: Child's Objections)*[97]. Earlier authorities should be treated with caution.

94 [2005] EWHC 733 (Fam), [2005] 2 FLR 878.
95 [2009] EWHC 3288 (Fam), [2010] 1 FLR 1342.
96 [2015] EWCA Civ 26, [2016] Fam 1, [2015] 2 FLR 1074.
97 [2015] EWCA Civ 1022, [2016] 1 FCR 168.

7.58 In *Re M*[98] Black LJ held that, in a number of the older authorities (in particular *Re T*[99]), the 'gateway' test had been set too high and over-complicated by the inclusion of factors relevant to the discretion stage instead, stating that[100] the gateway stage is confined to:

> *A straightforward and fairly robust examination of whether ...the child objects to being returned and has attained an age and degree of maturity at which it is appropriate to take account of his or her views. Sub-tests and technicality of all sorts should be avoided.*

7.59 The correct approach to the question of whether or not a child 'objects' can be illustrated as follows[101]:

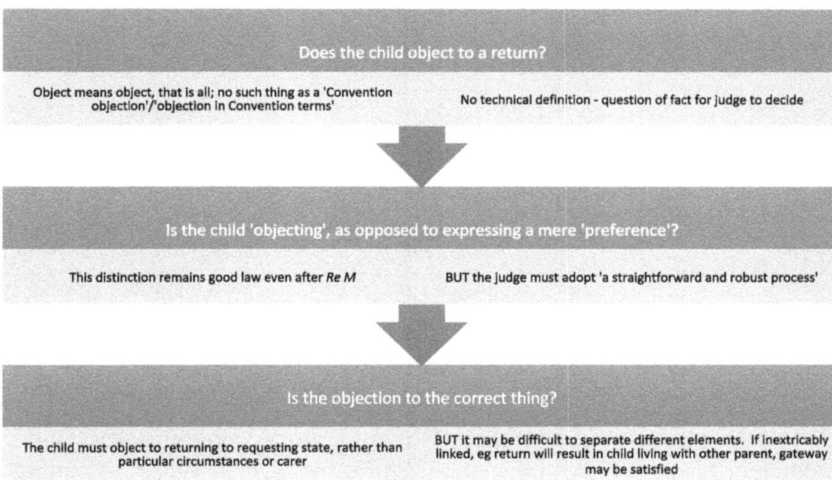

Age and degree of maturity appropriate to take account of views

7.60 HC80 does not lay down a minimum age before a child's objections can be taken into account: how to take the child's views into account, and the weight to be given to those views, is a decision for the judge in each individual case. In

98 [2015] EWCA Civ 26, [2016] Fam 1, [2015] 2 FLR 1074.
99 See *Re T (Children) (Abduction: Child's Objections to Return)* [2000] 2 FCR 159, [2000] 2 FLR 192, an example of the over-complicated approach to the gateway stage. *Re T* was expressly disapproved by Black LJ in *Re M.*
100 Paragraph 69.
101 See Black LJ in *Re M (Republic of Ireland) (Child's Objections) (Joinder of Children as Parties to Appeal)* [2015] EWCA Civ 26, [2016] Fam 1, [2015] 2 FLR 1074 at paras 38 and 41–45, and in *Re F (Abduction: Acquiescence: Child's Objections)* [2015] EWCA Civ 1022, [2016] 1 FCR 168. In *Re F*, she suggested that she would rather do away with the notion of 'preferences'; but felt bound by Lord Wilson in *Re LC* where he used the word without criticism.

the older cases decided before *Re D*[102], the exception was applied restrictively and generally confined to cases where mature adolescents were expressing forceful objections. Since *Re D*[103] the development of the general principle of '*hearing the voice of the child*' has led to a lowering of the age at which children's objections are taken into account.

7.61 The position has evolved significantly, to the point where children as young as 5 have had their views taken into account[104]. To '*take account of*' a child's views is not the same as acting in accordance with them, according to Baroness Hale in *Re D*[105]. Issues as to the rationality of a child's views and his or her precise degree of maturity are usually now considered at the discretion stage, rather than the gateway stage: see *Re M (Republic of Ireland) (Child's Objections) (Joinder of Children as Parties to Appeal)*[106].

7.62 In *Re M*[107], Black LJ cited with approval the following comments of Wilson LJ in *Re W (Minors)*[108]:

> *Earlier confusion ... about the meaning of ... 'to take account' ... has ... been eliminated. The phrase means no more than what it says so, albeit bounded of course by considerations of age and degree of maturity, it represents a fairly low threshold requirement. In particular it does not follow that the court should 'take account' of a child's objections only if they are so solidly based that they are likely to be determinative of the discretionary exercise which is to follow.*

7.63 It is relatively straightforward for the court to determine as a matter of fact whether or not a child 'objects' to return. In *Re M*[109], Black LJ tentatively gave the following guidance relevant to when the court may consider that the child's views do not to amount to an objection[110]:

102 [2006] UKHL 51, [2007] 1 AC 619, [2006] 3 WLR 989, [2007] 1 FLR 961.
103 [2006] UKHL 51, [2007] 1 AC 619, [2006] 3 WLR 989, [2007] 1 FLR 961.
104 See *Re W (Abduction: Child's Objections)* [2010] EWCA Civ 520, [2010] 2 FLR 1165, in which the CA upheld a decision to take account of the objections of children aged 8 and 6 (at the date of the appeal).
105 [2006] UKHL 51, [2007] 1 AC 619, [2006] 3 WLR 989, [2007] 1 FLR 961.
106 [2015] EWCA Civ 26, [2016] Fam 1, [2015] 2 FLR 1074.
107 [2015] EWCA Civ 26, [2016] Fam 1, [2015] 2 FLR 1074.
108 [2010] EWCA Civ 520; [2010] 2 FLR 1165.
109 [2015] EWCA Civ 26, [2016] Fam 1, [2015] 2 FLR 1074.
110 Paragraph 77.

- the child is merely parroting the views of a parent and does not personally object at all
- because of age or stage of development, the child will have nowhere near the sort of understanding that would be required
- it may not be an objection to the right thing; the objection may be to a return to the care of the other parent not the country
- it may not be an objection at all, but rather a wish or a preference

The exercise of discretion

7.64 Prior to *Re D*[111], the courts tended to adopt a robust approach, and would disregard the objections of children in all but the most exceptional cases. On the basis of the overriding policy of HC80[112], the courts held that there was a strong presumption in favour of return, and even older children would routinely have their objections overruled. This sometimes occurred in circumstances where younger siblings either did not object or were too young to have their views taken into account[113].

7.65 The robust approach to the exercise of discretion led to a number of cases where children took direct action, sometimes in dramatic fashion:

111 [2006] UKHL 51, [2007] 1 AC 619, [2006] 3 WLR 989, [2007] 1 FLR 961.

112 Defined in Art 1 as being '*to secure the prompt return of children wrongfully removed to or retained in any Contracting State*'.

113 See, for example, *Re HB (Abduction: Children's Objections)* [1997] 3 FCR 235, [1997] 1 FLR 392; see also *Re C (Abduction: Grave Risk of Physical or Psychological Harm)* [1999] 3 FCR 510, [1999] 2 FLR 478 and *S v B and Y* [2005] EWHC 733 (Fam), [2005] 2 FLR 878, in which the views of step-siblings were ignored; and *Vigreux v Michel* [2006] EWCA Civ 630, [2007] 3 FCR 196, [2006] 2 FLR 1180 where an extremely robust approach was taken, justified in particular by the requirements of BIIA.

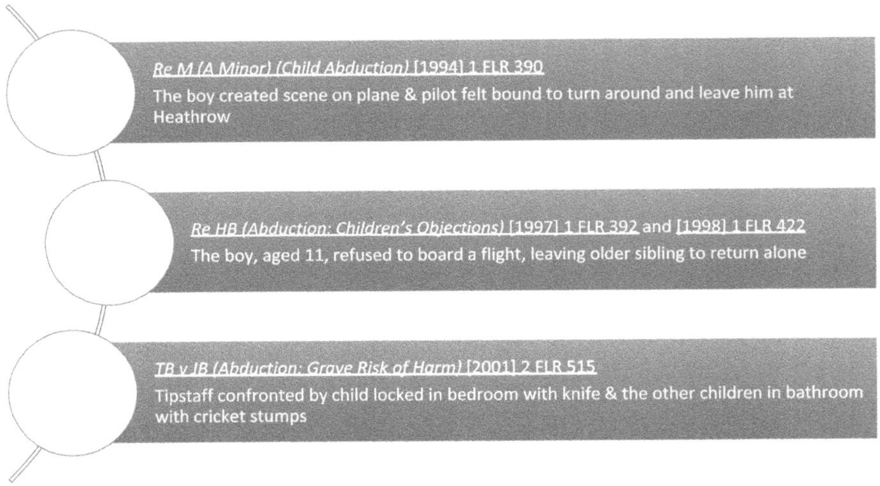

No 'exceptionality' test

7.66 In *Re M (Children) (Abduction: Rights of Custody)*[114] the House of Lords set out the proper approach to the exercise of discretion, both generally under HC80 and specifically in child objections cases; the previous '*exceptionality*' test was rejected. Baroness Hale pointed out that the exceptions to return are already '*exceptional*'; if a defence is made out, there is no need to add another layer of exceptionality at the discretion stage. The key principles identified in *Re M* relevant to the exercise of discretion under HC80 include:

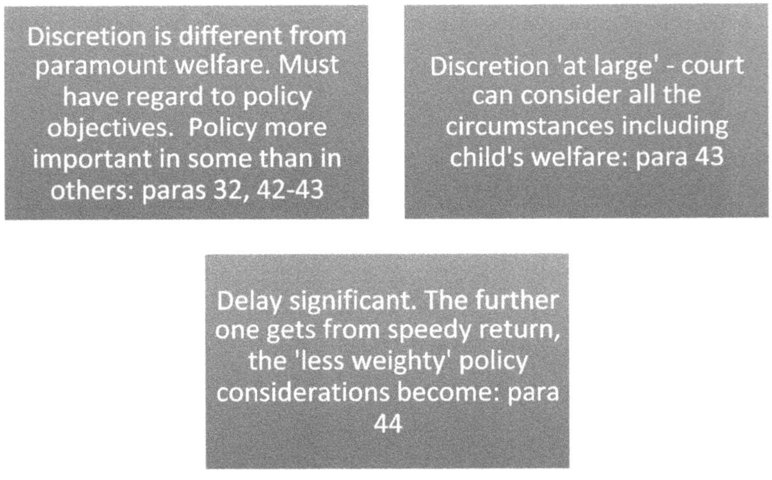

114 [2007] UKHL 55, [2008] 1 AC 1288, [2008] 1 FCR 536, [2008] 1 FLR 251.

The exercise of discretion in child objections cases

7.67 In *Re M*[115], Baroness Hale dealt specifically with the exercise of discretion in child objections cases[116]. She said that the '*range of considerations may be even wider than those in the other exceptions*' and referred to the increasing understanding of the need to hear the voice of the child, albeit that '*taking account of*' a child's views does not necessarily mean acting upon them. She gave a non-exhaustive list of factors relevant to discretion:

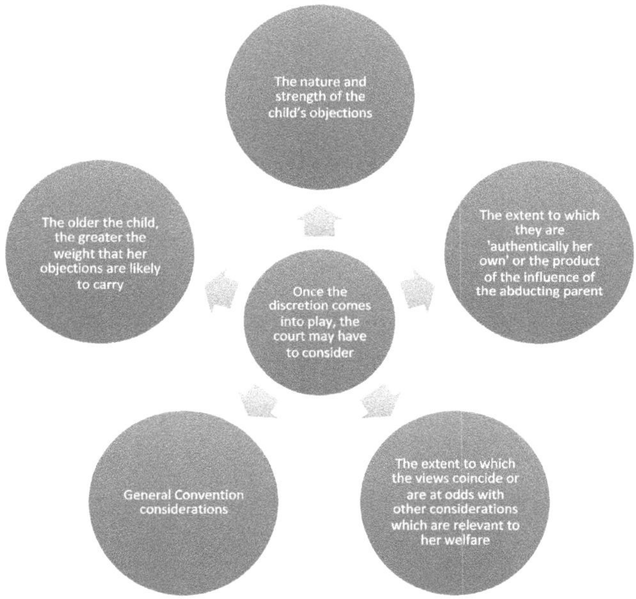

7.68

Case Summary: *Re S (Habitual Residence and Child's Objections: Brazil)*[117]

Facts:

The child (12) was born in the UK where she lived until 2013 when the parents separated. M was granted permission to relocate to Brazil with the child and her sibling. They returned to the UK during the summer holidays in 2014 and the child expressed a wish not to return to Brazil. The younger sibling did return.

115 [2007] UKHL 55, [2008] 1 AC 1288, [2008] 1 FCR 536, [2008] 1 FLR 251.
116 At para 46.
117 [2015] EWCA Civ 2, [2015] 2 FCR 92, [2015] 2 FLR 1338.

Hogg J determined that, at the time of her retention in England, the child was not habitually resident in Brazil: 'this child's strong feelings and sense of being English, is such that she did not acquire integration into Brazil'.

The retention was not, therefore, wrongful, and there was no power under HC80 to order a return. The judge went on to consider how she would have exercised her discretion if there had been a wrongful retention and concluded that it would not have been appropriate to order the child's return anyway. M appealed.

Held by the Court of Appeal:

The appeal was allowed in part but the child was allowed to remain in the UK.

The judge's finding on the child's habitual residence was set aside and replaced with a finding that the child had been habitually resident in Brazil.

The CA went on to consider the judge's alternative: that, based on the child's objections, she would have declined to order a return to Brazil if there had been a wrongful retention. On the basis of the strength of the child's views, there was no reason to interfere with the decision, even though it involved separating the siblings. The order refusing the child's return was upheld.

Relevant factors in the exercise of discretion

7.69 Although every case is fact-specific, in *Re M (Republic of Ireland) (Child's Objections) (Joinder of Children as Parties to Appeal)*[118] Black LJ explained what factors are likely to be relevant to discretion (as opposed to at the 'gateway' stage)[119].

The following graphic gives examples of factors that: (a) would usually support an order for return; (b) may or may not support a return order depending on the circumstances; and (c) would usually support a non-return order:

118 [2015] EWCA Civ 26, [2016] Fam 1, [2015] 2 FLR 1074.
119 See, in particular, para 71.

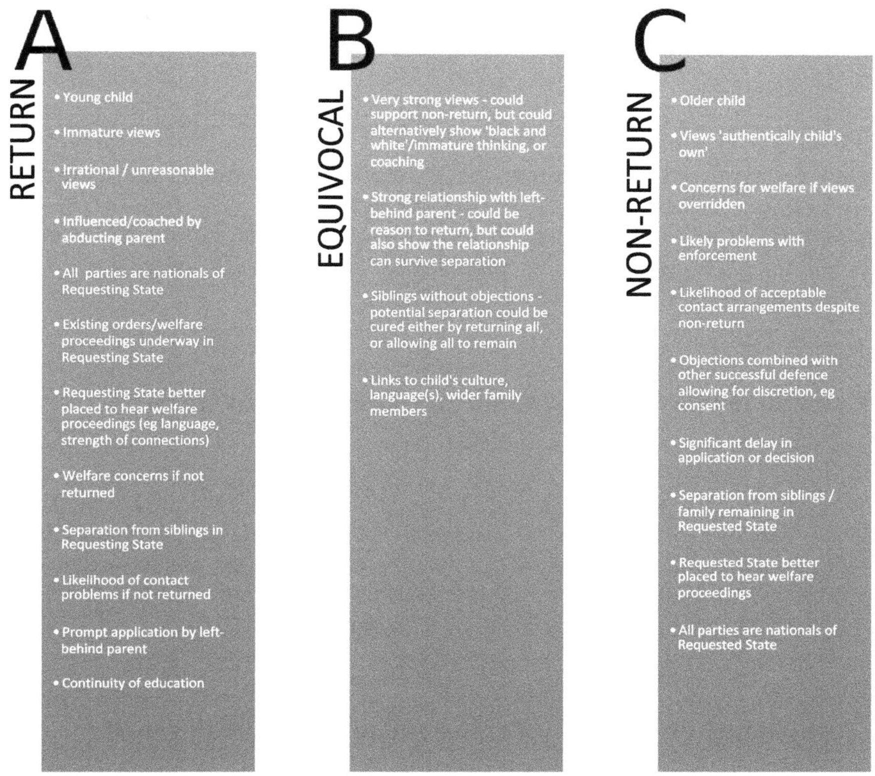

The competing positions of siblings

7.70 It is common for the court to be confronted with a child with relevant objections to a return and a sibling who does not object, or is too young for his or her views to be taken into account. The authorities dealing with the approach to be adopted in such cases are not easy to reconcile. In some cases the court has started from the proposition that there is no defence to the application in respect of the non-objecting child, and therefore the objections of the older child should be overruled; in other cases the court has determined first that the objecting child should not be returned and then held that to return the non-objecting child without a sibling would create an intolerable situation under Art 13(b). The divergent approaches can be illustrated by the following examples:

Case Snapshot: *Re HB (Abduction: Children's Objections)*[120]

Hale J considered the objections of children aged 13 and 11 to returning to Denmark. The objections of the younger child were insufficient to justify refusing a return order. The objections of the older child were more compelling. Nevertheless, she ordered his return in the exercise of her discretion so as to avoid splitting the siblings.

Case Snapshot: *TB v JB (Abduction: Grave Risk of Harm)*[121]

A 14-year-old girl objected to returning to New Zealand. She had three siblings: a boy (12) who expressed a positive wish to return, and two children who were too young for their views to be taken into account. The CA decided that the girl should be returned, citing with approval *Re HB*.

Case Snapshot: *Zaffino v Zaffino (Abduction: Child's Views)*[122]

A case involving six children aged between 5 and 14, four of whom had been wrongfully removed by M from Canada. The older two objected to returning but the younger two were too young to express a valid objection. Munby J ordered the return of the younger two children but upheld the objections of their older siblings. CA overturned his decision, holding that the discretion should have been exercised so as to avoid splitting the siblings.

120 [1997] 3 FCR 235, [1997] 1 FLR 392.
121 [2001] 2 FCR 497, [2001] 2 FLR 515.
122 [2005] EWCA Civ 1012, [2006] 1 FCR 387, [2006] 1 FLR 410.

Case Summary: *WF v RJ*[123]

Facts:

M wrongfully removed two children (13 and 11) from Germany to England. The younger child was functioning 12–18 months below his chronological age. F sought the summary return of both children.

Held by Baker J (refusing to return the children):

Judge considered the exercise of discretion in cases where siblings express distinctive wishes and feelings.

The older sibling was competent to instruct a solicitor; the younger was represented by a Cafcass officer – neither child was allowed to attend the hearing but the older child met the judge.

The older child was clear that she did not want to return. She feared that M would reunite with a violent partner. The child had 'a clear and unequivocal objection' and she was of an age and degree of maturity at which it was appropriate to take account of her views. The younger child did not want to return and had attained a degree of maturity whereby it was appropriate to take account of his views.

Splitting the siblings would place them in an intolerable situation and thus the Art 13(b) gateway was crossed.

The judge then considered the exercise of his discretion 'in the round', concluding that in the case of the older child the preponderance of the factors pointed against a summary return. The younger child's objections seemed to be less clear, less strong and less authentically his own; considered alongside the older child's objections, the judge found that to return the younger child alone would place the children in an intolerable position.

The impact of the UK's exit from the European Union ('Brexit')

7.71 The effect of Brexit upon HC80 proceedings generally is summarised in **Chapter 1**. In the context of the voice of the child, it should be noted that Art 11(2) of BIIA states that:

123 [2010] EWHC 2909 (Fam), [2011] 1 FLR 1153.

When applying Articles 12 and 13 of the 1980 Hague Convention, it shall be ensured that the child is given the opportunity to be heard during the proceedings unless this appears inappropriate having regard to his or her age or degree of maturity.

7.72 As noted above[124], Baroness Hale held in *Re D*[125] that the above principle is of universal application, and therefore it is not confined to intra-EU cases[126]. The Court of Appeal also confirmed in *Re D (A Child) (Recognition of Foreign Order) (Reunite Child Abduction Centre Intervening)*[127] that it is a fundamental principle of procedure of our domestic law that, in any proceedings concerning a child, the court must consider the question of whether (and, if so, how) the child should be heard. In that case, a Romanian order was not enforced pursuant to Art 23 of BIIA because the Romanian court had failed to canvass the child's views. Accordingly, the UK's impending exit from the European Union should not affect the principles or practice in HC80 cases, so far as 'hearing the voice of the child' is concerned.

7.73 BIIA is subject to amendment. The amended version of the Regulation ('BIIA Recast')[128] will come into effect in all EU Member States apart from Denmark on 1 August 2022. Article 21 of BIIA Recast (which applies to HC80 proceedings)[129] provides as follows:

> **'Article 21 Right of the child to express his or her views**
>
> 1. … the courts of the Member States shall … provide the child who is capable of forming his or her own views with a genuine and effective opportunity to express his or her views, either directly, or through a representative or an appropriate body.
> 2. … the court shall give due weight to the views of the child in accordance with his or her age and maturity.'

7.74 The courts may in due course consider whether the existing practice and procedure in HC80 cases in England and Wales is compatible with BIIA Recast. Although the new Regulation is unlikely to have effect in this jurisdiction, the courts may still take account of EU law and practice under HC80 to ensure that there is not significant divergence of approach.

124 See para **7.5**.

125 [2006] UKHL 51, [2007] 1 AC 619, [2007] 1 FCR 1, [2007] 1 FLR 961.

126 See para 58.

127 [2016] EWCA Civ 12, [2016] 1 WLR 2469, [2016] 2 FCR 1, [2016] 2 FLR 347.

128 Council Regulation (EU) No 2019/1111 of 25 June 2019 on jurisdiction and enforcement of decisions in matrimonial matters and the matters of parental responsibility, and on international child abduction (recast).

129 See Art 26 of BIIA Recast; guidance of the effect of Art 21 in the context of HC80 proceedings can be found in para 39 of the recitals to the Regulation.

7.75 English courts must strive to find the 'autonomous' meaning of HC80 when applying its terms – it is not only a matter of domestic law. The jurisprudence of our closest geographical neighbours in the EU is likely to be influential, even if decisions of the CJEU will no longer be binding.

7.76 Parties involved in proceedings in England and Wales may also be party to enforcement action in EU jurisdictions, or may be involved in proceedings in this jurisdiction concerning the enforcement of EU orders. Other EU Member States may well decline to recognise and enforce English orders (under any operative scheme for recognition and enforcement) if the proceedings in England and Wales do not conform to the new expected standard under BIIA Recast.

CHAPTER 8

Settlement

Content at a Glance:

A. INTRODUCTION

8.1 Where a child has been wrongfully removed or retained[1] and a period of less than a year has elapsed between the removal or retention and the date on which proceedings are commenced, Art 12(1) of the 1980 Hague Convention[2] ('HC80') provides that the court must order the return of the child forthwith unless the respondent can establish one of the exceptions in Art 13 of HC80[3].

8.2 Article 12(2) of HC80 addresses the situation where proceedings are commenced a year or more after the date of the wrongful removal or retention. It provides as follows:

1 For wrongful removals and retentions, see **Chapter 3**.

2 The Convention on the Civil Aspects of International Child Abduction signed at the Hague on 25 October 1980.

3 For the Art 13 exceptions, see **Chapter 4** (consent and acquiescence), **Chapter 6** (grave risk) and **Chapter 7** (child's objections).

Article 12(2) HC80

> 'The judicial or administrative authority, even where the proceedings have been commenced after the expiration of the period of one year referred to in the preceding paragraph, shall also order the return of the child, unless it is demonstrated that the child is now settled in its new environment.'

8.3 Thus, the court is required to order the return of an abducted child even where proceedings are commenced 12 months or more after the wrongful removal or retention, unless the respondent can demonstrate that the child is now settled in his or her new environment. This is often referred to as the 'settlement' exception. The settlement exception does not apply to cases where proceedings are issued before a year has elapsed since the date of the removal or retention.

8.4 Where the settlement exception is established, the court has a discretion whether to order the return of the child or not. However, in the majority of cases the court is likely to refuse a return. As Hale J explained in *Re HB (Abduction: Children's Objections) (No 2)*[4]:

> 'Once the time for a speedy return has passed, it must be questioned whether it is indeed in the best interests of a child for there to be a summary return after the very limited enquiry into the merits which is involved in these cases.'

An example of a case in which a return was ordered, despite settlement being established, is *F v M and N (Abduction: Acquiescence: Settlement)*[5].

Case Summary: *F v M and N (Abduction: Acquiescence: Settlement)*[6]

Facts:

The Polish M relocated to England for work, leaving the child in the care of F. F applied to the Polish courts for sole custody and a recommendation was made for the child to remain in his care. M then wrongfully removed the child to England.

4 [1999] 1 FCR 331, [1998] 1 FLR 564.
5 [2008] EWHC 1525 (Fam), [2008] 3 FCR 718, [2008] 2 FLR 1270.
6 [2008] EWHC 1525 (Fam), [2008] 3 FCR 718, [2008] 2 FLR 1270.

There was considerable delay in F's application under HC80 being brought and, by the time of the final hearing, the child had been living with M for 2 years. There was no concealment and M had been living in England openly with the child.

Held by Black J:

Despite being deprived of a relationship with F, with whom she had previously been close, the child had become settled in her new environment.

However, a return order was made as the Polish courts had been seised of the case since before the abduction and had gone a long way in their determination of what arrangements would be in the best interests of the child. The order was suspended to enable M time to seek interim leave to remove the child.

8.5 The application of the 'settlement' exception can be illustrated as follows:

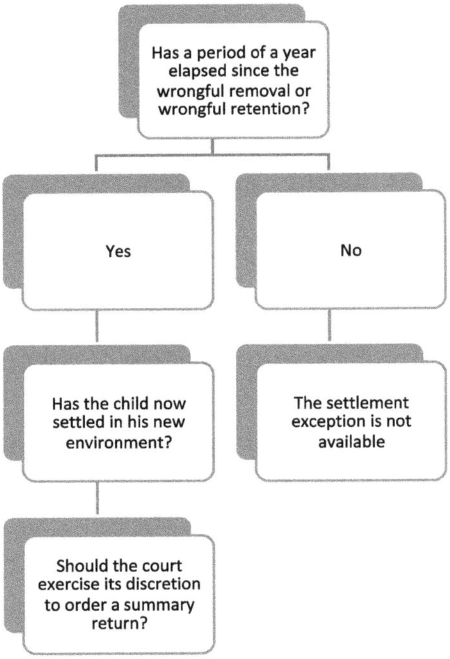

B. CALCULATING THE ONE-YEAR PERIOD

When does time start running?

8.6 For the purposes of Art 12(2), the clock only starts ticking on the date of the child's wrongful removal or retention.

8.7 Calculating the one-year period is a straightforward exercise in almost all cases involving a wrongful removal. The date of the removal is usually admitted or, if not admitted, easy to establish. In unusual cases the court may need to make a finding about the removal date if it will make a difference to whether settlement can be relied upon or not.

8.8 The position may be less clear in cases where the child has been subject to a wrongful retention. Very often in cases of wrongful retention, the retention may occur on the agreed date when the child was due to be returned to his home country; for example, in cases where a return flight had been purchased. However, as explained in **Chapter 3**[7], in cases of repudiatory retention the act of retention may occur earlier than the date on which the left-behind parent was made aware of the intention not to return the child. In such cases the court may need to resolve a substantial dispute about the date of retention in order to determine when time starts running[8].

When does time stop running?

8.9 The courts have been careful not to penalise the left-behind parent for any delay in a case being heard. Therefore, since *Re N (Minors) (Abduction)*[9], it has been accepted that the relevant date for deciding whether a child is settled in this jurisdiction is the date on which the application under HC80 was issued.

Case Summary: *Re N (Minors) (Abduction)*[10]

Facts:

F was an American citizen and M was a British citizen. They lived in Texas with their 2 children, aged 4 and 3. M unilaterally removed the children to England when the marriage broke down. She brought proceedings in England and the children were made wards of court.

F brought HC80 proceedings one year and two days following the children's removal.

Held by Bracewell J:

The meaning of 'now' in Art 12 refers to the date of the commencement of the proceedings, and not in the sense of 'today' in deciding the issue, as otherwise any delay in hearing the case may affect the outcome.

7 See para **3.10**.
8 See *Re C and another (Children) (International Centre for Family Law, Policy and Practice intervening)* [2018] UKSC 8, [2019] AC 1, [2018] 2 FCR 733, [2008] 1 FLR 861.
9 [1991] FCR 765, [1991] 1 FLR 413.
10 [1991] FCR 765, [1991] 1 FLR 413.

On the facts, the children were not settled and an order was made for their summary return to Texas.

The impact of concealment

8.10 In some cases the abducting parent will take steps to hide the whereabouts of the child such that it can take some time before the left-behind parent finds them. This has the potential to prejudice the left-behind parent, as the child could become settled in the new environment before he is found. In those circumstances, the question is: when should time start running for the purposes of establishing settlement?

8.11 In *Cannon v Cannon*[11], Thorpe LJ decided against an approach adopted by some jurisdictions which would see the time that the child was concealed '*subtracted from the total period of delay in order to ascertain whether or not the 12-month mark has been exceeded*'.

Case Summary: *Cannon v Cannon*[12]

Facts:

M removed the child from the USA to Ireland. An order was made by the Irish courts for the child's return to the USA. M then removed the child for a second time to England, where she lived under assumed names. She successfully concealed the child's whereabouts for many years. Four years later the father discovered M's whereabouts and brought HC80 proceedings.

Held by the Court of Appeal:

Thorpe LJ reviewed the approach of other jurisdictions to concealment. He concluded that '*a tolling rule that the period gained by concealment should be disregarded and therefore subtracted from the total period of delay in order to ascertain whether or not the 12-month mark has been exceeded*' would be '*too crude*'.

8.12 Thus, in England and Wales, the calculation of the 12-month period is not affected, even when the left-behind parent may not have known that the child was in England. However, concealment may be relevant to the factual question of whether a child is settled in a new environment. This is further discussed at paras **8.14** to **8.15** below.

11 [2004] EWCA Civ 1330; [2005] 1 WLR 32, [2005] 1 FLR 169.
12 [2004] EWCA Civ 1330; [2005] 1 WLR 32, [2005] 1 FLR 169.

C. THE MEANING OF 'SETTLED' IN A NEW ENVIRONMENT

8.13 In England and Wales, the meaning of the words 'settled in his/her new environment' have long been understood to require an analysis of the child's situation in relation to physical and emotional settlement[13]. The new environment includes the child's:

> 'place, home, school, people, friends, activities and opportunities but not, per se, the relationship with … [the abducting parent] which has always existed in a close, loving attachment. That can only be relevant insofar as it impinges on the new surroundings'[14].

In *Cannon v Cannon*[15], after a review of the domestic and international jurisprudence, Thorpe LJ concluded that it was not sufficient to have regard to the physical settlement of the child but that '*equal regard must be paid to the emotional and psychological elements*'. Thus, the components to settlement can be illustrated as follows:

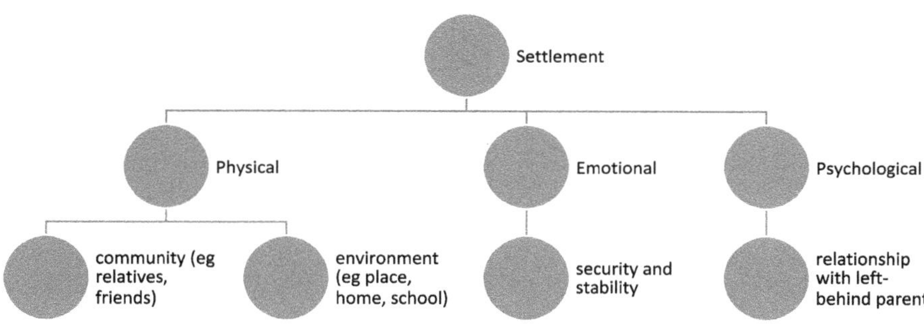

Concealment in the assessment of settlement

8.14 Concealment is relevant to the issue of whether the child is emotionally and psychologically settled in his new environment. While concealment cannot *prevent* a child from becoming settled, in *Cannon*[16] Thorpe LJ held that, where a child had been concealed from the left-behind parent, there is an increased burden on the abducting parent to establish that a child is emotionally and psychologically settled for the purposes of Art 12(2). In particular, he stated that judges should look critically at any alleged settlement that is built on concealment and deceit, especially if the respondent is a fugitive from criminal justice.

8.15 Cases where the abducted child has been living an entirely concealed existence are relatively rare. In those cases, it will be very difficult for the court

13 See *Re N (Minors) (Abduction)* [1991] FCR 765, [1991] 1 FLR 413.
14 *Re N (Minors) (Abduction)* [1991] FCR 765, [1991] 1 FLR 413.
15 [2004] EWCA Civ 1330, [2005] 1 WLR 32, [2005] 1 FLR 169.
16 [2004] EWCA Civ 1330, [2005] 1 WLR 32, [2005] 1 FLR 169.

to accept that a child of school age who has not been attending school and has not been part of the wider community is nevertheless settled.

How long does the child have to be settled for?

8.16 In *Re N*[17] the court held that it is not sufficient to establish settlement on a *transient* basis. It is necessary to demonstrate '*by a projection into the future, that the present position imports stability when looking into the future and is permanent in so far as anything in life can be said to be permanent*'.

8.17 Commentators have since suggested that to require the child's circumstances to be permanent to the extent '*that anything in life can be said to be permanent*' places the bar too high[18]. However, it remains the position that the court is not only concerned with the present but it also looks to the future. In *Re C (Child Abduction: Settlement)*[19], Sir Mark Potter, P held that the evidence must show that '*the present situation imports stability when looking into the future*'.

The 'new environment'

8.18 The new environment referred to in Art 12(2) is the environment to which the child has been removed. The Pérez-Vera report[20] suggests that the requirement to establish that the child is settled in its new environment opens up the possibility of longer proceedings than the summary process otherwise envisaged[21]. However, in this jurisdiction, proceedings involving alleged settlement closely follow a summary process.

8.19 The nature of the enquiry undertaken in settlement cases is dealt with at para **8.23** below. The relevant time for assessing whether the child is settled is not dealt with in the Pérez-Vera report, nor is it particularly addressed in any authority. However, as a Cafcass report is invariably ordered in all settlement cases, the time at which the child's settlement in his/her new environment is assessed will be the time when Cafcass conducts its investigation and reports to the court for the purposes of proceedings.

8.20 In *Re C (Child Abduction: Settlement)*[22], Sir Mark Potter considered that a child's new environment encompasses '*place, home, school, people, friends, activities and opportunities*'. Thus, a child's new environment is likely to depend on his/her age. The new environment of a child of school-going age will include his/her educational establishment and other activities, but the new environment of a toddler may only consist of immediate family, relatives and friends.

17 [1991] FCR 765, [1991] 1 FLR 413.
18 See *Dicey, Morris and Collins: The Conflict of Laws*, 15th edition (2012) at para 19-142.
19 [2006] EWHC 1229 (Fam), [2007] 1 FCR 649, [2006] 2 FLR 797.
20 Explanatory Report to HC80 by Professor Elisa Pérez-Vera.
21 Paragraph 109, page 47.
22 [2006] EWHC 1229 (Fam), [2007] 1 FCR 649, [2006] 2 FLR 797.

8.21 In *Re N*[23], Bracewell J did not consider the children sufficiently settled after they had spent 11 months in England living in the home of their grandmother, and only 3 months in their own home with their mother. Even though a child may have been away from his State of habitual residence for some time, he/she may not have lived in *the new environment* for a sufficiently long time or sufficiently stable circumstances to be considered settled.

8.22 A further example is the case of *M v M & Ors*[24], where Mrs Justice Black (as she then was) found that the children who had been living in England for over 12 months were not settled, as the father had deceived the Polish courts and the mother into believing that they had remained in Poland throughout that period.

Case Summary: *M v M & Ors*[25]

Facts:

The Polish F had retained the two children in this jurisdiction following an agreed holiday. M brought HC80 proceedings which concluded by consent and the children were returned to Poland. The consent order had included an undertaking by M that she would not separate the children from F pending a first inter partes hearing. M had some contact with the children following their return. While the Polish courts allowed the children to remain in the care of F pending conclusion of their proceedings, an order was made preventing F from removing the children from Poland and, following a request by the court, the children's passports were cancelled.

Unbeknown to M and the Polish courts, F managed to return with the children to England. The children resumed their life and schooling in England. M issued further HC80 proceedings.

Held by Black J:

The children had not settled in their environment despite the links that the family had made with their local area in this country. The children had done well enough in school and learnt to function adequately in English. However, the children had been caught up in F's influence and they had been aware that their situation in this country was far from settled, as F acknowledged that he had been waiting for the day that the police would knock on their door.

23 [1991] FCR 765, [1991] 1 FLR 413.
24 [2008] EWHC 2049 (Fam), [2008] 2 FLR 1884, [2008] Fam Law 1076.
25 [2008] EWHC 2049 (Fam), [2008] 2 FLR 1884, [2008] Fam Law 1076.

D. ESTABLISHING SETTLEMENT

Burden and standard of proof

8.23 There is no reference to the burden of proof in Art 12(2). The Explanatory Report to HC80 anticipated that the burden would fall on the parent opposing the return[26], and in practice this has been followed in England and Wales[27].

8.24 In *C v H (Abduction: Consent)*[28], Munby J (as he then was) held that the standard of proof in abduction cases is the ordinary civil standard, namely the balance of probabilities[29].

The nature of the enquiry

8.25 In accordance with the Practice Guidance[30] issued by Sir James Munby, P in March 2018, the court will expect consideration to be given to how the children will be heard at the earliest opportunity. In settlement cases, the separate point of view of the child will be particularly important[31].

8.26 While the proceedings retain their summary nature, settlement is the only exception which requires the court to direct that Cafcass prepares a report into the alleged settlement, regardless of the ages of the children, and (almost invariably) that the children are made parties to the proceedings[32]. The nature of the enquiry is broader than those undertaken under other exceptions such as child's objections. It usually comprises a 'home visit' in order to assess the physical settlement of the child and consideration is given to issues pertaining to the welfare of the child.

E. DISCRETION

8.27 Different jurisdictions have answered in different ways the question of whether a child who is settled could nevertheless be returned to their State of habitual residence. In *Re M (Children) (Abduction: Rights of Custody)*[33], the House of Lords conclusively settled this issue for England and Wales. It was considered that it may remain in the best interests of a child to be returned to his/her former home, regardless of the fact that they had been settled in their new

26 Paragraph 109, page 47.
27 See *Re N (Minors) (Abduction)* [1991] FCR 765, [1991] 1 FLR 413.
28 [2009] EWHC 2660 (Fam), [2010] 1 FLR 225.
29 See also the House of Lords decision in *Re B (Children) (Care Proceedings: standard of proof)* [2008] UKHL 35, [2009] 1 AC 11, [2008] 2 FCR 339, [2008] 2 FLR 141.
30 Case Management and Mediation of International Child Abduction Proceedings (13 March 2018).
31 See Practice Guidance at para 3.5.
32 See *Re M (Abduction: Rights of Custody)* [2007] UKHL 55, [2008] 1 AC 1288, [2008] 1 FCR 536, [2008] 1 FLR 251 at para 57.
33 [2007] UKHL 55, [2008] 1 AC 1288, [2008] 1 FCR 536, [2008] 1 FLR 251.

environment. As such, the Convention was read as including the power to order such a return.

8.28 Baroness Hale explained in *Re M* that, where the discretion to order a return arises, '*the discretion is at large*'. The court is entitled to take into account the various aspects of Convention policy, alongside the circumstances which gave rise to the court's discretion and wider considerations of the child's rights and welfare.

Case Summary: *Re M (Abduction: Rights of Custody)*[34]

Facts:

Following the parties' separation, the two children, aged 13 and 10, lived with F in Zimbabwe. During a contact visit they were removed to England by M. F discovered their whereabouts after approximately 6 months, but waited a year before approaching the Zimbabwean Central Authority. Proceedings under HC80 were issued more than 2 years following the wrongful removal.

Held by the House of Lords:

There was a judicial discretion to order the return of children, notwithstanding that settlement had been established under Art 12. This discretion was consistent with the aim of HC80 and recognised the flexibility in the concept of settlement. It also acknowledged that a late application might be the result of active concealment.

Baroness Hale stated that, where the discretion arises, it does so from the terms of HC80 itself and the discretion was 'at large'. Thus, the court was entitled to take into account the various aspects of HC80 policy, alongside the circumstances which gave rise to the discretion and wider considerations of the child's rights and welfare.

8.29 The considerations that fall to be taken into account when the court exercises its discretion can be illustrated as follows:

34 [2007] UKHL 55, [2008] 1 AC 1288, [2008] 1 FCR 536, [2008] 1 FLR 251.

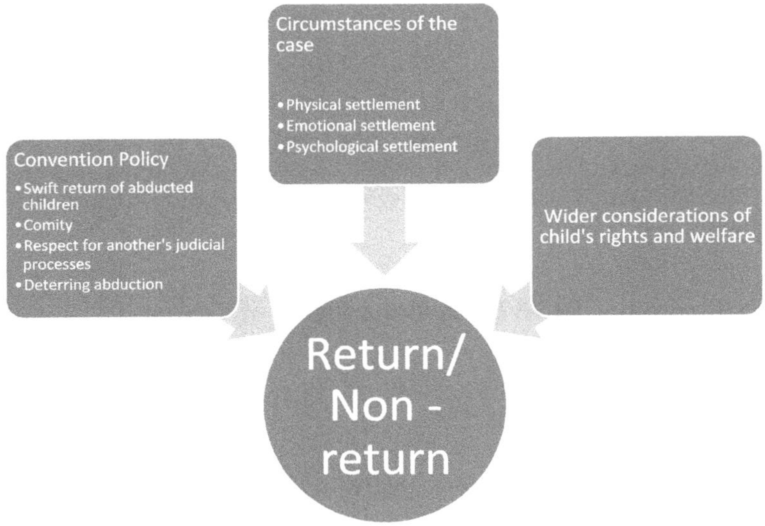

8.30 *Re O (Abduction: Settlement)*[35] is an example of how the balance between Hague Convention policy and the welfare of the child is struck in the exercise of the court's discretion.

Case Summary: *Re O (Abduction: Settlement)*[36]

Facts:

The Nigerian parents lived with their 2 children. When the children were aged 5 and 3, they were retained in Nigeria by M. F brought proceedings in the USA in which he made a number of unsubstantiated allegations and led the court to believe that M was in the USA. More than a year after the wrongful retention, M travelled to the UK with the children for a holiday. F issued HC80 proceedings here.

At first instance, the Judge found that the children were settled in Nigeria but nevertheless ordered their return to the USA. M appealed.

Held by the Court of Appeal (appeal allowed):

Black LJ found that the judge had been wrong in giving Hague policy considerations '*overriding significance in the hierarchy of factors in a way that Re M makes clear he should not have done*'. In a case which does not involve a hot pursuit, although not irrelevant, HC80 considerations are not as prominent as they would otherwise be.

35 [2011] EWCA Civ 128; [2011] 2 FLR 1307, [2011] 1 FCR 363.
36 [2011] EWCA Civ 128; [2011] 2 FLR 1307, [2011] 1 FCR 363.

The CA took various factors pertaining to the children's welfare into account, including the following:

- the children had lived in Nigeria for 16 months;
- they were happily settled there;
- they were fully integrated into their family, schools and community;
- the children found it hard to think about the possibility of returning to the USA imminently;
- they had patchy recollections of their life in the USA;
- they regarded Nigeria as their home;
- there was no concealment following the wrongful retention; and
- F had not sought return until the children travelled to England.

8.31 There are cases where the court has ordered a summary return despite settlement being established. However, they are very few and far between[37].

37 For an example of such a case, see para **8.4** above.

CHAPTER 9

The inherent jurisdiction

Content at a Glance:

A. INTRODUCTION

9.1 The inherent jurisdiction can be used in a variety of ways in child abduction proceedings. This chapter will focus mainly on its use for securing return orders in respect of abducted children. In the context of international child abduction, there are essentially three situations in which it may be necessary to bring *substantive* proceedings under the inherent jurisdiction[1]:

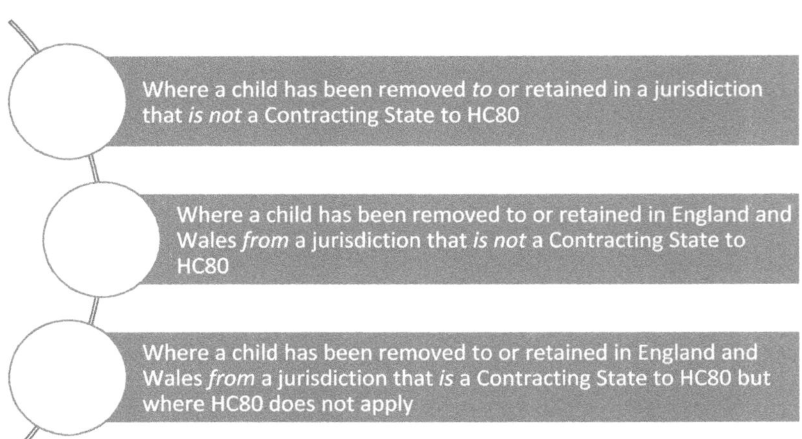

1 References to HC80 refer to the Convention on the Civil Aspects of International Child Abduction signed at the Hague on 25 October 1980.

9.2 Additionally, the High Court can make orders under the inherent jurisdiction in the context of existing proceedings (including applications under HC80) in order to locate a child or prevent a child from being abducted. Such orders are considered in **Chapter 12**.

9.3 Orders that may be made under the inherent jurisdiction in the context of international child abduction are summarised in the following graphic:

B. THE NATURE OF THE INHERENT JURISDICTION

9.4 The inherent jurisdiction of the High Court can be summarised as amounting to that which remains of its common-law powers. The High Court has very wide powers to safeguard the welfare of children. These can be exercised in relation to any child, except where such powers have been curtailed by statute or judicial intervention. For example, Children Act 1989 ('CA 1989'), s 100 prevents the court from making orders placing a child in care or requiring a child to be accommodated under the inherent jurisdiction.

9.5 Family Procedure Rules 2010 ('FPR 2010') PD 12D, para 1.1 provides that inherent jurisdiction proceedings '*should not be commenced unless it is clear that the issues concerning the child cannot be resolved under the Children Act 1989*'. However, practice directions do not have legislative force as they are not made under a statute – therefore, para 1.1 has no legal authority. Accordingly, it has been held by the Supreme Court[2] that, in the context of child abduction proceedings, orders *may* be made under the inherent jurisdiction even though similar orders could also be made under CA 1989; the fact that an order for the return of a child to or from another jurisdiction could be made as a specific issue order does not preclude a return order from being made pursuant to the inherent jurisdiction. This may be important in practice for two reasons:

- the court may have jurisdiction to make an order under the inherent jurisdiction but not under CA 1989, s 8 by virtue of the Family Law Act 1986 '(FLA 1986'): see paras **9.9–9.11** below; and
- public funding may be available for proceedings to be brought under the inherent jurisdiction but not under CA 1989.

9.6 It is important to remember that the question of whether the court *has* jurisdiction is separate from the question of whether the court should *exercise* its jurisdiction. It has a *power*, not a *duty*, to use its inherent jurisdiction[3]. Before any order can be made, the court must be satisfied of two things:

Does the court have jurisdiction?

Is it appropriate to use that jurisdiction?

9.7 The court must consider very critically the use of the inherent jurisdiction, particularly where there may be other bases upon which jurisdiction may be exercised. There may be good reasons for recourse to the inherent jurisdiction, but these need to be identified and highlighted. Although it may be useful to plead a case in the alternative where there are concerns about the applicability of HC80, it is important to establish the basis for use of the inherent jurisdiction. In *Re NY (A Child)*[4], it was suggested that the following might justify using the inherent jurisdiction:

2 *Re NY (A Child) (Reunite International and others intervening)* [2019] UKSC 49, [2019] 3 WLR 962, [2020] 1 FCR 56, [2019] 2 FLR 1247.

3 *A v A and another (Children: Habitual Residence) (Reunite International Child Abduction Centre intervening)* [2013] UKSC 60, [2014] AC 1, [2013] 3 FCR 559, [2014] 1 FLR 111; *Re NY (A Child) (Reunite International and others intervening)* [2019] UKSC 49, [2019] 3 WLR 962, [2020] 1 FCR 56, [2019] 2 FLR 1247.

4 *Re NY (A Child) (Reunite International and others intervening)* [2019] UKSC 49, [2019] 3 WLR 962, [2020] 1 FCR 56, [2019] 2 FLR 1247.

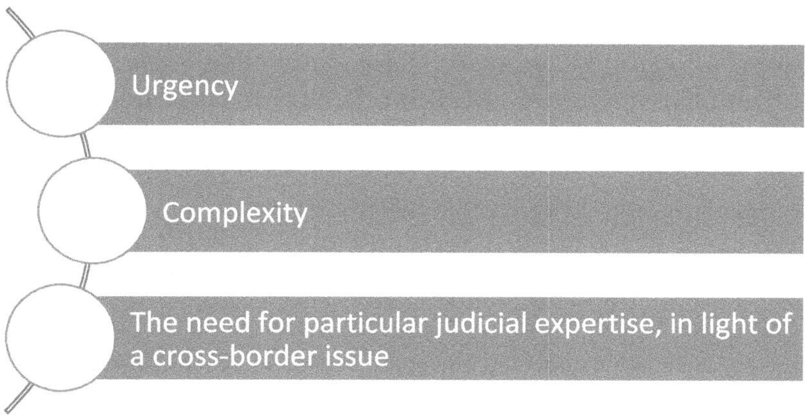

C. ESTABLISHING JURISDICTION IN CHILDREN PROCEEDINGS

9.8 The domestic law statute which governs jurisdiction in children proceedings is FLA 1986. This in turn cross-refers to two international instruments which regulate jurisdiction: (i) Council Regulation (EC) 2201/2003 ('BIIA')[5], and (ii) the 1996 Hague Convention[6] ('HC96').

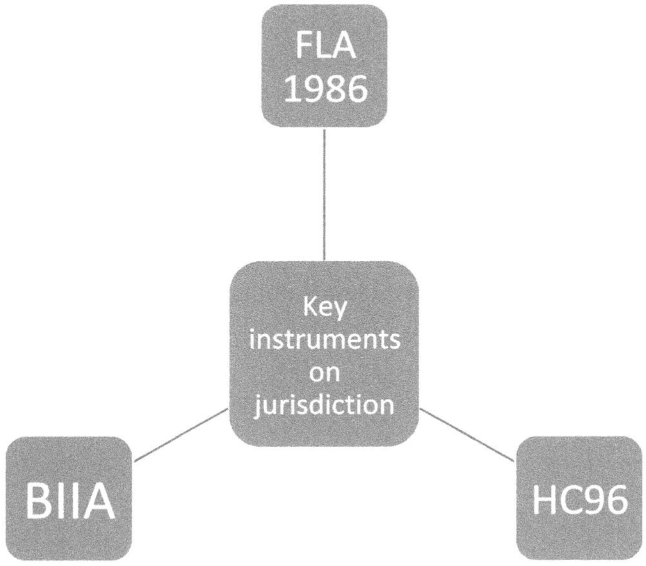

5 As a consequence of the United Kingdom's departure from the European Union, it is expected that BIIA will cease to apply when the implementation period provided for by the European Union (Withdrawal) Act 2018, s 3 ends on 31 December 2020 and that, with effect from 1 January 2021, the only international instrument governing jurisdiction within the United Kingdom will be HC96.

6 Convention of 19 October 1996 on Jurisdiction, Applicable Law, Recognition, Enforcement and Co-operation in Respect of Parental Responsibility and Measures for the Protection of Children.

9.9 FLA 1986, Part 1 contains provisions which limit the jurisdiction of the courts to make orders in relation to children. The Act restricts the courts' jurisdiction to make orders under CA 1989, s 8 (see FLA 1986, ss 1(1)(a) and 2(1)). It also limits the courts' jurisdiction to make certain categories of order under the inherent jurisdiction set out in FLA 1986, s 1(1)(d) ('section 1(1)(d) orders'). The section 1(1)(d) orders in question are:

– an order that gives the care of the child to any person;

– an order which provides for contact between the child and a person; and

– an order making provision for the child's education.

9.10 An order made under the inherent jurisdiction which requires a parent to return a child from another jurisdiction to England and Wales is not a section 1(1)(d) order and therefore falls outside the scope of Part 1 of FLA 1986[7]. Therefore, jurisdiction to make such an order is governed by common law rather than by statute.

9.11 If an order sought under the inherent jurisdiction is a section 1(1)(d) order, FLA 1986, s 2(3) provides that the court only has jurisdiction to make such an order if one of the following conditions is satisfied:

– the court has jurisdiction under BIIA or HC96; or

– neither BIIA nor HC96 applies and:
  - the condition in FLA 1986, s 3 is satisfied; or
  - the child is present on the relevant date and the court considers that the immediate exercise of its powers is necessary for the child's protection.

  Subject to certain exceptions where proceedings are continuing in Scotland or Northern Ireland, the condition in FLA 1986, s 3 is that on the relevant date[8] the child is:
  (a) habitually resident in England and Wales; or
  (b) present in England and Wales and not habitually resident in any part of the United Kingdom.

7 *A v A and another (Children: Habitual Residence) (Reunite International Child Abduction Centre intervening)* [2013] UKSC 60, [2014] AC 1, [2013] 3 FCR 559, [2014] 1 FLR 111.

8 The meaning of 'relevant date' can be found in FLA 1986, s 7(c). It means the date of the application to make or vary an order or, where no such application is made, the date on which the court is considering whether to make or vary the order.

Case Summary: *A (Children)*[9]

Facts:

The proceedings related to four children, the oldest three of whom were born in the UK. After the birth of the third child, the parents separated. M took the three children to Pakistan for a 3-week holiday. Under pressure from F and from family members, she agreed to reconcile with F on the basis that the family would return to England.

In fact, M and the children were forced to remain in Pakistan; the children were enrolled into local schools and F removed M's and the children's passports. M then became pregnant and was beaten, threatened and abused by F and his family.

Following the birth of the child, M managed to retrieve her passport and was able to return to England. F commenced custody proceedings in Pakistan.

On her arrival in the UK, M obtained an order from the English High Court for the immediate return of the children. The order was made in wardship, on the basis that all the children were habitually resident in England and Wales.

The Court of Appeal held that the youngest sibling was not habitually resident in England and Wales. The Court upheld the determination that the three older siblings remained habitually resident in England and Wales after being retained in Pakistan.

Held by the UKSC:

The wardship orders granted pursuant to the inherent jurisdiction did not fall within section 1(1)(a) or (d) of the Family Law Act 1986. However, they did fall within the wide definition of parental responsibility in Art 2(7) of BIIA. Article 14 of BIIA applied where no Member State court had jurisdiction, as was the case here. Accordingly, common law rules as to jurisdiction applied and the jurisdiction could be exercised on the basis of the child's nationality.

The Supreme Court also provided detailed guidance on the test for ascertaining a child's habitual residence, rejecting previous tests and adopting a simple test: a child is habitually resident in the place which reflects some degree of integration by the child in a social and family environment (see **Chapter 4** for habitual residence).

9 *A v A and another (Children: Habitual Residence) (Reunite International Child Abduction Centre intervening)* [2013] UKSC 60, [2014] AC 1, [2013] 3 WLR 76, [2013] 3 FCR 559, [2014] 1 FLR 111.

9.12 BIIA is a European Union Regulation which has direct effect in the domestic law of Member States which, until 31 January 2020, included the United Kingdom. Articles 8 to 13 of BIIA contain various provisions pursuant to which a Member State may have jurisdiction over issues of parental responsibility in relation to a child. As a consequence of the United Kingdom's departure from the European Union, it is expected that BIIA will cease to apply when the implementation period provided for by the European Union (Withdrawal) Act 2018, s 3 ends on 31 December 2020 and that, with effect from 1 January 2021, the only international instrument governing jurisdiction in respect of children proceedings within the United Kingdom will be HC96.

9.13 For so long as the provisions of BIIA continue to apply in England and Wales, the courts have jurisdiction to make welfare orders which fall outside the scope of FLA 1986, s 1(1)(d) on the basis of the child's nationality. This is because, if no Member State has jurisdiction under Arts 8 to 13 of BIIA, Art 14 enables jurisdiction to be established in accordance with the domestic law of the Member States. HC96 does not have an equivalent to Art 14 of BIIA providing for a residual jurisdiction in accordance with domestic law. It may therefore be arguable in future that the jurisdiction based upon a child's nationality no longer applies. For jurisdiction based upon HC96, see **Chapter 10**.

Summary

The inherent jurisdiction can be exercised based on the child's habitual residence or physical presence in England and Wales. In limited circumstances, it may also be exercised on the basis of a child's UK nationality, if no other EU Member State has jurisdiction.

D. SEEKING A SUMMARY RETURN UNDER THE INHERENT JURISDICTION

9.14 In this section we consider three situations in which it may be necessary to seek return orders under the inherent jurisdiction:

- where a child has been removed *to* or retained in a jurisdiction that *is not* a Contracting State to HC80;
- where a child has been removed to or retained in England and Wales *from* a jurisdiction that *is not* a Contracting State to HC80; and
- where a child has been removed to or retained in England and Wales from a jurisdiction that *is* a Contracting State to HC80 but where HC80 does not apply.

Returns to Hague Contracting States where HC80 does not apply

9.15 There are circumstances in which, even though a child has been removed from or retained away from a country that is a Contracting State to HC80, the Convention will not apply for one of three reasons:

- the child is aged 16 or over[10];
- the left-behind parent did not have rights of custody immediately prior to the removal or retention[11]; or
- the child was not habitually resident in the overseas State immediately prior to the removal or retention[12].

It may nevertheless be possible in such cases to obtain a return order under the inherent jurisdiction. Article 18 of HC80 provides that the relevant provisions of the Convention '*do not limit the power of a judicial or administrative authority to order the return of the child at any time*'.

Age of the child

9.16 HC80 ceases to apply when a child attains the age of 16 years[13]. However, a return order can be made in respect of a child aged 16 and above under the inherent jurisdiction.

Case Summary: Re Q *(A Child)*[14]

Facts:

M and F were Polish. They had two children, Q (17) and V (12). They separated in 2010 amidst significant hostility. The Polish court ordered that the children live with F. In early 2018, Q and V moved in with M. F issued proceedings to enforce the order for them to live with him. These were ongoing when M removed the children to England. F issued proceedings for the children's return. M argued that (i) the children were at grave risk of harm because F neglected their needs, (ii) they objected to a return, and (iii) returning Q against his wishes was not in his best interests.

10 *Re Q (Children) (1980 Hague Convention: Inherent Jurisdiction Summary Return)* [2019] EWHC 490 (Fam).

11 *Re W (Minors) (Abduction: Father's Rights); B (A Minor) (Abduction: Father's Rights)* [1999] Fam 1, [1998] 2 FCR 549, [1998] 2 FLR 146.

12 *Re L (A Child) (Custody: Habitual Residence) (Reunite International Child Abduction Centre intervening)* [2013] UKSC 75, [2014] AC 1017, [2014] 1 FCR 69, [2014] 1 FLR 772.

13 HC80, Art 4.

14 *Re Q (A Child) (1980 Hague Convention: Inherent Jurisdiction: Summary Return)* [2019] EWHC 490 (Fam).

Held by Williams J:

Both children returned to Poland: Q under the inherent jurisdiction and V under HC80. M had not established that F's care was so deficient as to constitute a grave risk of harm. The children's objections were not fundamental, but had been influenced by M. The parental conflict prevented Q from understanding his position fully.

No rights of custody

9.17 In order for the removal or retention of a child to be 'wrongful' under HC80, it must be in breach of rights of custody held under the law of the State of the child's habitual residence: see **Chapter 3**. Where no such rights of custody exist, the removal will not be wrongful and HC80 will not apply. The effect of Art 18 of HC80 is that the court may be able to make a return order under the inherent jurisdiction.

No habitual residence

9.18 The removal or retention of the child will not be wrongful under HC80 if the child was not habitually resident in the relevant overseas State immediately prior to the removal or retention[15]. For habitual residence, see **Chapter 4**. The effect of Art 18 is that, even if the removal is not wrongful, the court may be able to make a return order under the inherent jurisdiction[16]. However, there will be no jurisdiction to make an order under the inherent jurisdiction if the child is habitually resident in a jurisdiction that is a Contracting State to HC96 unless the case is one of urgency[17].

15 *Re C (Children) (International Centre for Family Law, Policy and Practice intervening)* [2018] UKSC 8, [2019] AC 1, [2018] 2 FCR 733, [2018] 1 FLR 861.

16 *Re K (Abduction: Consent: Forum Conveniens)* [1995] 3 FCR 697, [1995] 2 FLR 211; *Re L (A Child) (Custody: Habitual Residence) (Reunite International Child Abduction Centre intervening)* [2013] UKSC 75, [2014] AC 1017, [2014] 1 FCR 69, [2014] 1 FLR 772; *Re NY (A Child) (Reunite International and others intervening)* [2019] UKSC 49, [2019] 3 WLR 962, [2020] 1 FCR 56, [2019] 2 FLR 1247.

17 *Re J (A Child) (Reunite International Child Abduction Centre and others intervening)* [2015] UKSC 70, [2016] AC 1291, [2016] 1 FCR 481, [2016] 1 FLR 170; *Re IL (Children) (1996 Hague Child Protection Convention: Inherent Jurisdiction)* [2019] EWCA Civ 1956, [2020] 1 FCR 35.

Case Summary: *Re L (A Child)*[18]

Facts:

The proceedings concerned a child born in the USA. F was a US citizen; M had indefinite leave to remain in the UK. The parents entered into an agreement in Texas which provided that M had the authority to determine the child's residence 'without regard to geographic location'. M subsequently took the child to the UK.

In 2010, M took the child to Texas for court proceedings as a result of which the child stayed with F for 18 months. M appealed against an order that the F had custody of the child, but the appeal was never heard. M commenced proceedings in the Texas court under HC80 for the return of the child to the UK. She was successful and she was allowed to return to the UK with the child.

F's appeal against the Texas HC80 order was allowed; the Appeal court found that the child had remained habitually resident in the United States of America and that M had consented to the Texas court having jurisdiction to resolve the issue of custody[19]. M was ordered to return the child to F in the USA.

F brought proceedings in England, arguing that the removal of the child from Texas was wrongful in the light of the US Appeal court's ruling. These applications were dismissed[20]. F's appeal to the Court of Appeal was unsuccessful[21]. F was given permission to appeal to the Supreme Court.

Held by the UKSC:

The appeal was allowed and the child's return was ordered. The removal was not wrongful within the meaning of HC80 as the child was habitually resident in England and Wales on the relevant date. HC80 was thus not engaged.

However, the UKSC ordered a return under the inherent jurisdiction: it was in the child's best interests to return for the Texan court to make welfare determinations about his upbringing.

18 *Re L (A Child) (Custody: Habitual Residence) (Reunite International Child Abduction Centre intervening)* [2013] UKSC 75, [2014] AC 1017, [2014] 1 FCR 69, [2014] 1 FLR 722.

19 *Larbie v Larbie*, 690 F.3d 295 (5th Cir. 2012) [INCADAT Reference: HC/E/USf 1236].

20 *DL v EL (Hague Abduction Convention: Effect of Reversal of Return Order on Appeal)* [2013] EWHC 49 (Fam), [2013] 2 FLR 163.

21 *DL v EL (Hague Abduction Convention: Effect of Reversal of Return Order on Appeal)* [2013] EWCA Civ 865, [2013] 3 FCR 69, [2014] 1 FLR 570.

Case Summary: *Re I-L (Children)*[22]

Facts:

M (Russian) and F (British) had two children. The family had lived between England and Russia, but after the second child was born they went to live with M in Russia. F visited regularly. M issued divorce proceedings in Russia in 2017, but the arrangements continued.

The children remained in Russia without M for two months in 2019 while she went to the USA, as F did not consent to their going. They did not see F while M was away. In April 2019, F agreed to the children having a short holiday in the USA. The children then came to England with both parents, with the parties intending they would stay for several months.

In May 2019, F commenced proceedings under CA 1989. In response, M sought a return order under HC80 or alternatively the inherent jurisdiction. She asserted that F's commencement of proceedings amounted to a repudiatory wrongful retention (see **Chapter 3**).

Mr Geekie QC dismissed M's HC80 application, holding that F had not acted in the way asserted and so there had been no breach of M's rights of custody. He found that the children remained habitually resident in Russia. An order was made for the children to be returned to Russia under the inherent jurisdiction. F appealed and M cross-appealed.

Held by the Court of Appeal:

The children were habitually resident in Russia and there had been a Russian return order made. Accordingly, under HC96 the English court only had secondary jurisdiction to make supportive orders; it could not make orders which interfered with issues properly determined by the Russian court.

The purpose of HC96 would be defeated if the English court could assume jurisdiction under domestic law, despite having no jurisdiction under HC96.

Thus, the English court had no jurisdiction to make a welfare-based return order under the inherent jurisdiction. The appropriate route was for M to bring enforcement proceedings in respect of the Russian return order.

22 *Re IL (Children) (1996 Hague Child Protection Convention: Inherent Jurisdiction)* [2019] EWCA Civ 1956, [2020] 1 FCR 35.

Relevant principles on an application for summary return under the inherent jurisdiction

Welfare is paramount

9.19 An application for a summary return order under the inherent jurisdiction is decided differently from one made under HC80. The principles of HC80 should not be imported into the inquiry nor applied by analogy[23]. The child's welfare is the paramount consideration.

Case Summary: *Re J (A Child)*[24]

Facts:

F was a Saudi national; M was a dual British and Saudi national. They married in Saudi Arabia. The child was born in the USA but taken to live in Saudi Arabia shortly afterwards. He was a citizen of the USA, UK and Saudi Arabia. M brought the child to live in England for a short time when the marriage encountered difficulties, but she returned to Saudi Arabia to commence Sharia divorce proceedings. A term of the agreed divorce was that M should not remove the child from Saudi Arabia without F's consent. The parties then reconciled and remarried. M and the child came to England again, with F's consent, while M pursued a one-year Master's degree. F visited, but there were further difficulties and M resolved not to return. She sought a divorce in the English court and from the Muslim Council in London. F applied for a summary return of the child to Saudi Arabia.

Hughes J made a residence order in favour of M and contact to F. He held that, but for F's allegations of M's association with another man, the return would have been ordered. This was not so ordered because of the impact which those allegations would have on M under Sharia law.

The Court of Appeal allowed the appeal. Although it found no reason to criticise the judge's direction on the applicable principles, too much weight had been given to the risks stemming from F's allegations; such risks should not have had such decisive effect.

Held by the House of Lords:

Neither statute nor authority made provision for the principles of HC80 to be extended to countries not party to it. In such cases, the child's welfare was the deciding factor. A decision to return the child could be reached only on the basis that it was in the child's best interests. Although a summary order

23 *Re J (A Child) (Custody Rights: Jurisdiction)* [2005] UKHL 40, [2006] 1 AC 80, [2005] 2 FCR 381, [2005] 2 FLR 802.

24 *Re J (A Child) (Custody Rights: Jurisdiction)* [2005] UKHL 40, [2006] 1 AC 80, [2005] 2 FCR 381, [2005] 2 FLR 802.

could be made without a full investigation, that should not be the automatic reaction to any removal or retention of a child – there was no presumption to this effect.

Court must consider the welfare checklist

9.20 A welfare-based application for a summary return order can be made either under the inherent jurisdiction or by way of an application for a specific issue order under CA 1989, s 8[25]. In *Re NY (A Child)*[26] the Supreme Court held that the same principles should apply irrespective of the procedural route chosen. Accordingly, although the welfare checklist in CA 1989, s 1(3) does not expressly apply, the court must have regard to it in applications under the inherent jurisdiction. In cases involving allegations of domestic abuse, the court must also consider FPR 2010, PD 12J.

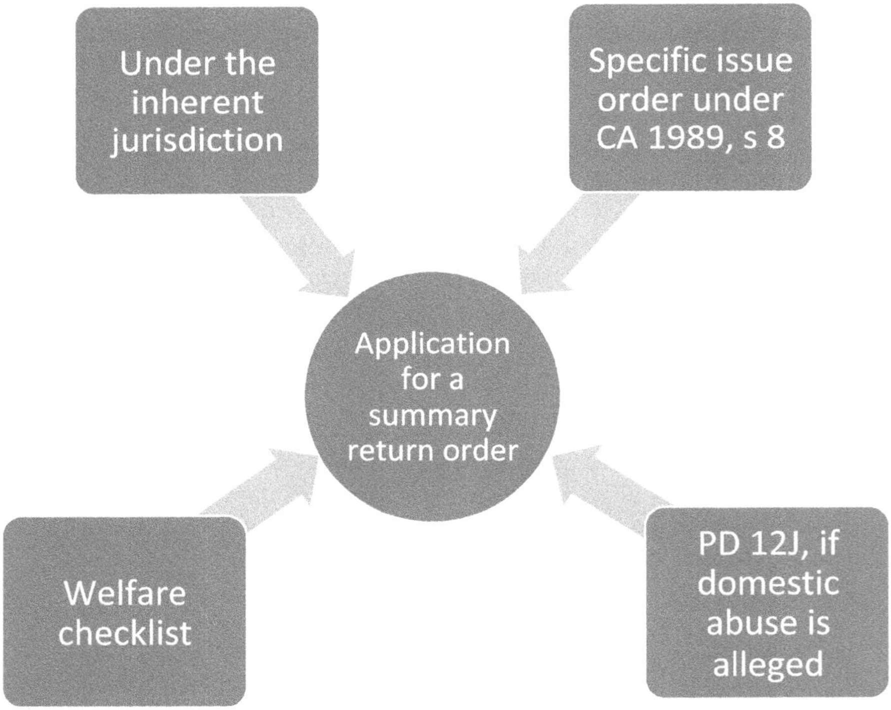

25 *Re NY (A Child) (Reunite International and others intervening)* [2019] UKSC 49, [2019] 3 WLR 962, [2020] 1 FCR 56, [2019] 2 FLR 1247.

26 *Re NY (A Child) (Reunite International and others intervening)* [2019] UKSC 49, [2019] 3 WLR 962, [2020] 1 FCR 56, [2019] 2 FLR 1247.

Case Summary: Re *NY (A Child)*[27]

Facts:

M and F lived in Israel with their child. They moved to England but the marriage broke down within two months. M remained with the child in England while F returned to Israel alone. He applied under HC80 for summary return of the child, asserting wrongful retention. M argued, among other matters, that the child was habitually resident in England and Wales at the relevant time.

MacDonald J rejected the contention that the child had become habitually resident in England and made a return order under HC80. He said that, even if he had found differently, he would have ordered return under the inherent jurisdiction.

The Court of Appeal dismissed M's appeal. The judge had been wrong to find wrongful retention and therefore to make an order under HC80. However, the judge had been entitled to make a return order under the inherent jurisdiction; therefore, the CA made an order in those terms.

Held by the UKSC:

Appeal allowed. Order set aside.

Neither CA 1989 nor case law precluded exercise of the inherent jurisdiction to make orders equivalent to those available under CA 1989, ss 8 and 10. FPR 2010, PD 12D para 1.1 (which suggested the contrary) had no legislative force.

A return order fell to be decided by reference to the child's welfare regardless of the jurisdictional basis. The welfare checklist was relevant whatever procedural route was chosen for the application. PD 12J should also be considered if there were relevant allegations of domestic abuse.

The CA should have considered a range of questions and issues by reference to the welfare checklist before making a return order under the inherent jurisdiction and, in failing to do so, had not properly considered the child's welfare.

Not necessarily a full welfare inquiry

9.21 The paramountcy of the child's welfare may not require a full welfare inquiry to be conducted.

27 *Re NY (A Child) (Reunite International and others intervening)* [2019] UKSC 49, [2019] 3 WLR 962, [2020] 1 FCR 56, [2019] 2 FLR 1247.

> 'The welfare of the child is the court's paramount consideration. But this does not mean that the court is obliged in every case to conduct a full-blown welfare-based inquiry into where the child should live.'[28]

9.22 There is no presumption in favour of a return order being made. At its highest, it has been said that the court can start from the proposition that:

> 'it is likely to be better for a child to return to his home country for any disputes about his future to be decided there.'[29]

However, this is not an absolute rule. The courts have consistently emphasised the need to focus on the particular child in the particular circumstances of the case.

9.23 In *Re NY (A Child)*[30] the Supreme Court identified questions that must be addressed, illustrated in the following graphic:

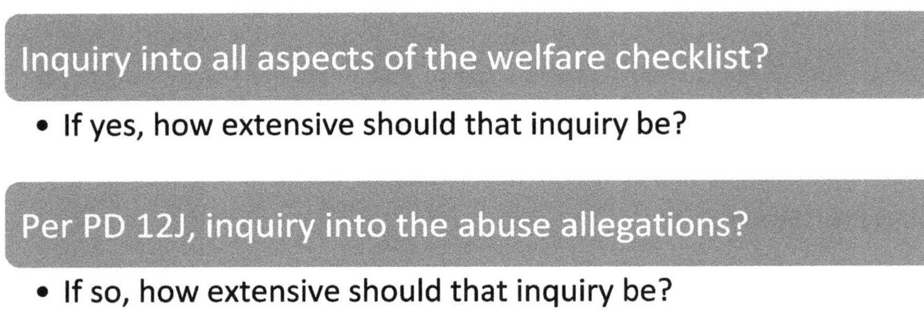

What factors should be considered?

9.24 In *Re J (A Child)*[31] Baroness Hale identified a range of factors which may be taken into account when considering whether a return should be ordered[32]. None of these is decisive, nor is it an exhaustive list. They can be summarised as follows:

28 *Re L (A Child) (Custody: Habitual Residence) (Reunite International Child Abduction Centre intervening)* [2013] UKSC 75, [2014] AC 1017, [2014] 1 FCR 69, [2014] 1 FLR 722.

29 *Re J (A Child) (Custody Rights: Jurisdiction)* [2005] UKHL 40, [2006] 1 AC 80, [2005] 2 FCR 381, [2005] 2 FLR 802.

30 *Re NY (A Child) (Reunite International and others intervening)* [2019] UKSC 49, [2019] 3 WLR 962, [2020] 1 FCR 56, [2019] 2 FLR 1247.

31 *Re J (A Child) (Custody Rights: Jurisdiction)* [2005] UKHL 40, [2006] 1 AC 80, [2005] 2 FCR 381, [2005] 2 FLR 802.

32 *Re J (A Child) (Custody Rights: Jurisdiction)* [2005] UKHL 40, [2006] 1 AC 80, [2005] 2 FCR 381, [2005] 2 FLR 802, paras 33–41.

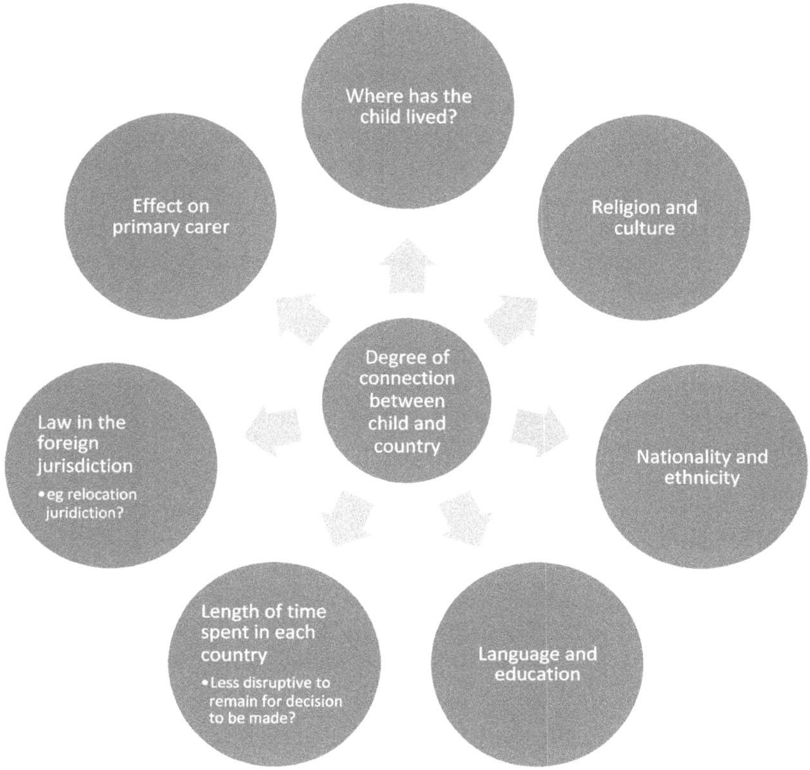

Degree of connection between child and country

9.25 This is intended to be common sense: what country would be considered the child's home? The suggested factors of language, nationality, where the child has lived, religion, culture and education will guide this inquiry.

Length of time spent in each country

9.26 Where a child is familiar with England and Wales and has been in the country for some time without opposition or other problems, it might be less disruptive for the child to remain in that same country while their longer-term future is decided[33]. However, being removed from a country which has for a long time been a child's home is likely also to have been disruptive and may not be in the child's best interests.

33 *Re J (A Child) (Custody Rights: Jurisdiction)* [2005] UKHL 40, [2006] 1 AC 80, [2005] 2 FCR 381, [2005] 2 FLR 802, at [34].

Law in the foreign jurisdiction

9.27 The extent to which this is relevant may differ depending on the facts of the case. The House of Lords in *Re J (A Child)*[34] was clear that it is not right to say that the future of *every* child whose case is before the English court must be decided according to our concept of welfare. However, the court also noted that, if the issue between the parents concerns the country in which a child should live and the other jurisdiction does not have a means by which this dispute can be resolved, it may be that such a dispute is better dealt with in England and Wales.

9.28 The burden is on the parent resisting return to demonstrate that the law in the foreign jurisdiction is relevant to the application for summary return[35]. It will need to be shown that the child's welfare will be prejudiced by a return to a jurisdiction which cannot hear the dispute.

Effect on the primary carer

9.29 Although the courts are reluctant to allow a person who has clandestinely removed or retained a child to benefit from this wrong, the effect of a return order on the carer of the child should be considered. It may be necessary to have regard to:

- whether it is reasonable to expect the carer to return;
- the sincerity of any refusal by the carer to return; and
- what will happen to the children if the carer will not return.

Voice of the child under the inherent jurisdiction

9.30 In *Re S (A Child) (Abduction: Hearing the Child)*[36], the Court of Appeal held that the principle that a child must have effective access to justice is equally applicable in abduction proceedings under the inherent jurisdiction, even where neither BIIA nor HC80 apply; a court must consider how the child can be heard.

34 *Re J (A Child) (Custody Rights: Jurisdiction)* [2005] UKHL 40, [2006] 1 AC 80, [2005] 2 FCR 381, [2005] 2 FLR 802.

35 *LM v DR* [2016] EWHC 1943 (Fam).

36 *Re S (A Child) (Abduction: Hearing the Child)* [2014] EWCA Civ 1557, [2015] Fam 263, [2015] 1 FCR 223, [2015] 2 FLR 588.

Case Summary: *Re S (A Child) (Abduction: Hearing the Child)*[37]

Facts:

The parents were Russian. The child had been born in the UK for medical reasons, although the family returned to Russia soon after. The parents separated when the child was 7. Both parents made applications for residence, which were ongoing. M formed a relationship with a political activist, who was seeking asylum in the UK. M and child followed him to the UK without F's permission; prior to this, the child had been having regular contact with F. M was by now pregnant by her new partner and stayed in England once the child was born; she said she would then return but did not. M obtained a without notice order prohibiting F removing the child from her care or from the child's school. F sought the child's return.

First instance decision: A summary return order under the inherent jurisdiction was granted, the judge having heard the matter as an urgent application under the impression that the issue of the child's voice had been dealt with at an earlier hearing.

Held by the Court of Appeal:

There was an obligation on the court to consider whether and how to hear the child concerned and this had both a procedural and substantive element. It could not be said that a child's voice was irrelevant to welfare where they were of an age and understanding to be heard. Nor could it be assumed that they would be heard through their parents. This had not been done because of the erroneous assumption it had already been addressed. The case was remitted for a rehearing.

E. OTHER INHERENT JURISDICTION ORDERS IN CHILD ABDUCTION CASES

Finding missing children

9.31 The court has wide powers to make a range of orders under the inherent jurisdiction which can be deployed to find and protect missing children. These can be used in substantive applications under the inherent jurisdiction and also in cases brought under HC80, HC96 or BIIA. The available orders to find missing children are summarised in the following graphic and addressed in more detail in **Chapter 12**:

37 [2014] EWCA Civ 1557, [2015] Fam 263, [2015] 1 FCR 223, [2015] 2 FLR 588.

Protecting missing children

9.32 If there are concerns for a child's welfare where they have been abducted, the court has powers under the inherent jurisdiction to protect them and safeguard their welfare during proceedings. As with orders designed to find missing children, these can be used in substantive applications under the inherent jurisdiction and also in cases brought under HC80, HC96 or BIIA. Such orders are summarised in the following graphic and addressed in more detail in **Chapter 12**:

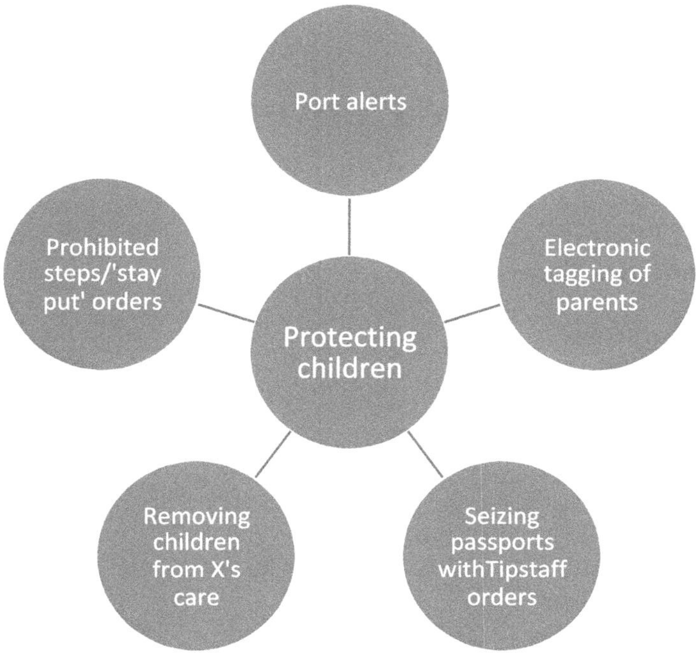
Port alerts
Prohibited steps/'stay put' orders
Electronic tagging of parents
Protecting children
Removing children from X's care
Seizing passports withTipstaff orders

CHAPTER 10

The 1996 Hague Convention

Content at a Glance:

A. INTRODUCTION

10.1 The full title of the 1996 Hague Convention ('HC96') is the 'Convention of 19 October 1996 on Jurisdiction, Applicable Law, Recognition, Enforcement and Co-operation in Respect of Parental Responsibility and Measures for the Protection of Children'. It is commonly known as the Welfare Convention. Both the title of the Convention and Art 1 clearly set out the five objects of the Convention:

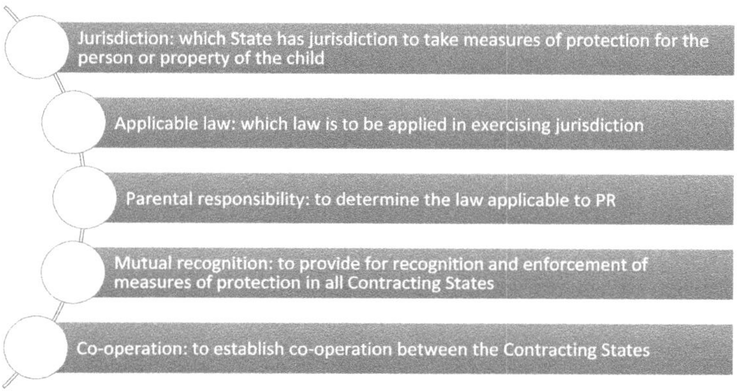

10.2 The term 'parental responsibility' includes parental authority, or any similar relationship of authority determining the rights, powers and responsibilities of parents, guardians or other legal representatives in relation to the person or the property of the child[1].

10.3 The term 'measures' must be construed broadly rather than narrowly[2] and includes undertakings; for a common law jurisdiction such as England and Wales to say that undertakings are not to be classed as measures would be erroneous and devoid of practical sense, according to Thorpe LJ[3]. Article 3 of HC96 sets out a list of measures which fall within the scope of the Convention:

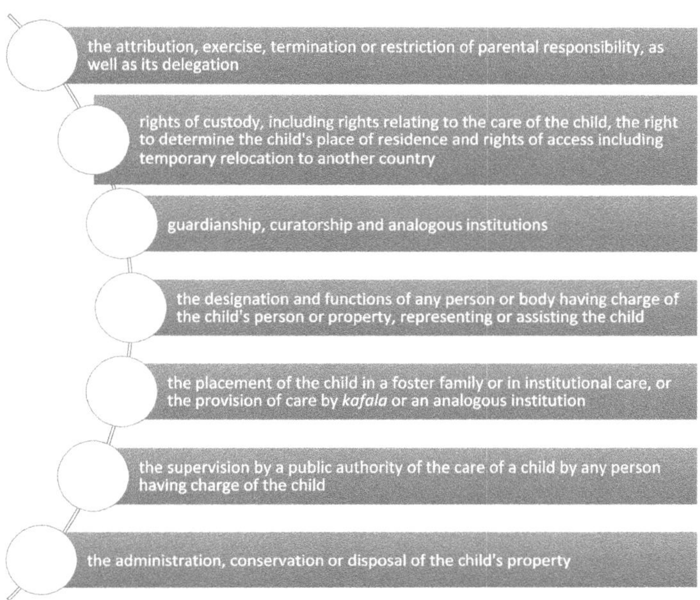

1 HC96, Art 1(2).
2 *Re Y (A Child)* [2013] EWCA Civ 129, [2013] 2 FLR 649.
3 *Re Y (A Child)* [2013] EWCA Civ 129, [2013] 2 FLR 649, at para 9.

Art 4 sets out matters falling outside the scope of HC96. HC96 does not apply to:

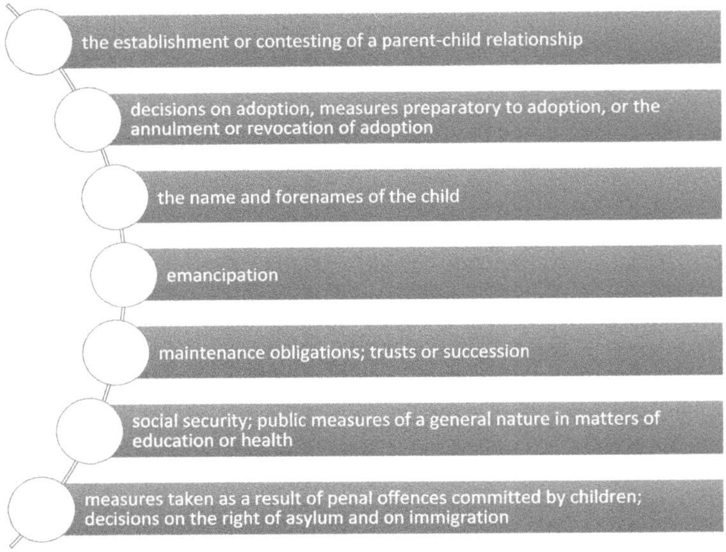

10.4 HC96 applies to children from birth to their 18th birthday. This contrasts with the 1980 Hague Convention on the Civil Aspects of International Child Abduction ('HC80') which ceases to have application on the child's 16th birthday[4].

10.5 HC96 came into force in England and Wales on 1 November 2012, and is directly effective as a matter of law. Additional provisions to facilitate the operation of HC96 in domestic law were made in the Parental Responsibility and Measures for the Protection of Children (International Obligations) (England and Wales and Northern Ireland) Regulations 2010 (SI 2010/1898).

The means by which HC96 was given effect in domestic law was the European Communities (Definition of Treaties) (1996 Hague Convention on Protection of Children etc) Order 2010 (SI 2010/232), s 2. This provides that HC96 is to be regarded as one of the 'EU Treaties' as defined in the European Communities Act 1972, s 1(2). Thus, the United Kingdom ('UK') became a party to HC96 by virtue of its membership of the European Union ('EU'). It is assumed that, following the UK's departure from the EU and the repeal of the European Communities Act 1972, steps will be taken to ensure that HC96 remains in force as a matter of domestic law, although at the time of writing such steps have not been taken.

4 Article 4 of HC80.

B. JURISDICTION

10.6 There are seven bases under which the court can acquire jurisdiction to take measures under HC96:

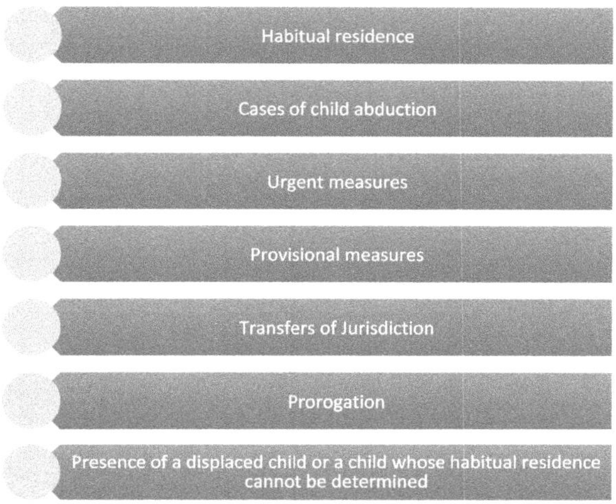

Habitual residence

10.7 Article 5 sets out the first jurisdictional test for taking any measures under HC96: that the child is habitually resident in the State where measures are taken. For the meaning of habitual residence, see **Chapter 4**.

Article 5

> '(1) The judicial or administrative authorities of the Contracting State of the habitual residence of the child have jurisdiction to take measures directed to the protection of the child's person or property.
>
> (2) Subject to Article 7, in case of a change of the child's habitual residence to another Contracting State, the authorities of the State of the new habitual residence have jurisdiction.'

10.8 Article 14 of HC96 makes it clear that a move from one Contracting State to another, and a change in the child's habitual residence, does not render an existing order obsolete. Rather, HC96 specifies that pre-existing orders continue to be valid despite a change of habitual residence. The Explanatory Report[5]

5 Explanatory Report to HC96 by Paul Lagarde, para 81.

suggests that a change to a child's habitual residence would not be a change of circumstances which justifies a challenge to a pre-existing order. Rather, existing measures should survive such a change in order to ensure, for the child, the maintenance in force of measures taken by the competent authority. This rule applies even when the basis for jurisdiction on the part of the authority taking the measures has subsequently disappeared, so long as the authorities which acquire jurisdiction following a change of habitual residence do not modify, replace or terminate them.

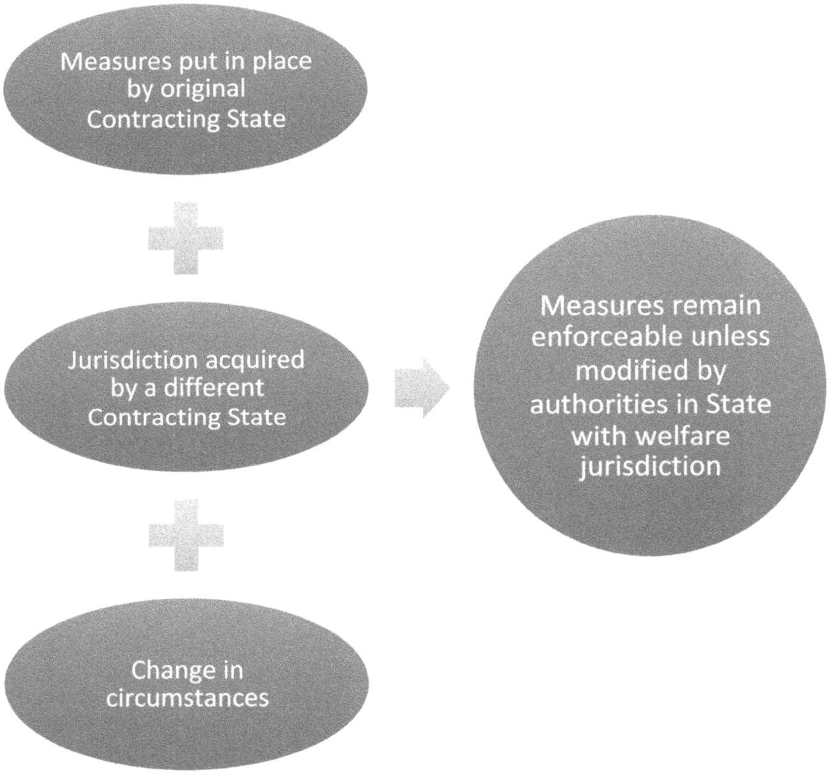

Article 14

> 'The measures taken in application of Articles 5 to 10 remain in force according to their terms, even if a change of circumstances has eliminated the basis upon which jurisdiction was founded, so long as the authorities which have jurisdiction under the Convention have not modified, replaced or terminated such measures.'

Child abduction

10.9 In child abduction cases, the authorities in the country of habitual residence immediately prior to the wrongful removal or retention of a child retain jurisdiction pursuant to Art 7, provided that (a) the child has not formed a new habitual residence[6], and (b) the child is not settled in a State in which they have lived for more than a year, their whereabouts being known to the left-behind parent. For the meaning of wrongful removal and retention, see **Chapter 3**.

The effects of Art 7(1) are illustrated by the following graphic:

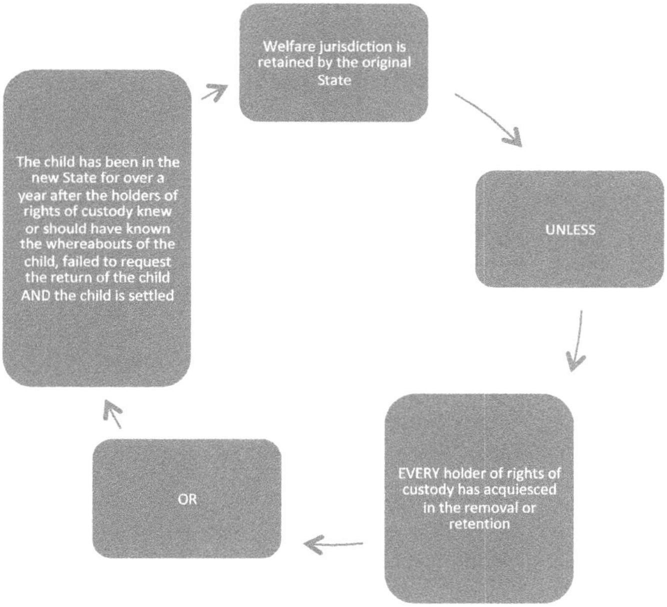

The effects of Art 7(2) are illustrated by the following graphic:

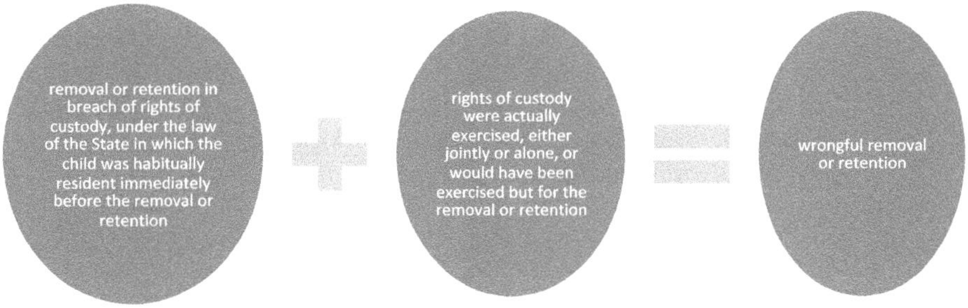

6 A child's habitual residence can change following an abduction; the former rule that one parent cannot bring about a change to habitual residence on a unilateral basis is no longer good law, following the decisions in *Re H (Children) (Reunite International Child Abduction Centre intervening)* [2014] EWCA Civ 1101, [2015] 1 WLR 863 and *AR v RN (Scotland)* [2015] UKSC 35.

Article 7

'(1) In case of wrongful removal or retention of the child, the authorities of the Contracting State in which the child was habitually resident immediately before the removal or retention keep their jurisdiction until the child has acquired a habitual residence in another State, and

(a) each person, institution or other body having rights of custody has acquiesced in the removal or retention; or

(b) the child has resided in that other State for a period of at least one year after the person, institution or other body having rights of custody has or should have had knowledge of the whereabouts of the child, no request for return lodged within that period is still pending, and the child is settled in his or her new environment.

(2) The removal or the retention of a child is to be considered wrongful where –

(a) it is in breach of rights of custody attributed to a person, an institution or any other body, either jointly or alone, under the law of the State in which the child was habitually resident immediately before the removal or retention; and

(b) at the time of removal or retention those rights were actually exercised, either jointly or alone, or would have been so exercised but for the removal or retention.

The rights of custody mentioned in sub-paragraph (a) above, may arise in particular by operation of law or by reason of a judicial or administrative decision, or by reason of an agreement having legal effect under the law of that State.

(3) So long as the authorities first mentioned in paragraph 1 keep their jurisdiction, the authorities of the Contracting State to which the child has been removed or in which he or she has been retained can take only such urgent measures under Article 11 as are necessary for the protection of the person or property of the child.'

Urgent measures

10.10 Under Art 7(3) the only jurisdiction in the State to which the child has been wrongfully removed, or in which the child has been wrongfully retained, is the jurisdiction to take '*such urgent measures as are necessary for the protection of the person or property of the child*' under Art 11.

Article 11

> '(1) In all cases of urgency, the authorities of any Contracting State in whose territory the child or property belonging to the child is present have jurisdiction to take any necessary measures of protection.
>
> (2) The measures taken under the preceding paragraph with regard to a child habitually resident in a Contracting State shall lapse as soon as the authorities which have jurisdiction under Articles 5 to 10 have taken the measures required by the situation.
>
> (3) The measures taken under paragraph 1 with regard to a child who is habitually resident in a non-Contracting State shall lapse in each Contracting State as soon as measures required by the situation and taken by the authorities of another State are recognised in the Contracting State in question.'

This is an important provision in relation to child abduction proceedings. The Explanatory Report specifically refers to the example of urgent measures taken in abduction proceedings which will remain in force until the situation is '*under the control of*' the authorities which normally have jurisdiction, and there is no longer any reason to maintain the jurisdiction of the authorities of the State of the child's presence[7].

The meaning of 'urgency' was considered by the Supreme Court in *Re J (A Child) (1996 Hague Convention: Cases of Urgency)*[8].

Case Summary: *Re J (A Child) (1996 Hague Convention: Cases of Urgency)*[9]

Facts:

Following the breakdown of the parents' marriage in 2011, the Moroccan courts granted custody to M and made an order for significant levels of direct contact between the child and F. In September 2013, M removed the child to England. F sought his return to Morocco. Wood J ordered the child's return, finding that the removal in September 2013 was wrongful.

7 Explanatory Report to HC96 by Paul Lagarde, paras 71–72.
8 [2016] 4 All ER 1084, UKSC.
9 [2016] 4 All ER 1084, UKSC.

The Court of Appeal concluded that an order for the return of the child *could* be considered as a measure of protection within the meaning of Art 11(1) of HC96 but the court would need to be satisfied that the case was urgent.

On the facts, it held that F could have made an application for a return order to the courts in Morocco (who held exclusive jurisdiction under Art 5 of HC96). The harm to the child currently was the absence of direct contact with F, which did not amount to a '*case of urgency*' within Art 11. As such, the English court had no jurisdiction to make a return order under HC96.

The Court of Appeal further considered that the inherent jurisdiction could not be invoked in this case. The purpose of the jurisdictional provisions of HC96 would be defeated if, notwithstanding an absence of jurisdiction under the Convention, a Contracting State could assume jurisdiction under a domestic rule.

Held by the UKSC (appeal allowed):

The Court of Appeal had set the bar too high. Most cases involving the abduction of a child will be 'urgent' for the purposes of Art 11.

Baroness Hale said: '*It would obviously place in jeopardy this valuable aspect of the HC96, in assisting the objectives of HC80, if the courts in the presence country could not invoke the article 11 jurisdiction without first assuring themselves that it was impossible for the courts of the home jurisdiction to take action*'.

At paras 38–39 she said: '*It would be extraordinary if, in a case to which HC80 did not apply, the question of whether to order the summary return of an abducted child were not a case of 'urgency' even if it was ultimately determined that it was not "necessary" to order the return of the child. While I would not, therefore, go so far as to say that such a case is invariably one of "urgency", I find it difficult to envisage a case in which the court should not consider it to be so, and then go on to consider whether it is appropriate to exercise the article 11 jurisdiction*'.

10.11 Under the automatic and reciprocal enforcement measures in Art 23 (see para **10.37** below), these measures will have effect in the country of habitual residence until the authorities in that State of habitual residence put in place their own measures.

10.12 Although Art 20 of HC96 states that '*the provisions of this Chapter apply even if the law designated by them is the law of a non-Contracting State*', in *Deticek v Sguelia*[10], the CJEU applied a restrictive interpretation to Art 11, stating that a delay in the enforcement of protective measures by the State of habitual residence would not justify the use of Art 20 if that would conflict with orders made by the court of primary jurisdiction.

10 Case C-403/09 PPU [2010] Fam 104, [2010] 1 FLR 1381, CJEU.

Provisional measures

10.13 The courts of a Contracting State in which a child is present may take *provisional* measures under Art 12, even where there is no urgency. The measures must not be incompatible with measures already taken in the State of habitual residence and will lapse once the authorities in the State of habitual residence have taken a substantive decision in relation to the child.

10.14 Article 12 cannot be used in a case where a child has been wrongfully removed or retained: see Art 12(1) and Art 7(3) which provides that only measures pursuant to Art 11 can be taken in those circumstances.

Transfer of jurisdiction

10.15 Articles 8 and 9 of HC96 contain a mechanism by which proceedings may be transferred from one Contracting State to another, provided both States agree to the transfer and the conditions in Art 8 are met. The process by which a transfer takes place begins with a request from the authorities in one Contracting State to those in another. In order for a transfer to take place, it is necessary to demonstrate that:

(i) the second State is 'better placed' in the particular case to assess the best interests of the child, and

(ii) the transfer is in the child's best interests.

These provisions permit what is essentially a '*forum conveniens*' basis for the transfer of jurisdiction, albeit the transfer must also accord with the best interests of the child concerned. A transfer cannot be based solely upon the second State being the more convenient or appropriate location for the litigation.

10.16 It is not permissible to transfer proceedings to *any* Contracting State. Article 8 provides that a transfer *from* the State of habitual residence can only take place to another State which falls into one of the following categories:

(a) State of which the child is a national;

(b) State in which property of the child is located;

(c) State whose authorities are seised of an application for divorce or legal separation of the child's parents; or

(d) State with which the child has a 'substantial connection'.

10.17 The process by which a transfer may take place under Art 8 is illustrated by the following graphic:

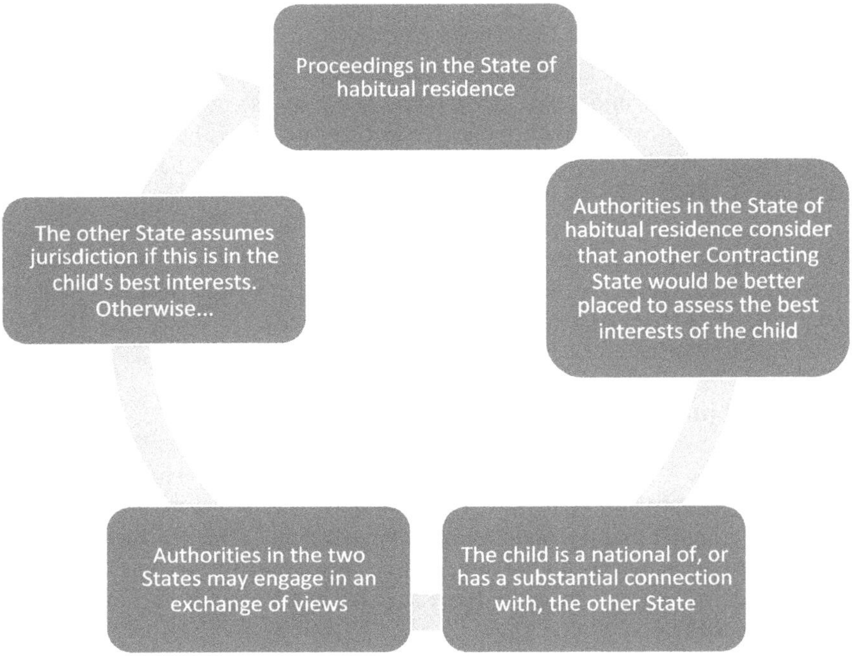

10.18 Article 9 allows a request to be made *to* the State of habitual residence requesting that the authorities in another State be authorised to exercise jurisdiction to take the measures of protection which they consider to be necessary. Article 9(1) provides that the request may be made by a State falling within one of the categories specified in Art 8(2), set out in paragraph **10.16** above.

10.19 The process by which a transfer may take place under Art 9 is illustrated by the following graphic:

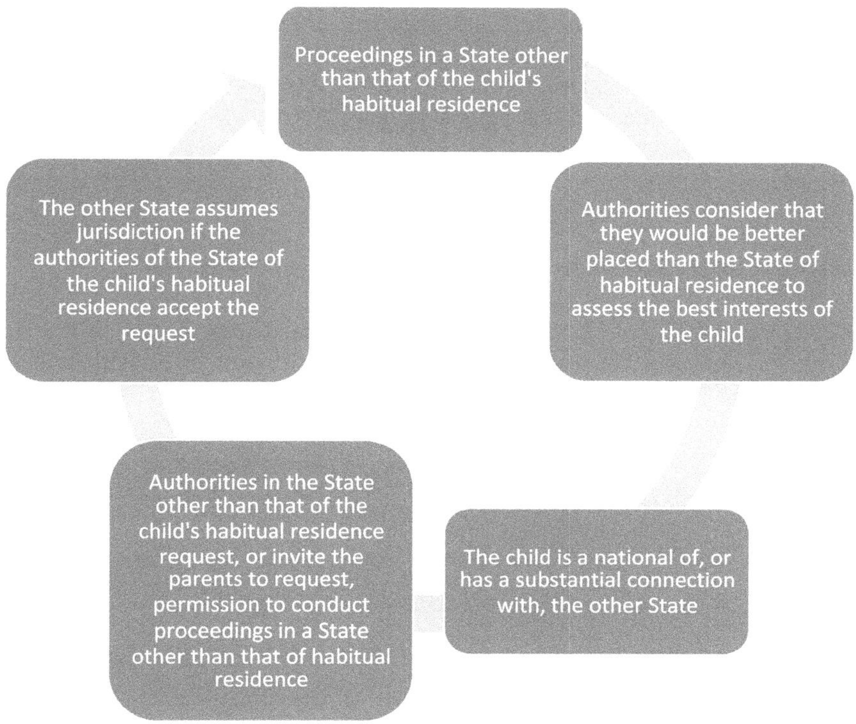

10.20

Case Summary: *Re M and L*[11]

Facts:

The parties had two children, one lived in the UK with F and the other in Norway with M; litigation was taking place in both countries. Baker J considered Arts 8 and 9 of HC96.

Held by Baker J:

The judge was satisfied that the power to submit a request under Art 9 of HC96, seeking the transfer of the proceedings in Norway to the English court, was available because the child who lived in Norway was a UK national and because the child had a 'substantial connection' with the UK.

The English and Norwegian courts were equally competent in general terms to determine issues about children. It was 'crucial' that proceedings relating to both children took place in the same court. Since M had not made a

11 [2016] EWHC 2535 (Fam), [2017] 1 FCR 33, [2017] 2 FLR 250.

request for the transfer of the English proceedings to Norway, the English court made the request to the Norwegian court to authorise the English court to exercise jurisdiction and make decisions in respect of the child's contact with F. Baker J indicated that he was prepared to discuss the issue with his Norwegian counterparts.

Transfers of proceedings under Arts 8 and 9 of HC96 in domestic law

10.21 Rules 12.61 to 12.68 of the Family Procedure Rules 2010 ('FPR 2010') set out the domestic rules under which the English court deals with transfers pursuant to HC96:

- Rule 12.62: applications for a transfer to or from another Contracting State made by a party to the proceedings under Art 8(1)
- Rule 12.63: applications by the court in another Contracting State for a transfer to that State under Art 15(2)(c)
- Rule 12.64: transfer of all or part of the proceedings to another Contracting State under Art 8
- Rule 12.66: request from the authorities in another Contracting State that jurisdiction should be assumed in England and Wales

Under FPR 2010, r 12.65 such applications must be heard on notice in the High Court.

Prorogation to a court dealing with divorce or legal separation proceedings

10.22 A court dealing with divorce or legal separation proceedings may take jurisdiction over matters connected with parental responsibility under Art 10, provided that all of the following conditions are met:

(a) one of the child's parents is habitually resident in the State concerned when proceedings are commenced;

(b) one of the child's parents has parental responsibility for the child when proceedings are commenced;

(c) the jurisdiction is accepted by both parents and by any other person who has parental responsibility for the child; and

(d) it is in the best interests of the child for the authorities in that State to assume jurisdiction.

Article 10

> '(1) Without prejudice to Articles 5 to 9, the authorities of a Contracting State exercising jurisdiction to decide upon an application for divorce or legal separation of the parents of a child habitually resident in another Contracting State, or for annulment of their marriage, may, if the law of their State so provides, take measures directed to the protection of the person or property of such child if:
>
> (a) at the time of commencement of the proceedings, one of his or her parents habitually resides in that State and one of them has parental responsibility in relation to the child, and
>
> (b) the jurisdiction of these authorities to take such measures has been accepted by the parents, as well as by any other person who has parental responsibility in relation to the child, and is in the best interests of the child.'

The circumstances in which a court can assume jurisdiction by agreement under Art 10 of HC96 are more limited than those set out in the equivalent provisions of Art 12 of Council Regulation (EC) 2201/2003 ('BIIA').

Presence of a displaced child or a child whose habitual residence cannot be determined

10.23 Article 6 of HC96 provides for Contracting States to have jurisdiction based on the presence of the child where:

- a child has left their home country as a refugee; or
- the habitual residence of the child cannot be determined

Article 6

> '(1) For refugee children and children who, due to disturbances occurring in their country, are internationally displaced, the authorities of the Contracting State on the territory of which these

children are present as a result of their displacement have the jurisdiction provided for in paragraph 1 of Article 5.

(2) The provisions of the preceding paragraph also apply to children whose habitual residence cannot be established.'

10.24 The jurisdiction under Art 6 will cease once a child acquires a new habitual residence. If the child's new habitual residence is in a Contracting State to HC96, then the authorities in that State will have exclusive jurisdiction under Art 5 (subject to Arts 7 to 12). If the child's new habitual residence is in a non-Contracting State, the authorities of the State in which the child is physically present will have jurisdiction for the limited purpose of taking urgent measures under Art 11 (see para **10.10** above).

Impact of the jurisdictional provisions of HC96

10.25 The impact of HC96 can be to limit the power of the English court to make orders using the inherent jurisdiction of the court. Where another Contracting State has welfare jurisdiction, the English court has no power to make orders other than under Art 11.

In *Re I-L (Children) (1996 Hague Child Protection Convention: Inherent Jurisdiction)*[12] the Court of Appeal considered whether the English court had jurisdiction to make orders in a case where the courts of another Contracting State (in this case, Russia) were already seised of proceedings in relation to the child.

Case Summary: *Re I-L (Children) (1996 Hague Child Protection Convention: Inherent Jurisdiction)*[13]

Facts:

The family was 'international', moving between Russia, the UK and the USA. Litigation had been ongoing in Russia for many years, and was continuing. Whilst the children were in England for a long holiday, F commenced Children Act 1989 proceedings in the Family Court. M issued an application under HC80 seeking the return of the children to Russia. During the English proceedings, the Russian court made an order that F return the children to M. M applied to enforce this order in England as an adjunct to the ongoing proceedings under HC80.

12 [2019] EWCA Civ 1956, [2020] 1 FCR 35.
13 [2019] EWCA Civ 1956, [2020] 1 FCR 35.

The HC80 proceedings were dismissed but the judge ordered the return of the children to Russia under the inherent jurisdiction of the court.

Held by the Court of Appeal (appeal allowed):

The judge had no power to make an order under the inherent jurisdiction: '*there was no gap in the scheme of HC96 to justify the exercise of the court's inherent powers*'.

Because the judge found that the children were habitually resident in Russia, England did not have substantive jurisdiction when F commenced proceedings. In addition, at the date of the hearing below, there were proceedings in Russia which were '*still under consideration*', within Art 13.

The English court only had a 'secondary' jurisdiction under Art 11. This was the only route by which it could potentially make a return order. It was not open to the court to make an order under the inherent jurisdiction and that order was set aside.

An order could not be made under Art 11. At para 39 of *Re J (A Child) (1996 Hague Convention: Cases of Urgency)* it was stated that it '*would obviously not be appropriate*' for the English court to exercise the Art 11 jurisdiction '*where the home country was already seised of the case and in a position to make effective orders to protect the child*'. M had already obtained a return order from the Russian court and should apply to enforce it; Art 11 was of no application.

C. APPLICABLE LAW

10.26 Chapter 3 of HC96 sets out the circumstances in which the laws of one country (i) may be applied and exercised by the courts of another country; and (ii) may be relevant to the application of the law in another country by reason of a child's move across a national border. Article 21(1) provides that, for the purposes of Chapter 3, 'law' means the law in force in a State other than its choice of law rules. This is subject to a limited exception in Art 21(2) where the applicable law under Art 16 is that of a non-Contracting State.

The applicable law rules can be refused only if an application of the rules would be manifestly contrary to public policy, taking into account the best interests of the child[14]. This is a very high threshold. In considering the same words in Art 23 of BIIA, Munby LJ stated:

> 'The use of the word "manifestly" connotes a very high degree of disparity between the order's effects if now enforced and the child's current welfare interests … The test is stringent, the bar, as I have said, is set high[15].'

14 Article 22 of HC96.
15 *Re L (BIIR) Appeal (CA)* [2013] 1 FLR 430.

Similarly, in *Re D (Recognition and Enforcement of Romanian Order)*[16] Ryder LJ described the public policy ground for non-recognition of a judgment under Art 23 of BIIA as 'an exceptional remedy', requiring '*something more*' than the breach of a fundamental principle.

10.27 Article 15(1) provides that, in exercising their jurisdiction under Arts 5–14 of HC96, the authorities of the Contracting States shall apply their own law. This provision may be unsurprising to lawyers practising in England and Wales but it is important to bear it in mind when dealing with a jurisdiction which may have applied the law of the nationality of the child (such as Spain). The only exception to this rule is provided for by Art 15(2) which allows the court, exceptionally, to take into consideration the law of another State '*with which the situation has a substantial connection*' in circumstances where it is required to do so to secure the protection of the person or the property of the child.

10.28 Article 16 is concerned with the applicable law for the attribution or extinction of parental responsibility. Its provisions can be summarised as follows:

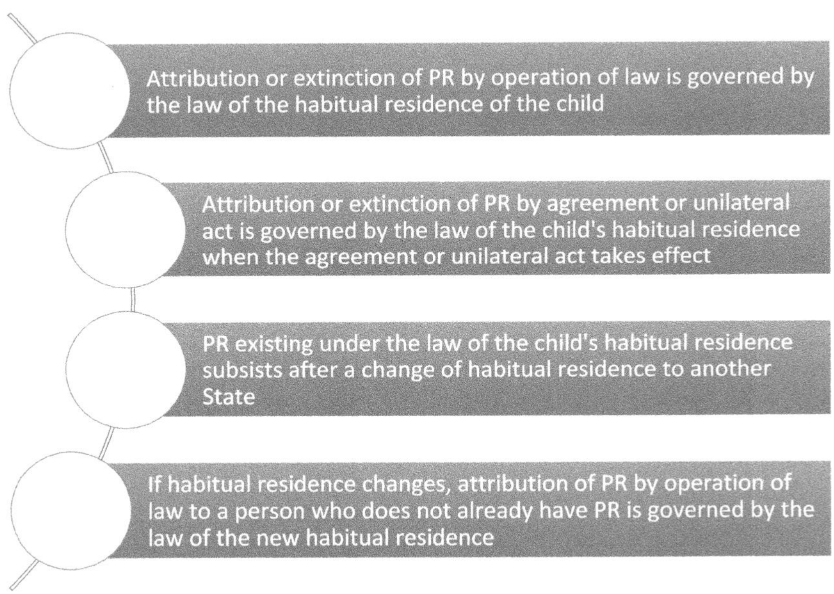

Article 18 provides that the parental responsibility may be terminated or its exercise modified by measures taken under HC96.

10.29 Article 17 is concerned with the *exercise* of parental responsibility (as opposed to its attribution or extinction). This is governed by the law of the State of the child's habitual residence. If the child's habitual residence changes, the exercise of parental responsibility is governed by the law of the State of the new habitual residence.

16 *Re D (Recognition and Enforcement of Romanian Order)* [2016] 1 WLR 2496.

10.30 Under Art 20 of HC96, the rules as to applicable law apply even if the law designated by them is the law of a non-Contracting State.

D. REINFORCEMENT OF THE 1980 HAGUE CONVENTION

10.31 An important purpose of HC96 is to support and supplement the effective operation of HC80. Providing an effective way to ensure that measures taken (including undertakings given) on the making of a return order is key to the operation of HC96. According to Thorpe LJ, '*it is simply unthinkable that an intention or an effect of the 1996 Convention was to diminish rather than to fortify the effect of undertakings and their use, as one of a number of mechanisms available to provide protection for the returning abductor and child*'[17].

Case Summary: *Re Y (A Child)*[18]

Facts:

F applied for a return order under HC80 in respect of his daughter, who had been abducted from Cyprus. M defended under Art 13(b), asserting a risk of domestic violence, and that the girl would be at risk of abuse from F. Parker J ordered the return of the girl subject to protective measures on the basis that adequate undertakings had been given to secure the protection of the child.

F's undertakings were drafted in the order on the basis that they would be valid in Cyprus under Art 23 of HC96. M's case was that F should obtain specific recognition of the order under Art 24 from the court in Cyprus. M appealed on this issue.

Held by the Court of Appeal (appeal dismissed):

'Measures' in HC96 included undertakings. It was unthinkable that it could have been intended that HC96 should diminish rather than fortify the effect of undertakings as a mechanism for protecting a returning abductor and child.

10.32 Under Art 50 of HC96, the substantive application of HC80 is not affected. A parent who alleges that their child has been abducted from, or retained outside, the State of habitual residence may bring proceedings under both Conventions: for a return order under HC80 made in the State to which the child has been taken; and for an order that the child must return, made in the State from which the child has been removed or retained.

17 *Re Y (A Child)* [2013] EWCA Civ 129, [2013] 2 FLR 649 at para 10.
18 [2013] EWCA Civ 129, [2013] 2 FLR 649.

Article 50

> 'This Convention shall not affect the application of the Convention of 25 October 1980 on the Civil Aspects of International Child Abduction, as between Parties to both Conventions. Nothing, however, precludes provisions of this Convention from being invoked for the purposes of obtaining the return of a child who has been wrongfully removed or retained or of organising access rights.'

10.33 HC96 reinforces HC80 by underlining the primary role played by the authorities of the child's habitual residence in deciding upon any measures which may be needed to protect the child in the long term. It also adds to the efficacy of any temporary protective measures ordered by a judge when returning a child to the country from which the child was taken, by making such orders enforceable in that country until such time as the authorities there are able themselves to put in place necessary protections.

10.34 HC96 also contains provisions which may assist when a judicial or administrative authority wishes to order the return of a child under HC80, but only if necessary protective measures are put in place to ensure the safe return of the child and to ensure the child's continued protection in the Requesting State until the authorities in that State can act to protect the child. In this regard, Art 11 of HC96 contains a specific ground of jurisdiction which, where the case is one of urgency, enables the Requested State to take '*necessary measures of protection*' regarding the child[19].

10.35 The ability to put in place measures (whether orders or by accepting undertakings) enables a judge who orders the return of a child to reduce any 'grave risk of harm' to the child which may otherwise exist. In *B v B*[20] Mostyn J concluded that he could put in place sufficient safeguards which would be enforceable in the courts of the child's habitual residence under Art 11 of HC96 on the return of the child so as to ensure that there is 'no risk' of the kind set out in Art 13(b) of HC80[21].

10.36 The Practical Handbook on the operation of HC96[22] envisages a situation[23] where a judge is faced with allegations that the father poses a risk of sexual harm to the child in abduction proceedings. The example supposes that the judge considers it necessary that any contact between the child and the

19 See Art 11, at para **10.10** above.
20 [2014] EWHC 1804 (Fam), Mostyn J.
21 For Article 13(b) of HC80, see **Chapter 6**.
22 Published by the Hague Conference on Private International Law Permanent Bureau, 2014.
23 Example 6(G), p 75.

father take place in a supervised environment until a decision on the merits of the custody issues, including contact, can be taken in the State of habitual residence. The judge therefore orders the return of the children but also takes an urgent measure to protect the children by providing that the father's contact with the children must be supervised until a decision on the matter can be taken in the State of habitual residence. This urgent measure will be recognised by operation of law but will lapse as soon as the State of habitual residence takes the necessary measures of protection required by the situation upon the return of the child.

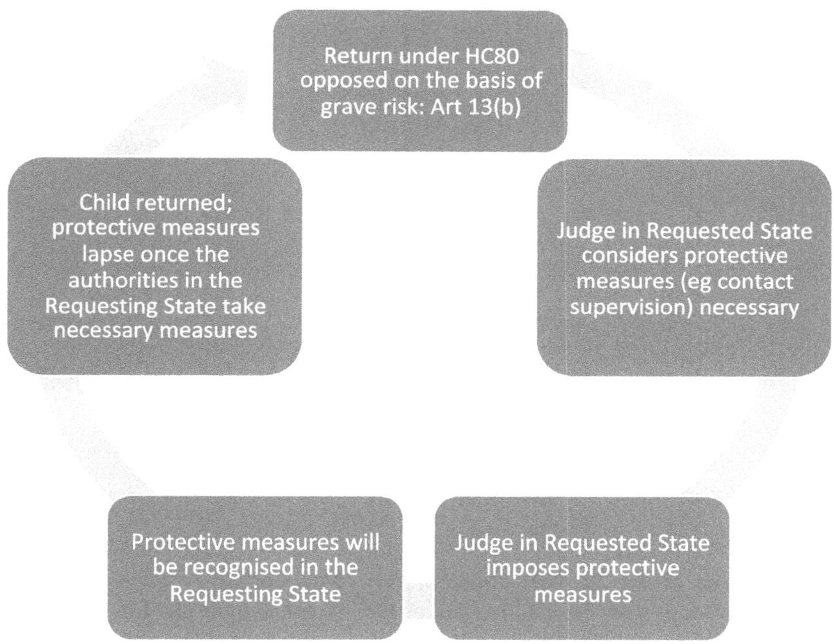

E. RECOGNITION AND ENFORCEMENT

Recognition and the grounds for the refusal of recognition

10.37 Article 23 of HC96 sets out the basic principle that a measures taken in one Contracting State shall be recognised by operation of law in all other Contracting States. This includes protective measures taken in child abduction proceedings and orders for contact/access made as part of relocation proceedings.

10.38 Recognition by operation of law means that no proceedings are required to obtain recognition. However, if a party seeks to *enforce* an order obtained in an overseas jurisdiction, this will require proceedings and, within these, another party may challenge recognition. In such proceedings, documents (including orders) are exempt from any requirement for legalisation or other analogous formality[24].

24 Article 43.

10.39 The authorities of the State in which recognition is sought are bound by any findings of fact made in the State where measures were taken[25]. The grounds upon which the court can refuse recognition are limited to those in Art 23(2):

- Measure taken by authority whose jurisdiction was not based on Arts 5-14
- Except in case of urgency, measure taken without child having opportunity to be heard, in violation of fundamental principles of procedure of the State in which recognition is sought
- Except in case of urgency, measure taken without a person whose PR is infringed without having opportunity to be heard
- Recognition manifestly contrary to public policy, taking into account best interests of the child
- Measure incompatible with later measure taken in non-Contracting State of child's habitual residence, where later measure fulfils requirements for recognition in the Requested State
- Procedure in Art 33 [relating to placement of a child in foster or institutional care] has not been complied with

The provisions of Art 23 were considered by MacDonald J in *Uhd v McKay*[26], albeit that the case was determined under HC80 rather than HC96.

Case Summary: *Uhd v McKay (Abduction: Publicity)*[27]

Facts:

The Australian courts were involved in lengthy welfare proceedings, within which M made allegations that F had been violent and abusive to her and to the child. Whilst the proceedings were ongoing, M removed the child to the UK. She accepted that this was a wrongful removal. On arrival in the UK, M and the child lived in a camper van and the child was home schooled.

25 Article 25.
26 *Uhd v McKay (Abduction: Publicity)* [2019] EWHC 1239 (Fam), [2019] 2 FLR 1159.
27 [2019] EWHC 1239 (Fam), [2019] 2 FLR 1559.

Following M leaving Australia, but at a hearing at which she was represented, the Australian court ordered that the child should be returned to Australia. Within the English proceedings, the father applied to enforce these orders.

M opposed enforcement, asserting that the exceptions in Art 23(2)(c) [no opportunity to be heard] and Art 23(2)(d) [public policy] were engaged. She also suggested that she had not been served with the Australian proceedings.

Held by MacDonald J:

M's submissions rejected. The relevant orders were made in 'a case of urgency', those orders being made in response to the abduction of the child. M had been represented at the hearings in Australia and the Australian court found that she had been served by email.

The orders for the return of the child to Australia and placing the child in F's care on an interim basis came '*nowhere near to engaging the public policy exception*' in the light of the welfare evidence upon which the Australian court made its decision.

10.40 It is very difficult to establish that an order made in a Contracting State is manifestly contrary to public policy. The same words have been considered on several occasions by the Court of Appeal in connection with appeals against the enforcement of orders under Art 23 of BIIA: see para **10.26** above. The remedy is said to be 'exceptional'[28].

10.41 The fact that orders made by courts in England and Wales are enforceable in other Contracting States under HC96 is of importance in applications seeking permission permanently to relocate children. The court can be satisfied that contact orders made in relocation proceedings will be enforced by the courts in the country to which the child is being taken.

Case Summary: *S v G*[29]

Facts:

An application was made for the permanent relocation of a child to Russia.

Held by Peter Jackson J:

Application allowed. Orders made on relocation, including orders for contact, would be enforceable in Russia under HC96.

The order allowing relocation to Russia specifically recited that:

28 *Re D (Recognition and Enforcement of Romanian Order)* [2016] EWCA Civ 12, [2016] 1 WLR 2469, [2016] 2 FCR 1, [2016] 2 FLR 347 at para 50.
29 [2015] EWFC 4.

'Article 23 of [HC96] provides that this order shall be recognised in the Russian Federation by operation of the laws of the Russian Federation.

Article 26 of [HC96] provides that this Order comes into force immediately upon the date that it is made and is therefore enforceable in the jurisdiction of England and Wales from this same date and shall upon the request of the mother or the father be declared enforceable in the Russian Federation.

Article 27 of [HC96] provides that there shall be no review of the merits of this order.'

Declaration of enforceability

10.42 Article 26 requires that each Contracting State must apply a '*simple and rapid process*'[30] to an application by any interested party for a declaration of enforceability. The requested court is not permitted to 'review' the merits of the decision taken[31]. Once habitual residence has transferred to the new Contracting State, that State may make orders based on its own substantive jurisdiction, even if those orders conflict with an earlier order in the State in which the child was formerly habitually resident.

10.43 Article 27 of HC96 provides that for the purposes of recognition or enforcement proceedings:

> 'Without prejudice to such review as is necessary in the application of the preceding Articles, there shall be no review of the merits of the measure taken.'

Enforcement

10.44 In an enforcement application, the measures to be enforced are treated as a domestic order[32]. If the measure has no equivalent in the law of the Requested State, the Requested State may adapt the measures to fit what can be achieved under domestic law.

10.45 Article 28 seems to introduce a welfare element to the decision on enforcement:

> 'enforcement takes place in accordance with the law of the requested State to the extent provided by such law, *taking into consideration the best interests of the child*.'

30 Article 26(2).
31 Article 27.
32 Article 28.

It is unlikely that this creates an unfettered discretion as to *whether* the order should be enforced; more likely the discretion relates to *how* to enforce the order.

Procedure

10.46 FPR 2010, Part 31 and PD 31A set out the domestic rules under which the English court deals with the recognition and enforcement of orders under HC96:

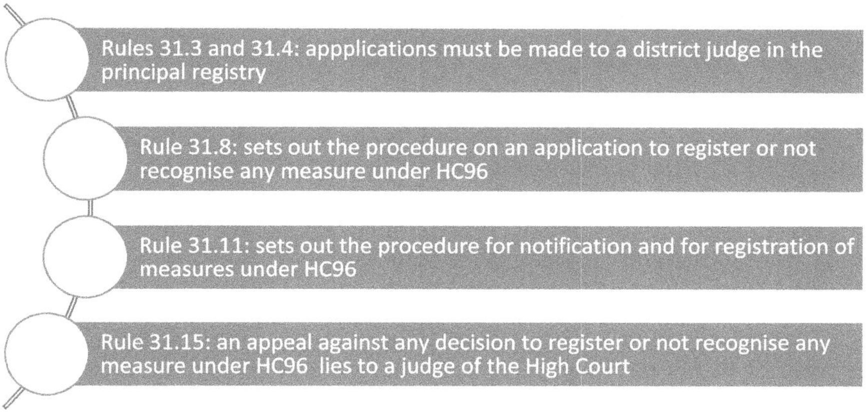

FPR 2010, PD 31A sets out detailed guidance as to the evidence required on an application for registration, recognition or non-recognition of a judgment generally[33] and specifically on applications under HC96[34].

F. CO-OPERATION

10.47 Chapter V of HC96 aims to improve the exchange of information between Contracting States. Two lines of communication are provided for by Arts 29 to 39:

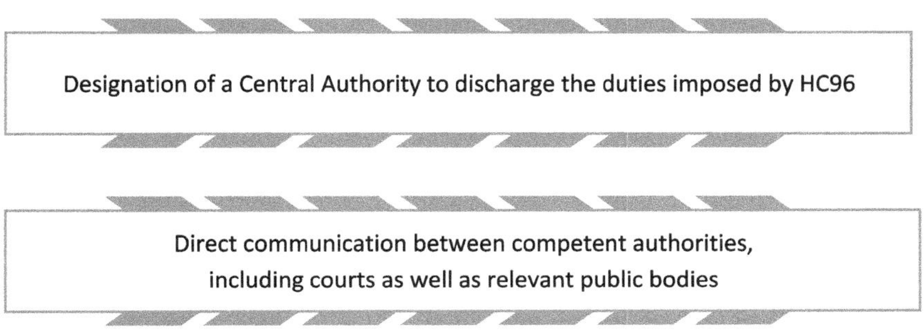

33 At para 2.
34 At para 4.

10.48 In the UK, the Central Authorities have been designated as follows:

England	• The Lord Chancellor
Wales	• The Welsh Ministers
Northern Ireland	• The Department of Justice
Scotland	• The Scottish Ministers

10.49 A Central Authority (or other competent authority) may make a request under Art 32 for a report on the situation of the child to another Central Authority in respect of a child who has a substantial connection with the Requesting State but who is habitually resident and present in the Requested State. In addition to the request for a report, the Requesting State may make a request of the State in which the child is habitually resident that protective measures are taken.

This would appear to cover relocation cases where the left-behind parent continues to live in the Requesting State and has lost contact with the child or has concerns over the situation of the child.

Implementation of access rights and other measures

10.50 The first part of Art 35 of HC96 appears to be an attempt to add teeth to Art 21 of HC80 in respect of access rights already secured in the State in which the child was formerly habitually resident.

10.51 The second part of Art 35 enables a left-behind parent who seeks access to his child (who is habitually resident in another Contracting State) to ask the authorities of his country to carry out an assessment of him for use in proceedings in the State of habitual residence. That report may both gather information and also assess the left-behind parent's suitability to have access and under what conditions. The report shall be admissible as evidence in proceedings over access in the other country. A court considering such an application may adjourn pending the outcome of a request under Art 35(2).

Article 35

'(1) The competent authorities of a Contracting State may request the authorities of another Contracting State to assist in the implementation of measures of protection taken under this Convention, especially in securing the effective exercise of rights of access as well as of the right to maintain direct contacts on a regular basis.

(2) The authorities of a Contracting State in which the child does not habitually reside may, on the request of a parent residing in that State who is seeking to obtain or to maintain access to the child, gather information or evidence and may make a finding on the suitability of that parent to exercise access and on the conditions under which access is to be exercised. An authority exercising jurisdiction under Articles 5 to 10 to determine an application concerning access to the child, shall admit and consider such information, evidence and finding before reaching its decision.

(3) An authority having jurisdiction under Articles 5 to 10 to decide on access may adjourn a proceeding pending the outcome of a request made under paragraph 2, in particular, when it is considering an application to restrict or terminate access rights granted in the State of the child's former habitual residence.

(4) Nothing in this Article shall prevent an authority having jurisdiction under Articles 5 to 10 from taking provisional measures pending the outcome of the request made under paragraph 2.'

CHAPTER 11

Procedure for incoming and outgoing applications

Content at a Glance:

A. INTRODUCTION

11.1 This chapter deals with the procedure for two types of application in child abduction proceedings:

- **'Incoming' applications**: proceedings for the recovery of children abducted from a foreign country to England and Wales; and
- **'Outgoing' applications**: proceedings for the recovery of children taken from this jurisdiction to a foreign country.

11.2 The procedure for *incoming* applications depends upon whether the abduction is from a 1980 Hague Convention[1] ('HC80') State, or from another

1 The 1980 Hague Convention on the Civil Aspects of International Child Abduction.

jurisdiction outside that Convention. In non-HC80 cases, an applicant will need to consider whether the 1996 Hague Convention[2] ('HC96') applies[3] and/or if proceedings should be issued seeking an order for the child's return under the inherent jurisdiction.

11.3 Where a child has been abducted from this jurisdiction to another HC80 Member State, usually the steps to be taken in this country will be limited. The left-behind parent will need to focus on launching an application for the child's return in the relevant foreign State. This is likely to involve contacting the English Central Authority (the International Child Abduction and Contact Unit, known informally as 'ICACU'[4]).

11.4 Where a child has been taken from this jurisdiction to a non-HC80 country, an application can be made in this jurisdiction, seeking an order for the child's return; but it is highly likely that the applicant parent will need to seek advice and pursue remedies in the foreign jurisdiction, in parallel to any English proceedings.

11.5 In the majority of outgoing cases involving other HC80 Contracting States, applications for 'chasing orders', ie orders of the English court requiring the child's return here, will probably not be necessary – but each case will turn on its own facts, and there is nothing to prevent an application being made where such an order might be appropriate[5].

11.6 The various procedural options that might apply where a child has been abducted are illustrated by the following chart:

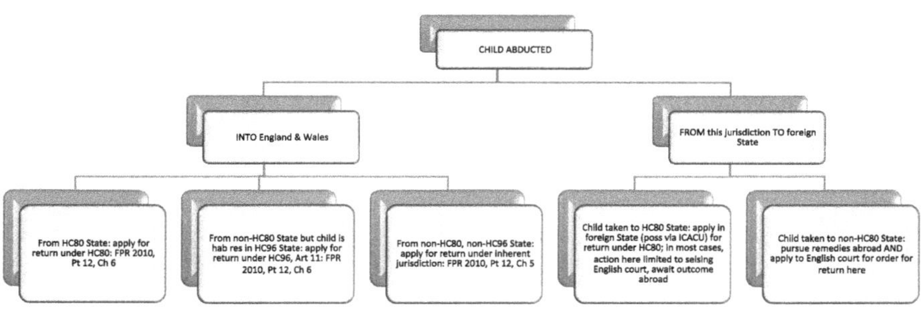

2 The 1996 Hague Convention of 19 October 1996 on Jurisdiction, Applicable Law, Recognition, Enforcement and Co-operation in Respect of Parental Responsibility and Measures for the Protection of Children.

3 See *Re J* [2015] UKSC 70, [2016] AC 1291, [2016] Fam Law 163, [2016] 1 FCR 481, [2016] 1 FLR 170 as to the use of Art 11 of HC96 to seek summary return of a child present here but habitually resident in another HC96 State, in that case Morocco. For HC96 generally, see **Chapter 10**.

4 For contact details of ICACU, see para **2.34** above.

5 *Re S (Abduction: Hague Convention or BIIA)* [2018] EWCA Civ 1226, [2018] 4 WLR 108, [2018] 2 FCR 819, [2018] 2 FLR 1405; see further at paras **11.63–11.86** below.

B. PROCEDURE FOR INCOMING APPLICATIONS UNDER HC80

The role of ICACU

11.7 Most incoming HC80 applications are made via the English Central Authority. Usually, ICACU will receive an application from the Central Authority in the Requesting State.

Upon receipt of an application from a foreign Central Authority, and provided ICACU is satisfied that there is a properly constituted application under the terms of HC80, the applicant parent will be referred to an accredited panel solicitor in the jurisdiction of England and Wales. PD 12F of the Family Procedure Rules 2010 ('FPR 2010') contains useful information about ICACU, including contact details[6].

11.8 It is possible for an application under HC80 to be made directly to the courts of England and Wales, without involving ICACU – it is not mandatory to use the Central Authority route. However, the advantage of making the application through ICACU is that such applicants are automatically entitled to legal aid which is not means-tested or merits-tested.

Legal aid

11.9 An important difference between the position of applicant and respondent to an incoming HC80 application is that applicant parents in this country are entitled to non-means-tested, non-merits-tested legal aid[7]. Respondents are not so entitled. As a consequence, it is common to see respondents appearing as litigants-in-person in HC80 cases; alternatively, respondents who can afford to do so have to pay privately for the proceedings, while their ex-partner enjoys the benefit of public funding. This obviously has the potential to create an inequality of arms, especially in light of the language / cultural barriers that are usually present, and the specialist nature of this area of the law.

11.10 The potential for seeking costs orders against the legally aided party at the conclusion of the case should be borne in mind, particularly where the applicant appears to be pursuing an unmeritorious case[8]. Where an application is brought by a wealthy litigant it may be possible for the respondent to apply against him or her for a legal funding order[9].

6 PD 12F, paras 2.6–2.9; see also para **2.34** above.
7 In order to qualify, the application must be made through ICACU.
8 See para **11.61** below on costs.
9 *Rubin v Rubin* [2014] EWHC 611 (Fam), [2014] 1 WLR 3289, [2014] 1 FLR 1018.

Procedural rules for incoming applications under HC80[10]

11.11 The procedure for applications under HC80 is contained within FPR 2010, Part 12, Chapter 6, and PD 12F. Chapter 6 covers proceedings under HC80 (as well as proceedings under Brussels IIA[11] ('BIIA'), the 1980 European Convention[12] ('EC80') and HC96)[13]. Parts of PD 12D and PD 12E are also relevant. It is essential to consider the procedural rules in conjunction with the Practice Guidance of March 2018[14] ('the 2018 Practice Guidance') which we consider at para **11.27** below.

The parties

11.12 The applicant may be:

> 'any person, institution or body who claims that a child has been removed or retained in breach of rights of custody or claims that there has been a breach of rights of access in relation to the child.'[15]

The respondent(s) must be[16]:

- Person alleged to have brought child to UK
- Person with whom child alleged to be
- Parent or guardian of child in UK
- Person in whose favour custody decision made
- Person with 'sufficient interest' in welfare of child.

10 Where an 'incoming' application needs to be made under the inherent jurisdiction, the relevant procedural rules are contained in FPR 2010, Part 12, Ch 5, rr 12.36–12.42, and PD 12D and PD 12F. However, the overarching Practice Guidance of 13 March 2018 applies to incoming international child abduction cases arising under the inherent jurisdiction, just as it does to HC80 cases. As to the use of the inherent jurisdiction in cases of international child abduction generally, see **Chapter 9**.

11 Council Regulation (EU) No 2201/2003 of 27 November 2003 concerning jurisdiction and the recognition and enforcement of judgments in matrimonial matters and matters of parental responsibility, repealing Regulation (EC) No 1347/2000.

12 The 1980 European Convention of 20 May 1980 on Recognition and Enforcement of Decisions Concerning Custody of Children.

13 Note that some of the general rules in FPR 2010, Part 12 also apply to HC80 proceedings, but there are some exclusions. For example, FPR 2010, r 12.16 'applications without notice' does not apply to Chapter 6 proceedings (Chapter 6 contains its own code on such applications, and see also the 2018 Practice Guidance as discussed at para **11.27** below).

14 *Practice Guidance 13 March 2018: Case Management and Mediation of International Child Abduction Proceedings.*

15 Article 3 of HC80 and FPR 2010, r 12.3.

16 FPR 2010, r 12.3.

11.13 Subject to FPR 2010, r 16.2 (joinder of children to proceedings), the court may at any time direct that any person or body be made a party to proceedings, or that a party be removed[17].

Which court?

11.14 Every application under HC80 must be made in the High Court and issued in the principal registry[18]. Applications are made in Form C67[19].

Applications must be heard by a Judge of the High Court (unless the application is to join a respondent, to dispense with service, or to extend the time for acknowledging service)[20].

Content of application

11.15 FPR 2010, PD 12F, paras 2.11–2.13 set out what information must be contained in an application, and the documents that must be attached to an application. If these are not attached, the court has discretion to fix a time for them to be produced, to accept equivalents, or to dispense with them[21].

11.16 The application should be accompanied by 'all relevant documents' including but not limited to[22]:

- an authenticated copy of any relevant decision or agreement; and
- a certificate or affidavit from the relevant Central Authority / other competent person in the State of habitual residence, concerning the law of that State.

Evidence in support

11.17 The evidence in support of the application will usually take the form of a witness statement by the applicant's solicitor[23], accompanied by a number of exhibits. Usually, a fuller narrative statement directly from the applicant is filed and served later in the proceedings, in response to the respondent's evidence.

The expected content of applications and supporting evidence is addressed in much greater detail in the 2018 Practice Guidance[24].

17 FPR 2010, r 12.3(3).
18 FPR 2010, r 12.45.
19 FPR 2010, PD 5A.
20 FPR 2010, r 12.45(b).
21 FPR 2010, r 12.46.
22 FPR 2010, PD 12F, para 2.12.
23 See FPR 2010, PD 12F, para 2.13.
24 *Practice Guidance 13 March 2018: Case Management and Mediation of International Child Abduction Proceedings*: see para **11.27** below.

Without notice applications

11.18 Without notice applications may be made in accordance with FPR 2010, r 12.47 which applies to the following applications:

- Applications commencing or in HC80 or EC80 proceedings
- Interim directions (CACA 1985, s 5 or 19)
- Disclosure of information and safeguarding welfare (FPR 2010, r 12.57)
- Disclosure of information re child whereabouts (CACA 1985, s 24A)
- Collection, location or passport order.

11.19 Where an application is made urgently by telephone, it must be filed the next working day; all other applications must be filed at the time of being made[25]. The applicant must serve a copy of the order as soon as practicable, unless otherwise directed[26].

The 2018 Practice Guidance[27] is essential reading where a without notice application is being considered; see further from para **11.27** below.

Directions

11.20 FPR 2010, r 12.48 states that '*as soon as practicable*' after an application has been made, the court may give directions as to a number of matters listed in the rule (the list is non-exhaustive).

The 2018 Practice Guidance contains further details of the way in which HC80 cases should be managed; see further from para **11.27** below. Of particular note is the relatively new mediation scheme, which now applies to *all* international child abduction cases as defined by the 2018 Practice Guidance.

25 FPR 2010, r 12.47(2). When appearing in the High Court applications list to make a without notice application, the convention is that the applicant's solicitors will usually undertake to issue and pay the necessary fee by no later than 4pm on the next working day.

26 FPR 2010, r 12.47(3); note that Tipstaff orders should be executed by the Tipstaff, and nothing should be served upon the respondent until execution by the Tipstaff has been successful (see **Chapter 12** on Tipstaff orders). Practice Directions 12E ('Urgent Business') and 12D (Inherent Jurisdiction including Wardship Proceedings) contain further relevant guidance.

27 *Practice Guidance 13 March 2018: Case Management and Mediation of International Child Abduction Proceedings*.

Proceedings to be conducted expeditiously

11.21 In HC80 proceedings it is of the utmost importance that delay is avoided[28]. There is a 6-week time limit in respect of proceedings to which BIIA applies[29] (although, in practice, this timetable is often exceeded).

An application should not be adjourned for a period of more than 21 days[30].

Welfare proceedings to be stayed

11.22 If there are already any substantive proceedings continuing at the time an HC80 application is issued, they must be stayed pending resolution of the HC80 application[31]. Practitioners with conduct of welfare proceedings have an obligation to bring any potential issues of child abduction to the attention of the court at the earliest opportunity[32].

The Answer and respondent's evidence in support

11.23 The respondent to an HC80 application is required to file and serve an Answer to the application within 7 days of service[33]. In practice, this timetable is often extended at the first on-notice directions hearing, whether because of late service, or due to inability of the respondent/their legal advisors to comply with the court's initial timetable (often due to a delay in the grant of legal aid).

11.24 The respondent 'may' file and serve evidence together with an Answer[34]. In practice, the respondent usually *does* file and serve a detailed narrative statement and evidence in support at the same time as their Answer, or very shortly thereafter.

11.25 The Answer should be a short document that clearly sets out the respondent's case in response to the application. The Answer should not contain detailed narrative material – it is a pleading, and should simply identify in clear and succinct terms what issues will be contested under the specific terms of HC80. An Answer will usually set out the respondent's case regarding each relevant article of HC80 – so it will highlight, for example, whether the case is

28 See HC80, Art 11 and paras **2.39–2.41** above.
29 Art 11(3) of BIIA.
30 FPR 2010, r 12.51.
31 See HC80, Art 16 and FPR 2010, r 12.52.
32 See *Re H (Abduction: Habitual Residence: Consent)* [2000] 3 FCR 412, [2000] 2 FLR 294 in which the lawyers were criticised for failing to do so; see also *R v R (Residence Order: Child Abduction)* [1995] Fam 209, [1995] 2 FLR 625 and *R v R (Jurisdiction and Acquiescence)* [2016] EWHC 1339 (Fam), [2018] 1 WLR 350, [2017] 1 FLR 1750, paras 8–15 where it was held that, in cases with a foreign dimension, issues of jurisdiction must be addressed at the outset of proceedings.
33 FPR 2010, r 12.49(1).
34 FPR 2010, r 12.50.

defended on the basis of Arts 3 and 4 (rights of custody / habitual residence), or whether the respondent relies upon any of the exceptions to return contained in Arts 12 and 13. The court direction will be as follows:

> 'In the event that the respondent intends to defend these proceedings the respondent shall by no later than [time and date] file and serve an answer, specifying the article[s] of HC80 upon which [he] / [she] intends to rely and the particulars of information [he] / [she] seeks to rely upon relating to each article.'

A draft answer might be phrased as follows:

> '1. The removal and/or retention of the child is not unlawful as the applicant did not have rights of custody in respect of the child, pursuant to Article 3 of HC80
>
> 2. On or before [date] when the applicant asserts that the child was wrongfully retained in England and Wales, the applicant had consented to the retention of the children pursuant to Article 13a of HC80
>
> 3. There is a grave risk that if the child was returned to the jurisdiction of [country] they would be exposed to physical or psychological harm or otherwise placed in an intolerable situation, pursuant to Article 13b of HC80'

Witness statements

11.26 When preparing evidence, care must be taken to confine statements to that which is truly relevant to the issues in HC80 proceedings. Parties, and their lawyers, may be criticised where the evidence has strayed off point[35]. The 2018 Practice Guidance has reinforced this message.

March 2018 Practice Guidance on the Case Management and Mediation of International Child Abduction Cases[36]

11.27 In March 2018, Sir James Munby, P published the *Practice Guidance 13 March 2018: Case Management and Mediation of International Child Abduction Proceedings* ('the 2018 Practice Guidance'). It applies to 'international

35 See, for example, the comments of Hayden J in *Re B (A Child) (Custody Rights: Habitual Residence)* [2016] EWHC 2174 (Fam), [2016] 4 WLR 156, at para 18.

36 The 2018 Practice Guidance is reproduced in full in the 'Materials' section of the book.

child abduction proceedings', defined as encompassing proceedings in which the return of a child is sought under[37]:

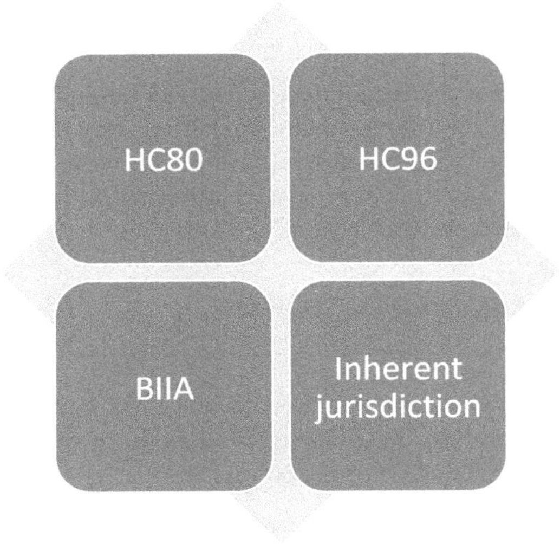

11.28 The 2018 Practice Guidance deals with:

(a) Case Management & Procedure

- without notice applications

(b) Case Management & Procedure

- on-notice applications

(c) Related Matters

- Mediation
- Identification of issues
- Child's participation
- Witness evidence
- Bundles
- Judicial liaison
- Orders
- Appeals and stays

Appendix

- Child Abduction Mediation Scheme

37 At para 1.1(a)–(d).

Without notice applications

11.29 The 2018 Practice Guidance was published following some judicial criticism of what had become fairly standard practice in the child abduction sphere[38]. There was a perception that those practising in this area did not adhere to the stringent rules applicable to without notice applications. Previously, it was the practice for *virtually all* HC80 applications to be commenced without notice with Tipstaff orders being made.

11.30 The 2018 Practice Guidance codified the principles on making without notice applications set out in cases such as *Re A*[39]. There is no longer any excuse for making unjustified without notice applications. Practitioners must carefully consider in every case whether the specific grounds are satisfied so as to justify a without notice application. If not, the case must be commenced using the on-notice procedure[40].

11.31 The 2018 Practice Guidance identified three categories of case in which a without notice application may be justified, and describes what the evidence in support must show in respect of each category[41]:

(a)
- Case of **exceptional urgency**;
- *Must show why it is exceptionally urgent*
- *Also explain why no notice, not even 'short informal', can be given*

(b)
- **Compelling case that the child's welfare will be compromised** if other party alerted in advance;
- *Must show **real risk** flowing from respondent being alerted, due to thwarting court's order or otherwise*
- *Must show magnitude of (i) risk, (ii) risk that respondent can evade protective measures, and (iii) consequences for child*

(c)
- **Whereabouts** of child and respondent **unknown**;
- *Must show steps taken to locate proposed respondent*
- *For disclosure orders, must explain why agency might hold information leading to child's location*
- *Court may require sequential service if more than one disclosure order granted*

Tipstaff orders

11.32 There are three Tipstaff orders that can be made to assist in finding a child and/or preventing the child from being subject to a further removal:

38 See, in particular, *Re A (A child)* [2016] EWCA Civ 572, [2016] 4 WLR 111, [2016] 3 FCR 85.

39 *Re A (A Child)* [2016] EWCA Civ 572, [2016] 4 WLR 111, [2016] 3 FCR 85.

40 For Covid-19 and the remote court, see para **1.21** onwards above and para **11.49** onwards below.

41 At paras 2.1–2.2.

location, collection and passport orders. The different types of Tipstaff order that can be made are considered in **Chapter 12**[42].

Tipstaff orders should not be made without prior liaison with the Tipstaff's office. They can be reached on 01622 858035.

11.33 The Tipstaff will usually require forms to be completed, containing relevant information to assist in their task, eg descriptions of the abducting parent and child, and the last known address. The court is responsible for drafting Tipstaff orders, and the Tipstaff will execute them (normally with the assistance of local police). Solicitors and counsel should not try to draw up or serve Tipstaff orders. Once a Tipstaff order has been executed, the Tipstaff will inform the applicant's solicitor, who can then arrange for the rest of the paperwork to be served. See **Chapter 12** which addresses in detail Tipstaff and disclosure orders.

Without notice case management procedure

11.34 The 2018 Practice Guidance states that, where an HC80 case is commenced by way of without notice application (whether or not a Tipstaff order is also made), the court will give case management directions 'to progress the matter' (albeit these may be 'varied and/or supplanted' at the first on-notice hearing)[43]; the guidance is in mandatory terms and says that the directions *will* include the following:

42 See paras **12.6** onwards below.
43 At para 2.5.

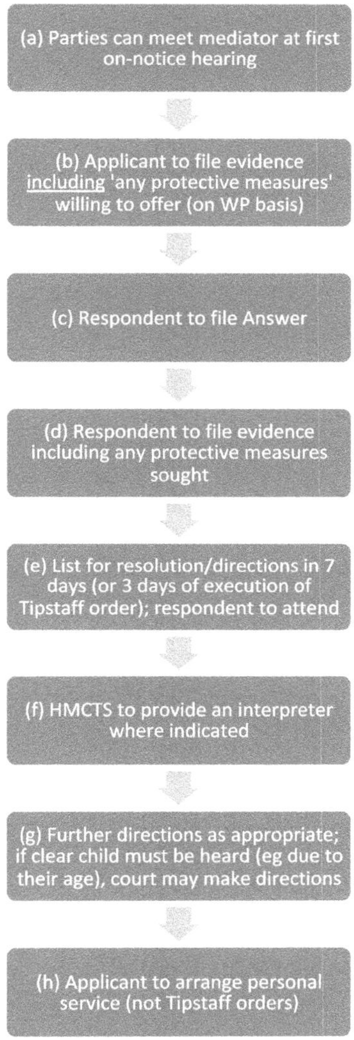

11.35 Paragraph 2.6 of the 2018 Practice Guidance emphasises:

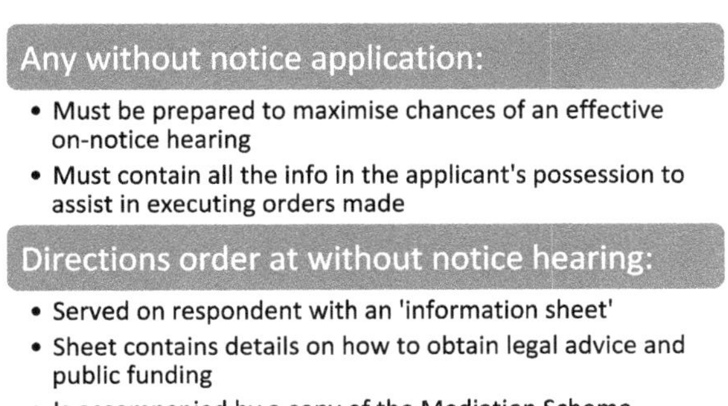

11.36 In practice, there is often a readjustment to the timetable set by a without notice order. This may occur because of late service of the papers, or the inability of a respondent/their lawyers to comply.

11.37 Paragraph (g) of the 2018 Practice Guidance permits the court to make '*such further* ***or other*** *directions*' as may be appropriate in the particular case. If it is clear that the respondent will not be able to comply with the directions and attend court within 7 days, it may be prudent to substitute a more realistic timetable in place of the standard directions (although practitioners must at all times be mindful of the urgent nature of HC80 cases).

On-notice applications

11.38 Due to the sea-change in practice and procedure with regard to the use of without notice applications, most HC80 cases are now issued using the on-notice procedure[44]. Applications are submitted on paper to the court, and an initial on-notice hearing is then listed at a later date. Practitioners should be mindful that the on-notice procedure can lead to significant time being lost between the issue of an application and the first on-notice hearing.

11.39 Paragraph 2.8 of the 2018 Practice Guidance refers to the minimum times for service of HC80 applications and those made under the inherent jurisdiction: 4 days and 14 days respectively[45].

11.40 The 2018 Practice Guidance contains a list of '*standard directions on issue*'[46], to be made by the court upon receipt of an on-notice application. These orders are made by a Judge on the papers, before any hearing has taken place. The Guidance states that the intention behind this practice is to minimise the risk that '*valuable time will be lost between issue and the first on-notice hearing*'[47].

11.41 The '*standard directions on issue*' are made of the court's own motion in accordance with FPR 2010, r 12.5(1)(b). The Guidance states that they are 'to include' a list of directions very similar to those listed in the without notice procedure, with some slight amendments and additions[48]:

44 For Covid-19 and the remote court, see para **1.21** onwards above and para **11.49** onwards below.

45 FPR 2010, Chapter 6 contains no rules for service specific to international child abduction proceedings. The rules in FPR 2010, r 12.8 and PD 12C therefore apply, subject always to the court's power to extend or shorten the time period. As referred to in the 2018 Practice Guidance, the minimum service period for an application under HC80 is 4 days; for an application under the inherent jurisdiction, it is 14 days.

46 These are reproduced in the 'Materials' section.

47 At para 2.9.

48 At para 2.5(a)–(h); see para 2.9(a)–(j) for the on-notice standard directions.

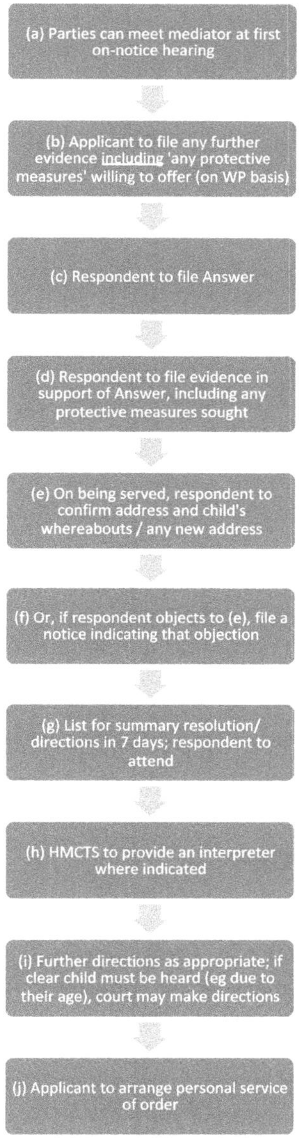

The respondent's evidence and Answer should be filed and served 'not less than' 2 days before the first on-notice hearing[49]. The respondent should also be required to file and serve a notice confirming their address and the whereabouts of the child[50].

49 At para 2.9(c), (d).

50 At para 2.9(e), (f) – para 2.9(f) permits the respondent to raise an objection to service upon the applicant, if appropriate, but the notice must always be filed at court pursuant to para 2.9(e).

Short informal notice

11.42 The 2018 Practice Guidance acknowledges the established practice of giving '*short informal notice*' of an application, instead of proceeding with a without notice hearing. This simply means giving less notice than the period required under the rules and/or giving notice by a means not specified in the rules (eg by text message or a phone call). Paragraph 2.8 emphasises that:

> where short, informal notice is given there must be evidence identifying why it was not possible to serve ... in accordance with the rules or to make an application to abridge time for service.

11.43 Although practitioners might be tempted to use the short informal notice procedure in preference to applying on notice, it is not intended to be the usual means of making an application. Moreover, changes in the administration of the High Court applications list mean that it is usually not possible to attend on the day to make a without notice or other urgent application. Practitioners attending court without a listing must be prepared to explain why the case falls within the new rubric, with evidence in support, or risk being turned away. The rubric on the court list states as follows:

> **'IMPORTANT NOTICE**
>
> 1. Unlisted applications may only be made to the Applications Court if they are **URGENT, AND the urgency arises from some very recent development or circumstance**. An application must not be made to the Applications Court simply because it is not on notice to the other party or parties, unless it is **URGENT** as defined above. All other applications, whether on notice or not, must first be issued, with a proper time estimate, and listed on a date given by the Clerk of the Rules.
> 2. Except in circumstances of extreme urgency, applications must be made at 10.30 am and not at any later time.
> 3. No application may be made to the High Court Applications Court which is capable of being made to a lower tier of judge.'

11.44 When an HC80 case is commenced without notice, or on short informal notice, it must still have a hearing date listed by the High Court[51], unless it also comes within the exceptional type of case for which the High Court urgent applications list is now reserved. Whether an application should be made without notice to the respondent is considered in detail in **Chapter 12**.

The first on-notice hearing

11.45 The parties must attend the first on notice hearing '*fully prepared to deal with the case management matters that have not been dealt with by the standard directions on issue or which have been so dealt with but require variation, together with any additional case management matters*'. This may include, for example: directions with regard to mediation; allocation; disclosure; further evidence including regarding protective measures; the need for expert evidence; possible applications for oral evidence; bundles; and directions for video-link[52].

Other case management directions

11.46 The 2018 Practice Guidance deals specifically with several aspects of case management in child abduction proceedings which commonly arise. In particular, both parties MUST deal with the issue of '*protective measures*'[53]:

> The applicant should clearly set out what is required, and the respondent whether this is accepted / if not, what is offered.

51 For most without notice / urgent hearings, representatives must now obtain a listing via the Clerk of the Rules office. Such cases will then usually be listed within a few days, but possibly longer, depending on court availability.

52 See para 2.11(a)–(k) of the 2018 Practice Guidance.

53 See **Chapter 6** on Article 13(b) regarding the importance of 'protective measures'.

11.47 The following graphic summarises the other points covered:

Review of the 2018 Practice Guidance

11.48 A review of the operation of the 2018 Practice Guidance is being conducted, led by MacDonald J. Practitioners have expressed concern about the delay that is often experienced under the on-notice procedure. It remains to be seen whether any changes will be made.

Covid-19 pandemic

11.49 At the time of writing, the Covid-19 pandemic has resulted in the court issuing temporary guidance[54] which makes amendments to the 2018 Practice Guidance discussed above. The following summarises the effect of that temporary guidance:

ICACU

- Working remotely
- All applications by email
- Documents sent by post, DX or fax will not be received

Legal Aid Agency

- Operating a normal service
- Provision of evidence to prove financial means has been amended

Issue Procedure - All Applications

- All applications issued as, in effect, without notice applications (paras 2.1, 2.2, 9 and 10 of the 2018 Practice Guidance suspended)
- Applications issued electronically and the email subject line should be: "URGENT: NEW 1980 HAGUE CONVENTION APPLICATION FOR ISSUE"
- All applications accompanied by proposed directions order in draft in Word document format

Service

- Permitted to serve orders prior to sealing, which have been endorsed by court
- Endorsed orders are effective without sealing
- Personal service only effected if safe. Service by email or posting through letterbox is sufficient in the first instance
- Copy of Temporary Guidance will be included with the order for service on the respondent

Child Abduction Mediation Scheme

- Suspended only insofar as to prevent face-to-face mediation at court
- Each party to contact reunite prior to first on-notice hearing: reunite@dircon.co.uk or 0116 2555 345

Child's Participation

- Children can be interviewed remotely by Cafcass High Court
- Cafcass can receive electronic papers
- Email: highcourtgm.cafcass.gov.uk

Hearings

- Take place in accordance with President's Guidance of 19 March 2020: "COVID 19: National Guidance for the Family Court"
- Each order must prominently state that the next hearing will take place 'remotely'
- Immediate steps must be taken to obtain/ensure access to technology for the next hearing
- No less than 48 hours before hearing, applicant's solicitor to contact respondent/solicitor to arrange remote hearing
- If respondent has no computer, hearing by telephone

Tipstaff

- Orders available in the usual way
- Tipstaff will discharge his responsibilities, subject to operational constraints imposed by Government
- Tipstaff requires sealed order to discharge port alerts and/or passport orders

Mediation

11.50 The Appendix to the 2018 Practice Guidance contains the Child Abduction Mediation Scheme. This scheme is operated from the Royal Courts

54 Covid-19: Temporary Amendments to the Practice Guidance on Case Management and Mediation of International Child Abduction Proceedings.

of Justice and is run by the well-known charity, *reunite International Child Abduction Centre*[55] ('*reunite*').

11.51 Mediation with *reunite* is intended to run in parallel with continuing HC80 proceedings, so that time is not lost if the mediation is unsuccessful. Hence all the usual directions should still be made, and should be complied with, even if the parties agree to attend mediation in the meantime[56]. Mediation is voluntary, and is confidential, so can be entered into without prejudice to either party's position in the proceedings[57].

11.52 The mediators will first perform an initial screening assessment, and there may be cases which are unsuitable – for example, where there are risks associated with domestic violence[58]. However, the mediator is able to perform this assessment themselves – domestic violence allegations do not, in and of themselves, mean that the court should not refer the parties at least to the initial screening stage. The scheme contains a detailed protocol for screening. It also states that a mediator might identify the need for a child's voice to be heard by the involvement of Cafcass[59].

11.53 Mediation is arranged on dates provided by *reunite*. It is possible to use technology such as video-link if one or more parties cannot come to this jurisdiction; interpreters can be arranged; and sometimes public funding may be available for flights and accommodation[60]. Parties can consult their legal advisors or other persons at any time[61] and, where mediation is successful, a Memorandum of Understanding will be created[62].

Interim applications

11.54 Section 5 of the Child Abduction and Custody Act 1985 ('CACA 1985') allows the court to make interim orders in HC80 proceedings. It provides:

> ... the court may ... give such interim directions as it thinks fit for the purpose of securing the welfare of the child concerned or of preventing changes in the circumstances relevant to the application.

55 Appendix, para 6.
56 Appendix, para 4(a).
57 Appendix, paras 4(b), (d)–(f), 8 and 11 – save that mediators must raise any safeguarding concerns if they arise (paras 23, 25).
58 Appendix, para 4(c) and paras 12–17.
59 Appendix, para 17.
60 Appendix, paras 18–21.
61 Appendix, para 22.
62 Appendix, para 24.

11.55 The power under CACA 1985, s 5 is frequently invoked to deal with issues of interim contact pending resolution of HC80 proceedings. It is a widely drawn power, and has many other potential uses. The chart below illustrates a number of examples of how the power may be used – but this list is by no means exhaustive[63]. There are limits, however – it has recently been held that it would '*stretch s 5 to breaking point*' to interpret it as allowing the court to defer a return order pending parenting assessments by the local authority[64].

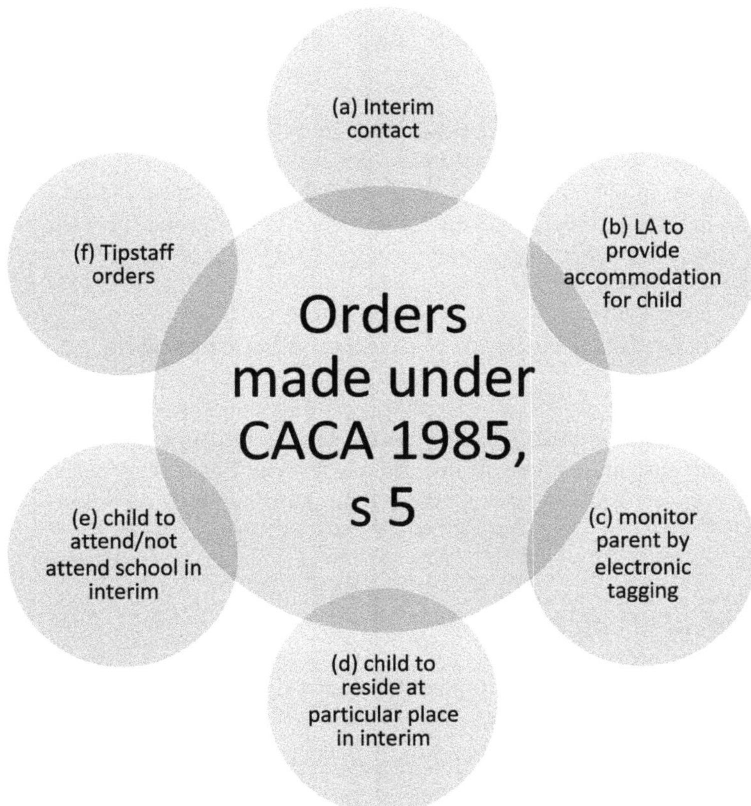

The conduct of the hearing

11.56 HC80 proceedings are summary in nature. Oral evidence is a rarity. Where an application for oral evidence is made, the applicant should be prepared to explain why oral evidence is necessary to resolve the proceedings justly.

63 Case references in the chart: (b) *Re A (abduction: interim directions: accommodation by local authority)* [2010] EWCA Civ 586, [2011] Fam 179, [2010] Fam Law 1256, [2010] 3 FCR 359, [2011] 1 FLR 1; (c) *Re C (interim directions: accommodation by local authority)* [2003] EWHC 3065 (Fam), [2004] 1 FLR 653; see also **Chapter 12** for further discussion of Tipstaff orders.

64 *Re E (Abduction: Article 13b Deferred Return Order)* [2019] EWHC 256 (Fam), [2019] 2 FLR 615.

11.57 The HC80 'defence' where oral evidence is more commonly heard is where Art 13(a) 'consent' is in issue[65]. Other than in consent cases, where the disputed issues of fact may be capable of resolution by limited and focused oral evidence, it is rare for the parties themselves to give evidence.

11.58 It is common, however, to hear oral evidence from Cafcass officers where a report to the court has been prepared. This usually, but not exclusively, occurs in cases concerning Art 13(2) child objections[66]. It is also possible that oral evidence might need to be heard from an expert instructed in the case, although usually any such evidence would be adduced by way of a report from a single joint expert.

11.59 In *Re K (Abduction: Case Management)*[67], Thorpe LJ expressed concern at a submission made by counsel to the effect that oral evidence was becoming more common in HC80 cases. He stressed that oral evidence should remain the exception in HC80 cases, and should very rarely be permitted from the parties in any circumstances other than a contested Art 13(a) case.

Strike-out or 'ultra-summary' disposal of applications

11.60 The summary nature of HC80 proceedings means that it should only be in rare cases that the court will dispose of a contested application at an interim stage. In the vast majority of cases, the court should at least proceed to hear a properly contested final hearing, rather than adopting such an 'ultra-summary' approach[68].

Withdrawal of applications

11.61 The withdrawal of an application under HC80 requires the permission of the court[69].

Costs

11.62 There are no rules within FPR 2010, Part 28 that are specific to HC80 proceedings. In *EC-L v DM (Child Abduction: Costs)*[70] Ryder J held that the

65 See **Chapter 5** on Article 13(a).

66 For child objections, see **Chapter 7**.

67 [2010] EWCA Civ 1546, [2011] 1 FLR 1268 at para 13.

68 *Re G* [1995] 2 FLR 410; *Re D (Children) (Child Abduction: Practice)* [2016] EWHC 504 (Fam), [2016] 4 WLR 62, [2017] 1 FLR 1125, FD; *Re A (A Child)* [2016] EWCA Civ 572, [2016] 4 WLR 111, [2016] 3 FCR 85; *Re S (A Child) (Abduction: Dismissal of Application)* [2018] EWCA Civ 1453, [2018] 3 FCR 394, [2019] 1 FLR 354 (which approved *Re D*).

69 FPR 2010, r 29.4; see *Ciccone v (Ritchie* [2016] EWHC 616 (Fam), [2016] 3 FCR 438, [2017] 1 FLR 812 for a discussion of the correct approach.

70 *EC-L v DM (Child Abduction: Costs)* [2005] EWHC 588 (Fam), [2005] 2 FLR 772.

general power to make costs orders should apply in HC80 proceedings as it does in other family proceedings. He said that there was nothing in the Convention preventing this, nor to prevent costs orders being made against unsuccessful publicly funded applicants[71]. He held that the principles to be applied were essentially the same as those in domestic children proceedings; a party would probably need to be responsible for some sort of unreasonable conduct for a costs order to be appropriate.

C. OUTGOING APPLICATIONS

11.63 This section covers the scenario where a child has been wrongfully removed from this jurisdiction and/or is being wrongfully retained in a foreign jurisdiction. What steps should the left-behind parent take to recover the child? The answer depends, to an extent, on whether the country in which the child is being retained is a Member State of HC80 and/or BIIA.

Abductions to another HC80 country

International Child Abduction and Contact Unit ('ICACU')

11.64 The first and most important step to take is to contact the English Central Authority (the International Child Abduction and Contact Unit – 'ICACU'). An application for the return of the child will normally be made via ICACU who will them transmit the application to the Central Authority of the foreign jurisdiction. That Central Authority will then take responsibility for making an application in the foreign courts for an order for the summary return of the child under HC80. The contact details for the ICACU are set out at para **2.34** above.

11.65 There is an official 'ICACU application form' which must be completed, which is accompanied by an 'ICACU Guide to Completing the Application Form'[72]. The following table provides a list of certain things which should be considered or included when completing the application form, drawn from the form itself and the guide; it is a non-exhaustive list and it is advisable in all circumstances to disclose *too much* information rather than *too little*:

71 Any such order would have to be made subject to the relevant public funding rules/regulations. Such an order was made in *K v K* [2016] EWHC 2002 (Fam), [2016] 4 WLR 143, [2017] 1 FCR 144.

72 Both the ICACU application form and the Guide to Completing the Form can be found online and downloaded in Word format at: www.gov.uk/government/publications/international-child-abduction-and-contact-unit-application-form.

Contacting ICACU

- By email to ICACU@ospt.gov.uk; see further details at para **2.34**
- A copy of the application form and accompanying documents <u>must</u> also be sent by post
- ICACU standard response time is 7 working days

Legal advice

- ICACU does not give legal advice
- A referral list of solicitors with expertise is available

The application form

- If completing by hand, ensure it is clearly legible
- It may need to be translated, so write in clear terms
- Some countries require certain documents to accompany the application form, so to avoid delay check with ICACU what those requirements are before sending the application
- Complete all the boxes on the form as fully as possible

Personal details

- Provide your personal contact details, even if you have a solicitor
- If you do not wish personal details to be disclosed to the respondent, include a covering letter to that effect

Whereabouts of the child?

- Provide as much info about the possible whereabouts of the child
- Include contact addresses, phone numbers, email etc. for the respondent and/or wider family

Flight risk?

- Identify in the application if you think the child is at risk of further removal
- Draw attention to the flight risk in the subject line of the email and covering letter

Habitual Residence

- Provide as much info that the child was habitually resident in England before removal
- See **Chapter 4** on habitual residence
- Relevant info: how long child in England, nationality, schooling, language, family and social relationships in England
- Provide any documentation to show social integration, eg letter from school, sports clubs etc.

Rights of Custody

- Were you exercising rights of custody at the time of the removal?
- See **Chapter 3** on rights of custody
- If you have parental responsibility under English law, that is sufficient
- Attach all relevant documentation, eg marriage / civil partnership certificate, court order, child's birth certificate

Arrangements for return

- Will you travel to the foreign country for a court hearing? Or to collect the child?
- If someone else is proposed to collect the child, who and what relation?
- If you cannot travel, why?

Mediation?

- Have you tried a 'voluntary return' by mediation?
- NB If there is a flight risk, this could be triggered by notifying the other party of an application

11.66 As is clear from the graphic above, an outgoing application made through the ICACU should include *as much information as possible* and attach *as much documentary evidence as possible*. Applicants should consider what the potential 'defences' to the application for a return might be (see **Chapters 5 to 8**), or whether there might be arguments about habitual residence (see **Chapter 4**) or rights of custody (see **Chapter 3**). The speed of information exchange between jurisdictions is often not very fast, and applicants should bear in mind that each document may have to be translated into a foreign language before it can be considered by the foreign Central Authority and courts. It is therefore advisable to front-load the disclosure with the application, rather than make the application and wait to hear what further evidence is needed.

11.67 An outgoing application for the return of a child made through the ICACU should be made *as quickly as possible* after the wrongful removal / retention has come to light. Any delay may prejudice the application in the same way that it might do so for an incoming application in this jurisdiction (see, for example, **Chapter 5** on 'acquiescence' and **Chapter 8** on 'settlement').

Issuing proceedings in this jurisdiction: 'chasing orders'

11.68 Even if the jurisdiction to which the child has been removed is another HC80 (or BIIA) State, it is nevertheless possible to issue proceedings in England. This is likely to be for two potential purposes:

(1) To ensure that the English court is seised of the substantive welfare jurisdiction

(2) A 'chasing order' to try to obtain the immediate return of the child

11.69 There is nothing wrong in law with issuing proceedings in this jurisdiction for purpose number (1). It may even be advisable to do so pending the outcome of the application under HC80 in the foreign country, so as to seek to ensure that England is seised of proceedings and thus its substantive welfare jurisdiction engaged.

11.70 Practitioners should be more cautious before making an application for a summary return order from the English court (pursuant to its jurisdiction under BIIA currently, or HC96 following IP completion day on 31 December 2020), as opposed to pursuing proceedings under HC80 in the foreign country. Such orders are often referred to as 'chasing orders'. Given that HC80 already provides a mechanism for seeking the summary return of a child, it is unlikely that the pursuit of a chasing order in this jurisdiction will be necessary or appropriate. If such an application is being considered, regard must be had to the decision of the Court of Appeal in *Re S*[73].

73 *Re S (A Child) (Abduction: Hague Convention or BIIa)* [2018] EWCA Civ 1226, [2018] 2 FCR 819, [2018] 2 FLR 1405.

Case Summary: *Re S (A Child) (Abduction: Hague Convention or BIIa)*[74]

Facts:

Since 2010 the parties' children had been living with M in England, pursuant to an English court order. F lived in the Netherlands. In 2017 the parties agreed the elder child would spend the summer holidays with F and return to England for school in early September 2017. F did not return the child on the agreed date. M issued proceedings in England. Knowles J made a return order at a hearing convened on short notice at which F attended in person by telephone.

M encountered difficulties enforcing the order and issued an application in the Netherlands under HC80. By the date of the appeal the HC80 proceedings were far advanced and a guardian had been appointed for the child. M accepted that the appeal should be allowed and the HC80 proceedings allowed to proceed. Nevertheless, the Court of Appeal gave a short judgment intended to be guidance for practitioners.

Held by the Court of Appeal (Moylan LJ):

(1) 'different considerations will arise when the other State is not a [EU] Member State and is not a party to any relevant international instrument …' (para 37).

(2) The court in England has the power to make a summary return order when it has substantive welfare jurisdiction (paras 44–45). The real question was *whether* the court should exercise that power:

> '47 … I do not …consider that a "particularly compelling reason" would be required before it would be appropriate for a court to make a return order summarily at the outset of proceedings. However, … absent a good reason to the contrary, the better course is for the court to defer making a return order until an application under [HC80] has been determined in the other Member State. As Black LJ said, this is how the return of a child is "expected to be dealt with"[75].'

(3) HC80 had 'real advantages': (1) a higher degree of direct assistance from the authorities of the foreign State; (2) the obligation under HC80 to determine applications within six weeks; and (3) Art 11(4) provides what happens if a non-return order is made. There is, therefore, a tailor-

74 [2018] EWCA Civ 1226, [2018] 2 FCR 819, [2018] 2 FLR 1405.

75 *Re A (A Child)* [2016] EWCA Civ 572, [2016] 3 FCR 85. This case is discussed by Moylan LJ at paras 34 and 35.

made procedure for inter-State engagement and enforcement under HC80 (para 48).

(4) 'There can be good reasons for starting proceedings, including to seek to ensure that the home State is seised of proceedings to make clear that its substantive jurisdiction is engaged. However, it does not follow from this that an order for summary return should be asked for or made, for the reasons given above …' (para 51).

11.71 The content and drafting of 'chasing orders' is discussed in para **11.72** below in relation to applications concerning non-HC80 countries.

Abductions to a non-HC80 country

11.72 If a child has been wrongfully removed from this jurisdiction and/or is being wrongfully retained in another jurisdiction that is not a signatory to HC80, the left-behind parent should obtain legal advice and pursue the remedies available in the foreign jurisdiction as quickly as possible. Such remedies are beyond the scope of this book.

11.73 In addition to pursuing remedies in the foreign jurisdiction, an application should be made in this country for declarations and/or orders granted pursuant to the court's inherent jurisdiction. An application can be made to make the child a ward of court and orders can be made within wardship proceedings[76]. Examples of orders that can be obtained are set out in the table below, but the appropriateness of each will depend on the circumstances of each case:

76 See Thorpe LJ at para 8 in *Re H (A Child) (Abduction: Habitual Residence: Agreement)* [2013] EWCA Civ 148, [2013] Fam Law 783, [2013] 2 FLR 1426, and Moylan LJ at para 37 in *Re S (A Child) (Abduction: Hague Convention or BIIa)* [2018] EWCA Civ 1226, [2018] 2 FCR 819, [2018] 2 FLR 1405, referred to at para **11.70** above.

Declaration: "The court was satisfied on a provisional basis of the evidence filed that..."

- The child was on [date of removal/retention] and remained on [date of application] habitually resident in the jurisdiction of England & Wales
- The child was wrongfully removed from the jurisdiction of England & Wales on [date] by [person]
- The child was and continues to be wrongfully retained in the jurisdiction of [country]
- The courts of England & Wales have jurisdiction in matters of parental responsibility over the child

The court respectfully requests:

- Any person not within the jurisdiction of this court who is in a position to do so to co-operate in assisting and securing the immediate return to England & Wales of the child

Orders:

- The child is and shall remain a Ward of this court during their minority or until further order
- The respondent shall return the child forthwith to England & Wales
- Every person within the jurisdiction of the court who is in a position to do so shall co-operate in assisting and securing the immediate return to England & Wales of the child
- The child shall be joined as a party to the proceedings

11.74 Practitioners should obtain advice from the foreign jurisdiction as to which orders or declarations from the English court, if any, are most likely to assist in securing the return of the child. In some cases the court may only be willing make the declarations and/or grant the orders listed in the paragraph above if there is evidence in the statement accompanying the application that such is likely to assist the applicant with obtaining the return of the child from the foreign jurisdiction.

11.75 Any order obtained pursuant to the paragraphs above should be sent to the Office of the Head of International Family Justice[77] and, if appropriate, to the Head of the Consular Division at the Foreign and Commonwealth Office[78].

77 Address: Office of the Head of International Family Justice, The Royal Courts of Justice, The Strand, London WC2A (DX4450 Strand RCJ; Fax 02079476408).

78 Address: Head of the Consular Division, Foreign and Commonwealth Office, Spring Gardens, London SW1A 2PA (Tel 0207008212, Fax 02070080152).

11.76 It is important to issue an application in this jurisdiction as soon as possible after the wrongful removal / retention so as to ensure that the English court continues to hold the jurisdiction to make substantive welfare decisions concerning the child.

11.77 If a return order has been made in England and Wales for a child to be returned here, but not complied with, consideration should then be given to taking further steps to secure the child's return. This could be committal proceedings against the non-returning parent, sequestration proceedings in respect of their property in this jurisdiction, or injunctive proceedings against other persons who may be able to assist in obtaining the return of the child. These are covered in more detail in **Chapter 13**, but below is a short summary of how they may assist when the left-behind parent remains in England and Wales.

Committal proceedings

11.78 If a return order has been made, but the child has not been returned, committal may be the next step. This involves an applicant proving, to the criminal standard, that the order has been deliberately breached. If proved, the court may sentence the respondent to a term of imprisonment for up to two years (which term may be suspended).

11.79 Applications for committal for contempt of court involve a two-stage process. Firstly, the court must be satisfied that the alleged contemnor is in contempt of court, ie they have deliberately breached the order[79]. Secondly, if proved, the court can proceed to consider sanction[80].

11.80 The contempt must be proved beyond reasonable doubt: it is a quasi-criminal remedy. It is important to remember that the contempt must be proved separately to the original abduction. The mere fact that the child has not been returned may not be sufficient to evidence contempt: what is required is proof of a deliberate breach of the order[81].

11.81 At this stage, the respondent's engagement may be in issue – especially if they have failed to comply with multiple orders. The respondent's non-attendance at a committal hearing is relatively unusual, but it is possible for the hearing to proceed in their absence. Cobb J in *Sanchez v Oboz*[82] set out the factors that should be considered in such circumstances:

79 *Re A (A Child) (Removal from Jurisdiction: Contempt of Court)* [2008] EWCA Civ 1138, [2009] 1 WLR 1482, [2009] 1 FLR 1.

80 The two stages do not have to take place in the same hearing; adjourning sentence may be a decision designed to encourage compliance, although it is for the court to decide whether to proceed directly to sanction: *Reilly v Shamrez* [2019] EWHC 3112 (Fam), [2016] 1 FLR 897.

81 *Re A (A Child) (Removal from Jurisdiction: Contempt of Court)* [2008] EWCA Civ 1138, [2009] 1 WLR 1482, [2009] 1 FLR 1.

82 [2015] EWHC 235 (Fam).

i) Whether the respondents have been served with the relevant documents, including the notice of the committal hearing

ii) Whether the respondents have had sufficient notice to enable them to prepare for the hearing

iii) Whether any reason has been advanced for the respondents' non-appearance

iv) Whether, by reference to the nature and circumstances of the respondents' behaviour, they have waived their right to be present

v) Whether an adjournment would be likely to secure the attendance of the respondents, or facilitate their representation

vi) The extent of the disadvantage to the respondents in not being able to present their account of events

vii) Whether undue prejudice would be caused to the applicant by any delay

viii) Whether undue prejudice would be caused to the forensic process if the application was to proceed in the absence of the respondents

ix) The terms of the overriding objective, including the obligation on the court to deal with the case 'justly', including doing so "*expeditiously and fairly*" (*r 1.1(2)*), and taking "*any ... step or make any ... order for the purposes of ... furthering the overriding objective*" (*r 4.1(3)(o)*).

Sequestration proceedings

11.82 Sequestration involves appointing sequestrators to take control of the contemnor's property until such time as the order is complied with[83]. During this time, the sequestrators can take possession of the property, let it out and raise money against it. The purpose of raising money against the property or selling

83 This was done in *A v A and another (Children: Habitual Residence) (Reunite International Child Abduction Centre intervening)* [2013] UKSC 60, [2014] AC 1, [2013] 3 FCR 559, [2014] 1 FLR 111.

the property can be two-fold: firstly, to encourage compliance with the order; and, secondly, to fund the applicant's legal fees to pursue further enforcement proceedings in the country to which the child has been taken. This may be by raising money against the property[84] or by selling it[85].

11.83 Sequestration proceedings can also be taken against a third party, where they have worked to frustrate and disobey an order to return the child[86]. This may be a useful option where a person in England and Wales is working with an abducting parent to frustrate the operation of a return order. However, it is likely to be only in exceptional circumstances, where the requisite knowledge of the order and involvement in frustrating it can be shown in respect of a non-party.

11.84 Applications for permission to issue a writ of sequestration must be made in the High Court to a single judge of the Family Division or in the Family Court to a judge of High Court level[87]. The procedure is set out in FPR 2010, Part 37 and Practice Direction 37A; an application must be made in accordance with FPR 2010, Part 18.

Applications against third parties

11.85 As is detailed in **Chapter 12** on locating children, orders against third parties can be utilised to establish the whereabouts of the child. Those who remain in England and Wales can be called upon to provide details of where the abducted child may be. This may be useful if the child is further removed after a return order is made.

11.86 It is important to be cautious as to the appropriate scope of such orders. In *Re B (A Child) (Wrongful Removal: Orders against Non-Parties)*[88], the Court of Appeal warned against using third party orders for coercive purposes. It was not appropriate to, for example, hold the passport of a third party in an attempt to encourage – or, rather, coerce – that third party to put pressure on the abducting parent to return.

84 *Richardson v Richardson* [1989] Fam 95, [1990] 1 FCR 232, [1990] 1 FLR 186 and *PM v KH* [2010] EWHC 870 (Fam), [2010] 2 FCR 639, [2010] 2 FLR 1057.
85 *Mir v Mir* [1992] Fam 79, [1992] 1 FCR 227, [1992] FLR 624.
86 *Re S (Minors) (Child Abduction: Sequestration)* [1995] 3 FCR 707, [1995] 1 FLR 858.
87 FPR 2010, r 37.25(1).
88 [2014] EWCA Civ 843, [2015] Fam 209, [2015] 1 FCR 75, [2015] 1 FLR 871.

CHAPTER 12

Locating children and preventing further abduction

Content at a Glance:

A. INTRODUCTION

12.1 When an application comes before the court for the return of a child to another jurisdiction, very often the whereabouts of the subject child and the abducting parent are unknown. This chapter will address the different options available to the applicant who seeks to locate the child, which are summarised in the following diagram:

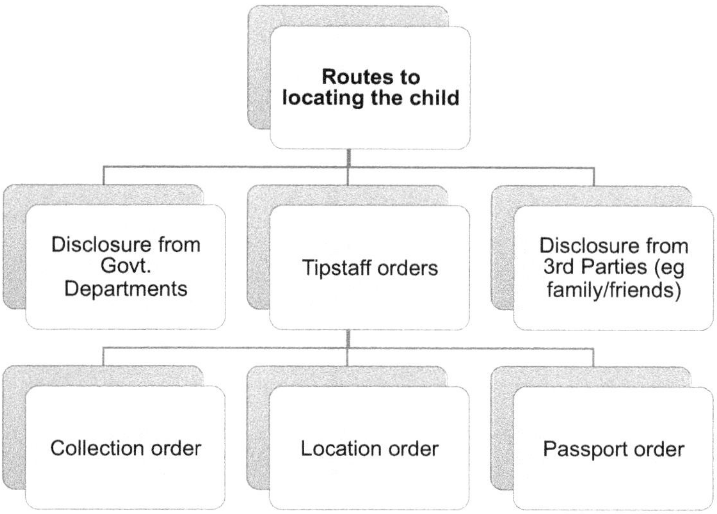

12.2 Careful thought must be given before making an application without notice. Until relatively recently, it was common practice to commence abduction proceedings with an application without notice to the respondent, whether or not their location was known or there was a risk they might flee the country if notice was given. This chapter should be read in conjunction with paras **11.18–11.19** and **11.29–11.31** above, which address the circumstances in which it may be appropriate to make an application to the court without notice. Those circumstances are increasingly rare. Practitioners should refer to the judgment of Munby, P in *Re A (A Child)*[1].

Case Summary: Re *A (A Child)*[2]

Facts:

M issued proceedings under the 1980 Hague Convention[3] ('HC80') for the return of the child, A (aged 4), to Sweden. The first hearing was without notice to F. MacDonald J granted a collection order on the basis that F posed '*an extreme flight risk given that this father seemingly has managed to move through so many jurisdictions with a child with the Swedish authorities hot on his tail*' (para 44).

1 [2016] 4 WLR 111, [2016] 3 FCR 85, particularly paras 57–70.
2 [2016] EWCA Civ 572, [2016] 4 WLR 111, [2016] 3 FCR 85.
3 The 1980 Hague Convention on the Civil Aspects of International Child Abduction.

Held by the Court of Appeal (Sir James Munby, P):

Upheld the *ex parte* collection order on the facts, but was sceptical about the process by which it had been obtained and endorsed these paragraphs from a previous judgment of Charles J[4]:

> '13. … I recognise that there is a natural temptation for applicants to seek, and for courts to grant, relief to protect the vulnerable, and, I add, to find children who it is alleged have been abducted. But this temptation, and the strong public interest in granting such relief, does not provide an excuse for failures to apply the correct approach in law to such applications … Naturally this applies to all without notice applications, but it can be said to have particular importance when Tipstaff orders are sought and granted because they can found a deprivation of liberty without further court involvement, and they do restrict freedom of movement.
>
> 14. In my view, a practice of granting and continuing Tipstaff orders in Hague Convention cases as a matter of course and without insisting on properly prepared, particularised and updating evidence is to be deprecated.'

12.3 If an applicant does not know the location of the respondent and child, that would seem a cast-iron ground for the first hearing being without notice; surely the respondent must be located before they can be served with the proceedings? However, that is not always right. Nowadays, short informal notice could be given by a number of means (email, text message, WhatsApp etc), so it is not as simple as saying: '*I do not know where they are living*'. This diagram sets out the issues which must be considered and addressed in any statement accompanying an application[5]:

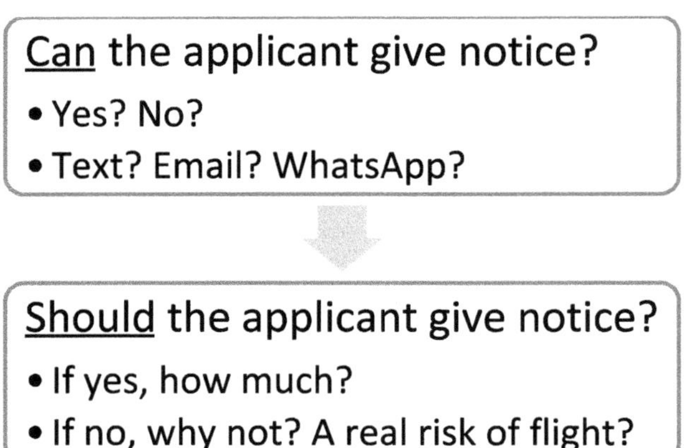

4 *B v A (Wasted Costs Order)* [2012] EWHC 3127 (Fam), [2013] 2 FLR 958 at paras 13–14.

5 See also **Chapter 11** on the procedure for making applications in both incoming and outgoing abductions.

12.4 Furthermore, the fact that the whereabouts of the child are unknown does not of itself mean that an application for a Tipstaff order will automatically be granted, if other less intrusive measures might be used to obtain information about their whereabouts expeditiously[6]. This must be assessed on a case-by-case basis, but if, for example, an applicant knows that the abducting parent has registered the child at a school, a disclosure order against the Department for Education might be more proportionate than a location order.

12.5 In summary, an applicant and their legal representatives must not only consider whether or not the initial application should be without notice, but must also think about the appropriate orders to seek at that hearing.

B. TIPSTAFF ORDERS

Who is the Tipstaff?

12.6 The Tipstaff is the Law Enforcement Officer to the Senior Courts, located at the Royal Courts of Justice in London. The role of the Tipstaff dates back several hundred years; it is the oldest law enforcement post in the jurisdiction of England and Wales. He has a deputy and assistants, and can authorise police officers or bailiffs (or, indeed, a member of the public) to assist in carrying out his enforcement duties. The Tipstaff can have very wide-ranging powers when these are authorised by an order of the court.

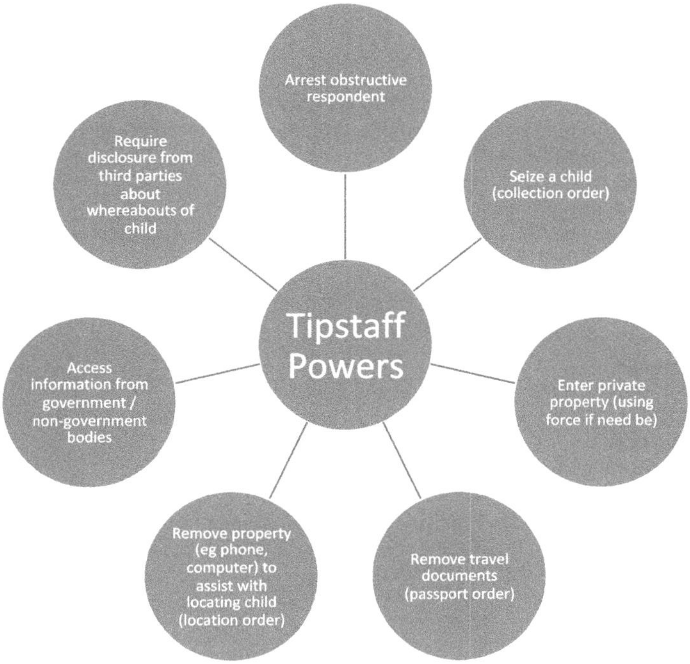

6 *Re A (A Child)* [2016] EWCA Civ 572, [2016] 4 WLR 111, [2016] 3 FCR 85 at para 58.

What are Tipstaff orders?

12.7 A Tipstaff order takes the form of an order addressed to the respondent, which the Tipstaff will enforce (an order will also be made containing directions to the Tipstaff as to steps he may take to enforce the terms of the order). The orders are drawn up by the court office.

12.8 The court has the option to make one of three Tipstaff orders: passport order, location order or collection order. Their essential features and the purpose behind each one are set out in the graphic below. If a respondent obstructs the Tipstaff in carrying out the provisions of the relevant order, they may be arrested[7].

Passport order

- **Features:**
  - Hand over any passport, ID card, ticket, travel warrant for the respondent/child to the Tipstaff. Prohibited from applying for / seeking to obtain further travel documents to enable the child or respondent to leave the jurisdiction
  - Respondent and child must not leave the jurisdiction
  - Inform the Tipstaff of the address where the child resides in E&W
  - Port Alert initiated
- **Purpose:**
  - To ensure the child and respondent cannot leave the jurisdiction pending determination of the application

Location order

- **Features:**
  - All features of the passport order
  - Any person served with the order must inform Tipstaff of the whereabouts of the child and give any information to assist with locating the child
  - The respondent must not cause/permit the child to stay overnight at an address other than that at which they have been located
- **Purpose:**
  - To assist with locating the child
  - To ensure the child and respondent cannot leave the jurisdiction pending determination of the application

Collection order

- **Features:**
  - All features of the passport order and location order
  - Child to be delivered up to the Tipstaff and placed in care of the applicant/local authority
  - Applicant not to remove the child from the jurisdiction
- **Purpose:**
  - To protect the child by removing them from the care of the respondent
  - To ensure the applicant cannot remove the child from the jurisdiction pending determination of the application

7 See, for example, *Re H* [2018] EWHC 3761 (Fam), [2019] 4 WLR 18, [2019] 1 FCR 641 in which the father had been arrested by the Tipstaff for failing to comply with a passport order.

12.9 Tipstaff orders can be used for a number of purposes, and are usually made at the commencement of proceedings. All three orders seek to prevent the child being removed from the jurisdiction of England and Wales until the conclusion of the proceedings. Tipstaff orders normally remain in force until further order of the court, save where the Tipstaff has been unable to enforce the order, in which case they expire six months after the order was made. The duration of orders is discussed at para **12.11** below. Further, revised wording has recently been published by the Tipstaff which must be included in all orders made during the course of proceedings so as to ensure the continued retention of travel documentation and continuation of the port alert; this is set out at para **12.38** below.

12.10 It is essential to note that these orders are granted to protect the subject child, as opposed to being coercive measures. Thus, a passport order granted in order to bring pressure to bear upon and influence the conduct of an abducting party (or, indeed, any third party) is an impermissible use of the court's powers[8].

Duration of orders

12.11 It is unclear whether a Tipstaff order should continue beyond the conclusion of proceedings. In *Re M (Children)*[9] the President indicated as follows in *obiter dictum* in relation to a passport order:

> 'If an order such as that … can ever be justified after the conclusion of proceedings, it is likely only to be in an unusual and probably quite extreme case where it can be demonstrated, after a close evaluation of the degree of risk to the children *and* of the harm to which they will be exposed if the risk becomes a reality, that such a serious invasion of the passport-holder's rights is proportionate and necessary …'

12.12 In *B v A*[10] Charles J made a wasted costs order against the applicant father's solicitors in circumstances where they had obtained a without notice location order without any time limit.

8 *Re B (A Child) (Wrongful Removal: Orders against Non-Parties)* [2014] EWCA Civ 843, [2015] Fam 209, [2015] 1 FCR 75, [2015] 1 FLR 871 at paras 18–35.

9 *Re M (Children) (Care Proceedings: Passport Order)* [2017] EWCA Civ 69, [2017] 4 WLR 41, [2017] 2 FCR 318 at para 14.

10 *B v A (Wasted Costs Order)* [2012] EWHC 3127 (Fam), [2013] 2 FLR 958.

Case Summary: *B v A (Wasted Costs Order)*[11]

Facts:

F and M were from Pakistan but lived in the United States during the marriage. F asserted that M abducted the child from the United States to Pakistan in 2008. M denied this. Nevertheless, M and the child lived in Pakistan from 2008.

On the basis of asserted '*credible information from an associate*' that M and her family had travelled to England, F obtained *ex parte* location and disclosure orders in 2011. After several hearings, with no further evidence being filed, M and the children were not located. Eventually, at the request of F's representatives, the judge adjourned the proceedings generally and continued the location order on an open-ended basis in case M returned.

Six months later, M travelled to England to visit her sister. The location order was executed. It transpired that she had not been in England since 2005 and was able to prove this (paras 44–50). M applied for costs including wasted costs.

Held by Charles J:

> '70.… in some cases, the grant of a location or passport order to effectively "catch" a Respondent or a child on arrival in this country is appropriate and proportionate … this should only be done on the basis of clear evidence and for defined periods.
>
> 71. … in this case the judge should not have continued the location order on 12 December 2011 at all, let alone on an open ended basis …
>
> 75. Even if there had been evidence before the court that founded a reasonable belief that the child might come to this jurisdiction with her mother, which there was not, I have the gravest doubt that it would have been appropriate to grant any continuation of the location order and it seems to me that an open ended continuation is very hard to justify.'

Port alert

12.13 An important feature of a Tipstaff order, contained in the directions to the Tipstaff, is the ability of the Tipstaff to initiate a 'port alert' at all points of entry into and exit from the UK. In principle, this should be initiated automatically

11 [2012] EWHC 3127 (Fam), [2013] 2 FLR 958.

under the directions to the Tipstaff. However, it is advisable to ask for this explicitly at court, on the basis that the risk of the child's further removal from the jurisdiction is 'real (ie not being sought merely by way of insurance)' and 'imminent (ie within 24 to 48 hours)'[12].

12.14 The mechanism of a port alert is not as failsafe as it might seem, and anecdotal evidence suggests a port alert does not always succeed in providing sufficient warning to the Tipstaff or police to prevent removal.

Passport orders

12.15 The obligations of a respondent or any person served with a passport order by the Tipstaff are set out in the following table:

Hand over to the Tipstaff:
• Every passport relating to the child and every ID card, ticket, travel warrant or other document enabling the child to leave E&W • Every passport relating to the respondent and every ID card, ticket, travel warrant or other document enabling the respondent to leave E&W
Must not:
• remove or knowingly cause or permit the removal of the child from the jurisdiction • (a) make any application for, (b) obtain, seek to obtain or (c) knowingly cause, permit, encourage or support any steps to obtain any passport, ID card, ticket, travel warrant or other document enabling the respondent or child to leave E&W
Must:
• Inform the Tipstaff of the address of the place at which the child resides in E&W, if known to him/her

12.16 Any travel documents seized will be kept in the Tipstaff's office in the Royal Courts of Justice, unless and until a court directs that they be released to the respondent or to one of the parties' respective solicitors to be held to the order of the court.

12.17 It is often overlooked, but a passport order can play a role in locating a child in addition to ensuring they cannot leave the jurisdiction, as the respondent or any person served with the order is required to reveal the address of the place at which the child resides in the jurisdiction if it is known to them. This obligation is not as wide-ranging as the equivalent obligation contained in a location order, but is nonetheless a useful tool. In a case where, for example, a child is suspected to be residing at a relative's address, a passport order may be sufficient to prevent further removal from the jurisdiction and confirmation of the address.

12 FPR 2010, PD 12F, para 4.6.

12.18 As noted in the graphic above, location orders and collection orders include passport orders; it is wrong in principle to make an application for both.

Location orders

12.19 A location order includes all of the provisions of a passport order (see paras **12.8** and **12.15** above), but imposes further obligations on the respondent or any person served with the order to assist the Tipstaff in locating the subject child:

Must immediately inform the Tipstaff of:

- The whereabouts of the child and of the place at which the child resides within E&W, if known to him/her
- All matters within their knowledge or understanding which might reasonably assist him to locate the child

Must not:

- Cause or permit the child to stay overnight at an address other than that at which they have been located

12.20 The location order is therefore the best tool for practitioners to locate a child whose whereabouts are entirely unknown; the Tipstaff can require any third party served with the order to disclose anything in their knowledge or understanding which may assist with locating the child. Munby J said this in *Re S (Ex Parte Orders)*[13]:

> 'In appropriate cases he may even be empowered to enter private property, if need be using force, for the purpose of searching for a missing child and, if the child cannot be found, removing and taking into custody anything which may throw light on the missing child's whereabouts.'

12.21 In practical terms, a location order will often be used in combination with disclosure orders against third parties (see paras **12.26–12.35** below). Typically, in the first instance, such orders may be made against public bodies; these may provide the Tipstaff with information to assist him in the search for a child[14].

Collection orders

12.22 A collection order includes the provisions of a passport order and a location order, but additionally contains directions to the respondent and

13 *Re S (A Child) (Family Division: Without Notice Orders)* [2001] 1 WLR 211, [2001] 1 FLR 308 at 320, referred to by Munby LJ in *PM v KH* [2010] EWHC 870 (Fam), [2010] 2 FCR 639, [2010] 2 FLR 1057 at para 38.

14 See Munby LJ at paras 36–38 in *PM v KH* [2010] EWHC 870 (Fam), [2010] 2 FCR 639, [2010] 2 FLR 1057.

Tipstaff which represent the most serious of the court's powers available in these circumstances:

The children must be:

- placed into the care of the applicant / accommodated by the appropriate local authority

The Tipstaff shall:

- take charge of the children as soon as practicable
- enter by force to search premises if necessary (a) if he suspects the child/respondent is/are present and (b) if he is unable to secure permission to enter

12.23 The collection order therefore has three inter-connected features:

12.24 When is a collection order appropriate, as opposed to a location order or a passport order? Collection orders are draconian as they involve the separation of a child from a parent and potentially temporary placement into local authority care. In *Re A (A Child)*[15] the President found that, whilst the first instance judge did not address the point explicitly:

> '... the judge must have had in mind and weighed in the balance the fact that his order would inevitably involve, even if only for a short period, the separation of A from his father. He was, in my judgment, entitled to conclude that the risk of harm resulting from that was outweighed by the risk of harm to A which would result from a further abduction.'

15 *Re A (A Child)* [2016] EWCA Civ 572, [2016] 4 WLR 111, [2016] 3 FCR 85 at para 72.

12.25 Some examples of cases in which a collection order has been granted are set out in the following table[16]:

PM v KH & Another	*Re A (A Child)*	*Bedford BC v Moutiq*
• Long proceedings before Munby J, who became Munby LJ • F removed adult lacking capacity from the UK to Israel in breach of a number of orders • Substantial psychiatric and social work evidence in the case • A collection order was made in case F tried to re-enter the jurisdiction clandestinely (para 24(v))	• In parties' home country of Sweden there had been social services' involvement due to domestic violence against the mother • F abducted the children to avoid Swedish police. He travelled via Malaysia, Morocco, Egypt, Germany and the UK • A collection order was made on account of the risk to the children posed by F and of the 'high flight risk' of F • Although the order was upheld on appeal, criticism was made of the unparticularised evidence	• Grave concerns about the welfare of the child (aged 3) • The court made an emergency protection order (EPO) and recovery order in care proceedings • The EPO and recovery order failed • A collection order was made

Thus it can be seen that, save in extreme circumstances whereby the subject child is (a) at risk of harm in the abductor's care and/or (b) there is a high flight risk, a collection order is unlikely to be an appropriate order to seek. A collection order must be justified by particularised evidence.

C. DISCLOSURE ORDERS AGAINST THIRD PARTIES

12.26 The Family Court has a statutory power to make orders directed to third parties who, there is reason to believe, may be able to provide information which may lead to the location of a missing child (see Family Law Act 1986, s 33 or Children Act 1989, s 50). The High Court has an inherent jurisdiction to make such orders which are invaluable for practitioners seeking to locate a missing child. The following are key features of disclosure orders made in the High Court[17]:

16 *PM v KH* [2010] EWHC 870 (Fam), [2010] 2 FCR 639, [2010] 2 FLR 1057; *Re A (A Child)* [2016] EWCA Civ 572, [2016] 4 WLR 111, [2016] 3 FCR 85; *Bedford Borough Council v Sarah Moutiq, A, I (A Minor) (by his Children's Guardian)* [2017] EWFC 22.

17 See Munby LJ at paras 36–38 in *PM v KH* [2010] EWHC 870 (Fam), [2010] 2 FCR 639, [2010] 2 FLR 1057.

12.27 The court's inherent jurisdiction to make disclosure orders against third parties in abduction proceedings is not limited by the principles derived from *Norwich Pharmacal Co v Customs and Excise Commissioners*[18]. This means that there is no need to establish that the third party against whom disclosure is sought has been involved in the abducting parent's wrongdoing, innocently or otherwise. It is sufficient that the third party may have information which could lead to the location of the missing child, acquired by whatever means[19].

Public bodies or corporate entities

12.28 As it is a feature of these orders that the applicant does not wish to 'tip off' the respondent parent while trying to ascertain the location of the child, orders for disclosure are normally first made against public bodies are opposed to third parties with a personal connection with the respondent (eg a parent, sibling, work colleague etc). It is usual to apply for orders against relatives or friends as a 'last resort' if orders against official bodies have proved fruitless. A degree of lateral thinking, depending on the facts of any particular case, may be required when considering the appropriate target of an order for disclosure, but some

18 *Norwich Pharmacal Co and Others v Customs and Excise Commissioners* [1974] AC 133.
19 See Munby LJ at para 38 in *PM v KH* [2010] EWHC 870 (Fam), [2010] 2 FCR 639, [2010] 2 FLR 1057 in which he refers to the case of *Ramsbotham v Senior* (1869) LR 8 Eq 575.

of the more ordinary targets (both public bodies and non-public bodies) are as follows:

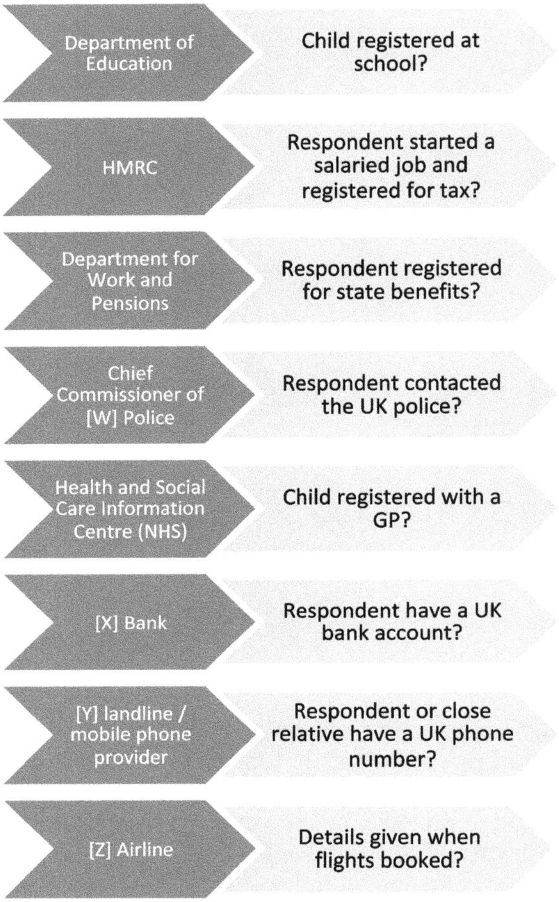

12.29 The possibilities are numerous. Careful thought needs to be given to the wording of any particular order and there are standardised draft disclosure orders[20] which assist in this regard, but each should be tailored to the specific third party so as to obtain the most information that may assist in locating the respondent or child.

12.30 Take, for example, an order against a bank. There is little point in seeking merely account numbers in the respondent's name; that would inevitably require a follow-up order to obtain more information. Far more useful in the first disclosure order would be to ask for the following:

20 HMCTS Compendium of Standard Orders, Volume 2, Draft Orders 13.1 to 13.4.

12.31 Another example is an order against a mobile phone provider. Nowadays, these providers often hold a huge amount of data on each particular user. The following graphic shows a selection of the orders which could be sought, although it may be that the court will not grant all of them in the first instance:

12.32 In practical terms, it is important to recognise that a court at a first hearing will not be likely to sanction a fishing expedition and grant an infinite raft of orders for disclosure against third parties, the costs of which are to be borne by the applicant's public funding certificate. It is tentatively suggested that, in an 'ordinary' case, a practitioner might be best advised to pick the strongest two or three targets at the first hearing. If they prove fruitless, at the return date further orders can be sought.

Other third parties

12.33 If more official avenues of disclosure have failed to locate the child, consideration can be given to involving any third parties who may have information. As above, the real fear in these circumstances can be that a friend or family member might tip off the respondent (in breach of an order) leading to the further abduction of the child. The threat of committing that person to prison for breach of the order will be scant consolation to the applicant if the child has left the jurisdiction.

12.34 In some cases, it can be appropriate to direct disclosure from a friend, relative, associate etc of the respondent. The court may require the attendance of that person at court to give oral evidence or provide relevant information. Compliance with these orders can be enforced, insofar as possible, with a penal notice on the face of the order. If the third party does not attend, or does not comply with the order for disclosure, a bench warrant can be issued for the arrest and compulsory production in court of the defaulting person[21]. Before ordering a person to attend court, it may be appropriate to obtain orders for the disclosure of their phone records so that they can be questioned about calls made to and from their phone.

Drafting of disclosure orders: undertakings and use of the information

12.35 A disclosure order must include certain undertakings given by the applicant (often given through their solicitor) and paragraphs in the order relating to the use and dissemination of any information obtained pursuant to the disclosure order.

Undertakings given by the applicant

- To indemnify the person / body for any reasonable costs incurred in complying with the order
- To use any info obtained under the order for no purpose other than to locate the parent and child
- Not to disclose any address / info obtained under the order to any third parties without the court's permission

Orders

- The person / body is prohibited from informing the respondent of the order
- Permission to the applicant to withhold service on the respondent
- Applicant's solicitors must not disclose any info obtained to the respondent, without the court's permission

D. PREVENTING FURTHER ABDUCTION OF A CHILD FROM THE JURISDICTION

12.36 In all cases involving an alleged abduction of a child, the court will want to ensure that the alleged abductor cannot take steps to remove the child from the jurisdiction pending the determination of the proceedings. There are several options:

21 See Munby LJ at para 36 in *PM v KH* [2010] EWHC 870 (Fam), [2010] Fam Law 935, [2010] 2 FCR 639, [2010] 2 FLR 1057.

Police assistance

- The police can issue a port alert without a court order if there is a 'real and imminent threat' that a child is about to be removed unlawfully from the country
- This request for assistance should be made with as much information as possible to maximise the chance of success
- See Family Procedure Rules 2010, PD 12F, Part 4 for full details

Passport Office

- If served with an order prohibiting the issue of any further UK passport for a named respondent and/or a child

Tipstaff orders: Passport, location and collection orders

- Each involves the removal and retention of passports and travel documentation by Tipstaff
- Each involves a prohibition against applying for / acquiring new travel documentation
- Each includes a port alert
- Each includes a prohibition against removing the child from the jurisdiction

Prohibited steps order or 'stay put' order

- Can prohibit removal of the child from the jurisdiction by either party

12.37 The most effective way of preventing the further abduction is to obtain a Tipstaff order: these require the removal from the respondent of all travel documents, prohibit any application for new travel documents, and mandate the Tipstaff to issue a port alert. It is, however, advisable when seeking a Tipstaff order expressly to ask the court to direct the initiation of a port alert by the Tipstaff on the grounds that the threat of further abduction is 'real' and 'imminent'; anecdotally, it is understood that the Tipstaff does not always initiate the port alert unless this is specifically raised.

12.38 At each subsequent hearing, the order should include two paragraphs that explicitly continue the operation of any port alert and passport order granted under any previous Tipstaff order[22]:

> '1. All passports, identity cards and/or travel documents currently held by the Tipstaff pursuant to the [passport / location / collection order] directed to the Tipstaff and issued on [date] in respect of [full names] do continue to be held by the Tipstaff until the conclusion of the

22 Revised wording sent by the Tipstaff's office on 7 February 2020, so as to ensure compliance with the Data Protection Act 2018, incorporating the General Data Protection Regulation (EU) 2016/679.

hearing on [date], at which the court will make further directions as to their continued retention or return.

2. The port alerts currently in place pursuant to the [passport /location/ collection order] directed to the Tipstaff and issued on [date] in respect of [names] do continue until the next hearing, at which the court will make further directions as to their continuance or discharge.'

12.39 In the event that a Tipstaff order has not been made, it is sensible to obtain at the very least a prohibited steps order (or an equivalent 'stay put' order under the inherent jurisdiction[23]) preventing removal of the child from the jurisdiction by either party pending final determination of the application by the court. Of course, whilst this order may be a deterrent and any penal notice attaching to it an even greater deterrent, it will not of itself put in place a practical barrier to a party physically removing a child from the jurisdiction absent a port alert or any other provision.

12.40 In a case where there is to be contact between one party and the child pending determination of the substantive proceedings but there is a risk of that parent abducting that child from the jurisdiction, the court has the power to order that party to be made subject to electronic tagging while spending time with the child. It is unlikely that such an order would be made in the absence of a proven risk of further abduction. The mechanism by which such an order may be made was discussed in *Re A (A Child) (Family Proceedings: Electronic Tagging)*[24] and there is now a standardised version of such an order, with a list of the information required as a schedule to the order[25].

23 A prohibited steps order is an order made under Children Act 1989, s 8; the same order can be made in abduction proceedings under the inherent jurisdiction of the court or pursuant to Child Abduction and Custody Act 1985, s 5.

24 *Re A (A Child) (Family Proceedings: Electronic Tagging)* [2009] EWHC 710 (Fam), [2009] Fam Law 482, [2009] 2 FLR 891.

25 HMCTS Compendium of Standard Orders, Volume 2, Draft Order 13.19.

CHAPTER 13

Enforcement of return orders

Content at a Glance:

A. INTRODUCTION

13.1 Where an order has been made for a child to be returned to an overseas jurisdiction at the conclusion of proceedings, as discussed in the preceding chapters of this book, enforcing that order can be problematic. This chapter addresses the principles and practical considerations surrounding the enforcement of that return order.

The Special Commission and the European Court of Human Rights

13.2 Considerable attention has been paid to the issue of swift enforcement of return orders in international guidance, most notably by the Special Commission established to review the operation of the 1980 Hague Convention[1] ('HC80').

1 The 1980 Convention on the Civil Aspects of International Child Abduction.

Fourth Review Special Commission – March 2001[2]

> '3.9 Delays in enforcement of return orders, or their non-enforcement, in certain Contracting States are matters of serious concern. The Special Commission calls upon Contracting States to enforce return orders promptly and effectively.
>
> 3.10 It should be made possible for courts, when making return orders, to include provisions to ensure that the order leads to the prompt and effective return of the child.
>
> 3.11 Efforts should be made by Central Authorities, or by other competent authorities, to track the outcome of return orders and to determine in each case whether enforcement is delayed or not achieved.'

13.3 In a number of decisions, the European Court of Human Rights has found that a Contracting State to the European Convention on Human Rights ('ECHR'), which is also a Contracting State to HC80, has failed in its positive obligation to take adequate, effective and sufficiently prompt measures to implement an order for the return of a child under HC80. This has led to a breach of the applicant parent's rights under the ECHR[3].

Case Summary: *Kaminska v Poland*[4]

Facts:

The child, A, was habitually resident in Ireland, where M lived. At the conclusion of an agreed holiday to Poland, F retained A.

2 Conclusions and Recommendations of the Fourth Meeting of the Special Commission to Review the Operation of the Hague Child Abduction Convention (22–28 March 2001). See also the preliminary document for the Fifth Review of the Special Commission in November 2006, titled 'Enforcement of Orders Made Under the 1980 Convention – Towards Principles of Good Practice' available at www.hcch.net.

3 See *Shaw v Hungary*, No 6457/09, [2012] 2 FLR 1314, for a review of the authorities; and more recently: *GN v Poland*, No 2171-14, (2016) ECHR 667; and *Kaminska v Poland*, No 28481/12, (2018) ECHR 70.

4 No 28481/12, (2018) ECHR 70.

The Irish court determined that A should live with M, ordered A's return to Ireland and issued a certificate under Art 42 of Brussels IIA[5] (annexe IV)[6].

After four years of proceedings in Ireland and Poland, A had not been returned. Eventually, M located A and travelled back to Ireland. M complained to the European Court of Human Rights that her rights under Arts 6 and 8 of ECHR had been breached by the Polish courts' failure to take all measures reasonably expected of them to enforce the Irish return orders.

Held by the European Court of Human Rights:

- Art 8 includes a parent's right to have measures taken with a view to being reunited with his or her child and an obligation on the national authorities to take such measures (para 83).
- The positive obligations imposed by Art 8 on the State must be interpreted in the light of HC80 (para 84).
- In cases of this kind, the adequacy of a measure is to be judged by the swiftness of its implementation (para 85).
- The Polish authorities failed to act swiftly to enforce the Irish judgments. The length of the proceedings did not result solely from the complexity of the case. The domestic courts issued contradictory decisions. The mother's Art 8 rights had been violated and she was awarded damages.

Practical issues

13.4 Despite the extent and clarity of the authorities above, which demand a swift implementation of an order for a child's return, there are numerous examples in domestic case-law of practical problems which have been and might be encountered in enforcing a return order, some of which ultimately resulted in a child remaining in this jurisdiction. This graphic is by no means a complete list of the potential problems which can occur[7].

5 Council Regulation (EC) No 2201/2003 of 27 November 2003 concerning jurisdiction and the recognition and enforcement of judgments in matrimonial matters and the matters of parental responsibility, repealing Regulation (EC) No 1347/2000.

6 A certificate of enforceability issued by the court of the Member State of the EU that has ordered the return of the child, in accordance with Art 42(1) BIIA.

7 Child misbehaving on a plane: *Re M (a Minor) (Child Abduction)* [1994] 2 FCR 750, [2014] 1 FLR 390; Entrenched views of 15-year-old: *Re C (Abduction: Setting Aside Return Order: Remission)* [2012] EWCA Civ 1144, [2013] 1 FLR 403; Children lock themselves in bathroom: *Re B (Children) (Abduction: New Evidence)* [2001] EWCA Civ 625, [2001] 2 FCR 531; Abductor refuses to co-operate and/or encourages the child to be obstructive: *Cambra v Jones* [2014] EWHC 2264 (Fam).

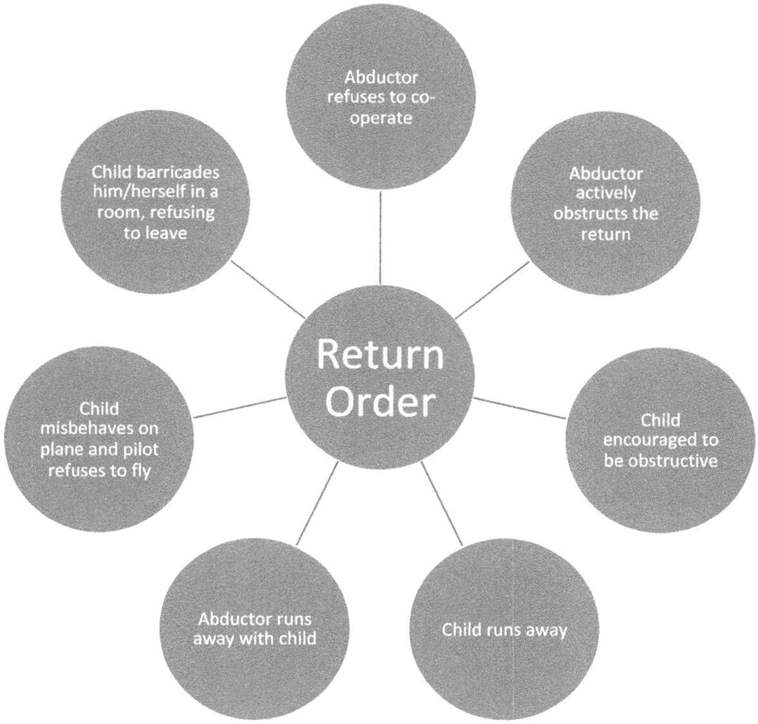

13.5 There is a significant tension between the court's positive obligation in principle to take all adequate, effective and sufficiently prompt measures to implement an order for the return of a child, and the practical difficulties inherent in ensuring a child's physical return to another jurisdiction.

B. DRAFTING OF THE RETURN ORDER

13.6 It is essential that the order for a return of the child to another jurisdiction is properly drafted. The same can be said for any subsequent orders implementing the return order, or imposing any mechanism for that return. Why? Because, in the event that a party needs to take steps to enforce that order (eg by way of committal proceedings, which are discussed below), the wording of the order must be clear and its meaning not open to alternative interpretation by a litigant seeking to escape the enforcement proceedings.

13.7 Three important principles emerge from the case of *The Solicitor General v Jones*[8] which are essential to note with regard to any prospective committal proceedings:

A mandatory order must specify a time for compliance:
eg the mother must return the child to the jurisdiction of Poland by [Time] on [Date]

Implied terms cannot be read into an order

An injunction must be drafted in clear, precise and unambiguous terms

Mechanics of the return

13.8 The court has the power to give any precise directions needed as to how a return order should be implemented, which will depend on the facts of any particular case. Therefore, proper thought should be given at the time of drafting to the mechanics by which a return order is to take effect, to minimise the need to come back to court to re-define the order before enforcement proceedings can be initiated. In general, the more specificity in the drafting, the better for enforcement.

13.9 Broadly, the mechanics of the return involves consideration of five inter-related issues as part of the drafting of an order:

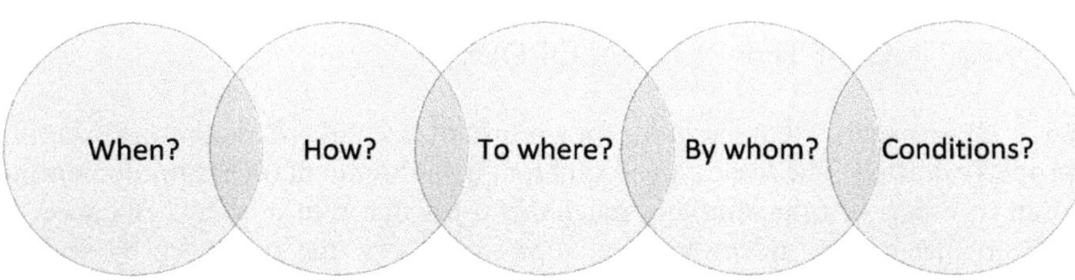

13.10 As a bare minimum, the return order must provide for a time (specify the time zone) and a date by which the child must have been returned to the relevant jurisdiction. As indicated in para **13.7** above, it is essential – if one wishes to enforce a mandatory order – that it contains a time by which the specified act must be done. There is a temptation amongst practitioners to draft an order providing that a child should be returned simply 'forthwith'. This should be resisted, as it is unlikely to be sufficient for any future enforcement proceedings.

> Example wording:
>
> 'The child, [name & d.o.b.], shall be returned to the jurisdiction of Italy by no later than 4pm (GMT) on Friday 13 December 2019 by [name].'

13.11 The need and extent to which the practitioner should consider including in any order the specific mechanics of how the return is to be effected is case-dependent. In some cases, it may be enough only to specify the time, date and person effecting the return. In others, it may be necessary to draft more detailed provisions. It is worth considering the following non-exhaustive list:

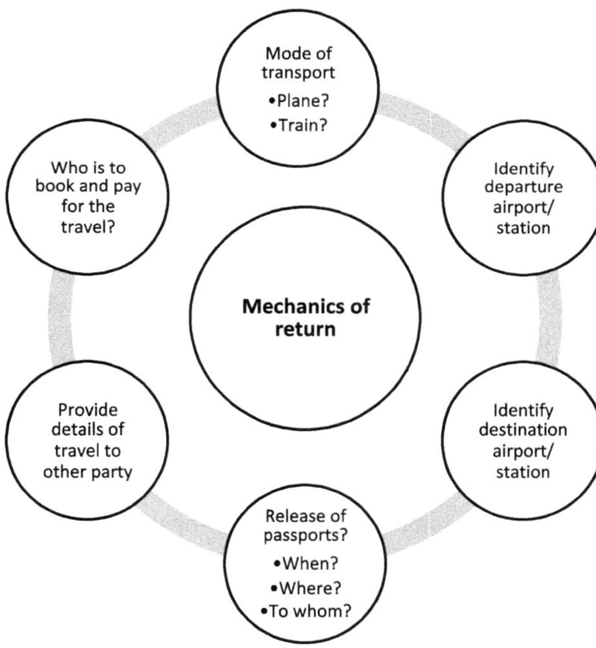

13.12 It can be seen from the graphic above that the question of 'how' a child is to be returned to another jurisdiction depends in part on the additional questions of 'to where' and 'by whom'.

To where and by whom?

13.13 The answer to these questions depends on the facts of the case. If the abducting parent is saying that he/she will not return *to live* in the jurisdiction from which he/she has abducted the child, the court does not have the power to order the abducting party to do so, although it may have the power to order the abductor to *accompany* the child on the return journey. The following graphic summarises the options available to the court:

Abductor to return the child to the other jurisdiction

Abductor to accompany the child on the return journey and hand over the child at the other end:
- handover location?
- how is handover time to be ascertained?

Abductor to deliver up the child at a time/place in the UK to enable the other parent to accompany the child on the return journey:
- To the Tipstaff (collection order) or the other parent

Conditions precedent on the return?

13.14 As has been discussed in **Chapter 6** of this book[9], the court may require additional measures to be put in place which relate to the mechanics of the abducting parent's return to the foreign jurisdiction. The most obvious and common example of this is the imposition of 'soft landing' provisions or measures imposed to avoid the risk of the child being exposed to a grave risk of harm under Art 13(b) of HC80. With an eye on any future proceedings to enforce the return order, consideration needs to be given as to how these additional provisions are drafted in the order; will they be conditions precedent to the return order taking effect, or not?

13.15 The following graphic illustrates some of the considerations that may arise in relation to the common requirement that the applicant parent is to provide suitable accommodation in the overseas jurisdiction in which the respondent and child can live on their return to that jurisdiction:

9 See also para **10.31** onwards above for protective measures under HC96.

Applicant to provide suitable accommodation for the respondent and child in the overseas jurisdiction:

1. Drafted as a "condition precedent" to the return order

- The respondent's compliance with the order to return is dependent on the applicant evidencing that he/she has secured the suitable accommodation
- If the applicant does not / subsequently cannot arrange the accommodation, a further application will have to be made to discharge/vary the condition before an application to enforce the return order can be made.

2. Not drafted as a condition

- Freestanding return order remains enforceable
- The applicant's failure to evidence the suitable accommodation <u>may</u> be a valid defence to any enforcement application
- Respondent may be left trying to enforce this order in the courts of the overseas jurisdiction.

13.16 Depending, therefore, on whether one represents the applicant or respondent, there can be a real benefit to either party in ensuring the order is drafted in a particular way.

Penal notice

13.17 In order to enforce an order by way of committal proceedings, there must be a valid penal notice on the **front** of the order[10]. The standardised precedent draft orders all comply with this and should be followed in this regard. The example wording given is as follows:

> **IMPORTANT WARNING TO [RESPONDENT NAME] OF [ADDRESS]**
>
> If you [RESPONDENT NAME] do not comply with this order you may be held to be in contempt of court and imprisoned or fined, or your assets may be seized
>
> If any other person who knows of this order and does anything which helps or permits you [RESPONDENT NAME] to breach the terms of this order they may be held to be in contempt of court and may be imprisoned, fined or have their assets seized

10 FPR 2010, r 17.9(1) and *Re DAD (Application to commit Muhammad Nawaz Chaudhry)* [2015] EWHC 2655 (Fam).

C. ENFORCEMENT OPTIONS

13.18 The appropriate steps to enforce an order to return will depend on the facts and the circumstances of any particular case. This graphic shows the available options:

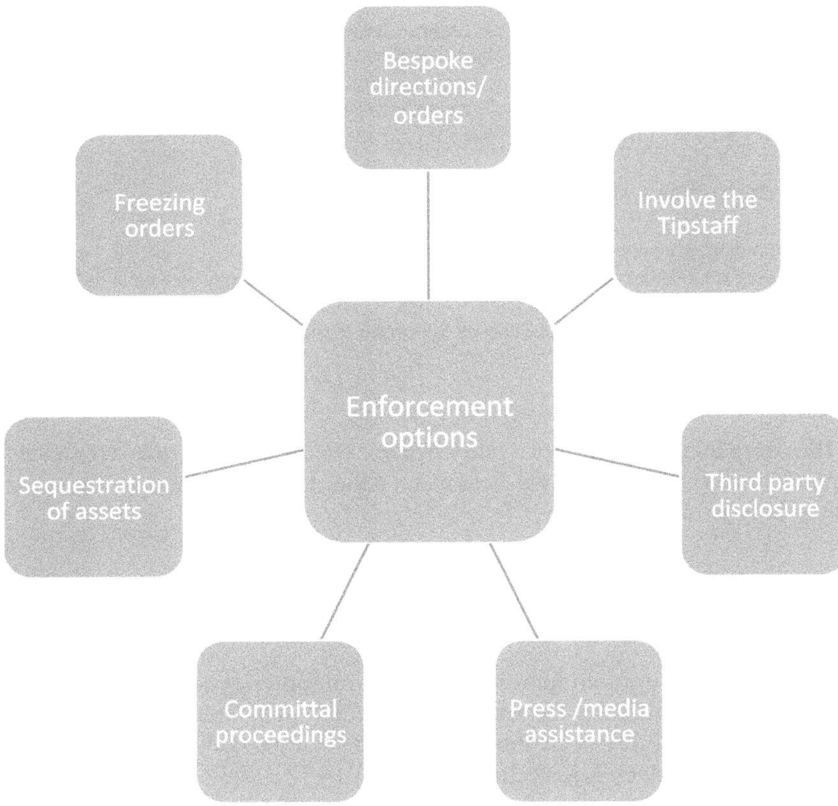

Further bespoke directions and/or orders

13.19 In practice, it is most likely that the first step towards enforcing an order will be to restore the matter before a judge of the High Court to seek orders either to define further the orders already made, or to obtain new orders to address any problems or circumstances which have arisen and which are preventing the return order being put into effect. Examples of such orders are those set out in paras **13.8–13.16** above.

Tipstaff orders and third party disclosure orders

13.20 If, on the making of a return order, the child has disappeared (whether with or without the assistance of the abductor), the court will need to locate the child and effect the return order. The options available to the court when trying to locate a child are discussed in **Chapter 12** and apply equally here, in particular the use of Tipstaff orders[11] and orders against third parties to disclose the whereabouts of the child and/or abductor[12].

13.21 In circumstances where the abductor is refusing to hand over the child or deliver up the child to the respondent, in breach of the court order, the court may make a collection order and directions to the Tipstaff to enforce that order. Collection orders are discussed more fully in **Chapter 12**[13], but include the following elements:

<u>Collection Order includes:</u>

Passport order

Location order

Child must be delivered into the care of the local authority or other named person

- Tipstaff must take charge of the child as soon as practicable
- Tipstaff may enter premises by force if necessary and search them for the child and/or information relating to the child's whereabouts

Press assistance

13.22 In a case where locating the child is particularly difficult, the court may seek assistance from the media or press in an attempt to obtain information as to the child's whereabouts. An example of this being used in practice was in the *Cambra v Jones* litigation, discussed at para **13.26** below, in which Roderic Wood J made a short statement to the press asking for assistance in locating the children and released a number of photographs[14]. Following extensive media coverage the respondent mother, her partner and the children were located. The mother and her partner were arrested and the children placed with local authority foster carers, the court having made a collection order. A more recent example is that of *Uhd v McKay*[15], in which Keehan J ordered that certain details of the case could be published in the media to assist with locating the child – for example, that the mother was thought to be in a camper van in the Outer Hebrides.

11 See paras **12.6–12.10** above.
12 See paras **12.26–12.35** above.
13 See paras **12.22–12.25** above.
14 *Cambra v Jones* [2013] EWHC 88 (Fam), [2014] 1 FLR 5 per Theis J at para 19.
15 [2019] EWHC 1239 (Fam), [2019] 2 FLR 1159.

Committal proceedings

13.23 As will be clear from what has already been set out in this chapter, it will sometimes be appropriate or necessary to seek to enforce a return order by way of an application to commit to prison the respondent or, indeed, a third party who has failed to comply with orders to disclose the whereabouts of the child[16].

13.24 The relevant rules applicable to committal proceedings are contained in Part 37 of the Family Procedure Rules 2010 ('FPR 2010') and the accompanying Practice Direction 37A. It is important to note that, whilst the court technically has the power to waive *some* of the formal procedural requirements by virtue of para 13.2 of PD 37A, it is absolutely essential that an applicant makes every attempt to comply with the procedural rules governing such an application[17].

13.25 This chapter does not provide a comprehensive analysis of the topic of committal, but the following diagram shows a chronological checklist of the most important procedural requirements which should be followed in all committal proceedings[18]:

16 See, for an example of this, *Egeneonu v Egeneonu* [2018] EWHC 3029 (Fam), [2019] 1 FCR 285, Cobb J.

17 *Re L (A Child)* [2016] EWCA Civ 173, [2017] 1 FLR 1135, CA; *H v T (Committal Appeal: Notices on Orders)* [2018] EWHC 1310 (Fam), [2018] 4 WLR 122, [2019] 1 FLR 700, Baker J; *Re H* [2018] EWHC 3761 (Fam), [2019] 4 WLR 18, [2019] 1 FCR 641, Mostyn J.

18 See the conclusion of the judgment in *Re L (A Child)* [2017] 1 FLR 1135, CA, and the cases listed in footnotes 16 and 17 above.

Contempt for breach of a court order

Has the order got a penal notice prominently displayed on its face? (FPR 2010, r 37.9)

Has the order been served on the respondent? (FPR 2010, r 37.5)

- Must be personally served (FPR 2010, r 37.6)
- Unless the court has dispensed with personal service (FPR 2010, r 37.8)

The committal application is made under the procedure prescribed by FPR 2010, Part 18

The application notice must (FPR 2010, r 37.10):

- Set out in full, separately and numerically the grounds of each alleged contempt
- Be accompanied by affidavit evidence
- Contain a notice about the consequences of a commital order (FPR 2010, PD 37A, para 10.2)

Have the application notice, affidavit evidence and notice of hearing been served on the respondent?

- Must be personally served (FPR 2010, r 37.10(4))
- Unless the court dispenses with personal service (FPR 2010, r 37.10(5))

Has the respondent been given the opportunity to secure legal representation?

- The respondent must be made aware of the availability of criminal legal aid (FPR 2010, PD 37A, para 12.5)

The hearing (no less than 14 days after service of the application - FPR 2010, PD 37A, para 12.2)

- Respondent cannot be compelled to give evidence
- Respondent must be warned about self-incrimination

A finding of any breach of the order must meet the criminal standard of proof (beyond all reasonable doubt)

The committal order must set out what findings have been made

13.26 The need to prove to the criminal standard that the respondent is in breach of the order to return the children can be very difficult in circumstances where the children are taking active steps to thwart the implementation of the order[19], as shown by this example:

Case Summary: *Cambra v Jones*[20]

Facts:

These were long-running child abduction proceedings. In October 2012, Hedley J ordered M to return five children to Spain. The oldest returned. M fled with the children (within the UK). She was located and the two younger children returned. The remaining two children (aged 15 and 13) refused to return.

The Solicitor General brought an initial committal application against M, following a failure to return them. The committal failed (*Solicitor General v JMJ (Contempt)*[21]), but the court made a further order requiring M to deliver up the children and return them to Spain (*Re Jones (No 2)*[22]).

They were not returned. F issued an application for committal against M.

Held by Sir James Munby, P:

- At a previous hearing before Theis J in November 2012:
  - The children were 'emphatic' and 'resolute' in their 'steadfastly' held view that there was no way they were going back to Spain.
  - The younger child had said 'you'd have to tie me up; you'd have to drug me'.
  - The experienced Cafcass High Court guardian had commented that their resistance was 'exceptional'.
- In 2012 and 2013, M had expressly said to the court that she would not accompany the children on a return and would not take any steps to comply with an order requiring her to encourage them to return.
- The judge found M to have engaged in a '*concerted campaign ... over a number of years to thwart and undermine the legitimate orders made ...*'
- M's defence to the committal application was that it was '*impossible*' to compel the children to return to Spain and that, as such, she was not in contempt.

19 In *Re M (a Minor) (Child Abduction)* [1994] 1 FLR 390, CA, the child's behaviour resulted in the aeroplane turning around on the runway and the pilot refusing to fly with the child on board. See also *Re C (Abduction: Setting Aside Return Order: Remission)* [2013] 1 FLR 403, CA, and *Cambra v Jones* [2014] EWHC 2264 (Fam), Sir James Munby, P.

20 [2014] EWHC 2264 (Fam).

21 [2013] EWHC 2579 (Fam), [2014] 2 FCR 354, [2014] 1 FLR 852.

22 [2013 EWHC 2730 (Fam).

- As a matter of law, it was for F to disprove this assertion to the criminal standard of proof, and not incumbent on M to prove it:

  '... before finding the defendant guilty of contempt the judge must be sure (a) that the defendant has not done what he was required to do and (b) that it was within the power of the defendant to do it.'

- The '*question of impossibility has to be determined by reference to the state of affairs as at the date fixed by the order for compliance ...*'
- Thus, whilst M had not made any positive attempts to comply with the order, F could not prove to the criminal standard (after hearing the oral evidence, including that of the oldest of the children in question) that it was possible for M to have returned the children to Spain.

The Court of Appeal dismissed F's appeal: *Cambra v Jones*[23].

13.27 If the court does commit the respondent to prison, it is important to have an eye on the potential need to commit him/her to prison again in the future for continued breach of the order to return the children (or, indeed, any other mandatory order). To this end, it is essential to remember to ask the court to make a fresh mandatory order with a new date in the future by which the respondent must comply. It is not possible to commit a respondent twice for breach of the same order, but it is possible to commit a respondent multiple times for repeated breaches of further orders, even if their terms are identical to those of which the respondent has been found in breach previously[24].

13.28

Case Summary: *Borg v El Zubaidy*[25]

Facts:

F had been ordered to return or cause the return of his two children from Libya, where he had left them. He failed to do so. M applied to commit him for breach of the return order (amongst other orders).

F argued that he could not contact the children and could not cause their return to England. He was found in contempt of a number of orders, including the order to return the children, by Moor J, who sentenced him to 9 months' imprisonment[26].

23 [2015] EWCA Civ 1019, [2016] 2 FCR 48, [2016] 2 FLR 1207.
24 *Wilkinson v Anjum* [2011] EWCA Civ 1196, [2012] 1 WLR 1036.
25 [2018] EWHC 432 (Fam).
26 [2017] EWFC 58.

Moor J made a further order that the children be returned from Libya and repeated other directions. F remained in breach. M applied to commit F a second time.

Held by Mostyn J:

- Found to the criminal standard that F was in contempt of court.
- 'It is established by … *Wilkinson v Anjum*[27] that it is not illegitimate or contrary to principle for a father who has already served a sentence for breach of an order requiring him to cause the return of children to the jurisdiction to be re-committed for breach of a later order seeking the same end, namely, the return of the children to the jurisdiction. To re-commit on a newer order does not involve a breach of the principle of double jeopardy; however, a time arises … when the court will eventually say that enough is enough' (para 16).
- Cited *Button v Salama*[28], in which the father had been repeatedly re-committed and served a total of 42 months in prison.
- Sentenced F to 12 months' immediate imprisonment, noting that the second offence was, if anything, an aggravating factor with regard to sentencing.

13.29 If a respondent remains in breach of an order to return and the intention is for there to be a further application for committal without the respondent spending a period of time out of prison, it is imperative that any further application to commit the respondent is issued well in advance of the end of the initial prison term, otherwise it will not be possible to follow proper procedure in time.

Sequestration of assets

13.30 In a case where a child cannot be found and/or there is obstruction to an order to return, the court has the jurisdiction to sequester a non-compliant party's assets and, in appropriate circumstances, to direct that those assets may be used by the applicant party to fund the enforcement litigation.

27 [2011] EWCA Civ 1196, [2012] 1 WLR 1036.
28 [2013] EWHC 2972 (Fam).

Case Summary: *PM v KH*[29]

Facts:

HM was an adult who lacked capacity (thus a protected person under the FPR 2010).

There was constant litigation for years, but at various stages her father ('F') had disobeyed residence orders and removed HM to Israel and refused to return her.

Munby LJ had made innumerable orders, including (paras 24 and 30):

- orders freezing certain monies owned by F;
- orders freezing certain assets in F's name and the names of various companies;
- orders permitting the mother to use funds in one of the frozen accounts in F's name to discharge her costs of the litigation in England; and
- orders inviting the Royal Courts of Jersey to assist with freezing F's assets.

Held by Munby LJ (paras 39–40):

> '... The court can make a freezing order to restrain the abducting parent's recourse to his assets and, where the parent has acted in breach of the court's order or breach of undertaking and is thus in contempt, the court can also make a sequestration order: see the decisions of Scott Baker J ... in *Richardson v Richardson*[30] and *Mir v Mir*[31]. Moreover, the court has power to direct that the sequestered funds be used to fund litigation brought in a foreign court with a view to securing the return to this jurisdiction of the abducted child: see *Richardson v Richardson* at 102–103.
>
> In that particular case, the sequestered property was land, so one can readily understand why a writ of sequestration was thought appropriate ... I can see no reason why the same power should not equally be exercisable in relation to other assets of the abducting parent which the court has seized or taken into its control by some means other than a writ of sequestration (or a garnishee order), for example, as in the present case, by means of the freezing and other orders I made, in particular those directed to X and DP.'

29 [2010] EWHC 870 (Fam), [2010] 2 FCR 639, [2010] 2 FLR 1057.
30 [1989] Fam 95, [1990] 2 FCR 186, [1990] 1 FLR 186.
31 [1992] Fam 79, [1992] 1 FCR 227, [1992] 1 FLR 624.

Failure to enforce

13.31 In some exceptional cases, it is ultimately not possible to enforce a return order to another jurisdiction. In those cases, the court might grant an appeal against the order[32], set the order aside[33], or simply impose a stay on the order for return[34].

32 For appeals, see **Chapter 14**. See also *Re M (A Minor) (Child Abduction)* [1994] 1 FLR 390.

33 For setting aside orders, see **Chapter 14** at paras **14.76–14.80**. See also *Re W (A Child) (Return Order: Power to Set Aside)* [2018] EWCA Civ 1904, [2018] 4 WLR 149.

34 *TB v JB (Abduction: Grave Risk of Harm)* [2001] 2 FLR 515 (see editor's footnote at the conclusion of the judgment); *Cambra v Jones* [2013] EWHC 88 (Fam), [2014] 1 FLR 5.

CHAPTER 14

Procedure for appeals and setting aside orders

Content at a Glance:

A. INTRODUCTION

14.1 This chapter will consider appeals in cases heard pursuant to the 1980 Hague Convention[1] ('HC80') and the inherent jurisdiction. It will also consider applications to set aside decisions made at first instance.

The venue for appeal

14.2 As proceedings relating to the international abduction and retention of children are heard in the High Court, appeals will lie to the Court of Appeal, with a further potential opportunity to appeal to the United Kingdom Supreme Court.

The relevant rules for appeals

14.3 The procedures which apply to appeals in family proceedings apply equally to proceedings involving international child abduction. They are contained in the Civil Procedure Rules ('CPR'), the Family Procedure Rules 2010 ('FPR 2010') and their Practice Directions ('PDs').

The relevant rules are as follows:

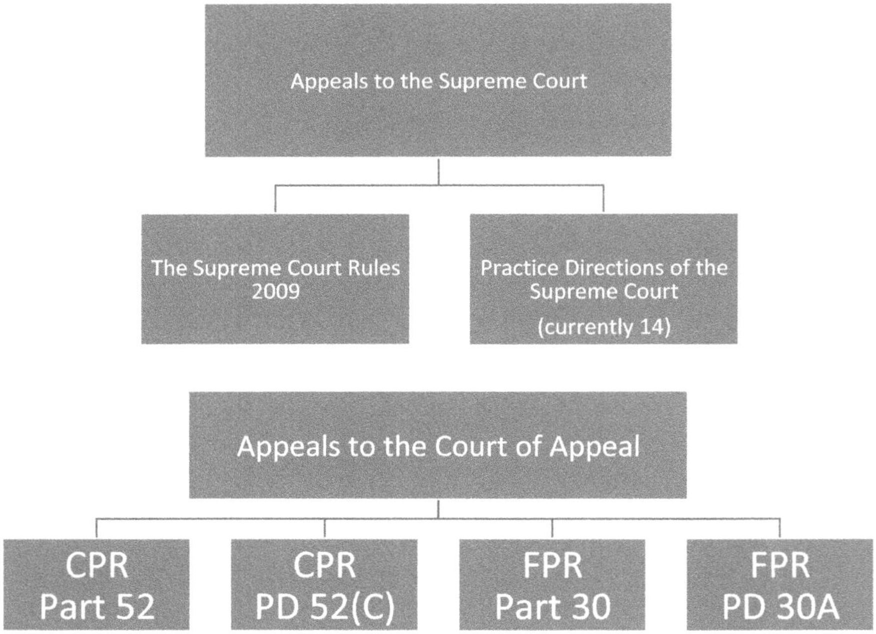

1 The 1980 Hague Convention on the Civil Aspects of International Child Abduction.

14.4 The need for expediency is crucial when dealing with an international child abduction case.

The test for permission to appeal

14.5 The test for an application for permission to appeal is the same, whether it is made to the High Court at first instance or to the Court of Appeal:

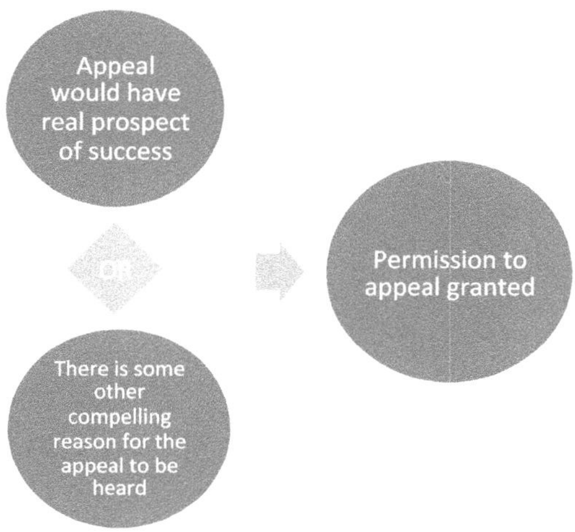

Principles particular to appeals in abduction proceedings

14.6 The most prominent feature of international cases is their urgent nature and the Convention obligations that flow from that. The two main consequences of that for appeals are:

The need to act expeditiously in seeking to appeal

The urgent need to consider whether to apply for a stay of execution of the return order

Time limits

14.7 The Court of Appeal has stressed that any appeal process must be accomplished urgently and with the Convention obligations firmly in mind.

CPR, r 52.12(2) provides a 21-day time limit from the date of the decision (*not* the order) for an appellant's notice to be filed. That general rule, applicable to all civil cases, should not be taken as the norm in child abduction proceedings.

14.8 Once a decision has been handed down, it is incumbent on the lawyers to act swiftly. The following principles should be followed:[2,3]

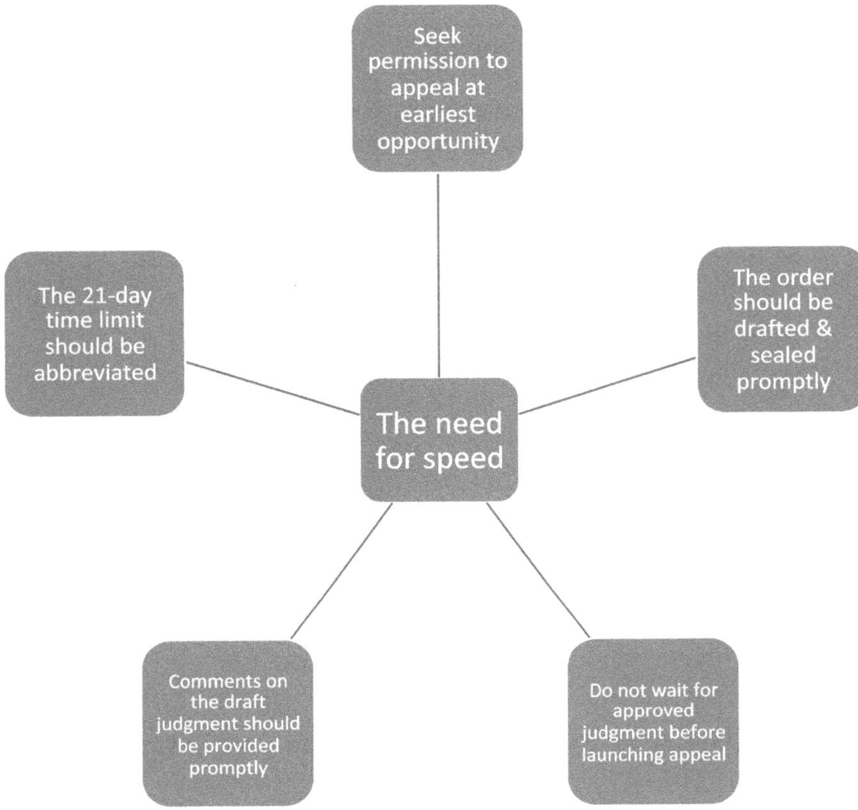

Case summary: *Klentzeris v Klentzeris*[4]

Facts:

After 5 months of living in Greece, the two children were surreptitiously removed to the UK by their elder sister and the following day joined by M. The children strongly objected to returning to Greece, with the younger child exhibiting panic attacks during the Cafcass interview. M also pleaded an Art 13(b) defence. Kirkwood J at first instance refused to return the child but granted the father permission to appeal.

2 Seal order promptly: *Re M (Abduction: Appeals)* [2007] EWCA Civ 1059, [2008] 1 FLR 699.

3 21-day limit should be abbreviated: *K v K* [2007] EWCA Civ 533, [2007] 3 FCR 580, [2007] 2 FLR 996.

4 [2007] EWCA Civ 533, [2007] 3 FCR 580, [2007] 2 FLR 996.

Held by the Court of Appeal:

The fact that the judge 'extended' F's time for lodging the notice of appeal to 21 days was criticised. That was not in fact an extension, as the CPR provided for a 21-day time limit. The CA held that a judge in every case should specifically address the minimum necessary period for the filing of the notice of the application. The court was required, pursuant to its BIIA[5] and Convention obligations, to issue its judgment no later than 6 weeks after the application is lodged. That provision clearly has most direct application to the process of trial. However, it is important that any appellate process should be completed in no less a period and, if the appellant is given 3 of the 6 weeks in which to put in the notice of appeal, the prospects of this court achieving completion within 6 weeks are heavily prejudiced. The court held that it was important that any judge dealing with an international abduction case should enquire at the conclusion whether either party wishes to appeal. If either party then makes an application, the judge should consider at once restricting the period of 21 days for lodging the notice of appeal. That period is completely inappropriate for international child cases where there is a Convention obligation to complete the case very quickly.

Applications for a stay of execution

14.9 Neither an application for permission to appeal, the grant of permission to appeal nor the listing of an appeal hearing acts as an automatic stay[6].

14.10 A stay of execution in relation to a return order must be considered and imposed, if appropriate, immediately upon the making of such an order by the first instance court, or the purpose of any appeal may well be defeated.

5 Council Regulation (EC) No 2201/2003 of 27 November 2003 concerning jurisdiction and the recognition and enforcement of judgments in matrimonial matters and the matters of parental responsibility, repealing Regulation (EC) No 1347/2000 ('BIIA').

6 CPR, r 52.16.

The cycle below will often take place within a matter of days:

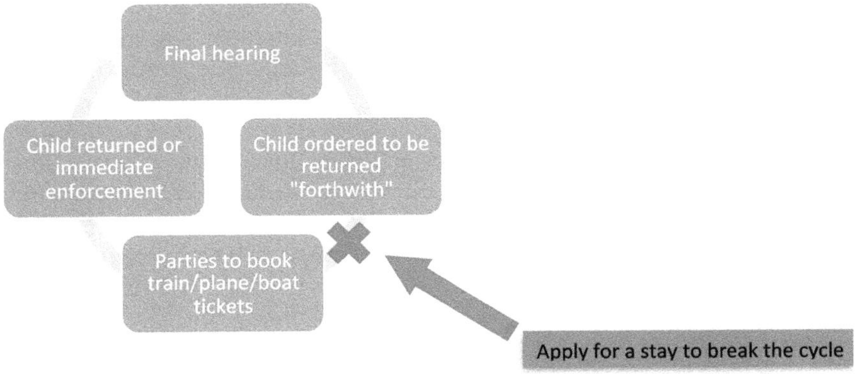

14.11 There are two opportunities to apply for a stay:

14.12 A Court of Appeal judge will ordinarily consider an application to stay, although exceptionally, when the Court of Appeal is not sitting or cannot conveniently be convened, a court officer assigned to the Civil Appeals Office who is a barrister or solicitor can order a temporary stay of execution of any order or decision of the lower court[7]. An application for a stay will usually be determined on paper, without the need for an oral hearing. For a summary of the principles relevant to an application for a stay, see *NB v Haringey LBC* [2011] EWHC 3544 (Fam), [2012] 2 FLR 125.

B. APPEAL PROCEDURE IN THE FIRST INSTANCE COURT

14.13 Permission to appeal must be obtained before an appeal can be launched[8]. As a first step, that permission *should* be sought from the court of first instance[9], orally at the hearing or later in writing.

7 CPR, r 52.24.
8 FPR 2010, PD 30A para 2.1.
9 FPR 2010, PD 30A para 4.2.

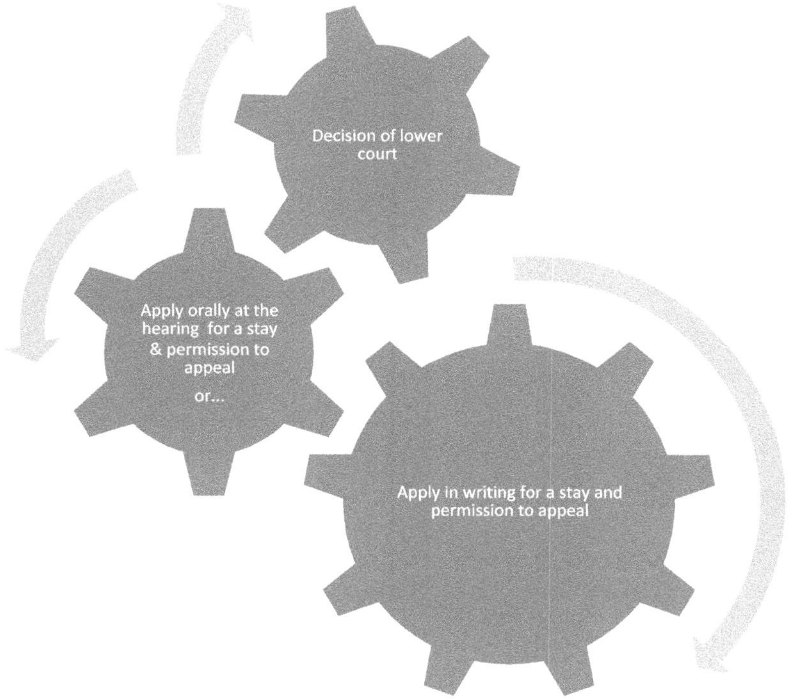

14.14 When considering whether to grant permission to appeal, the court will have to consider the test for permission to appeal[10] and, if satisfied that permission should be granted, it will make further directions.

Even if the court refuses to grant permission to appeal, it should separately consider the question of a stay, to give the appellant an opportunity to apply to the Court of Appeal for permission to appeal.

C. APPEAL PROCEDURE IN THE COURT OF APPEAL

14.15 This chapter considers the key procedural rules in relation to appeals to the Court of Appeal in international abduction cases. Not all procedures are addressed in detail; particular regard should be paid to CPR Part 52 and PD 52C.

Applications for permission to appeal

14.16 Applications to the Court of Appeal for permission to appeal are governed by CPR, r 52.5. The appellant must seek permission in the Appellant's

10 See para **14.5** above.

Notice[11], which must be served on all respondents as soon as practicable but in any event within 7 days of issue[12].

14.17

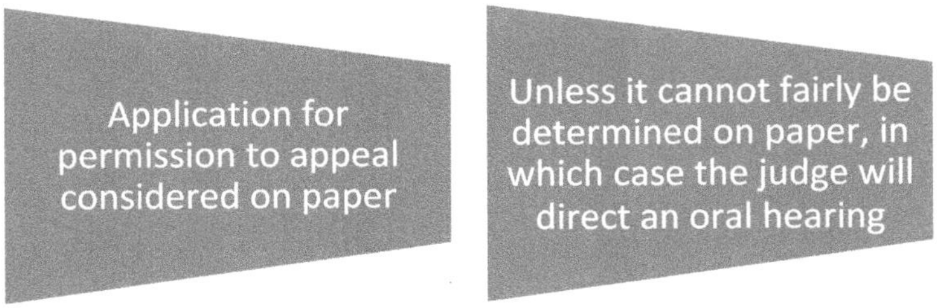

Respondent's Notice[13]

14.18 A respondent is under no obligation to file a Respondent's Notice. However, he must do so under certain circumstances:

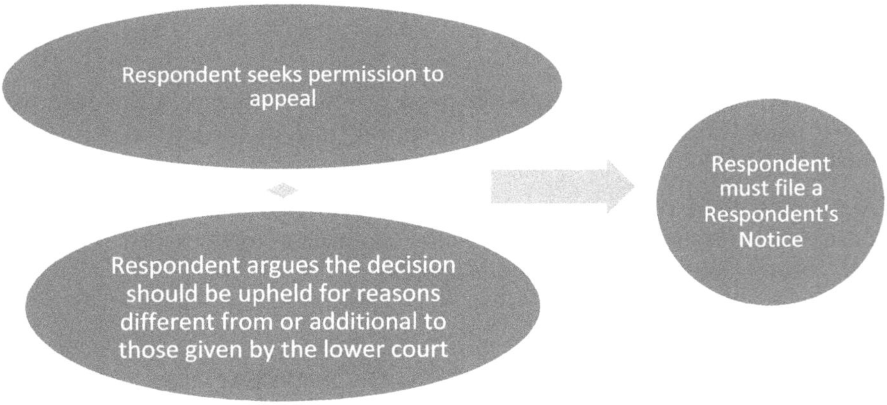

Time limits for Respondent's Notice

14.19 That notice must be filed within such period as may be directed by the court or, if there is no such direction[14]:

11 For time limits, see CPR, r 52.12 and the comments made at para **14.7** above.
12 CPR, r 52.12.
13 CPR, r 52.13.
14 CPR, r 52.13.

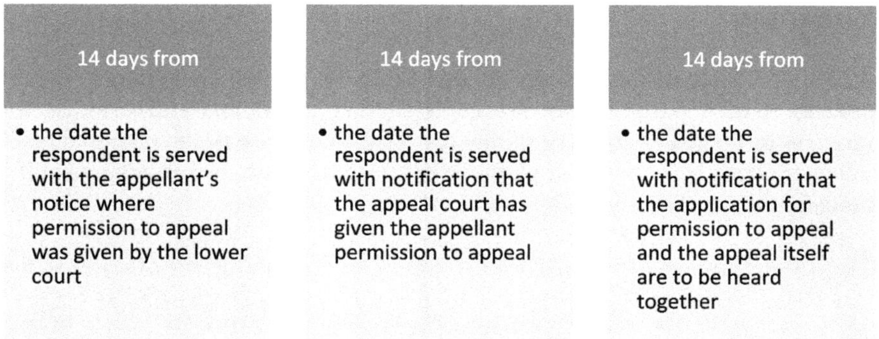

Service of the Respondent's Notice

14.20 The notice must be served on the appellant and all other respondents by the date directed by the court or, if none, within 7 days of it being filed[15].

14.21 If the judge considering the application for permission to appeal decides that an oral hearing is required to determine the application fairly, the following directions may also be given[16]:

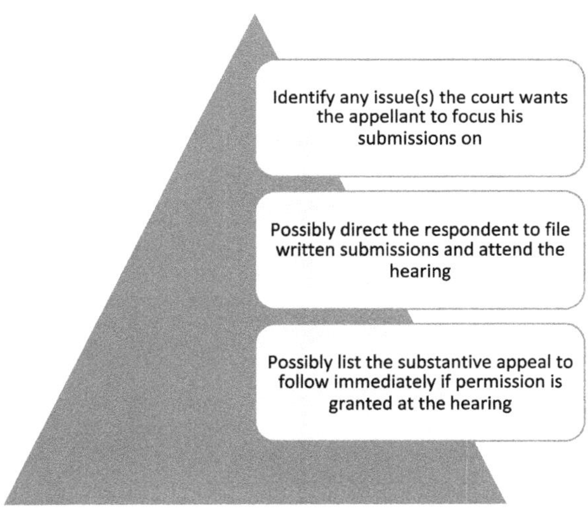

Permission to appeal granted

14.22 If permission to appeal is granted, the order giving permission may limit the issues to be heard and be made subject to conditions[17].

15 CPR, r 52.13.
16 CPR, rr 52.5 and 52.6.
17 CPR, r 52.6.

Transcripts[18]

14.23 The first instance court or the Court of Appeal may direct, on the application of a party to the proceedings, that an official transcript of the judgment of the lower court, or of any part of the evidence or the proceedings in the lower court, be obtained at public expense for the purposes of an appeal if it is satisfied that:

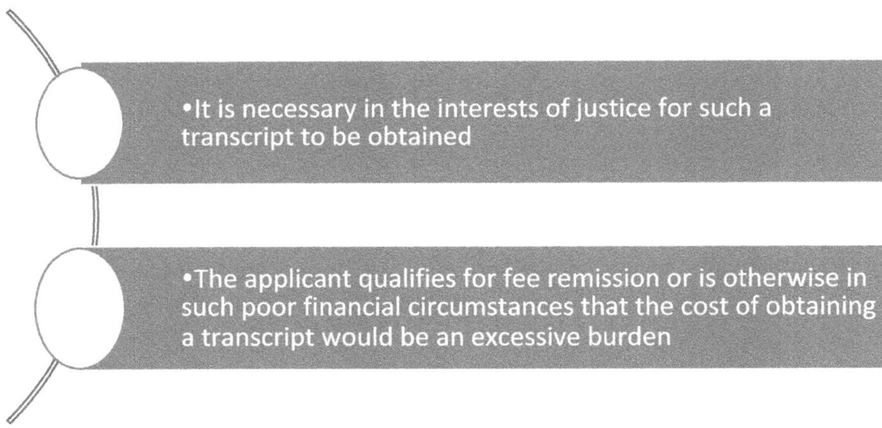

Powers of the Court of Appeal

14.24 The Court of Appeal has all the powers of the lower court and may[19]:

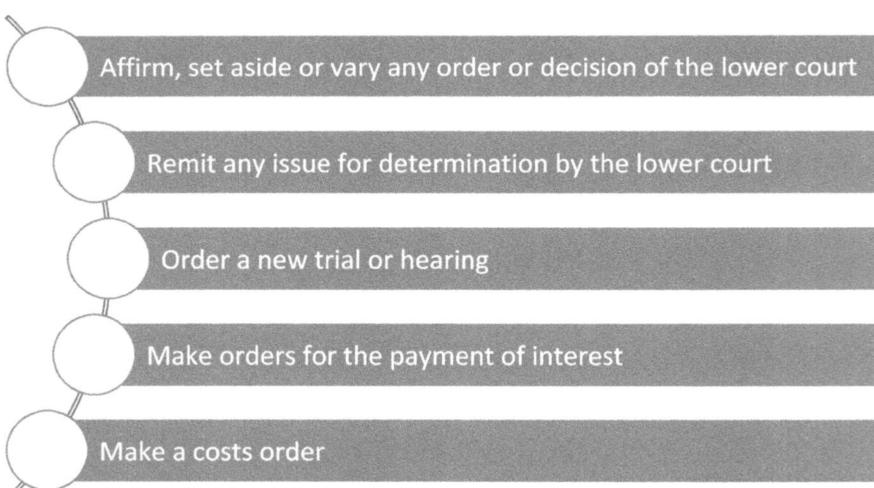

18 CPR, r 52.13.
19 CPR, r 52.20.

Test on appeal

14.25 For an appeal to be successful, the appellant must demonstrate that the judge at first instance was '*wrong*'. The Supreme Court affirmed this straightforward test in *Re B (A Child) (Care Proceedings: Appeal)*[20]. Lord Neuberger categorised the conclusions that an appellate court might reach:

Key citation: Lord Neuberger in *Re B*[21]

'93. … An appellate judge may conclude that the trial judge's conclusion on proportionality was (i) the only possible view, (ii) a view which she considers was right, (iii) a view on which she has doubts, but on balance considers was right, (iv) a view which she cannot say was right or wrong, (v) a view on which she has doubts, but on balance considers was wrong, (vi) a view which she considers was wrong, or (vii) a view which is unsupportable. The appeal must be dismissed if the appellate judge's view is in category (i) to (iv) and allowed if it is in category (vi) or (vii).

94. As to category (iv), there will be a number of cases where an appellate court may think that there is no right answer, in the sense that reasonable judges could differ in their conclusions. As with many evaluative assessments, cases raising an issue on proportionality will include those where the answer is in a grey area, as well as those where the answer is in a black or a white area. An appellate court is much less likely to conclude that category (iv) applies in cases where the trial judge's decision was not based on his assessment of the witnesses' reliability or likely future conduct. So far as category (v) is concerned, the appellate judge should think very carefully about the benefit the trial judge had in seeing the witnesses and hearing the evidence, which are factors whose significance depends on the particular case. However, if, after such anxious consideration, an appellate judge adheres to her view that the trial judge's decision was wrong, then I think that she should allow the appeal.'

14.26 Where what is under review by an appellate court is a decision based on the exercise of discretion, provided the decision-maker has not failed to take into account relevant matters and has not had regard to irrelevant factors and has not reached a decision that is plainly irrational, the review by an appellate court will not lead to the decision being overturned. In that instance, an appellate court which disagrees with the challenged decision of the judge will be constrained

20 [2013] UKSC 33, [2013] 1 WLR 1911, [2013] 2 FCR 525, [2013] 2 FLR 1075.
21 [2013] UKSC 33, [2013] 1 WLR 1911, [2013] 2 FCR 525, [2013] 2 FLR 1075.

to say that, even though it might have reached a different conclusion, it cannot interfere[22].

14.27 In *Re B*[23] the Court also emphasised that an appeal court will have due regard to the enormous benefit a first instance judge has in reading and hearing the evidence first-hand and it will not interfere with a decision unless that decision was wrong. It is inevitably very difficult therefore to successfully appeal findings of fact, which are almost wholly based on the evidence presented to the first instance judge.

D. APPEAL PROCEDURE IN THE SUPREME COURT

Introduction

14.28 Exceptionally, a case will merit an appeal from the Court of Appeal to the Supreme Court, which hears cases of the greatest public or constitutional importance affecting the whole population.

14.29 The procedure is governed by the Supreme Court Rules 2009 ('SCR 2009') and the Practice Directions issued by the Supreme Court (of which there are currently 14). This chapter does not cover every single rule in those documents, and due attention must be paid to those when filing or responding to an appeal.

14.30 The overriding objective of the Rules is to secure that the Court is '*accessible, fair and efficient*' and '*unnecessary disputes over procedural matters are discouraged*'[24].

14.31 If practitioners are in any doubt as to how to implement any part of the Rules or Practice Directions, the Supreme Court Registrar should be contacted for assistance.

The postal address of the Supreme Court
The Supreme Court of the United Kingdom
Parliament Square
London
SW1P 3BD

DX 157230 Parliament Square 4

The telephone numbers: 020 7960 1991 or 020 7960 1992

Email: registry@supremecourt.uk

22 *Re B (A Child) (Care Proceedings: Appeal)* [2013] UKSC 33, [2013] 1 WLR 1911, [2013] 2 FCR 525, [2013] 2 FLR 1075 per Lord Kerr at para 112.
23 [2013] UKSC 33, [2013] 1 WLR 1911, [2013] 2 FCR 525, [2013] 2 FLR 1075.
24 SCR 2009, r 2.

Rules and Practice Directions

Summary of Supreme Court Rules 2009

14.32 The SCR 2009 provide detailed information and guidance in respect of:

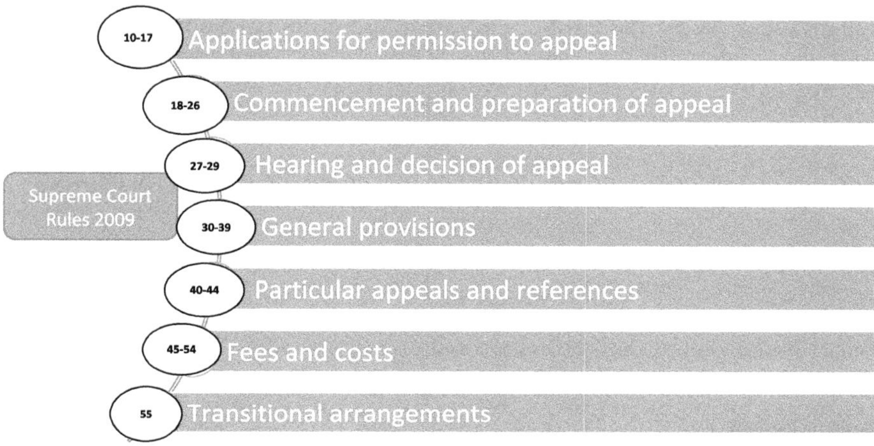

Summary of Supreme Court Practice Directions

14.33 The Practice Directions cover the following topics:

1. General Note & the Jurisdiction of the Supreme Court
2. The Registry of the Supreme Court
3. Applications for Permission to Appeal
4. Notice of Appeal
5. Papers for the Appeal Hearing
6. The Appeal Hearing
7. Applications, Documents, Forms & Orders
8. Miscellaneous Matters
9. The Human Rights Act 1998
10. Devolution Jurisdiction
11. The European Court of Justice
12. Criminal Proceedings
13. Costs
14. Filing Documents in the Registry of the Supreme Court by Electronic Means

Time limits

14.34 An application for permission to appeal must be filed within 28 days from the date of the order or decision of the court below[25].

However, Practice Direction 3 gives particular guidance in relation to cases brought under HC80 and BIIA[26]. The parties must inform the Registrar that the proceedings fall under the Convention or Regulation. The Court normally gives judgment within six weeks of the commencement of proceedings but '*this can only be achieved with the fullest co-operation of the parties*'.

14.35 PD 3 outlines a general guideline to the time limits for such appeals:

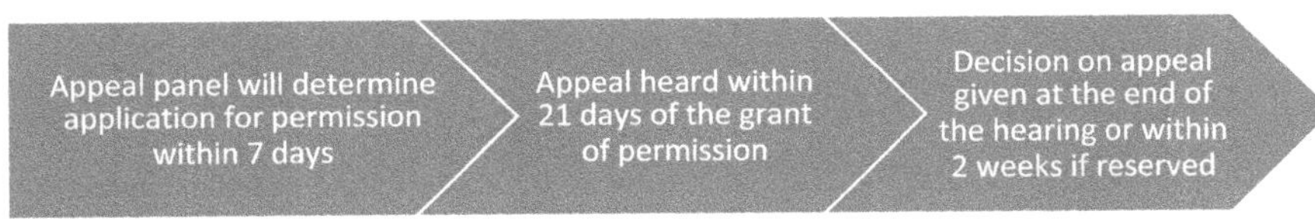

14.36 In order to achieve the above timetable, the Court will set aside or vary the time limits and Practice Directions that normally apply to applications and appeals.

Abridged procedures and special rules for the production of documents are applied to meet the circumstances of each application and appeal. The following timetable for the production of documents is therefore indicative only:

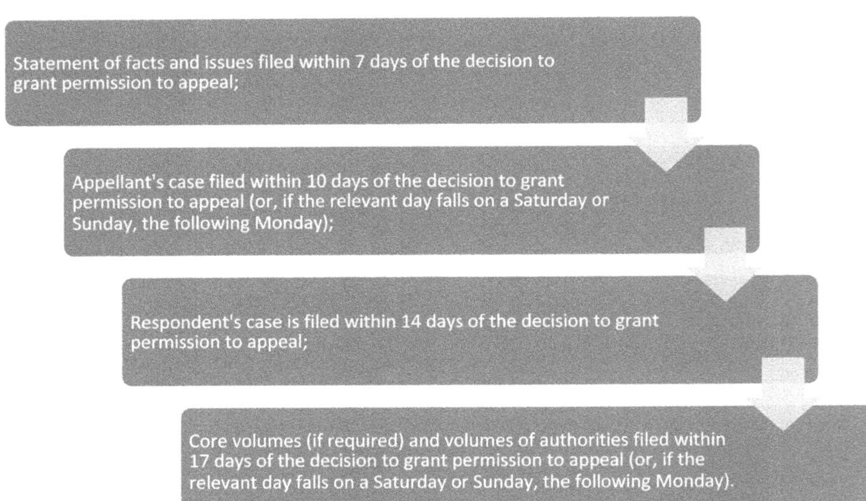

25 SCR 2009, r 11.

26 Council Regulation (EU) No 2201/2003 of 27 November 2003 concerning jurisdiction and the recognition and enforcement of judgments in matrimonial matters and matters of parental responsibility, repealing Regulation (EC) No 1347/2000.

The need for expediency

14.37 Whilst giving careful consideration to the Rules and relevant Practice Directions, the need for expediency in international abduction cases is crucial.

Requests for expedition are covered by SCR 2009, r 31:

> (1) Any request for urgent consideration of an application for permission to appeal or for an expedited hearing must be made to the Registrar.
>
> (2) Wherever possible the views of all parties should be obtained before such a request is made.

The Court has the power to alter any prescribed time limits pursuant to SCR 2009, r 5, whether on a party's application or of its own motion. A time limit may be extended after it has expired.

Leapfrog appeals

14.38 In certain cases, an appeal lies directly to the Supreme Court[27], bypassing the Court of Appeal. A certificate must first be obtained and the permission of the Supreme Court then given before the appeal may proceed. Such appeals are known as 'leapfrog' appeals and certain statutory grounds must be satisfied[28].

14.39 Section 13 of the Administration of Justice Act 1969 provides that an application for permission to appeal to the Supreme Court in a '*leapfrog appeal*' from the High Court must be filed within one month from the date on which the High Court judge grants a certificate under section 12.

Extension of time in publicly funded cases

14.40 Where a party has applied for public funding and the Registrar is informed of the application, the time limits in SCR 2009, rr 11 and 19 shall be extended until 28 days after the final determination of the application for public funding. However, in international abduction cases, a request to expedite the application for public funding should be made to the Legal Aid Agency.

Stay of execution

14.41 Any appellant who wishes to obtain a stay of execution of the order appealed from must seek it from the court below, and only in wholly exceptional circumstances will the Supreme Court grant a stay[29].

27 Paragraph 1.2.17 of Practice Direction 1.
28 The relevant statutory conditions are set out in Administration of Justice Act 1969, s 12(3), (3A).
29 SCR 2009, r 37.

Who can make procedural decisions?

14.42 SCR 2009, r 9 allows a single justice or the Registrar to exercise the powers of the Court without an oral hearing in respect of the following rules:

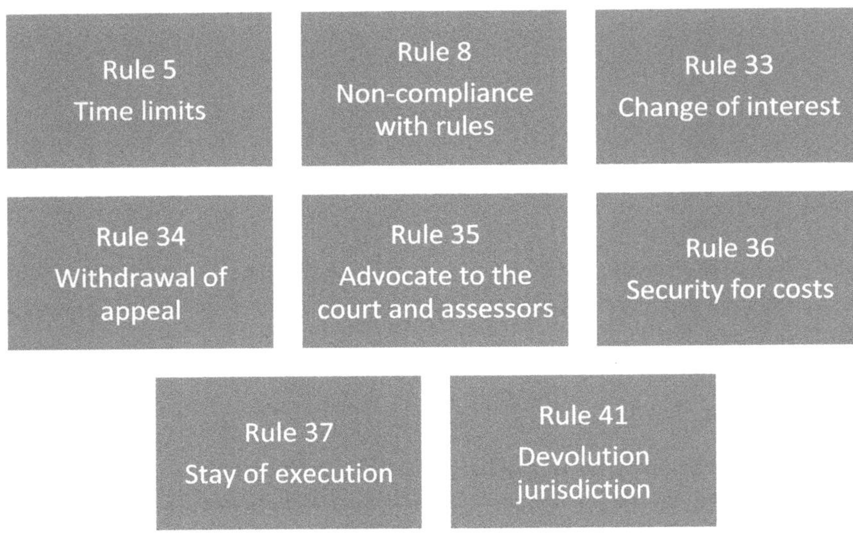

14.43 However, pursuant to SCR 2009, r 9:

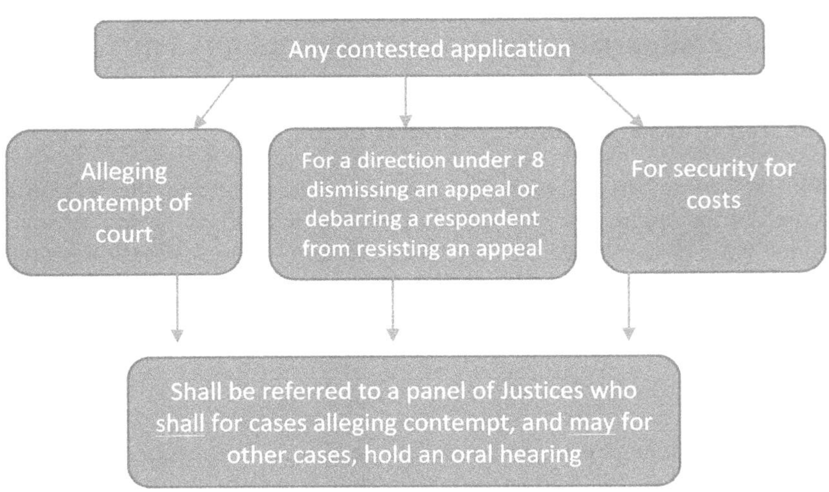

14.44 If any procedural question arises which is not dealt with by the SCR 2009, the Court or the Registrar may adopt any procedure that is consistent with the overriding objective, the Constitutional Reform Act 2005 and the rules.

Hearings on procedural matters

14.45 Subject to SCR 2009, r 27, oral hearings on procedural matters must be heard in open court or in a place to which the public is admitted.

Non-compliance with the Rules[30]

14.46 Failure to comply with the rules of any relevant practice direction does not have the effect of making the proceedings invalid. Where any provision in the SCR 2009 or any relevant practice direction is not complied with, the Court may give whatever directions appear appropriate, having regard to the seriousness of the non-compliance and generally to the circumstances of the case. Directions given *may* include the summary dismissal of an appeal or debarring a respondent from resisting an appeal[31].

Applications to the Supreme Court for permission to appeal

14.47 The application must first be made to the court below. The application may only be made to the Supreme Court if the court below has refused permission[32].

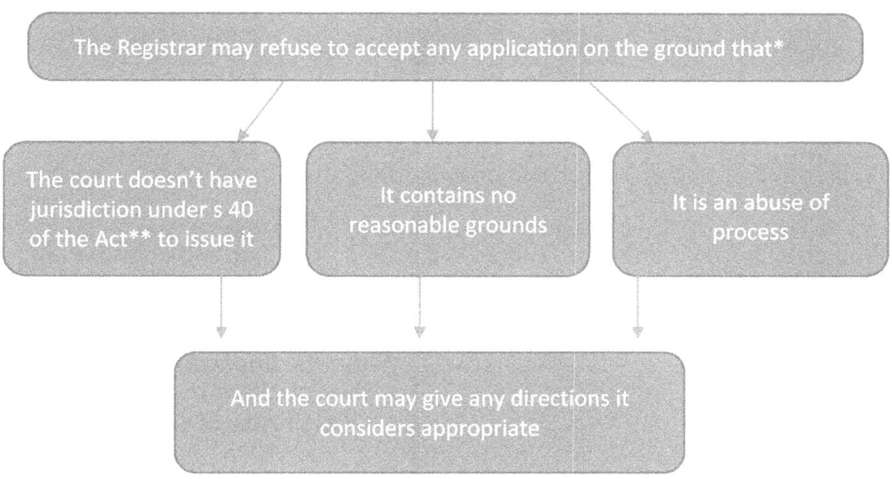

* SCR 2009, r 11.

** Constitutional Reform Act 2005.

30 SCR 2009, r 8.
31 SCR 2009, r 8.
32 SCR 2009, r 10.

The form

14.48 PD 3 specifically directs the forms that are to be used and what should be included.

Respondent's Notice[33]

14.49 Each respondent who wishes to object to the application must, within 14 days after service, file notice of objection in the appropriate form, together with a certificate of service.

Service of application[34]

14.50

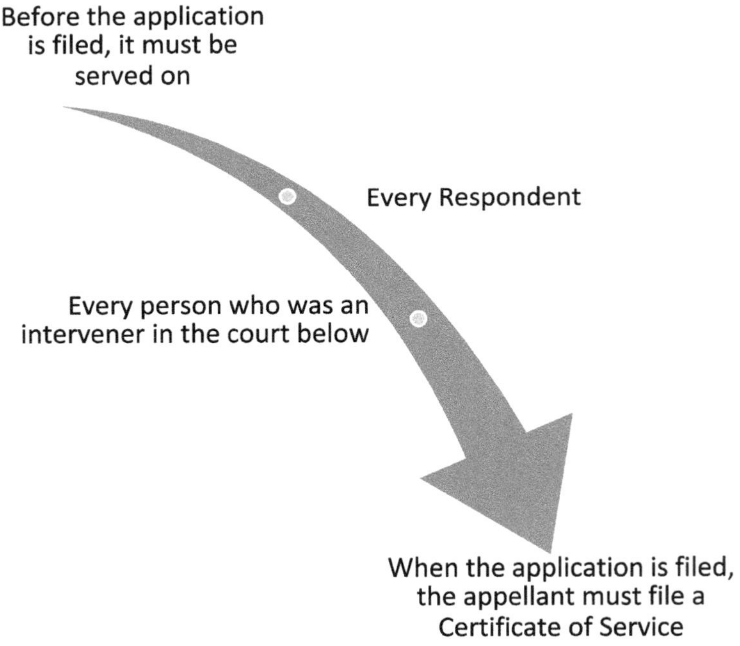

33 SCR 2009, r 13.
34 SCR 2009, r 12.

Service of Respondent's Notice[35]

14.51

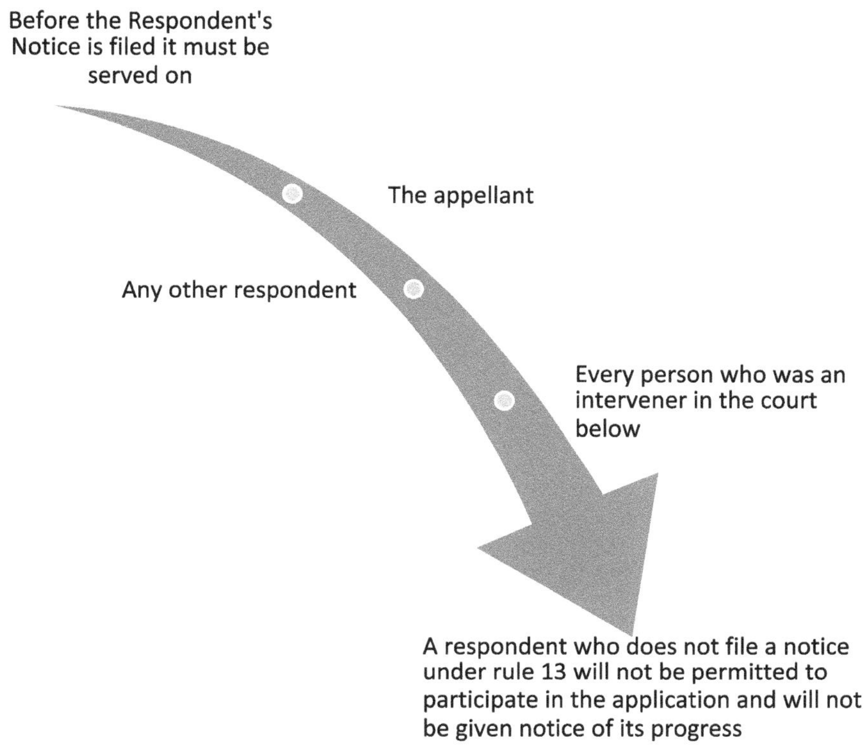

Interventions in applications[36]

14.52 Any person and in particular:

(a) any official body or non-governmental organisation seeking to make submissions in the public interest; or

(b) any person with an interest in proceedings by way of judicial review,

may make written submissions to the Court in support of an application for permission to appeal and request that the Court takes them into account.

Rules of service apply and submissions which are made shall be referred to the panel of Justices which considers the application for permission to appeal.

35 SCR 2009, r 13.
36 SCR 2009, r 15.

14.53 If permission to appeal is granted:

(a) a person whose submissions were taken into account by the panel will be notified but, if that person wishes to intervene in the appeal, an application must be made under rule 26; and

(b) the appellant must notify any person who was an intervener in the court below, whether or not that person made submissions under this rule.

Consideration on paper of application for permission to appeal[37]

14.54 Every admissible application for permission to appeal shall be considered on paper, without an oral hearing, by a panel of Justices.

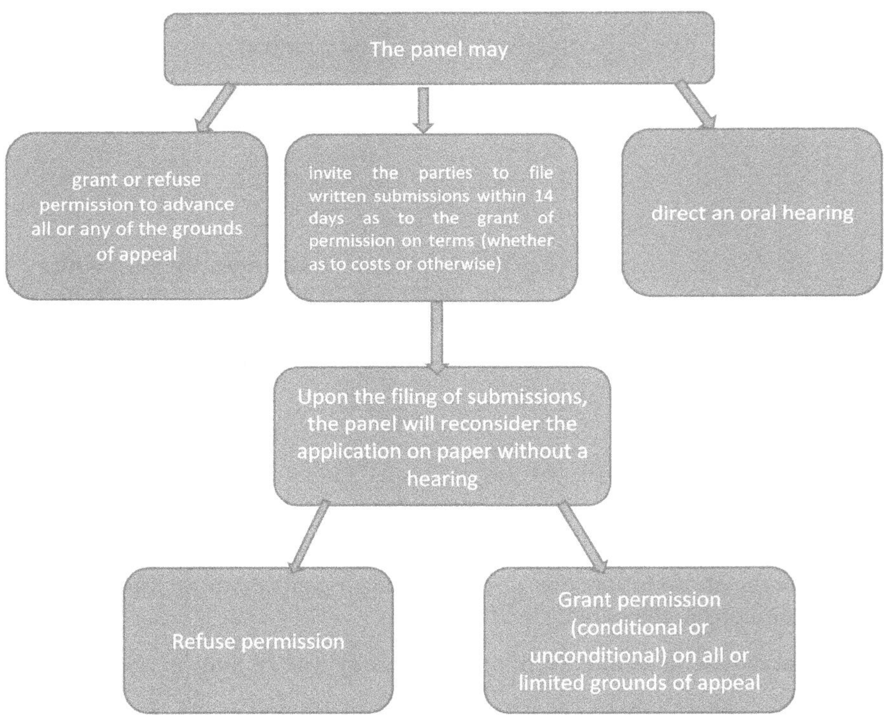

37 SCR 2009, r 16.

Oral hearing of application[38]

14.55 Where the panel has directed an oral hearing, the appellant and every respondent who has given notice under rule 13 will be informed of the date of the oral hearing.

Permission to appeal granted by the Supreme Court[39]

14.56 Permission to appeal is only granted for applications that, in the opinion of the Justices, raise an arguable point of law of general public importance which ought to be considered by the Supreme Court at that time, bearing in mind that the matter will already have been the subject of judicial decision and may have already been reviewed on appeal[40].

14.57 Where the Court grants permission to appeal:

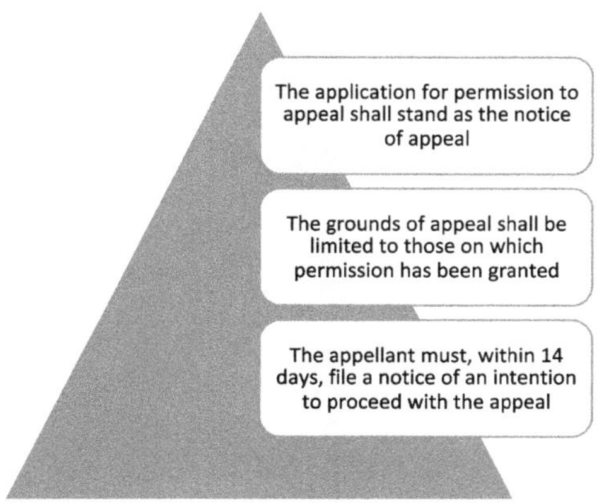

The appellant must then serve re-sealed copies of the application.

Permission to appeal granted by the lower court[41]

14.58 The appellant must file a notice of appeal, together with the requisite number of copies, within 42 days of the date of the order or decision of the court below.

14.59 The appellant must also file a copy of the order appealed from and (if separate) a copy of the order granting permission to appeal and, if the order appealed from is not immediately available, the notice of appeal must be filed without delay and the order filed as soon as it is available.

38 SCR 2009, r 17.
39 SCR 2009, r 18.
40 PD 3, para 3.3.3.
41 SCR 2009, r 19.

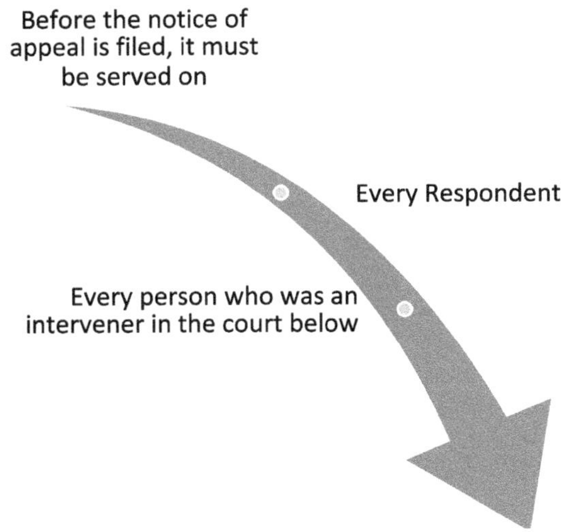

Respondents and interveners

Respondents who wish to participate in the appeal[42]

14.60 Each respondent who intends to participate in the appeal must, within 14 days after service under rule 18(2)(a) or 20, file notice in the appropriate form, together with a certificate of service.

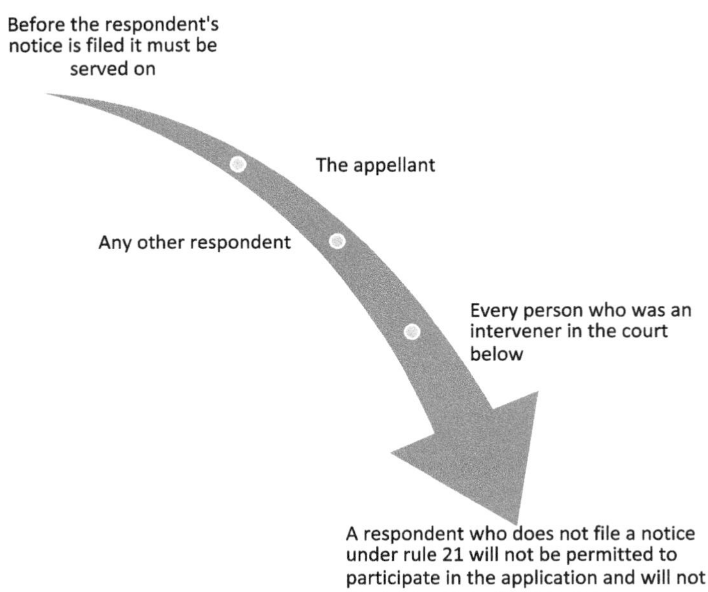

42 SCR 2009, r 21.

Upholding orders below on different grounds, and cross-appeals[43]

14.61 A respondent who wishes to argue that the order appealed from should be upheld on grounds different from those relied on by the court below must state that clearly in the respondent's written case (but need not cross-appeal).

14.62 With certain exceptions, a respondent who wishes to argue that the order appealed from should be varied must obtain permission from the Court to cross-appeal.

14.63 The rules relating to applications for permission to appeal (SCR 2009, rr 10–17) apply to an application to the Court for permission to cross-appeal, and (if practicable) applications for permission to appeal and to cross-appeal shall be considered together by the same panel of Justices.

Interventions

14.64 After permission to appeal has been granted by the Court or after a notice of appeal has been filed, any person and in particular:

(a) any official body or non-governmental organisation seeking to make submissions in the public interest;

(b) any person with an interest in proceedings by way of judicial review; or

(c) any person who was an intervener in the court below or whose submissions were taken into account under rule 15,

may apply to the Court for permission to intervene in the appeal.

14.65 Before the submissions are filed, a copy must be served on the appellant, every respondent and any person was an intervener in the court below. Four copies of the submissions must then be filed, together with a certificate of service.

14.66 Any submissions which are made are referred to the panel of Justices which considers the application for permission to appeal. Where the panel decides to take the submissions into account and grants permission to appeal, the person making them will be notified. If permission to appeal is granted, a formal application must be made under rule 26 if the intervener wishes to intervene in the appeal.

43 SCR 2009, r 25.

Preparation for the appeal hearing

Documents for appeal hearing[44]

14.67 SCR 2009, r 22 makes specific and detailed provision for what documents must be filed before the hearing.

PD 6 makes special provision for the way in which the volumes and authorities must be bound for the appeal. PD 14 provides for the filing of documents by electronic means. 'Oyez' is the major UK provider of the service to prepare those volumes.

14.68 Within 7 days after the filing of the statement and the appendix, every party must notify the Registrar that the appeal is ready for listing and specify the number of hours that their respective counsel estimate to be necessary for their oral submissions. The Registrar will subsequently inform the parties of the date fixed for the hearing.

14.69 The appellant and every respondent (and any intervener and advocate to the Court) must then sequentially exchange their respective written cases and file them, and every respondent (and any intervener and advocate to the Court) must for the purposes of SCR 2009, r 23 provide copies of their respective written cases, in compliance with the relevant practice direction.

The core volumes[45]

14.70 As soon as the parties' cases have been exchanged and in any event not later than 14 days before the date fixed for the hearing, the appellant must file the requisite number of core volumes and, if necessary, additional volumes containing further parts of the appendix, in compliance with the relevant practice direction.

Authorities[46]

14.71 The volumes of authorities that may be referred to during the hearing must be prepared in accordance with the relevant practice direction, and the requisite number of copies of the volumes of authorities must be filed by the appellant at the same time as the core volumes.

The hearing

14.72 The appeal is heard in open court, unless it is in the interests of justice or the interests of the public for part of the hearing to be heard in private. The

44 SCR 2009, r 22.
45 SCR 2009, r 23.
46 SCR 2009, r 24.

court may also exclude a party and his representative so that information is not disclosed contrary to the public interest, so long as a special advocate has been appointed to represent that party's interests. The court must announce publicly its reasons for sitting in private[47].

Powers of the Supreme Court

14.73 The Supreme Court has all the powers of the lower court and may:

- Affirm, set aside or vary any order or decision of the lower court
- Remit any issue for determination by the lower court
- Order a new trial or hearing
- Make orders for the payment of interest
- Make a costs order

The Supreme Court, like the Court of Appeal, will only allow the appeal if the lower court was 'wrong'[48].

Security for costs[49]

14.74 The Court may, on the application of a respondent, order an appellant to give security for the costs of the appeal. The court will determine the amount, the manner and the timing of the security.

14.75 An order made under this rule may require payment of the judgment debt (and costs) in the court below instead of, or in addition to, the amount ordered by way of security for costs.

E. SETTING ASIDE ORDERS

Setting aside a return order made pursuant to HC80

47 SCR 2009, r 27.
48 See para **14.24** above.
49 SCR 2009, r 36.

14.76 In certain cases, the appropriate remedy might be an application to set aside rather than an application for permission to appeal.

14.77 Following an order (including a consent order) to return a child pursuant to HC80, a party may apply to set aside that order pursuant to the Senior Courts Act 1981, s 17(2), FPR 2010, r 12.52A and PD 12F. The leading authority on the approach to be adopted is *Re B (A Child) (Abduction: article 13(b))* [2020] EWCA Civ 1057.

The following applies:

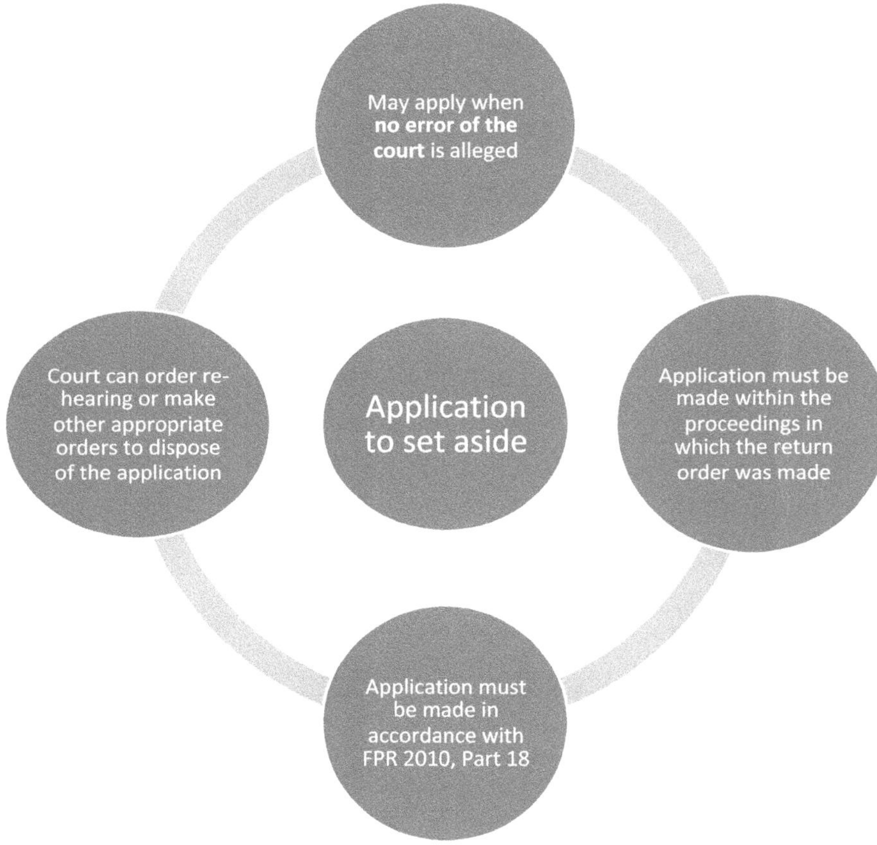

14.78 Even prior to FPR 2010, r 12.52A being introduced, the court had been prepared, in limited circumstances, to set aside return orders.

Case Summary: *Re F (a child) (return order: power to revoke)*[50]

Facts:

F's application for a summary return succeeded and M's appeal to the CA failed. Following her failed appeal, M had a dramatic change in her mental condition: a total psychological and psychiatric collapse. She made an application for the return order to be set aside based on the change in circumstances.

Held by Mostyn J:

The central issue was whether the judge had the power to set aside an order made by a judge of equivalent jurisdiction in family proceedings. The matter came before Mostyn J who satisfied himself that there was power to set aside an HC80 return order. He considered that the psychiatric evidence obtained since the original hearing (and the appeal to the CA) disclosed such a material change of circumstances that it represented 'a sea change' in the relevant evidence appertaining to M's mental health. Although there were other factors which amounted to material changes, the judge was of the opinion that the psychiatric evidence alone justified a finding of material change of circumstances. The original order was set aside.

The test for setting aside an order

14.79 In *Re W (A Child)*[51] (before the FPR rule) Moylan LJ (without deciding the point) was satisfied that there existed a power to set aside return orders but said the power should be restricted to cases '*when there has been a fundamental change of circumstances which undermines the basis on which the original order was made*'.

Setting aside a return order made pursuant to the inherent jurisdiction

14.80 The court may also set aside a return order made pursuant to the inherent jurisdiction pursuant to the Senior Courts Act 1981, s 17(2). FPR 2010, r 12.52A does not deal with inherent jurisdiction cases, but PD 12F, para 4 does envisage such applications.

50 [2014] EWHC 1780 (Fam), [2014] 1 WLR 4375, [2015] 1 FLR 861.
51 [2018] EWCA Civ 1904, [2018] 4 WLR 149, [2019] 1 FCR 216, [2019] 1 FLR 400.

Materials

CHILD ABDUCTION AND CUSTODY ACT 1985

(1985 C 60)

PART I:
INTERNATIONAL CHILD ABDUCTION

1 The Hague Convention

(1) In this Part of this Act 'the Convention' means the Convention on the Civil Aspects of International Child Abduction which was signed at The Hague on 25th October 1980.

(2) Subject to the provisions of this Part of this Act, the provisions of that Convention set out in Schedule 1 to this Act shall have the force of law in the United Kingdom.

[(3) But –
(a) those provisions of the Convention;
(b) this Part of this Act; and
(c) rules of court under section 10 of this Act,
are subject to Article 60 of the Council Regulation (by virtue of which the Regulation takes precedence over the Convention, in so far as it concerns matters governed by the Regulation).

(4) 'The Council Regulation' means Council Regulation (EC) No 2201/2003 of 27th November 2003 concerning jurisdiction and the recognition and enforcement of judgments in matrimonial matters and matters of parental responsibility.][1]

Amendment

1 Inserted by the European Communities (Jurisdiction and Judgments in Matrimonial and Parental Responsibility Matters) Regulations 2005, SI 2005/265, reg 6.

2 Contracting States

(1) For the purposes of the Convention as it has effect under this Part of this Act the Contracting States other than the United Kingdom shall be those for the time being specified by an Order in Council under this section.

(2) An Order in Council under this section shall specify the date of the coming into force of the Convention as between the United Kingdom and any State specified in the Order; and except where the Order otherwise provides, the Convention shall apply as between the United Kingdom and that State only in relation to wrongful removals or retentions occurring on or after that date.

(3) Where the Convention applies, or applies only, to a particular territory or particular territories specified in a declaration made by a Contracting State under Article 39 or 40 of the Convention references to that State in subsections (1) and (2) above shall be construed as references to that territory or those territories.

3 Central Authorities

(1) Subject to subsection (2) below, the functions under the Convention of a Central Authority shall be discharged –
  (a) in England and Wales ...[1] by the Lord Chancellor; and
  (b) in Scotland by the Secretary of State[; and
  (c) in Northern Ireland by the Department of Justice in Northern Ireland][2].

(2) Any application made under the Convention by or on behalf of a person outside the United Kingdom may be addressed to the Lord Chancellor as the Central Authority in the United Kingdom.

[(3) Where any such application relates to a function to be discharged under subsection (1) above by an authority ('the responsible authority') other than the authority to which the application is addressed, the authority to which the application is addressed shall transmit it to the responsible authority.][3]

Amendments

1 Repealed by the Northern Ireland Act 1998 (Devolution of Policing and Justice Functions) Order 2010, SI 2010/976, art 1(2), Sch 18, Pt 1, paras 35, 36(a).
2 Inserted by the Northern Ireland Act 1998 (Devolution of Policing and Justice Functions) Order 2010, SI 2010/976, art 1(2), Sch 18, Pt 1, paras 35, 36(b).
3 Substituted by the Northern Ireland Act 1998 (Devolution of Policing and Justice Functions) Order 2010, SI 2010/976, art 1(2), Sch 18, Pt 1, paras 35, 36(c).

4 Judicial authorities

The courts having jurisdiction to entertain applications under this Convention shall be –
  (a) in England and Wales or in Northern Ireland the High Court; and
  (b) in Scotland the Court of Session.

5 Interim powers

Where an application has been made to a court in the United Kingdom under the Convention, the court may, at any time before the application is determined, give such interim directions as it thinks fit for the purpose of securing the welfare of the child concerned or of preventing changes in the circumstances relevant to the determination of the application.

6 Reports

Where the Lord Chancellor[, the Department of Justice in Northern Ireland][1] or the Secretary of State is requested to provide information relating to a child under Article 7(d) of the Convention he may –
  (a) request a local authority or [an officer of the Service][2] [or a Welsh family proceedings officer][3] to make a report to him in writing with respect to any matter which appears to him to be relevant;

(b) request the Department of Health and Social Services for Northern Ireland to arrange for a suitably qualified person to make such a report to him;

(c) request any court to which a written report relating to the child has been made to send him a copy of the report;

and such a request shall be duly complied with.

Amendments

1 Inserted by the Northern Ireland Act 1998 (Devolution of Policing and Justice Functions) Order 2010, SI 2010/976, art 1(2), Sch 18, Pt 1, paras 35, 37.

2 Substituted by the Criminal Justice and Court Services Act 2000, s 74, Sch 7, paras 79, 80.

3 Inserted by the Children Act 2004, s 40, Sch 3, paras 2, 3.

7 Proof of documents and evidence

(1) For the purposes of Article 14 of the Convention a decision or determination of a judicial or administrative authority outside the United Kingdom may be proved by a duly authenticated copy of the decision or determination; and any document purporting to be such a copy shall be deemed to be a true copy unless the contrary is shown.

(2) For the purposes of subsection (1) above a copy is duly authenticated if it bears the seal, or is signed by a judge or officer, of the authority in question.

(3) For the purposes of Articles 14 and 30 of the Convention any such document as is mentioned in Article 8 of the Convention, or a certified copy of any such document, shall be sufficient evidence of anything stated in it.

8 Declarations by United Kingdom courts

The High Court or Court of Session may, on an application made for the purposes of Article 15 of the Convention by any person appearing to the court to have an interest in the matter, make a declaration or declarator that the removal of any child from, or his retention outside, the United Kingdom was wrongful within the meaning of Article 3 of the Convention.

9 Suspension of court's powers in cases of wrongful removal

The reference in Article 16 of the Convention to deciding on the merits of rights of custody shall be construed as a reference to –

(a) making, varying or revoking a custody order, or [a supervision order under section 31 of the Children Act 1989][1] or [Article 50 of the Children (Northern Ireland) Order 1995][2];

[(aa) enforcing under section 29 of the Family Law Act 1986 a custody order within the meaning of Chapter V of Part I of that Act][3];

(b) registering or enforcing a decision under Part II of this Act;

[(ba) registering or enforcing a decision under the Convention on Jurisdiction, Applicable Law, Recognition, Enforcement and Co-Operation in respect of Parental Responsibility and Measures for the Protection of Children that was signed at The Hague on 19 October 1996 ('the 1996

Convention'), except where provisions of the 1996 Convention are invoked in accordance with Article 50 of the 1996 Convention;][4]

(c) ...[5]

[(d) making, varying, amending or revoking a permanence order under section 80 of the Adoption and Children (Scotland) Act 2007 (including a deemed permanence order having effect by virtue of article 13(1) or 14(2) of the Adoption and Children (Scotland) Act 2007 (Commencement No. 4, Transitional and Savings Provisions) Order 2009 (S.S.I. 2009/267)).][6]

(e) ...[7]

Amendments

1 Substituted by the Children Act 1989, s 108(5), Sch 13, para 57(1).
2 Substituted by the Children (Northern Ireland Consequential Amendments) Order 1995, SI 1995/756, art 11(1), (2).
3 Paragraph inserted by the Family Law Act 1986, s 68(1), Sch 1, para 28.
4 Inserted by the Parental Responsibility and Measures for the Protection of Children (International Obligations) (England and Wales and Northern Ireland) Regulations 2010, SI 2010/1898, reg 17, Schedule, para 3.
5 Repealed by the Children Act 1989, s 108(7), Sch 15.
6 Substituted by the Adoption and Children (Scotland) Act 2007 (Consequential Modifications) Order 2011, SI 2011/1740, art 2, Sch 1, para 2(1), (2).
7 Repealed by the Children (Northern Ireland Consequential Amendments) Order 1995, SI 1995/756, art 15, Schedule.

10 Rules of court

(1) An authority having power to make rules of court may make such provision for giving effect to this Part of this Act as appears to that authority to be necessary or expedient.

(2) Without prejudice to the generality of subsection (1) above, rules of court may make provision –

(a) with respect to the procedure on applications for the return of a child and with respect to the documents and information to be furnished and the notices to be given in connection with any such application;

(b) for the transfer of any such application between the appropriate courts in the different parts of the United Kingdom;

(c) for the giving of notices by or to a court for the purposes of the provisions of Article 16 of the Convention and section 9 above and generally as respects proceedings to which those provisions apply;

(d) for enabling a person who wishes to make an application under the Convention in a Contracting State other than the United Kingdom to obtain from any court in the United Kingdom an authenticated copy of any decision of that court relating to the child to whom the application is to relate.

11 Cost of applications

The United Kingdom having made such a reservation as is mentioned in the third paragraph of Article 26 of the Convention, the costs mentioned in that paragraph shall not be borne by any Minister or other authority in the United Kingdom except so far as they fall to be so borne [by virtue of –

[(a) the provision of any civil legal services (within the meaning of Part 1 of the Legal Aid, Sentencing and Punishment of Offenders Act 2012) under arrangements made for the purposes of that Part of that Act,][1] or

(b) the grant of legal aid or legal advice and assistance under][2]

the Legal Aid (Scotland) Act 1967, Part I of the Legal Advice and Assistance Act 1972 or the Legal Aid Advice and Assistance (Northern Ireland) Order 1981.

Amendments

1 Substituted by the Legal Aid, Sentencing and Punishment of Offenders Act 2012, s 39, Sch 5, para 26.

2 Substituted by the Access to Justice Act 1999, s 24, Sch 4, para 31.

PART II: RECOGNITION AND ENFORCEMENT OF CUSTODY DECISIONS

12 The European Convention

(1) In this Part of this Act 'the Convention' means the European Convention on Recognition and Enforcement of Decisions concerning Custody of Children and on the Restoration of Custody of Children which was signed in Luxembourg on 20th May 1980.

(2) Subject to the provisions of this Part of this Act, the provisions of that Convention set out in Schedule 2 to this Act (which include Articles 9 and 10 as they have effect in consequence of a reservation made by the United Kingdom under Article 17) shall have the force of law in the United Kingdom.

[(3) But –

(a) those provisions of the Convention;

(b) this Part of this Act; and

(c) rules of court under section 24 of this Act,

are subject to Article 60 of the Council Regulation (by virtue of which the Regulation takes precedence over the Convention, in so far as it concerns matters governed by the Regulation).

(4) The Council Regulation' means Council Regulation (EC) No 2201/2003 of 27th November 2003 concerning jurisdiction and the recognition and enforcement of judgments in matrimonial matters and matters of parental responsibility.][1]

Amendment

1 Substituted by the European Communities (Jurisdiction and Judgments in Matrimonial and Parental Responsibility Matters) Regulations 2005, SI 2005/265, reg 7.

13 Contracting States

(1) For the purposes of the Convention as it has effect under this Part of this Act the Contracting States other than the United Kingdom shall be those for the time being specified by an Order in Council under this section.

(2) An Order in Council under this section shall specify the date of the coming into force of the Convention as between the United Kingdom and any State specified in the Order.

(3) Where the Convention applies, or applies only, to a particular territory or particular territories specified by a Contracting State under Article 24 or 25 of the Convention references to that State in subsections (1) and (2) above shall be construed as references to that territory or those territories.

14 Central Authorities

(1) Subject to subsection (2) below, the functions under the Convention of a Central Authority shall be discharged –
   (a) in England and Wales …[1] by the Lord Chancellor; and
   (b) in Scotland by the Secretary of State[; and
   (c) in Northern Ireland by the Department of Justice in Northern Ireland][2].

(2) Any application made under the Convention by or on behalf of a person outside the United Kingdom may be addressed to the Lord Chancellor as the Central Authority in the United Kingdom.

[(3) Where any such application relates to a function to be discharged under subsection (1) above by an authority ('the responsible authority') other than the authority to which the application is addressed, the authority to which the application is addressed shall transmit it to the responsible authority.][3]

Amendments

1 Repealed by the Northern Ireland Act 1998 (Devolution of Policing and Justice Functions) Order 2010, SI 2010/976, art 1(2), Sch 18, Pt 1, paras 35, 38(a).

2 Inserted by the Northern Ireland Act 1998 (Devolution of Policing and Justice Functions) Order 2010, SI 2010/976, art 1(2), Sch 18, Pt 1, paras 35, 38(b).

3 Substituted by the Northern Ireland Act 1998 (Devolution of Policing and Justice Functions) Order 2010, SI 2010/976, art 1(2), Sch 18, Pt 1, paras 35, 38(c).

15 Recognition of decisions

(1) Articles 7 and 12 of the Convention shall have effect in accordance with this section.

(2) A decision to which either of those Articles applies which was made in a Contracting State other than the United Kingdom shall be recognised in each part of the United Kingdom as if made by a court having jurisdiction to make it in that part but –

(a) the appropriate court in any part of the United Kingdom may, on the application of any person appearing to it to have an interest in the matter, declare on any of the grounds specified in Article 9 or 10 of the Convention that the decision is not to be recognised in any part of the United Kingdom; and

(b) the decision shall not be enforceable in any part of the United Kingdom unless registered in the appropriate court under section 16 below.

(3) The references in Article 9(1)(c) of the Convention to the removal of the child are to his improper removal within the meaning of the Convention.

16 Registration of decisions

(1) A person on whom any rights are conferred by a decision relating to custody made by an authority in a Contracting State other than the United Kingdom may make an application for the registration of the decision in an appropriate court in the United Kingdom.

(2) The Central Authority in the United Kingdom shall assist such a person in making such an application if a request for such assistance is made by him or on his behalf by the Central Authority of the Contracting State in question.

(3) An application under subsection (1) above or a request under subsection (2) above shall be treated as a request for enforcement for the purposes of Articles 10 and 13 of the Convention.

(4) The High Court or Court of Session shall refuse to register a decision if –

(a) the court is of the opinion that on any of the grounds specified in Article 9 or 10 of the Convention the decision should not be recognised in any part of the United Kingdom;

(b) the court is of the opinion that the decision is not enforceable in the Contracting State where it was made and is not a decision to which Article 12 of the Convention applies;

(c) an application in respect of the child under Part I of this Act is pending.

[(5) Where an authority mentioned in subsection (1) of section 14 above is requested to assist in making an application under this section to the appropriate court in a part of the United Kingdom ('the relevant part of the United Kingdom') other than the part in relation to which the authority has functions under that subsection, the authority shall transmit the request to the authority which has functions under that subsection in relation to the relevant part of the United Kingdom.][1]

(6) In this section 'decision relating to custody' has the same meaning as in the Convention.

Amendment

1 Substituted by the Northern Ireland Act 1998 (Devolution of Policing and Justice Functions) Order 2010, SI 2010/976, art 1(2), Sch 18, Pt 1, paras 35, 39.

17 Variation and revocation of registered decisions

(1) Where a decision which has been registered under section 16 above is varied or revoked by an authority in the Contracting State in which it was made, the person on whose behalf the application for registration of the decision was made shall notify the court in which the decision is registered of the variation or revocation.

(2) Where a court is notified under subsection (1) above of the revocation of a decision, it shall –
  (a) cancel the registration, and
  (b) notify such persons as may be prescribed by rules of court of the cancellation.

(3) Where a court is notified under subsection (1) above of the variation of a decision, it shall –
  (a) notify such persons as may be prescribed by rules of court of the variation; and
  (b) subject to any conditions which may be so prescribed, vary the registration.

(4) The court in which a decision is registered under section 16 above may also, on the application of any person appearing to the court to have an interest in the matter, cancel or vary the registration if it is satisfied that the decision has been revoked or, as the case may be, varied by an authority in the Contracting State in which it was made.

18 Enforcement of decisions

Where a decision relating to custody has been registered under section 16 above, the court in which it is registered shall have the same powers for the purpose of enforcing the decision as if it had been made by that court; and proceedings for or with respect to enforcement may be taken accordingly.

19 Interim powers

Where an application has been made to a court for the registration of a decision under section 16 above or for the enforcement of such a decision, the court may, at any time before the application is determined, give such interim directions as it thinks fit for the purpose of securing the welfare of the child concerned or of preventing changes in the circumstances relevant to the determination of the application or, in the case of an application for registration, to the determination of any subsequent application for the enforcement of the decision.

20 Suspension of court's powers

(1) Where it appears to any court in which such proceedings as are mentioned in subsection (2) below are pending in respect of a child that –

(a) an application has been made for the registration of a decision in respect of the child under section 16 above (other than a decision mentioned in subsection (3) below) or that such a decision is registered; and

(b) the decision was made in proceedings commenced before the proceedings which are pending,

the powers of the court with respect to the child in those proceedings shall be restricted as mentioned in subsection (2) below unless, in the case of an application for registration, the application is refused.

(2) Where subsection (1) above applies the court shall not –

(a) in the case of custody proceedings, make, vary or revoke any custody order, or [a supervision order under section 31 of the Children Act 1989][1] or [Article 50 of the Children (Northern Ireland) Order 1995][2];

[(aa) in the case of proceedings under section 29 of the Family Law Act 1986 for the enforcement of a custody order within the meaning of Chapter V of Part I of that Act, enforce that order][3]; [or][4]

(b) ...[5]

(b) ...[5]

[(d) in the case of proceedings for the making, varying, amending or revoking of a permanence order under section 80 of the Adoption and Children (Scotland) Act 2007 (including a deemed permanence order having effect by virtue of article 13(1) or 14(2) of the Adoption and Children (Scotland) Act 2007 (Commencement No. 4, Transitional and Savings Provisions) Order 2009 (S.S.I. 2009/267)), make, vary, amend or revoke such an order;][6] ...[7]

(e) ...[7]

[(2A) Where it appears to the Secretary of State –

(a) that an application has been made for the registration of a decision in respect of a child under section 16 above (other than a decision mentioned in subsection (3) below); or

(b) that such a decision is registered,

the Secretary of State shall not make, vary or revoke any custody order in respect of the child unless, in the case of an application for registration, the application is refused][8].

(3) The decision referred to in subsection (1) [or (2A)][8] above is a decision which is only a decision relating to custody within the meaning of section 16 of this Act by virtue of being a decision relating to rights of access.

(4) Paragraph (b) of Article 10(2) of the Convention shall be construed as referring to custody proceedings within the meaning of this Act.

(5) This section shall apply to a children's hearing [...[9]][10] as it does to a court.

[(6) In subsection (5), 'children's hearing' is to be construed in accordance with section 5 of the Children's Hearings (Scotland) Act 2011.][11]

Amendments

1 Substituted by the Children Act 1989, s 108(5), Sch 13, para 57(1).
2 Substituted by the Children (Northern Ireland Consequential Amendments) Order 1995, SI 1995/756, art 11(1), (2).
3 Inserted by the Family Law Act 1986, s 68(1), Sch 1, para 29.
4 Inserted by the Children (Northern Ireland Consequential Amendments) Order 1995, SI 1995/756, art 11(1), (3).
5 Repealed by the Children Act 1989, s 108(7), Sch 15.
6 Substituted by the Adoption and Children (Scotland) Act 2007 (Consequential Modifications) Order 2011, SI 2011/1740, art 2, Sch 1, para 2(1), (3).
7 Repealed by the Children (Northern Ireland Consequential Amendments) Order 1995, SI 1995/756, art 15, Schedule.
8 Inserted by the Family Law Act 1986, s 67(1)–(3).
9 Repealed by the Children's Hearings (Scotland) Act 2011 (Consequential and Transitional Provisions and Savings) Order 2013, SI 2013/1465, art 17(2), Sch 1, Pt 3.
10 Substituted by the Children (Scotland) Act 1995, s 105(4), Sch 4, para 37(1), (3).
11 Inserted by the Children's Hearings (Scotland) Act 2011 (Consequential and Transitional Provisions and Savings) Order 2013, SI 2013/1465, art 17(1), Sch 1, Pt 1, para 1(1), (2).

21 Reports

Where the Lord Chancellor[, the Department of Justice in Northern Ireland][1] or the Secretary of State is requested to make enquiries about a child under Article 15(1) (b) of the Convention he may –

(a) request a local authority or [an officer of the Service][2] [or a Welsh family proceedings officer][3] to make a report to him in writing with respect to any matter relating to the child concerned which appears to him to be relevant;

(b) request the Department of Health and Social Services for Northern Ireland to arrange for a suitably qualified person to make such a report to him;

(c) request any court to which a written report relating to the child has been made to send him a copy of the report;

and any such request shall be duly complied with.

Amendments

1 Inserted by the Northern Ireland Act 1998 (Devolution of Policing and Justice Functions) Order 2010, SI 2010/976, art 1(2), Sch 18, Pt 1, paras 35, 37.
2 Substituted by the Criminal Justice and Court Services Act 2000, s 74, Sch 7, Pt II, paras 79, 80.
3 Inserted by the Children Act 2004, s 40, Sch 3, paras 2, 3.

22 Proof of documents and evidence

(1) In any proceedings under this Part of this Act a decision of an authority outside the United Kingdom may be proved by a duly authenticated copy of the decision; and any document purporting to be such a copy shall be deemed to be a true copy unless the contrary is shown.

(2) For the purposes of subsection (1) above a copy is duly authenticated if it bears the seal, or is signed by a judge or officer, of the authority in question.

(3) In any proceedings under this Part of this Act any such document as is mentioned in Article 13 of the Convention, or a certified copy of any such document, shall be sufficient evidence of anything stated in it.

23 Decisions of United Kingdom courts

(1) Where a person on whom any rights are conferred by a decision relating to custody made by a court in the United Kingdom makes an application to the Lord Chancellor[, the Department of Justice in Northern Ireland][1] or the Secretary of State under Article 4 of the Convention with a view to securing its recognition or enforcement in another Contracting State, the Lord Chancellor[, the Department of Justice in Northern Ireland][1] or the Secretary of State may require the court which made the decision to furnish him with all or any of the documents referred to in Article 13(1)(b), (c) and (d) of the Convention.

(2) Where in any custody proceedings a court in the United Kingdom makes a decision relating to a child who has been removed from the United Kingdom, the court may also, on an application made by any person for the purposes of Article 12 of the Convention, declare the removal to have been unlawful if it is satisfied that the applicant has an interest in the matter and that the child has been taken from or sent or kept out of the United Kingdom without the consent of the person (or, if more than one, all the persons) having the right to determine the child's place of residence under the law of the part of the United Kingdom in which the child was habitually resident.

(3) In this section 'decision relating to custody' has the same meaning as in the Convention.

Amendments

1 Inserted by the Northern Ireland Act 1998 (Devolution of Policing and Justice Functions) Order 2010, SI 2010/976, art 1(2), Sch 18, Pt 1, paras 35, 37.

24 Rules of court

(1) An authority having power to make rules of court may make such provision for giving effect to this Part of this Act as appears to that authority to be necessary or expedient.

(2) Without prejudice to the generality of subsection (1) above, rules of court may make provision –
  (a) with respect to the procedure on applications to a court under any provision of this Part of this Act and with respect to the documents and information to be furnished and the notices to be given in connection with any such application;

(b) for the transfer of any such application between the appropriate courts in the different parts of the United Kingdom;
(c) for the giving of directions requiring the disclosure of information about any child who is the subject of proceedings under this Part of this Act and for safeguarding its welfare.

PART III: SUPPLEMENTARY

[24A Power to order disclosure of child's whereabouts

(1) Where –
  (a) in proceedings for the return of a child under Part I of this Act; or
  (b) on an application for the recognition, registration or enforcement of a decision in respect of a child under Part II of this Act,

  there is not available to the court adequate information as to where the child is, the court may order any person who it has reason to believe may have relevant information to disclose it to the court.

(2) A person shall not be excused from complying with an order under subsection (1) above by reason that to do so may incriminate him or his spouse [or civil partner][1] of an offence; but a statement or admission made in compliance with such an order shall not be admissible in evidence against either of them in proceedings for any offence other than perjury.][2]

Amendments

1 Inserted by the Civil Partnership Act 2004, s 261(1), Sch 27, para 110.
2 Inserted by the Family Law Act 1986, s 67(1), (4).

25 Termination of existing custody orders, etc

(1) Where –
  (a) an order is made for the return of a child under Part I of this Act; or
  (b) a decision with respect to a child (other than a decision mentioned in subsection (2) below) is registered under section 16 of this Act,

  any custody order relating to him shall cease to have effect.

(2) The decision referred to in subsection (1) (b) above is a decision which is only a decision relating to custody within the meaning of section 16 of this Act by virtue of being a decision relating to rights of access.

(3) …[1]

(4) …[2]

(5) …[1]

(6) …[3]

(7) …[2]

Amendments

1 Repealed by the Children Act 1989, s 108(7), Sch 15.
2 Repealed by the Children (Northern Ireland Consequential Amendments) Order 1995, SI 1995/756, art 15, Schedule.
3 Repealed by the Children (Scotland) Act 1995, s 105(4), Sch 4, para 37(1), (4).

26 Expenses

There shall be paid out of money provided by Parliament –

(a) any expenses incurred by the Lord Chancellor or the Secretary of State by virtue of this Act; and

(b) any increase attributable to this Act in the sums so payable under any other Act.

27 Interpretation

(1) In this Act 'custody order' means [(unless contrary intention appears)][1] any such order as is mentioned in Schedule 3 to this Act and 'custody proceedings' means proceedings in which an order within paragraphs 1, 2, 5, 6, 8 or 9 of that Schedule may be [made, varied or revoked][2].

(2) For the purposes of this Act 'part of the United Kingdom' means England and Wales, Scotland or Northern Ireland and 'the appropriate court', in relation to England and Wales or Northern Ireland means the High Court and, in relation to Scotland, the Court of Session.

(3) In this Act 'local authority' means –

(a) in relation to England and Wales, the council of a non-metropolitan county, a metropolitan district, a London borough or the Common Council of the City of London; and

(b) in relation to Scotland, [council constituted under section 2 of the Local Government etc (Scotland) Act 1994][3].

[(4) In this Act a decision relating to rights of access in England and Wales [or Scotland][4] [or Northern Ireland][5] means a decision as to the contact which a child may, or may not, have with any person][6].

[(5) In this Act 'officer of the Service' has the same meaning as in the Criminal Justice and Court Services Act 2000.][7]

[(5A) In this Act 'Welsh family proceedings officer' has the meaning given by section 35 of the Children Act 2004.][8]

Amendments

1 Inserted by the Family Law Act 1986, s 68(1), Sch 1, para 30.
2 Substituted by the Family Law Act 1986, s 67(1), (5).
3 Substituted by the Local Government etc (Scotland) Act 1994, s 180(1), Sch 13, para 139.
4 Inserted by the Children (Scotland) Act 1995, s 105(4), Sch 4, para 37(1), (5).
5 Inserted by the Children (Northern Ireland Consequential Amendments) Order 1995, SI 1995/756, art 11(1), (4).

6 Inserted by the Children Act 1989, s 108(5), Sch 13, para 57(2).
7 Inserted by the Criminal Justice and Court Services Act 2000, s 74, Sch 7, paras 79, 81.
8 Inserted by the Children Act 2004, s 40, Sch 3, paras 2, 4.

28 Application as respects British Islands and colonies

(1) Her Majesty may by Order in Council direct that any of the provisions of this Act specified in the Order shall extend, subject to such modifications as may be specified in the Order, to –
   (a) the Isle of Man,
   (b) any of the Channel Islands, and
   (c) any colony.

(2) Her Majesty may by Order in Council direct that this Act shall have effect in the United Kingdom as if any reference in this Act, or in any amendment made by this Act, to any order which may be made, or any proceedings which may be brought or any other thing which may be done, in, or in any part of, the United Kingdom included a reference to any corresponding order which may be made or, as the case may be, proceedings which may be brought or other thing which may be done in any of the territories mentioned in subsection (1) above.

(3) An Order in Council under this section may make such consequential, incidental and supplementary provision as Her Majesty considers appropriate.

(4) An Order in Council under this section shall be subject to annulment in pursuance of a resolution of either House of Parliament.

29 Short title, commencement and extent

(1) This Act may be cited as the Child Abduction and Custody Act 1985.

(2) This Act shall come into force on such day as may be appointed by an order made by statutory instrument by the Lord Chancellor and the Lord Advocate; and different days may be so appointed for different provisions.

(3) This Act extends to Northern Ireland.

SCHEDULE 1
CONVENTION ON THE CIVIL ASPECTS OF INTERNATIONAL CHILD ABDUCTION

Section 1(2)

CHAPTER I
SCOPE OF THE CONVENTION

Article 3

The removal or the retention of a child is to be considered wrongful where –

(a) it is in breach of rights of custody attributed to a person, an institution or any other body, either jointly or alone, under the law of the State in which the child was habitually resident immediately before the removal or retention; and

(b) at the time of removal or retention those rights were actually exercised, either jointly or alone, or would have been so exercised but for the removal or retention.

The rights of custody mentioned in sub-paragraph (a) above, may arise in particular by operation of law or by reason of a judicial or administrative decision, or by reason of an agreement having legal effect under the law of that State.

Article 4

The Convention shall apply to any child who was habitually resident in a Contracting State immediately before any breach of custody or access rights. The Convention shall cease to apply when the child attains the age of sixteen years.

Article 5

For the purposes of this Convention –

(a) 'rights of custody' shall include rights relating to the care of the person of the child and, in particular, the right to determine the child's place of residence;

(b) 'rights of access' shall include the right to take a child for a limited period of time to a place other than the child's habitual residence.

CHAPTER II
CENTRAL AUTHORITIES

Article 7

Central Authorities shall co-operate with each other and promote co-operation amongst the competent authorities in their respective States to secure the prompt return of children and to achieve the other objects of this Convention.

In particular, either directly or through any intermediary, they shall take all appropriate measures –

(a) to discover the whereabouts of a child who has been wrongfully removed or retained;

(b) to prevent further harm to the child or prejudice to interested parties by taking or causing to be taken provisional measures;

(c) to secure the voluntary return of the child or to bring about an amicable resolution of the issues;

(d) to exchange, where desirable, information relating to the social background of the child;

(e) to provide information of a general character as to the law of their State in connection with the application of the Convention;
(f) to initiate or facilitate the institution of judicial or administrative proceedings with a view to obtaining the return of the child, and in a proper case, to make arrangements for organizing or securing the effective exercise of rights of access;
(g) where the circumstances so require, to provide or facilitate the provision of legal aid and advice, including the participation of legal counsel and advisers;
(h) to provide such administrative arrangements as may be necessary and appropriate to secure the safe return of the child;
(i) to keep each other informed with respect to the operation of this Convention and, as far as possible, to eliminate any obstacles to its application.

CHAPTER III
RETURN OF CHILDREN

Article 8

Any person, institution or other body claiming that a child has been removed or retained in breach of custody rights may apply either to the Central Authority of the child's habitual residence or to the Central Authority of any other Contracting State for assistance in securing the return of the child.

The application shall contain –

(a) information concerning the identity of the applicant, of the child and of the person alleged to have removed or retained the child;
(b) where available, the date of birth of the child;
(c) the grounds on which the applicant's claim for return of the child is based;
(d) all available information relating to the whereabouts of the child and the identity of the person with whom the child is presumed to be.

The application may be accompanied or supplemented by –

(e) an authenticated copy of any relevant decision or agreement;
(f) a certificate or an affidavit emanating from a Central Authority, or other competent authority of the State of the child's habitual residence, or from a qualified person, concerning the relevant law of that State;
(g) any other relevant document.

Article 9

If the Central Authority which receives an application referred to in Article 8 has reason to believe that the child is in another Contracting State, it shall directly and without delay transmit the application to the Central Authority of that Contracting State and inform the requesting Central Authority, or the applicant, as the case may be.

Article 10

The Central Authority of the State where the child is shall take or cause to be taken all appropriate measures in order to obtain the voluntary return of the child.

Article 11

The Judicial or administrative authorities of Contracting States shall act expeditiously in proceedings for the return of children.

If the judicial or administrative authority concerned has not reached a decision within six weeks from the date of commencement of the proceedings, the applicant or the Central Authority of the requested State, on its own initiative or if asked by the Central Authority of the requesting State, shall have the right to request a statement of the reasons for the delay. If a reply is received by the Central Authority of the requested State, that Authority shall transmit the reply to the Central Authority of the requesting State, or to the applicant, as the case may be.

Article 12

Where a child has been wrongfully removed or retained in terms of Article 3 and, at the date of the commencement of the proceedings before the judicial or administrative authority of the Contracting State where the child is, a period of less than one year has elapsed from the date of the wrongful removal or retention, the authority concerned shall order the return of the child forthwith.

The judicial or administrative authority, even where the proceedings have been commenced after the expiration of the period of one year referred to in the preceding paragraph, shall also order the return of the child, unless it is demonstrated that the child is now settled in its new environment.

Where the judicial or administrative authority in the requested state has reason to believe that the child has been taken to another State, it may stay the proceedings or dismiss the application for the return of the child.

Article 13

Notwithstanding the provisions of the preceding Article, the judicial or administrative authority of the requested State is not bound to order the return of the child if the person, institution or other body which opposes its return establishes that –

(a) the person, institution or other body having the care of the person of the child was not actually exercising the custody rights at the time of removal or retention, or had consented to or subsequently acquiesced in the removal or retention; or

(b) there is a grave risk that his or her return would expose the child to physical or psychological harm or otherwise place the child in an intolerable situation.

The judicial or administrative authority may also refuse to order the return of the child if it finds that the child objects to being returned and has attained an age and degree of maturity at which it is appropriate to take account of its views.

In considering the circumstances referred to in this Article, the judicial and administrative authorities shall take into account the information relating to the social background of the child provided by the Central Authority or other competent authority of the child's habitual residence.

Article 14

In ascertaining whether there has been a wrongful removal or retention within the meaning of Article 3, the judicial or administrative authorities of the requested State may take notice directly of the law of, and of judicial or administrative decisions, formally recognised or not in the State of the habitual residence of the child, without recourse to the specific procedures for the proof of that law or for the recognition of foreign decisions which would otherwise be applicable.

Article 15

The judicial or administrative authorities of a Contracting State may, prior to the making of an order for the return of the child, request that the applicant obtain from the authorities of the State of the habitual residence of the child a decision or other determination that the removal or retention was wrongful within the meaning of Article 3 of the Convention, where such a decision or determination may be obtained in that State. The Central Authorities of the Contracting States shall so far as practicable assist applicants to obtain such a decision or determination.

Article 16

After receiving notice of a wrongful removal or retention of a child in the sense of Article 3, the judicial or administrative authorities of the Contracting State to which the child has been removed or in which it has been retained shall not decide on the merits of rights of custody until it has been determined that the child is not to be returned under this Convention or unless an application under this Convention is not lodged within a reasonable time following receipt of the notice.

Article 17

The sole fact that a decision relating to custody has been given in or is entitled to recognition in the requested State shall not be a ground for refusing to return a child under this Convention, but the judicial or administrative authorities of the requested State may take account of the reasons for that decision in applying this Convention.

Article 18

The provisions of this Chapter do not limit the power of a judicial or administrative authority to order the return of the child at any time.

Article 19

A decision under this Convention concerning the return of the child shall not be taken to be a determination on the merits of any custody issue.

CHAPTER IV
RIGHTS OF ACCESS

Article 21

An application to make arrangements for organising or securing the effective exercise of rights of access may be presented to the Central Authorities of the Contracting States in the same way as an application for the return of a child.

The Central Authorities are bound by the obligations of co-operation which are set forth in Article 7 to promote the peaceful enjoyment of access rights and the fulfilment of any conditions to which the exercise of those rights may be subject. The Central Authorities shall take steps to remove, as far as possible, all obstacles to the exercise of such rights. The Central Authorities, either directly or through intermediaries, may initiate or assist in the institution of proceedings with a view to organising or protecting these rights and securing respect for the conditions to which the exercise of these rights may be subject.

CHAPTER V
GENERAL PROVISIONS

Article 22

No security, bond or deposit, however described, shall be required to guarantee the payment of costs and expenses in the judicial or administrative proceedings falling within the scope of this Convention.

Article 24

Any application, communication or other document sent to the Central Authority of the requested State shall be in the original language, and shall be accompanied by a translation into the official language or one of the official languages of the requested State or, where that is not feasible, a translation into French or English.

Article 26

Each Central Authority shall bear its own costs in applying this Convention.

Central Authorities and other public services of Contracting States shall not impose any charges in relation to applications submitted under this Convention. In particular, they may not require any payment from the applicant towards the costs and expenses of the proceedings or, where applicable, those arising from the participation of legal counsel or advisers. However, they may require the payment of the expenses incurred or to be incurred in implementing the return of the child.

However, a Contracting State may, by making a reservation in accordance with Article 42, declare that it shall not be bound to assume any costs referred to in the preceding paragraph resulting from the participation of legal counsel or advisers or from court proceedings, except insofar as those costs may be covered by its system of legal aid and advice.

Upon ordering the return of a child or issuing an order concerning rights of access under this Convention, the judicial or administrative authorities may, where appropriate, direct the person who removed or retained the child, or who prevented the exercise of rights of access, to pay necessary expenses incurred by or on behalf of the applicant, including travel expenses, any costs incurred or payment made for locating the child, the costs of legal representation of the applicant, and those of returning the child.

Article 27

When it is manifest that the requirements of this Convention are not fulfilled or that the application is otherwise not well founded, a Central Authority is not bound to accept the application. In that case, the Central Authority shall forthwith inform the applicant or the Central Authority through which the application was submitted, as the case may be, of its reasons.

Article 28

A Central Authority may require that the application be accompanied by a written authorisation empowering it to act on behalf of the applicant, or to designate a representative so to act.

Article 29

This Convention shall not preclude any person, institution or body who claims that there has been a breach of custody or access rights within the meaning of

Article 3 or 21 from applying directly to the judicial or administrative authorities of a Contracting State, whether or not under the provisions of this Convention.

Article 30

Any application submitted to the Central Authorities or directly to the judicial or administrative authorities of a Contracting State in accordance with the terms of this Convention, together with documents and any other information appended thereto or provided by a Central Authority, shall be admissible in the courts or administrative authorities of the Contracting States.

Article 31

In relation to a State which in matters of custody of children has two or more systems of law applicable in different territorial units –

(a) any reference to habitual residence in that State shall be construed as referring to habitual residence in a territorial unit of that State;

(b) any reference to the law of the State of habitual residence shall be construed as referring to the law of the territorial unit in that State where the child habitually resides.

Article 32

In relation to a State which in matters of custody of children has two or more systems of law applicable to different categories of persons, any reference to the law of that State shall be construed as referring to the legal system specified by the law of that State.

SCHEDULE 2
EUROPEAN CONVENTION ON RECOGNITION AND ENFORCEMENT OF DECISIONS CONCERNING CUSTODY OF CHILDREN

Section 12(2)

Article 1

For the purposes of this Convention:

(a) 'child' means a person of any nationality, so long as he is under 16 years of age and has not the right to decide on his own place of residence under the law of his habitual residence, the law of his nationality or the internal law of the State addressed;

(b) 'authority' means a judicial or administrative authority;

(c) 'decision relating to custody' means a decision of an authority in so far as it relates to the care of the person of the child, including the right to decide on the place of his residence, or to the right of access to him;

(d) 'improper removal' means the removal of a child across an international frontier in breach of a decision relating to his custody which has been given in a Contracting State and which is enforceable in such a State; 'improper removal' also includes:
   (i) the failure to return a child across an international frontier at the end of a period of the exercise of the right of access to this child or at the end of any other temporary stay in a territory other than that where the custody is exercised;
   (ii) aremoval which is subsequently declared unlawful within the meaning of article 12.

Article 4

(1) Any person who has obtained in a Contracting State a decision relating to the custody of a child and who wishes to have that decision recognised or enforced in another Contracting State may submit an application for this purpose to the central authority in any Contracting State.

(2) The application shall be accompanied by the documents mentioned in Article 13.

(3) The central authority receiving the appplication, if it is not the central authority in the State addressed, shall send the document directly and without delay to that central authority.

(4) The central authority receiving the application may refuse to intervene where it is manifestly clear that the conditions laid down by this Convention are not satisfied.

(5) The central authority receiving the application shall keep the applicant informed without delay of the progress of his application.

Article 5

(1) The central authority in the State addressed shall take or cause to be taken without delay all steps which it considers to be appropriate, if necessary by instituting proceedings before its competent authorities, in order:
   (a) to discover the whereabouts of the child;
   (b) to avoid, in particular by any necessary provisional measures, prejudice to the interests of the child or of the applicant;
   (c) to secure the recognition or enforcement of the decision;
   (d) to secure the delivery of the child to the applicant where enforcement is granted;
   (e) to inform the requesting authority of the measures taken and their results.

(2) Where the central authority in the State addressed has reason to believe that the child is in the territory of another Contracting State it shall send the documents directly and without delay to the central authority of that State.

(3) With the exception of the cost of repatriation, each Contracting State undertakes not to claim any payment from an applicant in respect of any measures taken under paragraph (1) of this Article by the central authority of that State on the applicant's behalf, including the costs of proceedings and, where applicable, the costs incurred by the assistance of a lawyer.

(4) If recognition or enforcement is refused, and if the central authority of the State addressed considers that it should comply with a request by the applicant to bring in that State proceedings concerning the substance of the case, that authority shall use its best endeavours to secure the representation of the applicant in the proceedings under conditions no less favourable than those available to a person who is resident in and a national of that State and for this purpose it may, in particular, institute proceedings before its competent authorities.

Article 7

A decision relating to custody given in a Contracting State shall be recognised and, where it is enforceable in the State of origin, made enforceable in every other Contracting State.

Article 9

(1) (*Recognition and enforcement may be refused*) if:

(a) in the case of a decision given in the absence of the defendant or his legal representative, the defendant was not duly served with the document which instituted the proceedings or an equivalent document in sufficient time to enable him to arrange his defence; but such a failure to effect service cannot constitute a ground for refusing recognition or enforcement where service was not effected because the defendant had concealed his whereabouts from the person who instituted the proceedings in the State of origin;

(b) in the case of a decision given in the absence of the defendant or his legal representative, the competence of the authority giving the decision was not founded:

(i) on the habitual residence of the defendant; or

(ii) on the last common habitual residence of the child's parents, at least one parent being still habitually resident there, or

(iii) on the habitual residence of the child;

(c) the decision is incompatible with a decision relating to custody which became enforceable in the State addressed before the removal of the child, unless the child has had his habitual residence in the territory of the requesting State for one year before his removal.

(3) In no circumstances may the foreign decision be reviewed as to its substance.

Article 10

(1) (*Recognition and enforcement may also be refused*) on any of the following grounds:

(a) if it is found that the effects of the decision are manifestly incompatible with the fundamental principles of the law relating to the family and children in the State addressed;

(b) if it is found that by reason of a change in the circumstances including the passage of time but not including a mere change in the residence of the child after an improper removal, the effects of the original decision are manifestly no longer in accordance with the welfare of the child;

(c) if at the time when the proceedings were instituted in the State of origin:

(i) the child was a national of the State addressed or was habitually resident there and no such connection existed with the State of origin;

(ii) the child was a national both of the State of origin and of the State addressed and was habitually resident in the State addressed;

(d) if the decision is incompatible with a decision given in the State addressed or enforceable in that State after being given in a third State, pursuant to proceedings begun before the submission of the request for recognition or enforcement, and if the refusal is in accordance with the welfare of the child.

(2) Proceedings for recognition or enforcement may be adjourned on any of the following grounds:

(a) if an ordinary form of review of the original decision has been commenced;

(b) if proceedings relating to the custody of the child, commenced before the proceedings in the State of origin were instituted, are pending in the State addressed;

(c) if another decision concerning the custody of the child is the subject of proceedings for enforcement or of any other proceedings concerning the recognition of the decision.

Article 11

(1) Decisions on rights of access and provisions of decisions relating to custody which deal with the rights of access shall be recognised and enforced subject to the same conditions as other decisions relating to custody.

(2) However, the competent authority of the State addressed may fix the conditions for the implementation and exercise of the right of access taking into account, in particular, undertakings given by the parties on this matter.

(3) Where no decision on the right of access has been taken or where recognition or enforcement of the decision relating to custody is refused, the central authority of the State addressed may apply to its competent authorities for a decision on the right of access if the person claiming a right of access so requests.

Article 12

Where, at the time of the removal of a child across an international frontier, there is no enforceable decision given in a Contracting State relating to his custody, the provisions of this Convention shall apply to any subsequent decision, relating to the custody of that child and declaring the removal to be unlawful, given in a Contracting State at the request of any interested person.

Article 13

(1) A request for recognition or enforcement in another Contracting State of a decision relating to custody shall be accompanied by:
  (a) a document authorising the central authority of the State addressed to act on behalf of the applicant or to designate another representative for that purpose;
  (b) a copy of the decision which satisfies the necessary conditions of authenticity;
  (c) in the case of a decision given in the absence of the defendant or his legal representative, a document which establishes that the defendant was duly served with the document which instituted the proceedings or an equivalent document;
  (d) if applicable, any document which establishes that, in accordance with the law of the State of origin, the decision is enforceable;
  (e) if possible, a statement indicating the whereabouts or likely whereabouts of the child in the State addressed;
  (f) proposals as to how the custody of the child should be restored.

Article 15

(1) Before reaching a decision under paragraph (1) (b) of Article 10, the authority concerned in the State addressed:
  (a) shall ascertain the child's views unless this is impracticable having regard in particular to his age and understanding; and
  (b) may request that any appropriate enquiries be carried out.

(2) The cost of enquiries in any Contracting State shall be met by the authorities of the State where they are carried out.

Requests for enquiries and the results of enquiries may be sent to the authority concerned through the central authorities.

Article 26

(1) In relation to a State which has in matters of custody two or more systems of law of territorial application:
  (a) reference to the law of a person's habitual residence or to the law of a person's nationality shall be construed as referring to the system of law determined by the rules in force in that State or, if there are no such

rules, to the system of law with which the person concerned is most closely connected;

(b) reference to the State of origin or to the State addressed shall be construed as referring, as the case may be, to the territorial unit where the decision was given or to the territorial unit where recognition or enforcement of the decision or restoration of custody is requested.

(2) Paragraph (1) (a) of this Article also applies *mutatis mutandis* to States which have in matters of custody two or more systems of law of personal application.

SCHEDULE 3
CUSTODY ORDERS

Section 27(1)

PART I
ENGLAND AND WALES

[1

The following are the orders referred to in section 27(1) of this Act –

(a) a care order under the Children Act 1989 (as defined by section 31(11) of that Act, read with section 105(1) and Schedule 14);

[(b) a child arrangements order (as defined by section 8 of the Act of 1989) if the arrangements regulated by the order consist of, or include, arrangements relating to either or both of the following –

(i) with whom a child is to live, or

(ii) when a child is to live with any person;][1] …[2]

[(bb) a special guardianship order (within the meaning of the Act of 1989); and][3]

(c) any order made by a court in England and Wales under any of the following enactments –

(i) section 9(1), 10(1) (a) or 11(a) of the Guardianship of Minors Act 1971;

(ii) section 42(1) or (2) or 43(1) of the Matrimonial Causes Act 1973;

(iii) section 2(2)(b), (4)(b) or (5) of the Guardianship Act 1973 as applied by section 34(5) of the Children Act 1975;

(iv) section 8(2)(a), 10(1) or 19(1)(ii) of the Domestic Proceedings and Magistrates' Courts Act 1978;

(v) …[3]][4]

2

An order made by the High Court in the exercise of its jurisdiction relating to wardship so far as it gives the care and control of a child to any person.

3

...[5]

4

An authorisation given by the Secretary of State under section 26(2) of the Children and Young Persons Act 1969 (except where the relevant order, within the meaning of that section, was made by virtue of the court which made it being satisfied that the child was guilty of an offence).

Amendments

1 Substituted by the Children and Families Act 2014, s 12, Sch 2, para 48.
2 Repealed by the Adoption and Children Act 2002, s 139(1), (3), Sch 3, para 45, Sch 5.
3 Inserted by the Adoption and Children Act 2002, s 139(1), Sch 3, para 45.
4 Substituted by the Children Act 1989, s 108(5), Sch 13, para 57(3).
5 Repealed by the Children (Northern Ireland Consequential Amendments) Order 1995, SI 1995/756, art 15, Schedule.

PART II
SCOTLAND

5

An order made by a court of civil jurisdiction in Scotland under any enactment or rule of law with respect to the [residence, custody, care or control of a child or contact with or][1] access to a child, excluding –

(i) an order placing a child under the supervision of a local authority;
(ii) ...[2];
[(iia) ...[2]][3]
(iii) an order relating to the [guardianship][1] of a child;
(iv) an order made under section [86 of the Children (Scotland) Act 1995][1];
[(v) an order made, or warrant or authorisation granted, under or by virtue of Chapter 2 or 3 of Part II of the Children (Scotland) Act 1995 to remove the child to a place of safety or to secure accommodation, to keep him at such a place or in such accommodation, or to prevent his removal from a place where he is being accommodated (or an order varying or discharging any order, warrant or authorisation so made or granted);][1]
(vi) an order made in proceedings under this Act.
[(vii) an adoption order (as defined in section 28(1) of the Adoption and Children (Scotland) Act 2007 (asp 4);
(viii) a permanence order (as defined in subsection (2) of section 80 of that Act) which includes provision such as is mentioned in paragraph (c) of that subsection;][4]
[(ix) an order made, or warrant or authorisation granted, under or by virtue of the Children's Hearings (Scotland) Act 2011 to remove the child to a place of safety or to secure accommodation (those expressions having the meanings given by section 202(1) of that Act), to keep the child at

such a place or in such accommodation, or to prevent the removal of the child from a place where the child is being accommodated (or an order continuing, varying or discharging any order, warrant or authorisation so made or granted).][5]

[5A

The reference in paragraph 5(viii) to a permanence order includes a deemed permanence order having effect by virtue of article 13(1), 14(2), 17(1) or 19(2) of the Adoption and Children (Scotland) Act 2007 (Commencement No. 4, Transitional and Savings Provisions) Order 2009.][4]

[6

A compulsory supervision order (as defined in section 83 of the Children's Hearings (Scotland) Act 2011) and any order made by a court in England and Wales or in Northern Ireland which, by virtue section 190 of that Act has effect as if it were a compulsory supervision order.][5]

7

...[6]

Amendments

1 Substituted by the Children (Scotland) Act 1995, s 105(4), Sch 4, para 37(1), (6)(a).
2 Repealed by the Adoption and Children (Scotland) Act 2007, s 120(2), Sch 3 (extended to England, Wales and Northern Ireland by the Adoption and Children (Scotland) Act 2007 (Consequential Modifications) Order 2011, SI 2011/1740, art 3, Sch 2, Pt 3).
3 Inserted by the Family Law Act 1986, s 68(1), Sch 1, para 31.
4 Inserted by the Adoption and Children (Scotland) Act 2007, s 120(1), Sch 2, para 4 (extended to England, Wales and Northern Ireland by the Adoption and Children (Scotland) Act 2007 (Consequential Modifications) Order 2011, SI 2011/1740, art 3, Sch 2, Pt 1, para 1(1), (2)).
5 Inserted by the Children's Hearings (Scotland) Act 2011 (Consequential and Transitional Provisions and Savings) Order 2013, SI 2013/1465, art 17, Sch 1, Pt 1, para 1(1), (3).
6 Repealed by the Children (Scotland) Act 1995, s 105(4), (5), Sch 4, para 37(1), (6)(c), Sch 5.

PART III: NORTHERN IRELAND

[8

The following orders –

(a) a care order under the Children (Northern Ireland) Order 1995 (as defined by Article 49(1) of that Order read with Article 2(2) and Schedule 8);
(b) a residence order (as defined by Article 8 of that Order);
(c) any order made by a court in Northern Ireland under any of the following enactments –

(i) section 5 of the Guardianship of Infants Act 1886 (except so far as it relates to costs);
(ii) section 49 of the Mental Health Act (Northern Ireland) 1961;
(iii) Article 45(1) or (2) or 46 of the Matrimonial Causes (Northern Ireland) Order 1978;
(iv) Article 10(2)(a), 12(1) or 20(1)(ii) of the Domestic Proceedings (Northern Ireland) Order 1980;
(v) Article 27(1)(b) of the Adoption (Northern Ireland) Order 1987.][1]

9

An order made by the High Court in the exercise of its jurisdiction relating to wardship so far as it gives the care and control of a child to any person.

10

...[2]

Amendments

1 Substituted by the Children (Northern Ireland Consequential Amendments) Order 1995, SI 1995/756, art 11(1), (5).
2 Repealed by the Children (Northern Ireland Consequential Amendments) Order 1995, SI 1995/756, art 15, Schedule.

1980 Hague Convention on the Civil Aspects of International Child Abduction

(Concluded 25 October 1980)

The States signatory to the present Convention,

Firmly convinced that the interests of children are of paramount importance in matters relating to their custody,

Desiring to protect children internationally from the harmful effects of their wrongful removal or retention and to establish procedures to ensure their prompt return to the State of their habitual residence, as well as to secure protection for rights of access,

Have resolved to conclude a Convention to this effect, and have agreed upon the following provisions –

CHAPTER I – SCOPE OF THE CONVENTION

Article 1

The objects of the present Convention are –

a) to secure the prompt return of children wrongfully removed to or retained in any Contracting State; and

b) to ensure that rights of custody and of access under the law of one Contracting State are effectively respected in the other Contracting States.

Article 2

Contracting States shall take all appropriate measures to secure within their territories the implementation of the objects of the Convention. For this purpose they shall use the most expeditious procedures available.

Article 3

The removal or the retention of a child is to be considered wrongful where –

a) it is in breach of rights of custody attributed to a person, an institution or any other body, either jointly or alone, under the law of the State in which the child was habitually resident immediately before the removal or retention; and

b) at the time of removal or retention those rights were actually exercised, either jointly or alone, or would have been so exercised but for the removal or retention.

The rights of custody mentioned in sub-paragraph a) above, may arise in particular by operation of law or by reason of a judicial or administrative decision, or by reason of an agreement having legal effect under the law of that State.

Article 4

The Convention shall apply to any child who was habitually resident in a Contracting State immediately before any breach of custody or access rights. The Convention shall cease to apply when the child attains the age of 16 years.

Article 5

For the purposes of this Convention –

a) 'rights of custody' shall include rights relating to the care of the person of the child and, in particular, the right to determine the child's place of residence;
b) 'rights of access' shall include the right to take a child for a limited period of time to a place other than the child's habitual residence.

CHAPTER II – CENTRAL AUTHORITIES

Article 6

A Contracting State shall designate a Central Authority to discharge the duties which are imposed by the Convention upon such authorities.

Federal States, States with more than one system of law or States having autonomous territorial organisations shall be free to appoint more than one Central Authority and to specify the territorial extent of their powers. Where a State has appointed more than one Central Authority, it shall designate the Central Authority to which applications may be addressed for transmission to the appropriate Central Authority within that State.

Article 7

Central Authorities shall co-operate with each other and promote co-operation amongst the competent authorities in their respective States to secure the prompt return of children and to achieve the other objects of this Convention.

In particular, either directly or through any intermediary, they shall take all appropriate measures –

a) to discover the whereabouts of a child who has been wrongfully removed or retained;
b) to prevent further harm to the child or prejudice to interested parties by taking or causing to be taken provisional measures;
c) to secure the voluntary return of the child or to bring about an amicable resolution of the issues;
d) to exchange, where desirable, information relating to the social background of the child;
e) to provide information of a general character as to the law of their State in connection with the application of the Convention;
f) to initiate or facilitate the institution of judicial or administrative proceedings with a view to obtaining the return of the child and, in a proper case, to make arrangements for organising or securing the effective exercise of rights of access;
g) where the circumstances so require, to provide or facilitate the provision of legal aid and advice, including the participation of legal counsel and advisers;
h) to provide such administrative arrangements as may be necessary and appropriate to secure the safe return of the child;
i) to keep each other informed with respect to the operation of this Convention and, as far as possible, to eliminate any obstacles to its application.

CHAPTER III – RETURN OF CHILDREN

Article 8

Any person, institution or other body claiming that a child has been removed or retained in breach of custody rights may apply either to the Central Authority of the child's habitual residence or to the Central Authority of any other Contracting State for assistance in securing the return of the child. The application shall contain –

a) information concerning the identity of the applicant, of the child and of the person alleged to have removed or retained the child;
b) where available, the date of birth of the child;
c) the grounds on which the applicant's claim for return of the child is based;
d) all available information relating to the whereabouts of the child and the identity of the person with whom the child is presumed to be.

The application may be accompanied or supplemented by –

e) an authenticated copy of any relevant decision or agreement;
f) a certificate or an affidavit emanating from a Central Authority, or other competent authority of the State of the child's habitual residence, or from a qualified person, concerning the relevant law of that State;
g) any other relevant document.

Article 9

If the Central Authority which receives an application referred to in Article 8 has reason to believe that the child is in another Contracting State, it shall directly and without delay transmit the application to the Central Authority of that Contracting State and inform the requesting Central Authority, or the applicant, as the case may be.

Article 10

The Central Authority of the State where the child is shall take or cause to be taken all appropriate measures in order to obtain the voluntary return of the child.

Article 11

The judicial or administrative authorities of Contracting States shall act expeditiously in proceedings for the return of children.

If the judicial or administrative authority concerned has not reached a decision within six weeks from the date of commencement of the proceedings, the applicant or the Central Authority of the requested State, on its own initiative or if asked by the Central Authority of the requesting State, shall have the right to request a statement of the reasons for the delay. If a reply is received by the Central Authority of the requested State, that Authority shall transmit the reply to the Central Authority of the requesting State, or to the applicant, as the case may be.

Article 12

Where a child has been wrongfully removed or retained in terms of Article 3 and, at the date of the commencement of the proceedings before the judicial or administrative authority of the Contracting State where the child is, a period of less than one year has elapsed from the date of the wrongful removal or retention, the authority concerned shall order the return of the child forthwith.

The judicial or administrative authority, even where the proceedings have been commenced after the expiration of the period of one year referred to in the preceding paragraph, shall also order the return of the child, unless it is demonstrated that the child is now settled in its new environment.

Where the judicial or administrative authority in the requested State has reason to believe that the child has been taken to another State, it may stay the proceedings or dismiss the application for the return of the child.

Article 13

Notwithstanding the provisions of the preceding Article, the judicial or administrative authority of the requested State is not bound to order the return of the child if the person, institution or other body which opposes its return establishes that –

a) the person, institution or other body having the care of the person of the child was not actually exercising the custody rights at the time of removal or retention, or had consented to or subsequently acquiesced in the removal or retention; or
b) there is a grave risk that his or her return would expose the child to physical or psychological harm or otherwise place the child in an intolerable situation.

The judicial or administrative authority may also refuse to order the return of the child if it finds that the child objects to being returned and has attained an age and degree of maturity at which it is appropriate to take account of its views.

In considering the circumstances referred to in this Article, the judicial and administrative authorities shall take into account the information relating to the social background of the child provided by the Central Authority or other competent authority of the child's habitual residence.

Article 14

In ascertaining whether there has been a wrongful removal or retention within the meaning of Article 3, the judicial or administrative authorities of the requested State may take notice directly of the law of, and of judicial or administrative decisions, formally recognised or not in the State of the habitual residence of the child, without recourse to the specific procedures for the proof of that law or for the recognition of foreign decisions which would otherwise be applicable.

Article 15

The judicial or administrative authorities of a Contracting State may, prior to the making of an order for the return of the child, request that the applicant obtain from the authorities of the State of the habitual residence of the child a decision or other determination that the removal or retention was wrongful within the meaning of Article 3 of the Convention, where such a decision or determination may be obtained in that State. The Central Authorities of the Contracting States shall so far as practicable assist applicants to obtain such a decision or determination.

Article 16

After receiving notice of a wrongful removal or retention of a child in the sense of Article 3, the judicial or administrative authorities of the Contracting State to which the child has been removed or in which it has been retained shall not decide on the merits of rights of custody until it has been determined that the child is not to be returned under this Convention or unless an application under this Convention is not lodged within a reasonable time following receipt of the notice.

Article 17

The sole fact that a decision relating to custody has been given in or is entitled to recognition in the requested State shall not be a ground for refusing to return a child under this Convention, but the judicial or administrative authorities of the requested State may take account of the reasons for that decision in applying this Convention.

Article 18

The provisions of this Chapter do not limit the power of a judicial or administrative authority to order the return of the child at any time.

Article 19

A decision under this Convention concerning the return of the child shall not be taken to be a determination on the merits of any custody issue.

Article 20

The return of the child under the provisions of Article 12 may be refused if this would not be permitted by the fundamental principles of the requested State relating to the protection of human rights and fundamental freedoms.

CHAPTER IV – RIGHTS OF ACCESS

Article 21

An application to make arrangements for organising or securing the effective exercise of rights of access may be presented to the Central Authorities of the Contracting States in the same way as an application for the return of a child.

The Central Authorities are bound by the obligations of co-operation which are set forth in Article 7 to promote the peaceful enjoyment of access rights and the fulfilment of any conditions to which the exercise of those rights may be subject. The Central Authorities shall take steps to remove, as far as possible, all obstacles to the exercise of such rights.

The Central Authorities, either directly or through intermediaries, may initiate or assist in the institution of proceedings with a view to organising or protecting these rights and securing respect for the conditions to which the exercise of these rights may be subject.

CHAPTER V – GENERAL PROVISIONS

Article 22

No security, bond or deposit, however described, shall be required to guarantee the payment of costs and expenses in the judicial or administrative proceedings falling within the scope of this Convention.

Article 23

No legalisation or similar formality may be required in the context of this Convention.

Article 24

Any application, communication or other document sent to the Central Authority of the requested State shall be in the original language, and shall be accompanied by a translation into the official language or one of the official languages of the requested State or, where that is not feasible, a translation into French or English.

However, a Contracting State may, by making a reservation in accordance with Article 42, object to the use of either French or English, but not both, in any application, communication or other document sent to its Central Authority.

Article 25

Nationals of the Contracting States and persons who are habitually resident within those States shall be entitled in matters concerned with the application of this Convention to legal aid and advice in any other Contracting State on the same conditions as if they themselves were nationals of and habitually resident in that State.

Article 26

Each Central Authority shall bear its own costs in applying this Convention.

Central Authorities and other public services of Contracting States shall not impose any charges in relation to applications submitted under this Convention. In particular, they may not require any payment from the applicant towards the costs and expenses of the proceedings or, where applicable, those arising from the participation of legal counsel or advisers. However, they may require the payment of the expenses incurred or to be incurred in implementing the return of the child.

However, a Contracting State may, by making a reservation in accordance with Article 42, declare that it shall not be bound to assume any costs referred to in the preceding paragraph resulting from the participation of legal counsel or advisers or from court proceedings, except insofar as those costs may be covered by its system of legal aid and advice.

Upon ordering the return of a child or issuing an order concerning rights of access under this Convention, the judicial or administrative authorities may, where appropriate, direct the person who removed or retained the child, or who prevented the exercise of rights of access, to pay necessary expenses incurred by or on behalf of the applicant, including travel expenses, any costs incurred or payments made for locating the child, the costs of legal representation of the applicant, and those of returning the child.

Article 27

When it is manifest that the requirements of this Convention are not fulfilled or that the application is otherwise not well founded, a Central Authority is not bound to accept the application. In that case, the Central Authority shall forthwith inform the applicant or the Central Authority through which the application was submitted, as the case may be, of its reasons.

Article 28

A Central Authority may require that the application be accompanied by a written authorisation empowering it to act on behalf of the applicant, or to designate a representative so to act.

Article 29

This Convention shall not preclude any person, institution or body who claims that there has been a breach of custody or access rights within the meaning of Article 3 or 21 from applying directly to the judicial or administrative authorities of a Contracting State, whether or not under the provisions of this Convention.

Article 30

Any application submitted to the Central Authorities or directly to the judicial or administrative authorities of a Contracting State in accordance with the terms of this Convention, together with documents and any other information appended thereto or provided by a Central Authority, shall be admissible in the courts or administrative authorities of the Contracting States.

Article 31

In relation to a State which in matters of custody of children has two or more systems of law applicable in different territorial units –

a) any reference to habitual residence in that State shall be construed as referring to habitual residence in a territorial unit of that State;

b) any reference to the law of the State of habitual residence shall be construed as referring to the law of the territorial unit in that State where the child habitually resides.

Article 32

In relation to a State which in matters of custody of children has two or more systems of law applicable to different categories of persons, any reference to the law of that State shall be construed as referring to the legal system specified by the law of that State.

Article 33

A State within which different territorial units have their own rules of law in respect of custody of children shall not be bound to apply this Convention where a State with a unified system of law would not be bound to do so.

Article 34

This Convention shall take priority in matters within its scope over the Convention of 5 October 1961 concerning the powers of authorities and the law applicable in respect of the protection of minors, as between Parties to both Conventions. Otherwise the present Convention shall not restrict the application of an international instrument in force between the State of origin and the State addressed or other law of the State addressed for the purposes of obtaining the return of a child who has been wrongfully removed or retained or of organising access rights.

Article 35

This Convention shall apply as between Contracting States only to wrongful removals or retentions occurring after its entry into force in those States.

Where a declaration has been made under Article 39 or 40, the reference in the preceding paragraph to a Contracting State shall be taken to refer to the territorial unit or units in relation to which this Convention applies.

Article 36

Nothing in this Convention shall prevent two or more Contracting States, in order to limit the restrictions to which the return of the child may be subject, from agreeing among themselves to derogate from any provisions of this Convention which may imply such a restriction.

CHAPTER VI – FINAL CLAUSES

Article 37

The Convention shall be open for signature by the States which were Members of the Hague Conference on Private International Law at the time of its Fourteenth Session.

It shall be ratified, accepted or approved and the instruments of ratification, acceptance or approval shall be deposited with the Ministry of Foreign Affairs of the Kingdom of the Netherlands.

Article 38

Any other State may accede to the Convention.

The instrument of accession shall be deposited with the Ministry of Foreign Affairs of the Kingdom of the Netherlands.

The Convention shall enter into force for a State acceding to it on the first day of the third calendar month after the deposit of its instrument of accession.

The accession will have effect only as regards the relations between the acceding State and such Contracting States as will have declared their acceptance of the accession. Such a declaration will also have to be made by any Member State ratifying, accepting or approving the Convention after an accession. Such declaration shall be deposited at the Ministry of Foreign Affairs of the Kingdom of the Netherlands; this Ministry shall forward, through diplomatic channels, a certified copy to each of the Contracting States.

The Convention will enter into force as between the acceding State and the State that has declared its acceptance of the accession on the first day of the third calendar month after the deposit of the declaration of acceptance.

Article 39

Any State may, at the time of signature, ratification, acceptance, approval or accession, declare that the Convention shall extend to all the territories for the international relations of which it is responsible, or to one or more of them. Such a declaration shall take effect at the time the Convention enters into force for that State.

Such declaration, as well as any subsequent extension, shall be notified to the Ministry of Foreign Affairs of the Kingdom of the Netherlands.

Article 40

If a Contracting State has two or more territorial units in which different systems of law are applicable in relation to matters dealt with in this Convention, it may at the time of signature, ratification, acceptance, approval or accession declare that this Convention shall extend to all its territorial units or only to one or more of them and may modify this declaration by submitting another declaration at any time.

Any such declaration shall be notified to the Ministry of Foreign Affairs of the Kingdom of the Netherlands and shall state expressly the territorial units to which the Convention applies.

Article 41

Where a Contracting State has a system of government under which executive, judicial and legislative powers are distributed between central and other authorities within that State, its signature or ratification, acceptance or approval of, or accession to this Convention, or its making of any declaration in terms of Article 40 shall carry no implication as to the internal distribution of powers within that State.

Article 42

Any State may, not later than the time of ratification, acceptance, approval or accession, or at the time of making a declaration in terms of Article 39 or 40, make one or both of the reservations provided for in Article 24 and Article 26, third paragraph. No other reservation shall be permitted.

Any State may at any time withdraw a reservation it has made. The withdrawal shall be notified to the Ministry of Foreign Affairs of the Kingdom of the Netherlands.

The reservation shall cease to have effect on the first day of the third calendar month after the notification referred to in the preceding paragraph.

Article 43

The Convention shall enter into force on the first day of the third calendar month after the deposit of the third instrument of ratification, acceptance, approval or accession referred to in Articles 37 and 38.

Thereafter the Convention shall enter into force –

(1) for each State ratifying, accepting, approving or acceding to it subsequently, on the first day of the third calendar month after the deposit of its instrument of ratification, acceptance, approval or accession;

(2) for any territory or territorial unit to which the Convention has been extended in conformity with Article 39 or 40, on the first day of the third calendar month after the notification referred to in that Article.

Article 44

The Convention shall remain in force for five years from the date of its entry into force in accordance with the first paragraph of Article 43 even for States which subsequently have ratified, accepted, approved it or acceded to it.

If there has been no denunciation, it shall be renewed tacitly every five years.

Any denunciation shall be notified to the Ministry of Foreign Affairs of the Kingdom of the Netherlands at least six months before the expiry of the five year period. It may be limited to certain of the territories or territorial units to which the Convention applies.

The denunciation shall have effect only as regards the State which has notified it. The Convention shall remain in force for the other Contracting States.

Article 45

The Ministry of Foreign Affairs of the Kingdom of the Netherlands shall notify the States Members of the Conference, and the States which have acceded in accordance with Article 38, of the following –

(1) the signatures and ratifications, acceptances and approvals referred to in Article 37;
(2) the accessions referred to in Article 38;
(3) the date on which the Convention enters into force in accordance with Article 43;
(4) the extensions referred to in Article 39;
(5) the declarations referred to in Articles 38 and 40;
(6) the reservations referred to in Article 24 and Article 26, third paragraph, and the withdrawals referred to in Article 42;
(7) the denunciations referred to in Article 44.

In witness whereof the undersigned, being duly authorised thereto, have signed this Convention.

Done at The Hague, on the 25th day of October, 1980, in the English and French languages, both texts being equally authentic, in a single copy which shall be deposited in the archives of the Government of the Kingdom of the Netherlands, and of which a certified copy shall be sent, through diplomatic channels, to each of the States Members of the Hague Conference on Private International Law at the date of its Fourteenth Session.

1996 Hague Convention on Jurisdiction, Applicable Law, Recognition, Enforcement and Co-operation in Respect of Parental Responsibility and Measures for the Protection of Children

(Concluded 19 October 1996)

The States signatory to the present Convention,

Considering the need to improve the protection of children in international situations,

Wishing to avoid conflicts between their legal systems in respect of jurisdiction, applicable law, recognition and enforcement of measures for the protection of children,

Recalling the importance of international co-operation for the protection of children,

Confirming that the best interests of the child are to be a primary consideration,

Noting that the Convention of 5 October 1961 concerning the powers of authorities and the law applicable in respect of the protection of minors is in need of revision,

Desiring to establish common provisions to this effect, taking into account the United Nations Convention on the Rights of the Child of 20 November 1989,

Have agreed on the following provisions –

CHAPTER I – SCOPE OF THE CONVENTION

Article 1

(1) The objects of the present Convention are –

a) to determine the State whose authorities have jurisdiction to take measures directed to the protection of the person or property of the child;
b) to determine which law is to be applied by such authorities in exercising their jurisdiction;
c) to determine the law applicable to parental responsibility;
d) to provide for the recognition and enforcement of such measures of protection in all Contracting States;

e) to establish such co-operation between the authorities of the Contracting States as may be necessary in order to achieve the purposes of this Convention.

(2) For the purposes of this Convention, the term 'parental responsibility' includes parental authority, or any analogous relationship of authority determining the rights, powers and responsibilities of parents, guardians or other legal representatives in relation to the person or the property of the child.

Article 2

The Convention applies to children from the moment of their birth until they reach the age of 18 years.

Article 3

The measures referred to in Article 1 may deal in particular with –

a) the attribution, exercise, termination or restriction of parental responsibility, as well as its delegation;
b) rights of custody, including rights relating to the care of the person of the child and, in particular, the right to determine the child's place of residence, as well as rights of access including the right to take a child for a limited period of time to a place other than the child's habitual residence;
c) guardianship, curatorship and analogous institutions;
d) the designation and functions of any person or body having charge of the child's person or property, representing or assisting the child;
e) the placement of the child in a foster family or in institutional care, or the provision of care by kafala or an analogous institution;
f) the supervision by a public authority of the care of a child by any person having charge of the child;
g) the administration, conservation or disposal of the child's property.

Article 4

The Convention does not apply to –

a) the establishment or contesting of a parent-child relationship;
b) decisions on adoption, measures preparatory to adoption, or the annulment or revocation of adoption;
c) the name and forenames of the child;
d) emancipation;
e) maintenance obligations;
f) trusts or succession;
g) social security;
h) public measures of a general nature in matters of education or health;
i) measures taken as a result of penal offences committed by children;
j) decisions on the right of asylum and on immigration.

CHAPTER II – JURISDICTION

Article 5

(1) The judicial or administrative authorities of the Contracting State of the habitual residence of the child have jurisdiction to take measures directed to the protection of the child's person or property.

(2) Subject to Article 7, in case of a change of the child's habitual residence to another Contracting State, the authorities of the State of the new habitual residence have jurisdiction.

Article 6

(1) For refugee children and children who, due to disturbances occurring in their country, are internationally displaced, the authorities of the Contracting State on the territory of which these children are present as a result of their displacement have the jurisdiction provided for in paragraph 1 of Article 5.

(2) The provisions of the preceding paragraph also apply to children whose habitual residence cannot be established.

Article 7

(1) In case of wrongful removal or retention of the child, the authorities of the Contracting State in which the child was habitually resident immediately before the removal or retention keep their jurisdiction until the child has acquired a habitual residence in another State, and
  a) each person, institution or other body having rights of custody has acquiesced in the removal or retention; or
  b) the child has resided in that other State for a period of at least one year after the person, institution or other body having rights of custody has or should have had knowledge of the whereabouts of the child, no request for return lodged within that period is still pending, and the child is settled in his or her new environment.

(2) The removal or the retention of a child is to be considered wrongful where –
  a) it is in breach of rights of custody attributed to a person, an institution or any other body, either jointly or alone, under the law of the State in which the child was habitually resident immediately before the removal or retention; and
  b) at the time of removal or retention those rights were actually exercised, either jointly or alone, or would have been so exercised but for the removal or retention.

The rights of custody mentioned in sub-paragraph a above, may arise in particular by operation of law or by reason of a judicial or administrative decision, or by reason of an agreement having legal effect under the law of that State.

(3) So long as the authorities first mentioned in paragraph 1 keep their jurisdiction, the authorities of the Contracting State to which the child has been removed or in which he or she has been retained can take only such urgent measures under Article 11 as are necessary for the protection of the person or property of the child.

Article 8

(1) By way of exception, the authority of a Contracting State having jurisdiction under Article 5 or 6, if it considers that the authority of another Contracting State would be better placed in the particular case to assess the best interests of the child, may either
— request that other authority, directly or with the assistance of the Central Authority of its State, to assume jurisdiction to take such measures of protection as it considers to be necessary, or
— suspend consideration of the case and invite the parties to introduce such a request before the authority of that other State.

(2) The Contracting States whose authorities may be addressed as provided in the preceding paragraph are
a) a State of which the child is a national,
b) a State in which property of the child is located,
c) a State whose authorities are seised of an application for divorce or legal separation of the child's parents, or for annulment of their marriage,
d) a State with which the child has a substantial connection.

(3) The authorities concerned may proceed to an exchange of views.

(4) The authority addressed as provided in paragraph 1 may assume jurisdiction, in place of the authority having jurisdiction under Article 5 or 6, if it considers that this is in the child's best interests.

Article 9

(1) If the authorities of a Contracting State referred to in Article 8, paragraph 2, consider that they are better placed in the particular case to assess the child's best interests, they may either
— request the competent authority of the Contracting State of the habitual residence of the child, directly or with the assistance of the Central Authority of that State, that they be authorised to exercise jurisdiction to take the measures of protection which they consider to be necessary, or
— invite the parties to introduce such a request before the authority of the Contracting State of the habitual residence of the child.

(2) The authorities concerned may proceed to an exchange of views.

(3) The authority initiating the request may exercise jurisdiction in place of the authority of the Contracting State of the habitual residence of the child only if the latter authority has accepted the request.

Article 10

(1) Without prejudice to Articles 5 to 9, the authorities of a Contracting State exercising jurisdiction to decide upon an application for divorce or legal separation of the parents of a child habitually resident in another Contracting State, or for annulment of their marriage, may, if the law of their State so provides, take measures directed to the protection of the person or property of such child if

a) at the time of commencement of the proceedings, one of his or her parents habitually resides in that State and one of them has parental responsibility in relation to the child, and

b) the jurisdiction of these authorities to take such measures has been accepted by the parents, as well as by any other person who has parental responsibility in relation to the child, and is in the best interests of the child.

(2) The jurisdiction provided for by paragraph 1 to take measures for the protection of the child ceases as soon as the decision allowing or refusing the application for divorce, legal separation or annulment of the marriage has become final, or the proceedings have come to an end for another reason.

Article 11

(1) In all cases of urgency, the authorities of any Contracting State in whose territory the child or property belonging to the child is present have jurisdiction to take any necessary measures of protection.

(2) The measures taken under the preceding paragraph with regard to a child habitually resident in a Contracting State shall lapse as soon as the authorities which have jurisdiction under Articles 5 to 10 have taken the measures required by the situation.

(3) The measures taken under paragraph 1 with regard to a child who is habitually resident in a non-Contracting State shall lapse in each Contracting State as soon as measures required by the situation and taken by the authorities of another State are recognised in the Contracting State in question.

Article 12

(1) Subject to Article 7, the authorities of a Contracting State in whose territory the child or property belonging to the child is present have jurisdiction to take measures of a provisional character for the protection of the person or property of the child which have a territorial effect limited to the State in question, in so far as such measures are not incompatible with measures already taken by authorities which have jurisdiction under Articles 5 to 10.

(2) The measures taken under the preceding paragraph with regard to a child habitually resident in a Contracting State shall lapse as soon as the authorities

which have jurisdiction under Articles 5 to 10 have taken a decision in respect of the measures of protection which may be required by the situation.

(3) The measures taken under paragraph 1 with regard to a child who is habitually resident in a non-Contracting State shall lapse in the Contracting State where the measures were taken as soon as measures required by the situation and taken by the authorities of another State are recognised in the Contracting State in question.

Article 13

(1) The authorities of a Contracting State which have jurisdiction under Articles 5 to 10 to take measures for the protection of the person or property of the child must abstain from exercising this jurisdiction if, at the time of the commencement of the proceedings, corresponding measures have been requested from the authorities of another Contracting State having jurisdiction under Articles 5 to 10 at the time of the request and are still under consideration.

(2) The provisions of the preceding paragraph shall not apply if the authorities before whom the request for measures was initially introduced have declined jurisdiction.

Article 14

The measures taken in application of Articles 5 to 10 remain in force according to their terms, even if a change of circumstances has eliminated the basis upon which jurisdiction was founded, so long as the authorities which have jurisdiction under the Convention have not modified, replaced or terminated such measures.

CHAPTER III – APPLICABLE LAW

Article 15

(1) In exercising their jurisdiction under the provisions of Chapter II, the authorities of the Contracting States shall apply their own law.

(2) However, in so far as the protection of the person or the property of the child requires, they may exceptionally apply or take into consideration the law of another State with which the situation has a substantial connection.

(3) If the child's habitual residence changes to another Contracting State, the law of that other State governs, from the time of the change, the conditions of application of the measures taken in the State of the former habitual residence.

Article 16

(1) The attribution or extinction of parental responsibility by operation of law, without the intervention of a judicial or administrative authority, is governed by the law of the State of the habitual residence of the child.

(2) The attribution or extinction of parental responsibility by an agreement or a unilateral act, without intervention of a judicial or administrative authority, is governed by the law of the State of the child's habitual residence at the time when the agreement or unilateral act takes effect.

(3) Parental responsibility which exists under the law of the State of the child's habitual residence subsists after a change of that habitual residence to another State.

(4) If the child's habitual residence changes, the attribution of parental responsibility by operation of law to a person who does not already have such responsibility is governed by the law of the State of the new habitual residence.

Article 17

The exercise of parental responsibility is governed by the law of the State of the child's habitual residence. If the child's habitual residence changes, it is governed by the law of the State of the new habitual residence.

Article 18

The parental responsibility referred to in Article 16 may be terminated, or the conditions of its exercise modified, by measures taken under this Convention.

Article 19

(1) The validity of a transaction entered into between a third party and another person who would be entitled to act as the child's legal representative under the law of the State where the transaction was concluded cannot be contested, and the third party cannot be held liable, on the sole ground that the other person was not entitled to act as the child's legal representative under the law designated by the provisions of this Chapter, unless the third party knew or should have known that the parental responsibility was governed by the latter law.

(2) The preceding paragraph applies only if the transaction was entered into between persons present on the territory of the same State.

Article 20

The provisions of this Chapter apply even if the law designated by them is the law of a non-Contracting State.

Article 21

(1) In this Chapter the term 'law' means the law in force in a State other than its choice of law rules.

(2) However, if the law applicable according to Article 16 is that of a non-Contracting State and if the choice of law rules of that State designate the law of another non-Contracting State which would apply its own law, the law of the latter State applies. If that other non-Contracting State would not apply its own law, the applicable law is that designated by Article 16.

Article 22

The application of the law designated by the provisions of this Chapter can be refused only if this application would be manifestly contrary to public policy, taking into account the best interests of the child.

CHAPTER IV – RECOGNITION AND ENFORCEMENT

Article 23

(1) The measures taken by the authorities of a Contracting State shall be recognised by operation of law in all other Contracting States.

(2) Recognition may however be refused –
   a) if the measure was taken by an authority whose jurisdiction was not based on one of the grounds provided for in Chapter II;
   b) if the measure was taken, except in a case of urgency, in the context of a judicial or administrative proceeding, without the child having been provided the opportunity to be heard, in violation of fundamental principles of procedure of the requested State;
   c) on the request of any person claiming that the measure infringes his or her parental responsibility, if such measure was taken, except in a case of urgency, without such person having been given an opportunity to be heard;
   d) if such recognition is manifestly contrary to public policy of the requested State, taking into account the best interests of the child;
   e) if the measure is incompatible with a later measure taken in the non-Contracting State of the habitual residence of the child, where this later measure fulfils the requirements for recognition in the requested State;
   f) if the procedure provided in Article 33 has not been complied with.

Article 24

Without prejudice to Article 23, paragraph 1, any interested person may request from the competent authorities of a Contracting State that they decide on the recognition or non-recognition of a measure taken in another Contracting State. The procedure is governed by the law of the requested State.

Article 25

The authority of the requested State is bound by the findings of fact on which the authority of the State where the measure was taken based its jurisdiction.

Article 26

(1) If measures taken in one Contracting State and enforceable there require enforcement in another Contracting State, they shall, upon request by an interested party, be declared enforceable or registered for the purpose of enforcement in that other State according to the procedure provided in the law of the latter State.

(2) Each Contracting State shall apply to the declaration of enforceability or registration a simple and rapid procedure.

(3) The declaration of enforceability or registration may be refused only for one of the reasons set out in Article 23, paragraph 2.

Article 27

Without prejudice to such review as is necessary in the application of the preceding Articles, there shall be no review of the merits of the measure taken.

Article 28

Measures taken in one Contracting State and declared enforceable, or registered for the purpose of enforcement, in another Contracting State shall be enforced in the latter State as if they had been taken by the authorities of that State. Enforcement takes place in accordance with the law of the requested State to the extent provided by such law, taking into consideration the best interests of the child.

CHAPTER V – CO-OPERATION

Article 29

(1) A Contracting State shall designate a Central Authority to discharge the duties which are imposed by the Convention on such authorities.

(2) Federal States, States with more than one system of law or States having autonomous territorial units shall be free to appoint more than one Central Authority and to specify the territorial or personal extent of their functions. Where a State has appointed more than one Central Authority, it shall designate the Central Authority to which any communication may be addressed for transmission to the appropriate Central Authority within that State.

Article 30

(1) Central Authorities shall co-operate with each other and promote co-operation amongst the competent authorities in their States to achieve the purposes of the Convention.

(2) They shall, in connection with the application of the Convention, take appropriate steps to provide information as to the laws of, and services available in, their States relating to the protection of children.

Article 31

The Central Authority of a Contracting State, either directly or through public authorities or other bodies, shall take all appropriate steps to –

a) facilitate the communications and offer the assistance provided for in Articles 8 and 9 and in this Chapter;

b) facilitate, by mediation, conciliation or similar means, agreed solutions for the protection of the person or property of the child in situations to which the Convention applies;

c) provide, on the request of a competent authority of another Contracting State, assistance in discovering the whereabouts of a child where it appears that the child may be present and in need of protection within the territory of the requested State.

Article 32

On a request made with supporting reasons by the Central Authority or other competent authority of any Contracting State with which the child has a substantial connection, the Central Authority of the Contracting State in which the child is habitually resident and present may, directly or through public authorities or other bodies,

a) provide a report on the situation of the child;

b) request the competent authority of its State to consider the need to take measures for the protection of the person or property of the child.

Article 33

(1) If an authority having jurisdiction under Articles 5 to 10 contemplates the placement of the child in a foster family or institutional care, or the provision of care by kafala or an analogous institution, and if such placement or such provision of care is to take place in another Contracting State, it shall first consult with the Central Authority or other competent authority of the latter State. To that effect it shall transmit a report on the child together with the reasons for the proposed placement or provision of care.

(2) The decision on the placement or provision of care may be made in the requesting State only if the Central Authority or other competent authority of the requested State has consented to the placement or provision of care, taking into account the child's best interests.

Article 34

(1) Where a measure of protection is contemplated, the competent authorities under the Convention, if the situation of the child so requires, may request any authority of another Contracting State which has information relevant to the protection of the child to communicate such information.

(2) A Contracting State may declare that requests under paragraph 1 shall be communicated to its authorities only through its Central Authority.

Article 35

(1) The competent authorities of a Contracting State may request the authorities of another Contracting State to assist in the implementation of measures of protection taken under this Convention, especially in securing the effective exercise of rights of access as well as of the right to maintain direct contacts on a regular basis.

(2) The authorities of a Contracting State in which the child does not habitually reside may, on the request of a parent residing in that State who is seeking to obtain or to maintain access to the child, gather information or evidence and may make a finding on the suitability of that parent to exercise access and on the conditions under which access is to be exercised. An authority exercising jurisdiction under Articles 5 to 10 to determine an application concerning access to the child, shall admit and consider such information, evidence and finding before reaching its decision.

(3) An authority having jurisdiction under Articles 5 to 10 to decide on access may adjourn a proceeding pending the outcome of a request made under paragraph 2, in particular, when it is considering an application to restrict or terminate access rights granted in the State of the child's former habitual residence.

(4) Nothing in this Article shall prevent an authority having jurisdiction under Articles 5 to 10 from taking provisional measures pending the outcome of the request made under paragraph 2.

Article 36

In any case where the child is exposed to a serious danger, the competent authorities of the Contracting State where measures for the protection of the child have been taken or are under consideration, if they are informed that the child's residence has changed to, or that the child is present in another State, shall inform the authorities of that other State about the danger involved and the measures taken or under consideration.

Article 37

An authority shall not request or transmit any information under this Chapter if to do so would, in its opinion, be likely to place the child's person or property in danger, or constitute a serious threat to the liberty or life of a member of the child's family.

Article 38

(1) Without prejudice to the possibility of imposing reasonable charges for the provision of services, Central Authorities and other public authorities of Contracting States shall bear their own costs in applying the provisions of this Chapter.

(2) Any Contracting State may enter into agreements with one or more other Contracting States concerning the allocation of charges.

Article 39

Any Contracting State may enter into agreements with one or more other Contracting States with a view to improving the application of this Chapter in their mutual relations. The States which have concluded such an agreement shall transmit a copy to the depositary of the Convention.

CHAPTER VI – GENERAL PROVISIONS

Article 40

(1) The authorities of the Contracting State of the child's habitual residence, or of the Contracting State where a measure of protection has been taken, may deliver to the person having parental responsibility or to the person entrusted with protection of the child's person or property, at his or her request, a

certificate indicating the capacity in which that person is entitled to act and the powers conferred upon him or her.

(2) The capacity and powers indicated in the certificate are presumed to be vested in that person, in the absence of proof to the contrary.

(3) Each Contracting State shall designate the authorities competent to draw up the certificate.

Article 41

Personal data gathered or transmitted under the Convention shall be used only for the purposes for which they were gathered or transmitted.

Article 42

The authorities to whom information is transmitted shall ensure its confidentiality, in accordance with the law of their State.

Article 43

All documents forwarded or delivered under this Convention shall be exempt from legalisation or any analogous formality.

Article 44

Each Contracting State may designate the authorities to which requests under Articles 8, 9 and 33 are to be addressed.

Article 45

(1) The designations referred to in Articles 29 and 44 shall be communicated to the Permanent Bureau of the Hague Conference on Private International Law.

(2) The declaration referred to in Article 34, paragraph 2, shall be made to the depositary of the Convention.

Article 46

A Contracting State in which different systems of law or sets of rules of law apply to the protection of the child and his or her property shall not be bound to apply the rules of the Convention to conflicts solely between such different systems or sets of rules of law.

Article 47

In relation to a State in which two or more systems of law or sets of rules of law with regard to any matter dealt with in this Convention apply in different territorial units –

(1) any reference to habitual residence in that State shall be construed as referring to habitual residence in a territorial unit;

(2) any reference to the presence of the child in that State shall be construed as referring to presence in a territorial unit;

(3) any reference to the location of property of the child in that State shall be construed as referring to location of property of the child in a territorial unit;

(4) any reference to the State of which the child is a national shall be construed as referring to the territorial unit designated by the law of that State or, in the absence of relevant rules, to the territorial unit with which the child has the closest connection;

(5) any reference to the State whose authorities are seised of an application for divorce or legal separation of the child's parents, or for annulment of their marriage, shall be construed as referring to the territorial unit whose authorities are seised of such application;

(6) any reference to the State with which the child has a substantial connection shall be construed as referring to the territorial unit with which the child has such connection;

(7) any reference to the State to which the child has been removed or in which he or she has been retained shall be construed as referring to the relevant territorial unit to which the child has been removed or in which he or she has been retained;

(8) any reference to bodies or authorities of that State, other than Central Authorities, shall be construed as referring to those authorised to act in the relevant territorial unit;

(9) any reference to the law or procedure or authority of the State in which a measure has been taken shall be construed as referring to the law or procedure or authority of the territorial unit in which such measure was taken;

(10) any reference to the law or procedure or authority of the requested State shall be construed as referring to the law or procedure or authority of the territorial unit in which recognition or enforcement is sought.

Article 48

For the purpose of identifying the applicable law under Chapter III, in relation to a State which comprises two or more territorial units each of which has its own system of law or set of rules of law in respect of matters covered by this Convention, the following rules apply –

a) if there are rules in force in such a State identifying which territorial unit's law is applicable, the law of that unit applies;
b) in the absence of such rules, the law of the relevant territorial unit as defined in Article 47 applies.

Article 49

For the purpose of identifying the applicable law under Chapter III, in relation to a State which has two or more systems of law or sets of rules of law applicable to different categories of persons in respect of matters covered by this Convention, the following rules apply –

a) if there are rules in force in such a State identifying which among such laws applies, that law applies;
b) in the absence of such rules, the law of the system or the set of rules of law with which the child has the closest connection applies.

Article 50

This Convention shall not affect the application of the Convention of 25 October 1980 on the Civil Aspects of International Child Abduction, as between Parties to both Conventions. Nothing, however, precludes provisions of this Convention from being invoked for the purposes of obtaining the return of a child who has been wrongfully removed or retained or of organising access rights.

Article 51

In relations between the Contracting States this Convention replaces the Convention of 5 October 1961 concerning the powers of authorities and the law applicable in respect of the protection of minors, and the Convention governing the guardianship of minors, signed at The Hague 12 June 1902, without prejudice to the recognition of measures taken under the Convention of 5 October 1961 mentioned above.

Article 52

(1) This Convention does not affect any international instrument to which Contracting States are Parties and which contains provisions on matters governed by the Convention, unless a contrary declaration is made by the States Parties to such instrument.

(2) This Convention does not affect the possibility for one or more Contracting States to conclude agreements which contain, in respect of children habitually resident in any of the States Parties to such agreements, provisions on matters governed by this Convention.

(3) Agreements to be concluded by one or more Contracting States on matters within the scope of this Convention do not affect, in the relationship of such

States with other Contracting States, the application of the provisions of this Convention.

(4) The preceding paragraphs also apply to uniform laws based on special ties of a regional or other nature between the States concerned.

Article 53

(1) The Convention shall apply to measures only if they are taken in a State after the Convention has entered into force for that State.

(2) The Convention shall apply to the recognition and enforcement of measures taken after its entry into force as between the State where the measures have been taken and the requested State.

Article 54

(1) Any communication sent to the Central Authority or to another authority of a Contracting State shall be in the original language, and shall be accompanied by a translation into the official language or one of the official languages of the other State or, where that is not feasible, a translation into French or English.

(2) However, a Contracting State may, by making a reservation in accordance with Article 60, object to the use of either French or English, but not both.

Article 55

(1) A Contracting State may, in accordance with Article 60,

a) reserve the jurisdiction of its authorities to take measures directed to the protection of property of a child situated on its territory;

b) reserve the right not to recognise any parental responsibility or measure in so far as it is incompatible with any measure taken by its authorities in relation to that property.

(2) The reservation may be restricted to certain categories of property.

Article 56

The Secretary General of the Hague Conference on Private International Law shall at regular intervals convoke a Special Commission in order to review the practical operation of the Convention.

CHAPTER VII – FINAL CLAUSES

Article 57

(1) The Convention shall be open for signature by the States which were Members of the Hague Conference on Private International Law at the time of its Eighteenth Session.

(2) It shall be ratified, accepted or approved and the instruments of ratification, acceptance or approval shall be deposited with the Ministry of Foreign Affairs of the Kingdom of the Netherlands, depositary of the Convention.

Article 58

(1) Any other State may accede to the Convention after it has entered into force in accordance with Article 61, paragraph 1.

(2) The instrument of accession shall be deposited with the depositary.

(3) Such accession shall have effect only as regards the relations between the acceding State and those Contracting States which have not raised an objection to its accession in the six months after the receipt of the notification referred to in sub-paragraph b of Article 63. Such an objection may also be raised by States at the time when they ratify, accept or approve the Convention after an accession. Any such objection shall be notified to the depositary.

Article 59

(1) If a State has two or more territorial units in which different systems of law are applicable in relation to matters dealt with in this Convention, it may at the time of signature, ratification, acceptance, approval or accession declare that the Convention shall extend to all its territorial units or only to one or more of them and may modify this declaration by submitting another declaration at any time.

(2) Any such declaration shall be notified to the depositary and shall state expressly the territorial units to which the Convention applies.

(3) If a State makes no declaration under this Article, the Convention is to extend to all territorial units of that State.

Article 60

(1) Any State may, not later than the time of ratification, acceptance, approval or accession, or at the time of making a declaration in terms of Article 59, make one or both of the reservations provided for in Articles 54, paragraph 2, and 55. No other reservation shall be permitted.

(2) Any State may at any time withdraw a reservation it has made. The withdrawal shall be notified to the depositary.

(3) The reservation shall cease to have effect on the first day of the third calendar month after the notification referred to in the preceding paragraph.

Article 61

(1) The Convention shall enter into force on the first day of the month following the expiration of three months after the deposit of the third instrument of ratification, acceptance or approval referred to in Article 57.

(2) Thereafter the Convention shall enter into force –
  a) for each State ratifying, accepting or approving it subsequently, on the first day of the month following the expiration of three months after the deposit of its instrument of ratification, acceptance, approval or accession;
  b) for each State acceding, on the first day of the month following the expiration of three months after the expiration of the period of six months provided in Article 58, paragraph 3;
  c) for a territorial unit to which the Convention has been extended in conformity with Article 59, on the first day of the month following the expiration of three months after the notification referred to in that Article.

Article 62

(1) A State Party to the Convention may denounce it by a notification in writing addressed to the depositary. The denunciation may be limited to certain territorial units to which the Convention applies.

(2) The denunciation takes effect on the first day of the month following the expiration of twelve months after the notification is received by the depositary. Where a longer period for the denunciation to take effect is specified in the notification, the denunciation takes effect upon the expiration of such longer period.

Article 63

The depositary shall notify the States Members of the Hague Conference on Private International Law and the States which have acceded in accordance with Article 58 of the following –
  a) the signatures, ratifications, acceptances and approvals referred to in Article 57;
  b) the accessions and objections raised to accessions referred to in Article 58;
  c) the date on which the Convention enters into force in accordance with Article 61;

d) the declarations referred to in Articles 34, paragraph 2, and 59;
e) the agreements referred to in Article 39;
f) the reservations referred to in Articles 54, paragraph 2, and 55 and the withdrawals referred to in Article 60, paragraph 2;
g) the denunciations referred to in Article 62.

In witness whereof the undersigned, being duly authorised thereto, have signed this Convention.

Done at The Hague, on the 19th day of October 1996, in the English and French languages, both texts being equally authentic, in a single copy which shall be deposited in the archives of the Government of the Kingdom of the Netherlands, and of which a certified copy shall be sent, through diplomatic channels, to each of the States Members of the Hague Conference on Private International Law at the date of its Eighteenth Session.

Contracting States to the 1980 Hague Convention

Albania
Andorra
Argentina
Armenia
Australia
Austria
Bahamas
Barbados
Belarus
Belgium
Belize
Bolivia
Bosnia and Herzegovina
Brazil
Bulgaria
Burkina Faso
Canada
Chile
China, People's Republic of
Colombia
Costa Rica
Croatia
Cuba
Cyprus
Czech Republic
Denmark
Dominican Republic
Ecuador
El Salvador
Estonia
Fiji
Finland
France
Gabon
Georgia
Germany
Greece
Guatemala
Guinea
Guyana
Honduras
Hungary
Iceland
Iraq
Ireland
Israel
Italy
Jamaica
Japan
Kazakhstan
Korea, Republic of
Latvia
Lesotho
Lithuania
Luxembourg
Malta

Mauritius
Mexico
Monaco
Montenegro
Morocco
Netherlands
New Zealand
Nicaragua
Norway
Pakistan
Panama
Paraguay
Peru
Philippines
Poland
Portugal
Republic of Moldova
Republic of North Macedonia
Romania
Russian Federation
Saint Kitts and Nevis
San Marino
Serbia
Seychelles
Singapore
Slovakia
Slovenia
South Africa
Spain
Sri Lanka
Sweden
Switzerland
Thailand
Trinidad and Tobago
Tunisia
Turkey
Turkmenistan
Ukraine
United Kingdom of Great Britain and Northern Ireland
United States of America
Uruguay
Uzbekistan
Venezuela
Zambia
Zimbabwe

Contracting States to the 1996 Hague Convention

Albania
Argentina
Armenia
Australia
Austria
Barbados
Belgium
Bulgaria
Canada
Croatia
Cuba
Cyprus
Czech Republic
Denmark
Dominican Republic
Ecuador
Estonia
Fiji
Finland
France
Georgia
Germany
Greece
Guyana
Honduras
Hungary
Ireland
Italy
Latvia
Lesotho
Lithuania
Luxembourg
Malta
Monaco
Montenegro
Morocco
Netherlands
Nicaragua
Norway
Paraguay
Poland
Portugal
Republic of North Macedonia
Romania
Russian Federation
Serbia
Slovakia
Slovenia
Spain
Sweden
Switzerland
Turkey
Ukraine
United Kingdom of Great Britain and Northern Ireland
United States of America
Uruguay

Family Law Act 1986

(1986 C 55)

PART I: CHILD CUSTODY

Chapter I: Preliminary

1 Orders to which Part I applies

(1) Subject to the following provisions of this section, in this Part '[Part I order][1]' means –

[(a) a section 8 order made by a court in England and Wales under the Children Act 1989, other than an order varying or discharging such an order][2];

[(aa) a special guardianship order made by a court in England and Wales under the Children Act 1989;

(ab) an order made under section 26 of the Adoption and Children Act 2002 (contact), other than an order varying or revoking such an order;][3]

[(ac) an order made under section 51A of the Adoption and Children Act 2002 (post-adoption contact), other than an order varying or revoking such an order;][4]

(b) an order made by a court of civil jurisdiction in Scotland under any enactment or rule of law with respect to the [residence, custody, care or control of a child, contact with or][5] access to a child or the education or upbringing of a child, excluding –

(i) an order committing the care of a child to a local authority or placing a child under the supervision of a local authority;

(ii) …[6]

(iii) …[6]

(iv) an order [giving parental responsibilities and parental rights in relation to][5] a child made in the course of proceedings for the adoption of the child (other than an order made following the making of a direction under section 53(1) of the Children Act 1975);

(v) an order made under the Education (Scotland) Act 1980;

(vi) an order made under Part II or III of the Social Work (Scotland) Act 1968;

(vii) an order made under the Child Abduction and Custody Act 1985;

(viii) an order for the delivery of a child or other order for the enforcement of a [Part I order][1];

(ix) an order relating to the [guardianship][7] of a child;

[(x) an adoption order (as defined in section 28(1) of the Adoption and Children (Scotland) Act 2007 (asp 4);
(xi) a permanence order (as defined in subsection (2) of section 80 of that Act) which includes provision such as is mentioned in paragraph (c) of that subsection.][8]

[(c) an Article 8 order made by a court in Northern Ireland under the Children (Northern Ireland) Order 1995, other than an order varying or discharging such an order][9];

[(d) an order made by a court in England and Wales in the exercise of the inherent jurisdiction of the High Court with respect to children –
(i) so far as it gives care of a child to any person or provides for contact with, or the education of, a child; but
(ii) excluding an order varying or revoking such an order;

[(e) an order made by the High Court in Northern Ireland in the exercise of its inherent jurisdiction with respect to children –
(i) so far as it gives care of a child to any person or provides for contact with, or the education of, a child; but
(ii) excluding an order varying or discharging such an order.][9]][2]

(2) In this Part '[Part I order][1]' does not include –
(a) …[10]
(b) …[1]
(c) …[10]

[(3) In this Part, 'Part I order' –
(a) includes any order which would have been a custody order by virtue of this section in any form in which it was in force at any time before its amendment by the Children Act 1989 [or the Children (Northern Ireland) Order 1995, as the case may be][11]; and
(b) (subject to sections 32 and 40 of this Act) excludes any order which would have been excluded from being a custody order by virtue of this section in any such form.][2]

[(3A) In subsection (1)(b)(xi) 'permanence order' includes a deemed permanence order having effect by virtue of article 13(1), 14(2), 17(1) or 19(2) of the Adoption and Children (Scotland) Act 2007 (Commencement No. 4, Transitional and Savings Provisions) Order 2009.][12]

(6) Provision may be made by act of sederunt prescribing, in relation to orders within subsection (1) (b) above, what constitutes an application for the purposes of this Part.

Amendments

1 Substituted by the Children Act 1989, s 108(5), Sch 13, para 62(1), (2)(a).
2 Substituted by the Children Act 1989, s 108(5), Sch 13, para 63(1), (3).
3 Inserted by the Adoption and Children Act 2002, s 139(1), Sch 3, paras 46, 47.
4 Inserted by the Children and Families Act 2014, s 9(5).
5 Substituted by the Children (Scotland) Act 1995, s 105(4), Sch 4, para 41(1), (2).
6 Repealed by the Adoption and Children (Scotland) 2007, s 120(2), Sch 3 (extended to England, Wales and Northern Ireland by the Adoption and Children (Scotland) Act 2007 (Consequential Modifications) Order 2011, SI 2011/1740, art 3, Sch 2, Pt 3).

7 Substituted by the Age of Legal Capacity (Scotland) Act 1991, s 10, Sch 1, para 44.
8 Inserted by the Adoption and Children (Scotland) 2007, s 120(1), Sch 2, para 5 (extended to England, Wales and Northern Ireland by the Adoption and Children (Scotland) Act 2007 (Consequential Modifications) Order 2011, SI 2011/1740, art 3, Sch 2, Pt 1, para 2(1), (2)).
9 Substituted by the Children (Northern Ireland Consequential Amendments) Order 1995, SI 1995/756, art 12(1), (2)(a).
10 Repealed by the Children (Northern Ireland Consequential Amendments) Order 1995, SI 1995/756, art 15, Schedule.
11 Inserted by the Children (Northern Ireland Consequential Amendments) Order 1995, SI 1995/756, art 12(1), (2)(b).
12 Inserted in relation to England, Wales and Northern Ireland by the Adoption and Children (Scotland) Act 2007 (Consequential Modifications) Order 2011, SI 2011/1740, art 3, Sch 2, Pt 1, para 2(1), (3).

Chapter II: Jurisdiction of Courts in England and Wales

[2 Jurisdiction: general

[(1) A court in England and Wales shall not make a section 1(1)(a) order with respect to a child unless –
- (a) it has jurisdiction under the Council Regulation [or the Hague Convention][1], or
- (b) [neither the Council Regulation nor the Hague Convention applies][2] but –
  - (i) the question of making the order arises in or in connection with matrimonial proceedings [or civil partnership proceedings][3] and the condition in section 2A of this Act is satisfied, or
  - (ii) the condition in section 3 of this Act is satisfied.][4]

[(2A) A court in England and Wales shall not have jurisdiction to make a special guardianship order under the Children Act 1989 unless the condition in section 3 of this Act is satisfied.

(2B) A court in England and Wales shall not have jurisdiction to make an order under section 26 of the Adoption and Children Act 2002 unless the condition in section 3 of this Act is satisfied.][5]

[(2C) A court in England and Wales shall not have jurisdiction to make an order under section 51A of the Adoption and Children Act 2002 unless –
- (a) it has jurisdiction under the Council Regulation or the Hague Convention, or
- (b) neither the Council Regulation nor the Hague Convention applies but the condition in section 3 of this Act is satisfied.][6]

[(3) A court in England and Wales shall not make a section 1(1)(d) order unless –
- (a) it has jurisdiction under the Council Regulation [or the Hague Convention][1], or
- (b) [neither the Council Regulation nor the Hague Convention applies][2] but –
  - (i) the condition in section 3 of this Act is satisfied, or

(ii) the child concerned is present in England and Wales on the relevant date and the court considers that the immediate exercise of its powers is necessary for his protection.][4]][7]

Amendments

1 Inserted by the Parental Responsibility and Measures for the Protection of Children (International Obligations) (England and Wales and Northern Ireland) Regulations 2010, SI 2010/1898, reg 17, Schedule, paras 4, 5(a), (c).
2 Substituted by the Parental Responsibility and Measures for the Protection of Children (International Obligations) (England and Wales and Northern Ireland) Regulations 2010, SI 2010/1898, reg 17, Schedule, paras 4, 5(b), (d).
3 Inserted by the Civil Partnership (Family Proceedings and Housing Consequential Amendments) Order 2005, SI 2005/3336, arts 4, 5.
4 Substituted by the European Communities (Jurisdiction and Judgments in Matrimonial and Parental Responsibility Matters) Regulations 2005, SI 2005/265, reg 8.
5 Inserted by the Adoption and Children Act 2002, s 139(1), Sch 3, paras 46, 48.
6 Inserted by the Children and Families Act 2014, s 9(6).
7 Substituted by the Children Act 1989, s 108, Sch 13, para 64.

[2A Jurisdiction in or in connection with matrimonial proceedings [or civil partnership proceedings][1]

(1) The condition referred to in section 2(1) of this Act is that the …[2] proceedings are proceedings in respect of the marriage [or civil partnership][3] of the parents of the child concerned and –
- (a) the proceedings –
  - (i) are proceedings for divorce or nullity of marriage[, or dissolution or annulment of a civil partnership][3], and
  - (ii) are continuing;
- (b) the proceedings –
  - (i) are proceedings for judicial separation [or legal separation of civil partners][3],
  - (ii) are continuing,

and the jurisdiction of the court is not excluded by subsection (2) below; or
- (c) the proceedings have been dismissed after the beginning of the trial but –
  - (i) the section 1(1)(a) order is being made forthwith, or
  - (ii) the application for the order was made on or before the dismissal.

[(2) For the purposes of subsection (1)(b) above, the jurisdiction of the court is excluded if –
- (a) after the grant of a decree of judicial separation, on the relevant date, proceedings for divorce or nullity in respect of the marriage, or
- (b) after the making of a separation order, on the relevant date, proceedings for dissolution or annulment in respect of the civil partnership,

are continuing in Scotland or Northern Ireland.][1]

(3) Subsection (2) above shall not apply if the court in which the other proceedings there referred to are continuing has made –

(a) an order under section 13(6) or [19A(4)][4] of this Act (not being an order made by virtue of section 13(6)(a)(i)), or

(b) an order under section 14(2) or 22(2) of this Act which is recorded as being made for the purpose of enabling Part I proceedings to be taken in England and Wales with respect to the child concerned.

(4) Where a court –

(a) has jurisdiction to make a section 1(1)(a) order [by virtue of section 2(1)(b)(i) of this Act][5], but

(b) considers that it would be more appropriate for Part I matters relating to the child to be determined outside England and Wales,

the court may by order direct that, while the order under this subsection is in force, no section 1(1)(a) order shall be made by any court [by virtue of section 2(1)(b)(i) of this Act][5]][6].

Amendments

1 Inserted by the Civil Partnership (Family Proceedings and Housing Consequential Amendments) Order 2005, SI 2005/3336, arts 4, 6, 7(1), (3).

2 Repealed by the Civil Partnership (Family Proceedings and Housing Consequential Amendments) Order 2005, SI 2005/3336, arts 4, 7(1), (2)(a).

3 Substituted by the Civil Partnership (Family Proceedings and Housing Consequential Amendments) Order 2005, SI 2005/3336, arts 4, 7(1), (2)(b)–(d).

4 Substituted by the Children (Northern Ireland Consequential Amendments) Order 1995, SI 1995/756, art 12(1), (5)(b).

5 Substituted by the European Communities (Jurisdiction and Judgments in Matrimonial and Parental Responsibility Matters) Regulations 2005, SI 2005/265, reg 9.

6 Substituted by the Children Act 1989, s 108, Sch 13, para 64.

3 Habitual residence or presence of child

(1) The condition referred to in [section 2(1)(b)(ii)][1] of this Act is that on the relevant date the child concerned –

(a) is habitually resident in England and Wales, or

(b) is present in England and Wales and is not habitually resident in any part of the United Kingdom,

and, in either case, the jurisdiction of the court is not excluded by subsection (2) below.

(2) For the purposes of subsection (1) above, the jurisdiction of the court is excluded if, on the relevant date, [matrimonial proceedings][2] [or civil partnership proceedings][3] are continuing in a court in Scotland ot Northern Ireland in respect of the marriage [or civil partnership][3] of the parents of the child concerned.

(3) Subsection (2) above shall not apply if the court in which the other proceedings there referred to are continuing has made –

(a) an order under section 13(6) or [19A(4)][4] of this Act (not being an order made by virtue of section 13(6)(a)(i)), or

(b) an order under section 14(2) or 22(2) of this Act which is recorded as made for the purpose of enabling [Part I proceedings with respect to][5] the child concerned to be taken in England and Wales,

and that order is in force.

(4)–(6) …[6]

Amendments

1 Substituted by the European Communities (Jurisdiction and Judgments in Matrimonial and Parental Responsibility Matters) Regulations 2005, SI 2005/265, reg 10.

2 Substituted by the Children Act 1989, s 108(5), Sch 13, para 65.

3 Inserted by the Civil Partnership (Family Proceedings and Housing Consequential Amendments) Order 2005, SI 2005/3336, arts 4, 8.

4 Substituted by the Children (Northern Ireland Consequential Amendments) Order 1995, SI 1995/756, art 12(1), (5)(b).

5 Substituted by the Children Act 1989, s 108(5), Sch 13, para 62(1), (2)(b).

6 Repealed by the Children Act 1989, s 108(7), Sch 15.

4 …[1]

…[1]

Amendment

1 Repealed by the Children Act 1989, s 108(7), Sch 15.

5 Power of court to refuse application or stay proceedings

(1) A court in England and Wales which has jurisdiction to make a [Part I order][1] may refuse an application for the order in any case where the matter in question has already been determined in proceedings outside England and Wales.

(2) Where, at any stage of the proceedings on an application made to a court in England and Wales for a [Part I order][1], or for the variation of a [Part I order][1], …[2] it appears to the court –

(a) that proceedings with respect to the matters to which the application relates are continuing outside England and Wales, …[3]

(b) that it would be more appropriate for those matters to be determined in proceedings to be taken outside England and Wales, […[3]

(c) that it should exercise its powers under Article 15 of the Council Regulation (transfer to a court better placed to hear the case),][4][or

(d) that it should exercise its powers under Article 8 of the Hague Convention (request to authority in another Contracting State to assume jurisdiction),][5] the court may stay the proceedings on the application [or (as the case may be) exercise its powers under Article 15 [of the Council Regulation or Article 8 of the Hague Convention][5]][4].

[(2A) If the proceedings on the application are proceedings in which [an][6] activity direction has been made under section 11A of the Children Act 1989 (or an enforcement order has been made under section 11J of that Act), the court may when granting a stay under or by virtue of subsection (2) also suspend [the][6] activity direction (or the enforcement order).][7]

(3) The court may remove a stay granted [by virtue of subsection (2)(a) or (b) above][8] in accordance with subsection (2) above if it appears to the court that there has been unreasonable delay in the taking or prosecution of the other proceedings referred to in that subsection, or that those proceedings are stayed, sisted or concluded.

[(3A) The court may remove a stay granted under Article 15 of the Council Regulation only in accordance with that Article.][4]

[(3AA) The court may remove a stay granted in order for it to exercise its powers under Article 8 of the Hague Convention, and withdraw any request made by it to an authority in another Contracting State to assume jurisdiction, if –

(a) the authority in the other Contracting State does not assume jurisdiction within the period for which the court granted the stay, or
(b) the parties do not, within the period specified by the court, request the authority in the other Contracting State to assume jurisdiction.][5]

[(3B) If the stay removed under subsection (3)[, (3A) or (3AA)][9] is a stay in relation to which the court suspended [an][6] activity direction made under section 11A of the Children Act 1989 (or an enforcement order made under section 11J of that Act), the court may when removing the stay under subsection (3) or (3A) also bring the suspension to an end.][7]

(4) Nothing in this section [so far as it relates to proceedings not governed by the Council Regulation][4] shall affect any power exercisable apart from this section to refuse an application or to grant or remove a stay.

Amendments

1 Substituted by the Children Act 1989, s 108, Sch 13, para 62(1), (2)(a).
2 Repealed by the European Communities (Jurisdiction and Judgments in Matrimonial and Parental Responsibility Matters) Regulations 2005, SI 2005/265, reg 11(1), (2).
3 Repealed by the Parental Responsibility and Measures for the Protection of Children (International Obligations) (England and Wales and Northern Ireland) Regulations 2010, SI 2010/1898, reg 17, Schedule, paras 4, 6(1)(a), (b).
4 Inserted by the European Communities (Jurisdiction and Judgments in Matrimonial and Parental Responsibility Matters) Regulations 2005, SI 2005/265, reg 11(1), (3), (4), (6), (7).
5 Inserted by the Parental Responsibility and Measures for the Protection of Children (International Obligations) (England and Wales and Northern Ireland) Regulations 2010, SI 2010/1898, reg 17, Schedule, paras 4, 6(1)(c), (d), (2).
6 Substituted by the Children and Families Act 2014, s 12, Sch 2, paras 49, 50.
7 Inserted by the Children and Adoption Act 2006, s 15(1), Sch 2, paras 2, 3.

8 Substituted by the European Communities (Jurisdiction and Judgments in Matrimonial and Parental Responsibility Matters) Regulations 2005, SI 2005/265, reg 11(1), (5).

9 Substituted by the Parental Responsibility and Measures for the Protection of Children (International Obligations) (England and Wales and Northern Ireland) Regulations 2010, SI 2010/1898, reg 17, Schedule, paras 4, 6(3).

6 Duration and variation of [Part I orders][1]

(1) If a [Part I order][1] made by a court in Scotland or Northern Ireland (or a variation of such an order) comes into force with respect to a child at a time when a [Part I order][1] made by a court in England and Wales has effect with respect to him, the latter order shall cease to have effect so far as it makes provision for any matter for which the same or different provision is made by (or by the variation of) the order made by the court in Scotland or Northern Ireland.

(2) Where by virtue of subsection (1) above a [Part I order][1] has ceased to have effect so far as it makes provision for any matter, a court in England or Wales shall not have jurisdiction to vary that order so as to make provision for that matter.

[(3) A court in England and Wales shall not have jurisdiction to vary a Part I order if, on the relevant date, matrimonial proceedings [or civil partnership proceedings][2] are continuing in Scotland or Northern Ireland in respect of the marriage [or civil partnership][2] of the parents of the child concerned.

[(3A) Subsection (3) shall not apply if –

(a) the Part 1 order was made in or in connection with proceedings –

(i) for divorce or nullity in England and Wales in respect of the marriage of the parents of the child concerned; or

(ii) for dissolution or annulment in England and Wales in respect of the civil partnership of the parents of the child concerned; and

(b) those proceedings are continuing.

(3B) Subsection (3) shall not apply if –

(a) the Part 1 order was made in or in connection with proceedings –

(i) for judicial separation in England and Wales; or

(ii) for a separation order in England and Wales; and

(b) those proceedings are continuing; and

(c) as the case may be, the decree of judicial separation has not yet been granted or the separation order has not yet been made.][3]][4]

(4) Subsection (3) above shall not apply if the court in which the proceedings there referred to are continuing has made –

(a) an order under section 13(6) or [19A(4)][5] of this Act (not being an order made by virtue of section 13(6)(a)(i)), or

(b) an order under section 14(2) or 22(2) of this Act which is recorded as made for the purpose of enabling [Part I proceedings with respect to][1] the child concerned to be taken in England and Wales, and that order is in force.

(5) Subsection (3) above shall not apply in the case of a [variation of a section 1(1)(d) order if the child concerned][4] is present in England and Wales on the relevant date and the court considers that the immediate exercise of its powers is necessary for his protection.

[(5A) Subsection (7) below applies where a Part I order which is a child arrangements order (within the meaning of section 8(1) of the Children Act 1989) ceases by virtue of subsection (1) above to name a person as someone with whom a child is to live.][6]

[(6) Subsection (7) below [also][6] applies where a Part I order which is –

(a) …[7]

(b) an order made in the exercise of the High Court's inherent jurisdiction with respect to children by virtue of which a person has care of a child, or

(c) an order –

(i) of a kind mentioned in section 1(3)(a) of this Act,

(ii) under which a person is entitled to the actual possession of a child,

ceases to have effect in relation to that person by virtue of subsection (1) above.

(7) Where this subsection applies, any family assistance order made under section 16 of the Children Act 1989 with respect to the child shall also cease to have effect.

(8) For the purposes of subsection (7) above the reference to a family assistance order under section 16 of the Children Act 1989 shall be deemed to include a reference to an order for the supervision of a child made under –

(a) section 7(4) of the Family Law Reform Act 1969,

(b) section 44 of the Matrimonial Causes Act 1973,

(c) section 2(2)(a) of the Guardianship Act 1973,

(d) section 34(5) or 36(3)(b) of the Children Act 1975, or

(e) section 9 of the Domestic Proceedings and Magistrates' Courts Act 1978;

but this subsection shall cease to have effect once all such orders for the supervision of children have ceased to have effect in accordance with Schedule 14 to the Children Act 1989.][4]

Amendments

1 Substituted by the Children Act 1989, s 108, Sch 13, paras 62(1), (2)(a), (b).

2 Inserted by the Civil Partnership (Family Proceedings and Housing Consequential Amendments) Order 2005, SI 2005/3336, arts 4, 9(1), (2).

3 Substituted by the Civil Partnership (Family Proceedings and Housing Consequential Amendments) Order 2005, SI 2005/3336, arts 4, 9(1), (3).

4 Substituted by the Children Act 1989, s 108, Sch 13, paras 62, 66.

5 Substituted by the Children (Northern Ireland Consequential Amendments) Order 1995, SI 1995/756, art 12(1), (5)(b).

6 Inserted by the Children and Families Act 2014, s 12, Sch 2, paras 49, 51(1), (2), (3)(a).
7 Repealed by the Children and Families Act 2014, s 12, Sch 2, paras 49, 51(1), (3)(b).

[7 Interpretation of Chapter II

In this Chapter –

(a) 'child' means a person who has not attained the age of eighteen;

[(aa) 'civil partnership proceedings' means proceedings for the dissolution or annulment of a civil partnership or for legal separation of the civil partners;][1]

(b) 'matrimonial proceedings' means proceedings for divorce, nullity of marriage or judicial separation;

(c) 'the relevant date' means, in relation to the making or variation of an order –

(i) where an application is made for an order to be made or varied, the date of the application (or first application, if two or more are determined together), and

(ii) where no such application is made, the date on which the court is considering whether to make or, as the case may be, vary the order; and

(d) 'section 1(1)(a) order' and 'section 1(1)(d) order' mean orders falling within section 1(1)(a) and (d) of this Act respectively.][2]

Amendments

1 Inserted by the Civil Partnership (Family Proceedings and Housing Consequential Amendments) Order 2005, SI 2005/3336, arts 4, 10
2 Substituted by the Children Act 1989, s 108, Sch 13, para 67.

Chapter V: Recognition and Enforcement

25 Recognition of [Part I orders][1]: general

(1) Where a [Part I order][1] made by a court in any part of the United Kingdom is in force with respect to a child who has not attained the age of sixteen, then, subject to subsection (2) below, the order shall be recognised in any other part of the United Kingdom as having the same effect in that other part as if it had been made by the appropriate court in that other part and as if that court had had jurisdiction to make it.

(2) Where a [Part I order][1] includes provision as to the means by which rights conferred by the order are to be enforced, subsection (1) above shall not apply to that provision.

(3) A court in a part of the United Kingdom in which a [Part I order][1] is recognised in accordance with subsection (1) above shall not enforce the order unless it has been registered in that part of the United Kingdom under section 27 of this Act and proceedings for enforcement are taken in accordance with section 29 of this Act.

Amendments

1 Substituted by the Children Act 1989, s 108, Sch 13, para 62(1), (2)(a).

27 Registration

(1) Any person on whom any rights are conferred by a [Part I order][1] may apply to the court which made it for the order to be registered in another part of the United Kingdom under this section.

(2) An application under this section shall be made in the prescribed manner and shall contain the prescribed information and be accompanied by such documents as may be prescribed.

(3) On receiving an application under this section the court which made the [Part I order][1] shall, unless it appears to the court that the order is no longer in force, cause the following documents to be sent to the appropriate court in the part of the United Kingdom specified in the application, namely –

- (a) a certified copy of the order, and
- (b) where the order has been varied, prescribed particulars of any variation which is in force, and
- (c) a copy of the application and of any accompanying documents.

(4) Where the prescribed officer of the appropriate court receives a certified copy of a [Part I order][1] under subsection (3) above he shall forthwith cause the order, together with particulars of any variation, to be registered in that court in the prescribed manner.

(5) An order shall not be registered under this section in respect of a child who has attained the age of sixteen, and the registration of an order in respect of a child who has not attained the age of sixteen shall cease to have effect on the attainment by the child of that age.

Amendments

1 Substituted by the Children Act 1989, s 108, Sch 13, para 62(1), (2)(a).

28 Cancellation and variation of registration

(1) A court which revokes, recalls or varies an order registered under section 27 of this Act shall cause notice of the revocation, recall or variation to be given in the prescribed manner to the prescribed officer of the court in which it is registered and, on receiving the notice, the prescribed officer –

- (a) in the case of the revocation or recall of the order, shall cancel the registration, and
- (b) in the case of the variation of the order, shall cause particulars of the variation to be registered in the prescribed manner.

(2) Where –
  (a) an order registered under section 27 of this Act ceases (in whole or in part) to have effect in the part of the United Kingdom in which it was made, otherwise than because of its revocation, recall or variation, or
  (b) an order registered under section 27 of this Act in Scotland ceases (in whole or in part) to have effect there as a result of the making of an order in proceedings outside the United Kingdom,

the court in which the order is registered may, of its own motion or on the application of any person who appears to the court to have an interest in the matter, cancel the registration (or, if the order has ceased to have effect in part, cancel the registration so far as it relates to the provisions which have ceased to have effect).

29 Enforcement

(1) Where a [Part I order][1] has been registered under section 27 of this Act, the court in which it is registered shall have the same powers for the purpose of enforcing the order [(including, where an order with respect to contact is registered in England and Wales, the powers under section 110 of the Children Act 1989)][2] as it would have if it had itself made the order and had jurisdiction to make it; and proceedings for or with respect to enforcement may be taken accordingly.

(2) Where an application has been made to any court for the enforcement of an order registered in that court under section 27 of this Act, the court may, at any time before the application is determined, give such interim directions as it thinks fit for the purpose of securing the welfare of the child concerned or of preventing changes in the circumstances relevant to the determination of the application.

(3) The references in subsection (1) above to a [Part I order][1] do not include references to any provision of the order as to the means by which rights conferred by the order are to be enforced.

Amendments

1 Substituted by the Children Act 1989, s 108, Sch 13, para 62(1), (2)(a).
2 Inserted by the Children and Adoption Act 2006, s 15(1), Sch 2, paras 2, 4.

30 Staying or sisting of enforcement proceedings

(1) Where in accordance with section 29 of this Act proceedings are taken in any court for the enforcement of an order registered in that court, any person who appears to the court to have an interest in the matter may apply for the proceedings to be stayed or sisted on the ground that he has taken or intends to take other proceedings (in the United Kingdom or elsewhere) as a result of which the order may cease to have effect, or may have a different effect, in the part of the United Kingdom in which it is registered.

[(1A) No application may be made under subsection (1) for proceedings to be stayed or sisted if the proceedings are proceedings on an application for an order under section 11O(2) of the Children Act 1989.][1]

(2) If after considering an application under subsection (1) above the court considers that the proceedings for enforcement should be stayed or sisted in order that other proceedings may be taken or concluded, it shall stay or sist the proceedings for enforcement accordingly.

(3) The court may remove a stay or recall a sist granted in accordance with subsection (2) above if it appears to the court –
  (a) that there has been unreasonable delay in the taking or prosecution of the other proceedings referred to in that subsection, or
  (b) that those other proceedings are concluded and that the registered order, or a relevant part of it, is still in force.

(4) Nothing in this section shall affect any power exercisable apart from this section to grant, remove or recall a stay or sist.

Amendment

1 Inserted by the Children and Adoption Act 2006, s 15(1), Sch 2, paras 2, 5.

31 Dismissal of enforcement proceedings

(1) Where in accordance with section 29 of this Act proceedings are taken in any court for the enforcement of an order registered in that court, any person who appears to the court to have an interest in the matter may apply for those proceedings to be dismissed on the ground that the order has (in whole or in part) ceased to have effect in the part of the United Kingdom in which it was made.

[(1A) No application may be made under subsection (1) for proceedings to be dismissed if the proceedings are proceedings on an application for an order under section 11O(2) of the Children Act 1989.][1]

(2) Where in accordance with section 29 of this Act proceedings are taken in the Court of Session for the enforcement of an order registered in that court, any person who appears to the court to have an interest in the matter may apply for those proceedings to be dismissed on the ground that the order has (in whole or in part) ceased to have effect in Scotland as a result of the making of an order in proceedings outside the United Kingdom.

(3) If, after considering an application under subsection (1) or (2) above, the court is satisfied that the registered order has ceased to have effect, it shall dismiss the proceedings for enforcement (or, if it is satisfied that the order has ceased to have effect in part, it shall dismiss the proceedings so far as they relate to the enforcement of provisions which have ceased to have effect).

Amendment

1 Inserted by the Children and Adoption Act 2006, s 15(1), Sch 2, paras 2, 6.

32 Interpretation of Chapter V

(1) In this Chapter –

'the appropriate court', in relation to England and Wales or Northern Ireland, means the High Court and, in relation to Scotland, means the Court of Session;

'[Part I order][1]' includes (except where the context otherwise requires) any order within section 1(3) of this Act which, on the assumptions mentioned in subsection (3) below –

(a) could have been made notwithstanding the provisions of this Part;

(b) would have been a [Part I order][1] for the purposes of this Part; and

(c) would not have ceased to have effect by virtue of section 6, 15 or 23 of this Act.

(2) In the application of this Chapter to Scotland, '[Part I order][1]' also includes (except where the context otherwise requires) any order within section 1(3) of this Act which, on the assumptions mentioned in subsection (3) below –

(a) would have been a [Part I order][1] for the purposes of this Part; and

(b) would not have ceased to have effect by virtue of section 6 or 23 of this Act,

and which, but for the provisions of this Part, would be recognised in Scotland under any rule of law.

(3) The said assumptions are –

(a) that this Part had been in force at all material times; and

(b) that any reference in section 1 of this Act to any enactment included a reference to any corresponding enactment previously in force.

Amendments

1 Substituted by the Children Act 1989, s 108, Sch 13, para 62(1), (2)(a).

Chapter VI: Miscellaneous and Supplemental

33 Power to order disclosure of child's whereabouts

(1) Where in proceedings for or relating to a [Part I order][1] in respect of a child there is not available to the court adequate information as to where the child is, the court may order any person who it has reason to believe may have relevant information to disclose it to the court.

(2) A person shall not be excused from complying with an order under subsection (1) above by reason that to do so may incriminate him or his spouse [or civil partner][2] of an offence; but a statement or admission made in compliance with such an order shall not be admissible in evidence against either of them in proceedings for any offence other than perjury.

(3) A court in Scotland before which proceedings are pending for the enforcement of an order [relating to parental responsibilities or parental rights in relation to][3] a child made outside the United Kingdom which is recognised in Scotland shall have the same powers as it would have under subsection (1) above if the order were its own.

Amendments

1 Substituted by the Children Act 1989, s 108, Sch 13, para 62(1), (2)(a).

2 Inserted by the Civil Partnership Act 2004, s 261(1), Sch 27, para 124.

3 Substituted by the Children (Scotland) Act 1995, s 105(4), Sch 4, para 41(1), (7).

34 Power to order recovery of child

(1) Where –

(a) a person is required by a [Part I order][1], or an order for the enforcement of a [Part I order][1], to give up a child to another person ('the person concerned'), and

(b) the court which made the order imposing the requirement is satisfied that the child has not been given up in accordance with the order,

the court may make an order authorising an officer of the court or a constable to take charge of the child and deliver him to the person concerned.

(2) The authority conferred by subsection (1) above includes authority –

(a) to enter and search any premises where the person acting in pursuance of the order has reason to believe the child may be found, and

(b) to use such force as may be necessary to give effect to the purpose of the order.

(3) Where by virtue of –

[(a) section 14 of the Children Act 1989][2], or

[(b) Article 14 (enforcement of residence orders) of the Children (Northern Ireland) Order 1995,][3]

a [Part I order][1] (or a provision of a [Part I order][1]) may be enforced as if it were an order requiring a person to give up a child to another person, subsection (1) above shall apply as if the [Part I order][1] had included such a requirement.

(4) This section is without prejudice to any power conferred on a court by or under any other enactment or rule of law.

Amendments

1 Substituted by the Children Act 1989, s 108, Sch 13, para 62(1), (2)(a).

2 Substituted by the Children Act 1989, s 108, Sch 13, para 70.

3 Substituted by the Children (Northern Ireland Consequential Amendments) Order 1995, SI 1995/756, art 12(1), (3).

35 Powers to restrict removal of child from jurisdiction

(1) ...[1]

(2) ...[2]

(3) A court in Scotland –

(a) at any time after the commencement of proceedings in connection with which the court would have jurisdiction to make a [Part I order][3], or

(b) in any proceedings in which it would be competent for the court to grant an interdict prohibiting the removal of a child from its jurisdiction,

may, on an application by any of the persons mentioned in subsection (4) below, grant interdict or interim interdict prohibiting the removal of the child from the United Kingdom or any part of the United Kingdom, or out of the control of the person in [whose care][4] the child is.

(4) The said persons are –

(a) any party to the proceedings,

(b) the [guardian][5] of the child concerned, and

(c) any other person who has or wishes to obtain the ...[6] care of the child.

(5) In subsection (3) above 'the court' means the Court of Session or the sheriff; and for the purposes of subsection (3) (a) above, proceedings shall be held to commence –

(a) in the Court of Session, when a summons is signeted or a petition is presented;

(b) in the sheriff court, when the warrant of citation is signed.

Amendments

1 Repealed by the Children Act 1989, s 108(7), Sch 15.

2 Repealed by the Children (Northern Ireland) Order 1995, SI 1995/755, art 185(2), Sch 10.

3 Substituted by the Children Act 1989, s 108(5), Sch 13, para 62(1), (2)(a).

4 Substituted by the Children (Scotland) Act 1995, s 105(4), Sch 4, para 41(1), (8).

5 Substituted by the Age of Legal Capacity (Scotland) Act 1991, s 10, Sch 1, para 47.

6 Repealed by the Children (Scotland) Act 1995, s 105(5), Sch 5.

36 Effect of orders restricting removal

(1) This section applies to any order made by a court in the United Kingdom prohibiting the removal of a child from the United Kingdom or from any specified part of it.

(2) An order to which this section applies shall have effect in each part of the United Kingdom other than the part in which it was made –

(a) as if it had been made by the appropriate court in the other part, and

(b) in the case of an order which has the effect of prohibiting the child's removal to that other part, as if it had included a prohibition on his further removal to any place except one to which he could be removed consistently with the order.

(3) The references in subsections (1) and (2) above to prohibitions on a child's removal include references to prohibitions subject to exceptions; and in a case where removal is prohibited except with the consent of the court, nothing in subsection (2) above shall be construed as affecting the identity of the court whose consent is required.

(4) In this section 'child' means a person who has not attained the age of sixteen; and this section shall cease to apply to an order relating to a child when he attains the age of sixteen.

37 Surrender of passports

(1) Where there is in force an order prohibiting or otherwise restricting the removal of a child from the United Kingdom or from any specified part of it, the court by which the order was in fact made, or by which it is treated under section 36 of this Act as having been made, may require any person to surrender any United Kingdom passport which has been issued to, or contains particulars of, the child.

(2) In this section 'United Kingdom passport' means a current passport issued by the Government of the United Kingdom.

38 Automatic restriction on removal of wards of court

(1) The rule of law which (without any order of the court) restricts the removal of a ward of court from the jurisdiction of the court shall, in a case to which this section applies, have effect subject to the modifications in subsection (3) below.

(2) This section applies in relation to a ward of court if –

(a) proceedings for divorce, nullity or judicial separation in respect of the marriage of his parents are continuing in a court in another part of the United Kingdom (that is to say, in a part of the United Kingdom outside the jurisdiction of the court of which he is a ward), or

[(aa) proceedings for dissolution or annulment or legal separation in respect of the civil partnership of his parents are continuing in a court in another part of the United Kingdom (that is to say, in a part of the United Kingdom outside the jurisdiction of the court of which he is a ward), or][1]

(b) he is habitually resident in another part of the United Kingdom,

except where that other part is Scotland and he has attained the age of sixteen.

(3) Where this section applies, the rule referred to in subsection (1) above shall not prevent –

(a) the removal of the ward of court, without the consent of any court, to the other part of the United Kingdom mentioned in subsection (2) above, or

(b) his removal to any other place with the consent of either the approriate court in that other part of the United Kingdom or the court mentioned in subsection [(2)(a) or (aa) above][2].

Amendments

1 Inserted by the Civil Partnership (Family Proceedings and Housing Consequential Amendments) Order 2005, SI 2005/3336, arts 4, 18(1).

2 Substituted by the Civil Partnership (Family Proceedings and Housing Consequential Amendments) Order 2005, SI 2005/3336, arts 4, 18(2).

39 Duty to furnish particulars of other proceedings

Parties to proceedings for or relating to a [Part I order][1] shall, to such extent and in such manner as may be prescribed, give particulars of other proceedings known to them which relate to the child concerned (including proceedings instituted abroad and proceedings which are no longer continuing).

Amendment

1 Substituted by the Children Act 1989, s 108, Sch 13, para 62(1), (2)(a).

40 Interpretation of Chapter VI

(1) In this Chapter –

'the appropriate court' has the same meaning as in Chapter V;

'[Part I order][1]' includes (except where the context otherwise requires) any such order as is mentioned in section 32(1) of this Act.

(2) In the application of this Chapter to Scotland, '[Part I order][1]' also includes (except where the context otherwise requires) any such order as is mentioned in section 32(2) of this Act.

Amendments

1 Substituted by the Children Act 1989, s 108, Sch 13, para 62(1), (2)(a).

41 Habitual residence after removal without consent, etc

(1) Where a child who –

(a) has not attained the age of sixteen, and

(b) is habitually resident in a part of the United Kingdom,

becomes habitually resident outside that part of the United Kingdom in consequence of circumstances of the kind specified in subsection (2) below, he shall be treated for the purposes of this Part as continuing to be habitually resident in that part of the United Kingdom for the period of one year beginning with the date on which those circumstances arise.

(2) The circumstances referred to in subsection (1) above exist where the child is removed from or retained outside, or himself leaves or remains outside, the part of the United Kingdom in which he was habitually resident before his change of residence –
(a) without the agreement of the person or all the persons having, under the law of that part of the United Kingdom, the right to determine where he is to reside, or
(b) in contravention of an order made by a court in any part of the United Kingdom.

(3) A child shall cease to be treated by virtue of subsection (1) above as habitually resident in a part of the United Kingdom if, during the period there mentioned –
(a) he attains the age of sixteen, or
(b) he becomes habitually resident outside that part of the United Kingdom with the agreement of the person or persons mentioned in subsection (2)(a) above and not in contravention of an order made by a court in any part of the United Kingdom.

42 General interpretation of Part I

(1) In this Part –
'certified copy', in relation to an order of any court, means a copy certified by the prescribed officer of the court to be a true copy of the order or of the official record of the order;
['parental responsibilities' and 'parental rights' have the meanings respectively given by sections 1(3) and 2(4) of the Children (Scotland) Act 1995;][1]
'part of the United Kingdom' means England and Wales, Scotland or Northern Ireland;
'prescribed' means prescribed by rules of court or act of sederunt;
['the Council Regulation' means Council Regulation (EC) No 2201/2003 of 27th November 2003 concerning jurisdiction and the recognition and enforcement of judgments in matrimonial matters and matters of parental responsibility.][2]
['the Hague Convention' means the Convention on Jurisdiction, Applicable Law, Recognition, Enforcement and Co-Operation in respect of Parental Responsibility and Measures for the Protection of Children that was signed at The Hague on 19 October 1996.][3]

(2) For the purposes of this Part proceedings in England and Wales or in Northern Ireland for divorce, nullity or judicial separation in respect of the marriage of the parents of a child shall, unless they have been dismissed, be treated as continuing until the child concerned attains the age of eighteen (whether or not a decree has been granted and whether or not, in the case

of a decree of divorce or nullity of marriage, that decree has been made absolute).

[(2A) For the purposes of this Part proceedings in England and Wales or in Northern Ireland for dissolution, annulment or legal separation in respect of the civil partnership of the parents of the child shall, unless they have been dismissed, be treated as continuing until the child concerned attains the age of eighteen (whether or not a dissolution, nullity or separation order has been made and whether or not, in the case of a dissolution or nullity order, that order has been made final).][4]

(3) For the purposes of this Part, matrimonial [or civil partnership][5] proceedings [or civil partnership proceedings][4] in a court in Scotland which has jurisdiction in those proceedings to make a [Part I order][6] with respect to a child shall, unless they have been dismissed or decree of absolvitor has been granted therein, be treated as continuing until the child concerned attains the age of sixteen.

(4) Any reference in this Part to proceedings in respect of the marriage [or civil partnership][5] of the parents of a child shall, in relation to a child who, although not a child of both parties to the marriage [or civil partnership][5], is a child of the family of those parties, be construed as a reference to proceedings in respect of that marriage; and for this purpose 'child of the family' –

(a) if the proceedings are in England and Wales, means any child who has been treated by both parties as a child of their family, except a child who [is placed with those parties as foster parents][7] by a local authority or a voluntary organisation;

(b) if the proceedings are in Scotland, means any child [who has been treated by both parties as a child of their family, except a child who has been placed with those parties as foster parents by a local authority or a voluntary organisation][8];

(c) if the proceedings are in Northern Ireland, means any child who has been treated by both parties as a child of their family, except a child who [is placed with those parties as foster parents by an authority within the meaning of the Children (Northern Ireland) Order 1995][9].

[(4A) Any reference in this Part to proceedings in respect of the civil partnership of the parents of a child shall, in relation to a child who, although not a child of the civil partners, is a child of the family of the civil partners, be construed as a reference to proceedings in respect of that civil partnership; and for this purpose 'child of the family' has the meaning given in paragraphs (a) to (c) of subsection (4) (but substituting references to the civil partners for references to the parties to the marriage).][4]

(5) References in this Part to [Part I orders][6] include (except where the context otherwise requires) references to [Part I orders][6] as varied.

(6) For the purposes of this Part each of the following orders shall be treated as varying the [Part I order][6] to which it relates –

(a) an order which provides for a person [to be allowed contact with or][10] to be given access to a child who is the subject of a [Part I order][6], or which makes provision for the education of such a child,

(b) ...[11]

[(7) In this Part –

(a) references to Part I proceedings in respect of a child are references to any proceedings for a Part I order or an order corresponding to a Part I order and include, in relation to proceedings outside the United Kingdom, references to proceedings before a tribunal or other authority having power under the law having effect there to determine Part I matters; and

(b) references to Part I matters are references to matters that might be determined by a Part I order or an order corresponding to a Part I order][12]

Amendments

1 Inserted by the Children (Scotland) Act 1995, s 105(4), Sch 4, para 41(1), (9)(a).

2 Substituted in relation to England, Wales and Northern Ireland by the European Communities (Jurisdiction and Judgments in Matrimonial and Parental Responsibility Matters) Regulations 2005, SI 2005/265, reg 16, and in relation to Scotland by the European Communities (Matrimonial and Parental Responsibility Jurisdiction and Judgments) (Scotland) Regulations 2005, SSI 2005/42, reg 4(1), (5).

3 Inserted in relation to England, Wales and Northern Ireland by the Parental Responsibility and Measures for the Protection of Children (International Obligations) (England and Wales and Northern Ireland) Regulations 2010, SI 2010/1898, reg 17, Schedule, paras 4, 9, and in relation to Scotland by the Parental Responsibility and Measures for the Protection of Children (International Obligations) (Scotland) Regulations 2010, SSI 2010/213, reg 15, Schedule, paras 2, 5.

4 Inserted in relation to England and Wales by the Civil Partnership (Family Proceedings and Housing Consequential Amendments) Order 2005, SI 2005/3336, arts 4, 19.

5 Inserted in relation to Scotland by the Civil Partnership Act 2004 (Consequential Amendments) (Scotland) Order 2005, SSI 2005/623, arts 12, 17.

6 Substituted by the Children Act 1989, s 108(5), Sch 13, para 62(1), (2)(a).

7 Substituted by the Children Act 1989, s 108(5), Sch 13, para 71(1).

8 Substituted by the Children (Scotland) Act 1995, s 105(4), Sch 4, para 41(1), (9)(b).

9 Substituted by the Children (Northern Ireland Consequential Amendments) Order 1995, SI 1995/756, art 12(1), (4).

10 Inserted by the Children Act 1989, s 108(5), Sch 13, para 71(2).

11 Repealed by the Children (Northern Ireland Consequential Amendments) Order 1995, SI 1995/756, art 15, Schedule.

12 Substituted by the Children Act 1989, s 108(5), Sch 13, para 62(1), (3).

43 Application of Part I to dependent territories

(1) Her Majesty may by Order in Council make provision corresponding to or applying any of the foregoing provisions of this Part, with such modifications as appear to Her Majesty to be appropriate, for the purpose of regulating –

(a) in any dependent territory;

(b) as between any dependent territory and any part of the United Kingdom; or
(c) as between any dependent territory and any other such territory,

the jurisdiction of courts to make [Part I orders][1], or orders corresponding to [Part I orders][1], and the recognition and enforcement of such orders.

(2) In subsection (1) above 'dependent territory' means any of the following territories –
(a) the Isle of Man,
(b) any of the Channel Islands, and
(c) any colony.

(3) An Order in Council under subsection (1) above may contain such consequential, incidental and supplementary provisions as appear to Her Majesty to be necessary or expedient.

(4) An Order in Council under subsection (1)(b) above which makes provision affecting the law of any part of the United Kingdom shall be subject to annulment in pursuance of a resolution of either House of Parliament.

Amendments

1 Substituted by the Children Act 1989, s 108, Sch 13, para 62(1), (2)(a).

Family Procedure Rules 2010

(SI 2010/2955)

PART 12:
[CHILDREN PROCEEDINGS][1] EXCEPT PARENTAL ORDER PROCEEDINGS AND PROCEEDINGS FOR APPLICATIONS IN ADOPTION, PLACEMENT AND RELATED PROCEEDINGS

CHAPTER 6:
PROCEEDINGS UNDER THE 1980 HAGUE CONVENTION, THE EUROPEAN CONVENTION, THE COUNCIL REGULATION, AND THE 1996 HAGUE CONVENTION

12.43 Scope

This Chapter applies to –

(a) [children proceedings][1] under the 1980 Hague Convention or the European Convention; and

(b) applications relating to the Council Regulation or the 1996 Hague Convention in respect of children.

Amendment

1 Substituted by the Family Procedure (Amendment) (No.5) Rules 2012, SI 2012/3061, rr 2, 5.

Section 1: Proceedings under the 1980 Hague Convention or the European Convention

12.44 Interpretation

In this section –

'the 1985 Act' means the Child Abduction and Custody Act 1985;

'Central Authority' means, in relation to England and Wales, the Lord Chancellor;

'Contracting State' has the meaning given in –

(a) section 2 of the 1985 Act in relation to the 1980 Hague Convention; and

(b) section 13 of the 1985 Act in relation to the European Convention; and

'decision relating to custody' has the same meaning as in the European Convention.

('the 1980 Hague Convention' and the 'the European Convention' are defined in rule 2.3.)

12.45 Where to start proceedings

Every application under the 1980 Hague Convention or the European Convention must be –

- (a) made in the High Court and issued in the principal registry; and
- (b) heard by a Judge of the High Court unless the application is –
  - (i) to join a respondent; or
  - (ii) to dispense with service or extend the time for acknowledging service.

12.46 Evidence in support of application

Where the party making an application under this section does not produce the documents referred to in Practice Direction 12F, the court may –

- (a) fix a time within which the documents are to be produced;
- (b) accept equivalent documents; or
- (c) dispense with production of the documents if the court considers it has sufficient information.

12.47 Without-notice applications

(1) This rule applies to applications –

- (a) commencing or in proceedings under this section;
- (b) for interim directions under section 5 or 19 of the 1985 Act;
- (c) for the disclosure of information about the child and for safeguarding the child's welfare, under rule 12.57;
- (d) for the disclosure of relevant information as to where the child is, under section 24A of the 1985 Act; or
- (e) for a collection order, location order or passport order.

(2) Applications under this rule may be made without notice, in which case the applicant must file the application –

- (a) where the application is made by telephone, the next business day after the making of the application; or
- (b) in any other case, at the time when the application is made.

(3) Where an order is made without notice, the applicant must serve a copy of the order on the other parties as soon as practicable after the making of the order, unless the court otherwise directs.

(4) Where the court refuses to make an order on an application without notice, it may direct that the application is made on notice.

(5) Where any hearing takes place outside the hours during which the court office is usually open –

- (a) if the hearing takes place by telephone, the applicant's solicitors will, if practicable, arrange for the hearing to be recorded; and
- (b) in all other cases, the court or court officer will take a note of the proceedings.

(Practice Direction 12E (Urgent Business) provides further details of the procedure for out of hours applications. See also Practice Direction 12D (Inherent Jurisdiction (including Wardship Proceedings)).)

12.48 Directions

(1) As soon as practicable after an application to which this section applies has been made, the court may give directions as to the following matters, among others –
 (a) whether service of the application may be dispensed with;
 (b) whether the proceedings should be transferred to another court under rule 12.54;
 (c) expedition of the proceedings or any part of the proceedings (and any direction for expedition may specify a date by which the court must issue its final judgment in the proceedings or a specified part of the proceedings);
 (d) the steps to be taken in the proceedings and the time by which each step is to be taken;
 (e) whether the child or any other person should be made a party to the proceedings;
 (f) if the child is not made a party to the proceedings, the manner in which the child's wishes and feelings are to be ascertained, having regard to the child's age and maturity and in particular whether an officer of the Service or a Welsh family proceedings officer should report to the court for that purpose;
 (g) where the child is made a party to the proceedings, the appointment of a children's guardian for that child unless a children's guardian has already been appointed;
 (h) the attendance of the child or any other person before the court;
 (i) the appointment of a litigation friend for a child or for any protected party, unless a litigation friend has already been appointed;
 (j) the service of documents;
 (k) the filing of evidence including expert evidence; and
 (l) whether the parties and their representatives should meet at any stage of the proceedings and the purpose of such a meeting.

(Rule 16.2 provides for when the court may make the child a party to the proceedings and rule 16.4 for the appointment of a children's guardian for the child who is made a party. Rule 16.5 (without prejudice to rule 16.6) requires a child who is a party to the proceedings but not the subject of those proceedings to have a litigation friend.)

(2) Directions of a court which are in force immediately prior to the transfer of proceedings to another court under rule 12.54 will continue to apply following the transfer subject to –
 (a) any changes of terminology which are required to apply those directions to the court to which the proceedings are transferred; and
 (b) any variation or revocation of the directions.

(3) The court or court officer will –
  (a) take a note of the giving, variation or revocation of directions under this rule; and
  (b) as soon as practicable serve a copy of the directions order on every party.

12.49 Answer

(1) Subject to paragraph (2) and to any directions given under rule 12.48, a respondent must file and serve on the parties an answer to the application within 7 days beginning with the date on which the application is served.

(2) The court may direct a longer period for service where the respondent has been made a party solely on one of the following grounds –
  (a) a decision relating to custody has been made in the respondent's favour; or
  (b) the respondent appears to the court to have sufficient interest in the welfare of the child.

12.50 Filing and serving written evidence

(1) The respondent to an application to which this section applies may file and serve with the answer a statement verified by a statement of truth, together with any further evidence on which the respondent intends to rely.

(2) The applicant may, within 7 days beginning with the date on which the respondent's evidence was served under paragraph (1), file and serve a statement in reply verified by a statement of truth, together with any further evidence on which the applicant intends to rely.

12.51 Adjournment

The court will not adjourn the hearing of an application to which this section applies for more than 21 days at any one time.

12.52 Stay of proceedings upon notification of wrongful removal etc.

(1) In this rule and in rule 12.53 –
  (a) 'relevant authority' means –
    (i) the High Court;
    (ii) [the family court][1];
    (iii) …[2]
    (iv) the Court of Session;
    (v) a sheriff court;
    (vi) a children's hearing within the meaning of section 93 of the Children (Scotland) Act 1995;
    (vii) the High Court in Northern Ireland;

(viii) a county court in Northern Ireland;
(ix) a court of summary jurisdiction in Northern Ireland;
(x) the Royal Court of Jersey;
(xi) a court of summary jurisdiction in Jersey;
(xii) the High Court of Justice of the Isle of Man;
(xiii) a court of summary jurisdiction in the Isle of Man; or
(xiv) the Secretary of State; and

(b) 'rights of custody' has the same meaning as in the 1980 Hague Convention.

(2) Where a party to proceedings under the 1980 Hague Convention knows that an application relating to the merits of rights of custody is pending in or before a relevant authority, that party must file within the proceedings under the 1980 Hague Convention a concise statement of the nature of that application, including the relevant authority in or before which it is pending.

(3) On receipt of a statement filed in accordance with paragraph (2) above, a court officer will notify the relevant authority in or before which the application is pending and will subsequently notify the relevant authority of the result of the proceedings.

(4) On receipt by the relevant authority of a notification under paragraph (3) from the High Court or equivalent notification from the Court of Session, the High Court in Northern Ireland or the High Court of Justice of the Isle of Man –

(a) all further proceedings in the action will be stayed(GL) unless and until the proceedings under the 1980 Hague Convention in the High Court, Court of Session, the High Court in Northern Ireland or the High Court of Justice of the Isle of Man are dismissed; and

(b) the parties to the action will be notified by the court officer of the stay(GL) and dismissal.

Amendments

1 Substituted by the Family Procedure (Amendment No.3) Rules 2013, SI 2013/3204, rr 2, 52(a).
2 Repealed by the Family Procedure (Amendment No.3) Rules 2013, SI 2013/3204, rr 2, 52(b).

[12.52A Application to set aside a return order under the 1980 Hague Convention

(1) In this rule –

'return order' means an order for the return or non-return of a child made under the 1980 Hague Convention and includes a consent order;

'set aside' means to set aside a return order pursuant to section 17(2) of the Senior Courts Act 1981 and this rule.

(2) A party may apply under this rule to set aside a return order where no error of the court is alleged.

(3) An application under this rule must be made within the proceedings in which the return order was made.

(4) An application under this rule must be made in accordance with the Part 18 procedure, subject to the modifications contained in this rule.

(5) Where the court decides to set aside a return order, it shall give directions for a rehearing or make such other orders as may be appropriate to dispose of the application.

(6) This rule is without prejudice to any power the High Court has to vary, revoke, discharge or set aside other orders, declarations or judgments which are not specified in this rule and where no error of the court is alleged.][1]

Amendment

1 Inserted by the Family Procedure (Amendment) Rules 2020, SI 2020/135, rr 2, 18.

12.53 Stay of proceedings where application made under s.16 of the 1985 Act (registration of decisions under the European Convention)

(1) A person who –
- (a) is a party to –
  - (i) proceedings under section 16 of the 1985 Act; or
  - (ii) proceedings as a result of which a decision relating to custody has been registered under section 16 of the 1985 Act; and
- (b) knows that an application is pending under –
  - (i) section 20(2) of the 1985 Act;
  - (ii) Article 21(2) of the Child Abduction and Custody (Jersey) Law 2005; or
  - (iii) section 42(2) of the Child Custody Act 1987 (an Act of Tynwald),

must file within the proceedings under section 16 of the 1985 Act a concise statement of the nature of the pending application.

(2) On receipt of a statement filed in accordance with paragraph (1) above, a court officer will notify the relevant authority in or before which the application is pending and will subsequently notify the relevant authority of the result of the proceedings.

(3) On receipt by the relevant authority of a notification under paragraph (2) from the High Court or equivalent notification from the Court of Session, the High Court in Northern Ireland or the High Court of Justice of the Isle of Man, the court officer will notify the parties to the action.

12.54 Transfer of proceedings

(1) At any stage in proceedings under the 1985 Act the court may –
- (a) of its own initiative; or
- (b) on the application of a party with a minimum of two days' notice;

order that the proceedings be transferred to a court listed in paragraph (4).

(2) Where the court makes an order for transfer under paragraph (1) –

(a) the court will state its reasons on the face of the order;

(b) a court officer will send a copy of the order, the application and the accompanying documents (if any) and any evidence to the court to which the proceedings are transferred; and

(c) the costs of the proceedings both before and after the transfer will be at the discretion of the court to which the proceedings are transferred.

(3) Where proceedings are transferred to the High Court from a court listed in paragraph (4), a court officer will notify the parties of the transfer and the proceedings will continue as if they had been commenced in the High Court.

(4) The listed courts are the Court of Session, the High Court in Northern Ireland, the Royal Court of Jersey or the High Court of Justice of the Isle of Man.

12.55 Revocation and variation of registered decisions

(1) This rule applies to decisions which –

(a) have been registered under section 16 of the 1985 Act; and

(b) are subsequently varied or revoked by an authority in the Contracting State in which they were made.

(2) The court will, on cancelling the registration of a decision which has been revoked, notify –

(a) the person appearing to the court to have care of the child;

(b) the person on whose behalf the application for registration of the decision was made; and

(c) any other party to the application.

(3) The court will, on being informed of the variation of a decision, notify –

(a) the party appearing to the court to have care of the child; and

(b) any party to the application for registration of the decision;

and any such person may apply to make representations to the court before the registration is varied.

(4) Any person appearing to the court to have an interest in the proceedings may apply for the registration of a decision for the cancellation or variation of the decision referred to in paragraph (1).

12.56 The central index of decisions registered under the 1985 Act

A central index of decisions registered under section 16 of the 1985 Act, together with any variation of those decisions made under section 17 of that Act, will be kept by the principal registry.

12.57 *Disclosure of information in proceedings under the European Convention*

At any stage in proceedings under the European Convention the court may, if it has reason to believe that any person may have relevant information about the child who is the subject of those proceedings, order that person to disclose such information and may for that purpose order that the person attend before it or file affidavit(GL) evidence

Section 2: Applications relating to the Council Regulation and the 1996 Hague Convention

12.58 *Interpretation*

(1) In this section –

. . .[1]

'Contracting State' means a State party to the 1996 Hague Convention;

['domestic Central Authority' means –

(a) where the matter relates to the Council Regulation, the Lord Chancellor;

(b) where the matter relates to the 1996 Hague Convention in England, the Lord Chancellor;

(c) where the matter relates to the 1996 Hague Convention in Wales, the Welsh Ministers;][2]

'judgment' has the meaning given in Article 2(4) of the Council Regulation;

'Member State' means a Member State bound by the Council Regulation or a country which has subsequently adopted the Council Regulation;

'parental responsibility' has the meaning given in –

(a) Article 2(7) of the Council Regulation in relation to proceedings under that Regulation; and

(b) Article 1(2) of the 1996 Hague Convention in relation to proceedings under that Convention; and

'seised' has the meaning given in Article 16 of the Council Regulation.

(2) In rules 12.59 to 12.70, references to the court of another member State or Contracting State include authorities within the meaning of 'court' in Article 2(1) of the Council Regulation, and authorities of Contracting States which have jurisdiction to take measures directed to the protection of the person or property of the child within the meaning of the 1996 Hague Convention.

Amendments

1 Repealed by the Family Procedure (Amendment No. 3) Rules 2012, SI 2012/2046, rr 2, 4(a).

2 Inserted by the Family Procedure (Amendment No. 3) Rules 2012, SI 2012/2046, rr 2, 4(b).

12.59 Procedure under Article 11(6) of the Council Regulation where the court makes a non-return order under Article 13 of the 1980 Hague Convention

(1) Where the court makes an order for the non-return of a child under Article 13 of the 1980 Hague Convention, it must immediately transmit the documents referred to in Article 11(6) of the Council Regulation –
  (a) directly to the court with jurisdiction or the central authority in the Member State where the child was habitually resident immediately before the wrongful removal to, or wrongful retention in, England and Wales; or
  (b) to the [domestic Central Authority][1] for onward transmission to the court with jurisdiction or the central authority in the other Member State mentioned in sub-paragraph (a).

(2) The documents required by paragraph (1) must be transmitted by a method which, in the case of direct transmission to the court with jurisdiction in the other Member State, ensures and, in any other case, will not prevent, their receipt by that court within one month of the date of the non-return order.

Amendment

1 Substituted by the Family Procedure (Amendment No. 3) Rules 2012, SI 2012/2046, rr 2, 5.

12.60 Procedure under Article 11(7) of the Council Regulation where the court receives a non-return order made under Article 13 of the 1980 Hague Convention by a court in another Member State

(1) This rule applies where the court receives an order made by a court in another Member State for the non-return of a child.

(2) In this rule, the order for non-return of the child and the papers transmitted with that order from the court in the other Member State are referred to as 'the non-return order'.

(3) Where, at the time of receipt of the non-return order, the court is already seised of a question of parental responsibility in relation to the child, –
  (a) the court officer shall immediately –
    (i) serve copies of the non-return order on each party to the proceedings in which a question of parental responsibility in relation to the child is at issue; and
    (ii) where the non-return order was received directly from the court or the central authority in the other Member State, transmit to the [domestic Central Authority][1] a copy of the non-return order.
  (b) the court shall immediately invite the parties to the 1980 Hague Convention proceedings to file written submissions in respect of the question of custody by a specified date, or to attend a hearing to consider the future conduct of the proceedings in the light of the non-return order.

(4) Where, at the time of receipt of the non-return order, the court is not already seised of the question of parental responsibility in relation to the child, it shall immediately –

  (a) open a court file in respect of the child and assign a court reference to the file;

  (b) serve a copy of the non-return order on each party to the proceedings before the court in the Member State which made that order;

  (c) invite each party to file, within 3 months of notification to that party of receipt of the non-return order, submissions in the form of –

    (i) an application for an order under –

      (aa) the 1989 Act; or

      (bb) (in the High Court only) an application under the inherent jurisdiction in respect of the child; or

    (ii) where permission is required to make an application for the order in question, an application for that permission;

  (d) where the non-return order was received directly from the court or central authority in the other Member State, transmit to the [domestic Central Authority][1] a copy of the non-return order.

(5) In a case to which paragraph (4) applies where no application is filed within the 3 month period provided for by paragraph (4)(c) the court must close its file in respect of the child.

(Enforcement of a subsequent judgment requiring the return of the child, made under Article 11(8) by a court examining custody of the child under Article 11(7), is dealt with in Part 31 below.)

Amendment

1 Substituted by the Family Procedure (Amendment No. 3) Rules 2012, SI 2012/2046, rr 2, 5.

12.61 Transfer of proceedings under Article 15 of the Council Regulation or under Article 8 of the 1996 Hague Convention

(1) Where the court is considering the transfer of proceedings to the court of another Member State or Contracting State under rules 12.62 to 12.64 it will –

  (a) fix a date for a hearing for the court to consider the question of transfer; and

  (b) give directions as to the manner in which the parties may make representations.

(2) The court may, with the consent of all parties, deal with the question of transfer without a hearing.

(3) Directions which are in force immediately prior to the transfer of proceedings to a court in another Member State or Contracting State under rules 12.62 to 12.64 will continue to apply until the court in that other State accepts jurisdiction in accordance with the provisions of the Council

Regulation or the 1996 Hague Convention (as appropriate), subject to any variation or revocation of the directions.

(4) The court or court officer will –
  (a) take a note of the giving, variation or revocation of directions under this rule; and
  (b) as soon as practicable serve a copy of the directions order on every party.

(5) A register of all applications and requests for transfer of jurisdiction to or from another Member State or Contracting State will be kept by the principal registry.

12.62 Application by a party for transfer of the proceedings

(1) A party may apply to the court under Article 15(1) of the Council Regulation or under Article 8(1) of the 1996 Hague Convention –
  (a) to stay(GL) the proceedings or a specified part of the proceedings and to invite the parties to introduce a request before a court of another Member State or Contracting State; or
  (b) to make a request to a court of another Member State or another Contracting State to assume jurisdiction for the proceedings, or a specified part of the proceedings.

(2) An application under paragraph (1) must be made –
  (a) to the court in which the relevant parental responsibility proceedings are pending; and
  (b) using the Part 18 procedure.

(3) The applicant must file the application notice and serve it on the respondents –
  (a) where the application is also made under Article 11 of the Council Regulation, not less than 5 days, and
  (b) in any other case, not less than 42 days,

before the hearing of the application.

12.63 Application by a court of another Member State or another Contracting State for transfer of the proceedings

(1) This rule applies where a court of another Member State or another Contracting State makes an application under Article 15(2)(c) of the Council Regulation or under Article 9 of the 1996 Hague Convention that the court having jurisdiction in relation to the proceedings transfer the proceedings or a specific part of the proceedings to the applicant court.

(2) When the court receives the application, the court officer will –
  (a) as soon as practicable, notify the [domestic Central Authority][1] of the application; and

(b) serve the application, and notice of the hearing on all other parties in England and Wales not less than 5 days before the hearing of the application.

Amendment

1 Substituted by the Family Procedure (Amendment No. 3) Rules 2012, SI 2012/2046, rr 2, 5.

12.64 Exercise by the court of its own initiative of powers to seek to transfer the proceedings

(1) The court having jurisdiction in relation to the proceedings may exercise its powers of its own initiative under Article 15 of the Council Regulation or Article 8 of the 1996 Hague Convention in relation to the proceedings or a specified part of the proceedings.

(2) Where the court proposes to exercise its powers, the court officer will give the parties not less than 5 days' notice of the hearing.

12.65 Application to High Court to make request under Article 15 of the Council Regulation or Article 9 of the 1996 Hague Convention to request transfer of jurisdiction

(1) An application for the court to request transfer of jurisdiction in a matter concerning a child from another Member State or another Contracting State under Article 15 of the Council Regulation, or Article 9 of the 1996 Hague Convention (as the case may be) must be made to the principal registry and heard in the High Court.

(2) An application must be made without notice to any other person and the court may give directions about joining any other party to the application.

(3) Where there is agreement between the court and the court or competent authority to which the request under paragraph (1) is made to transfer the matter to the courts of England and Wales, the court will consider with that other court or competent authority the specific timing and conditions for the transfer.

(4) Upon receipt of agreement to transfer jurisdiction from the court or other competent authority in the Member State, or Contracting State to which the request has been made, the court officer will serve on the applicant a notice that jurisdiction has been accepted by the courts of England and Wales.

(5) The applicant must attach the notice referred to in subparagraph (3) to any subsequent application in relation to the child.

(6) Nothing in this rule requires an application with respect to a child commenced following a transfer of jurisdiction to be made to or heard in the High Court.

(7) Upon allocation, the court to which the proceedings are allocated must immediately fix a directions hearing to consider the future conduct of the case.

12.66 Procedure where the court receives a request from the authorities of another Member State or Contracting State to assume jurisdiction in a matter concerning a child

(1) Where any court other than the High Court receives a request to assume jurisdiction in a matter concerning a child from a court or other authority which has jurisdiction in another Member State or Contracting State, that court must immediately refer the request to a Judge of the High Court for a decision regarding acceptance of jurisdiction to be made.

(2) Upon the High Court agreeing to the request under paragraph (1), the court officer will notify the parties to the proceedings before the other Member State or Contracting State of that decision, and the case must be allocated as if the application had been made in England and Wales.

(3) Upon allocation, the court to which the proceedings are allocated must immediately fix a directions hearing to consider the future conduct of the case.

(4) The court officer will serve notice of the directions hearing on all parties to the proceedings in the other Member State or Contracting State no later than 5 days before the date of that hearing.

12.67 Service of the court's order or request relating to transfer of jurisdiction under the Council Regulation or the 1996 Hague Convention

The court officer will serve an order or request relating to transfer of jurisdiction on all parties, the Central Authority of the other Member State or Contracting State, and the [domestic Central Authority][1].

Amendment

1 Substituted by the Family Procedure (Amendment No. 3) Rules 2012, SI 2012/2046, rr 2, 5.

12.68 Questions as to the court's jurisdiction or whether the proceedings should be stayed

(1) If at any time after issue of the application it appears to the court that under any of Articles 16 to 18 of the Council Regulation it does not or may not have jurisdiction to hear an application, or that under Article 19 of the Council Regulation or Article 13 of the 1996 Hague Convention it is or may be required to stay[(GL)] the proceedings or to decline jurisdiction, the court must –

(a) stay[(GL)] the proceedings; and

(b) fix a date for a hearing to determine jurisdiction or whether there should be a stay[(GL)] or other order.

(2) The court officer will serve notice of the hearing referred to at paragraph (1)(b) on the parties to the proceedings.

(3) The court must, in writing –
(a) give reasons for its decision under paragraph (1); and
(b) where it makes a finding of fact, state such finding.

(4) The court may with the consent of all the parties deal with any question as to the jurisdiction of the court, or as to whether the proceedings should be stayed(GL), without a hearing.

12.69 Request for consultation as to contemplated placement of child in England and Wales

(1) This rule applies to a request made –
(a) under Article 56 of the Council Regulation, by a court in another Member State; or
(b) under Article 33 of the 1996 Hague Convention by a court in another Contracting State

for consultation on or consent to the contemplated placement of a child in England and Wales.

(2) Where the court receives a request directly from a court in another Member State or Contracting State, the court shall, as soon as practicable after receipt of the request, notify the [domestic Central Authority][1] of the request and take the appropriate action under paragraph (4).

(3) Where it appears to the court officer that no proceedings relating to the child are pending before a court in England and Wales, the court officer must inform the [domestic Central Authority][1] of that fact and forward to the Central Authority all documents relating to the request sent by the court in the other Member State or Contracting State.

(4) Where the court receives a request forwarded by the [domestic Central Authority][1], the court must, as soon as practicable after receipt of the request, either –
(a) where proceedings relating to the child are pending before the court, fix a directions hearing; or
(b) where proceedings relating to the child are pending before another court in England and Wales, send a copy of the request to that court.

Amendment

1 Substituted by the Family Procedure (Amendment No. 3) Rules 2012, SI 2012/2046, rr 2, 5.

12.70 Request made by court in England and Wales for consultation as to contemplated placement of child in another Member State or Contracting State

(1) This rule applies where the court is contemplating the placement of a child in another Member State under Article 56 of the Council Regulation or

another Contracting State under Article 33 of the 1996 Hague Convention, and proposes to send a request for consultation with or for the consent of the central authority or other authority having jurisdiction in the other State in relation to the contemplated placement.

(2) In this rule, a reference to 'the request' includes a reference to a report prepared for purposes of Article 33 of the 1996 Hague Convention where the request is made under that Convention.

(3) Where the court sends the request directly to the central authority or other authority having jurisdiction in the other State, it shall at the same time send a copy of the request to the [domestic Central Authority][1].

(4) The court may send the request to the [domestic Central Authority][1] for onward transmission to the central authority or other authority having jurisdiction in the other Member State.

(5) The court should give consideration to the documents which should accompany the request.

(See Chapters 1 to 3 of this Part generally, for the procedure governing applications for an order under paragraph 19(1) of Schedule 2 to the 1989 Act permitting a local authority to arrange for any child in its care to live outside England and Wales.)

(Part 14 sets out the procedure governing applications for an order under section 84 (giving parental responsibility prior to adoption abroad) of the Adoption and Children Act 2002.)

Amendment

1 Substituted by the Family Procedure (Amendment No. 3) Rules 2012, SI 2012/2046, rr 2, 5.

12.71 Application for a declaration as to the extent, or existence, of parental responsibility in relation to a child under Article 16 of the 1996 Hague Convention

(1) Any interested person may apply for a declaration –
   (a) that a person has, or does not have, parental responsibility for a child; or
   (b) as to the extent of a person's parental responsibility for a child,

   where the question arises by virtue of the application of Article 16 of the 1996 Hague Convention.

(2) An application for a declaration as to the extent, or existence of a person's parental responsibility for a child by virtue of Article 16 of the 1996 Hague Convention must be made in the principal registry and heard in the High Court.

(3) An application for a declaration referred to in paragraph (1) may not be made where the question raised is otherwise capable of resolution in any other family proceedings in respect of the child.

PRACTICE DIRECTION 12D – INHERENT JURISDICTION (INCLUDING WARDSHIP) PROCEEDINGS

This Practice Direction supplements FPR Part 12, Chapter 5

The nature of inherent jurisdiction proceedings

1.1 It is the duty of the court under its inherent jurisdiction to ensure that a child who is the subject of proceedings is protected and properly taken care of. The court may in exercising its inherent jurisdiction make any order or determine any issue in respect of a child unless limited by case law or statute. Such proceedings should not be commenced unless it is clear that the issues concerning the child cannot be resolved under the Children Act 1989.

1.2 The court may under its inherent jurisdiction, in addition to all of the orders which can be made in family proceedings, make a wide range of injunctions for the child's protection of which the following are the most common –

(a) orders to restrain publicity;

(b) orders to prevent an undesirable association;

(c) orders relating to medical treatment;

(d) orders to protect abducted children, or children where the case has another substantial foreign element; and

(e) orders for the return of children to and from another state.

1.3 The court's wardship jurisdiction is part of and not separate from the court's inherent jurisdiction. The distinguishing characteristics of wardship are that –

(a) custody of a child who is a ward is vested in the court; and

(b) although day to day care and control of the ward is given to an individual or to a local authority, no important step can be taken in the child's life without the court's consent.

Transfer of proceedings to [family][1] court

2.1 Whilst [the family court does][1] not have jurisdiction to deal with applications that a child be made or cease to be a ward of court, consideration should be given to transferring the case in whole or in part to [the family][1] court where a direction has been given confirming the wardship and directing that the child remain a ward of court during his minority or until further order.

2.2 The [family][1] court must transfer the case back to the High Court if a decision is required as to whether the child should remain a ward of court.

2.3 The following proceedings in relation to a ward of court will be dealt with in the High Court unless the nature of the issues of fact or law makes them more suitable for hearing in the [family][1] court –

(a) those in which an officer of the Cafcass High Court Team or the Official Solicitor is or becomes the litigation friend or children's guardian of the ward or a party to the proceedings;
(b) those in which a local authority is or becomes a party;
(c) those in which an application for paternity testing is made;
(d) those in which there is a dispute about medical treatment;
(e) those in which an application is opposed on the grounds of lack of jurisdiction;
(f) those in which there is a substantial foreign element;
(g) those in which there is an opposed application for leave to take the child permanently out of the jurisdiction or where there is an application for temporary removal of a child from the jurisdiction and it is opposed on the ground that the child may not be duly returned.

Amendments

1 Substituted by the FPR Update, April 2014.

Parties

3.1 Where the child has formed or is seeking to form an association, considered to be undesirable, with another person, that other person should not be made a party to the application. Such a person should be made a respondent only to an application within the proceedings for an injunction or committal. Such a person should not be added to the title of the proceedings nor allowed to see any documents other than those relating directly to the proceedings for the injunction or committal. He or she should be allowed time to obtain representation and any injunction should in the first instance extend over a few days only.

Removal from jurisdiction

4.1 A child who is a ward of court may not be removed from England and Wales without the court's permission. Practice Direction 12F (International Child Abduction) deals in detail with locating and protecting children at risk of unlawful removal.

Criminal Proceedings

[5.1 Case law establishes that:

1. There is no requirement for the police or any other agency carrying out statutory powers of investigation or enforcement to seek the permission of the court to interview a child who is a ward of court. The fact that a child is a ward of court does not affect the powers and duties of the police or other statutory agencies in relation to their investigations. Provided that the relevant statutory requirements are complied with, the police or other

agencies are under no duty to take any special steps in carrying out their functions in relation to a child who is a ward of court.

2. Where a child has been interviewed by the police in connection with contemplated criminal proceedings and the child is, or subsequently becomes, a ward of court, the permission of the court is not required for the child to be called as a witness in the criminal proceedings.

For a full review of the relevant case law and principles, see *In the matter of a Ward of Court* [2017] EWHC 1022 (Fam).

5.2 Where the police or other statutory agencies take any action in relation to a child who is a ward of court, the person(s) with day to day care and control of the child, or where applicable the local authority, should bring the relevant information to the attention of the court as soon as practicable. Where wardship proceedings are continuing, any children's guardian appointed for the child must be informed of the situation by the other parties.][1]

Amendment

1 Substituted by the President's Circular, 16 June 2017.

Applications to the Criminal Injuries Compensation Authority

6.1 Where a child who is a ward of court has a right to make a claim for compensation to the Criminal Injuries Compensation Authority ('CICA'), an application must be made by the child's guardian, or, if no guardian has been appointed, the person with care and control of the child, for permission to apply to CICA and disclose such documents on the wardship proceedings file as are considered necessary to establish whether or not the child is eligible for an award plus, as appropriate, the amount of the award.

6.2 Any order giving permission should state that any award made by CICA should normally be paid into court immediately upon receipt and, once that payment has been made, application should made to the court as to its management and administration. If it is proposed to invest the award in any other way, the court's prior approval must be sought

The role of the tipstaff

7.1 The tipstaff is the enforcement officer for all orders made in the High Court. The tipstaff's jurisdiction extends throughout England and Wales. Every applicable order made in the High Court is addressed to the tipstaff in children and family matters (eg 'The Court hereby directs the Tipstaff of the High Court of Justice, whether acting by himself or his assistants or a police officer as follows…').

7.2 The tipstaff may effect an arrest and then inform the police. Sometimes the local bailiff or police will detain a person in custody until the tipstaff arrives to collect that person or give further directions as to the disposal of the matter. The tipstaff may also make a forced entry although there will generally be a uniformed police officer standing by to make sure there is no breach of the peace.

7.3 There is only one tipstaff (with two assistants) but the tipstaff can also call on any constable or bailiff to assist in carrying out the tipstaff's duties.

7.4 The majority of the tipstaff's work involves locating children and taking them into protective custody, including cases of child abduction abroad.

[Application to set aside an inherent jurisdiction order

8.1 As set out in rule 12.42B, the Part 18 procedure applies to set aside an inherent jurisdiction order. Where such an application was made before rule 12.42B came into force, the Part 18 procedure will still apply subject to any directions that the court might make for the purpose of ensuring that the proceedings are dealt with fairly.

8.2 An application under rule 12.42B should be dealt with by the same level of judge that dealt with the original application. Where reasonably possible, the application should be dealt with by the same judge that dealt with the original application.

8.3 The application should be made promptly upon the party becoming aware of the information or upon the circumstances occurring that give rise to the application.

8.4 An application to set aside an inherent jurisdiction order should only be made where no error of the court is alleged (unless the circumstances set out in rule 18.11 apply). If an error of the court is alleged, an application for permission to appeal under Part 30 should be considered. The grounds on which an inherent jurisdiction order may be set aside are and will remain a matter for decisions by judges. The grounds may include: (i) fraud; (ii) material non-disclosure; (iii) certain limited types of mistake; (iv) a fundamental change in circumstances which undermines the basis on which the order was made; and (v) the welfare of the child requires it.

8.5 The effect of rules 12.42B(1)(a) and (2) is that an application may be made to set aside all or only part of an inherent jurisdiction order, including an inherent jurisdiction order that has been made by consent.

Inherent jurisdiction orders are defined in the rule and include any order, declaration or judgment made under the inherent jurisdiction, including but not limited to orders making a child a ward of court, orders regarding medical treatment of a child and orders for the return or non-return of a child made under the inherent jurisdiction. Inherent jurisdiction orders do not include return orders made under the 1980 Hague Convention (for those orders, see rule 12.42B and paragraphs 4.1A – 4.1B of Practice Direction 12F), but can include orders where the basis to exercise jurisdiction is found in other instruments, such as the 1996 Hague Convention (though the source of power for the return order remains the inherent jurisdiction). Inherent jurisdiction orders do not include orders or judgments made within inherent jurisdiction proceedings for which the power to make such an order or judgment is found in statute (such as the power to make return orders under section 8 of the Children Act 1989) or these Rules (and not the inherent jurisdiction). The power to set aside any such orders would, if it exists, derive either from relevant statutory provisions or form the power to vary or revoke in rule 4.1(6), or from any inherent power of the High Court to set aside its own orders. Rule 12.42B(6) clarifies that any such other power to revoke, discharge or set aside is not ousted by the rule.

8.6 In applications under rule 12.42B, the starting point is that the order which one party is seeking to have set aside was properly made. A mere allegation e.g. that it was obtained by fraud, is not sufficient for the court to set aside the order; evidence must be provided. Only once the ground for setting aside the order has been established (or admitted) can the court set aside the order and rehear the original application. The court has a full range of case management powers and considerable discretion as to how to determine an application to set aside an inherent jurisdiction order, including where appropriate the power to strike out or summarily dispose of an application to set aside. If and when a ground for setting aside has been established, the court may decide to set aside the whole or part of the order there and then, or may delay doing so. Ordinarily, once the court has decided to set aside an inherent jurisdiction order, the court would give directions for a full rehearing to re-determine the original application. However, if the court is satisfied that it has sufficient information to do so, it may proceed to re-determine the original application at the same time as setting aside the inherent jurisdiction order.][1]

Amendment

1 Inserted by the Practice Direction, April 2020.

PRACTICE DIRECTION 12E – URGENT BUSINESS

This Practice Direction supplements FPR Part 12

Introduction

1.1 This Practice Direction describes the procedure to be followed in respect of urgent and out of hours cases in the Family Division of the High Court. For the avoidance of doubt, it does not relate to cases in respect of adults.

1.2 Urgent or out of hours applications, particularly those which have become urgent because they have not been pursued sufficiently promptly, should be avoided. A judge who has concerns that the urgent or out of hours facilities may have been abused may require a representative of the applicant to attend at a subsequent directions hearing to provide an explanation.

1.3 Urgent applications should whenever possible be made within court hours. The earliest possible liaison is required with the Clerk of the Rules who will attempt to accommodate genuinely urgent applications (at least for initial directions) in the Family Division applications court, from which the matter may be referred to another judge.

1.4 When it is not possible to apply within court hours, contact should be made with the security office at the Royal Courts of Justice (020 7947 6000 or 020 7947 6260) who will refer the matter to the urgent business officer. The urgent business officer can contact the duty judge. The judge may agree to hold a hearing, either convened at court or elsewhere, or by telephone.

1.5 When the hearing is to take place by telephone it should, unless not practicable, be by tape-recorded conference call arranged (and paid for in the first instance) by the applicant's solicitors. Solicitors acting for potential applicants should consider having standing arrangements with their telephone service providers under which such conference calls can be arranged. All parties (especially the judge) should be informed that the call is being recorded by the service provider. The applicant's solicitors should order a transcript of the hearing from the service provider. Otherwise the applicant's legal representative should prepare a note for approval by the judge.

General Issues

2.1 Parents, carers or other necessary respondents should whenever possible be given the opportunity to have independent legal advice or at least to have access to support or counselling.

2.2 In suitable cases, application may be made for directions providing for anonymity of the parties and others involved in the matter in any order or subsequent listing of the case. Exceptionally, a reporting restriction order may be sought.

2.3 Either the Official Solicitor or Cafcass, or CAFCASS Cymru, as the case may be, may be invited by the court to be appointed as advocate to the court.

Medical treatment and press injunction cases

3.1 It may be desirable for a child who is the subject of such proceedings to be made a party and represented through a children's guardian (usually an officer of Cafcass or a Welsh Family Proceedings Officer). Cafcass and CAFCASS Cymru stand ready to arrange for an officer to accept appointment as a children's guardian. They should be contacted at the earliest opportunity where an urgent application is envisaged. For urgent out of hours applications, the urgent business officer will contact a representative of Cafcass. CAFCASS Cymru is not able to deal with cases that arise out of office hours and those cases should be referred to Cafcass who will deal with the matter on behalf of CAFCASS Cymru until the next working day. A child of sufficient understanding to instruct his or her own solicitor should be made a party and given notice of any application.

3.2 Interim declarations/orders under the wardship jurisdiction or Children Act 1989 may be made on application either by an NHS trust, a local authority, an interested adult (where necessary with the leave of the court) or by the child if he or she has sufficient understanding to make the application.

Consultation with Cafcass, CAFCASS Cymru and Official Solicitor

4.1 Cafcass, CAFCASS Cymru and members of the Official Solicitor's legal staff are prepared to discuss cases before proceedings are issued. In all cases in which the urgent and out of hours procedures are to be used it would be helpful if the Official Solicitor, Cafcass or CAFCASS Cymru have had some advance notice of the application and its circumstances.

[4.2 Enquiries about children cases should be directed to the High Court Team Duty Manager at Cafcass National Office, 3rd Floor, 21 Bloomsbury Street, London, WC1B 3HF. DX: Cafcass DX 310101 Bloomsbury 11. Telephone 01753 235273 (Cafcass High Court Team) or 01753 235295 (Cafcass Legal Duty Lawyer). Email HighCourtGM@Cafcass.gsi.gov.uk (office hours only). Enquiries should be marked 'F.A.O. High Court Team' or 'F.A.O. HCT'.][1]

4.3 Enquiries about children cases in Wales should be directed to:
Social Care Team
Legal Services
Welsh Assembly Government
Cathays Park
Cardiff
CF10 3NQ
[telephone 02920 370888
fax 0872 437 7306.][1].

4.4 Medical and welfare cases relating to an adult lacking capacity in relation to their medical treatment or welfare are brought in the Court of Protection. [Enquiries about adult medical and welfare cases should be addressed to the Court of Protection Healthcare and Welfare Team, Office of the Official Solicitor, Victory House, 30-34 Kingsway, London, WC2B 6EX, telephone 020 3681 2751, fax 020 3681 2762, email enquiries@offsol.gsi.gov.uk.][1]

Reference should also be made to Practice Direction E, accompanying Part 9 of the Court of Protection Rules 2007, and to Practice Direction B accompanying Part 10 of those Rules. Information for parties and practitioners is available on the website of the Ministry of Justice www.justice.gov.uk and general information for members of the public is available on www.direct.gov.uk.

Amendment

1 Substituted by the FPR Update, July 2015.

PRACTICE DIRECTION 12F – INTERNATIONAL CHILD ABDUCTION

This Practice Direction supplements FPR Part 12, Chapters 5 and 6

Part 1 – Introduction

1.1 This Practice Direction explains what to do if a child has been brought to, or kept in, England and Wales without the permission of anyone who has rights of custody in respect of the child in the country where the child was habitually resident immediately before the removal or retention. It also explains what to do if a child has been taken out of, or kept out of, England and Wales[(a)] without the permission of a parent or someone who has rights of custody in respect of the child. These cases are called 'international child abduction cases' and are dealt with in the High Court. This Practice Direction also explains what to do if you receive legal papers claiming that you have abducted a child. You can find the legal cases which are mentioned in this Practice Direction, and other legal material, on the website http://www.bailii.org (British and Irish Legal Information Institute).

(a) The child must be taken or kept out of the United Kingdom without the permission of a parent or someone who has rights of custody for it to be an international child abduction. This practice direction relates to the law as it applies in England and Wales. If the child has been taken or kept out of the United Kingdom when the child was habitually resident in Scotland, you should contact the Central Authority for Scotland, Scottish Government Justice Directorate, Civil Law Division, St Andrew's House, Regent Road, Edinburgh EH1 3DG Tel: +44 (0) 131 244 4827/4832 Fax: +44 (0)131 244 4848 Website: [http://www.gov.scot/Topics/Justice/law/17867/fm-children-root/18533][1]

If the child has been taken or kept out of the United Kingdom when the child was habitually resident in Northern Ireland, you should contact the Central Authority for Northern Ireland, Northern Ireland Courts and Tribunals Service, Civil Policy and Tribunal Reform Division, 3rd Floor Laganside House, 23-27 Oxford Street, Belfast BT1 3LA [Tel: + 44 (0)28 9072 8808 or + 44 (0) 28 9072 8819; fax +44 (0) 28 9072 8945][1]

Website: http://www.nics.gov.uk or http://www.courtsni.gov.uk/en-GB/Services/ChildAbduction.

1.2 If you have rights of custody in respect of a child and the child has been brought to England or Wales without your permission, or has been brought here with your permission but the person your child is staying with is refusing to return the child, then you can apply to the High Court of Justice, which covers all of England and Wales, for an order for the return of the child.

1.3 How you make an application to the High Court, what evidence you need to provide and what orders you should ask the court to make are all explained in this Practice Direction.

1.4 If your child is under 16 years of age and has been brought to England or Wales from a country which is a party (a 'State party') to the 1980 Hague Convention on the Civil Aspects of International Child Abduction ('the 1980 Hague Convention') then you can make an application to the High Court for an order under that Convention for the return of your child to the State in which he or she was habitually resident immediately before being removed or being kept away. This is explained in Part 2 below.

1.5 If your child is over 16 years of age and under 18, or has been brought to England or Wales from a country which is not a State party to the 1980 Hague Convention, then you can make an application for the return of your child under the inherent jurisdiction of the High Court with respect to children. In exercising this jurisdiction over children, the High Court will make your child's welfare its paramount consideration. How to make an application under the inherent jurisdiction of the High Court with respect to children is explained in Part 3 below.

1.6 It might be necessary for you to make an urgent application to the court if you are not sure where your child is, or you think that there is a risk that the person who is keeping your child away from you might take the child out of the United Kingdom or hide them away. Part 4 below explains how to make an urgent application to the High Court for orders to protect your child until a final decision can be made about returning the child and also how to ask for help from the police and government agencies if you think your child might be taken out of the country.

Rights of Access

1.7 Rights of access to children (also called contact or visitation) may be enforced in England and Wales. Access orders made in other Member States of the European Union can be enforced under EU law, and the 1980 Hague Convention expects State parties to comply with orders and agreements concerning access as well as rights of custody. If you have an access order and you want to enforce it in England or Wales, you should read Part 5 below.

Amendments

1 Substituted by the FPR Update, July 2015.

Part 2 – Hague Convention Cases

2.1 States which are party to the 1980 Hague Convention have agreed to return children who have been either wrongfully removed from, or wrongfully retained away from, the State where they were habitually resident immediately before the wrongful removal or retention. There are very limited exceptions to this obligation.

2.2 'Wrongfully removed' or 'wrongfully retained' means removed or retained in breach of rights of custody in respect of the child attributed to a person or a body or an institution. 'Rights of custody' are interpreted very widely (see paragraph 2.16 below).

2.3 The text of the 1980 Hague Convention and a list of Contracting States (that is, State parties) can be found on the website of the Hague Conference on Private International Law at http://www.hcch.net. All Member States of the European Union are State parties to the 1980 Hague Convention, and all but Denmark are bound by an EU Regulation which supplements the operation of the 1980 Hague Convention between the Member States of the EU (Council Regulation (EC) No 2201/2003, see paragraph 2.6).

2.4 In each State party there is a body called the Central Authority whose duty is to help people use the 1980 Hague Convention.

2.5 If you think that your child has been brought to, or kept in, England or Wales, and your State is a State party to the 1980 Hague Convention, then you should get in touch with your own Central Authority who will help you to send an application for the return of your child to the Central Authority for England and Wales. However, you are not obliged to contact your own Central Authority. You may contact the Central Authority for England and Wales directly, or you may simply instruct lawyers in England or Wales to make an application for you. The advantage of making your application through the Central Authority for England and Wales if you are applying from outside the United Kingdom is that you will get public funding ('legal aid') to make your application, regardless of your financial resources.

The Central Authority for England and Wales

2.6 The Child Abduction and Custody Act 1985 brings the 1980 Hague Convention into the law of England and Wales and identifies the Lord Chancellor as the Central Authority. His duties as the Central Authority are carried out by the International Child Abduction and Contact Unit (ICACU). ICACU also carries out the duties of the Central Authority for two other international instruments. These are the European Convention on Recognition and Enforcement of Decisions concerning Custody of Children signed at Luxembourg on 20 May 1980 (called 'the European Convention' in this Practice Direction but sometimes also referred to as 'the Luxembourg Convention') and the European Union Council Regulation (EC) No 2201/2003 of 27 November 2003 on jurisdiction and the recognition and enforcement of judgments in matrimonial matters and in matters of parental responsibility ('the Council Regulation[(b)]'). The Council Regulation has direct effect in the law of England and Wales.

(b) The Council Regulation (EC) No 2201/2003 of 27 November 2003 concerning jurisdiction and the recognition and enforcement of judgments in matrimonial matters and the matters of parental responsibility, repealing Regulation (EC) No 1347/2000 is also known as Brussels IIa, or Brussels II Revised, or Brussels II bis.

2.7 ICACU is open Mondays to Fridays from 9.00 a.m. to 5.00 p.m. It is located in the Office of the Official Solicitor and Public Trustee and its contact details are as follows:
[International Child Abduction and Contact Unit
Office of the Official Solicitor
Victory House
30–34 Kingsway
London WC2B 6EX
Email: ICACU@offsol.gsi.gov.uk
Tel: + 44 (20) 3681 2608 (10.00am to 4.00pm)
Fax: +44 (20) 3681 2763][1]

In an emergency (including out of normal working hours) contact should be made with the Royal Courts of Justice on one of the following telephone numbers:
+ 44 (0)20 7947 6000, or
+ 44 (0) 20 7947 6260.

In addition, in an emergency or outside normal working hours advice on international child abduction can be sought from reunite International Child Abduction Centre on +44 (0)1162 556 234. Outside office hours you will be directed to the 24 hour emergency service. You can also see information on Reunite's website http://www.reunite.org.

What ICACU Will Do

2.8 When ICACU receives your application for the return of your child, unless you already have a legal representative in England and Wales whom you want to act for you, it will send your application to a solicitor whom it knows to be experienced in international child abduction cases and ask them to take the case for you. You will then be the solicitor's client and the solicitor will make an application for public funding to meet your legal costs. The solicitor will then apply to the High Court for an order for the return of your child.

2.9 You can find out more about ICACU and about the 1980 Hague Convention and the other international instruments mentioned at paragraph 2.6 on two websites: Information for parties and practitioners is available on http://www.justice.gov.uk and general information for members of the public is available on http://[www.gov.uk][1].

Applying to the High Court – the Form and Content of Application

2.10 An application to the High Court for an order under the 1980 Hague Convention must be made in the Principal Registry of the Family Division in Form C67. If the Council Regulation applies, then the application must be headed both 'in the matter of the Child Abduction and Custody Act 1985' and 'in the matter of Council Regulation (EC) 2201/2003'. This is to ensure that the application is handled quickly (see paragraph 2.14 below) and to draw the court's attention to its obligations under the Council Regulation.

2.11 The application must include –

(a) the names and dates of birth of the children;

(b) the names of the children's parents or guardians;

(c) the whereabouts or suspected whereabouts of the children;

(d) the interest of the applicant in the matter (e.g. mother, father, or person with whom the child lives and details of any order placing the child with that person);

(e) the reasons for the application;

(f) details of any proceedings (including proceedings not in England or Wales, and including any legal proceedings which have finished) relating to the children;

(g) where the application is for the return of a child, the identity of the person alleged to have removed or retained the child and, if different, the identity of the person with whom the child is thought to be;

(h) in an application to which the Council Regulation also applies, any details of measures of which you are aware that have been taken by courts or authorities to ensure the protection of the child after its return to the Member State of habitual residence.

2.12 The application should be accompanied by all relevant documents including (but not limited to) –

(a) an authenticated copy of any relevant decision or agreement;

(b) a certificate or an affidavit from a Central Authority, or other competent authority of the State of the child's habitual residence, or from a qualified person, concerning the relevant law of that State.

2.13 As the applicant you may also file a statement in support of the application, although usually your solicitor will make and file a statement for you on your instructions. The statement must contain and be verified by a statement of truth in the following terms:

> 'I make this statement knowing that it will be placed before the court, and I confirm that to the best of my knowledge and belief its contents are true.'

(Further provisions about statements of truth are contained in Part 17 of these Rules and in Practice Direction 17A).

The Timetable for the Case

2.14 Proceedings to which the Council Regulation applies must be completed in 6 weeks 'except where exceptional circumstances make this impossible'. The following procedural steps are intended to ensure that applications under the 1980 Hague Convention and the Council Regulation are handled quickly –

(a) the application must be headed both 'in the matter of the Child Abduction and Custody Act 1985' and 'in the matter of Council Regulation (EC) 2201/2003';

(b) the court file will be marked to –

  (i) draw attention to the nature of the application; and

  (ii) state the date on which the 6 week period will expire (the 'hear-by date');

(c) listing priority will, where necessary, be given to such applications;

(d) the trial judge will expedite the transcript of the judgment and its approval and ensure that it is sent to the Central Authority without delay.

(The above is taken from the judgment of the Court of Appeal, Civil Division in *Vigreux v Michel & anor* [2006] EWCA Civ 630, [2006] 2 FLR 1180).

Applications for Declarations

2.15 If a child has been taken from England and Wales to another State party, the judicial or administrative authorities of that State may ask for a declaration that the removal or retention of the child was wrongful. Or it might be thought that a declaration from the High Court that a child has been wrongfully removed or retained away from the United Kingdom would be helpful in securing his return. The High Court can make such declarations under section 8 of the Child Abduction and Custody Act 1985. An application for a declaration is made in the same way as an application for a return order, the only difference being that the details of relevant legal proceedings in respect of which the declaration is sought (if any), including a copy of any order made relating to the application, should be included in the documentation.

Rights of Custody

2.16 'Rights of custody' includes rights relating to the care of the person of the child and, in particular, the right to determine the child's place of residence. Rights of custody may arise by operation of law (that is, they are conferred on someone automatically by the legal system in which they are living) or by a judicial or administrative decision or as a result of an agreement having legal effect. The rights of a person, an institution or any other body are a matter for the law of the State of the child's habitual residence, but it is for the State which is being asked to return the child to decide: if those rights amount to rights of custody for the purposes of the 1980 Hague Convention; whether at the time of the removal or retention those rights were actually being exercised; and whether there has been a breach of those rights.

2.17 In England and Wales a father who is not married to the mother of their child does not necessarily have 'rights of custody' in respect of the child. An unmarried father in England and Wales who has parental responsibility for a child has rights of custody in respect of that child. In the case of an unmarried father without parental responsibility, the concept of rights of custody may include more than strictly legal rights and where immediately before the removal or retention of the child he was exercising parental functions over a substantial period of time as the only or main carer for the child he may have rights of custody. An unmarried father can ask ICACU or his legal representative for advice on this. It is important to remember that it will be for the State which is being asked to return the child to decide if the father's circumstances meet that State's requirements for the establishment of rights of custody.

2.18 Sometimes, court orders impose restrictions on the removal of children from the country in which they are living. These can be orders under the Children Act 1989 ('section 8' orders) or orders under the inherent jurisdiction of the High Court (sometimes called 'injunctions'). Any removal of a child in breach of an order imposing such a restriction would be wrongful under the 1980 Hague Convention.

2.19 The fact that court proceedings are in progress about a child does not of itself give rise to a prohibition on the removal of the child by a mother with sole parental responsibility from the country in which the proceedings are taking place unless –

(a) the proceedings are Wardship proceedings in England and Wales (in which case removal would breach the rights of custody attributed to the High Court and fathers with no custody rights could rely on that breach); or

(b) the court is actually considering the custody of the child, because then the court itself would have rights of custody.

Particular provisions for European Convention applications

2.20 The European Convention provides for the mutual recognition and enforcement of decisions relating to custody and access, so if a child has been brought here or retained here in breach of a custody order, then that order can be enforced. The European Convention has now been superseded to a very great extent by the Council Regulation. If however you want to make an application under the European Convention, then you make it in the same way as is described in paragraphs 2.10 and 2.11 above, but in addition you must include a copy of the decision relating to custody (or rights of access – see paragraph 5.1 below) which you are seeking to register or enforce, or about which you are seeking a declaration by the court.

Defending Abduction Proceedings

2.21 If you are served with an application – whether it is under the 1980 Hague or the European Convention or the inherent jurisdiction of the High Court

– you must not delay. You must obey any directions given in any order with which you have been served, and you should seek legal advice at the earliest possible opportunity, although neither you nor the child concerned will automatically be entitled to legal aid.

2.22 It is particularly important that you tell the court where the child is, because the child will not be permitted to live anywhere else without the permission of the court, or to leave England and Wales, until the proceedings are finished.

2.23 It is also particularly important that you present to the court any defence to the application which you or the child might want to make at the earliest possible opportunity, although the orders with which you will have been served are likely to tell you the time by which you will have to do this.

2.24 If the child concerned objects to any order sought in relation to them, and if the child is of an age and understanding at which the court will take account of their views, the court is likely to direct that the child is seen by an officer of the Children and Family Court Advisory and Support Service (Cafcass) or in Wales CAFCASS Cymru. You should cooperate in this process. Children are not usually made parties to abduction cases, but in certain exceptional circumstances the court can make them parties so that they have their own separate legal representation. These are all matters about which you should seek legal advice.

(Provisions about the power of the court to join parties are contained in rule 12.3 and provisions about the joining and representation of children are contained in Part 16 of these Rules and the Practice Direction 16A (Representation of Children).

Amendments

1 Substituted by the FPR Update, July 2015.

Part 3 – Non-Convention Cases

3.1 Applications for the return of children wrongfully removed or retained away from States which are not parties to the 1980 Hague Convention or in respect of children to whom that Convention does not apply, can be made to the High Court under its inherent jurisdiction with respect to children. Such proceedings are referred to as 'non-Convention' cases. In proceedings under the inherent jurisdiction of the High Court with respect to children, the child's welfare is the court's paramount consideration. The extent of the court's enquiry into the child's welfare will depend on the circumstances of the case; in some cases the child's welfare will be best served by a summary hearing and, if necessary, a prompt return to the State from which the child has been removed or retained. In other cases a more detailed enquiry may be necessary (see *Re J (Child Returned Abroad: Convention Rights)* [2005] UKHL 40; [2005] 2 FLR 802).

3.2 Every application for the return of a child under the inherent jurisdiction must be made in the Principal Registry of the Family Division and heard in the High Court.

Provision about the inherent jurisdiction is made at Chapter 5 of Part 12 of the Rules and in Practice Direction 12D (Inherent Jurisdiction (including Wardship) Proceedings).

The Form and content of the application

3.3 An application for the return of a child under the inherent jurisdiction must be made in Form C66 and must include the information in paragraph 2.11 above.

3.4 You must file a statement in support of your application, which must exhibit all the relevant documents. The statement must contain and be verified by a statement of truth in the following terms:

> 'I make this statement knowing that it will be placed before the court, and confirm that to the best of my knowledge and belief its contents are true.'

(Further provisions about statements of truth are contained in Part 17 of these Rules and Practice Direction 17A).

Timetable for Non-Convention Cases

3.5 While the 6 week deadline referred to in paragraph 2.14 is set out in the 1980 Hague Convention and in the Council Regulation, non-Convention child abduction cases must similarly be completed in 6 weeks except where exceptional circumstances make this impossible. Paragraph 2.14 applies to these cases as appropriate for a non-Convention case.

Part 4 – General Provisions

Urgent applications, or applications out of business hours

4.1 Guidance about urgent and out of hours applications is in Practice Direction 12E (Urgent Business).

[Challenging a return order or non-return order

4.1A If you are a party to a return case and you believe that the court has made an error, it is possible to apply for permission to appeal (see Part 30 of the Rules and Practice Direction 30A).

In rare circumstances, the court might also 'set aside' its own order where it has not made an error but where new information comes to light which fundamentally changes the basis on which the order was made. The threshold for the court to set aside its decision is high, and evidence will be required – not just assertions or allegations.

If the return order or non-return order was made under the 1980 Hague Convention, the court might set aside its decision where there has been fraud, material nondisclosure or mistake (which all essentially mean that there was information that the court needed to know in order to make its decision, but was not told), or where there has been a fundamental change in circumstances which undermines the basis on which the order was made. If you have evidence of such circumstances and wish to apply to the court to set aside its decision, you should use the procedure in Part 18 of the Rules.

If the return order or non-return order was made under the inherent jurisdiction (see Part 3 of this Practice Direction), the court might set aside its decision for similar reasons as with return-non-return orders under the 1980 Hague Convention, but it also might set aside its decision because the welfare of the child or children requires it. If you have evidence of such circumstances and wish to apply to the court to set aside its decision, you should use the procedure in Part 18 of the Rules.

Any such application should be made promptly and the court will also aim to deal with the application as expeditiously as possible.

4.1B If the court has ordered the immediate implementation of the return order and you wish to apply for permission to appeal that return order or for that order to be set aside, you should also consider an application to the court for a 'stay' of the return order, or stop it being implemented.][1]

Amendment

1 Inserted by the Practice Direction, April 2020.

Police assistance to prevent removal from England and Wales

4.2 The Child Abduction Act 1984 sets out the circumstances in which the removal of a child from this jurisdiction is a criminal offence. The police provide the following 24 hour service to prevent the unlawful removal of a child –

(a) they inform ports directly when there is a real and imminent threat that a child is about to be removed unlawfully from the country; and
(b) they liaise with Immigration Officers at the ports in an attempt to identify children at risk of removal.

4.3 Where the child is under 16, it is not necessary to obtain a court order before seeking police assistance. The police do not need an order to act to protect the child. If an order has already been obtained it should however be produced to the police. Where the child is between 16 and 18, an order must be obtained restricting or restraining removal before seeking police assistance.

4.4 Where the child is a ward of court (see Practice Direction 12D (Inherent Jurisdiction (including Wardship) Proceedings) the court's permission is needed to remove that child from the jurisdiction. When the court has not given that permission and police assistance is sought to prevent the removal of the ward, the applicant must produce evidence that the child is a ward such as –

(a) an order confirming wardship;
(b) an injunction; or
(c) where the matter is urgent and no order has been made, a certified copy of the wardship application.

4.5 The application for police assistance must be made by the applicant or his legal representative to the applicant's local police station except that applications may be made to any police station –

(a) in urgent cases;
(b) where the wardship application has just been issued; or
(c) where the court has just made the order relied on.

4.6 The police will, if they consider it appropriate, institute the 'port alert' system (otherwise known as 'an all ports warning') to try to prevent removal from the jurisdiction where the danger of removal is –

(a) real (ie not being sought merely by way of insurance); and
(b) imminent (ie within 24 to 48 hours).

4.7 The request for police assistance must be accompanied by as much of the following information as possible –

(a) *the child:* the name, sex, date of birth, physical description, nationality and passport number; if the child has more than one nationality or passport, provide details;
(b) *the person likely to remove:* the name, age, physical description, nationality, passport number, relationship to the child, and whether the child is likely to assist him or her; if the person has more than one nationality or passport, provide details;
(c) *person applying for a port alert:* the name, relationship to the child, nationality, telephone number and (if appropriate) solicitor's or other legal representative's name and contact details; if the person has more than one nationality, provide details;
(d) likely destination;
(e) likely time of travel and port of embarkation and, if known, details of travel arrangements;
(f) grounds for port alert (as appropriate) –
    (i) suspected offence under section 1 or section 2 of the Child Abduction Act 1984;
    (ii) the child is subject to a court order.
(g) details of person to whom the child should be returned if intercepted.

4.8 If the police decide that the case is one in which the port-alert system should be used, the child's name will remain on the stop list for **four weeks**. After that time it will be removed automatically unless a further application is made.

[HM Passport Office][1]

4.9 Where the court makes an order prohibiting or otherwise restricting the removal of a child from the United Kingdom, or from any specified part of it, or from a specified dependent territory, the court may make an order under section 37 of the Family Law Act 1986 requiring any person to surrender any UK passport which has been issued to, or contains particulars of, the child.

4.10 [HM Passport Office ('HMPO')][1] will take action to prevent a United Kingdom passport or replacement passport being issued only where [HMPO][1] has been served with a court order expressly requiring a United Kingdom passport to be surrendered, or expressly prohibiting the issue of any further United Kingdom passport facilities to the child without the consent of the court, or the holder of such an order. Accordingly, in every case in which such an order has been made, [HMPO][1] must be served the same day if possible, or at the latest the following day, with a copy of the order. It is the responsibility of the applicant to do this. The specimen form of letter set out below should be used and a copy of the court order must be attached to the letter. Delay in sending the letter to [HMPO][1] must be kept to an absolute minimum.

'Intelligence Hub
Her Majesty's Passport Office
3 Northgate
96 Milton Street
Glasgow
G4 0BT][1]

Dear Sir/Madam

.........................v.....................

Case no: ....

This is to inform you that the court has today made an order

*prohibiting the issue of a passport/passports to [name(s)] [date of birth (if known)] of [address] without the consent of the holder of the order.

*requiring [name(s)] [date of birth (if known)] of [address] to surrender the passport(s) issued to him/her/them/the following child[ren] / or which contain(s) particulars of the following child[ren]:

Name Date of Birth

*and has granted an injunction/*made an order restraining the removal of the child[ren] from the jurisdiction.

(*Delete as appropriate)

Please add these names to your records to prevent the issue of further passport facilities for the child[ren]. I enclose a copy of the court order.

Yours faithfully

Applicant's name / Applicant's Solicitor's name'

4.11 Following service on [HMPO][1] of an order either expressly requiring a United Kingdom passport to be surrendered by, or expressly prohibiting the issue of any further United Kingdom passport facilities to the child, [HMPO][1] will maintain a prohibition on issuing a passport, or further passport facilities until the child's 16th birthday. The order should state that a passport must not be granted/applied for without the consent of the court or the holder of the order.

Note: These requests may also be sent to any of the regional Passport Offices.

4.12 Further information on communicating with [HMPO][1] where the court has made a request of, or an order against, [HMPO][1], may be found in [The President's Guidance reissued in October 2014: Communicating with the Home Office in Family Proceedings. Annex 1 to this Practice Direction contains that Guidance and Annex 2 contains the current version (as at June 2015) of the relevant court form.][1]

4.13 Information about other circumstances, in which [HMPO][1] will agree not to issue a passport to a child if [HMPO][1] receives an application, or an order in more general terms than set out at 4.11 above, from a person who claims to have parental responsibility for the child, is available from [HMPO][1] or at [www.gov.uk][1].

The Home Office

4.14 Information about communicating with the Home Office, where a question of the immigration status of a party arises in family proceedings, may be found in the Protocol: Communicating with the Home Office in Family Proceedings (revised and re-issued October 2010).

Press Reporting

4.15 When a child has been abducted and a judge considers that publicity may help in tracing the child, the judge may adjourn the case for a short period to enable representatives of the Press to attend to give the case the widest possible publicity.

4.16. If a Child Rescue Alert has been used concerning a child, within the UK or abroad, it will give rise to media publicity. The court should be informed that this has happened. If there are already court proceedings concerning a child, it is advisable to obtain the agreement of the court before there is publicity to trace a missing child. If the court has not given its permission for a child who is the subject of children proceedings to be identified as the subject of proceedings, to do so would be contempt of court.

Other Assistance

4.17 The Missing Persons Bureau will be participating for the UK in the European Union wide 116 000 hotline for missing children. Parents and children can ring this number for assistance. (It is primarily intended to deal with criminal matters, for example stranger kidnapping.)

4.18 It may also be possible to trace a child by obtaining a court order under the inherent jurisdiction or the wardship jurisdiction of the High Court addressed to certain government departments, as set out in Practice Direction 6C.

Amendments

1 Substituted by the FPR Update, July 2015.

Part 5 – Applications about rights of access

5.1 Access orders made in another Member State of the European Union (except Denmark) can be enforced in England or Wales under the Council Regulation.

5.2 Chapter III of the Council Regulation sets out provision for recognition and enforcement of parental responsibility orders, which include orders for custody and access ([child arrangements][1]) between Member States. Under Article 41 of the Council Regulation you can enforce an access order in your favour from another Member State directly, provided you produce the certificate given under Article 41(2) by the court which made the order. This is a quick procedure. The unsuccessful party is not allowed to oppose recognition of the order.

5.3 The rules on recognition and enforcement of parental responsibility orders are in Part 31. You should apply to the High Court using Form C69. Rule 31.8 covers applications for Article 41 of the Council Regulation. You can make the application without notice.

5.4 If the Council Regulation does not apply, and the access order was made by a State party to the European Convention, an application can be made to enforce the order under Article 11 of the European Convention. Paragraph 2.20 above gives further information about how to make the application.

5.5 Article 21 of the 1980 Hague Convention requires the States parties to respect rights of access. However, in the case of *Re G (A Minor) (Hague Convention: Access)* [1993] 1 FLR 669, the Court of Appeal took the view that Article 21 conferred no jurisdiction to determine matters relating to access, or to recognise or enforce foreign access orders (see Practice Note of 5 March 1993: Child Abduction Unit: Lord Chancellor's Department set out in [Annex 3][2] to this Practice Direction). (The Child Abduction Unit is now called ICACU see paragraph 2.6.) An access order which does not fall within the Council Regulation or the (very limited) application of the European Convention may only be enforced by applying for a ['child arrangements order'][1] under section 8 of the Children Act 1989.

5.6 This means that if, during the course of proceedings under the 1980 Hague Convention for a return order, the applicant decides to ask for access (contact) instead of the return of the child, but no agreement can be reached, a separate application for a contact order will have to be made, or the court invited to make a [child arrangements order][1] without an application being made (Children Act 1989, s 10(1)(b)).

Amendments

1 Substituted by the FPR Update, April 2014.
2 Substituted by the FPR Update, July 2015.

Part 6 – Child abduction cases between the United Kingdom and Pakistan

6.1 A consensus was reached in January 2003 between the President of the Family Division and the Hon. Chief Justice of Pakistan as to the principles to be applied in resolving child abduction cases between the UK and Pakistan.

The Protocol setting out that consensus can be accessed at:

http://www.fco.gov.uk/resources/en/pdf/2855621/3069133

[Annex 1 Communicating with the UK Visas and Immigration (UKVI) in family proceedings

Protocol agreed between the President of the Family Division and the Home Office issued on 16 May 2018

1 This Protocol enables the family courts (the Family Division of the High Court of Justice and the Family Court) to communicate with UK VISAS AND IMMIGRATION (UKVI), the relevant division of the Home Office, to obtain immigration and visa information for use in family court proceedings. Although it replaces and supersedes the previous guidance issued in 2002, 2004, 2006, 2010 and 2014, in particular to reflect new UKVI processes and contact details, it does not alter the nature or purpose of the Protocol.

2 There are three parts of the process:

(1) HMCTS form EX660 (rev 04/18), a copy of which is annexed to this Protocol, must be completed by the parties and approved by the judge.

  (a) The EX660 must be typed, not handwritten.

  (b) The EX660 must be completed in full, specifying the details of the relevant family members and their relationship to the child(ren).

Details of both mother and father/adoptive parents if known should be provided, whether or not they are involved in the proceedings, as this enables UKVI to trace the child(ren)'s records.

(c) The EX660 and the order must specify the questions the court wishes to be answered by UKVI.

(d) The EX660 must contain the name and contact details of someone who has agreed and is able to provide further information if needed.

(e) The EX660 must clearly state the time by which the information is required. Failure to do this may cause delay in the time it takes UKVI to process the request.

(2) An order in the relevant form, a copy of which is annexed to this Protocol, must be drawn up, approved by the judge and sealed by the court.

(a) The order must clearly state the time by which the information is required.

(b) The order must specify any additional information or documents, such as a synopsis, which it wishes UKVI to have and set out in the order that the leave of the court to make disclosure to UKVI has been given. (Note that it may be a contempt of court to disclose this information otherwise.)

(3) The UKVI SVEC pro-forma must be completed by the court staff utilising the information in the EX660 and the order.

(a) All relevant fields in the SVEC pro-forma must be completed:

i. Section A – All fields to be completed if known
ii. Section B – Enquiry Type – Select Standard
iii. Section C – Select Subject 1 and complete all fields.
iv. Section D – Enter "Y" in "Other " field only.
v. Section E – Enter " Please refer to court order and EX660".
vi. For more than one subject, select subject 2 and so on, completing steps C-E for each one.

(b) In Section B there are two fields, "Court date" and "required date", which must be completed. In both fields the date the information is required should be entered, not the court date. These fields generate the target date on UKVI systems and, as the information ordered by the court will be required before the date of the court hearing, this will ensure that the information is provided in time.

3 The EX660 and the order must contain sufficient information to enable UKVI to understand the nature of the case, to identify whether the case involves an adoption, and to identify whether the immigration issues raised relate to an asylum or a non- asylum application.

4 In order to comply with the agreed four (4) week period for UKVI to provide a response to the court, the sealed order should be available to be sent by the court staff to UKVI on the same day that the order is made. Where that is not possible, the court, when stating the required date of receipt by the court of the information requested, must allow any additional time necessary for the preparation, sealing and sending of the order. This is

to ensure that UKVI has four (4) weeks to provide a response from the time it receives the order.

5 The sealed order, completed EX660 and SVEC pro-forma should be sent immediately by the court to ICESSVECWorkflow@homeoffice.gsi.gov.uk including EEREQUEST on the subject line of the email. The request for information will be rejected by UKVI if either the sealed order or the SVEC pro-forma is not provided.

6 Where the court wishes to progress a case that may be delayed, it may send an email to SVECManagement@homeoffice.gsi.gov.uk

7 The UKVI official will be personally responsible for either:
   (i) answering the query themselves, by retrieving the file and preparing a statement for the court; or
   (ii) forwarding to a caseworker or relevant official with carriage of the particular file.

8 UKVI will ensure that their information is received by the court in time, as instructed by the judge or court making the request.

Amendment

1 Inserted by the FPR Update, July 2015.

Annex 2 Court request for information to the Home Office

Annex 2

Court request for information to the Home Office

UK Visas & Immigration (UKVI)

Please note that information provided in this form will be forwarded to the Home Office

Name of court	
Case no.	
Serial no.	
Date	

In the matter of the Act

In the matter of

To the judge: Each of the following fields must be completed to assist the Home Office find the relevant records. Once completed pass the form to your Court Clerk. The Court Clerk will then produce a separate order directed to the Home Office and using the information provided on this form, complete the Home Office application form SVEC.

Name of Judge:					
Full name of each party, including relationship to child(ren)	Female/Male (please tick)	Date of birth	Country of origin	Date arrived in UK:	All relevant Home Office reference no's:
	☐ Female ☐ Male				
	☐ Female ☐ Male				
	☐ Female ☐ Male				
	☐ Female ☐ Male				
	☐ Female ☐ Male				

	☐ Female ☐ Male				

What questions would you like the UKVI to answer?	
Please provide a brief summary of case and any other information which will be useful to the UKVI in dealing with the request e.g. any details relating to immigration: (Please attach any documents, such as Case Summaries, in respect of which the Court has given leave to disclose to the Home Office).	

Has the court in the order given leave to disclose any supporting documentation to the Home Office?	☐ Yes ☐ No
Contact details of person from whom additional information can be sought:	
By what date is the information required? (Please allow a minimum of 4 weeks from the date of sending to the Home Office Liaison Team)	

Amendment

1 Inserted by the FPR Update, July 2015.

[Annex 3][1]

See paragraph 5.5

Practice Note

5 March 1993

Citations: [1993] 1 FLR 804

Child Abduction Unit: Lord Chancellor's Department

Duties of the Central Authority for England and Wales under Article 21 of the Hague Convention on the Civil Aspects of International Child Abduction

CHILD ABDUCTION AND CUSTODY ACT 1985

In the case of *R G (A Minor) (Hague Convention: Access)* [1993] 1 FLR 669 the Court of Appeal considered the duties of the Central Authority for England and Wales on receiving an application in respect of rights of access under Art 21 of the Hague Convention.

The Court of Appeal took the view that Art 21 conferred no jurisdiction to determine matters relating to access, or to recognise or enforce foreign access orders. It provides, however, for executive co-operation in the enforcement of such recognition as national law allows.

Accordingly, the duty of the Central Authority is to make appropriate arrangements for the applicant by providing solicitors to act on his behalf in applying for legal aid and instituting proceedings in the High Court under s 8 of the Children Act 1989.

If, during the course of proceedings under Art 21 of the Convention, the applicant decides to seek access instead of the return of the child, but no agreement can be reached and the provisions of the European Convention on the Recognition and Enforcement of Decisions Concerning Custody of Children and on Restoration of Custody of Children are not available, a separate application under s 8 of the Children Act 1989 will have to be made.

Central Authority for England and Wales

NOTE: The Child Abduction Unit is now called ICACU, see paragraph 2.6.

Amendment

1 Renumbered by the FPR Update, July 2015.

[PRACTICE DIRECTION 12J – CHILD ARRANGEMENTS AND CONTACT ORDERS: DOMESTIC ABUSE AND HARM

This Practice Direction supplements FPR Part 12, and incorporates and supersedes the President's Guidance in Relation to Split Hearings (May 2010) as it applies to proceedings for child arrangements orders.

Summary

1 This Practice Direction applies to any family proceedings in the Family Court or the High Court under the relevant parts of the Children Act 1989 or the relevant parts of the Adoption and Children Act 2002 in which an application is made for a child arrangements order, or in which any question arises about where a child should live, or about contact between a child and a parent or other family member, where the court considers that an order should be made.

2 The purpose of this Practice Direction is to set out what the Family Court or the High Court is required to do in any case in which it is alleged or admitted, or there is other reason to believe, that the child or a party has experienced domestic abuse perpetrated by another party or that there is a risk of such abuse.

3 For the purpose of this Practice Direction –

'domestic abuse' includes any incident or pattern of incidents of controlling, coercive or threatening behaviour, violence or abuse between those aged 16 or over who are or have been intimate partners or family members regardless of gender or sexuality. This can encompass, but is not limited to, psychological, physical, sexual, financial, or emotional abuse. Domestic abuse also includes culturally specific forms of abuse including, but not limited to, forced marriage, honour-based violence, dowry-related abuse and transnational marriage abandonment;

'abandonment' refers to the practice whereby a husband, in England and Wales, deliberately abandons or 'strands' his foreign national wife abroad, usually without financial resources, in order to prevent her from asserting matrimonial and/or residence rights in England and Wales. It may involve children who are either abandoned with, or separated from, their mother;

'coercive behaviour' means an act or a pattern of acts of assault, threats, humiliation and intimidation or other abuse that is used to harm, punish, or frighten the victim;

'controlling behaviour' means an act or pattern of acts designed to make a person subordinate and/or dependent by isolating them from sources of support, exploiting their resources and capacities for personal gain, depriving them of the means needed for independence, resistance and escape and regulating their everyday behaviour;

'development' means physical, intellectual, emotional, social or behavioural development;

'harm' means ill-treatment or the impairment of health or development including, for example, impairment suffered from seeing or hearing the ill-treatment of another, by domestic abuse or otherwise;
'health' means physical or mental health;
'ill-treatment' includes sexual abuse and forms of ill-treatment which are not physical; and
'judge' includes salaried and fee-paid judges and lay justices sitting in the Family Court and, where the context permits, can include a [justices' legal adviser][1] in the Family Court.

Amendment

1 Substituted by the Practice Direction, April 2020.

General principles

4 Domestic abuse is harmful to children, and/or puts children at risk of harm, whether they are subjected to domestic abuse, or witness one of their parents being violent or abusive to the other parent, or live in a home in which domestic abuse is perpetrated (even if the child is too young to be conscious of the behaviour). Children may suffer direct physical, psychological and/or emotional harm from living with domestic abuse, and may also suffer harm indirectly where the domestic abuse impairs the parenting capacity of either or both of their parents.

5 The court must, at all stages of the proceedings, and specifically at the First Hearing Dispute Resolution Appointment ('FHDRA'), consider whether domestic abuse is raised as an issue, either by the parties or by Cafcass or CAFCASS Cymru or otherwise, and if so must –

- identify at the earliest opportunity (usually at the FHDRA) the factual and welfare issues involved;
- consider the nature of any allegation, admission or evidence of domestic abuse, and the extent to which it would be likely to be relevant in deciding whether to make a child arrangements order and, if so, in what terms;
- give directions to enable contested relevant factual and welfare issues to be tried as soon as possible and fairly;
- ensure that where domestic abuse is admitted or proven, any child arrangements order in place protects the safety and wellbeing of the child and the parent with whom the child is living, and does not expose either of them to the risk of further harm; and
- ensure that any interim child arrangements order (i.e. considered by the court before determination of the facts, and in the absence of admission) is only made having followed the guidance in paragraphs 25–27 below.

In particular, the court must be satisfied that any contact ordered with a parent who has perpetrated domestic abuse does not expose the child and/or other parent to the risk of harm and is in the best interests of the child.

6 In all cases it is for the court to decide whether a child arrangements order accords with Section 1(1) of the Children Act 1989; any proposed child arrangements order, whether to be made by agreement between the parties or otherwise must be carefully scrutinised by the court accordingly. The court must not make a child arrangements order by consent or give permission for an application for a child arrangements order to be withdrawn, unless the parties are present in court, all initial safeguarding checks have been obtained by the court, and an officer of Cafcass or CAFCASS Cymru has spoken to the parties separately, except where it is satisfied that there is no risk of harm to the child and/or the other parent in so doing.

7 In proceedings relating to a child arrangements order, the court presumes that the involvement of a parent in a child's life will further the child's welfare, unless there is evidence to the contrary. The court must in every case consider carefully whether the statutory presumption applies, having particular regard to any allegation or admission of harm by domestic abuse to the child or parent or any evidence indicating such harm or risk of harm.

8 In considering, on an application for a child arrangements order by consent, whether there is any risk of harm to the child, the court must consider all the evidence and information available. The court may direct a report under Section 7 of the Children Act 1989 to be provided either orally or in writing, before it makes its decision; in such a case, the court must ask for information about any advice given by the officer preparing the report to the parties and whether they, or the child, have been referred to any other agency, including local authority children's services. If the report is not in writing, the court must make a note of its substance on the court file and a summary of the same shall be set out in a Schedule to the relevant order.

Before the FHDRA

9 Where any information provided to the court before the FHDRA or other first hearing (whether as a result of initial safeguarding enquiries by Cafcass or CAFCASS Cymru or on form C1A or otherwise) indicates that there are issues of domestic abuse which may be relevant to the court's determination, the court must ensure that the issues are addressed at the hearing, and that the parties are not expected to engage in conciliation or other forms of dispute resolution which are not suitable and/or safe.

10 If at any stage the court is advised by any party (in the application form, or otherwise), by Cafcass or CAFCASS Cymru or otherwise that there is a need for special arrangements to protect the party or child attending any hearing, the court must ensure so far as practicable that appropriate arrangements are made for the hearing (including the waiting arrangements at court prior to the hearing, and arrangements for entering and exiting the court building) and for all subsequent hearings in the case, unless it is advised and considers that these are no longer necessary. Where practicable, the court should enquire of the alleged victim of domestic abuse how best she/he wishes to participate.

First hearing / FHDRA

11 At the FHDRA, if the parties have not been provided with the safeguarding letter/report by Cafcass/CAFCASS Cymru, the court must inform the parties of the content of any safeguarding letter or report or other information which has been provided by Cafcass or CAFCASS Cymru, unless it considers that to do so would create a risk of harm to a party or the child.

12 Where the results of Cafcass or CAFCASS Cymru safeguarding checks are not available at the FHDRA, and no other reliable safeguarding information is available, the court must adjourn the FHDRA until the results of safeguarding checks are available. The court must not generally make an interim child arrangements order, or orders for contact, in the absence of safeguarding information, unless it is to protect the safety of the child, and/or safeguard the child from harm (see further paragraphs 25-27 below).

13 There is a continuing duty on the Cafcass Officer/Welsh FPO which requires them to provide a risk assessment for the court under section 16A Children Act 1989 if they are given cause to suspect that the child concerned is at risk of harm. Specific provision about service of a risk assessment under section 16A of the 1989 Act is made by rule 12.34 of the FPR 2010.

14 The court must ascertain at the earliest opportunity, and record on the face of its order, whether domestic abuse is raised as an issue which is likely to be relevant to any decision of the court relating to the welfare of the child, and specifically whether the child and/or parent would be at risk of harm in the making of any child arrangements order.

Admissions

15 Where at any hearing an admission of domestic abuse toward another person or the child is made by a party, the admission must be recorded in writing by the judge and set out as a Schedule to the relevant order. The court office must arrange for a copy of any order containing a record of admissions to be made available as soon as possible to any Cafcass officer or officer of CAFCASS Cymru or local authority officer preparing a report under section 7 of the Children Act 1989.

Directions for a fact-finding hearing

16 The court should determine as soon as possible whether it is necessary to conduct a fact-finding hearing in relation to any disputed allegation of domestic abuse –

(a) in order to provide a factual basis for any welfare report or for assessment of the factors set out in paragraphs 36 and 37 below;
(b) in order to provide a basis for an accurate assessment of risk;
(c) before it can consider any final welfare-based order(s) in relation to child arrangements; or

(d) before it considers the need for a domestic abuse-related Activity (such as a Domestic Violence Perpetrator Programme (DVPP)).

17 In determining whether it is necessary to conduct a fact-finding hearing, the court should consider –
(a) the views of the parties and of Cafcass or CAFCASS Cymru;
(b) whether there are admissions by a party which provide a sufficient factual basis on which to proceed;
(c) if a party is in receipt of legal aid, whether the evidence required to be provided to obtain legal aid provides a sufficient factual basis on which to proceed;
(d) whether there is other evidence available to the court that provides a sufficient factual basis on which to proceed;
(e) whether the factors set out in paragraphs 36 and 37 below can be determined without a fact-finding hearing;
(f) the nature of the evidence required to resolve disputed allegations;
(g) whether the nature and extent of the allegations, if proved, would be relevant to the issue before the court; and
(h) whether a separate fact-finding hearing would be necessary and proportionate in all the circumstances of the case.

18 Where the court determines that a finding of fact hearing is not necessary, the order must record the reasons for that decision.

19 Where the court considers that a fact-finding hearing is necessary, it must give directions as to how the proceedings are to be conducted to ensure that the matters in issue are determined as soon as possible, fairly and proportionately, and within the capabilities of the parties. In particular it should consider –
(a) what are the key facts in dispute;
(b) whether it is necessary for the fact-finding to take place at a separate (and earlier) hearing than the welfare hearing;
(c) whether the key facts in dispute can be contained in a schedule or a table (known as a Scott Schedule) which sets out what the applicant complains of or alleges, what the respondent says in relation to each individual allegation or complaint; the allegations in the schedule should be focused on the factual issues to be tried; and if so, whether it is practicable for this schedule to be completed at the first hearing, with the assistance of the judge;
(d) what evidence is required in order to determine the existence of coercive, controlling or threatening behaviour, or of any other form of domestic abuse;
(e) directing the parties to file written statements giving details of such behaviour and of any response;
(f) whether documents are required from third parties such as the police, health services or domestic abuse support services and giving directions for those documents to be obtained;
(g) whether oral evidence may be required from third parties and if so, giving directions for the filing of written statements from such third parties;

(h) where (for example in cases of abandonment) third parties from whom documents are to be obtained are abroad, how to obtain those documents in good time for the hearing, and who should be responsible for the costs of obtaining those documents;

(i) whether any other evidence is required to enable the court to decide the key issues and giving directions for that evidence to be provided;

(j) what evidence the alleged victim of domestic abuse is able to give and what support the alleged victim may require at the fact-finding hearing in order to give that evidence;

(k) in cases where the alleged victim of domestic abuse is unable for reasons beyond their control to be present at the hearing (for example, abandonment cases where the abandoned spouse remains abroad), what measures should be taken to ensure that that person's best evidence can be put before the court. Where video-link is not available, the court should consider alternative technological or other methods which may be utilised to allow that person to participate in the proceedings;

(l) what support the alleged perpetrator may need in order to have a reasonable opportunity to challenge the evidence; and

(m) whether a pre-hearing review would be useful prior to the fact-finding hearing to ensure directions have been complied with and all the required evidence is available.

20 Where the court fixes a fact-finding hearing, it must at the same time fix a Dispute Resolution Appointment to follow. Subject to the exception in paragraph 31 below, the hearings should be arranged in such a way that they are conducted by the same judge or, wherever possible, by the same panel of lay justices; where it is not possible to assemble the same panel of justices, the resumed hearing should be listed before at least the same chairperson of the lay justices. Judicial continuity is important.

Reports under Section 7

21 In any case where a risk of harm to a child resulting from domestic abuse is raised as an issue, the court should consider directing that a report on the question of contact, or any other matters relating to the welfare of the child, be prepared under section 7 of the Children Act 1989 by an Officer of Cafcass or a Welsh family proceedings officer (or local authority officer if appropriate), unless the court is satisfied that it is not necessary to do so in order to safeguard the child's interests.

22 If the court directs that there shall be a fact-finding hearing on the issue of domestic abuse, the court will not usually request a section 7 report until after that hearing. In that event, the court should direct that any judgment is provided to Cafcass/CAFCASS Cymru; if there is no transcribed judgment, an agreed list of findings should be provided, as set out at paragraph 29.

23 Any request for a section 7 report should set out clearly the matters the court considers need to be addressed.

Representation of the child

24 Subject to the seriousness of the allegations made and the difficulty of the case, the court must consider whether it is appropriate for the child who is the subject of the application to be made a party to the proceedings and be separately represented. If the court considers that the child should be so represented, it must review the allocation decision so that it is satisfied that the case proceeds before the correct level of judge in the Family Court or High Court.

Interim orders before determination of relevant facts

25 Where the court gives directions for a fact-finding hearing, or where disputed allegations of domestic abuse are otherwise undetermined, the court should not make an interim child arrangements order unless it is satisfied that it is in the interests of the child to do so and that the order would not expose the child or the other parent to an unmanageable risk of harm (bearing in mind the impact which domestic abuse against a parent can have on the emotional well-being of the child, the safety of the other parent and the need to protect against domestic abuse including controlling or coercive behaviour).

26 In deciding any interim child arrangements question the court should–

(a) take into account the matters set out in section 1(3) of the Children Act 1989 or section 1(4) of the Adoption and Children Act 2002 ('the welfare check-list'), as appropriate; and

(b) give particular consideration to the likely effect on the child, and on the care given to the child by the parent who has made the allegation of domestic abuse, of any contact and any risk of harm, whether physical, emotional or psychological, which the child and that parent is likely to suffer as a consequence of making or declining to make an order.

27 Where the court is considering whether to make an order for interim contact, it should in addition consider –

(a) the arrangements required to ensure, as far as possible, that any risk of harm to the child and the parent who is at any time caring for the child is minimised and that the safety of the child and the parties is secured; and in particular:

(i) whether the contact should be supervised or supported, and if so, where and by whom; and (ii) the availability of appropriate facilities for that purpose;

(b) if direct contact is not appropriate, whether it is in the best interests of the child to make an order for indirect contact; and

(c) whether contact will be beneficial for the child.

The fact-finding hearing or other hearing of the facts where domestic abuse is alleged

28 While ensuring that the allegations are properly put and responded to, the fact-finding hearing or other hearing can be an inquisitorial (or investigative) process, which at all times must protect the interests of all involved. At the fact-finding hearing or other hearing –

- each party can be asked to identify what questions they wish to ask of the other party, and to set out or confirm in sworn evidence their version of the disputed key facts; and
- the judge should be prepared where necessary and appropriate to conduct the questioning of the witnesses on behalf of the parties, focusing on the key issues in the case.

29 The court should, wherever practicable, make findings of fact as to the nature and degree of any domestic abuse which is established and its effect on the child, the child's parents and any other relevant person. The court must record its findings in writing in a Schedule to the relevant order, and the court office must serve a copy of this order on the parties. A copy of any record of findings of fact or of admissions must be sent by the court office to any officer preparing a report under Section 7 of the 1989 Act.

30. At the conclusion of any fact-finding hearing, the court must consider, notwithstanding any earlier direction for a section 7 report, whether it is in the best interests of the child for the court to give further directions about the preparation or scope of any report under section 7; where necessary, it may adjourn the proceedings for a brief period to enable the officer to make representations about the preparation or scope of any further enquiries. Any section 7 report should address the factors set out in paragraphs 36 and 37 below, unless the court directs otherwise.

31 Where the court has made findings of fact on disputed allegations, any subsequent hearing in the proceedings should be conducted by the same judge or by at least the same chairperson of the justices. Exceptions may be made only where observing this requirement would result in delay to the planned timetable and the judge or chairperson is satisfied, for reasons which must be recorded in writing, that the detriment to the welfare of the child would outweigh the detriment to the fair trial of the proceedings.

In all cases where domestic abuse has occurred

32 The court should take steps to obtain (or direct the parties or an Officer of Cafcass or a Welsh family proceedings officer to obtain) information about the facilities available locally (to include local domestic abuse support services) to assist any party or the child in cases where domestic abuse has occurred.

33 Following any determination of the nature and extent of domestic abuse, whether or not following a fact-finding hearing, the court must, if considering any form of contact or involvement of the parent in the child's life, consider –

(a) whether it would be assisted by any social work, psychiatric, psychological or other assessment (including an expert safety and risk assessment) of any party or the child and if so (subject to any necessary consent) make directions for such assessment to be undertaken and for the filing of any consequent report. Any such report should address the factors set out in paragraphs 36 and 37 below, unless the court directs otherwise;

(b) whether any party should seek advice, treatment or other intervention as a precondition to any child arrangements order being made, and may (with the consent of that party) give directions for such attendance.

34 Further or as an alternative to the advice, treatment or other intervention referred to in paragraph 33(b) above, the court may make an Activity Direction under section 11A and 11B Children Act 1989. Any intervention directed pursuant to this provision should be one commissioned and approved by Cafcass. It is acknowledged that acceptance on a DVPP is subject to a suitability assessment by the service provider, and that completion of a DVPP will take time in order to achieve the aim of risk-reduction for the long-term benefit of the child and the parent with whom the child is living.

Factors to be taken into account when determining whether to make child arrangements orders in all cases where domestic abuse has occurred

35 When deciding the issue of child arrangements the court should ensure that any order for contact will not expose the child to an unmanageable risk of harm and will be in the best interests of the child.

36 In the light of any findings of fact or admissions or where domestic abuse is otherwise established, the court should apply the individual matters in the welfare checklist with reference to the domestic abuse which has occurred and any expert risk assessment obtained. In particular, the court should in every case consider any harm which the child and the parent with whom the child is living has suffered as a consequence of that domestic abuse, and any harm which the child and the parent with whom the child is living is at risk of suffering, if a child arrangements order is made. The court should make an order for contact only if it is satisfied that the physical and emotional safety of the child and the parent with whom the child is living can, as far as possible, be secured before during and after contact, and that the parent with whom the child is living will not be subjected to further domestic abuse by the other parent.

37 In every case where a finding or admission of domestic abuse is made, or where domestic abuse is otherwise established, the court should consider the conduct of both parents towards each other and towards the child and the impact of the same. In particular, the court should consider –

(a) the effect of the domestic abuse on the child and on the arrangements for where the child is living;
(b) the effect of the domestic abuse on the child and its effect on the child's relationship with the parents;
(c) whether the parent is motivated by a desire to promote the best interests of the child or is using the process to continue a form of domestic abuse against the other parent;
(d) the likely behaviour during contact of the parent against whom findings are made and its effect on the child; and
(e) the capacity of the parents to appreciate the effect of past domestic abuse and the potential for future domestic abuse.

Directions as to how contact is to proceed

38 Where any domestic abuse has occurred but the court, having considered any expert risk assessment and having applied the welfare checklist, nonetheless considers that direct contact is safe and beneficial for the child, the court should consider what, if any, directions or conditions are required to enable the order to be carried into effect and in particular should consider –

(a) whether or not contact should be supervised, and if so, where and by whom;
(b) whether to impose any conditions to be complied with by the party in whose favour the order for contact has been made and if so, the nature of those conditions, for example by way of seeking intervention (subject to any necessary consent);
(c) whether such contact should be for a specified period or should contain provisions which are to have effect for a specified period; and
(d) whether it will be necessary, in the child's best interests, to review the operation of the order; if so the court should set a date for the review consistent with the timetable for the child, and must give directions to ensure that at the review the court has full information about the operation of the order.

Where a risk assessment has concluded that a parent poses a risk to a child or to the other parent, contact via a supported contact centre, or contact supported by a parent or relative, is not appropriate.

39 Where the court does not consider direct contact to be appropriate, it must consider whether it is safe and beneficial for the child to make an order for indirect contact.

The reasons of the court

40 In its judgment or reasons the court should always make clear how its findings on the issue of domestic abuse have influenced its decision on the issue of arrangements for the child. In particular, where the court has found domestic abuse proved but nonetheless makes an order which results

in the child having future contact with the perpetrator of domestic abuse, the court must always explain, whether by way of reference to the welfare check-list, the factors in paragraphs 36 and 37 or otherwise, why it takes the view that the order which it has made will not expose the child to the risk of harm and is beneficial for the child.][1]

Amendment

1 Substituted by the President's Circular 14 September 2017.

PART 16: REPRESENTATION OF CHILDREN AND REPORTS IN PROCEEDINGS INVOLVING CHILDREN

Chapter 1: Application of this Part

16.1 Application of this Part

This Part –
- (a) sets out when the court will make a child a party in family proceedings; and
- (b) contains special provisions which apply in proceedings involving children.

Chapter 2: Child as Party in Family Proceedings

16.2 When the court may make a child a party to proceedings

(1) The court may make a child a party to proceedings if it considers it is in the best interests of the child to do so.

(2) This rule does not apply to a child who is the subject of proceedings –
- (a) which are specified proceedings; or
- (b) to which Part 14 applies.

(The Practice Direction 16A sets out the matters which the court will take into consideration before making a child a party under this rule.)

Chapter 3: When a Children's Guardian or Litigation Friend will be Appointed

16.3 Appointment of a children's guardian in specified proceedings or proceedings to which Part 14 applies

(1) Unless it is satisfied that it is not necessary to do so to safeguard the interests of the child, the court must appoint a children's guardian for a child who is –
- (a) the subject of; and
- (b) a party to,

proceedings –

(i) which are specified proceedings; or
(ii) to which Part 14 applies.

(Rules 12.6 and 14.6 set out the point in the proceedings when the court will appoint a children's guardian in specified proceedings and proceedings to which Part 14 respectively.)

(2) At any stage in the proceedings –
(a) a party may apply, without notice to the other parties unless the court directs otherwise, for the appointment of a children's guardian; or
(b) the court may of its own initiative appoint a children's guardian.

(3) Where the court refuses an application under paragraph (2)(a) it will give reasons for the refusal and the court or a court officer will –
(a) record the refusal and the reasons for it; and
(b) as soon as practicable, notify the parties and either the Service or the Assembly of a decision not to appoint a children's guardian.

(4) When appointing a children's guardian the court will consider the appointment of anyone who has previously acted as a children's guardian of the same child.

(5) Where the court appoints a children's guardian in accordance with this rule, the provisions of Chapter 6 of this Part apply.

16.4 Appointment of a children's guardian in proceedings not being specified proceedings or proceedings to which Part 14 applies

(1) [Except in proceedings under section 55A of the 1986 Act and without][1] prejudice to rule 8.42 or 16.6, the court must appoint a children's guardian for a child who is the subject of proceedings, which are not proceedings of a type referred to in rule 16.3(1), if –
(a) the child is an applicant in the proceedings;
(b) a provision in these rules provides for the child to be a party to the proceedings; or
(c) the court has made the child a party in accordance with rule 16.2.

[(1A) Without prejudice to rule 16.6, in proceedings under section 55A of the 1986 Act, the court must appoint a children's guardian for a child where –
(a) the court has made the child a party in accordance with rule 16.2; and
(b) the child is the person whose parentage is in dispute in those proceedings.][2]

(2) The provisions of Chapter 7 of this Part apply where the appointment of a children's guardian is required in accordance with paragraph (1) [or paragraph (1A)][2].

('children's guardian' is defined in rule 2.3.)

Amendments

1 Substituted by the Family Procedure (Amendment No. 2) Rules 2016, SI 2016/901, rr 2, 5(a).
2 Inserted by the Family Procedure (Amendment No. 2) Rules 2016, SI 2016/901, rr 2, 5(b), (c).

16.5 Requirement for a litigation friend

(1) [Except in proceedings under section 55A of the 1986 Act and without][1] prejudice to rule 16.6, where a child is –
(a) a party to proceedings; but
(b) not the subject of those proceedings,

the child must have a litigation friend to conduct proceedings on the child's behalf.

[(1A) Without prejudice to rule 16.6, where a child is –
(a) a party to proceedings under section 55A of the 1986 Act; but
(b) not the person whose parentage is in dispute in those proceedings,

the child must have a litigation friend to conduct proceedings on the child's behalf.][2]

(2) The provisions of Chapter 5 of this Part apply where a litigation friend is required in accordance with paragraph (1) [or paragraph (1A)][2].

Amendments

1 Substituted by the Family Procedure (Amendment No. 2) Rules 2016, SI 2016/901, rr 2, 6(a).
2 Inserted by the Family Procedure (Amendment No. 2) Rules 2016, SI 2016/901, rr 2, 6(b), (c).

Chapter 6: Children's Guardian Appointed under Rule 16.3

16.16 Application of this Chapter

This Chapter applies where the court must appoint a children's guardian in accordance with rule 16.3.

16.17 Who may be a children's guardian

Where the court is appointing a children's guardian under rule 16.3 it will appoint an officer of the Service or a Welsh family proceedings officer.

16.18 What the court or a court officer will do once the court has made a decision about appointing a children's guardian

(1) Where the court appoints a children's guardian under rule 16.3 a court officer will record the appointment and, as soon as practicable, will –
(a) inform the parties and either the Service or the Assembly; and
(b) unless it has already been sent, send the children's guardian a copy of the application and copies of any document filed with the court in the proceedings.

(2) A court officer has a continuing duty to send the children's guardian a copy of any other document filed with the court during the course of the proceedings.

16.19 Termination of the appointment of the children's guardian

(1) The appointment of a children's guardian under rule 16.3 continues for such time as is specified in the appointment or until terminated by the court.

(2) When terminating an appointment in accordance with paragraph (1), the court will give reasons for doing so, a note of which will be taken by the court or a court officer.

16.20 Powers and duties of the children's guardian

(1) The children's guardian is to act on behalf of the child upon the hearing of any application in proceedings to which this Chapter applies with the duty of safeguarding the interests of the child.

(2) The children's guardian must also provide the court with such other assistance as it may require.

(3) The children's guardian, when carrying out duties in relation to specified proceedings, other than placement proceedings, must have regard to the principle set out in section 1(2) and the matters set out in section 1(3)(a) to (f) of the 1989 Act as if for the word 'court' in that section there were substituted the words 'children's guardian'.

(4) The children's guardian, when carrying out duties in relation to proceedings to which Part 14 applies, must have regard to the principle set out in section 1(3) and the matters set out in section 1(4)(a) to (f) of the 2002 Act as if for the word 'court' in that section there were substituted the words 'children's guardian'.

(5) The children's guardian's duties must be exercised in accordance with Practice Direction 16A.

(6) A report to the court by the children's guardian is confidential.

16.21 Where the child instructs a solicitor or conducts proceedings on the child's own behalf

(1) Where it appears to the children's guardian that the child –
   (a) is instructing a solicitor direct; or
   (b) intends to conduct and is capable of conducting the proceedings on that child's own behalf,

   the children's guardian must inform the court of that fact.

(2) Where paragraph (1) applies the children's guardian –
   (a) must perform such additional duties as the court may direct;
   (b) must take such part in the proceedings as the court may direct; and
   (c) may, with the permission of the court, have legal representation in the conduct of those duties.

Chapter 7: Children's Guardian Appointed under Rule 16.4

16.22 Application of this Chapter

This Chapter applies where the court must appoint a children's guardian under rule 16.4.

16.23 Stage of proceedings at which a children's guardian becomes necessary

(1) This rule does not apply in relation to a child who is conducting proceedings without a children's guardian in accordance with rule 16.6.

(2) A person may not without the permission of the court take any step in proceedings except –
- (a) filing an application form; or
- (b) applying for the appointment of a children's guardian under rule 16.24,

until the child has a children's guardian.

(3) Any step taken before a child has a children's guardian has no effect unless the court orders otherwise.

16.24 Appointment of a children's guardian

(1) The court may make an order appointing as a children's guardian, an officer of the Service or a Welsh family proceedings officer or, if the person to be appointed consents –
- (a) a person other than the Official Solicitor; or
- (b) the Official Solicitor.

(2) An order appointing a children's guardian may be made by the court of its own initiative or on the application of –
- (a) a person who wishes to be a children's guardian; or
- (b) a party to the proceedings.

(3) The court may at any time direct that a party make an application for an order under paragraph (2).

(4) An application for an order appointing a children's guardian must be supported by evidence.

(5) The court may not appoint a children's guardian under this rule unless it is satisfied that that person –
- (a) can fairly and competently conduct proceedings on behalf of the child;
- (b) has no interest adverse to that of the child; and
- (c) subject to paragraph (6), undertakes to pay any costs which the child may be ordered to pay in relation to the proceedings, subject to any right that person may have to be repaid from the assets of the child.

(6) Paragraph (5)(c) does not apply to the Official Solicitor, an officer of the Service or a Welsh family proceedings officer.

(7) This rule is without prejudice to rule 16.6 and rule 9.11.

(Rule 9.11 provides for a child to be separately represented in certain applications for a financial remedy.)

16.25 Court's power to change children's guardian and to prevent person acting as children's guardian

(1) The court may –

- (a) direct that a person may not act as a children's guardian;
- (b) terminate the appointment of a children's guardian; or
- (c) appoint a new children's guardian in substitution for an existing one.

(2) An application for an order or direction under paragraph (1) must be supported by evidence.

(3) Subject to rule 16.24(6), the court may not appoint a children's guardian under this rule unless it is satisfied that the person to be appointed complies with the conditions specified in rule 16.24(5).

16.26 Appointment of children's guardian by court order – supplementary

(1) A copy of the application for an order under rule 16.24 or 16.25 must be sent by a court officer to every person on whom, in accordance with rule 6.28, the application form should be served.

(2) A copy of an application for an order under rule 16.25 must also be sent to –

- (a) the person who is the children's guardian, or who is purporting to act as the children's guardian when the application is made; and
- (b) the person, if not the applicant, who it is proposed should be the children's guardian.

16.27 Powers and duties of children's guardian

(1) The children's guardian –

- (a) has the powers and duties set out in Practice Direction 16A; and
- (b) must exercise those powers and duties in accordance with Practice Direction 16A.

(2) Where the children's guardian is an officer of the Service or a Welsh family proceedings officer, rule 16.20 applies to a children's guardian appointed in accordance with this Chapter as it applies to a children's guardian appointed in accordance with Chapter 6.

16.28 Procedure where appointment of children's guardian comes to an end

(1) When a child reaches the age of 18, the appointment of a children's guardian comes to an end.

(2) A court officer will send a notice to the other parties stating that the appointment of the child's children's guardian to act has ended.

Chapter 8: Duties of Solicitor Acting for the Child

16.29 Solicitor for child

(1) Subject to paragraphs (2) and (4), a solicitor appointed –
- (a) under section 41(3) of the 1989 Act; or
- (b) by the children's guardian in accordance with the Practice Direction 16A,

must represent the child in accordance with instructions received from the children's guardian.

(2) If a solicitor appointed as mentioned in paragraph (1) considers, having taken into account the matters referred to in paragraph (3), that the child –
- (a) wishes to give instructions which conflict with those of the children's guardian; and
- (b) is able, having regard to the child's understanding, to give such instructions on the child's own behalf,

the solicitor must conduct the proceedings in accordance with instructions received from the child.

(3) The matters the solicitor must take into account for the purposes of paragraph (2) are –
- (a) the views of the children's guardian; and
- (b) any direction given by the court to the children's guardian concerning the part to be taken by the children's guardian in the proceedings.

(4) Where –
- (a) no children's guardian has been appointed; and
- (b) the condition in section 41(4)(b) of the 1989 Act is satisfied,

a solicitor appointed under section 41(3) of the 1989 Act must represent the child in accordance with instructions received from the child.

(5) Where a solicitor appointed as mentioned in paragraph (1) receives no instructions under paragraphs (1), (2) or (4), the solicitor must represent the child in furtherance of the best interests of the child.

(6) A solicitor appointed under section 41(3) of the 1989 Act or by the children's guardian in accordance with Practice Direction 16A must serve documents, and accept service of documents, on behalf of the child in accordance with rule 6.31 and, where the child has not been served separately and has sufficient understanding, advise the child of the contents of any document so served.

(7) Where the child wishes an appointment of a solicitor –

(a) under section 41(3) of the 1989 Act; or

(b) by the children's guardian in accordance with the Practice Direction 16A,

to be terminated –

(i) the child may apply to the court for an order terminating the appointment; and

(ii) the solicitor and the children's guardian will be given an opportunity to make representations.

(8) Where the children's guardian wishes an appointment of a solicitor under section 41(3) of the 1989 Act to be terminated –

(a) the children's guardian may apply to the court for an order terminating the appointment; and

(b) the solicitor and, if of sufficient understanding, the child, will be given an opportunity to make representations.

(9) When terminating an appointment in accordance with paragraph (7) or (8), the court will give its reasons for so doing, a note of which will be taken by the court or a court officer.

(10) The court or a court officer will record the appointment under section 41(3) of the 1989 Act or the refusal to make the appointment.

PRACTICE DIRECTION 16A – REPRESENTATION OF CHILDREN

This Practice Direction supplements FPR Part 16

Part 1: General

Reference in title of proceedings

1.1 Where a litigation friend represents a child in family proceedings in accordance with rule 16.5 and Chapter 5 of Part 16, the child should be referred to in the title of the proceedings as 'A.B. (a child by C.D. his/her litigation friend).

1.2 Where a children's guardian represents a child in family proceedings in accordance with rule 16.4 and Chapter 7 of Part 16, the child should be referred to in the title as 'A.B. (a child by C.D. his/her children's guardian).

1.3 A child who is conducting proceedings on that child's own behalf should be referred to in the title as 'A.B. (a child).'

Part 2: Litigation Friend

Duties of the litigation friend

2.1 It is the duty of a litigation friend fairly and competently to conduct proceedings on behalf of the child. The litigation friend must have no interest in the proceedings adverse to that of the child and all steps and decisions the litigation friend takes in the proceedings must be taken for the benefit of the child.

2.2 …[1]

Becoming a litigation friend without a court order

3.1 In order to become a litigation friend without a court order the person who wishes to act as litigation friend must file a certificate of suitability –
(a) stating that the litigation friend consents to act;
(b) stating that the litigation friend knows or believes that the [applicant] [respondent] is a child to whom rule 16.5 and Chapter 5 of Part 16 apply;
(c) stating that the litigation friend can fairly and competently conduct proceedings on behalf of the child and has no interest adverse to that of the child;
(d) undertaking to pay any costs which the child may be ordered to pay in relation to the proceedings, subject to any right the litigation friend may have to be repaid from the assets of the child; and
(e) which the litigation friend has verified by a statement of truth.

3.2 Paragraph 3.1 does not apply to the Official Solicitor, an officer of the Service or a Welsh family proceedings officer.

3.3 The court officer will send the certificate of suitability to one of the child's parents or guardians or, if there is no parent or guardian, to the person with whom the child resides or in whose care the child is.

3.4 The litigation friend must file the certificate of suitability at a time when the litigation friend first takes a step in the proceedings on behalf of the child.

Application for a court order appointing a litigation friend

4.1 An application for a court order appointing a litigation friend should be made in accordance with Part 18 and must be supported by evidence.

4.2 The court officer must serve the application notice on the persons referred to in paragraph 3.3.

4.3 The evidence in support must satisfy the court that the proposed litigation friend –
(a) consents to act;
(b) can fairly and competently conduct proceedings on behalf of the child;

(c) has no interest adverse to that of the child; and

(d) undertakes to pay any costs which the child may be ordered to pay in relation to the proceedings, subject to any right the litigation friend may have to be repaid from the assets of the child.

4.4 Paragraph 4.3(d) does not apply to the Official Solicitor, an officer of the Service of a Welsh family proceedings officer.

4.5 The proposed litigation friend may be one of the persons referred to in paragraph 3.3 where appropriate, or otherwise may be the Official Solicitor, an officer of the Service or a Welsh family proceedings officer. Where it is sought to appoint the Official Solicitor, an officer of the Service or a Welsh family proceedings officer, provision should be made for payment of that person's charges.

Change of litigation friend and prevention of person acting as litigation friend

5.1 Where an application is made for an order under rule 16.12, the application must set out the reasons for seeking it and the application must be supported by evidence.

5.2 Subject to paragraph 4.4, if the order sought is substitution of a new litigation friend for an existing one, the evidence must satisfy the court of the matters set out in paragraph 4.3.

5.3 The court officer will serve the application notice on –

(a) the persons referred to in paragraph 3.3; and

(b) the litigation friend or person purporting to act as litigation friend.

Amendment

1 Repealed by the FPR Update, October 2016.

Part 3: Children's Guardian Appointed under Rule 16.3

How the children's guardian exercises duties – investigations and appointment of solicitor

6.1 The children's guardian must make such investigations as are necessary to carry out the children's guardian's duties and must, in particular –

(a) contact or seek to interview such persons as the children's guardian thinks appropriate or as the court directs; and

(b) obtain such professional assistance as is available which the children's guardian thinks appropriate or which the court directs be obtained.

6.2 The children's guardian must –

(a) appoint a solicitor for the child unless a solicitor has already been appointed;

(b) give such advice to the child as is appropriate having regard to that child's understanding; and

(c) where appropriate instruct the solicitor representing the child on all matters relevant to the interests of the child arising in the course of proceedings, including possibilities for appeal.

6.3 Where the children's guardian is authorised in the terms mentioned by and in accordance with section 15(1) of the Criminal Justice and Court Services Act 2000 or section 37(1) of the Children Act 2004 (right of officer of the Service or Welsh family proceedings officer to conduct litigation or exercise a right of audience), paragraph 6.2(a) will not apply if the children's guardian intends to have conduct of the proceedings on behalf of the child unless –

(a) the child wishes to instruct a solicitor direct; and

(b) the children's guardian or the court considers that the child is of sufficient understanding to do so.

6.4 Where rule 16.21 (Where the child instructs a solicitor or conducts proceedings on the child's own behalf) applies, the duties set out in paragraph 6.2(a) and (c) do not apply.

How the children's guardian exercises duties – attendance at court, advice to the court and reports

6.5 The children's guardian or the solicitor appointed under section 41(3) of the 1989 Act or in accordance with paragraph 6.2(a) must attend all directions hearings unless the court directs otherwise.

6.6 The children's guardian must advise the court on the following matters –

(a) whether the child is of sufficient understanding for any purpose including the child's refusal to submit to a medical or psychiatric examination or other assessment that the court has the power to require, direct or order;

(b) the wishes of the child in respect of any matter relevant to the proceedings including that child's attendance at court;

(c) the appropriate forum for the proceedings;

(d) the appropriate timing of the proceedings or any part of them;

(e) the options available to it in respect of the child and the suitability of each such option including what order should be made in determining the application; and

(f) any other matter on which the court seeks advice or on which the children's guardian considers that the court should be informed.

6.7 The advice given under paragraph 6.6 may, subject to any direction of the court, be given orally or in writing. If the advice is given orally, a note of it must be taken by the court or the court officer.

6.8 The children's guardian must –

(a) unless the court directs otherwise, file a written report advising on the interests of the child in accordance with the timetable set by the court; and

(b) in proceedings to which Part 14 applies, where practicable, notify any person the joining of whom as a party to those proceedings would be likely, in the opinion of the children's guardian, to safeguard the interests of the child, of the court's power to join that person as a party under rule 14.3 and must inform the court –

  (i) of any notification;

  (ii) of anyone whom the children's guardian attempted to notify under this paragraph but was unable to contact; and

  (iii) of anyone whom the children's guardian believes may wish to be joined to the proceedings.

(Part 18 sets out the procedure for making an application to be joined as a party in proceedings.)

How the children's guardian exercises duties – service of documents and inspection of records

6.9 The children's guardian must serve and accept service of documents on behalf of the child in accordance with rule 6.31 and, where the child has not himself been served and has sufficient understanding, advise the child of the contents of any document so served.

6.10 Where the children's guardian inspects records of the kinds referred to in –

(a) section 42 of the 1989 Act (right to have access to local authority records); or

(b) section 103 of the 2002 Act (right to have access to adoption agency records)

the children's guardian must bring all records and documents which may, in the opinion of the children's guardian, assist in the proper determination of the proceedings to the attention of –

(i) the court; and

(ii) unless the court directs otherwise, the other parties to the proceedings.

How the children's guardian exercises duties – communication of a court's decision to the child

6.11 The children's guardian must ensure that, in relation to a decision made by the court in the proceedings –

(a) if the children's guardian considers it appropriate to the age and understanding of the child, the child is notified of that decision; and

(b) if the child is notified of the decision, it is explained to the child in a manner appropriate to that child's age and understanding.

Part 4: Appointment of Children's Guardian under Rule 16.4

Section 1 – When a child should be made a party to proceedings

7.1 Making the child a party to the proceedings is a step that will be taken only in cases which involve an issue of significant difficulty and consequently will occur in only a minority of cases. Before taking the decision to make the child a party, consideration should be given to whether an alternative route might be preferable, such as asking an officer of the Service or a Welsh family proceedings officer to carry out further work or by making a referral to social services or, possibly, by obtaining expert evidence.

7.2 The decision to make the child a party will always be exclusively that of the court, made in the light of the facts and circumstances of the particular case. The following are offered, solely by way of guidance, as circumstances which may justify the making of such an order –

(a) where an officer of the Service or Welsh family proceedings officer has notified the court that in the opinion of that officer the child should be made a party;

(b) where the child has a standpoint or interest which is inconsistent with or incapable of being represented by any of the adult parties;

(c) where there is an intractable dispute over residence or contact, including where all contact has ceased, or where there is irrational but implacable hostility to contact or where the child may be suffering harm associated with the contact dispute;

(d) where the views and wishes of the child cannot be adequately met by a report to the court;

(e) where an older child is opposing a proposed course of action;

(f) where there are complex medical or mental health issues to be determined or there are other unusually complex issues that necessitate separate representation of the child;

(g) where there are international complications outside child abduction, in particular where it may be necessary for there to be discussions with overseas authorities or a foreign court;

(h) where there are serious allegations of physical, sexual or other abuse in relation to the child or there are allegations of domestic violence not capable of being resolved with the help of an officer of the Service or Welsh family proceedings officer;

(i) where the proceedings concern more than one child and the welfare of the children is in conflict or one child is in a particularly disadvantaged position;

(j) where there is a contested issue about scientific testing.

7.3 It must be recognised that separate representation of the child may result in a delay in the resolution of the proceedings. When deciding whether to direct that a child be made a party, the court will take into account the risk of delay or other facts adverse to the welfare of the child. The court's primary consideration will be the best interests of the child.

7.4 When a child is made a party and a children's guardian is to be appointed –

(a) consideration should first be given to appointing an officer of the Service or Welsh family proceedings officer. Before appointing an officer, the court will cause preliminary enquiries to be made of Cafcass or CAFCASS Cymru. For the relevant procedure, reference should be made to the practice note issued by Cafcass in June 2006 and any modifications of that practice note.

(b) If Cafcass or CAFCASS Cymru is unable to provide a children's guardian without delay, or if for some other reason the appointment of an officer of the Service of Welsh family proceedings officer is not appropriate, rule 16.24 makes further provision for the appointment of a children's guardian.

7.5 …[1]

Amendments

1 Repealed by the FPR Update, April 2014.

Section 2 – Children's guardian appointed under rule 16.4

Duties of the children's guardian

7.6 It is the duty of a children's guardian fairly and competently to conduct proceedings on behalf of the child. The children's guardian must have no interest in the proceedings adverse to that of the child and all steps and decisions the children's guardian takes in the proceedings must be taken for the benefit of the child.

7.7 A children's guardian who is an officer of the Service or a Welsh family proceedings officer has, in addition, the duties set out in Part 3 of this Practice Direction and must exercise those duties as set out in that Part.

Becoming a children's guardian without a court order

7.8 In order to become a children's guardian without a court order the person who wishes to act as children's guardian must file a certificate of suitability –

(a) stating that the children's guardian consents to act;

(b) stating that the children's guardian knows or believes that the [applicant][respondent] is a child to whom rule 16.4 and Chapter 7 of Part 16 apply;

(c) stating that the children's guardian can fairly and competently conduct proceedings on behalf of the child and has no interest adverse to that of the child;

(d) undertaking to pay any costs which the child may be ordered to pay in relation to the proceedings, subject to any right the children's guardian may have to be repaid from the assets of the child; and

(e) which the children's guardian has verified by a statement of truth.

7.9 Paragraph 7.8 does not apply to the Official Solicitor, an officer of the Service or a Welsh family proceedings officer.

7.10 The court officer will send the certificate of suitability to one of the child's parents or guardians or, if there is no parent or guardian, to the person with whom the child resides or in whose care the child is.

7.11 The children's guardian must file either the certificate of suitability at a time when the children's guardian first takes a step in the proceedings on behalf of the child.

Application for a court order appointing a children's guardian

7.12 An application for a court order appointing a children's guardian should be made in accordance with Part 18 and must be supported by evidence.

7.13 The court officer must serve the application notice on the persons referred to in paragraph 7.10.

7.14 The evidence in support must satisfy the court that the proposed children's guardian –

(a) consents to act;

(b) can fairly and competently conduct proceedings on behalf of the child;

(c) has no interest adverse to that of the child; and

(d) undertakes to pay any costs which the child may be ordered to pay in relation to the proceedings, subject to any right the children's guardian may have to be repaid from the assets of the child.

7.15 Paragraph 7.14 does not apply to the Official Solicitor, an officer of the Service of a Welsh family proceedings officer.

7.16 The proposed children's guardian may be one of the persons referred to in paragraph 7.10 where appropriate, or otherwise may be the Official Solicitor, an officer of the Service or a Welsh family proceedings officer. Where it is sought to appoint the Official Solicitor, an officer of the Service or a Welsh family proceedings officer, provision should be made for payment of that person's charges.

Change of children's guardian and prevention of person acting as children's guardian.

7.17 Where an application is made for an order under rule 16.25, the application must set out the reasons for seeking it and must be supported by evidence.

7.18 Subject to paragraph 7.15, if the order sought is substitution of a new children's guardian for an existing one, the evidence must satisfy the court of the matters set out in paragraph 7.14.

7.19 The court officer will serve the application notice on –

(a) the persons referred to in paragraph 7.10; and

(b) the children's guardian or person purporting to act as children's guardian.

Part 5: Reporting Officer

How the reporting officer exercises duties

8.1 The reporting officer must –
  (a) ensure so far as reasonably practicable that the parent or guardian is –
    (i) giving consent unconditionally to the placing of the child for adoption or to the making of an adoption order (as defined in section 46 of the Adoption and Children Act 2002) or a section 84 order; and
    (ii) with full understanding of what is involved;
  (b) investigate all the circumstances relevant to a parent's or guardian's consent; and
  (c) on completing the investigations the reporting officer must –
    (i) make a report in writing to the court in accordance with the timetable set by the court, drawing attention to any matters which, in the opinion of the reporting officer, may be of assistance to the court in considering the application; or
    (ii) make an interim report to the court if a parent or guardian of the child is unwilling to consent to the placing of the child for adoption or to the making of an adoption order or section 84 order.

8.2 On receipt of an interim report under paragraph 8.1(1)(c)(ii) a court officer must inform the applicant that a parent or guardian of the child is unwilling to consent to the placing of the child for adoption or to the making of an adoption order or section 84 order.

8.3 The reporting officer may at any time before the final hearing make an interim report to the court if the reporting officer considers it necessary and ask the court for directions.

8.4 The reporting officer must attend hearings as directed by the court.

Part 6: Children and Family Reporter and Welfare Officer

How the children and family reporter or welfare officer exercises powers and duties

9.1 In this Part, the person preparing the welfare report in accordance with rule 16.33 is called 'the officer'.

9.2 The officer must make such investigations as may be necessary to perform the officer's powers and duties and must, in particular –
  (a) contact or seek to interview such persons as appear appropriate or as the court directs; and
  (b) obtain such professional assistance as is available which the children and family reporter thinks appropriate or which the court directs be obtained.

9.3 The officer must –
  (a) notify the child of such contents of the report (if any) as the officer considers appropriate to the age and understanding of the child,

including any reference to the child's own views on the application and the recommendation; and
(b) if the child is notified of any contents of the report, explain them to the child in a manner appropriate to the child's age and understanding.

9.4 The officer must –
(a) attend hearings as directed by the court;
(b) advise the court of the child's wishes and feelings;
(c) advise the court if the officer considers that the joining of a person as a party to the proceedings would be likely to safeguard the interests of the child;
(d) consider whether it is in the best interests of the child for the child to be made a party to the proceedings, and if so, notify the court of that opinion together with the reasons for that opinion; and
(e) where the court has directed that a written report be made –
(i) file the report; and
(ii) serve a copy on the other parties and on any children's guardian,

in accordance with the timetable set by the court.

Part 7: Parental Order Reporter

How the parental order reporter exercises duties – investigations and reports

10.1 The parental order reporter must make such investigations as are necessary to carry out the parental order reporter's duties and must, in particular –
(a) contact or seek to interview such persons as the parental order reporter thinks appropriate or as the court directs; and
(b) obtain such professional assistance as is available which the parental order reporter thinks appropriate or which the court directs be obtained.

How the parental order reporter exercises duties – attendance at court, advice to the court and reports

10.2 The parental order reporter must attend all directions hearings unless the court directs otherwise.

10.3 The parental order reporter must advise the court on the following matters –
(a) the appropriate forum for the proceedings;
(b) the appropriate timing of the proceedings or any part of them;
(c) the options available to it in respect of the child and the suitability of each such option including what order should be made in determining the application; and
(d) any other matter on which the court seeks advice or on which the parental order reporter considers that the court should be informed.

10.4 The advice given under paragraph 10.3 may, subject to any direction of the court, be given orally or in writing. If the advice is given orally, a note of it must be taken by the court or the court officer.

10.5 The parental order reporter must –
- (a) unless the court directs otherwise, file a written report advising on the interests of the child in accordance with the timetable set by the court; and
- (b) where practicable, notify any person the joining of whom as a party to those proceedings would be likely, in the opinion of the parental order reporter, to safeguard the interests of the child, of the court's power to join that person as a party under rule 13.3 and must inform the court –
  - (i) of any notification;
  - (ii) of anyone whom the parental order reporter attempted to notify under this paragraph but was unable to contact; and
  - (iii) of anyone whom the parental order reporter believes may wish to be joined to the proceedings.

(Part 18 sets out the procedure for making an application to be joined as a party in proceedings.)

Part 8: Officers of the Service, Welsh Family Proceedings Officers and Local Authority Officers: Further Duties

How officers of the Service, Welsh family proceedings officers and local authority officers exercise certain further duties

11.1 This Part applies when an officer of the Service, a Welsh family proceedings officer or a local authority officer is acting under a duty referred to in rule 16.38(1). In this Part, the person acting under a duty referred to in rule 16.38(1) is referred to as 'the officer'.

11.2 The officer must make such investigations as may be necessary to perform the officer's duties and must, in particular –
- (a) contact or seek to interview such persons as the officer thinks appropriate or as the court directs; and
- (b) obtain such professional assistance as the officer thinks appropriate or which the court directs.

11.3 The officer must –
- (a) notify the child of such (if any) of the contents of any report or risk assessment as the officer considers appropriate to the age and understanding of the child;
- (b) if the child is notified of any contents of a report or risk assessment, explain them to the child in a manner appropriate to the child's age and understanding;
- (c) consider whether to recommend in any report or risk assessment that the court lists a hearing for the purposes of considering the report or risk assessment;
- (d) consider whether it is in the best interests of the child for the child to be made a party to the proceedings, and, if so, notify the court of that opinion together with the reasons for that opinion.

11.4 When making a risk assessment, the officer must, if of the opinion that the court should exercise its discretion under rule 12.34(2), state in the risk assessment –

(a) the way in which the officer considers the court should exercise its discretion (including the officer's view on the length of any suggested delay in service); and

(b) the officer's reasons for that reaching that view.

11.5 The officer must file any report or risk assessment with the court –

(a) at or by the time directed by the court;

(b) in the absence of any direction, at least 14 days before a relevant hearing; or

(c) where there has been no direction from the court and there is no relevant hearing listed, as soon as possible following the completion of the report or risk assessment.

11.6 In paragraph 11.5, a hearing is relevant if the court officer has given the officer notice that a report prepared by the officer is to be considered at it.

11.7 A copy of any report prepared as a result of acting under a duty referred to in rule 16.38(1)(a)(i) to (vi) or (b) (but not any risk assessment) must, as soon as practicable, be served by the officer on the parties.

(Rule 12.34 makes provision for the service of risk assessments.)

PART 31: REGISTRATION OF ORDERS UNDER THE COUNCIL REGULATION, THE CIVIL PARTNERSHIP (JURISDICTION AND RECOGNITION OF JUDGMENTS) REGULATIONS 2005[, THE MARRIAGE (SAME SEX COUPLES) (JURISDICTION AND RECOGNITION OF JUDGMENTS) REGULATIONS 2014][1] AND UNDER THE HAGUE CONVENTION 1996

31.1 Scope

This Part applies to proceedings for the recognition, non-recognition and registration of –

(a) judgments to which the Council Regulation applies;

(b) measures to which the 1996 Hague Convention applies; …[2]

(c) judgments to which the Jurisdiction and Recognition of Judgments Regulations apply, and which relate to dissolution or annulment of overseas relationships entitled to be treated as a civil partnership, or legal separation of the same[; and][1]

[(d) judgments to which the 2014 Regulations apply and which relate to divorce, or annulment of a marriage of a same sex couple or the judicial separation of the same.][1]

Amendments

1 Inserted by the Family Procedure (Amendment) Rules 2014, SI 2014/524, rr 2, 5, 6(c).

2 Repealed by the Family Procedure (Amendment) Rules 2014, SI 2014/524, rr 2, 6(a), (b).

31.2 Interpretation

(1) In this Part –
  (a) 'judgment' is to be construed –
    (i) in accordance with the definition in Article 2(4) of the Council Regulation where it applies;
    (ii) in accordance with regulation 6 of the Jurisdiction and Recognition of Judgments Regulations where those Regulations apply; …[1]
    (iii) as meaning any measure taken by an authority with jurisdiction under Chapter II of the 1996 Hague Convention where that Convention applies; [or][2]
    [(iv) in accordance with regulation 4(1)(a) of The Marriage (Same Sex Couples) (Jurisdiction and Recognition of Judgments) Regulations 2014 where those Regulations apply;][2]
  (b) 'the Jurisdiction and Recognition of Judgments Regulations' means the Civil Partnership (Jurisdiction and Recognition of Judgments) Regulations 2005;
  [(ba) 'the 2014 Regulations' means the Marriage (Same Sex Couples) (Jurisdiction and Recognition of Judgments) Regulations 2014;][2]
  (c) 'Member State' means –
    (i) where registration, recognition or non-recognition is sought of a judgment under the Council Regulation, a Member State of the European Union which is bound by that Regulation or a country which has subsequently adopted it;
    (ii) where recognition is sought of a judgment to which the Jurisdiction and Recognition of Judgments Regulations apply, a Member State of the European Union to which Part II of those Regulations applies;
    [(iii) where recognition is sought of a judgment to which the 2014 Regulations apply, a member State of the European Union to which Part II of those Regulations applies;][2]
  (d) 'Contracting State' means a State, other than a Member State within the meaning of (c) above, in relation to which the 1996 Hague Convention is in force as between that State and the United Kingdom; and
  (e) 'parental responsibility' –
    (i) where the Council Regulation applies, has the meaning given in Article 2(7) of that Regulation; and
    (ii) where the 1996 Hague Convention applies, has the meaning given in Article 1(2) of that Convention.

(2) References in this Part to registration are to the registration of a judgment in accordance with the provisions of this Part.

Amendments

1 Repealed by the Family Procedure (Amendment) Rules 2014, SI 2014/524, rr 2, 7(a).

2 Inserted by the Family Procedure (Amendment) Rules 2014, SI 2014/524, rr 2, 7(b)–(e).

31.3 Where to start proceedings

(1) Every application under this Part, except for an application under rule 31.18 for a certified copy of a judgment, or under rule 31.20 for rectification of a certificate issued under Articles 41 or 42, must be made to the principal registry.

(2) Nothing in this rule prevents the determination of an issue of recognition as an incidental question by any court in proceedings, in accordance with Article 21(4) of the Council Regulation.

(3) Notwithstanding paragraph (1), where recognition of a judgment is raised as an incidental question in proceedings under the 1996 Hague Convention[,][1] ...[2] the Jurisdiction and Recognition of Judgments Regulations [or the 2014 Regulations][1] the court hearing those proceedings may determine the question of recognition.

Amendments

1 Inserted by the Family Procedure (Amendment) Rules 2014, SI 2014/524, rr 2, 8.
2 Repealed by the Family Procedure (Amendment) Rules 2014, SI 2014/524, rr 2, 8(a).

31.4 Application for registration, recognition or non-recognition of a judgment

(1) Any interested person may apply to the court for an order that the judgment be registered, recognised or not recognised.

(2) Except for an application under rule 31.7, an application for registration, recognition or non-recognition must be –
   (a) made to a district judge of the principal registry; and
   (b) in the form, and supported by the documents and the information required by a practice direction.

31.5 Documents – supplementary

(1) Except as regards a copy of a judgment required by Article 37(1)(a) of the Council Regulation, where the person making an application under this Part does not produce the documents required by rule 31.4(2)(b) the court may –
   (a) fix a time within which the documents are to be produced;
   (b) accept equivalent documents; or
   (c) dispense with production of the documents if the court considers it has sufficient information.

(2) This rule does not apply to applications under rule 31.7.

31.6 Directions

(1) As soon as practicable after an application under this Part has been made, the court may (subject to the requirements of the Council Regulation)

give such directions as it considers appropriate, including as regards the following matters –

(a) whether service of the application may be dispensed with;

(b) expedition of the proceedings or any part of the proceedings (and any direction for expedition may specify a date by which the court must give its decision);

(c) the steps to be taken in the proceedings and the time by which each step is to be taken;

(d) the service of documents; and

(e) the filing of evidence.

(2) The court or court officer will –

(a) record the giving, variation or revocation of directions under this rule; and

(b) as soon as practicable serve a copy of the directions order on every party.

31.7 Recognition and enforcement under the Council Regulation of a judgment given in another Member State relating to rights of access or under Article 11(8) for the return of the child to that State

(1) This rule applies where a judgment has been given in another Member State –

(a) relating to rights of access: or

(b) under Article 11(8) of the Council Regulation for the return of a child to that State,

which has been certified, in accordance with Article 41(2) or 42(2) as the case may be, by the judge in the court of origin.

(2) An application for recognition or enforcement of the judgment must be –

(a) made in writing to a district judge of the principal registry; and

(b) accompanied by a copy of the certificate issued by the judge in the court of origin.

(3) The application may be made without notice.

(4) Rules 31.5 and 31.8 to 31.17 do not apply to an application made under this rule.

(5) Nothing in this rule shall prevent a holder of parental responsibility from seeking recognition and enforcement of a judgment in accordance with the provisions of rules 31.8 to 31.17.

31.8 Registration for enforcement or order for non-recognition of a judgment

(1) This rule applies where an application is made for an order that a judgment given in another Member State, or a Contracting State, should be registered, or should not be recognised, except where rule 31.7 applies.

(2) Where the application is made for an order that the judgment should be registered –
  (a) upon receipt of the application, and subject to any direction given by the court under rule 31.6 the court officer will serve the application on the person against whom registration is sought;
  (b) the court will not accept submissions from either the person against whom registration is sought or any child in relation to whom the judgment was given.

(3) Where the application is for an order that the judgment should not be recognised –
  (a) upon receipt of the application, and subject to any direction given by the court under rule 31.6, the court officer will serve the application on the person in whose favour judgment was given;
  (b) the person in whose favour the judgment was given must file an answer to the application and serve it on the applicant –
    (i) within 1 month of service of the application; or
    (ii) if the applicant is habitually resident in another Member State, within two months of service of the application.

(4) In cases to which the 1996 Hague Convention applies and the Council Regulation does not apply, the court may extend the time set out in subparagraph (3)(b)(ii) on account of distance.

(5) The person in whose favour the judgment was given may request recognition or registration of the judgment in their answer, and in that event must comply with 31.4(2)(b) to the extent that such documents, information and evidence are not already contained in the application for non-recognition.

(6) If, in a case to which the Council Regulation applies, the person in whose favour the judgment was given fails to file an answer as required by paragraph (3), the court will act in accordance with the provisions of Article 18 of the Council Regulation.

(7) If, in a case to which the 1996 Hague Convention applies and the Service Regulation does not, the person in whose favour the judgment was given fails to file an answer as required by paragraph (3) –
  (a) where the Hague Convention of 15th November 1965 on the service abroad of judicial and extrajudicial documents in civil or commercial matters applies, the court shall apply Article 15 of that Convention; and
  (b) in all other cases, the court will not consider the application unless –
    (i) it is proved to the satisfaction of the court that the person in whose favour judgment was given was served with the application within a reasonable period of time to arrange his or her response; or
    (ii) the court is satisfied that the circumstances of the case justify proceeding with consideration of the application.

(8) In a case to which the Jurisdiction and Recognition of Judgments Regulations [or the 2014 Regulations][1] apply, if the person in whose favour

judgment was given fails to file an answer as required by paragraph (3), the court will apply the Service Regulation where that regulation applies, and if it does not –

(a) where the Hague Convention of 15th November 1965 on the service abroad of judicial and extrajudicial documents in civil or commercial matters applies, the court shall apply Article 15 of that Convention; and

(b) in all other cases, the court will apply the provisions of paragraph (7)(b).

Amendment

1 Inserted by the Family Procedure (Amendment) Rules 2014, SI 2014/524, rr 2, 9.

31.9 Stay of recognition proceedings by reason of an appeal

Where recognition or non-recognition of a judgment given in another Member State or Contracting State is sought, or is raised as an incidental question in other proceedings, the court may stay the proceedings –

(a) if an ordinary appeal against the judgment has been lodged; or

(b) if the judgment was given in the Republic of Ireland, if enforcement of the judgment is suspended there by reason of an appeal.

31.10 Effect of refusal of application for a decision that a judgment should not be recognised

Where the court refuses an application for a decision that a judgment should not be recognised, the court may –

(a) direct that the decision to refuse the application is to be treated as a decision that the judgment be recognised; or

(b) treat the answer under paragraph (3)(b) of rule 31.8 as an application that the judgment be registered for enforcement if paragraph (5) of that rule is complied with and order that the judgment be registered for enforcement in accordance with rule 31.11.

31.11 Notification of the court's decision on an application for registration or non-recognition

(1) Where the court has –

(a) made an order on an application for an order that a judgment should be registered for enforcement; or

(b) refused an application that a judgment should not be recognised and ordered under rule 31.10 that the judgment be registered for enforcement,

the court officer will as soon as practicable take the appropriate action under paragraph (2) or (3).

(2) If the court refuses the application for the judgment to be registered for enforcement, the court officer will serve the order on the applicant and the person against whom judgment was given in the state of origin.

(3) If the court orders that the judgment should be registered for enforcement, the court officer will –

(a) register the judgment in the central index of judgments kept by the principal registry;

(b) confirm on the order that the judgment has been registered; and

(c) serve on the parties the court's order endorsed with the court officer's confirmation that the judgment has been registered.

(4) A sealed order of the court endorsed in accordance with paragraph (3)(b) will constitute notification that the judgment has been registered under Article 28(2) of the Council Regulation or under Article 26 of the 1996 Hague Convention, as the case may be, and in this Part 'notice of registration' means a sealed order so endorsed.

(5) The notice of registration must state –

(a) full particulars of the judgment registered and the order for registration;

(b) the name of the party making the application and his address for service within the jurisdiction;

(c) the right of the person against whom judgment was given to appeal against the order for registration; and

(d) the period within which an appeal against the order for registration may be made.

31.12 Effect of registration under rule 31.11

Registration of a judgment under rule 31.11 will serve for the purpose of Article 21(3) of the Council Regulation, Article 24 of the 1996 Hague Convention[,][1] …[2] regulation 7 of the Jurisdiction and Recognition of Judgments Regulations [or regulation 5 of the 2014 Regulations][1] (as the case may be) as a decision that the judgment is recognised.

Amendments

1 Inserted by the Family Procedure (Amendment) Rules 2014, SI 2014/524, rr 2, 10.
2 Repealed by the Family Procedure (Amendment) Rules 2014, SI 2014/524, rr 2, 10(a).

31.13 The central index of judgments registered under rule 31.11

The central index of judgments registered under rule 31.11 will be kept by the principal registry.

31.14 Decision on recognition of a judgment only

(1) Where an application is made seeking recognition of a judgment only, the provisions of rules 31.8 and 31.9 apply to that application as they do to an application for registration for enforcement.

(2) Where the court orders that the judgment should be recognised, the court officer will serve a copy of the order on each party as soon as practicable.

(3) A sealed order of the court will constitute notification that the judgment has been recognised under Article 21(3) of the Council Regulation, Article 24 of the 1996 Hague convention[,][1] ...[2] regulation 7 of the Jurisdiction and Recognition of Judgments Regulations [or regulation 5 of the 2014 Regulations][1], as the case may be.

(4) The sealed order shall indicate –
 (a) full particulars of the judgment recognised;
 (b) the name of the party making the application and his address for service within the jurisdiction;
 (c) the right of the person against whom judgment was given to appeal against the order for recognition; and
 (d) the period within which an appeal against the order for recognition may be made.

Amendments

1 Inserted by the Family Procedure (Amendment) Rules 2014, SI 2014/524, rr 2, 11.
2 Repealed by the Family Procedure (Amendment) Rules 2014, SI 2014/524, rr 2, 11(a).

31.15 Appeal against the court's decision under rules 31.10, 31.11 or 31.14

(1) An appeal against the court's decision under rules 31.10, 31.11 or 31.14 must be made to a judge of the High Court –
 (a) within one month of the date of service of the notice of registration; or
 (b) if the party bringing the appeal is habitually resident in another Member State, or a Contracting State, within two months of the date of service.

(2) The court may not extend time for an appeal on account of distance unless the matter is one to which the 1996 Hague Convention applies and the Council Regulation does not apply.

(3) If, in a case to which the 1996 Hague Convention applies and the Service Regulation does not, the appeal is brought by the applicant for a declaration of enforceability or registration and the respondent fails to appear –
 (a) where the Hague Convention of 15th November 1965 on the service abroad of judicial and extrajudicial documents in civil or commercial matters applies, the court shall apply Article 15 of that Convention; and
 (b) in all other cases, the court will not consider the appeal unless –
  (i) it is proved to the satisfaction of the court that the respondent was served with notice of the appeal within a reasonable period of time to arrange his or her response; or
  (ii) the court is satisfied that the circumstances of the case justify proceeding with consideration of the appeal.

(4) This rule is subject to rule 31.16.

(The procedure for applications under rule 31.15 is set out in Practice Direction 30A (Appeals).)

31.16 Stay of enforcement where appeal pending in state of origin

(1) A party against whom enforcement is sought of a judgment which has been registered under rule 31.11 may apply to the court with which an appeal is lodged under rule 31.15 for the proceedings to be stayed where –
  (a) that party has lodged an ordinary appeal in the Member State or Contracting State of origin; or
  (b) the time for such an appeal has not yet expired.

(2) Where an application for a stay is filed in the circumstances described in paragraph (1)(b), the court may specify the time within which an appeal must be lodged.

31.17 Enforcement of judgments registered under rule 31.11

(1) [Subject to paragraph (1A)][1] the court will not enforce a judgment registered under rule 31.11 until after –
  (a) the expiration of any applicable period under rules 31.15 or 31.16; or
  (b) if that period has been extended by the court, the expiration of the period so extended.

[(1A) The court may enforce a judgment registered under rule 31.11 before the expiration of a period referred to in paragraph (1) where urgent enforcement of the judgment is necessary to secure the welfare of the child to whom the judgment relates.][1]

(2) A party applying to the court for the enforcement of a registered judgment must produce to the court a certificate of service of –
  (a) the notice of registration of the judgment; and
  (b) any order made by the court in relation to the judgment.

(Service out of the jurisdiction, including service in accordance with the Service Regulation, is dealt with in chapter 4 of Part 6 and in Practice Direction 6B.)

Amendments

1 Inserted by the Family Procedure (Amendment) (No.2) Rules 2012, SI 2012/1462, rr 2, 3.

31.18 Request for a certificate or a certified copy of a judgment

(1) An application for a certified copy of a judgment, or for a certificate under Articles 39, 41 or 42 of the Council Regulation, must be made to the court which made the order or judgment in respect of which certification is sought and without giving notice to any other party.

(2) The application must be made in the form, and supported by the documents and information required by a practice direction.

(3) The certified copy of the judgment will be an office copy sealed with the seal of the court and signed by [a court officer][1]. It will be issued with a certified copy of any order which has varied any of the terms of the original order.

(4) Where the application is made for the purposes of applying for recognition or recognition and enforcement of the order in another Contracting State, the court must indicate on the certified copy of the judgment the grounds on which it based its jurisdiction to make the order, for the purposes of Article 23(2)(a) of the 1996 Hague Convention.

Amendment

1 Substituted by the Family Procedure (Amendment No.3) Rules 2013, SI 2013/3204, rr 2, 75.

31.19 Certificates issued in England and Wales under Articles 41 and 42 of the Council Regulation

The court officer will serve –

(a) a certificate issued under Article 41 or 42; or

(b) a certificate rectified under rule 31.20,

on all parties and will transmit a copy to the Central Authority for England and Wales.

31.20 Rectification of certificate issued under Article 41 or 42 of the Council Regulation

(1) Where there is an error in a certificate issued under Article 41 or 42, an application to rectify that error must be made to the court which issued the certificate.

(2) A rectification under paragraph (1) may be made –

(a) by the court of its own initiative; or

(b) on application by –

(i) any party to the proceedings; or

(ii) the court or Central Authority of another Member State.

(3) An application under paragraph (2)(b) may be made without notice being served on any other party.

31.21 Authentic instruments and agreements under Article 46 of the Council Regulation

This Chapter applies to an authentic instrument and an agreement to which Article 46 of the Council Regulation applies as it applies to a judgment.

31.22 Application for provisional, including protective measures

An application for provisional, including protective, measures under Article 20 of the Council Regulation or Articles 11 or 12 of the 1996 Hague Convention may be made notwithstanding that the time for appealing against an order for registration of a judgment has not expired or that a final determination of any issue relating to enforcement of the judgment is pending.

PRACTICE DIRECTION 31A – REGISTRATION OF ORDERS UNDER THE COUNCIL REGULATION, THE CIVIL PARTNERSHIP (JURISDICTION AND RECOGNITION OF JUDGMENTS) REGULATIONS 2005[, THE MARRIAGE (SAME SEX COUPLES) (JURISDICTION AND RECOGNITION OF JUDGMENTS) REGULATIONS 2014][1] AND UNDER THE 1996 HAGUE CONVENTION

This Practice Direction supplements FPR Part 31

Amendments

1 Inserted by the FPR Update, April 2014.

Form of application

1.1 An application under rule 31.4 must be made using the Part 19 procedure, except that the provisions of rules 31.8 to 31.14 and of this Practice Direction shall apply in place of rules 19.4 to 19.9.

1.2 Where the application is for recognition only of an order, it should be made clear that the application does not extend to registration for enforcement.

Evidence in support of all applications for registration, recognition or non-recognition

2.1 The requirements for information and evidence for applications differ according to whether the application is made under the Council Regulation, the Jurisdiction and Recognition of Judgments Regulations, [the 2014 Regulations,][1] or the 1996 Hague Convention.

2.2 All applications to which rule 31.4(2) applies must be supported by a statement that is sworn to be true or an affidavit, exhibiting the judgment, or a verified, certified or otherwise duly authenticated copy of the judgment. In the case of an application under the Jurisdiction and Recognition of Judgments Regulations[, the 2014 Regulations][1] or under the 1996 Hague Convention, a translation of the judgment should be supplied.

2.3 Where any other document required by this Practice Direction or by direction of the court under rule 31.5 is not in English, the applicant must supply a translation of that document into English certified by a notary public or a person qualified for the purpose, or accompanied by witness statement or affidavit confirming that the translation is accurate.

Amendments

1 Inserted by the FPR Update, April 2014.

Evidence required in support of application for registration, recognition or non-recognition of a judgment under the Council Regulation

3.1 An application for a judgment to be registered, recognised or not recognised under the Council Regulation must be accompanied by a witness statement or an affidavit exhibiting the following documents and giving the information required by 3.2 or 3.3 below, as appropriate.

3.2 In the case of an application for recognition or registration –

(a) the certificate in the form set out in Annex I or Annex II of the Council Regulation, issued by the Member State in which judgment was given;

(b) in the case of a judgment given in default, the documents referred to in Article 37(2);

(c) whether the judgment provides for the payment of a sum or sums of money;

(d) whether interest is recoverable on the judgment or part of the judgment in accordance with the law of the State in which the judgment was given, and if that is the case, the rate of interest, the date from which interest is recoverable, and the date on which interest ceases to accrue;

(e) an address within the jurisdiction of the court for service of process on the party making the application and stating, in so far as is known to the applicant, the name and usual or last known address or place of business of the person against whom judgment was given; and

(f) where appropriate, whether Article 56 has been complied with, and the identity and address of the authority or authorities from whom consent has been obtained, together with evidence of that consent.

3.3 In the case of an application for an order that a judgment should not be recognised under Article 21(3) –

(a) the certificate referred to at paragraph 3.2(a);

(b) in relation to the documents identified at paragraph 3.2(b), those documents or a statement that no such service or acceptance occurred if that is the case;

(c) an address within the jurisdiction of the court for service of process on the applicant and stating, in so far as is known to the applicant, the name and usual or last known address or place of business of the person in whose favour judgment was given; and

(d) a statement of the ground or grounds under Articles 22 or 23 (as the case may be) on which it is requested that the judgment should not be recognised, the reasons why the applicant asserts that such ground or grounds is, or are, made out, and any documentary evidence on which the applicant relies.

Evidence required in support of an application for registration, recognition or non-recognition of a judgment under the 1996 Hague Convention.

4.1 An application for an order for a judgment to be registered under Article 26 or not recognised under Article 24 of the 1996 Hague Convention must be accompanied by a witness statement or affidavit exhibiting the following documents and giving the information required by 4.2, 4.3 or 4.4 below as appropriate.

4.2 In the case of an application for registration –

(a) those documents necessary to show that the judgment is enforceable according to the law of the Contracting State in which it was given;

(b) a description of the opportunities provided by the authority which gave the judgment in question for the child to be heard, except where that judgment was given in a case of urgency;

(c) where the judgment was given in a case of urgency, a statement as to the circumstances of the urgency that led to the child not having the opportunity to be heard;

(d) details of any measures taken in the non-Contracting State of the habitual residence of the child, if applicable, specifying the nature and effect of the measure, and the date on which it was taken;

(e) in as far as not apparent from the copy of the judgment provided, a statement of the grounds on which the authority which gave the judgment based its jurisdiction, together with any documentary evidence in support of that statement;

(f) where appropriate, a statement regarding whether Article 33 of the 1996 Hague Convention has been complied with, and the identity and address of the authority or authorities from which consent has been obtained, together with evidence of that consent; and

(g) the information referred to at 3.2(c) to (e) above.

4.3 In the case of an application for an order that a judgment should not be recognised –

(a) a statement of the ground or grounds under Article 23 of the 1996 Hague Convention on which it is requested that the judgment be not recognised, the reasons why the applicant asserts that such ground or grounds is or are made out, and any documentary evidence on which the Applicant relies; and

(b) an address within the jurisdiction of the court for service of process on the applicant and stating, in so far as is known to the applicant, the name and usual or last known address or place of business of the person in whose favour judgment was given.

4.4 Where is it sought to apply for recognition only of a judgment under the 1996 Hague Convention, the provisions of paragraph 4.2 apply with the exception that the applicant is not required to produce the document referred to in subparagraph 4.2(a).

Evidence required in support of an application for recognition or non-recognition of a judgment under the Jurisdiction and Recognition of Judgments Regulations [or the 2014 Regulations][1]

5.1 An application for recognition of a judgment under regulation 7 of the Jurisdiction and Recognition of Judgments Regulations [or under regulation 4 of the 2014 Regulations][1] or for non-recognition of a judgment under regulation 8 [of the Jurisdiction and Recognition of Judgments Regulations or regulation 5 of the 2014 Regulations][1] must be accompanied by a witness statement or affidavit exhibiting the following documents and giving the information at 5.2 or 5.3 below, as appropriate.

5.2 In the case of an application for recognition of a judgment –

(a) where applicable, details of any decision determining the question of the substance or validity of the civil partnership [or marriage][1] previously given by a court of civil jurisdiction in England and Wales, or by a court elsewhere;

(b) where the judgment was obtained otherwise than by means of proceedings –

(i) an official document certifying that the judgment is effective under the law of the country in which it was obtained;

(ii) where either civil partner [or spouse][1] was domiciled in another country from that in which the judgment was obtained at the relevant date, an official document certifying that the judgment is recognised as valid under the law of that country; or

(iii) a verified, certified or otherwise duly authenticated copy of the document at (i) or (ii) above, as appropriate;

(c) in relation to a judgment obtained by means of proceedings and given in default, the original or a certified true copy of the document which establishes that the party who did not respond was served with the document instituting the proceedings or with an equivalent document, or any document indicating that the respondent has accepted the judgment unequivocally; and

(d) the information referred to at paragraph 3.2(c) to (e) above.

5.3 In the case of an application for non-recognition of a judgment –

(a) an address within the jurisdiction of the court for service of process on the applicant and stating, in so far as is known to the applicant, the name and usual or last known address or place of business of the person in whose favour judgment was given;

(b) a statement of the ground or grounds under regulation 8 of the Jurisdiction and Recognition of Judgments Regulations [or regulation 5 of the 2014 Regulations][1] on which it is requested that the judgment should not be recognised together with any documentary evidence on which the applicant relies; and

(c) where the judgment was obtained by means of proceedings, the document referred to at paragraph 5.2(c) or a statement that no such service or acceptance occurred if that is the case.

Amendments

1 Inserted by the FPR Update, April 2014.

Evidence in support of application for a certificate under Articles 39, 41 or 42 of the Council Regulation, or for a certified copy of a judgment

6.1 The procedure described in the following paragraphs should be used where the application for the certified copy of the judgment or relevant certificate under the Council Regulation has not been made at the conclusion of the proceedings to which it relates.

6.2 An application for a certified copy of a judgment, or for a certificate under Articles 39, 41 or 42 of the Council Regulation must be made by witness statement or affidavit, containing the information and attaching the documents required under paragraph 6.3, and paragraphs 6.4, 6.5 or 6.6 below, as appropriate.

6.3 All applications must –

(a) provide details of the proceedings in which the judgment was obtained;

(b) attach a copy of the application by which the proceedings were begun;

(c) attach a copy of all statements of case filed in the proceedings; and

(d) state –

(i) whether the judgment provides for the payment of a sum of money; and

(ii) whether interest is recoverable on the judgment or part of it and if so, the rate of interest, the date from which interest is recoverable, and the date on which interest ceases to accrue.

Further, where the application relates to the Council Regulation, the applicant must attach a document showing that he or she benefitted from legal aid in the proceedings to which the judgment relates, if that is the case.

6.4 An application for a certified copy of the judgment and a certificate under Article 41 or 42 of the Council Regulation must –

(a) contain a statement of whether the certificate is sought under Article 41 or Article 42;

(b) attach a document evidencing the service of the application by which the proceedings were begun on all respondents, and if no such service occurred, details of all opportunities provided to each respondent to put their case before the court;

(c) provide information regarding the age of the child at the time of the judgment and the opportunities given during the proceedings, if any, for the child's wishes and feelings to be ascertained;

(d) state the full names, addresses and dates and places of birth (where available) of all persons holding parental responsibility in relation to the child or children to whom the judgment relates; and

(e) state the full names and dates of birth of each child to whom the judgment relates.

6.5 An application for a certified copy of the judgment and a certificate under Article 39 of the Council Regulation must –

(a) state whether the certificate sought relates to a parental responsibility matter or a matrimonial matter;
(b) in relation to a parental responsibility matter, attach evidence that the judgment has been served on the respondent;
(c) in the case of a judgment given in default, attach a document which establishes that the respondent was served with the petition or application by which the proceedings were commenced, or a document indicating that the respondent accepted the judgment unequivocally;
(d) state that the time for appealing has expired, or give the date on which it will expire, as appropriate, and state whether a notice of appeal against the judgment has been given;
(e) in relation to a matrimonial matter, give the full name, address, country and place of birth, and date of birth of each party, and the country, place and date of the marriage;
(f) in relation to a parental responsibility matter, give the full name, address, place and date of birth of each person who holds parental responsibility ;
(g) as appropriate, give the name, address, and date and place of birth of the person with access rights, or to whom the child is to be returned.

6.6 An application for a certified copy of a judgment for the purposes of recognition and enforcement of the judgment under the 1996 Hague Convention must –

(a) provide a statement of the grounds on which the court based its jurisdiction to make the orders in question;
(b) indicate the age of the child at the time of the judgment and the measures taken, if any, for the child's wishes and feelings to be ascertained; and
(c) indicate which persons were provided with notice of the proceedings and, where such persons were served with the proceedings, attach evidence of such service.

President's Practice Guidance: Case Management and Mediation of International Child Abduction Proceedings

13 March 2018

1. INTRODUCTION

1.1. For the purposes of this Practice Guidance, 'international child abduction proceedings' are proceedings in which the return of a child is sought under any of the following:

(a) The Convention on the Civil Aspects of International Child Abduction of 25 October 1980 ('the 1980 Hague Convention');

(b) The Convention on Jurisdiction, Applicable Law, Recognition, Enforcement and Cooperation in Respect of Parental Responsibility and Measures for the Protection of Children ('the 1996 Hague Convention');

(c) Council Regulation (EC) No 2201/2003 of 27 November 2003 on jurisdiction and the recognition and enforcement of judgments in matrimonial matters and matters of parental responsibility ('the Council Regulation');

(d) The High Court's power to make an order returning the child to another jurisdiction or to make an order for the return of the child to this jurisdiction ('the inherent jurisdiction')

1.2. International child abduction proceedings dealt with under the 1980 Hague Convention must be completed within six weeks of the date of the application. FPR PD12F paragraph 3.5 applies the same time limit to non-Convention cases under the inherent jurisdiction, save where exceptional circumstances make this impossible. This Practice Guidance is issued to ensure all applications are case managed in a manner that facilitates these time limits, both in cases that commence with a without notice application and cases that commence on notice.

1.3. Chapter 6 of Part 12 of the FPR 2010 and PD12F provide the procedural framework for proceedings under the 1980 Hague Convention, the 1996 Hague Convention and the Council Regulation. The rules provide for case management directions in child abduction proceedings to be given 'as soon as practicable' after the application has been made. In particular, the rules provide for:

(a) Directions for the production of the applicant's evidence (r. 12.46)

(b) The giving of case management directions generally (r 12.48)

(c) The filing and service of an answer (r 12.49)
(d) The filing and service of written evidence (r 12.50)

2. CASE MANAGEMENT – PROCEDURE

(a) Without notice applications

Use of without notice applications

2.1. Commencing proceedings by way of a without notice application pursuant to FPR r 12.47 will be justified *only* where (a) the case is one of exceptional urgency or (b) there is a compelling case that the child's welfare will be compromised if the other party is alerted in advance or (c) where the whereabouts of the child and the proposed respondent are unknown.

An urgent out of hours without notice application will be justified only where an order is necessary to regulate the position between the moment the order is made and the next available sitting of the court.

Evidence in support of without notice applications

2.2. The evidence in support of a without notice application must be as detailed and precise as possible having regard to the material provided by the applicant and transmitted by the Central Authority of the Requesting State. Unparticularised generalities will not suffice. Sources of hearsay must be identified and expressions of opinion must be supported by evidence and proper reasoning. The evidence should set out the orders sought, together with fully particularised reasons. Specifically, with respect to the narrow circumstances justifying a without notice application set out in para 2.1 above:

(a) Where the justification for proceeding without notice is said to be exceptional urgency, the evidence in support of the without notice application *must* identify why the case is exceptionally urgent and why no notice, even short informal notice, can be given to the respondent (with respect to short, informal notice see para 2.8 below).
(b) Where the justification for proceeding without notice is said to be a compelling case that the child's welfare will be compromised if notice is given, the evidence in support of the without notice application *must* demonstrate a real risk that if the respondent is alerted in advance the welfare of the child will be compromised, whether by the respondent thwarting the court's order or otherwise. Where the risk is said to be removal of the child from the jurisdiction, the evidence must address (i) the magnitude of the risk that the respondent will be minded to remove, (ii) the magnitude of the risk that, if the respondent is minded to remove, he or she will be able to evade protective measures put in place by the court and (iii) the magnitude of the consequences for the children if the protective measures are evaded.

(c) Where the justification for proceeding without notice is said to be that the whereabouts of the child and the proposed respondent are unknown, the evidence in support of the without notice application *must* explain what steps have been taken to locate them, what disclosure orders are required against an identified agency and why there is reason to believe that that agency may be able to provide information which may lead to the location of the child.

Without notice orders

2.3. Before seeking a without notice Tipstaff order the applicant or their legal representative must speak to the Tipstaff. The Tipstaff can be contacted by telephone on 01622 858035.

2.4. Passport orders, location orders and collection orders constitute an interference with the child's and the respondent's fundamental rights. On a without notice application, parties should only seek, and the court can only be expected to grant, such orders as are necessary and proportionate having regard to the risks assessed to exist on the evidence. Where a court makes more than one disclosure order, it may provide for the sequential service of those orders.

Case management directions at without notice hearings

2.5. Where a without notice application is justified and the court grants a Tipstaff or other substantive order, or where a without notice application is justified but the court refuses to grant a Tipstaff or other substantive order on the merits, the court will in each case proceed to give case management directions to progress the matter, which directions may be varied and/or supplemented at the first on notice hearing where appropriate. The directions given will include the following:

(a) A direction that at the first on notice hearing the applicant and the respondent shall each be given the opportunity to speak separately with a mediator, who will be present at the Royal Courts of Justice, to enable the mediator to discuss with the parties the possibility of mediation under the Child Abduction Mediation Scheme and, where appropriate, undertake a screening interview.

(b) A direction pursuant to FPR r 12.46(a) for the filing of any further evidence to be relied on by the applicant in support of the application including, where it is not already contained in the evidence supporting the application, a description of any protective measures (including orders that may be subject to a declaration of enforceability or registration under Art 11 of the 1996 Hague Convention or, where appropriate, undertakings) the applicant is prepared, without prejudice to his or her case, to offer for the purpose of securing the child's return.

(c) A direction pursuant to FPR r 12.50(2)(a) for the filing and serving of the respondent's answer.

(d) A direction pursuant to FPR r 12.50(1) for the filing of the respondent's evidence in support of the answer, to include details of any protective measures the respondent seeks (including, where appropriate, undertakings) in the event that the court orders the child's return.

(e) An order listing the matter for hearing for summary resolution, or in the alternative, further directions, no more than seven days from the date on which the without notice order is made (where a collection order is made the Tipstaff will return the matter to court within 3 days of the order being executed) with a direction that the respondent shall attend this hearing.

(f) A direction for the provision by HMCTS of an interpreter for the hearing where Section 11 of Form C67 indicates that the respondent does not speak English and indicates the language and dialect spoken by the respondent.

(g) Such further or other case management directions that are appropriate in the circumstances of the case. Where it is clear on the face of the application and supporting evidence that it will be appropriate for the child to be heard during the proceedings the court may make directions to ensure the child is given the opportunity to be heard (see paragraph 3.5 below).

(h) Unless the court directs otherwise, a direction pursuant to FPR r 12.47(3) that the applicant is to effect personal service of the standard directions order together with a record of the without notice hearing (note that where an order provides for service by the Tipstaff it is not sufficient for the order to be served by the applicant).

2.6. It is important that any without notice application is prepared in a manner that maximises the chances of the on notice hearing being effective. To this end, the without notice application and the evidence in support must contain *all* the information in the possession of the applicant that will or may assist in the prompt execution of any orders made. To further assist in achieving an effective on notice hearing, the directions order resulting from the without notice hearing will be served together with an information sheet, detailing how the respondent can obtain legal advice, public funding from the Legal Aid Agency and, if necessary, *pro bono* assistance, and a copy of the Child Abduction Mediation Scheme.

2.7. Where the application has been commenced by way of a without notice hearing, at the first effective on notice hearing the court will make further case management directions with input from both parties with a view to addressing each of the matters set out in paragraph 2.11 of this Practice Guidance where those matters have not already been dealt with by way of directions at the without notice hearing.

(b) On notice applications

Notice periods for on notice applications

2.8. FPR r 12.8 and PD12C provide that, in proceedings under the 1980 Hague Convention, service of the application on the respondent must be effected a minimum of 4 days before the first hearing and that, in proceedings under the inherent jurisdiction, service on the respondent must be effected a minimum of 14 days before the first hearing. Pursuant to PD12C para 2.2 the court may extend or shorten these periods for service. Whilst the courts have endorsed the practice of giving short, informal notice of proceedings in preference to proceeding without notice, where short, informal notice is given there *must* be evidence identifying why it was not possible to serve the application in accordance with the rules or to make an application to abridge time for service.

Standard directions on issue

2.9. Where the application is made on notice (and, accordingly, there is no without notice hearing immediately following the issuing of the application) there is a risk that valuable time will be lost between issue and the first on notice hearing. To minimise this risk, upon the court issuing an on notice application the court will, of its own motion, make standard directions upon issue pursuant to FPR r 12.5(1)(b), to include:

(a) A direction that at the first on notice hearing the applicant and the respondent shall each be given the opportunity to speak separately with the mediator present at the Royal Courts of Justice to enable the mediator to discuss with the parties the possibility of mediation under the Child Abduction Mediation Scheme and, where appropriate, undertake a screening interview.

(b) A direction pursuant to FPR r 12.46(a) for the filing of any further evidence to be relied on by the applicant in support of the application including, where it is not already contained in the evidence supporting the application, a description of any protective measures (including orders that may be subject to registration under Art 11 of the 1996 Hague Convention or, where appropriate, undertakings) the applicant is prepared, without prejudice to his or her case, to offer for the purpose of securing the child's return.

(c) A direction pursuant to FPR r 12.50(2)(a) for the filing and serving of the respondent's answer not less than 2 days prior to the first hearing.

(d) A direction pursuant to FPR r 12.50(1) for the filing of the respondent's evidence in support of the answer, to include details of any protective measures the respondent seeks (including, where appropriate, undertakings) in the event that the court orders the child's return not less than 2 days prior to the first hearing.

(e) A direction that upon service of the application the respondent file with the court a notice confirming the respondent's address and the whereabouts of the child (or that they are unaware of the child's whereabouts) and, where the respondent subsequently changes his or her address or becomes aware of any change in the child's whereabouts, a notice of the new address or of the new whereabouts of the child.

(f) A direction that upon service of the application the respondent serve on the applicant the notice confirming the respondent's address and the whereabouts of the child (or that they are unaware of the child's whereabouts) *or* file with the court a notice indicating that the respondent objects to serving on the applicant with notice confirming the respondent's address and the whereabouts of the child and the reasons for that objection.

(g) An order listing the matter for hearing for summary resolution or in the alternative further directions, seven days from the date the application is issued with a direction that the respondent shall attend this hearing.

(h) A direction for the provision by HMCTS of an interpreter for the hearing where Section 11 of Form C67 indicates that the respondent does not speak English and indicates the language and dialect spoken by the respondent.

(i) Such further or other case management directions that are appropriate in the circumstances of the case. Where it is clear on the face of the application and supporting evidence that it will be appropriate for the child to be heard during the proceedings the court may make directions to ensure the child is given the opportunity to be heard (see paragraph 3.5 below).

(j) A direction that the applicant is to effect personal service of the standard directions order.

2.10. The resulting directions order will be served together with an information sheet, detailing how the respondent can obtain legal advice, public funding from the Legal Aid Agency and, if necessary, *pro bono* assistance, and a copy of the Child Abduction Mediation Scheme.

Directions at first on notice hearing

2.11. At the first hearing, the parties should attend fully prepared to deal with the case management matters that have not been dealt with by way of standard directions upon issue or which have been so dealt with but require variation, together with any additional case management matters that may arise in the circumstances of the case. The court will expect the parties to be able to deal with the following case management issues if applicable:

(a) Further directions with respect to mediation or other non-court dispute resolution procedure.

(b) Allocation.

(c) Any directions required to deal with further disclosure.

(d) Any further directions with respect to the filing and service of an answer and evidence in support, to include details of any protective measures the respondent seeks (including, where appropriate, undertakings) in the event that the court orders the child's return.

(e) Any further directions with respect to the filing and service of the applicant's evidence in reply to the answer, including, where it is not already contained in the evidence supporting the application, a description of any protective measures (including orders that may be subject to a declaration of enforceability or registration under Art 11 of the 1996 Hague Convention or, where appropriate, undertakings) the applicant is prepared, without prejudice to his or her case, to offer to secure the child's return. Where the respondent's answer raises a defence under Art 13(b) the applicant should give immediate consideration to, and take steps, in the most expeditious way available, to ensure that information is obtained, whether from the Central Authority of the Requesting State or otherwise, as to the protective measures that are available, or could be put in place to meet the alleged identified risks.

(f) Directions in respect of expert evidence, if appropriate. Where a party seeks to adduce expert evidence, that party must comply with the requirements of FPR Part 25.

(g) Directions in respect of oral evidence, if appropriate (in respect of directions for oral evidence see para 3.8 below).

(h) Directions with respect to ensuring that the child is given the opportunity to be heard during the proceedings, unless this appears inappropriate having regard to his or her age or degree of maturity, including consideration of joinder and separate representation (see paragraph 3.5 below). Any application for joinder and separate representation should be made on notice prior to the first on notice hearing, to be dealt with at that hearing.

(i) The timetabling of the final hearing prior to the expiry of the six-week deadline, including the appropriate time estimate for the hearing, incorporating time for judicial reading and judgment writing.

(j) The arrangements for the provision of a court bundle that complies with FPR 2010 PD27A.

(k) The arrangements for the provision, where appropriate, of skeleton arguments and an agreed bundle of authorities in compliance with PD27A.

(l) Ancillary directions making provision where necessary for the attendance of a party not in the jurisdiction, the provision of video-links and the provision for interpreters at the final hearing. Where a video-link it sought, it is the responsibility of the parties to ensure appropriate arrangements are made for the video link and that the connection is made to the court via an ISDN line or, where an ISDN line is not available, that a 'bridging link' is arranged to ensure that a connection with the court can take place.

3. CASE MANAGEMENT – RELATED MATTERS

(a) Child Abduction Mediation Scheme

3.1. The requirement in FPR r 1.4(2)(f)) that case management includes encouraging the parties to use a non-court dispute resolution procedure if the court considers that appropriate and facilitating the use of such procedure, and the obligation imposed by FPR r 3.3(1) to consider whether non-court dispute resolution is appropriate at every stage of the proceedings, applies to international child abduction proceedings. The Lord Chancellor has set out in regulations provision on the of grant of non-means non-merit tested legal aid for mediation for applicant parents in cases under the 1980 Hague Convention.

3.2 Within this context, the court will, where appropriate, encourage the parties to engage in mediation of their dispute through participation in the Child Abduction Mediation Scheme (see Appendix). In any case where it is alleged or admitted, or there is other reason to believe, that the child or a parent has experienced domestic abuse or that there is a risk of such abuse, the court will have regard to these matters when deciding whether it is appropriate to encourage the parties to mediate. Participation in the Child Abduction Mediation Scheme is voluntary and without prejudice to the parties' right to invite the court to determine the issues between them. An unwillingness to enter into mediation will not have an effect on the outcome of the proceedings. It is important that parties and their representatives note that entering into a process of mediation will not ground a defence of acquiescence (see *In Re H (Minors) (Abduction: Acquiescence)* [1998] AC 72 at 88-89).

3.3. The Child Abduction Mediation Scheme will operate in parallel with, but independent from, the proceedings. Where parties agree to enter into mediation, the court will give any directions required to facilitate the mediation. The parties or the parties' representatives must be in a position to address the court on the question of mediation at the relevant hearing to enable the court to consider the appropriateness of such directions. The mediation will proceed with the aim of completing that mediation within the applicable timescales. Where the mediation is successful, the resulting Memorandum of Understanding will be drawn up into a consent order for approval by the court. If the mediation is not successful, the court will proceed to determine the application.

(b) Issue Identification

3.4. Key to ensuring that the final hearing is dealt with in a manner commensurate with the summary nature of most international child abduction hearings is the identification at the case management stage of what matters are truly in issue between the parties. It is particularly important that the directions hearing(s) preceding the final hearing be used to identify the real issues in the case, so that the judge can give firm and focused case management directions, including as to the form that the hearing will take. Parties can expect the court to be rigorous and robust at the case management stage in requiring parties to consider and identify the issues that the court is required to determine and to make concessions in respect of issues that are capable of agreement.

(b) Participation of the Child

3.5. Art 11(3) of the Council Regulation requires the court to ensure that child is given the opportunity to be heard during the proceedings unless this appears inappropriate having regard to his or her age or degree of maturity. Where it is clear on the face of the application and supporting evidence that it will be appropriate for the child to be heard during the proceedings the court may give directions to facilitate this at a without notice hearing or by way of standard directions on issue. Where directions have not already been given, the question of whether the child is to be given an opportunity to be heard in proceedings having regard to his or her age and degree of maturity, and if so how, must be considered and determined at the first on notice hearing. The methods by which a child may be heard during the proceedings comprise a report from an Officer of the Cafcass High Court Team or party status with legal representation. In most cases where it is appropriate for the child to be given an opportunity to be heard in proceedings an interview of the child by an officer of the Cafcass High Court Team will be sufficient to ensure that the child's wishes and feelings are placed before the court. In only a very few cases will party status be necessary. Where the exception relied on is that of settlement pursuant to Art 12 of the 1980 Hague Convention, the separate point of view of the child will be particularly important. The court should record on the face of any final order the manner in which the child has been heard in the proceedings.

(c) Witness Statements

3.6. Paragraph 2.13 of Practice Direction PD12F recognises that, to avoid delay, the *initial* statement in support of the application may be in the form of a statement given by the applicant's solicitor based on information transmitted by the Central Authority of the Requesting State. The applicant's initial statement of evidence *must* however, include the applicant's evidence establishing the necessary requirements for a return, a description of any protective measures (including orders that may be subject to a declaration of enforceability or registration under Art 11 of the 1996 Hague Convention or, where appropriate, undertakings) the applicant is prepared, without prejudice to his or her case, to offer for the purpose of securing the child's return and full details of any proceedings in the Requesting State or in England and Wales of which the applicant is aware.

3.7. Witness statements filed in support of the answer and in reply to the answer should be as economical as possible and should deal only with those factual matters relevant to the issues raised in the answer. The court will rarely be assisted by a detailed account of the history of the parents' relationship. Appropriate translations of exhibits should be provided with the statement. Where the maker of the statement does not speak English, the statement should be prepared and served in the maker's own language and then certified translation into English provided by the party concerned.

(d) Oral Evidence

3.8. The court will rarely make a direction for oral evidence to be given. Any party seeking such direction for oral evidence will need to demonstrate to the satisfaction of the court that oral evidence is necessary to assist the court to resolve the proceedings justly. Any party seeking to rely on oral evidence should raise the issue at the earliest available opportunity and no later than the pre-hearing review.

(e) Bundles

3.9. The court bundle for any hearing must comply with FPR PD 27A. PD27A limits the size of the bundle to a single file containing no more than 350 pages (PD 27A para 5.1). The limit of 350 pages includes the skeleton arguments. Only those documents which are relevant to the hearing and which it is necessary for the court to read, or which will be referred to during the hearing, may be included (PD 27A para 4.1). It will not generally be necessary to include in the bundle the application sent from the home country's Central Authority to ICACU. Where an issue arises as to the inclusion of this document, that issue will be dealt with by direction of the court. Skeleton arguments and other preliminary materials prepared for use in relation to earlier hearings should be excluded. Any separate bundle of all authorities relied on for any hearing must comply with PD 27A para 4.3. Each authority relied on must be provided with the relevant passages highlighted by means of a vertical line in the margin. Skeleton arguments must be filed by no later than 11am on the working day before the hearing (PD 27A para 6.4).

3.10. The time limits set out in FPR PD 27A para 6 for preparing and delivering the bundle and case management documents represent the *minimum* time limits applicable to this task. Where the hearing is on notice and the respondent is a litigant in person, the applicant should prepare and deliver the bundle pursuant to PD27A para 6 in a timeframe that ensures that the bundle and the case management documents are provided to the litigant in person at least three working days prior to the hearing.

(f) Time estimates

3.11. The time estimate for the final hearing should make reasonable allowance for judicial reading time and judgment writing. In those cases where permission for oral evidence has been given a witness template for the final hearing should also be completed at the time that the direction for oral evidence is made to ensure that the time estimate for the final hearing is accurate.

(g) International Judicial Liaison

3.12. The following matters may appropriately be the subject of direct international judicial liaison: (a) information concerning the scheduling of the case in the foreign jurisdiction, (b) seeking to establish whether protective measures are available for the child or other parent in the State to which the child would be returned, (c) ascertaining whether the foreign court can accept and enforce orders made or undertakings offered by the parties in the initiating jurisdiction, (d) ascertaining whether the foreign court can make a 'mirror order', (e) confirming whether orders were made by the foreign court and (f) verifying whether findings about domestic violence were made by the foreign court. This is not an exhaustive list. It is important to remember that international judicial liaison is not intended to be a substitute for obtaining legal advice, a means to avoid having to seek expert evidence as to foreign law or procedure, a mechanism for judges to settle welfare disputes or a means of making submissions to a foreign court. All requests for international judicial liaison should be made through the International Family Justice Office (IFJOffice@hmcts.gsi.gov.uk) and should be accompanied by a (preferably agreed) concise case summary and a set of focused questions to be put to the network judge which ask for information of a practical and non-legal nature, phrased in a neutral, non-tactical way.

(h) Final Hearing

3.13. Article 11 of the 1980 Hague Convention requires the judicial or administrative authorities of Contracting States to act expeditiously in proceedings for the return of children. Article 11(3) of the Council Regulation also requires a court to which a return application is made to act expeditiously and stipulates that, unless exceptional circumstances make this impossible, the court must issue its judgment no later than six weeks after the application is lodged. Within this context, whilst the quantity and nature of the evidential material required to reach a proper determination of the application at final hearing will depend on the individual case, as will the format of the final hearing, including the extent to which oral evidence is permitted, the final hearing will be dealt with *summarily* and in most cases based on the written material then available to the court.

(i) Orders

3.14. The Tipstaff passport, location and collection orders are in a standard format that has been arrived at after careful consultation and revision. It is for the court to draw the relevant Tipstaff order once granted. Legal representatives should *not* provide a draft of the passport order, location order or collection order sought. Legal representatives should provide drafts of any disclosure orders sought and a separate draft of the case management directions sought alongside the Tipstaff and/or disclosure order(s) applied for. Orders which discharge Tipstaff orders, including orders for the release of passports held by the Tipstaff, will only be accepted by the Tipstaff if they are sealed.

3.15. Where one of the parties is a litigant in person, the advocate for the represented party will need to ensure that any case management and disclosure orders made by court are drafted and submitted for approval by the judge. When the solicitor for the represented party sends a copy of the order to the litigant in person, the solicitor should highlight in writing to the litigant in person any case management steps that the order requires them to take. Counsel instructed on a Direct Access basis cannot conduct litigation on behalf of their client. The obligation on Direct Access counsel ends once the order has been submitted to the court. Case management directions made against the client must accordingly be met by them as a litigant in person.

3.16. Where an order refusing the return of the child (a 'non-return' order) has been made in respect of an applicant from an EU member state on the grounds set out in Art 13 of the 1980 Hague Convention, the procedure set out in Art 11(6) of the Council Regulation, requiring the transmission of certain documents to the court with jurisdiction or Central Authority in the Member State where the child was habitually resident within one month of the date of the nonreturn order, must be complied with.

(j) Appeals and Applications for Stay

3.17. Any application for a stay pending an application for permission to appeal and the application for permission to appeal should be made expeditiously. Any application for permission to appeal and any stay should be made to the judge if possible and, if not possible or if refused, to the Court of Appeal. The filing of the notice of appeal should not be delayed until the appellant has received a copy of the approved transcript of the judgment under appeal.

Sir James Munby President of the Family Division

13 March 2018

APPENDIX
CHILD ABDUCTION MEDIATION SCHEME

Introduction

1. The requirement in FPR r 1.4(2)(f)) that case management includes encouraging the parties to use a non-court dispute resolution procedure if the court considers that appropriate and facilitating the use of such procedure, and the obligation imposed by FPR r 3.3(1) to consider whether non-court dispute resolution is appropriate at every stage of the proceedings, applies to international child abduction proceedings. The 1980 Hague Convention itself, by Arts 7(c) and 10, places weight on the desirability of a negotiated or voluntary return or the amicable resolution of the issues.

2. In 2006, a child abduction Mediation Pilot Scheme run by Reunite, with funding from the Nuffield Foundation, found, in the context of twenty-eight cases which progressed to a concluded mediation, that there is a clear role for mediation in resolving cases of alleged child abduction and that parents were willing to embrace the use of mediation. Seventy-five percent of cases resulted in the parents concerned reaching a Memorandum of Understanding.

3. The Child Abduction Mediation Scheme is a mediation scheme that aims to ensure that parties engaged in child abduction proceedings are able, in an appropriate case, to access a mediation service as an integral part of the court process and in parallel with, but independent from, the proceedings. Whilst mediation will not be appropriate, or suitable, in every case, it is an option that should be explored by the court in all cases of alleged international child abduction.

Child Abduction Mediation Scheme – Key Principles

4. The Child Abduction Mediation Scheme is an independent mediation scheme run with the assistance of Reunite, which organisation provides mediators with specialised knowledge of international child abduction, trained and experienced in mediating cases of this nature. The following key principles apply to the operation of the Child Abduction Mediation Scheme:
   (a) The mediation will run in parallel with, but independent from, the proceedings in court, with the aim of completing the mediation within the timescale applicable to the proceedings.
   (b) Mediation is voluntary and will only be undertaken with the consent of both parents. An unwillingness to enter into mediation will not have an effect on the outcome of the proceedings.
   (c) Mediation will only be undertaken if the mediator considers that it is appropriate and safe to do so, and following an assessment of the parties and their situation during the required screening stage.

(d) Participation by the parties in mediation is without prejudice to the applicant's right to pursue the return of the child, and without prejudice to the respondent's right to defend the proceedings.
(e) Participation by the parties in mediation does not prevent the parties from requesting that the court determine the issues between them.
(f) If the mediation is not successful in resolving the issues then the matter will return to the court arena for determination.

5. The Child Abduction Mediation Scheme complements the proceedings and is only embarked upon once proceedings have been issued (Reunite also runs a mediation scheme that operates independent of court proceedings. Full details of this scheme can be found at http://www.reunite.org/pages/mediation.asp).

6. The operation of the Child Abduction Mediation Scheme will be facilitated by the presence at the Royal Courts of Justice of mediators from Reunite with specialised knowledge of international child abduction who will be available to speak with parties on child abduction matters.

Child Abduction Mediation Scheme – Operation

7. The scheme has three key stages, namely (i) identification, (ii) screening and (iii) mediation. The three key stages operate as follows:

Identification

8. Participation in the Child Abduction Mediation Scheme is voluntary. Mediation will only be undertaken with the consent of both parents and where it can be undertaken safely. However, it is also important that parties to child abduction proceedings are aware of, and have the proper opportunity to indicate their willingness to participate in the Child Abduction Mediation Scheme.

9. Within this context, the following steps will be taken by the court in each case, with a view to identifying those cases in which the parties are willing to consider mediation of their dispute:
(a) At the first without notice hearing, or by way of standard directions following an on notice application, the court will, where appropriate, direct that the applicant and the respondent shall each be given the opportunity at the first on notice hearing to speak with a mediator.
(b) At the first on notice hearing, the court will, where appropriate, encourage the parties to consider the option of mediation and, in an appropriate case, will invite the parties to speak with a mediator.
(c) Where the parties agree to speak with the mediator, the mediator will discuss with the parties the possibility of participating in mediation under the Child Abduction Mediation Scheme and will carry out an initial screening interview (see paragraph 11 below).

(d) Where the parties consent to mediate *and* the case is suitable for mediation, the court will give any directions necessary to facilitate the mediation and will record on the face of the order the proposed outline timetable for the mediation, in consultation with the parties and the mediator.

10. Where one party is outside the jurisdiction, the steps set out at Paragraph 9 will be accomplished by telephone at the first on notice hearing. Where this is not possible, for example due to a time difference, they will be accomplished on an agreed date shortly after the hearing. If these steps are accomplished on an agreed date shortly after the hearing, the parties will inform the court of the outcome and, where necessary, the court will either approve agreed directions to facilitate any agreement to mediate or list the matter for the purposes of giving any such directions. In any event, the mediator will ensure that the required screening and assessment is carried out prior to the mediation commencing.

11. It is important to note that entering into a process of mediation will not ground a defence of acquiescence (see In *Re H (Minors) (Abduction: Acquiescence)* [1998] AC 72 at 88-89).

Screening

12. In addition to the parents being willing to mediate, the case must be suitable for mediation. Mediators have a responsibility to ensure that the parents take part in any mediation process willingly, and without fear of violence or harm. The mediator will undertake a screening procedure to confirm that this can be achieved. The mediator will have particular regard to the welfare of the child or children. The mediator will also have particular regard to any allegation or admission of domestic abuse (as defined in FPR PD12J paragraph 3), or other reason to believe that the child or a parent has experienced domestic abuse or is at risk of such abuse.

13. Within this context, an initial screening interview will be undertaken individually with each of the parents prior to undertaking mediation, in order to ensure that the parent is willing to take part in mediation and to assess whether the case is suitable and safe for mediation. The screening interview will also allow the mediator to confirm to each parent at the conclusion of the interview whether it is appropriate for mediation to be offered and, if so, to ensure that each parent understand the purpose of the mediation and to provide an opportunity for any concerns relevant to mediation to be further discussed.

14. As provided for at paragraphs 8(c) and 10, where possible, the screening interviews will take place at the first on notice hearing when the parents speak with the mediator, either in person or by telephone. However, where the screening interview takes place at a later agreed date, the parties will inform the court of the outcome and, where necessary, the court will either approve agreed directions to facilitate any agreement to mediate or list the matter for the purposes of giving any such directions.

15. Where both parents indicate a willingness to engage in mediation, during the screening interview the mediator will deal with the following matters:
    (a) Whether or not the case is one that is suitable for mediation.
    (b) Whether or not both parents are willing to mediate and to attend mediation with an open mind.
    (c) Whether or not the subject child appears to be of an age and level of maturity at which their voice should be heard.
    (d) Provide information about the mediation and how the mediation process will work in parallel with, but independent from, the proceedings.
    (e) Address any concerns that either parent may have relevant to the conduct of the mediation.

16. Within the context of the matters set out in paragraph 12, the assessment of the suitability of a case for mediation will include an assessment of whether the mediation can be conducted safely. In any case in which the parents are willing to mediate but it is alleged or admitted, or there is other reason to believe, that the child or a parent has experienced domestic abuse (as defined in FPR PD12J paragraph 3) or that there is a risk of such abuse, the mediator will assess, through the screening procedure, whether a mediation can be conducted safely having regard to the matters set out in FPR PD12B paragraphs 5.1 and 5.2 and FPR PD12J. A mediation will take place in such circumstances only after the mediator has undertaken a risk assessment and is satisfied that appropriate measures are in place to protect the safety of those participating in the mediation process.

17. If, during the screening interview, it is identified that the subject child appears to be of an age and level of maturity at which their voice should be heard, the court will direct that the child be interviewed by a member of the Cafcass High Court Team and a report filed with the court and provided to the parents and mediators.

Mediation

18. Where the parties agree to mediate and the case is suitable for mediation, the mediation will be timetabled so as to ensure that the timescales applicable to the proceedings are met.

19. Reunite will contact both parents to arrange appropriate dates for mediation. Where it proves impossible for an applicant to come to this jurisdiction for the purposes of mediation, the mediator will conduct the mediation with the applicant attending by way of a telecommunications application such as Skype.

20. In some circumstances public funding from the Legal Aid Agency may be available to cover the costs of flights and hotel for the applicant parent to come to this jurisdiction for the purposes of mediation, in which case Reunite will co-ordinate travel and accommodation arrangements.

21. Where the parent has requested the services of an interpreter, this will be provided throughout the mediation session(s).

22. Parents are free at any stage during the course of the mediation to consult their respective legal representatives in this jurisdiction or overseas, or any other individual they wish to consult and the mediator may encourage them, as appropriate, to consult.

23. Where a safeguarding issue concerning a child or an adult arises during the course of the mediation, the mediator will, where appropriate, terminate the mediation and will notify the relevant agencies.

24. Where the mediation is successful, the agreement reached between the parents will be set down in the form of a Memorandum of Understanding. Parents will be encouraged to seek advice on the Memorandum of Understanding from their respective legal representatives if they have them. The court will be informed of the outcome of the mediation and the Memorandum of Understanding will be reduced to a consent order which will be placed before the court for approval. Any consent order will explain how the child has been heard in the context of the mediation process.

25. Where the mediation is not successful, the court will proceed to determine the case. Ordinarily, there will be no further reference to the mediation or to anything said during the mediation, save where child protection concerns have been revealed or a report has been prepared by the Cafcass High Court Team pursuant to paragraph 17 above.

13 March 2018

Guidelines for Judges Meeting Children who are subject to Family Proceedings

Produced by the Family Justice Council and approved by the President of the Family Division. April 2010

In these Guidelines –

- All references to 'child or 'children' are intended to include a young person or young people the subject of proceedings under the Children Act 1989.
- 'Family proceedings' includes both public and private law cases.
- 'Judge' includes magistrates.
- Cafcass includes CAFCASS CYMRU.

PURPOSE

The purpose of these Guidelines is to encourage Judges to enable children to feel more involved and connected with proceedings in which important decisions are made in their lives and to give them an opportunity to satisfy themselves that the Judge has understood their wishes and feelings and to understand the nature of the Judge's task.

PREAMBLE

- In England and Wales in most cases a child's needs, wishes and feelings are brought to the court in written form by a Cafcass officer. Nothing in this guidance document is intended to replace or undermine that responsibility.
- It is Cafcass practice to discuss with a child in a manner appropriate to their developmental understanding whether their participation in the process includes a wish to meet the Judge. If the child does not wish to meet the Judge discussions can centre on other ways of enabling the child to feel a part of the process. If the child wishes to meet the Judge, that wish should be conveyed to the Judge where appropriate.
- The primary purpose of the meeting is to benefit the child. However, it may also benefit the Judge and other family members.

GUIDELINES

1. The Judge is entitled to expect the lawyer for the child and/or the Cafcass officer:
   (i) to advise whether the child wishes to meet the Judge;
   (ii) if so, to explain from the child's perspective, the purpose of the meeting;
   (iii) to advise whether it accords with the welfare interests of the child for such a meeting take place; and
   (iv) to identify the purpose of the proposed meeting as perceived by the child's professional representative/s.

2. The other parties shall be entitled to make representations as to any proposed meeting with the Judge before the Judge decides whether or not it shall take place.

3. In deciding whether or not a meeting shall take place and, if so, in what circumstances, the child's chronological age is relevant but not determinative. Some children of 7 or even younger have a clear understanding of their circumstances and very clear views which they may wish to express.

4. If the child wishes to meet the Judge but the Judge decides that a meeting would be inappropriate, the Judge should consider providing a brief explanation in writing for the child.

5. If a Judge decides to meet a child, it is a matter for the discretion of the Judge, having considered representations from the parties –
   (i) the purpose and proposed content of the meeting;
   (ii) at what stage during the proceedings, or after they have concluded, the meeting should take place;
   (iii) where the meeting will take place;
   (iv) who will bring the child to the meeting;
   (v) who will prepare the child for the meeting (this should usually be the Cafcass officer);
   (vi) who shall attend during the meeting – although a Judge should never see a child alone;
   (vii) by whom a minute of the meeting shall be taken, how that minute is to be approved by the Judge, and how it is to be communicated to the other parties.

   It cannot be stressed too often that the child's meeting with the judge is not for the purpose of gathering evidence. That is the responsibility of the Cafcass officer. The purpose is to enable the child to gain some understanding of what is going on, and to be reassured that the judge has understood him/her.

6. If the meeting takes place prior to the conclusion of the proceedings –
   (i) The Judge should explain to the child at an early stage that a Judge cannot hold secrets. What is said by the child will, other than in

exceptional circumstances, be communicated to his/her parents and other parties.

(ii) The Judge should also explain that decisions in the case are the responsibility of the Judge, who will have to weigh a number of factors, and that the outcome is never the responsibility of the child.

(iii) The Judge should discuss with the child how his or her decisions will be communicated to the child.

(iv) The parties or their representatives shall have the opportunity to respond to the content of the meeting, whether by way of oral evidence or submissions.

Index

[All references are to paragraph numbers]

B

S

www.ingramcontent.com/pod-product-compliance
Ingram Content Group UK Ltd.
Pitfield, Milton Keynes, MK11 3LW, UK
UKHW051416150926
475561UK00005B/200

9 781526 512826